Oxford Primary Thesaurus

Chief Editor: Susan Rennie

OXFORD
UNIVERSITY PRESS

Great Clarendon Street, Oxford, OX2 6DP, United Kingdom

Oxford University Press is a department of the University of Oxford. It furthers the University's objective of excellence in research, scholarship, and education by publishing worldwide. Oxford is a registered trade mark of Oxford University Press in the UK and in certain other countries

First published 1993
Second edition 1998
Revised second edition 2002
Third edition 2005
Fourth edition 2007
Fifth illustrated edition 2012

This new edition 2018

British Library Cataloguing in Publication Data

Data available

ISBN: 978-0-19-276717-2
10 9 8 7 6

Printed in India

Paper used in the production of this book is a natural, recyclable product made from wood grown in sustainable forests. The manufacturing process conforms to the environmental regulations of the country of origin.

You can trust this book to be up to date, relevant and engaging because it is powered by the Oxford Corpus, a unique living database of children's and adults' language.

Contents

Preface

The Oxford Primary Thesaurus has been specially written for primary school children aged 8+. It is designed to address school and curriculum needs and has been checked by teachers. It is also designed to complement the Oxford Primary Dictionary which is aimed at the same age range.

A special feature of this edition are the literary quotations that show how words in the thesaurus have been used by children's authors. There is also a special **Become a Word Explorer** section at the back of the thesaurus. This includes advice on using synonyms and other types of language, and tips on how to make writing more varied and colourful through the use of a thesaurus.

Introduction

What is a thesaurus for?

Here are three good reasons to use your thesaurus:

- **to find a more interesting word**

What words can you use besides *kick* for striking a football? Look up **kick** and **ball** to find some other verbs to describe footwork.

- **to find the right word**

What do you call the home of a fox? Is a young otter known as a *cub* or a *pup*? Look up **animal** to find the answers.

- **to give you ideas for writing**

Imagine you are describing a giant's castle. Look up **castle** for ideas for the setting, then **big** to find adjectives to describe how *colossal* and *mammoth* everything is in a giant's world.

What is the difference between a thesaurus and a dictionary?

A **dictionary** tells you what a word means, whereas a **thesaurus** tells you what other words have the same meaning, or are related to the word in some way. A dictionary gives you a *definition* of a word; a **thesaurus** gives you *synonyms* of a word.

For example, if you look up **clothes** in a dictionary, it will tell you that clothes are things that you wear. But a thesaurus will give you some other words for clothes (**garments, dress, attire**) and will list particular types of clothes (**jeans, kilt, pyjamas**).

You often use a dictionary to check the meaning of something you have read or heard. You use a thesaurus to find ways to write or say something yourself.

How to use your thesaurus

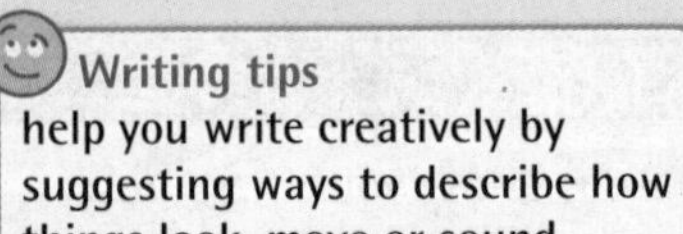

literary quotation shows you how an author has used a word in a story or poem

highlighted letter shows which letter you are on

alphabet on every page to help you find your way around the thesaurus easily

numbered sense if a word has more than one meaning, they are numbered

Word web gives words that are related to the headword and are useful for project work and story writing

---

bird to bit

A B C D E F G H I J K L M N O P Q R S T U V W X Y Z

SEA AND WATER BIRDS:

• albatross, auk, bittern, coot, cormorant, crane, curlew, duck, gannet, goose, guillemot, gull, heron, kingfisher, kittiwake, lapwing, mallard, moorhen, oystercatcher, peewit, pelican, penguin, puffin, seagull, snipe, stork, swan, teal

BIRDS FROM OTHER COUNTRIES:

• bird of paradise, budgerigar, canary, cockatoo, flamingo, hummingbird, ibis, kookaburra, macaw, mynah bird, parakeet, parrot, toucan

BIRDS WHICH CANNOT FLY:

• emu, kiwi, ostrich, peacock, penguin

PARTS OF A BIRD'S BODY:

• beak, bill, claw, talon, breast, crown, throat, crest, feather, down, plumage, plume, wing
see also feather

SOME TYPES OF BIRD HOME:

• nest, nesting box, aviary, coop, roost

SOUNDS MADE BY BIRDS:

• cackle, caw, cheep, chirp, chirrup, cluck, coo, crow, gabble, honk, peep, pipe, quack, screech, squawk, trill, tweet, twitter, warble
A turkey **gobbles**.
An owl **hoots**.

SPECIAL NAMES:

A female peacock is a **peahen**.
A young duck is a **duckling**.
A young goose is a **gosling**.
A young puffin is a **puffling**.
A young swan is a **cygnet**.
An eagle's nest is an **eyrie**.
A place where rooks nest is a **rookery**.
for groups of birds see group

WRITING TIPS

You can use these words to describe a bird:

TO DESCRIBE HOW A BIRD MOVES:

• circle, dart, flit, flutter, fly, glide, hop, hover, peck, perch, preen, skim, soar, swoop, waddle, wheel
The post owls arrived, swooping down through rain-flecked windows, scattering everyone with droplets of water.—HARRY POTTER AND THE HALF-BLOOD PRINCE, J. K. Rowling

TO DESCRIBE A BIRD'S FEATHERS:

• bedraggled, downy, drab, fluffy, gleaming, iridescent, ruffled, smooth, speckled
*The peacock displayed its **iridescent** tail.*

bit *NOUN*

1 *Mum divided the cake into eight **bits**.*
• piece, portion, part, section, segment, share, slice

2 *These jeans are a **bit** long for me.*
• a little, slightly, rather, fairly, somewhat, quite

OVERUSED WORD

Try to vary the words you use for bit. Here are some other words you could use.

FOR A LARGE BIT OF SOMETHING:

• chunk, lump, hunk, wedge, slab
And they all went over to the tunnel entrance and began scooping out great chunks of juicy, golden-coloured peach flesh.—JAMES AND THE GIANT PEACH, Road Dahl

FOR A SMALL BIT OF SOMETHING:

• fragment, scrap, chip, particle, speck, sliver, pinch, touch, dab, atom, iota (*informal*) smidgen
*The map was drawn on a **scrap** of old paper.*

38

---

cross reference points you to another headword in this thesaurus where you will find further useful words or information

Overused word offers more interesting alternatives for common words such as **big**, **bit**, **happy**, **nice** and **sad**

label
tells you that certain synonyms are only for *informal* or *formal* use

guide words
show the first and last word on a page

special synonyms
words that are similar in meaning to the headword, but can only be used in special cases

bite to blaze

FOR A BIT OF FOOD:
• morsel, crumb, bite, nibble, taste, mouthful
Please try a ***morsel*** *of chocolate mousse.*

FOR A BIT OF LIQUID:
• drop, dash, dribble, splash, spot
Add a ***splash*** *of vinegar to the sauce.*

bite *VERB* **bites, biting, bit, bitten**
❶ *I* ***bit*** *a chunk out of my apple.*
• munch, nibble, chew, crunch, gnaw
(informal) chomp
for other ways to eat see eat
❷ *Take care. These animals can* ***bite.***
• nip, pinch, pierce, wound
When an animal tries to bite you it **snaps** at you.
When an insect bites you it **stings** you.
A fierce animal **mauls** or **savages** its prey.

bitter *ADJECTIVE*
❶ *The medicine had a* ***bitter*** *taste.*
• sour, sharp, acid, acrid, tart
OPPOSITE sweet
❷ *His brother was still* ***bitter*** *about the quarrel.*
• resentful, embittered, disgruntled, aggrieved
OPPOSITE contented
❸ *The wind blowing in from the sea was* ***bitter.***
• biting, cold, freezing, icy, piercing, raw, wintry
(informal) perishing
OPPOSITE mild

bizarre *ADJECTIVE*
'Whiskers' is a ***bizarre*** *name for a goldfish!*
• odd, strange, peculiar, weird, extraordinary, outlandish
OPPOSITE ordinary

black *ADJECTIVE, NOUN*
The pony had a shiny ***black*** *coat.*
• coal-black, jet-black, pitch-black, ebony, raven

You can also describe a black night as **pitch-dark.**
Someone in a bad mood is said to look **as black as thunder.**
Common similes are **as black as coal** and **as black as night.**

blame *VERB*
Don't ***blame*** *me if you miss the bus.*
• accuse, criticise, condemn, reproach, scold

bland *ADJECTIVE*
This cheese has a really ***bland*** *taste.*
• mild, dull, weak, insipid
OPPOSITES strong, pungent

blank *ADJECTIVE*
❶ *There are no* ***blank*** *pages left in my jotter.*
• empty, bare, clean, plain, unmarked, unused
❷ *The old woman gave us a* ***blank*** *look.*
• expressionless, faceless, vacant

blank *NOUN*
Fill in the ***blanks*** *to complete the sentence.*
• space, break, gap

blanket *NOUN*
❶ *The baby was wrapped in a woollen* ***blanket.***
• cover, sheet, quilt, rug, throw
❷ *A* ***blanket*** *of snow covered the lawn.*
• covering, layer, film, sheet, mantle

blast *NOUN*
❶ *A* ***blast*** *of cold air came through the door.*
• gust, rush, draught, burst
❷ *They heard the* ***blast*** *of a trumpet.*
• blare, noise, roar
❸ *Many people were injured in the* ***blast.***
• explosion, shock

blatant *ADJECTIVE*
Do you expect me to believe such a ***blatant*** *lie?*
• barefaced, flagrant, obvious, shameless, brazen, unabashed

blaze *NOUN*
Firefighters fought the ***blaze*** *for hours.*
• fire, flames, inferno

a b c d e f g h i j k l m n o p q r s t u v w x y z

39

headword
is in blue; it is the word you look up and is in alphabetical order

synonyms
words that mean the same, or nearly the same, as the headword

example sentence
shows you how you might use a word; each meaning of a word has a separate example

word class
tells you what type of word it is, for example *NOUN*, *VERB*, *ADJECTIVE* or *ADVERB*

opposite
words that are opposite in meaning to the headword; they are also called antonyms

Special panels

Throughout this thesaurus, you will see special tinted boxes which give extra help on finding and using words. There are three types of panel, each marked by a special symbol:

Overused words  Writing tips  Word webs 

OVERUSED WORD

The **Overused word** panels offer more interesting alternatives for common words like **big**, **happy**, **nice** and **sad**. If you use these words too often, your writing will seem dull and boring.

Here is a complete list of all the **overused word panels** in this thesaurus:

bad	**good**	**look**	**sad**
beautiful	**happy**	**lovely**	**say**
big	**hard**	**move**	**small**
bit	**like**	**nice**	**strong**
eat	**little**	**old**	**walk**

WRITING TIPS

Writing tips can help you to create more colourful descriptions by suggesting ways to describe how people, things or animals look, move or sound. Other **writing tips** offer suggestions for creating dialogue or for using idioms. Here is a list of all the **writing tips** in this thesaurus:

afraid	**building**	**hair**	**sound**
angry	**clothes**	**light**	**surprised**
animal	**colour**	**nose**	**tooth**
ball	**exclamation**	**planet**	**un-**
bell	**eye**	**river**	**voice**
bird	**face**	**sea**	**water**
boat	**feel**	**sky**	**weather**
body	**food**	**smell**	**writing**

WORD WEBS

As well as exploring *alternative* words, you can explore *related* words. The **Word web** panels give lists of words related to a topic word, such as **animal** or **castle**. These can be useful for both project work and for story writing.

accommodation
aircraft
alien
amphibian
animal
anniversary
armed forces
armour
art
artist
astronaut
athletics
bear
bee
bicycle
bird
blue
boat
body
bone
book
brown
building
car
card
castle
cat
cave
cheese
chess
church
clothes
coin
colour
communication
competition
computer
cook
cricket
criminal
crockery
cutlery
dance
day
desert
detective
dinosaur
disaster
dog
dragon
drawing
drink
drum
education
entertainer
explorer
expression
eye
fabric
fairy
family
farm
fighter
figure of speech
fish
flower
food
football
fossil
fruit
furniture
game
ghost
glasses
green
group
hair
hat
herb
horse
hospital
house
ice
illness
injury
insect
island

jewel
jewellery
job
jungle
kitchen
knife
knight
light
magic
mathematics
meal
measurement
meat
medicine
metal
moon
mountain
museum
music
myth
needlework
nut
ocean
paint
paper
park
party
pasta
pattern
pet
photograph
pirate
planet
plant
poem
polar
politics
pottery
poultry
prehistoric
punctuation
pyramid
railway
red
religion
reptile
restaurant
road
robot
rock
room
royalty
ruler
school
science
sea
seashore
seaside
shape
shellfish
shoe
shop
sing
snake
song
sound
space
spice
sport
spy
story
superhero
sweet
swim
sword
tennis
tent
theatre
time
tool
tooth
toy
transport
travel
tree
vegetable
vehicle
water
weapon
weather
wedding
white
wood
writing
yellow
zodiac

abandon *VERB*
❶ *The robbers **abandoned** the stolen car.*
• leave, desert, forsake, leave behind, strand
(informal) dump, ditch
❷ *We **abandoned** our picnic because of the rain.*
• cancel, give up, scrap, drop, abort, discard

abduct *VERB*
*The pirates **abducted** two members of the crew.*
• kidnap

ability *NOUN*
*Skin has a natural **ability** to heal itself.*
• capability, competence, aptitude, talent, expertise, skill

able *ADJECTIVE*
❶ *Will you be **able** to come to my party?*
• allowed, permitted, free, willing
OPPOSITE unable
❷ *Penguins are very **able** swimmers.*
• competent, capable, accomplished, expert, skilful, proficient, talented, gifted
OPPOSITE incompetent

abnormal *ADJECTIVE*
*It's **abnormal** to have snow in June.*
• unusual, exceptional, extraordinary, peculiar, odd, strange, weird, bizarre, unnatural, freak
OPPOSITE normal

abolish *VERB*
*I wish someone would **abolish** homework!*
• get rid of, do away with, put an end to, eliminate
OPPOSITE create

about *PREPOSITION*
*There are **about** two hundred pupils in the school.*
• approximately, roughly, close to, around

➤ **to be about something**
*The film is **about** a dog called Scruff.*
• concern, deal with, involve

above *PREPOSITION*
*The witch flew **above** the rooftops on her broom.*
• over, higher than

abroad *ADVERB*
*We're planning to go **abroad** next summer.*
• overseas, to a foreign country

abrupt *ADJECTIVE*
❶ *The book came to a very **abrupt** end.*
• sudden, hurried, hasty, quick, unexpected
OPPOSITE gradual
❷ *The sales assistant had a very **abrupt** manner.*
• blunt, curt, sharp, rude, gruff, impolite, tactless, unfriendly
OPPOSITE polite

absence *NOUN*
*There's an **absence** of salt in the soup.*
• lack, want, need, deficit
OPPOSITE presence

absent *ADJECTIVE*
*Why were you **absent** from school yesterday?*
• away, missing
To be absent from school without a good reason is to **play truant**.
OPPOSITE present

absent-minded *ADJECTIVE*
*The **absent-minded** witch had forgotten the spell.*
• forgetful, careless, inattentive, vague
OPPOSITE alert

absolute *ADJECTIVE*
*The hypnotist asked for **absolute** silence.*
• complete, total, utter, perfect

absolutely *ADVERB*
*This floor is **absolutely** filthy!*
• completely, thoroughly, totally, utterly, wholly, entirely

absorb *VERB*
A sponge ***absorbs*** *water.*
• soak up, suck up, take in, fill up with, hold, retain

absorbed *ADJECTIVE*
➤ to be absorbed in something
I was so ***absorbed in*** *my book that I forgot the time.*
• be engrossed in, be interested in, be preoccupied with, concentrate on, think about

absorbing *ADJECTIVE*
'101 Dalmatians' is an ***absorbing*** *book.*
• interesting, fascinating, intriguing, gripping, enthralling, engrossing, captivating

absurd *ADJECTIVE*
The idea that little green men live on Mars is ***absurd.***
• ridiculous, silly, ludicrous, preposterous, foolish, laughable, nonsensical, idiotic, senseless, stupid, unreasonable, illogical
(informal) daft
OPPOSITES sensible, reasonable

abundant *ADJECTIVE*
Birds have an ***abundant*** *supply of food in the summer.*
• ample, plentiful, generous, profuse, lavish, liberal
OPPOSITES meagre, scarce

abuse *VERB*
❶ *The rescued dog had been* ***abused*** *by its owners.*
• mistreat, maltreat, hurt, injure, damage, harm, misuse
❷ *The referee was* ***abused*** *by players from both teams.*
• be rude to, insult, swear at
(informal) call someone names

abuse *NOUN*
❶ *They campaigned against the* ***abuse*** *of animals.*
• mistreatment, misuse, damage, harm, injury
❷ *A spectator yelled* ***abuse*** *at the referee.*
• insults, name-calling, swear words

accelerate *VERB*
The bus ***accelerated*** *when it reached the motorway.*
• go faster, speed up, pick up speed
OPPOSITE slow down

accent *NOUN*
❶ *My mum speaks English with a Jamaican* ***accent.***
• pronunciation, intonation, tone
❷ *Play the first note of each bar with a strong* ***accent.***
• beat, stress, emphasis, rhythm, pulse

accept *VERB*
❶ *I* ***accepted*** *the offer of a lift to the station.*
• take, receive, welcome
OPPOSITE reject
❷ *The club* ***accepted*** *my application for membership.*
• approve, agree to, consent to
OPPOSITE reject
❸ *Do you* ***accept*** *responsibility for the damage?*
• admit, acknowledge, recognise, face up to
OPPOSITE deny
❹ *They had to* ***accept*** *the umpire's decision.*
• agree to, go along with, tolerate, put up with, resign yourself to

acceptable *ADJECTIVE*
❶ *Would a pound be* ***acceptable*** *as a tip?*
• welcome, agreeable, appreciated, pleasant, pleasing, worthwhile
❷ *She said my handwriting was not* ***acceptable.***
• satisfactory, adequate, appropriate, permissible, suitable, tolerable, passable
OPPOSITE unacceptable

access *NOUN*
The ***access*** *to the lighthouse is over those rocks.*
• entrance, way in, approach

access *VERB*
*Can I **access** my email on this computer?*
• get at, obtain, reach, make use of

accident *NOUN*
❶ *There has been an **accident** at a fireworks display.*
• misfortune, mishap, disaster, calamity, catastrophe
A person who is always having accidents is **accident-prone**.
❷ *A motorway **accident** is causing traffic delays.*
• collision, crash, smash
An accident involving a lot of vehicles is a **pile-up**.
A railway accident may involve a **derailment**.
❸ *It was pure **accident** that led us to the secret passage.*
• chance, luck, a fluke
➤ **by accident**
*I found the piece of paper **by accident**.*
• by chance, accidentally, coincidentally, unintentionally

accidental *ADJECTIVE*
❶ *The damage to the building was **accidental**.*
• unintentional, unfortunate, unlucky
❷ *The professor made an **accidental** discovery.*
• unexpected, unforeseen, unplanned, fortunate, lucky, chance
OPPOSITE deliberate

accommodate *VERB*
❶ *The hotel can **accommodate** thirty guests.*
• house, shelter, lodge, provide for, cater for, put up, take in, hold
❷ *If you need anything, we'll try to **accommodate** you.*
• serve, assist, help, aid, oblige, supply, please

accommodation *NOUN*
*Have you booked your holiday **accommodation** yet?*
• housing, lodgings, quarters, premises, shelter, rooms

WORD WEB

PLACES WHERE PEOPLE NORMALLY LIVE:
• bedsit, flat, house

KINDS OF HOLIDAY ACCOMMODATION:
• apartment, bed and breakfast, boarding house, chalet, guest house, hotel, motel, self-catering, timeshare, youth hostel
Accommodation for students is in a **hall of residence** or *(informal)* **digs**.
Accommodation for the armed services is in **barracks** or a **billet**.
see also **building, house**

accompany *VERB*
*A guide **accompanied** us through the jungle.*
• escort, go with, follow, attend, travel with, tag along with

accomplish *VERB*
*She **accomplished** her goal of sailing round the world.*
• achieve, finish, complete, carry out, perform, succeed in, fulfil

account *NOUN*
❶ *I wrote an **account** of our camping trip in my diary.*
• report, record, description, history, narrative, story, chronicle, log
(informal) write-up
❷ *Money was of no **account** to him.*
• importance, significance, consequence, interest, value
➤ **to account for**
*Can you **account for** your strange behaviour?*
• explain, give reasons for, justify, make excuses for

accumulate *VERB*
❶ *Our family has **accumulated** a lot of rubbish.*
• collect, gather, amass, assemble, heap up, pile up, hoard
OPPOSITE scatter

❷ *Dust had **accumulated** on the mantelpiece.*
• build up, grow, increase, multiply
OPPOSITE **decrease**

accurate *ADJECTIVE*
❶ *The detective took **accurate** measurements of the room.*
• careful, correct, exact, meticulous, minute, precise
OPPOSITES **inexact, rough**
❷ *Is this an **accurate** account of what happened?*
• faithful, true, reliable, truthful, factual
OPPOSITES **inaccurate, false**

accuse *VERB*
➤ **accuse of**
*Miss Sharp **accused** her opponent **of** cheating.*
• charge with, blame for, condemn for, denounce for
OPPOSITE **defend**

accustomed *ADJECTIVE*
➤ **accustomed to**
*Desert plants are not **accustomed to** rain.*
• acclimatised to, familiar with, used to

ache *NOUN*
*The **ache** in my tooth is getting worse.*
• pain, soreness, throbbing, discomfort, pang, twinge, pain

ache *VERB*
*My legs **ached** from the long walk.*
• hurt, be painful, be sore, throb, pound, smart

achieve *VERB*
❶ *He **achieved** his ambition to play rugby for Wales.*
• accomplish, attain, succeed in, carry out, fulfil
❷ *The singer **achieved** success with her first CD.*
• acquire, win, gain, earn, get, score

achievement *NOUN*
*To climb Mount Everest would be an **achievement**.*
• accomplishment, attainment, success, feat, triumph

acknowledge *VERB*
❶ *The queen did not **acknowledge** her cousin's claim to the throne.*
• admit, accept, concede, grant, recognise
OPPOSITE **deny**
❷ *Please **acknowledge** my email.*
• answer, reply to, respond to

acquire *VERB*
*Where can I **acquire** a copy of this book?*
• get, get hold of, obtain
To acquire something by paying for it is to **buy** or **purchase** it.

across *PREPOSITION*
*We could see their camp **across** the river.*
• on the other side of, over, beyond

act *NOUN*
❶ *Rescuing the boy from the river was a brave **act**.*
• action, deed, feat, exploit, operation
❷ *The best **act** at the circus involved three clowns.*
• performance, sketch, item, turn

act *VERB*
❶ *We must **act** as soon as we hear the signal.*
• do something, take action
❷ *Give the medicine time to **act**.*
• work, take effect, have an effect, function
❸ *Stop **acting** like a baby!*
• behave, carry on
❹ *I **acted** the part of a pirate in the play.*
• perform, play, portray, represent, appear as

action *NOUN*
❶ *The driver's **action** prevented an accident.*
• act, deed, effort, measure, feat
❷ *The fruit ripens through the **action** of the sun.*
• working, effect, mechanism
❸ *The film was packed with **action**.*
• drama, excitement, activity, liveliness, energy, vigour, vitality
❹ *He was killed in **action** in the Second World War.*
• battle, fighting

active *ADJECTIVE*
❶ *Mr Aziz is very **active** for his age.*
• **energetic, lively, dynamic, vigorous, busy**
❷ *My uncle is an **active** member of the football club.*
• **enthusiastic, devoted, committed, dedicated, hard-working**
OPPOSITE **inactive**

activity *NOUN*
❶ *The town centre was full of **activity**.*
• **action, life, busyness, liveliness, excitement, movement, animation**
❷ *My mum's favourite **activity** is gardening.*
• **hobby, interest, pastime, pursuit, job, occupation, task**

actor or **actress** *NOUN*
*A company of **actors** performed a play in the school hall.*
• **performer, player**
The most important actor in a play or film is the **lead** or the **star**.
The other actors are the **supporting actors**.
All the actors in a play or film are the **cast** or the **company**.

actual *ADJECTIVE*
*Did you see the **actual** crime?*
• **real, true, genuine, authentic**
OPPOSITES **imaginary, supposed**

actually *ADVERB*
*What did the teacher **actually** say to you?*
• **really, truly, definitely, certainly, genuinely, in fact**

acute *ADJECTIVE*
❶ *She felt an **acute** pain in her knee.*
• **intense, severe, sharp, piercing, sudden, violent**
OPPOSITES **mild, slight**
❷ *There is an **acute** shortage of food.*
• **serious, urgent, crucial, important, vital**
OPPOSITE **unimportant**
❸ *Clearly the aliens had an **acute** intelligence.*
• **keen, quick, sharp, clever, intelligent, shrewd, smart, alert**
OPPOSITE **stupid**

adapt *VERB*
❶ *I'll **adapt** the goggles so that they fit you.*
• **alter, change, modify, convert, reorganise, transform**
❷ *Our family **adapted** quickly to life in the country.*
• **become accustomed, adjust, acclimatise**

add *VERB*
*The poet **added** an extra line in the last verse.*
• **join on, attach, append, insert**
➤ **to add to**
*The herbs **add to** the flavour of the stew.*
• **improve, enhance, increase**
➤ **to add up**
❶ *Can you **add up** these figures for me?*
• **count up, find the sum of, find the total of**
(informal) **tot up**
❷ *Her story just doesn't **add up**.*
• **be convincing, make sense**

additional *ADJECTIVE*
*There are **additional** toilets downstairs.*
• **extra, further, more, supplementary**

address *VERB*
*The head **addressed** us in assembly.*
• **speak to, talk to, make a speech to, lecture to**

adequate *ADJECTIVE*
❶ *A sandwich will be **adequate**, thank you.*
• **enough, sufficient, ample**
❷ *Your work is **adequate**, but I'm sure you can do better.*
• **satisfactory, acceptable, tolerable, competent, passable, respectable**
OPPOSITE **inadequate**

adjust *VERB*
❶ *You need to **adjust** the TV picture.*
• **correct, modify, put right, improve, tune**
❷ *She **adjusted** the central heating thermostat.*
• **alter, change, set, vary, regulate**

➤ to adjust to
I found it hard ***to adjust to*** *my new school at first.*
• adapt to, get used to, get accustomed to, become acclimatised to, settle in to

admiration *NOUN*
I'm full of ***admiration*** *for her work.*
• praise, respect, approval
OPPOSITE contempt

admire *VERB*
❶ *I* ***admire*** *her skill with words.*
• think highly of, look up to, value, have a high opinion of, respect, applaud, approve of, esteem
OPPOSITE despise
❷ *The travellers stopped to* ***admire*** *the view.*
• enjoy, appreciate, be delighted by

admission *NOUN*
❶ *We were surprised by his* ***admission*** *of guilt.*
• confession, declaration, acknowledgement, acceptance
OPPOSITE denial
❷ ***Admission*** *to the castle is by ticket only.*
• entrance, entry, access, admittance

admit *VERB*
❶ *The hospital* ***admitted*** *all the victims of the accident.*
• receive, take in, accept, allow in, let in
OPPOSITE exclude
❷ *Did he* ***admit*** *that he told a lie?*
• acknowledge, agree, accept, confess, grant, own up
OPPOSITE deny

adopt *VERB*
❶ *Our school has* ***adopted*** *a healthy eating policy.*
• take up, accept, choose, follow, embrace
❷ *We have* ***adopted*** *a stray kitten.*
• foster, take in

adore *VERB*
❶ *Rosie* ***adores*** *her big sister.*
• love, worship, idolise, dote on
❷ *(informal) I* ***adore*** *chocolate milkshakes!*
• love, like, enjoy
OPPOSITES hate, detest

adult *ADJECTIVE*
An ***adult*** *zebra can run at 80km an hour.*
• grown-up, mature, full-size, fully grown
OPPOSITES young, immature

adult *NOUN*
Adults *are not allowed in our club.*
• grown-up
OPPOSITES young person, child

advance *NOUN*
❶ *You can't stop the* ***advance*** *of science.*
• progress, development, growth, evolution
❷ *This computer is a great* ***advance*** *on our old one.*
• improvement

advance *VERB*
❶ *As the army* ***advanced****, the enemy fled.*
• move forward, go forward, proceed, approach, come near, press on, progress, forge ahead, gain ground, make headway, make progress
OPPOSITE retreat
❷ *Mobile phones have* ***advanced*** *in the last few years.*
• develop, grow, improve, evolve, progress

advantage *NOUN*
We had the ***advantage*** *of the wind behind us.*
• assistance, benefit, help, aid, asset
OPPOSITES disadvantage, drawback

adventure *NOUN*
❶ *He told us about his latest* ***adventure****.*
• enterprise, exploit, venture, escapade
❷ *They travelled the world in search of* ***adventure****.*
• excitement, danger, risk, thrills

adventurous *ADJECTIVE*
❶ *I dreamed of being an* ***adventurous*** *explorer.*
• bold, daring, heroic, enterprising, intrepid

❷ *She has led a very **adventurous** life.*
• exciting, eventful, dangerous, challenging, risky
OPPOSITE unadventurous

advertise *VERB*
*We made a poster to **advertise** the cake sale.*
• publicise, promote, announce, make known
(informal) plug

advice *NOUN*
*The website gives **advice** on building a bird table.*
• guidance, help, directions, recommendations, suggestions, tips, pointers

advise *VERB*
❶ *What did the doctor **advise**?*
• recommend, suggest, advocate, prescribe
❷ *He **advised** me to rest.*
• counsel, encourage, urge

aeroplane *NOUN*
see **aircraft**

affair *NOUN*
*The theft of the jewels was a mysterious **affair**.*
• event, happening, incident, occurrence, occasion, thing
➤ **affairs**
*I don't discuss my private **affairs** on the phone.*
• business, matters, concerns, questions, subjects, topics

affect *VERB*
❶ *Global warming will **affect** our climate.*
• have an effect or impact on, influence, change, modify, alter
❷ *The bad news **affected** us deeply.*
• disturb, upset, concern, trouble, worry

affectionate *ADJECTIVE*
*She gave him an **affectionate** kiss.*
• loving, tender, caring, fond, friendly, devoted
OPPOSITE unfriendly

afford *VERB*
*I can't **afford** a new bike just now.*
• have enough money for, pay for, manage, spare

afraid *ADJECTIVE*
❶ *We felt **afraid** as we approached the haunted house.*
• frightened, scared, terrified, petrified, alarmed, fearful, anxious, apprehensive
OPPOSITE brave
❷ *Don't be **afraid** to ask questions.*
• hesitant, reluctant, shy
➤ **to be afraid of**
*Luke was **afraid of** large hairy spiders.*
• be frightened of, be scared of, fear, dread

WRITING TIPS

SOMEONE WHO FEELS AFRAID MIGHT:

• blanch, go or turn pale, have goose pimples or goosebumps, quake in their boots, shudder, stand frozen or rooted to the spot, tremble like a leaf

SOMETHING WHICH MAKES YOU AFRAID MIGHT:

• give you goose pimples or goosebumps, make your hair stand on end, make your knees tremble, strike fear into you or your heart
The hairs stood up stiff with terror in the nape of Slightly's neck.—PETER PAN, J. M. Barrie

again *ADVERB*
*Would you like to come round **again** next week?*
• another time, once more, once again

against *PREPOSITION*
*I signed a petition **against** cruelty to animals.*
• in opposition to, opposed to, hostile to

age *NOUN*
*The book is set in the **age** of the Vikings.*
• period, time, era, epoch, days

A B C D E F G H I J K L M N O P Q R S T U V W X Y Z

age *VERB*
❶ *The woman had* ***aged*** *since we last saw her.*
• **become older, look older**
❷ *The wine is left to* ***age*** *in the cellar.*
• **mature, develop**

agent *NOUN*
for secret agents see **spy**

aggressive *ADJECTIVE*
Bats are not ***aggressive*** *creatures.*
• **hostile, violent, provocative, quarrelsome, bullying, warlike**
OPPOSITE **friendly**

agile *ADJECTIVE*
Mountain goats are extremely ***agile****.*
• **nimble, graceful, sure-footed, sprightly, acrobatic, supple, swift**
OPPOSITES **clumsy, stiff**

agitated *ADJECTIVE*
I felt ***agitated*** *before my music exam.*
• **nervous, anxious, edgy, restless, fidgety, flustered, ruffled, disturbed, upset, unsettled**
OPPOSITE **calm, cool**

agony *NOUN*
He screamed in ***agony*** *when he broke his leg.*
• **pain, suffering, torture, torment, anguish, distress**

agree *VERB*
❶ *I'm glad that we* ***agree****.*
• **be united, think the same, concur**
OPPOSITE **disagree**
❷ *I* ***agree*** *that you are right.*
• **accept, acknowledge, admit, grant, allow**
OPPOSITE **disagree**
❸ *I* ***agree*** *to pay my share.*
• **consent, promise, be willing, undertake**
OPPOSITE **refuse**
➤ **to agree on**
We ***agreed on*** *a price.*
• **decide, fix, settle, choose, establish**
➤ **to agree with**
❶ *I don't* ***agree with*** *animal testing.*
• **support, advocate, argue for, defend**
❷ *Onions don't* ***agree with*** *me.*
• **suit**

agreement *NOUN*
❶ *There was* ***agreement*** *on the need for longer holidays.*
• **consensus, unanimity, unity, consent, harmony, sympathy, conformity**
OPPOSITE **disagreement**
❷ *The two sides signed an* ***agreement****.*
• **alliance, treaty**
An agreement to end fighting is an **armistice** or **truce**.
A business agreement is a **bargain, contract** or **deal**.

ahead *ADVERB*
❶ *They sent a messenger* ***ahead*** *with the news.*
• **in advance, in front, before**
❷ *I stared* ***ahead****, trying to see through the mist.*
• **forwards, to the front**

aid *NOUN*
❶ *We can climb out with the* ***aid*** *of this rope.*
• **help, support, assistance, backing, cooperation**
❷ *They agreed to send more* ***aid*** *to the poorer countries.*
• **donations, subsidies, contributions**

aid *VERB*
The local people ***aided*** *the police in their investigation.*
• **help, assist, support, back, collaborate with, cooperate with, contribute to, lend a hand to, further, promote, subsidise**

aim *NOUN*
What was the ***aim*** *of the experiment?*
• **ambition, desire, dream, goal, hope, intention, objective, purpose, target, wish**

aim *VERB*
❶ *She* ***aims*** *to be a professional dancer.*
• **intend, mean, plan, propose, want, wish, seek**

❷ *He **aimed** his bow and arrow at the target.*
• point, direct, take aim with, line up, level, train, focus

air *NOUN*
❶ *We shouldn't pollute the **air** we breathe.*
• atmosphere
❷ *This room needs some **air**.*
• fresh air, ventilation
❸ *She was singing a traditional **air**.*
• song, tune, melody
❹ *There was an **air** of mystery about the place.*
• feeling, mood, look, appearance, sense

air *VERB*
❶ *He opened the window to **air** the room.*
• freshen, refresh, ventilate
❷ *I have a right to **air** my opinions.*
• express, make known, make public, reveal, voice

aircraft *NOUN*

WORD WEB

SOME TYPES OF AIRCRAFT:
• aeroplane, airliner, airship, biplane, bomber, drone, fighter, glider, helicopter, hot-air balloon, jet, jumbo jet, seaplane

PARTS OF AIRCRAFT:
• cabin, cargo hold, cockpit, engine, fin, flap, flight deck, fuselage, joystick, passenger cabin, propeller, rotor, rudder, tail, tailplane, undercarriage, wing

PLACES WHERE AIRCRAFT TAKE OFF AND LAND:
• aerodrome, airfield, airport, airstrip, helipad, heliport, landing strip, runway

PEOPLE WHO FLY IN AIRCRAFT:
• pilot, aviator, balloonist; co-pilot, cabin crew, flight attendant; passengers

air force *NOUN*
see **armed forces**

airy *ADJECTIVE*
*Our hotel room was pleasantly light and **airy**.*
• fresh, breezy, ventilated
OPPOSITES stuffy, close

alarm *VERB*
*The barking dog **alarmed** the sheep.*
• frighten, startle, scare, panic, agitate, distress, shock, surprise, upset, worry
OPPOSITE reassure

alarm *NOUN*
❶ *Did you hear the **alarm**?*
• signal, alert, warning, siren
❷ *The sudden noise filled me with **alarm**.*
• fright, fear, panic, anxiety, apprehension, distress, nervousness, terror, uneasiness

alarming *ADJECTIVE*
*We have received some **alarming** news.*
• frightening, scary, terrifying, shocking, startling

alert *ADJECTIVE*
*The guards were told to stay **alert** at all times.*
• vigilant, watchful, sharp, observant, attentive, awake, careful, on the alert, on the lookout, ready, wary, wide awake
A phrase meaning 'to stay alert' is to keep your eyes peeled.
OPPOSITE inattentive

alert *VERB*
*We **alerted** them to the danger.*
• make aware, warn, notify, inform, signal, tip off

alien *ADJECTIVE*
❶ *The desert landscape looked **alien** to us.*
• strange, foreign, unfamiliar, different, exotic
OPPOSITE familiar
❷ *Could those be the lights of an **alien** spacecraft?*
• extraterrestrial

alien *NOUN*
*I wrote a story about **aliens** from another galaxy.*
• extraterrestrial, alien life-form

WORD WEB

AN ALIEN FROM ANOTHER PLANET MIGHT BE:

• humanoid, insect-like, lizard-like, reptilian, intelligent, primitive, super-intelligent, telepathic

BODY PARTS AN ALIEN MIGHT HAVE:

• antenna, blotches, scales, slime, sucker, tentacle, webbing

TRANSPORT AN ALIEN MIGHT USE:

• alien vessel, flying saucer, mothership, pod, spacecraft, spaceship, starship, time machine, transporter beam

An alien might call someone from Earth an **Earthling**.

see also **planet, space**

alight *ADJECTIVE*

*The bonfire was still **alight**.*

• burning, lit, on fire, ignited

alike *ADJECTIVE*

*All the houses in the street looked **alike**.*

• similar, the same, identical, indistinguishable, comparable, uniform

alive *ADJECTIVE*

*Fortunately, my goldfish was still **alive**.*

• living, live, existing, in existence, surviving, breathing, flourishing

OPPOSITE dead

alliance *NOUN*

*The two countries formed an **alliance**.*

• partnership, union, association, federation, league

An alliance between political parties is a **coalition**.

allocate *VERB*

*I **allocated** some pocket money for buying presents.*

• allot, assign, set aside, reserve, earmark

allow *VERB*

❶ *They don't **allow** skateboards in the playground.*

• permit, let, authorise, approve of, agree to, consent to, give permission for, license, put up with, stand, support, tolerate

OPPOSITE forbid

❷ *Have you **allowed** enough time for the journey?*

• allocate, set aside, assign, grant, earmark

all right *ADJECTIVE*

❶ *The survivors appeared to be **all right**.*

• well, unhurt, unharmed, uninjured, safe

❷ *The food in the hotel was **all right**.*

• satisfactory, acceptable, adequate, reasonable, passable

❸ *Is it **all right** to play music in here?*

• acceptable, permissible

ally *NOUN*

*The two countries work together as **allies**.*

• friend, partner

OPPOSITE enemy

almost *ADVERB*

❶ *I have **almost** finished the crossword.*

• nearly, practically, just about, virtually, all but, as good as, not quite

❷ ***Almost** a hundred people came to the concert.*

• about, approximately, around

alone *ADJECTIVE, ADVERB*

❶ *Did you go to the party **alone**?*

• on your own, by yourself, unaccompanied

❷ *Zoe had no friends and felt very **alone**.*

• lonely, friendless, isolated, solitary, lonesome, desolate

also *ADVERB*

*We need some bread, and **also** more butter.*

• in addition, besides, additionally, too, furthermore, moreover

alter *VERB*

*They have **altered** the route for the cycle race.*

• change, adjust, adapt, modify, transform, amend, make different, revise, vary

alternative *NOUN*
I lost my bus money and had no ***alternative*** *but to walk.*
• choice, option

altogether *ADVERB*
❶ *I'm not* ***altogether*** *satisfied.*
• completely, entirely, absolutely, quite, totally, utterly, wholly, fully, perfectly, thoroughly
❷ *Our house has five rooms* ***altogether.***
• in all, in total, all told

always *ADVERB*
❶ *The sea is* ***always*** *in motion.*
• constantly, continuously, endlessly, eternally, for ever, perpetually, unceasingly
❷ *This bus is* ***always*** *late.*
• consistently, continually, invariably, persistently, regularly, repeatedly

amateur *NOUN*
All the players in this team are unpaid ***amateurs.***
OPPOSITE professional

amaze *VERB*
It ***amazes*** *me to think that the Earth is billions of years old.*
• astonish, astound, startle, surprise, stun, shock, stagger, dumbfound
(informal) flabbergast

amazed *ADJECTIVE*
I was ***amazed*** *by the number of emails I received.*
• astonished, astounded, stunned, surprised, dumbfounded, speechless, staggered
(informal) flabbergasted

amazing *ADJECTIVE*
The Northern Lights are an ***amazing*** *sight.*
• astonishing, astounding, staggering, remarkable, surprising, extraordinary, incredible, breathtaking, phenomenal, sensational, stupendous, tremendous, wonderful, mind-boggling

ambition *NOUN*
❶ *She had great* ***ambition*** *when she was young.*
• drive, enthusiasm, enterprise, push, zeal
❷ *My* ***ambition*** *is to play tennis at Wimbledon.*
• goal, aim, intention, objective, target, desire, dream, wish, hope, aspiration

ambitious *ADJECTIVE*
❶ *If you're* ***ambitious****, you will probably succeed.*
• enterprising, enthusiastic, committed, go-ahead, keen
OPPOSITE unambitious
❷ *I think your plan is too* ***ambitious.***
• grand, big, large-scale

amend *VERB*
I ***amended*** *the letter to make it clearer.*
• change, alter, adjust, modify, revise

among *PREPOSITION*
We played hide-and-seek ***among*** *the bushes.*
• between, amid, in, in the middle of, surrounded by

amount *NOUN*
❶ *Mum wrote a cheque for the correct* ***amount.***
• sum, total, whole
❷ *There's a large* ***amount*** *of paper in the cupboard.*
• quantity, measure, supply, volume, mass, bulk

amount *VERB*
➤ **to amount to**
What does the bill ***amount to?***
• add up to, come to, total, equal, make

amphibian *NOUN*

WORD WEB
SOME ANIMALS WHICH ARE AMPHIBIANS:
• bullfrog, frog, newt, salamander, toad, tree frog
for other animals see **animal**

A B C D E F G H I J K L M N O P Q R S T U V W X Y Z

ample *ADJECTIVE*
❶ *The car has an **ample** boot.*
• big, large, spacious, roomy
OPPOSITE small
❷ *We had an **ample** supply of food.*
• abundant, plentiful, generous, substantial, considerable, profuse, lavish, liberal
OPPOSITE meagre
❸ *No more juice, thanks—that's **ample**.*
• plenty, sufficient, lots, more than enough
(informal) heaps, masses, loads, stacks
OPPOSITE insufficient

amuse *VERB*
*I think this joke will **amuse** you.*
• make you laugh, entertain, cheer up, divert
(informal) tickle

amusement *NOUN*
❶ *What's your favourite **amusement**?*
• pastime, recreation, entertainment, diversion, game, hobby, interest, leisure activity, sport
❷ *We tried not to show our **amusement**.*
• merriment, hilarity, laughter, mirth

amusing *ADJECTIVE*
*I didn't find his jokes very **amusing**.*
• funny, witty, humorous, comic, comical, hilarious, diverting, entertaining
OPPOSITES unamusing, serious

analyse *VERB*
*We **analysed** the results of our experiment.*
• examine, study, investigate, scrutinise

ancestor *NOUN*
*Our family's **ancestors** came from France.*
• forebear, forefather, predecessor
OPPOSITE descendant

ancestry *NOUN*
*She was proud of her African **ancestry**.*
• origins, descent, heredity, heritage, blood, extraction, pedigree, stock

ancient *ADJECTIVE*
❶ *Does that **ancient** camera still work?*
• old, old-fashioned, antiquated, out of date, obsolete
❷ *In **ancient** times, our ancestors were hunters.*
• early, primitive, prehistoric, remote, long past, olden
The times before written records were kept are **prehistoric** times.
The ancient Greeks and Romans lived in **classical** times.
OPPOSITES modern, contemporary
see also **museum, pyramid**

anger *NOUN*
*I was filled with **anger** when I read her letter.*
• rage, fury, indignation, ire
(old use) wrath
An outburst of anger is a **tantrum** or a **fit of temper**.

anger *VERB*
*His cruelty towards his dog **angered** me.*
• enrage, infuriate, incense, madden, annoy, irritate, exasperate, antagonise, provoke
(informal) make your blood boil, make you see red
OPPOSITE pacify

angle *NOUN*
❶ *He wore a top hat set at a slight **angle**.*
• slope, slant, tilt
❷ *Let's look at the problem from a different **angle**.*
• viewpoint, point of view, perspective

angry *ADJECTIVE*
*Miss Potts turns purple when she gets **angry**.*
• cross, furious, enraged, infuriated, irate, livid, annoyed, incensed, exasperated, fuming, indignant, raging, seething
(informal) mad
(old use) wrathful
To become angry and lose control is to **lose your temper**.
OPPOSITE calm

angry *ADJECTIVE*

WRITING TIPS

SOMEONE WHO GETS ANGRY MIGHT:

• **blow a fuse, blow their top, fly off the handle, have a face like thunder, have steam coming out of their ears, hit the roof, see red**
Well, that did it! I saw red. And before I was able to stop myself, I did something I never meant to do. I PUT THE MAGIC FINGER ON THEM ALL!—THE MAGIC FINGER, Roald Dahl
for things an angry person might say see **exclamation**

animal *NOUN*
Wild **animals** *roam freely in the safari park.*
• **creature, beast, brute**

WORD WEB

A word for wild animals in general is **wildlife.**
A scientific word for animals is **fauna.**

VARIOUS KINDS OF ANIMAL:

• **amphibian, arachnid, bird, fish, insect, invertebrate, mammal, marsupial, mollusc, reptile, rodent, vertebrate**
An animal that eats meat is a **carnivore.**
An animal that eats plants is a **herbivore.**
An animal that eats many things is an **omnivore.**
Animals that sleep most of the winter are **hibernating animals.**
Animals that are active at night are **nocturnal animals.**

SOME ANIMALS THAT LIVE ON LAND:

• **aardvark, anteater, antelope, ape, armadillo, baboon, badger, bat, bear, beaver, bison, boar, buffalo, camel, cheetah, chimpanzee, chinchilla, chipmunk, deer, dormouse, echidna, elephant, elk, fox, gazelle, gibbon, giraffe, gnu, gorilla, grizzly bear, hare, hedgehog, hippopotamus** or *(informal)* **hippo, hyena, jackal, jaguar, kangaroo, koala, lemming, lemur, leopard, lion, llama, lynx, meerkat, mongoose, monkey, moose, mouse, ocelot, opossum, orangutan, otter, panda, pangolin, panther, platypus, polar bear, porcupine, rabbit, rat, reindeer, rhinoceros** or *(informal)* **rhino, skunk, snow leopard, squirrel, stoat, tapir, tiger, vole, wallaby, warthog, weasel, wildebeest, wolf, wolverine, wombat, yak, zebra**
for animals commonly kept as pets see **pet, amphibian, bird, fish, insect, reptile**

SOME ANIMALS THAT LIVE IN THE SEA:

• **dolphin, killer whale** or **orca, manatee** or **sea cow, narwhal, porpoise, seal, sea lion, walrus, whale**

SOME EXTINCT ANIMALS:

• **dinosaur, dodo, mammoth, quagga, sabre-toothed cat** or **smilodon**
see also **dinosaur**

PARTS OF AN ANIMAL'S BODY:

• **antler, claw, fang, foreleg, hind leg, hoof, horn, jaws, mane, muzzle, paw, snout, tail, trotter, tusk, whisker, fur, coat, fleece, hide, pelt**

MALE AND FEMALE ANIMALS:

A male elephant or whale is a **bull** and a female is a **cow.**
A male fox is a **dog** and a female is a **vixen.**
A male goat is a **billy goat** and a female is a **nanny goat.**
A male hare or rabbit is a **buck** and a female is a **doe.**
A male horse is a **stallion** and a female is a **mare.**
A female lion is a **lioness.**
A female pig is a **sow.**
A male sheep is a **ram** and a female is a **ewe.**
A female tiger is a **tigress.**
A male wolf is a **dog** and a female is a **bitch.**
see also **cat, cattle, deer, dog**

YOUNG ANIMALS:

A young beaver is a **kit**.
A young bear, fox or lion is a **cub**.
A young goat is a **kid**.
A young hare is a **leveret**.
A young horse is a **foal**, **colt** (male) or **filly** (female).
A young pig is a **piglet**.
A young otter or seal is a **pup**.
A young sheep is a **lamb**.
see also **cat, cattle, deer, dog**

HOMES OF WILD ANIMALS:

• **den, lair**
A badger lives in a **sett**.
A beaver lives in a **lodge**.
A fox lives in an **earth**.
An otter lives in a **holt**.
A rabbit lives in a **burrow** or **warren**.
A squirrel lives in a **drey**.

SOUNDS MADE BY ANIMALS:

• **bark, bay, bellow, buzz, gnash, growl, grunt, hiss, howl, jabber, oink, purr, roar, snap, snarl, snort, snuffle, squeak, trumpet, whimper, whine, woof, yap, yelp, yowl**
A sheep **bleats**.
A donkey **brays**.
A frog **croaks**.
Cattle **low** or **moo**.
A cat **mews** or **miaows**.
A horse **neighs** or **whinnies**.
for groups of animals see **group**

WRITING TIPS

You can use these words to describe an animal:

TO DESCRIBE HOW AN ANIMAL MOVES:

• **bound, creep, crouch, dart, gallop, gambol, leap, lumber, nuzzle, pad, paw, pounce, roam, scuttle, skip, slink, slither, spring, stamp, stampede, trot, waddle**
The hounds started to spread out in a circle around him. They were growling and snapping, looking for a chance to pounce.
—HERE BE MONSTERS, Alan Snow

TO DESCRIBE AN ANIMAL'S BODY:

• **agile, nimble, sinewy, wiry; lumbering, majestic, mighty, muscular, powerful**
*The cheetah stretched its long, **sinewy** body.*

TO DESCRIBE AN ANIMAL'S SKIN OR COAT:

• **coarse, fluffy, furry, glistening, glossy, hairy, leathery, matted, prickly, scaly, shaggy, shiny, silky, sleek, slimy, slippery, smooth, spiky, thick, thorny, tough, wiry, woolly; dappled, mottled, piebald, spotted, striped**
She was a strong, well-made animal, of a bright dun colour, beautifully dappled, and with a dark-brown mane and tail.—BLACK BEAUTY, Anna Sewell

anniversary *NOUN*

WORD WEB

The anniversary of the day you were born is your **birthday**.
The anniversary of the day someone was married is their **wedding anniversary**.

SPECIAL ANNIVERSARIES:

• **centenary** (100 years), **sesquicentenary** (150 years), **bicentenary** (200 years), **tercentenary** (300 years), **quatercentenary** (400 years), **quincentenary** (500 years), **millenary** (1000 years)

SPECIAL WEDDING ANNIVERSARIES:

• **silver wedding** (25 years), **ruby wedding** (40 years), **golden wedding** (50 years), **diamond wedding** (60 years)

announce *VERB*

❶ *The head **announced** that sports day was cancelled.*
• **declare, state, proclaim, report**
❷ *The DJ **announced** the next record.*
• **present, introduce, lead into**

announcement *NOUN*
❶ *The head reads the* ***announcements*** *in assembly.*
• notice
❷ *The prime minister issued an* ***announcement.***
• statement, declaration, proclamation, pronouncement
❸ *I heard the* ***announcement*** *on TV.*
• report, bulletin, newsflash

annoy *VERB*
❶ *I was* ***annoyed*** *that I missed the bus.*
• irritate, bother, displease, exasperate, anger, upset, vex, trouble, worry
OPPOSITE please
❷ *Please don't* ***annoy*** *me while I'm working.*
• pester, bother, harass, badger, nag, plague, trouble, try
(informal) bug

annoyance *NOUN*
❶ *Mrs Grant's face showed her* ***annoyance.***
• irritation, anger, exasperation, vexation
❷ *Is the dog an* ***annoyance*** *to you?*
• nuisance, bother, trouble, worry

annoying *ADJECTIVE*
My brother has a lot of ***annoying*** *habits.*
• irritating, exasperating, maddening, provoking, tiresome, trying, vexing, troublesome

anonymous *ADJECTIVE*
❶ *An* ***anonymous*** *donor gave the school some money.*
• unnamed, nameless, unidentified, unknown
❷ *I received an* ***anonymous*** *letter.*
• unsigned

answer *NOUN*
❶ *Did you get an* ***answer*** *to your letter?*
• reply, response, acknowledgement, reaction
A quick or angry answer is a **retort**
❷ *The* ***answers*** *to the quiz are on the next page.*
• solution, explanation

answer *VERB*
❶ *You haven't* ***answered*** *my question.*
• give an answer to, reply to, respond to, react to, acknowledge
❷ *'I'm quite well,' I* ***answered.***
• reply, respond, return
To answer quickly or angrily is to **retort**.
➤ **to answer back**
She doesn't like it when I ***answer back.***
• argue, protest, object

anthology *NOUN*
see **collection**

anticipate *VERB*
I ***anticipate*** *that the result will be a draw.*
• expect, predict, forecast, foretell

antique *ADJECTIVE*
The palace was full of ***antique*** *furniture.*
• old, old-fashioned
Antique cars are **veteran** or **vintage** cars.

anxiety *NOUN*
❶ *We waited for news with a growing sense of* ***anxiety.***
• apprehension, concern, worry, fear, nervousness, dread, tension, strain, stress, uncertainty, doubt
OPPOSITES calmness, calm
❷ *In his* ***anxiety*** *to win, he started before the gun went off.*
• eagerness, keenness, desire, impatience, enthusiasm

anxious *ADJECTIVE*
❶ *Are you* ***anxious*** *about your exams?*
• nervous, worried, apprehensive, concerned, uneasy, fearful, edgy, fraught, tense, troubled
(informal) uptight, jittery
OPPOSITE calm
❷ *I'm* ***anxious*** *to do my best.*
• eager, keen, impatient, enthusiastic, willing

apologetic *ADJECTIVE*
The shopkeeper was ***apologetic*** *about his mistake.*
• sorry, repentant, remorseful, regretful, penitent, contrite
OPPOSITE unrepentant

apologise *VERB*
*The ogre **apologised** for being rude.*
• make an apology, say sorry, express regret, repent, be penitent

appal *VERB*
*They were **appalled** by conditions in the prison.*
• disgust, revolt, shock, sicken, horrify, distress

appalling *ADJECTIVE*
❶ *He suffered **appalling** injuries in the accident.*
• distressing, dreadful, frightful, gruesome, horrible, horrific, horrifying, shocking, sickening, revolting
❷ *This handwriting is **appalling**—I can barely read it.*
• bad, awful, terrible, deplorable, disgraceful, unsatisfactory, atrocious
(informal) abysmal

apparent *ADJECTIVE*
*There was no **apparent** reason for the crash.*
• obvious, evident, clear, noticeable, detectable, perceptible, recognisable, conspicuous, visible
OPPOSITES concealed, unclear

appeal *VERB*
➤ **to appeal for**
*The prisoners **appealed for** our help.*
• request, beg for, plead for, cry out for, entreat, ask earnestly for, pray for
➤ **to appeal to**
*That kind of music doesn't **appeal to** me.*
• attract, interest, fascinate, tempt

appeal *NOUN*
❶ *Did you hear their **appeal** for help?*
• request, call, cry, entreaty
An appeal signed by a lot of people is a petition.
❷ *Baby animals always have great **appeal**.*
• attractiveness, interest, charm, fascination

appear *VERB*
❶ *Snowdrops **appear** in the spring.*
• come out, emerge, become visible, come into view, develop, occur, show, crop up, spring up, surface
❷ *Our visitors didn't **appear** until midnight.*
• arrive, come, turn up
(informal) show up
❸ *It **appears** that the baby is asleep.*
• seem, look
❹ *I once **appeared** in a musical.*
• act, perform, take part, feature

appearance *NOUN*
❶ *They were startled by the **appearance** of the ghost.*
• approach, arrival, entrance, entry
❷ *Mr Hogweed had a grim **appearance**.*
• air, aspect, bearing, look

appetising *ADJECTIVE*
*The **appetising** smell of baking filled the house.*
• delicious, tasty, tempting, mouthwatering food

appetite *NOUN*
❶ *When I was ill, I completely lost my **appetite**.*
• desire to eat, hunger
❷ *Explorers have a great **appetite** for adventure.*
• hunger, desire, eagerness, enthusiasm, passion, keenness, wish, urge, taste, thirst, longing, yearning, craving, lust, zest

applaud *VERB*
*The audience laughed and **applauded**.*
• clap, cheer
OPPOSITE boo

application *NOUN*
❶ *Have you sent in our **application** for a refund?*
• request, claim
❷ *The job needs a lot of patience and **application**.*
• effort, commitment, dedication, perseverance, persistence, devotion

apply *VERB*
❶ *The nurse told me to **apply** the ointment generously.*
• administer, put on, lay on, spread

❷ *My brother has **applied** for a new job.*
• make an application for, ask for, request
❸ *The rules **apply** to all our members.*
• be relevant, relate, refer
❹ *The vet **applied** all her skill to save the animal's life.*
• use, employ, exercise, utilise

appoint *VERB*
❶ *The school governors **appointed** a new teacher.*
• choose, select, elect, vote for, settle on
❷ *We **appointed** a time for our meeting.*
• arrange, decide on, fix, settle, determine

appointment *NOUN*
❶ *I have an **appointment** to meet the bank manager.*
• arrangement, engagement, date
❷ *The team are waiting for the **appointment** of a new captain.*
• naming, selection, choice, choosing, election
❸ *My uncle got a new **appointment** overseas.*
• job, post, position, situation

appreciate *VERB*
❶ *He **appreciates** good music.*
• enjoy, like, love
❷ *I **appreciate** her good qualities.*
• admire, respect, regard highly, approve of, value, esteem
OPPOSITE despise
❸ *I **appreciate** that you can't afford much.*
• realise, recognise, understand, comprehend, know, see
❹ *Dad hopes that the value of our house will **appreciate**.*
• grow, increase, go up, mount, rise

apprehensive *ADJECTIVE*
*Are you **apprehensive** about your exams?*
• worried, anxious, nervous, tense, edgy, uneasy, troubled, frightened, fearful

approach *VERB*
❶ *The lioness **approached** her prey.*
• draw near to, move towards, come near to, advance on
❷ *I **approached** the head to ask if we could have a party.*
• speak to, contact, go to
❸ *The volunteers **approached** their work cheerfully.*
• begin, undertake, embark on, set about

approach *NOUN*
❶ *We could hear the **approach** of heavy footsteps.*
• arrival, advance, coming
❷ *Dad made an **approach** to the bank manager for a loan.*
• application, appeal, proposal
❸ *I like her positive **approach**.*
• attitude, manner, style, way
❹ *The easiest **approach** to the castle is from the west.*
• access, entry, entrance, way in

appropriate *ADJECTIVE*
*It's not **appropriate** to wear jeans to a wedding.*
• suitable, proper, fitting, apt, right, tactful, tasteful, well-judged
OPPOSITE inappropriate

approval *NOUN*
❶ *We cheered to show our **approval**.*
• appreciation, admiration, praise, high regard, acclaim, respect, support
OPPOSITE disapproval
❷ *The head gave her **approval** to our plan.*
• agreement, consent, authorisation, assent, go-ahead, permission, support, blessing
OPPOSITE refusal

approve *VERB*
*The head **approved** my request for a day off school.*
• agree to, consent to, authorise, allow, accept, pass, permit, support, back
OPPOSITE refuse
➤ **to approve of**
*Her family did not **approve of** her marriage.*
• like, favour, welcome, appreciate, admire, value, praise, commend, applaud, respect, esteem
OPPOSITE condemn

approximate *ADJECTIVE*
*What is the **approximate** length of the journey?*
• estimated, rough, inexact, near
OPPOSITE exact

approximately *ADVERB*
*The film will finish at **approximately** five o'clock.*
• roughly, about, around, round about, close to, nearly, more or less

apt *ADJECTIVE*
❶ *He is **apt** to be careless with money.*
• likely, liable, inclined, prone
❷ *Your comments on my essay were very **apt**.*
• appropriate, suitable, proper, fitting, right, well-judged, pertinent
(informal) spot on

aptitude *NOUN*
*He has a remarkable **aptitude** for music.*
• talent, gift, ability, skill, expertise, potential, bent

arch *VERB*
*The cat **arched** its back.*
• curve, bend, bow

arch *NOUN*
*They saw the **arch** of a rainbow in the sky.*
• curve, arc, bend, bow

archer *NOUN*
see **arrow**

Arctic *ADJECTIVE*
see **polar**

area *NOUN*
❶ *From the plane we saw a big **area** of desert.*
• expanse, stretch, tract
A small area is a **patch**.
An area of water or ice is a **sheet**.
❷ *I live in an urban **area**.*
• district, locality, neighbourhood, region, zone, vicinity

arena *NOUN*
for places where sport takes place see **sport**

argue *VERB*
❶ *You two are always **arguing** over something.*
• quarrel, disagree, differ, fall out, fight, have an argument, squabble, wrangle, bicker
OPPOSITE agree
❷ *We **argued** over the price of the cloth.*
• bargain, haggle
OPPOSITE agree
❸ *He **argued** that it was my turn to walk the dog.*
• claim, assert, try to prove, maintain, reason, suggest

➤ **to argue about something**
*We could **argue** for hours **about** football.*
• debate, discuss

argument *NOUN*
❶ *They had an **argument** over who should pay.*
• disagreement, quarrel, dispute, row, clash, controversy, debate, difference, fight, squabble, altercation
❷ *Did you follow the **argument** of the book?*
• line of reasoning, theme, outline, gist

arid *ADJECTIVE*
*No plants could grow in the **arid** soil.*
• dry, parched, barren, waterless, lifeless, infertile, sterile, unproductive

arise *VERB*
❶ *We can phone for help if the need **arises**.*
• occur, emerge, develop, ensue, appear, come into existence, come up, crop up, happen
❷ *(old use) '**Arise**, Sir Lancelot!' said the King.*
• stand up, get up

arm *NOUN*
*The skeleton held out a bony **arm**.*
for parts of your body see **body**

arm *VERB*
*The boys **armed** themselves with sticks.*
• equip, supply, provide

armed forces *PLURAL NOUN*

WORD WEB

THE PRINCIPAL ARMED FORCES ARE:

• **air force, army, navy**
Men and women in the armed forces are **troops**.
A new member of the armed forces is a **recruit**.
A young person training to be in the armed forces is a **cadet**.

VARIOUS GROUPS IN THE ARMED FORCES:

• **battalion, brigade, company, corps, fleet, garrison, legion, patrol, platoon, regiment, squad, squadron**

MEMBERS OF THE ARMED FORCES INCLUDE:

• **aircraftman, aircraftwoman, commando, marine, paratrooper, serviceman, servicewoman, sailor, soldier**
see also **soldier**

armour *NOUN*

WORD WEB

PARTS OF A MEDIEVAL KNIGHT'S ARMOUR:

• **breastplate, gauntlet, greave** (shin guard), **habergeon** (sleeveless coat), **helmet, visor**
Armour made of linked rings is **chain mail**.
An outfit of armour is a **suit of armour**.
see also **knight**

arms *PLURAL NOUN*
The bandits were equipped with ***arms****.*
• **weapons, guns, firearms, ammunition**

army *NOUN*
see **armed forces**

aroma *NOUN*
The ***aroma*** *of lavender filled the air.*
• **smell, scent, odour, fragrance, perfume**

around *PREPOSITION*
❶ *The mermaid wore a coral necklace* ***around*** *her neck.*
• **about, round, encircling, surrounding**
❷ *There were* ***around*** *a hundred people in the audience.*
• **about, approximately, roughly, more or less**

arouse *VERB*
The plan to build a supermarket ***aroused*** *strong feelings.*
• **cause, generate, evoke, stir up, excite, stimulate, incite, provoke, lead to, produce, set off, whip up**
OPPOSITES **calm, quell**

arrange *VERB*
❶ *The books are* ***arranged*** *in alphabetical order.*
• **sort, order, put in order, group, organise, categorise, classify, collate, display, sort out, set out, lay out, line up**
❷ *Do you need any help* ***arranging*** *the party?*
• **plan, organise, prepare, set up, see to**

arrangement *NOUN*
❶ *They have improved the* ***arrangement*** *of the garden.*
• **layout, organisation, design, planning**
❷ *Did you change the* ***arrangement*** *of my CDs?*
• **order, grouping, display, distribution, spacing**
❸ *We have an* ***arrangement*** *to use the swimming pool.*
• **agreement, deal, bargain, contract, scheme**

arrest *VERB*
❶ *The police* ***arrested*** *two men yesterday.*
• **seize, capture, detain, apprehend, hold, take prisoner, take into custody, catch** *(informal)* **nick**
❷ *Doctors are trying to* ***arrest*** *the spread of the disease.*
• **stop, prevent, halt, hinder, check, delay**

A B C D E F G H I J K L M N O P Q R S T U V W X Y Z

arrive *VERB*
*When is the train due to **arrive**?*
• **appear, come, turn up, show up, get in**
When a plane arrives, it **lands** or **touches down.**
➤ **to arrive at**
*We **arrived at** the castle before midnight.*
• **get to, reach**

arrogant *ADJECTIVE*
*His **arrogant** manner annoys me.*
• **boastful, conceited, proud, haughty, self-important, bumptious, pompous, snobbish, superior, vain**
(informal) **cocky, snooty, stuck-up**
OPPOSITE **modest**

arrow *NOUN*
The spine of an arrow is the **shaft**.
The point of an arrow is the **arrowhead**.
Arrows are shot using a **bow**.
A holder for several arrows is a **quiver**.
The sport of shooting arrows at a target is **archery**.
Someone who practises archery is an **archer**.

art *NOUN*
❶ *The **art** of writing letters is disappearing fast.*
• **skill, craft, technique, talent, knack, trick**
❷ *She took a course in **art** and design.*
• **artwork, fine art**

WORD WEB

SOME TYPES OF ART, CRAFT AND DESIGN:

• **animation, basketry, batik, beadwork, carpentry, ceramics, collage, crochet, cross stitch, digital art, drawing, embroidery, enamelling, engraving, etching, fine art, graphics, illustration, jewellery, knitting, metalwork, modelling, mosaics, needlework, origami, painting, paper sculpture, patchwork, photography, pottery, printing, quilting, screen printing, sculpture, sewing, sketching, spinning, stained glass, stamping, stencilling, tapestry, textiles, watercolour, weaving, woodwork**
for people who work in arts and design see **artist**

article *NOUN*
❶ *Have you any **articles** for the jumble sale?*
• **item, object, thing**
❷ *Did you read my **article** in the magazine?*
• **essay, report, piece of writing**

artificial *ADJECTIVE*
❶ *Organic gardeners don't use **artificial** fertilisers.*
• **man-made, synthetic, unnatural, manufactured**
OPPOSITE **natural**
❷ *She had an **artificial** flower in her buttonhole.*
• **fake, false, imitation, unreal, bogus, counterfeit**
OPPOSITES **genuine, real**
❸ *Captain Hook gave us an **artificial** smile.*
• **pretended, sham, affected, simulated**
(informal) **put on**
OPPOSITES **genuine, natural**

artist *NOUN*

WORD WEB

SOME ARTISTS AND CRAFTSPEOPLE:

• **animator, blacksmith, carpenter, cartoonist, designer, draughtsman, draughtswoman, embroiderer, engraver, goldsmith, graphic designer, illustrator, jeweller, knitter, mason, painter, photographer, potter, printer, quilter, sculptor, silversmith, textile designer, weaver**
for performing artists see **entertainer**

artistic *ADJECTIVE*
*Mum's flower arrangements are very **artistic**.*
• **creative, imaginative, aesthetic, attractive, beautiful, tasteful**
OPPOSITE **ugly**

ascend *VERB*
❶ *It took the rescuers a long time to **ascend** the mountain.*
• climb, go up, mount, move up, scale
❷ *The plane began to **ascend**.*
• lift off, take off
❸ *The eagle **ascended** into the air.*
• fly up, rise, soar
OPPOSITE descend

ascent *NOUN*
*The bus moved slowly up the steep **ascent**.*
• climb, rise, slope, hill, gradient, incline, ramp
OPPOSITE descent

ashamed *ADJECTIVE*
*He was **ashamed** because of what he had done.*
• sorry, remorseful, repentant, embarrassed, shamefaced, abashed, mortified, apologetic, penitent
(informal) red-faced
OPPOSITES unashamed, unrepentant

ashes *PLURAL NOUN*
*Next morning, the **ashes** of the bonfire were still glowing.*
• embers, cinders

ask *VERB*
❶ *I **asked** them to be careful with the parcel.*
• beg, entreat, appeal to, implore, plead with
❷ *'Are you ready?' I **asked**.*
• demand, enquire, inquire, query, question
❸ *I'm going to **ask** you to my party.*
• invite
(formal) request the pleasure of your company

asleep *ADJECTIVE*
*I didn't hear the phone because I was **asleep**.*
• sleeping, dozing, having a nap, napping
(old use) slumbering
A patient asleep for an operation is **anaesthetised** or **under sedation**.
An animal asleep for the winter is **hibernating**.
OPPOSITE awake

➤ **to fall asleep**
*We waited until the giant **fell asleep**.*
• drop off, doze, nod off
To fall asleep quickly is to **go out like a light**.

aspect *NOUN*
❶ *The book describes some **aspects** of life in ancient Rome.*
• part, feature, element, angle, detail, side, facet
❷ *The ruined tower had an unfriendly **aspect**.*
• appearance, look, manner, air, expression, face, countenance
❸ *The front room has a southern **aspect**.*
• outlook, view, prospect

assault *NOUN*
*The old lady was the victim of a serious **assault**.*
• attack, mugging

assault *VERB*
*It's a serious crime to **assault** a policeman.*
• attack, strike, hit, beat up, mug

assemble *VERB*
❶ *A crowd **assembled** to watch the rescue.*
• gather, come together, converge, accumulate, crowd together, flock together, meet, convene
OPPOSITE disperse
❷ *We **assembled** our luggage at the front door.*
• collect, gather, bring together, pile up, put together
❸ *The general **assembled** his troops.*
• round up, rally, muster

assembly *NOUN*
*There was a large **assembly** of people in the market square.*
• gathering, meeting, crowd, throng
An assembly for worship is a **service**.
A large assembly to show support for something, often out of doors, is a **rally**.
An assembly to discuss political matters is a **council** or **parliament**.

An assembly to discuss and learn about a particular topic is a **conference** or **congress**.

assent *NOUN*
*The pirates gave their **assent** to the plan.*
• agreement, approval, consent, go-ahead, permission
OPPOSITE refusal

assert *VERB*
*The prisoner **asserted** that he was innocent.*
• state, claim, contend, declare, argue, insist, maintain, proclaim, insist, protest, swear, testify

assess *VERB*
*The test will **assess** your knowledge of French.*
• evaluate, determine, judge, estimate, measure, gauge, value, weigh up

asset *NOUN*
*Good health is a great **asset**.*
• advantage, benefit, help, blessing

assign *VERB*
*He **assigned** the difficult jobs to the older children.*
• allocate, allot, give, consign, hand over, distribute, share out

assignment *NOUN*
*The spy was given a tough **assignment**.*
• job, task, piece of work, mission, project, duty, responsibility

assist *VERB*
*We were asked to **assist** the gardener with the weeding.*
• help, aid, support, cooperate with, collaborate with
OPPOSITE hinder

assistance *NOUN*
❶ *Do you need **assistance** with your luggage?*
• help, aid, support, encouragement
❷ *We bought new sports equipment with the **assistance** of a local firm.*
• backing, collaboration, cooperation, sponsorship, subsidy, support

assistant *NOUN*
*The magician was training a new **assistant**.*
• helper, partner, colleague, associate, supporter

associate *VERB*
➤ **to associate one thing with another**
*I **associate** Christmas **with** holly and snow.*
• connect with, identify with, link with, relate to
➤ **to associate with someone**
*I don't think you should **associate with** those people!*
• be friends with, go about with, mix with

association *NOUN*
❶ *We have started a junior tennis **association**.*
• club, society, group, league, fellowship, partnership, union, alliance
A political association is a **party**.
A business association is a **company** or **organisation**.
❷ *The **association** between the two men lasted many years.*
• friendship, relationship, link, partnership, closeness

assorted *ADJECTIVE*
*I bought a bag of sweets with **assorted** flavours.*
• various, different, mixed, diverse, miscellaneous, several

assortment *NOUN*
*There was an **assortment** of sandwiches to choose from.*
• variety, mixture, selection, array, choice, collection, diversity

assume *VERB*
❶ *I **assume** you'd like some chocolate.*
• suppose, presume, imagine, believe, guess, expect, gather, suspect, think
❷ *The bandit **assumed** a disguise.*
• put on, adopt, dress up in, wear

assure *VERB*
I ***assure*** *you that I will take care of your dog.*
• **promise, give your word to**

astonish *VERB*
It ***astonished*** *us to learn that the house was haunted.*
• **amaze, astound, surprise, stagger, shock, dumbfound, leave speechless, startle, stun, take aback, take by surprise**
(informal) **flabbergast, take your breath away**

astonishing *ADJECTIVE*
The volcano was an ***astonishing*** *sight.*
• **amazing, astounding, staggering, remarkable, surprising, extraordinary, incredible, breathtaking, phenomenal, sensational, stupendous, tremendous, wonderful**

astound *VERB*
see **astonish**

astounding *ADJECTIVE*
see **astonishing**

astronaut *NOUN*
The ***astronauts*** *climbed aboard the spacecraft.*
• **spaceman or spacewoman**

WORD WEB

THINGS AN ASTRONAUT MIGHT USE OR WEAR:
• **jet pack, oxygen tank, moon boots or space boots, space helmet, spacesuit, visor**

PLACES AN ASTRONAUT MIGHT VISIT:
• **alien planet, moon base, space lab, space station, star base**
see also **moon, planet, space**

astronomy *NOUN*
for words used in astronomy see **space**

ate *past tense see* **eat**

athlete *NOUN*
for events in which athletes take part
see **athletics**

athletic *ADJECTIVE*
You need to be ***athletic*** *to run in a marathon.*
• **fit, active, energetic, strong, muscular, powerful, robust, sturdy, vigorous, well-built**
(informal) **sporty**
OPPOSITES **feeble, puny**

athletics *PLURAL NOUN*

WORD WEB

SOME ATHLETIC EVENTS:
• **cross-country, decathlon, discus, heptathlon, high jump, hurdles, javelin, long jump, marathon, pentathlon, pole vault, relay race, running, shot-put, sprinting, steeplechase, triathlon, triple jump**
for other sports see **sport**

atmosphere *NOUN*
❶ *The* ***atmosphere*** *on Mars is unbreathable.*
• **air, sky**
❷ *There was a happy* ***atmosphere*** *at the party.*
• **feeling, mood, spirit**

atrocious *ADJECTIVE*
Everyone was shocked by the ***atrocious*** *crime.*
• **wicked, terrible, dreadful, abominable, brutal, savage, barbaric, bloodthirsty, callous, cruel, diabolical, evil, fiendish, horrifying, merciless, outrageous, sadistic, terrible, vicious, villainous**

attach *VERB*
Attach *this label to the parcel.*
• **fasten, fix, join, tie, bind, secure, connect, link, couple, stick, affix, add, append**
OPPOSITE **detach**

attached *ADJECTIVE*
➤ **attached to**
*The twins are very **attached to** each other.*
• **fond of, close to, dear to, devoted to, loyal to, affectionate towards, friendly towards, loving towards**
OPPOSITE **not close to**

attack *NOUN*
❶ *The pirates' **attack** took us by surprise.*
• **assault, strike, charge, rush, raid, ambush, invasion, onslaught**
An attack with big guns or bombs is a **blitz** or **bombardment.**
An attack by planes is an **air raid.**
❷ *The newspaper published an **attack** on his character.*
• **criticism, outburst, abuse, tirade**
❸ *I had a sneezing **attack** in assembly.*
• **bout, fit, spasm**
(informal) **turn**

attack *VERB*
❶ *The travellers were **attacked** by highwaymen.*
• **assault, beat up, mug, set on, assail**
To attack someone else's territory is to **invade** or **raid** it.
To attack someone from a hidden place is to **ambush** them.
To attack the enemy with bombs or heavy guns is to **bombard** them.
To attack by rushing at the enemy is to **charge.**
To attack a place suddenly is to **storm** it.
If an animal attacks you, it might **savage** you.
❷ *He **attacked** her reputation.*
• **abuse, criticise, denounce**
OPPOSITE **defend**

attain *VERB*
*The team **attained** a total of twelve gold medals.*
• **get, obtain, reach, achieve, accomplish, gain**

attempt *VERB*
*They will **attempt** to reconstruct a Viking ship.*
• **try, endeavour, strive, seek, aim, make an effort**

attempt *NOUN*
*The pole vaulter cleared the bar at the first **attempt**.*
• **try, effort**
(informal) **shot, go**

attend *VERB*
*Are you going to **attend** the end-of-term concert?*
• **go to, appear at, be present at**
➤ **to attend to**
❶ *Please **attend** carefully **to** my instructions.*
• **listen to, pay attention to, follow carefully, heed, mark, mind, note, notice, observe, think about**
❷ *Who will **attend to** the washing up?*
• **deal with, see to**
❸ *The nurses **attended to** the wounded.*
• **take care of, care for, look after, help, mind, tend**

attention *NOUN*
❶ *Please give your full **attention** to the teacher.*
• **concentration, consideration, thought, observation, awareness, heed, concern**
❷ *The survivors need urgent medical **attention**.*
• **treatment, care**

attentive *ADJECTIVE*
*Drivers should be **attentive** at all times.*
• **alert, paying attention, watchful, vigilant, observant, careful, listening, on the alert, on the lookout, sharp-eyed, wary, wide awake**

attitude *NOUN*
*I'm trying to take a more positive **attitude** to life.*
• **outlook, approach, behaviour, stance, frame of mind, disposition, view, position, manner, mood**

attract *VERB*
❶ *Do you think our exhibition will **attract** people?*
• **interest, appeal to, fascinate, tempt, entice**
❷ *Baby animals **attract** big crowds at the zoo.*
• **draw, pull in**
OPPOSITE **repel**

attractive *ADJECTIVE*
❶ *Miranda was a very **attractive** young woman.*
• beautiful, pretty, good-looking, handsome, gorgeous, glamorous, striking, fetching, charming, lovely, delightful, pleasing, fascinating, captivating, enchanting
see also **beautiful**
OPPOSITES unattractive, repulsive
❷ *There are some **attractive** bargains in the sale.*
• appealing, agreeable, interesting, desirable, tempting, irresistible

audible *ADJECTIVE*
see **hear**

audience *NOUN*
*The **audience** were enthralled by the jugglers.*
• crowd, spectators
The audience for a TV programme is the **viewers**. The audience for a radio programme is the **listeners**.

authentic *ADJECTIVE*
❶ *That is an **authentic** painting by Picasso.*
• genuine, real, actual
OPPOSITE counterfeit
❷ *The book is an **authentic** account of life at sea.*
• accurate, truthful, reliable, true, honest, dependable, factual
OPPOSITE false

author *NOUN*
see **writer**

authority *NOUN*
❶ *I have the head's **authority** to go home early.*
• permission, consent, approval
❷ *The king had the **authority** to execute the prisoners.*
• power, right, influence
❸ *My uncle is an **authority** on steam trains.*
• expert, specialist

automatic *ADJECTIVE*
❶ *We took our car through the **automatic** car wash.*
• automated, mechanical, programmed, computerised
❷ *My sneezing was an **automatic** response to the pepper.*
• instinctive, involuntary, impulsive, spontaneous, reflex, natural, unconscious, unthinking

available *ADJECTIVE*
❶ *There are no more seats **available**.*
• obtainable, free
❷ *Is there a phone **available** in the library?*
• accessible, ready, usable, at hand, handy, within reach, convenient
OPPOSITE unavailable

average *ADJECTIVE*
*It was an **average** kind of day at school.*
• everyday, ordinary, normal, typical, usual, regular, commonplace, familiar
OPPOSITES unusual, extraordinary

avid *ADJECTIVE*
*My sister is an **avid** reader.*
• keen, eager, enthusiastic, passionate, ardent, fervent, zealous

avoid *VERB*
❶ *The driver tried hard to **avoid** the collision.*
• get out of the way of, avert, dodge, keep clear of, steer clear of, fend off, shun
❷ *The outlaws **avoided** capture for months.*
• elude, evade, run away from, escape from
❸ *How did you manage to **avoid** the washing up?*
• get out of, dodge, shirk

await *VERB*
*I **await** your reply to my letter.*
• wait for, look out for, be ready for, expect, hope for

awake *ADJECTIVE*
*Hester lay **awake** all night worrying.*
• wide awake, restless, sleepless, conscious, astir
Not being able to sleep is to be suffering from **insomnia**.
OPPOSITE asleep

A
B
C
D
E
F
G
H
I
J
K
L
M
N
O
P
Q
R
S
T
U
V
W
X
Y
Z

awaken VERB
❶ *Mum* ***awakened*** *us at seven.*
• **wake, waken, rouse, arouse, call, alert**
❷ *The dragon will* ***awaken*** *at dawn.*
• **wake up, become conscious, stir**

award NOUN
Kirsty got a national ***award*** *for gymnastics.*
• **prize, trophy, medal**

award VERB
My friend was ***awarded*** *first prize in the competition.*
• **give, present, grant**

aware ADJECTIVE
➤ **aware of**
The spy was ***aware of*** *the dangers of the mission.*
• **acquainted with, conscious of, familiar with, informed about**
OPPOSITE **ignorant of**

awful ADJECTIVE
❶ *The weather was* ***awful*** *last weekend.*
• **bad, dreadful, terrible, appalling, dire, abysmal**
(informal) **rubbish, lousy**
❷ *The teacher complained about our* ***awful*** *behaviour.*
• **disgraceful, shameful, disobedient, naughty**
❸ *Cinderella's stepmother was an* ***awful*** *woman.*
• **unpleasant, disagreeable, nasty, horrid, detestable, unkind, unfriendly**
❹ *The country was shocked by the* ***awful*** *crime.*
• **horrifying, shocking, atrocious, abominable, outrageous**
❺ *I feel* ***awful*** *about forgetting your birthday.*
• **sorry, ashamed, embarrassed, guilty, remorseful**
for other ways to describe something bad see **bad**

awkward ADJECTIVE
❶ *The parcel was an* ***awkward*** *shape.*
• **bulky, inconvenient, unmanageable, unwieldy**
OPPOSITE **convenient**
❷ *The giant was very* ***awkward*** *with his knife and fork.*
• **clumsy, unskilful, bungling**
OPPOSITE **skilful**
❸ *We found ourselves in a very* ***awkward*** *situation.*
• **difficult, troublesome, trying, perplexing, tough**
OPPOSITES **straightforward, easy**
❹ *Are you trying to be* ***awkward****?*
• **obstinate, stubborn, uncooperative, unhelpful, exasperating**
OPPOSITE **cooperative**
❺ *I felt* ***awkward*** *as I didn't know anyone at the party.*
• **embarrassed, uncomfortable, uneasy, out of place**
OPPOSITES **comfortable, at ease**

Bb

baby NOUN
• **infant, child**
A baby who has just been born is a **newborn**.
A baby just learning to walk is a **toddler**.
The time when someone is a baby is their **babyhood**.
for names of baby animals see **animal**

babyish ADJECTIVE
My brother thinks that dolls are ***babyish****.*
• **childish, immature, infantile**
OPPOSITES **grown-up, mature**

back NOUN
We always sit at the ***back*** *of the bus.*
• **end, rear, tail end**
The back of a ship is the **stern**.
The back of a piece of paper is the **reverse**.

The back of an animal is the **hindquarters, rear** or **rump.**
A fin or spine on the back of an animal is a **dorsal fin** or **spine.**
OPPOSITE front

back *ADJECTIVE*
*The **back** door of the cabin was locked.*
• end, rear, tail
The back legs of an animal are its **hind** legs.
OPPOSITE front

back *VERB*
❶ *A big lorry was **backing** into our driveway.*
• go backwards, reverse
❷ *I'm **backing** the blue team to win the race.*
• bet on, put money on
❸ *The council is **backing** the plan to build a skate park.*
• support, sponsor, endorse
➤ **to back away**
*When the dog growled, the robber **backed away.***
• back off, retreat, give way, retire, recoil
OPPOSITE approach
➤ **to back out of something**
*The injured player may have to **back out of** the final.*
• drop out of, withdraw from
➤ **to back someone up**
*Will you **back me up** if I need help?*
• support, second

background *NOUN*
❶ *I drew a mermaid with the sea in the **background.***
OPPOSITE foreground
❷ *The first chapter deals with the **background** to the war.*
• circumstances (of), history (of), lead-up (to)
❸ *My mother's family has a Swedish **background.***
• tradition, upbringing, ancestry

bad *ADJECTIVE*
*This has been a **bad** week for all of us.*
• awful, horrible, terrible
OPPOSITES good, fine, excellent

OVERUSED WORD

Try to vary the words you use for **bad**. Here are some other words you could use.

FOR A BAD PERSON OR BAD CREATURE:

• **wicked, evil, cruel, malevolent, malicious, vicious, villainous, mean, nasty, beastly, monstrous, corrupt, deplorable, detestable, immoral, infamous, shameful, sinful**
Beedle the Bard... rather liked Muggles, whom he regarded as ignorant rather than malevolent.—THE TALES OF BEEDLE THE BARD, J. K. Rowling
A bad person is a **scoundrel, rogue** or **rascal.**
A bad character in a story or film is a **villain** or *(informal)* **baddy.**
OPPOSITES good, virtuous

FOR A BAD ACCIDENT OR BAD ILLNESS:

• **serious, severe, grave, distressing, acute**
*Ingrid has a **severe** case of chickenpox.*
OPPOSITE minor

FOR BAD BEHAVIOUR:

• **naughty, mischievous, disobedient, disgraceful, wrong**
*That **mischievous** kitten drank my milk!*
OPPOSITES exemplary, angelic

FOR A BAD EXPERIENCE OR BAD NEWS:

• **unpleasant, unwelcome, disagreeable, horrible, awful, terrible, dreadful, horrific, appalling, shocking, hideous, disastrous, ghastly, frightful, abominable, diabolical**
*The letter contained **disagreeable** news.*
Another word for a bad experience is an **ordeal.**
OPPOSITES good, excellent

FOR A BAD HABIT OR SOMETHING THAT IS BAD FOR YOU:

• **harmful, damaging, dangerous, undesirable, detrimental, injurious**
*Fizzy drinks can be **harmful** to your teeth.*

A B C D E F G H I J K L M N O P Q R S T U V W X Y Z

FOR A BAD PERFORMANCE OR BAD WORK:

• poor, inferior, weak, unsatisfactory, inadequate, incompetent, awful, hopeless, terrible, useless, worthless, abysmal, shoddy
(informal) rubbish
The worst part of the film is the ***incompetent*** *acting.*

FOR A BAD SMELL OR BAD TASTE:

• disgusting, revolting, repulsive, sickening, nauseating, repugnant, foul, loathsome, offensive, vile
A ***nauseating*** *smell wafted from the kitchen.*
OPPOSITES pleasant, appetising

FOR BAD TIMING:

• inconvenient, unsuitable, unfortunate, inappropriate
You've caught me at an ***inconvenient*** *moment.*
OPPOSITES convenient, opportune

FOR BAD WEATHER:

• harsh, hostile, unfavourable, adverse, miserable
(informal) lousy
Penguins face ***hostile*** *weather in the Antarctic.*
OPPOSITES fine, favourable

FOR FOOD THAT HAS GONE BAD:

• mouldy, rotten, off, decayed, sour, spoiled, rancid
The strawberries have started to go ***mouldy.***
OPPOSITE fresh

TO FEEL BAD ABOUT SOMETHING:

• guilty, ashamed, sorry, remorseful, repentant
Scrooge feels ***repentant*** *by the end of the story.*
OPPOSITES unashamed, unrepentant

bad-tempered *ADJECTIVE*
Trolls are always ***bad-tempered*** *before breakfast.*
• cross, grumpy, irritable, moody, quarrelsome, fractious, ill-tempered, short-tempered, cantankerous, crotchety, snappy, testy, sullen
OPPOSITES good-tempered, cheerful

bag *NOUN*
I put my wet clothes in a plastic ***bag.***
• sack, carrier, holdall, satchel, handbag, shoulder bag
A bag you carry on your back is a **backpack** or **rucksack.**

baggage *NOUN*
We loaded our ***baggage*** *on to a trolley.*
• luggage, bags, cases, suitcases, belongings, things
(informal) gear, stuff

baggy *ADJECTIVE*
The clown wore a pair of ***baggy*** *trousers.*
• loose, loose-fitting, roomy

bake *VERB*
for ways to cook things see **cook**

balance *NOUN*
➤ **to lose your balance**
Rick ***lost his balance*** *and fell off the branch.*
• totter, wobble

bald *ADJECTIVE*
The ogre had a ***bald*** *patch on the top of his head.*
• bare, hairless
OPPOSITE hairy

ball *NOUN*
❶ *Wind the string into a* ***ball.***
• sphere, globe, orb
A small ball of something is a **pellet** or **globule.**
❷ *We kicked a* ***ball*** *about in the playground.*
for games played with a ball see **sport**

WRITING TIPS

You can use these words to describe how a ball moves or how you hit or throw a ball:
• arc, bounce, bowl, dribble, drive, fling, header, hurl, kick, lob, pitch, scoop, spin, strike, swerve, toss, volley; belt, blast, smash, sock, swipe, wham
*The ball **dribbled** into the back of the net.*
*Murray **smashed** the ball across the court.*

ban *VERB*
*Rollerblades are **banned** from the playground.*
• forbid, prohibit, bar, exclude, outlaw
OPPOSITES allow, permit

band *NOUN*
❶ *The king was surrounded by a **band** of courtiers.*
• company, group, gang, party, troop, crew
❷ *I play piano in the junior jazz **band**.*
• group, ensemble, orchestra
❸ *She wore a **band** of velvet ribbon.*
• strip, stripe, ring, line, belt, hoop

bandage *NOUN*
*You need a **bandage** on that knee.*
• dressing, plaster, gauze, lint

bandit *NOUN*
***Bandits** used to live in these mountains.*
• robber, brigand, thief, outlaw, desperado, highwayman, pirate, buccaneer

bang *NOUN*
❶ *There was a loud **bang** as the balloon burst.*
• blast, boom, crash, thud, thump, pop, explosion, report
for other types of noise see **sound**
❷ *He got a **bang** on the head from the low ceiling.*
• bump, blow, hit, knock, thump, punch, smack, whack, clout
(informal) wallop

bang *VERB*
*Miss Crabbit **banged** her fist on the desk and scowled.*
• hit, thump, strike, bash, slam, wham

banish *VERB*
*The king's brother was **banished** forever.*
• exile, expel, deport, send away, eject

bank *NOUN*
❶ *The temple was built on the **banks** of the River Nile.*
• edge, side, shore, margin, brink
❷ *We rolled our Easter eggs down a grassy **bank**.*
• slope, mound, ridge, embankment

banner *NOUN*
*The turrets were decorated with colourful **banners**.*
• flag, standard, streamer, pennant

banquet *NOUN*
*There was a **banquet** on the queen's birthday.*
• dinner, feast

bar *NOUN*
❶ *Did you eat the whole **bar** of chocolate?*
• block, slab, chunk, wedge
A bar of gold or silver is an **ingot**.
A bar of soap is a **cake**.
❷ *The window had iron **bars** across it.*
• rod, pole, rail, stake, beam, girder

bar *VERB*
❶ *Two athletes were **barred** from competing in the race.*
• ban, prohibit, exclude, keep out
❷ *A fallen tree **barred** our way.*
• block, hinder, impede, obstruct, stop, check

bare *ADJECTIVE*
❶ *I put suncream on my **bare** arms and legs.*
• naked, nude, exposed, uncovered, unclothed, undressed
❷ *The wolf had a **bare** patch on its back.*
• bald, hairless

a b c d e f g h i j k l m n o p q r s t u v w x y z

A B C D E F G H I J K L M N O P Q R S T U V W X Y Z

❸ *We slept outside on the **bare** mountain.*
• **barren, bleak, treeless**
❹ *Inside, the dungeon was cold and **bare**.*
• **empty, unfurnished, vacant**
❺ *There wasn't a **bare** patch of wall left.*
• **blank, plain, clear, empty**
❻ *There is only room to pack the **bare** essentials.*
• **basic, minimum**

barely *ADVERB*
*We **barely** had time to get dressed.*
• **hardly, scarcely, only just**

bargain *NOUN*
❶ *We made a **bargain** with the captain to take us ashore.*
• **deal, agreement, promise, pact**
❷ *That camera you bought was a **bargain**.*
• **good buy, special offer**
(informal) **snip, steal**

bargain *VERB*
*He refused to **bargain** with the pirates for his life.*
• **argue, do a deal, haggle, negotiate**

barge *VERB*
➤ **to barge into**
❶ *A woman **barged into** me with her shopping trolley.*
• **bump into, collide with, veer into**
❷ *A messenger **barged** breathlessly **into** the room.*
• **push into, rush into, storm into**

bark *VERB*
*The guard dog began to **bark** fiercely.*
• **woof, yap, yelp, growl**
for other animal noises see **animal**

barrel *NOUN*
*The smugglers carried **barrels** of gunpowder.*
• **cask, drum, tub, keg, butt**

barren *ADJECTIVE*
*Pictures show the surface of Mars as a **barren** landscape.*
• **dry, dried-up, arid, bare, waste, lifeless, infertile, sterile**
OPPOSITES **fertile, lush**

barrier *NOUN*
❶ *Spectators were asked to stay behind the **barrier**.*
• **wall, fence, railing, barricade**
A barrier across a road is a **roadblock**.
❷ *His shyness was a **barrier** to making friends.*
• **obstacle, hurdle, drawback, handicap, hindrance, stumbling block**

base *NOUN*
❶ *The footprints stop at the **base** of the pyramid.*
• **bottom, foot**
❷ *The doll's house comes with a wooden **base**.*
• **foundation, support**
A base under a statue is a **pedestal** or **plinth**.
❸ *The mountaineers returned to their **base**.*
• **headquarters, camp, depot**

basement *NOUN*
• **cellar, vault**
A room underneath a church is a **crypt**.
An underground cell in a castle is a **dungeon**.
for other parts of a building see **building**

basic *ADJECTIVE*
❶ *These are the **basic** moves in ice-skating.*
• **main, chief, principal, key, central, essential, fundamental, crucial**
❷ *My knowledge of French is very **basic**.*
• **elementary, simple**
OPPOSITE **advanced**

basically *ADVERB*
***Basically**, I think you're right.*
• **essentially, in essence, at heart, fundamentally**

basin *NOUN*
*Fill a **basin** with soapy water.*
• **sink, bowl, dish**

basis *NOUN*
*What is the **basis** of your argument?*
• **base, core, foundation**

basket *NOUN*
A basket of food is a **hamper**.
A basket on a bicycle is a **pannier**.
A small basket of strawberries is a **punnet**.

bat *NOUN*
*A **bat** is used to hit the ball in cricket and baseball.*
In golf, you hit the ball with a **club**.
In snooker, you hit it with a **cue**.
In tennis, you hit it with a **racket**.
In hockey, you hit it with a **stick**.

batch *NOUN*
*Mum made a fresh **batch** of pancakes.*
• **lot, bunch, amount, quantity**

bathe *VERB*
❶ *It was too cold to **bathe** in the sea.*
• **swim, go swimming, splash about, take a dip**
To walk about in shallow water is to **paddle**.
To walk through deep water is to **wade**.
❷ *The nurse gently **bathed** the wound.*
• **clean, cleanse, wash, rinse**

batter *VERB*
*The prisoner **battered** his fists against the door.*
• **beat, pound, thump, pummel**

battle *NOUN*
*The **battle** raged for many months.*
• **fight, clash, conflict, action, engagement, hostilities, struggle**

bay *NOUN*
*Dolphins were swimming in the **bay**.*
• **cove, inlet, gulf, harbour, sound**

be *VERB* **am, are, is; was, were; being, been**
❶ *I'll **be** at home all morning.*
• **stay, continue, remain**
❷ *The concert will **be** in March.*
• **take place, happen, come about, occur**
❸ *She wants to **be** a famous writer.*
• **become, develop into**

beach *NOUN*
*We found these shells on the **beach**.*
• **sands, seashore, seaside, shore**
for things you might see or do on a beach see also **seashore, seaside**

bead *NOUN*
❶ *Sylvia wore a string of coral **beads**.*
for items of jewellery see **jewel**
❷ *The explorer wiped **beads** of sweat from his brow.*
• **blob, drop, droplet, drip, pearl**

beam *NOUN*
❶ *Wooden **beams** ran across the ceiling.*
• **bar, timber, joist, plank, post, rafter, spar, strut, support**
❷ *A **beam** of sunlight entered the cave.*
• **ray, shaft, stream, gleam**
A strong narrow beam of light used in various devices is a **laser**.

beam *VERB*
❶ *In the photo, we are all **beaming** at the camera.*
• **smile, grin**
OPPOSITES **frown, scowl**
❷ *The satellite will **beam** a signal back to Earth.*
• **transmit, send out, broadcast, emit**

bean *NOUN*
see **vegetable**

bear *NOUN*

WORD WEB

SOME TYPES OF BEAR:
• **black bear, brown bear, grizzly bear, polar bear**
A young bear is a **cub**.
A bear lives in a **den** and **hibernates** in winter.
Animals rather like bears are the **koala** and **giant panda**.
A toy bear is a **teddy bear**.
for other animals see **animal**

A B C D E F G H I J K L M N O P Q R S T U V W X Y Z

bear *VERB* **bears, bearing, bore, born** or **borne**
❶ *The rope won't* **bear** *my weight.*
• **carry, support, hold, take**
❷ *The messenger* **bore** *a letter from the king.*
• **bring, carry, convey, transport, take, transfer**
❸ *The gravestone* **bears** *an old inscription.*
• **display, show, have**
❹ *The stench in the cave was too much to* **bear**.
• **put up with, cope with, stand, suffer, tolerate, endure, abide**
❺ *The lioness has* **borne** *three cubs.*
• **give birth to**

bearable *ADJECTIVE*
The temperature at midday is high, but **bearable**.
• **tolerable, endurable, acceptable**
OPPOSITE **unbearable**

beast *NOUN*
In the darkness, they heard a wild **beast** *howl.*
• **animal, creature**
You might call a large or frightening beast a **brute** or **monster**.
for mythological beasts see **myth**

beat *VERB* **beats, beating, beat, beaten**
❶ *It's cruel to* **beat** *an animal with a stick.*
• **hit, strike, thrash, batter, whip, lash, flog**
(informal) **whack, wallop**
for other ways of hitting see **hit**
❷ *I* **beat** *my brother at chess for the first time.*
• **defeat, conquer, vanquish, win against, get the better of, overcome, overwhelm, rout, thrash, trounce**
(informal) **hammer**
❸ **Beat** *the eggs, milk and sugar together.*
• **whisk, whip, blend, mix, stir**
❹ *Can you feel your heart* **beating**?
• **pound, thump, palpitate**
➤ **to beat someone up**
The bully threatened to **beat me up**.
• **assault, attack**

beat *NOUN*
❶ *Can you feel the* **beat** *of your heart?*
• **pulse, throb**
❷ *Reggae music has a strong* **beat**.
• **rhythm, accent, stress**

beautiful *ADJECTIVE*

OVERUSED WORD

Try to vary the words you use for **beautiful**. Here are some other words you could use.

FOR A BEAUTIFUL PERSON:

• **attractive, good-looking, pretty, gorgeous, glamorous, radiant, elegant, enchanting, dazzling, stunning, magnificent, resplendent**
This balcony belonged to an attractive middle-aged lady called Mrs Silver … And although she didn't know it, it was she who was the object of Mr Hoppy's secret love.
—ESIO TROT, Roald Dahl
A man who is pleasing to look at is **good-looking** or **handsome**.
OPPOSITES **ugly, unattractive**

FOR A BEAUTIFUL DAY OR BEAUTIFUL WEATHER:

• **fine, excellent, glorious, marvellous, sunny, superb, splendid, wonderful**
It was a **glorious** *day for a bicycle trip.*
OPPOSITES **dull, gloomy, drab**

FOR A BEAUTIFUL SIGHT:

• **glorious, magnificent, splendid, spectacular, picturesque, scenic**
The Northern Lights are a **spectacular** *sight.*

FOR A BEAUTIFUL SOUND:

• **harmonious, melodious, mellifluous, sweet-sounding**
The nightingale has a **sweet-sounding** *song.*
OPPOSITE **grating**

beauty *NOUN*
The film star was famous for her ***beauty****.*
• **attractiveness, prettiness, loveliness, charm, allure, magnificence, radiance, splendour**
OPPOSITE **ugliness**

beckon *VERB*
The guard was ***beckoning*** *me to approach.*
• **signal, gesture, motion, gesticulate**

become *VERB* **becomes, becoming, became, become**
❶ *I soon* ***became*** *frustrated with the video game.*
• **begin to be, turn, get**
❷ *Eventually, the tadpoles will* ***become*** *frogs.*
• **grow into, change into, develop into, turn into**
❸ *That style of hat* ***becomes*** *you.*
• **look good on, suit, flatter**

bed *NOUN*
❶ *The children slept on hard, wooden* ***beds****.*
• **bunk, mattress**
A bed for a baby is a **cot, cradle** or **crib**.
Two single beds one above the other are **bunk beds**.
A bed on a ship or train is a **berth**.
A bed made of net or cloth hung up above the ground is a **hammock**.
❷ *We planted daffodils in the flower* ***beds****.*
• **plot, patch, border**
❸ *These creatures feed on the* ***bed*** *of the ocean.*
• **bottom, floor**
OPPOSITE **surface**

bedraggled *ADJECTIVE*
After its swim, the puppy was wet and ***bedraggled****.*
• **messy, scruffy, untidy, dishevelled, dirty, wet**
OPPOSITES **smart, spruced up**

bee *NOUN*

WORD WEB

SOME TYPES OF BEE:
• **bumblebee, drone, honeybee, worker, queen**
A young bee after it hatches is a **larva**.
A group of bees is a **swarm** or a **colony**.
A place where bees live is a **hive**.
A person who owns bees and collects their honey is a **beekeeper**.
for other insects see **insect**

before *ADVERB*
❶ *Have you used a camera* ***before****?*
• **previously, in the past, earlier, sooner**
OPPOSITE **later**
❷ *Those people were* ***before*** *us in the queue.*
• **in front of, ahead of, in advance of**
OPPOSITE **after**

beg *VERB*
He ***begged*** *me not to let go of the rope.*
• **ask, plead with, entreat, implore, beseech**

begin *VERB* **begins, beginning, began, begun**
❶ *The hunters* ***began*** *their search at dawn.*
• **start, commence, embark on, set about**
OPPOSITES **end, finish, conclude**
❷ *When did the trouble* ***begin****?*
• **start, commence, arise, emerge, appear, originate, spring up**
OPPOSITES **end, stop, cease**

beginner *NOUN*
This swimming class is for ***beginners****.*
• **learner, starter, novice**
A beginner in a trade or a job is an **apprentice** or **trainee**.
A beginner in the police or armed services is a **cadet** or **recruit**.

beginning *NOUN*
The house was built at the ***beginning*** *of the last century.*

A B C D E F G H I J K L M N O P Q R S T U V W X Y Z

• start, opening, commencement, introduction, establishment, foundation, initiation, launch, dawn
The beginning of the day is **dawn** or **daybreak**.
The beginning of a journey is the **starting point**.
The beginning of a stream or river is the **origin** or **source**.
A piece of writing at the beginning of a book is an **introduction, preface** or **prologue**.
A piece of music at the beginning of a musical or opera is a **prelude** or **overture**.
OPPOSITES end, conclusion

behave *VERB*
*Our neighbour is **behaving** very strangely.*
• act, react
➤ **to behave yourself**
*We promised to **behave ourselves** in the car.*
• be good, be on your best behaviour

behaviour *NOUN*
*I give my puppy treats for good **behaviour**.*
• actions, conduct, manners, attitude

being *NOUN*
*They looked like **beings** from another planet.*
• creature, individual, person, entity

belch *VERB*
*The chimney **belched** clouds of black smoke.*
• discharge, emit, send out, gush, spew

belief *NOUN*
❶ *She was a woman of strong religious beliefs.*
• faith, principle, creed, doctrine
❷ *It is my **belief** that he stole the money.*
• opinion, view, conviction, feeling, notion, theory

believable *ADJECTIVE*
*None of the characters in the book is **believable**.*
• credible, plausible
OPPOSITES unbelievable, implausible

believe *VERB*
❶ *I don't **believe** anything he says.*
• accept, have faith in, rely on, trust
OPPOSITES disbelieve, doubt
❷ *I **believe** they used to live in Canada.*
• think, assume, feel, presume, reckon, suppose

bell *NOUN*

WRITING TIPS

You can use these words to describe how a bell sounds:
• chime, clang, jangle, jingle, peal, ring, tinkle, toll
The front-door bell clanged loudly, and the Rat, who was very greasy with buttered toast, sent Billy, the smaller hedgehog, to see who it might be.—THE WIND IN THE WILLOWS, Kenneth Grahame

belong *VERB*
❶ *This ring **belonged** to my grandmother.*
• be owned by
❷ *Do you **belong** to the sports club?*
• be a member of, be connected with

belongings *PLURAL NOUN*
*Don't leave any **belongings** on the bus.*
• possessions, property, goods, things

below *PREPOSITION*
❶ *We saw goldfish swimming **below** the surface.*
• under, underneath, beneath
❷ *The temperature never fell **below** 20 degrees.*
• less than, lower than
OPPOSITE above

belt *NOUN*
❶ *The prince wore a **belt** of pure gold.*
• girdle, sash, strap, band
❷ *We walked through a **belt** of woodland.*
• strip, band, line, stretch

bench *NOUN*
We sat on a ***bench*** *in the park.*
• seat, form
A long seat in a church is a **pew**.
for other types of seat see **seat**

bend *VERB*
This drinking straw ***bends*** *in the middle.*
• curve, turn, twist, curl, coil, loop, arch, warp, wind
A word to describe things which bend easily is **flexible** or *(informal)* **bendy**.
OPPOSITE **straighten**
➤ **to bend down**
I ***bent down*** *to tie my shoelaces.*
• stoop, bow *(rhymes with* **cow***)*, crouch, duck, kneel

bend *NOUN*
Watch out for the sharp ***bend*** *in the road.*
• curve, turn, angle, corner, twist, zigzag

beneath *PREPOSITION*
The tunnel ran ***beneath*** *the castle.*
• under, underneath, below
OPPOSITES **above, over**

beneficial *ADJECTIVE*
Drinking water is ***beneficial*** *to your health.*
• favourable, useful, advantageous, salutary
OPPOSITES **harmful, detrimental**

benefit *NOUN*
What are the ***benefits*** *of regular exercise?*
• advantage, reward, gain, good point
OPPOSITES **disadvantage, drawback**

benefit *VERB*
The rainy weather will ***benefit*** *gardeners.*
• help, aid, assist, be good for, profit
OPPOSITES **hinder, harm**

benevolent *ADJECTIVE*
The lady greeted us with a ***benevolent*** *smile.*
• friendly, kind, warm-hearted, sympathetic, generous, charitable, benign
OPPOSITE **malevolent**

bent *ADJECTIVE*
❶ *After the crash, the car was a mass of* ***bent*** *metal.*
• curved, twisted, coiled, looped, buckled, crooked, arched, folded, warped
(informal) **wonky**
❷ *The witch had a* ***bent*** *back and walked with a stick.*
• crooked, hunched, curved, arched, bowed *(rhymes with* **loud***)*
OPPOSITE **straight**

beside *PREPOSITION*
You can sit ***beside*** *me if you like.*
• next to, alongside, by, close to, near
➤ **beside the point**
The fact that you're ill is ***beside the point****.*
• irrelevant, neither here nor there, unimportant

besides *ADVERB*
❶ *No-one knows the secret,* ***besides*** *you and me.*
• as well as, in addition to, apart from, other than
❷ *It's too cold to go out.* ***Besides****, it's dark now.*
• also, in addition, additionally, furthermore, moreover

besiege *VERB*
❶ *The Greeks* ***besieged*** *Troy for 10 long years.*
• blockade, cut off, isolate
❷ *The film star was* ***besieged*** *by reporters.*
• surround, mob, plague, harass

best *ADJECTIVE*
❶ *She is our* ***best*** *goalkeeper.*
• top, leading, finest, foremost, supreme, star, outstanding, unequalled, unrivalled
OPPOSITE **worst**
❷ *We did what we thought was* ***best****.*
• most suitable, most appropriate

bet *NOUN*
I had a ***bet*** *that our team would win.*
• gamble, wager
(informal) **flutter**

a b c d e f g h i j k l m n o p q r s t u v w x y z

A B C D E F G H I J K L M N O P Q R S T U V W X Y Z

bet *VERB* **bets, betting, bet** or **betted**
❶ *I* ***bet*** *you 50 pence that it will snow tomorrow.*
• **gamble, wager, stake, risk**
❷ *I bet my brother forgets my birthday.*
• **feel sure, be certain, expect**

betray *VERB*
❶ *He* ***betrayed*** *us by telling the enemy our plan.*
• **be disloyal to, be a traitor to, cheat, conspire against, double-cross**
Someone who betrays you is a **traitor**.
To betray your country is to commit **treason**.
❷ *The look in her eyes* ***betrayed*** *her true feelings.*
• **reveal, show, indicate, disclose, divulge, expose, tell**

better *ADJECTIVE*
❶ *Which of these songs do you think is better?*
• **superior, finer, preferable**
❷ *I had a cold, but I'm* ***better*** *now.*
• **recovered, cured, healed, improved, well**

between *PREPOSITION*
Let's divide the chocolate ***between*** *us.*
• **among, amongst**

beware *VERB*
Beware! There are thieves about.
• **be careful, watch out, look out, take care, be on your guard**
➤ **beware of**
Beware of the bull.
• **watch out for, avoid, mind, heed, keep clear of**

bewilder *VERB*
We were ***bewildered*** *by the directions on the map.*
• **confuse, puzzle, baffle, bemuse, mystify, perplex, fox**
(informal) **flummox**

beyond *PREPOSITION*
The village lies just ***beyond*** *those hills.*
• **after, past, the other side of**

biased *ADJECTIVE*
A referee should not make a ***biased*** *decision.*
• **prejudiced, partial, one-sided, partisan, unfair**
OPPOSITE **impartial**

bicycle *NOUN*
(informal) **bike, push bike**

WORD WEB

A person who rides a bicycle is a **cyclist**.
An indoor arena for bicycle racing is a **velodrome**.

SOME TYPES OF BICYCLE:

• **mountain bike, racing bike, reclining** or **recumbent bike, road bike, tandem, trailer bike**
A cycle with one wheel is a **unicycle**.
A cycle with three wheels is a **tricycle** or *(informal)* **trike**.
A cycle without pedals is a **scooter**.
A type of bicycle used in the past was a **penny-farthing**.

THE MAIN PARTS OF A BICYCLE ARE:

• **brakes, brake lever, chain, crossbar, gear shift, handlebars, pedals, saddle**

bid *NOUN*
❶ *There were several* ***bids*** *for the painting at the auction.*
• **offer, price, tender**
❷ *His* ***bid*** *to beat the world record failed.*
• **attempt, effort, try, go**

big *ADJECTIVE*

OVERUSED WORD

Try to vary the words you use for **big**. Here are some other words you could use.

FOR SOMETHING BIG IN SIZE OR WEIGHT:

• **large, huge, enormous, massive, great, gigantic, colossal, mammoth, overgrown**
(informal) **whopping, ginormous, humungous**
OPPOSITES **small, little, tiny**
The Dragon Stoorworm ... was absolutely ginormous and almost completely covered Scotland, from the top to the bottom, and all the way across from side to side.—THE DRAGON STOORWORM, Theresa Breslin

FOR A BIG PERSON OR BIG CREATURE:

• **giant, hefty, hulking, burly, mighty, monstrous, towering**
The Trunchbull, this mighty female giant, stood there in her green breeches, quivering like a blancmange.—MATILDA, Road Dahl

FOR A BIG DISTANCE OR BIG AREA:

• **immense, vast, infinite**
A ***vast*** *stretch of ocean lay before them.*

FOR SOMETHING BIG INSIDE:

• **roomy, spacious, sizeable**
Inside, the spaceship was surprisingly ***roomy****.*
OPPOSITE **cramped**

FOR A BIG AMOUNT OR BIG HELPING:

• **ample, considerable, substantial**
We each got an ***ample*** *helping of porridge.*
OPPOSITES **meagre, paltry**

FOR A BIG DECISION OR BIG MOMENT:

• **important, significant, serious, grave**
Yesterday was the most ***significant*** *day in my short life.*
OPPOSITES **unimportant, minor**

bill *NOUN*

My granny offered to pay the ***bill****.*
• **account, invoice, statement, charges**

billow *VERB*

❶ *Smoke* ***billowed*** *from the mouth of the cave.*
• **pour, swirl, spiral**
❷ *The sheets on the washing line* ***billowed*** *in the wind.*
• **swell, bulge, puff, balloon**

bind *VERB* **binds, binding, bound**

We ***bound*** *the sticks together with some rope.*
• **attach, fasten, tie, secure, join, connect, lash, rope**

bird *NOUN*

WORD WEB

A female bird is a **hen**.
A male bird is a **cock**.
A young bird is a **chick, fledgling** or **nestling**.
A family of chicks is a **brood**.
A group of birds is a **colony** or **flock**.
A group of flying birds is a **flight** or **skein**.
A person who studies birds is an **ornithologist**.

SOME COMMON BRITISH BIRDS:

• **blackbird, blue tit, bullfinch, bunting, chaffinch, crow, cuckoo, dove, greenfinch, jackdaw, jay, lark, linnet, magpie, martin, nightingale, pigeon, raven, robin, rook, skylark, sparrow, starling, swallow, swift, thrush, tit, wagtail, waxwing, woodpecker, wren, yellowhammer**

BIRDS OF PREY:

• **buzzard, eagle, falcon, hawk, kestrel, kite, merlin, osprey, owl, sparrowhawk, vulture**

FARM AND GAME BIRDS:

• **chicken, duck, goose, grouse, partridge, pheasant, quail, turkey**
Birds kept by farmers are called **poultry**.

SEA AND WATER BIRDS:

• **albatross, auk, bittern, coot, cormorant, crane, curlew, duck, gannet, goose, guillemot, gull, heron, kingfisher, kittiwake, lapwing, mallard, moorhen, oystercatcher, peewit, pelican, penguin, puffin, seagull, snipe, stork, swan, teal**

BIRDS FROM OTHER COUNTRIES:

• **bird of paradise, budgerigar, canary, cockatoo, flamingo, hummingbird, ibis, kookaburra, macaw, mynah bird, parakeet, parrot, toucan**

BIRDS WHICH CANNOT FLY:

• **emu, kiwi, ostrich, peacock, penguin**

PARTS OF A BIRD'S BODY:

• **beak, bill, claw, talon, breast, crown, throat, crest, feather, down, plumage, plume, wing**
see also **feather**

SOME TYPES OF BIRD HOME:

• **nest, nesting box, aviary, coop, roost**

SOUNDS MADE BY BIRDS:

• **cackle, caw, cheep, chirp, chirrup, cluck, coo, crow, gabble, honk, peep, pipe, quack, screech, squawk, trill, tweet, twitter, warble**
A turkey **gobbles**.
An owl **hoots**.

SPECIAL NAMES:

A female peacock is a **peahen**.
A young duck is a **duckling**.
A young goose is a **gosling**.
A young puffin is a **puffling**.
A young swan is a **cygnet**.
An eagle's nest is an **eyrie**.
A place where rooks nest is a **rookery**.
for groups of birds see **group**

WRITING TIPS

You can use these words to describe a **bird**:

TO DESCRIBE HOW A BIRD MOVES:

• **circle, dart, flit, flutter, fly, glide, hop, hover, peck, perch, preen, skim, soar, swoop, waddle, wheel**
The post owls arrived, swooping down through rain-flecked windows, scattering everyone with droplets of water.—HARRY POTTER AND THE HALF-BLOOD PRINCE, J. K. Rowling

TO DESCRIBE A BIRD'S FEATHERS:

• **bedraggled, downy, drab, fluffy, gleaming, iridescent, ruffled, smooth, speckled**
The peacock displayed its ***iridescent*** *tail.*

bit *NOUN*

❶ *Mum divided the cake into eight* ***bits****.*
• **piece, portion, part, section, segment, share, slice**
❷ *These jeans are a* ***bit*** *long for me.*
• **a little, slightly, rather, fairly, somewhat, quite**

OVERUSED WORD

Try to vary the words you use for **bit**. Here are some other words you could use.

FOR A LARGE BIT OF SOMETHING:

• **chunk, lump, hunk, wedge, slab**
And they all went over to the tunnel entrance and began scooping out great chunks of juicy, golden-coloured peach flesh.—JAMES AND THE GIANT PEACH, Road Dahl

FOR A SMALL BIT OF SOMETHING:

• **fragment, scrap, chip, particle, speck, sliver, pinch, touch, dab, atom, iota** *(informal)* **smidgen**
The map was drawn on a ***scrap*** *of old paper.*

FOR A BIT OF FOOD:

• **morsel, crumb, bite, nibble, taste, mouthful**
Please try a ***morsel*** *of chocolate mousse.*

FOR A BIT OF LIQUID:

• **drop, dash, dribble, splash, spot**
Add a ***splash*** *of vinegar to the sauce.*

bite *VERB* **bites, biting, bit, bitten**
❶ *I* ***bit*** *a chunk out of my apple.*
• **munch, nibble, chew, crunch, gnaw**
(informal) **chomp**
for other ways to eat see **eat**
❷ *Take care. These animals can* ***bite.***
• **nip, pinch, pierce, wound**
When an animal tries to bite you it **snaps** at you.
When an insect bites you it **stings** you.
A fierce animal **mauls** or **savages** its prey.

bitter *ADJECTIVE*
❶ *The medicine had a* ***bitter*** *taste.*
• **sour, sharp, acid, acrid, tart**
OPPOSITE **sweet**
❷ *His brother was still* ***bitter*** *about the quarrel.*
• **resentful, embittered, disgruntled, aggrieved**
OPPOSITE **contented**
❸ *The wind blowing in from the sea was* ***bitter.***
• **biting, cold, freezing, icy, piercing, raw, wintry**
(informal) **perishing**
OPPOSITE **mild**

bizarre *ADJECTIVE*
'Whiskers' is a ***bizarre*** *name for a goldfish!*
• **odd, strange, peculiar, weird, extraordinary, outlandish**
OPPOSITE **ordinary**

black *ADJECTIVE, NOUN*
The pony had a shiny ***black*** *coat.*
• **coal-black, jet-black, pitch-black, ebony, raven**

You can also describe a black night as **pitch-dark.**
Someone in a bad mood is said to look **as black as thunder.**
Common similes are **as black as coal** and **as black as night.**

blame *VERB*
Don't ***blame*** *me if you miss the bus.*
• **accuse, criticise, condemn, reproach, scold**

bland *ADJECTIVE*
This cheese has a really ***bland*** *taste.*
• **mild, dull, weak, insipid**
OPPOSITES **strong, pungent**

blank *ADJECTIVE*
❶ *There are no* ***blank*** *pages left in my jotter.*
• **empty, bare, clean, plain, unmarked, unused**
❷ *The old woman gave us a* ***blank*** *look.*
• **expressionless, faceless, vacant**

blank *NOUN*
Fill in the ***blanks*** *to complete the sentence.*
• **space, break, gap**

blanket *NOUN*
❶ *The baby was wrapped in a woollen* ***blanket.***
• **cover, sheet, quilt, rug, throw**
❷ *A* ***blanket*** *of snow covered the lawn.*
• **covering, layer, film, sheet, mantle**

blast *NOUN*
❶ *A* ***blast*** *of cold air came through the door.*
• **gust, rush, draught, burst**
❷ *They heard the* ***blast*** *of a trumpet.*
• **blare, noise, roar**
❸ *Many people were injured in the* ***blast.***
• **explosion, shock**

blatant *ADJECTIVE*
Do you expect me to believe such a ***blatant*** *lie?*
• **barefaced, flagrant, obvious, shameless, brazen, unabashed**

blaze *NOUN*
Firefighters fought the ***blaze*** *for hours.*
• **fire, flames, inferno**

A B C D E F G H I J K L M N O P Q R S T U V W X Y Z

blaze *VERB*
Within a few minutes the campfire was blazing.
• **burn brightly, flare up**

bleak *ADJECTIVE*
❶ *The countryside was **bleak** and barren.*
• **bare, barren, desolate, empty, exposed, stark**
❷ *The future looks **bleak** for the club.*
• **gloomy, hopeless, depressing, dismal, grim, miserable**
OPPOSITE **promising**

blemish *NOUN*
*This peach has a **blemish** on the skin.*
• **fault, flaw, defect, imperfection, mark, spot, stain**

blend *VERB*
❶ ***Blend** the flour with a tablespoon of water.*
• **beat together, mix, stir together, whip, whisk**
❷ *The paint colours **blend** well with each other.*
• **go together, match, fit, harmonise**
OPPOSITE **clash**

blessing *NOUN*
❶ *The author gave the film her **blessing**.*
• **approval, backing, support, consent, permission**
OPPOSITE **disapproval**
❷ *A warm hat is a **blessing** in cold weather.*
• **benefit, advantage, gift, asset, comfort**
OPPOSITES **curse, evil**

blew *past tense see* **blow**

blight *NOUN*
*The tower block is a **blight** on the landscape.*
• **menace, nuisance, affliction, curse, evil, plague**

blind *ADJECTIVE*
*Polar bear cubs are born **blind**.*
• **sightless, unsighted, unseeing**
A common simile is **as blind as a bat**.
OPPOSITES **sighted, seeing**

➤ **blind to**
*The captain was **blind to** his own faults.*
• **ignorant of, unaware of, oblivious to**
OPPOSITE **aware of**

bliss *NOUN*
*Having a whole day off school was sheer **bliss**.*
• **joy, delight, pleasure, happiness, heaven, ecstasy**
OPPOSITE **misery**

blob *NOUN*
*The alien left **blobs** of green slime on the carpet.*
• **drop, lump, spot, dollop, daub, globule**

block *NOUN*
❶ *A **block** of ice fell from the glacier.*
• **chunk, hunk, lump, piece**
❷ *There must be a **block** in the drainpipe.*
• **blockage, jam, obstacle, obstruction**

block *VERB*
❶ *A tall hedge **blocked** our view of the house.*
• **obstruct, hamper, hinder, interfere with**
❷ *A mass of leaves had **blocked** the drain.*
• **clog, choke, jam, plug, stop up, congest** *(informal)* **bung up**

blockage *NOUN*
*Dad spent ages clearing the **blockage** in the drain.*
• **block, obstacle, obstruction, jam**

bloodshed *NOUN*
*In ancient times, this was a scene of **bloodshed**.*
• **killing, massacre, slaughter, butchery, carnage**

bloodthirsty *ADJECTIVE*
*The **bloodthirsty** pirates rattled their swords.*
• **brutal, cruel, barbaric, murderous, inhuman, pitiless, ruthless, savage, vicious**

bloom *NOUN*
*The pear tree was covered in white **blooms**.*
• **flower, blossom, bud**
WHICH WORD? Note that a **bloom** is a single flower. A mass of flowers is **blossom**.

bloom *VERB*
*The daffodils **bloomed** early this year.*
• blossom, flower, open
OPPOSITE fade

blossom *NOUN*
*I love to see the cherry **blossom** in spring.*
• blooms, buds, flowers
WHICH WORD? Note that **blossom** usually means a mass of flowers. A single flower is a **bloom**.

blot *NOUN*
*The old map was covered with ink **blots**.*
• spot, blotch, mark, blob, splodge, smudge, smear, stain

blot *VERB*
➤ **to blot something out**
*The new tower block **blots out** the view.*
• conceal, hide, mask, obliterate, obscure

blotch *NOUN*
*The dragon had green skin with purple **blotches**.*
• patch, blot, spot, mark, blob, splodge, splash, stain

blow *NOUN*
❶ *He was knocked out by a **blow** on the head.*
• knock, bang, bash, hit, punch, clout, slap, smack, swipe, thump
(informal) wallop, whack
❷ *Losing the hockey match was a terrible **blow**.*
• shock, upset, setback, disappointment, catastrophe, misfortune, disaster, calamity

blow *VERB* **blows, blowing, blew, blown**
*The wind was **blowing** from the east.*
• blast, gust, puff, fan
To make a shrill sound by blowing is to **whistle**.
➤ **to blow out**
*I **blew out** the candles on my birthday cake.*
• extinguish
➤ **to blow up**
❶ *I need to **blow up** the tyres on my bike.*
• inflate, pump up, swell, fill out
❷ *The soldiers tried to **blow up** the enemy hideout.*
• blast, bomb, destroy
❸ *Do you think they could **blow up** this photograph?*
• enlarge

blue *ADJECTIVE, NOUN*

WORD WEB

SOME SHADES OF BLUE:
• azure, cobalt, indigo, navy blue, sapphire, sky-blue, turquoise

blunder *NOUN*
*Forgetting her birthday was a terrible **blunder**.*
• mistake, error, fault, slip, slip-up, gaffe
(informal) howler

blunt *ADJECTIVE*
❶ *This pencil is **blunt**.*
• dull, worn, unsharpened
OPPOSITES sharp, pointed
❷ *Her reply to my question was very **blunt**.*
• abrupt, frank, direct, outspoken, plain, tactless
OPPOSITE tactful

blur *VERB*
❶ *The steamy windows **blurred** the view.*
• cloud, darken, obscure, smear
❷ *The accident **blurred** her memory.*
• confuse, muddle

blurred *ADJECTIVE*
*The background of the photograph is all **blurred**.*
• indistinct, vague, blurry, fuzzy, hazy, out of focus
OPPOSITES clear, distinct

blush *VERB*
*The actor **blushed** with embarrassment.*
• flush, go red, colour

blustery *ADJECTIVE*
It was a typical, ***blustery*** *day in autumn.*
• gusty, windy, blowy, squally
OPPOSITE calm

board *NOUN*
The tabletop was made from a wooden ***board.***
• plank, panel, beam, timber
for board games see **game**

board *VERB*
We ***boarded*** *the plane for New York.*
• get on, enter, embark

boast *VERB*
The knight was always ***boasting*** *about his fencing skills.*
• brag, show off, crow, gloat, swagger
(informal) **blow your own trumpet**

boastful *ADJECTIVE*
Giants are ***boastful*** *creatures and brag about everything.*
• arrogant, big-headed, conceited, vain, bumptious
(informal) **cocky, swanky**
OPPOSITES **modest, humble**

boat *NOUN*
Several fishing ***boats*** *were moored in the harbour.*
• ship, craft, vessel

WORD WEB

SOME TYPES OF BOAT OR SHIP:

• barge, canoe, catamaran, cruise liner, dhow, dinghy, dugout, ferry, freighter, gondola, hovercraft, hydrofoil, junk, kayak, launch, lifeboat, motorboat, oil tanker, punt, raft, rowing boat, schooner, skiff, speedboat, steamship, tanker, trawler, tug, yacht

MILITARY BOATS OR SHIPS:

• aircraft carrier, battleship, destroyer, frigate, gunboat, minesweeper, submarine, warship

SOME BOATS USED IN THE PAST:

• brigantine, clipper, coracle, cutter, galleon, galley, longship, man-of-war, paddle steamer, schooner, trireme, windjammer

WORDS FOR PARTS OF A BOAT OR SHIP:

• boom, bridge, bulwark, cabin, crow's nest, deck, engine room, funnel, galley, helm, hull, keel, mast, poop, porthole, propeller, quarterdeck, rigging, rudder, sail, tiller

SPECIAL NAMES:

The front part of a boat is the **bow** or **prow**.
The back part of a boat is the **stern**.
The part below deck where the crew live is called the **fo'c'sle**.
The left-hand side of a boat is called **port**.
The right-hand side of a boat is called **starboard**.
A shed where boats are stored is a **boathouse**.

WRITING TIPS

You can use these words to describe **how a boat moves**:
• cut through the waves or water, drift, float, glide, lurch, pitch, roll, sail, steam, tack
So the boat was left to drift down the stream as it would, till it glided gently in among the waving rushes.—ALICE THROUGH THE LOOKING-GLASS, Lewis Carroll

bob *VERB*
A plastic duck ***bobbed*** *up and down in the water.*
• bounce, dance, toss, wobble

body *NOUN*

WORD WEB

The study of the human body is **anatomy**.
The main part of your body except your head, arms and legs is your **trunk** or **torso**.
The shape of your body is your **build**, **figure** or **physique**.
The dead body of a person is a **corpse**.
The dead body of an animal is a **carcass**.

OUTER PARTS OF THE HUMAN BODY:

• abdomen, ankle, arm, armpit, breast, buttocks, calf, cheek, chest, chin, ear, elbow, eye, finger, foot, forehead, genitals, groin, hand, head, heel, hip, instep, jaw, knee, kneecap, knuckle, leg, lip, mouth, navel, neck, nipple, nose, pores, shin, shoulder, skin, stomach, temple, thigh, throat, waist, wrist

INNER PARTS OF THE HUMAN BODY:

• arteries, bladder, bowels, brain, eardrum, glands, gullet, gums, guts, heart, intestines, kidneys, larynx, liver, lung, muscles, nerves, ovaries, pancreas, prostate, sinews, stomach, tendons, tongue, tonsil, tooth, uterus, veins, windpipe, womb

for bones in your body see **bone**

for parts of animal bodies see **animal**

WRITING TIPS

You can use these words to describe a person's **body**:

TO DESCRIBE A LARGE, HEAVY OR STRONG BODY:

• athletic, beefy, brawny, burly, dumpy, fat, hefty, hulking, muscular, sinewy, squat, stocky, stout, thickset, flabby, plump, rotund, well-rounded

Aunt Agatha was a stout woman, and Stella thought the outfit made her look rather like a giant violet frog.—THE POLAR BEAR EXPLORERS' CLUB, Alex Bell

TO DESCRIBE A SMALL OR WEAK BODY:

• petite, short, slender, slight, slim, svelte, thin, bony, gangly, gaunt, lanky, tall, puny, scraggy, scrawny, skinny, spindly, wiry

Hiccup was just absolutely average, the kind of unremarkable, skinny, freckled boy who was easy to overlook in a crowd.—HOW TO BE A PIRATE, Cressida Cowell

bog *NOUN*

We felt our boots sinking into the ***bog****.*

• swamp, quagmire, quicksand, fen

boil *VERB*

❶ *Would you like your egg* ***boiled*** *or fried?*

for ways to cook food see **cook**

❷ *The water must be* ***boiling*** *before you add the pasta.*

• bubble, seethe, steam

bold *ADJECTIVE*

❶ *It was a* ***bold*** *move to attack the fortress.*

• brave, courageous, daring, adventurous, audacious, confident, enterprising, fearless, heroic, valiant, intrepid, plucky

OPPOSITE cowardly

❷ *The poster uses large letters in* ***bold*** *colours.*

• striking, strong, bright, loud, showy, conspicuous, eye-catching, noticeable, prominent

OPPOSITES inconspicuous, subtle

bolt *VERB*

❶ *Did you remember to* ***bolt*** *the door?*

• fasten, latch, lock, secure, bar

❷ *The horses* ***bolted*** *when they heard the thunder.*

• dash away, dart, flee, sprint, run away, rush off

❸ *Don't* ***bolt*** *your food.*

• gobble, gulp, guzzle, wolf down

for other ways to eat see **eat**

bond *NOUN*

❶ *The prisoner tried to escape from his* ***bonds****.*

• chains, fetters, ropes, handcuffs, manacles, shackles, restraints

❷ *There was a special* ***bond*** *between the twins.*

• attachment, connection, tie, link, relationship

bone *NOUN*

WORD WEB

The bones of your body are your **skeleton**.

SOME BONES IN THE HUMAN BODY:

• backbone or spine, collarbone, cranium or skull, pelvis, ribs, shoulder blade, vertebrae

A B C D E F G H I J K L M N O P Q R S T U V W X Y Z

bonus *NOUN*
*I got a **bonus** on top of my pocket money last week.*
• **extra, supplement, reward, tip, handout**

book *NOUN*

WORD WEB

A book with hard covers is a **hardback**.
A book with soft covers is a **paperback**.
A book which is typed or handwritten but not printed is a **manuscript**.
A thin book in paper covers is a **booklet**, **leaflet** or **pamphlet**.
A book which is part of a set is a **volume**.
A large heavy book is a **tome**.
The person who writes a book is the **author**.
A book which sells a lot of copies is a **bestseller**.

SOME TYPES OF BOOK:

• **album, annual, anthology, atlas, audiobook, comic book, dictionary, e-book, encyclopedia, graphic novel, guidebook, manual, novel, picture book, reading book, reference book, story book, textbook, thesaurus**

BOOKS YOU CAN WRITE OR DRAW IN:

• **diary, exercise book, jotter, notebook, scrapbook, sketchbook**

SOME PARTS OF A BOOK:

• **appendix, bibliography, blurb, chapters, contents page, cover, foreword, illustrations, index, introduction, preface, prologue, title page**
for ways to describe a book or story see **writing**

book *VERB*
*Have you **booked** a seat on the train?*
• **order, reserve, engage**

boom *VERB*
❶ *Miss Barker's voice **boomed** along the corridor.*
• **shout, roar, bellow, blast, thunder, resound, reverberate**
❷ *Business was **booming** in the Riverbank Cafe.*
• **be successful, do well, expand, flourish, grow, prosper, thrive**

boost *VERB*
*Winning the cup really **boosted** the team's morale.*
• **raise, uplift, improve, increase, bolster, help, encourage, enhance**
OPPOSITES **lower, dampen**

boot *NOUN*
for types of shoe or boot see **shoe**

border *NOUN*
❶ *The town is on the **border** between France and Germany.*
• **boundary, frontier**
❷ *I drew a thin line around the **border** of the picture.*
• **edge, margin, perimeter**
A decorative border round the top of a wall is a **frieze**.
A border round the bottom of a skirt is a **hem**.
A decorative border on fabric is a **frill**, **fringe** or **trimming**.

bore *past tense see* **bear**

bore *VERB*
*They **bored** a hole right through the outer wall.*
• **drill, pierce, sink, tunnel**

boring *ADJECTIVE*
*The film was so **boring** I fell asleep.*
• **dull, dreary, tedious, tiresome, unexciting, uninteresting, dry, monotonous, uninspiring, insipid, unimaginative, uneventful, humdrum**
OPPOSITES **interesting, exciting**

borrow *VERB*
*Can I **borrow** your pencil?*
• **use, take, obtain, acquire**
(informal) **cadge, scrounge**
OPPOSITE **lend**

boss *NOUN*
*There is a new **boss** at the football club.*
• **head, chief, manager, leader, director**
(informal) **gaffer**

bossy *ADJECTIVE*
*Stop being so **bossy** towards your sister.*
• **domineering, bullying, dictatorial, officious, tyrannical**
An informal name for a bossy person is **bossy boots.**

bother *VERB*
❶ *Would it **bother** you if I played some music?*
• **disturb, trouble, upset, annoy, irritate, pester, worry, vex, exasperate**
(informal) **bug, hassle**
❷ *Don't **bother** to phone tonight.*
• **make an effort, take the trouble, concern yourself, care, mind**

bother *NOUN*
*It's such a **bother** to remember the password.*
• **nuisance, annoyance, irritation, inconvenience, pest, trouble, difficulty, problem**
(informal) **hassle**

bottle *NOUN*
*Bring a **bottle** of water with you.*
• **flask, flagon, jar, pitcher**
A bottle for serving water or wine is a **carafe** or **decanter.**
A small bottle for perfume or medicine is a **phial.**

bottle *VERB*
➤ **to bottle something up**
*It's not healthy to **bottle up** your anger.*
• **hold in, cover up, conceal, suppress**
OPPOSITES **show, express**

bottom *NOUN*
❶ *We camped at the **bottom** of the mountain.*
• **foot, base**
OPPOSITES **top, peak**
❷ *The wreck sank to the **bottom** of the sea.*
• **bed, floor**
OPPOSITE **surface**
❸ *A wasp stung me on the **bottom**.*
• **backside, behind, buttocks, rear, rump, seat**
(informal) **bum**

bottom *ADJECTIVE*
*I got the **bottom** mark in the maths test.*
• **least, lowest**
OPPOSITE **top**

bough *NOUN*
*The robin perched on a **bough** of the tree.*
• **branch, limb**

bought *past tense see* **buy**

bounce *VERB*
*The ball **bounced** twice before it reached the net.*
• **rebound, ricochet, spring, leap**

bound *past tense see* **bind**

bound *ADJECTIVE*
❶ *It's **bound** to rain at the weekend.*
• **certain, sure**
❷ *I felt **bound** to invite my cousin to the party.*
• **obliged, duty-bound, committed, compelled, forced, required**
❸ *The accident was **bound** to happen.*
• **destined, doomed, fated**
➤ **bound for**
*The space rocket was **bound for** Mars.*
• **going to, heading for, making for, travelling towards, off to**

bound *VERB*
*The puppies **bounded** across the lawn.*
• **leap, bounce, jump, spring, skip, gambol, caper, frisk**

boundary *NOUN*
*The lamp post marks the **boundary** of Narnia.*
• **border, frontier, edge, end, limit, perimeter, dividing line**

bout *NOUN*
❶ *She's recovering from a **bout** of flu.*
• **attack, fit, period, spell**
(informal) **turn**

❷ *A judo* **bout** *is between two contestants.*
• **contest, match, round, fight, battle, combat**

bow *NOUN (rhymes with* **go***)*
The archer raised his **bow** *and arrow.*
for words to do with archery see **arrow**

bow *NOUN (rhymes with* **cow***)*
The captain stood at the **bow** *of the ship.*
• **front, prow**
for other parts of a boat or ship see **boat**

bow *VERB (rhymes with* **cow***)*
❶ *The prisoner* **bowed** *his head in shame.*
• **lower, bend, duck**
❷ *The knight knelt and* **bowed** *in front of the king.*
The corresponding movement of a woman is to **curtsy**.

bowl *NOUN*
There was a **bowl** *of fresh fruit on the table.*
• **basin, dish, vessel**
A large bowl for serving soup is a **tureen**.

bowl *VERB*
Can you **bowl** *a faster ball next time?*
• **throw, pitch, fling, hurl, toss**
for other ways to throw a ball see **ball**

box *NOUN*
• **case, chest, crate, carton, packet**
A small box for jewellery or treasure is a **casket**.
A large box for luggage is a **trunk**.

boy *NOUN*
• **lad, youngster, youth**
(informal) **kid**

brag *VERB*
Flo is still **bragging** *about her swimming medal.*
• **show off, boast, gloat, crow**
(informal) **blow your own trumpet**
A person who is always bragging is a **braggart**.

brain *NOUN*
You'll need to use your **brain** *to solve this riddle.*
• **intelligence, intellect, mind, reason, sense, wit**

branch *NOUN*
❶ *A robin perched on a* **branch** *of the tree.*
• **bough, limb**
❷ *I've joined the local* **branch** *of the Kennel Club.*
• **section, division, department, wing**

branch *VERB*
Follow the track until it **branches** *into two.*
• **divide, fork**

brand *NOUN*
Which **brand** *of ice cream do you like?*
• **make, kind, sort, type, variety, label**
The sign of a particular brand of goods is a **trademark**.

brandish *VERB*
Captain Hook **brandished** *his cutlass at the crew.*
• **flourish, wield, flaunt, wave**

brave *ADJECTIVE*
It was **brave** *of you to save the cat from drowning.*
• **courageous, heroic, valiant, fearless, daring, gallant, intrepid, plucky**
A common simile is **as brave as a lion**.
OPPOSITE **cowardly**

bravery *NOUN*
The police dog was awarded a medal for **bravery**.
• **courage, heroism, valour, fearlessness, daring, nerve, gallantry, grit, pluck**
(informal) **guts, bottle**
OPPOSITE **cowardice**

brawl *NOUN*
We could hear a **brawl** *on the street outside.*
• **fight, quarrel, scuffle, tussle**
(informal) **scrap**

breach *NOUN*
❶ *Handling the ball is a* **breach** *of the rules.*
• **breaking, violation**

You can also talk about an offence against the rules.

❷ *The storm caused a **breach** in the sea wall.*

• **break, split, crack, gap, hole, opening, fracture, rupture, fissure**

break *NOUN*

❶ *Can you see any **breaks** in the chain?*

• **breach, crack, hole, gap, opening, split, rift, puncture, rupture, fracture, fissure**

❷ *Let's take a **break** for coffee.*

• **interval, pause, rest, lull, timeout**
(informal) **breather**

break *VERB* **breaks, breaking, broke, broken**

❶ *The vase fell off the shelf and **broke**.*

• **smash, shatter, fracture, chip, crack, split, snap, splinter**
(informal) **bust**

❷ *The burglar was arrested for **breaking** the law.*

• **disobey, disregard, violate, flout**

❸ *In her last race, she **broke** the world record.*

• **beat, better, exceed, surpass, outdo**

➤ **to break down**

*Our car **broke down** on the motorway.*

• **fail, go wrong, stop working**
(informal) **pack in, conk out**

➤ **to break off**

*We'll **break off** for lunch at one o'clock.*

• **have a rest, pause, stop**

➤ **to break out**

*A flu epidemic **broke out** just after Christmas.*

• **begin, spread, start**

➤ **to break out of**

*The prisoner tried to **break out of** jail.*

• **escape from, break loose from, abscond from**

➤ **to break up**

*After the speeches, the crowd began to **break up**.*

• **disperse, scatter, separate, split up, disintegrate**

breakable *ADJECTIVE*

*Be careful! The parcel has **breakable** things in it.*

• **fragile, delicate, brittle, frail**

OPPOSITE **unbreakable**

breakdown *NOUN*

❶ *There has been a **breakdown** in the peace talks.*

• **failure, collapse, fault**

❷ *Can you give me a **breakdown** of the figures?*

• **analysis**

break-in *NOUN*

*There was a **break-in** at the local bank.*

• **burglary, robbery, theft, raid**

breakthrough *NOUN*

*Scientists have made a **breakthrough** in medicine.*

• **advance, leap forward, discovery, development, revolution, progress**

OPPOSITE **setback**

breath *NOUN*

*There wasn't a **breath** of wind in the air.*

• **breeze, puff, waft, whiff, whisper, sigh**

breathe *VERB*

To breathe in is to **inhale**.
To breathe out is to **exhale**.
To breathe heavily when you have been running is to **pant** or **puff**.
The formal word for breathing is **respiration**.

breathless *ADJECTIVE*

*Leo was **breathless** after the race.*

• **out of breath, gasping, panting, puffing, tired out, wheezing**

breed *VERB*

❶ *Salmon swim upstream to **breed** every year.*

• **reproduce, have young, multiply, procreate, spawn**

❷ *Bad hygiene **breeds** disease.*

• **cause, produce, generate, encourage, promote, cultivate, induce**

breed *NOUN*

*What **breed** of dog is that?*

• **kind, sort, type, variety**

The evidence of how a dog has been bred is its **pedigree**.

breezy *ADJECTIVE*
This morning the weather was bright and breezy.
• **windy, blowy, blustery, gusty, fresh, draughty**
see also **weather**

brew *VERB*
❶ *I'm just going to* **brew** *some tea.*
• **make, prepare**
When you brew beer it **ferments.**
❷ *It looks like a storm is* **brewing.**
• **develop, form, loom, build up, gather, threaten**

brew *NOUN*
The wizard stirred an evil-smelling **brew.**
• **mixture, concoction**

bridge *NOUN*
A bridge you can walk over is a **footbridge.**
A bridge to carry water is an **aqueduct.**
A long bridge carrying a road or railway is a **viaduct.**

brief *ADJECTIVE*
❶ *We paid a* **brief** *visit to our cousins on the way home.*
• **short, quick, hasty, fleeting, temporary**
❷ *Give me a* **brief** *account of what happened.*
• **short, concise, abbreviated, condensed, compact, succinct**
OPPOSITES **long, lengthy**

bright *ADJECTIVE*
❶ *We saw the* **bright** *lights of the town in the distance.*
• **shining, brilliant, blazing, dazzling, glaring, gleaming**
OPPOSITES **dull, dim, weak**
❷ **Bright** *colours will make the poster stand out.*
• **strong, intense, vivid**
Colours that shine in the dark are **luminous** colours.
OPPOSITES **dull, faded, muted**
❸ *Her teachers thought she was very* **bright.**
• **clever, intelligent, gifted, sharp, quick-witted**
(informal) **brainy**
A common simile is **as bright as a button.**
OPPOSITES **stupid, dull-witted**
❹ *Miranda gave me a* **bright** *smile.*
• **cheerful, happy, lively, merry, jolly, radiant**
OPPOSITES **sad, gloomy**
❺ *The day was cold, but* **bright.**
• **sunny, fine, fair, clear, cloudless**
OPPOSITES **dull, cloudy, overcast**

brighten *VERB*
It was a cloudy morning, but it **brightened** *after lunch.*
• **become sunny, clear up, improve**
➤ **to brighten up**
A new coat of paint will **brighten up** *the room.*
• **cheer up, light up, enliven**

brilliant *ADJECTIVE*
❶ *The fireworks gave off a* **brilliant** *light.*
• **bright, blazing, dazzling, glaring, gleaming, glittering, glorious, shining, splendid, vivid**
OPPOSITES **dim, dull**
❷ *Brunel was a* **brilliant** *engineer.*
• **clever, exceptional, outstanding, gifted, talented**
OPPOSITES **incompetent, talentless**
❸ *(informal) I saw a* **brilliant** *film last week.*
• **excellent, marvellous, outstanding, wonderful, superb**
(informal) **fantastic, fabulous**
see also **good**

brim *NOUN*
I filled my glass to the **brim.**
• **top, rim, edge, brink, lip**

bring *VERB* **brings, bringing, brought**
❶ *Can you* **bring** *the shopping in from the car?*
• **carry, fetch, deliver, bear, transport**
❷ *You can* **bring** *a friend to the party.*
• **invite, conduct, escort, guide, lead**

❸ *The war has **brought** great sorrow to our people.*
• cause, produce, lead to, result in, generate

➤ **to bring something about**
*The new coach **brought about** some changes.*
• cause, effect, create, introduce, be responsible for

➤ **to bring someone up**
*In the story, Tarzan is **brought up** by apes.*
• rear, raise, care for, foster, look after, nurture, educate, train

➤ **to bring something up**
*I wish you hadn't **brought up** the subject of money.*
• mention, talk about, raise, broach

brink *NOUN*
*We stood on the **brink** of a deep crater.*
• edge, lip, rim, verge, brim

brisk *ADJECTIVE*
❶ *Mr Hastie went for a **brisk** walk every evening.*
• lively, fast-paced, energetic, invigorating, vigorous, refreshing, bracing
OPPOSITES slow, leisurely
❷ *The flower shop does a **brisk** trade around Easter.*
• busy, lively, bustling, hectic
OPPOSITES quiet, slack, slow

brittle *ADJECTIVE*
*The bones of the skeleton were dry and **brittle**.*
• breakable, fragile, delicate, frail
OPPOSITES soft, flexible

broad *ADJECTIVE*
❶ *The streets in the city were **broad** and straight.*
• wide, open, large, roomy, spacious, vast, extensive
OPPOSITE narrow
❷ *Just give me a **broad** outline of what happened.*
• general, rough, vague, loose, indefinite, imprecise
OPPOSITES specific, detailed

broaden *VERB*
*I'm **broadening** my interests by listening to jazz.*
• widen, extend, enlarge, expand, increase, develop, diversify

brochure *NOUN*
*We got some holiday **brochures** from the travel agent.*
• leaflet, pamphlet, booklet, catalogue

broke *past tense see* **break**

broken *ADJECTIVE*
❶ *Don't use that computer—it's **broken**.*
• faulty, defective, damaged, out of order
OPPOSITE working
❷ *After losing all his money, Forbes was a **broken** man.*
• crushed, defeated, beaten, spiritless

brood *VERB*
❶ *The hen was **brooding** her clutch of eggs.*
• hatch, incubate, sit on
❷ *He was still **brooding** over what I had said.*
• fret, mope, worry, dwell on

brought *past tense see* **bring**

brown *ADJECTIVE, NOUN*

WORD WEB

SOME SHADES OF BROWN:

• beige, bronze, buff, chestnut, chocolate, dun, fawn, khaki, russet, sepia, tan, tawny

browse *VERB*
❶ *I like **browsing** through toy catalogues.*
• flick through, leaf through, scan, skim
❷ *The cattle were **browsing** in the meadow.*
• graze, feed

bruise *VERB*
I fell and ***bruised*** *my knee.*
• mark, hurt, injure
for other types of injury see **injury**

brush *VERB*
❶ *Jill spent ages* ***brushing*** *her hair for the party.*
• groom, comb, tidy
❷ *A bird* ***brushed*** *against my cheek as it flew past.*
• touch, contact, rub, scrape
➤ **to brush up**
I must ***brush up*** *my French before we go to Paris.*
• revise, improve, go over, refresh your memory of
(informal) swot up

brutal *ADJECTIVE*
The bandits launched a ***brutal*** *attack.*
• savage, vicious, cruel, barbaric, bloodthirsty, callous, ferocious, inhuman, merciless, pitiless, ruthless, sadistic
OPPOSITES gentle, humane

bubble *NOUN*
The bubbles in a fizzy drink are **effervescence**.
The bubbles made by soap or detergent are **lather** or **suds**.
Bubbles on top of a liquid are **foam** or **froth**.
The bubbles on top of beer are the **head**.

bubble *VERB*
A green liquid ***bubbled*** *in the witch's cauldron.*
• boil, seethe, gurgle, froth, foam

bubbly *ADJECTIVE*
❶ ***Bubbly*** *drinks get up my nose.*
• fizzy, sparkling, effervescent
❷ *Sophie has a bright and* ***bubbly*** *personality.*
• cheerful, lively, vivacious, spirited, animated

bucket *NOUN*
We took ***buckets*** *and spades to the seaside.*
• pail, can

buckle *NOUN*
The pirate wore a belt with a large silver ***buckle****.*
• clasp, fastener, fastening, clip, catch

buckle *VERB*
❶ *Please* ***buckle*** *your seat belts.*
• fasten, secure, clasp, clip, do up, hook up
❷ *The bridge* ***buckled*** *when the giant stepped on to it.*
• bend, warp, twist, crumple, cave in, collapse

bud *NOUN*
Buds *are appearing on the apple trees.*
• shoot, sprout

budge *VERB*
The window was stuck and wouldn't ***budge****.*
• give way, move, shift, stir

budget *VERB*
➤ **to budget for**
Have you ***budgeted for*** *a holiday this year?*
• allow for, plan for, provide for

bug *NOUN*
❶ *Birds help to control* ***bugs*** *in the garden.*
• insect, pest
❷ *(informal) I can't get rid of this stomach* ***bug****.*
• infection, virus, germ, disease, illness
❸ *There are a few* ***bugs*** *in the computer program.*
• fault, error, defect, flaw
(informal) gremlin

bug *VERB*
❶ *The spy* ***bugged*** *their phone conversations.*
• tap, listen in to, intercept
❷ *(informal) I wish you'd stop* ***bugging*** *me with questions.*
• bother, annoy, pester, trouble, harass

build *VERB* **builds, building, built**
Dad is going to ***build*** *a shed in the garden.*
• construct, erect, put together, put up, set up, assemble
➤ **to build up**
❶ *I'm* ***building up*** *a collection of DVDs.*
• accumulate, assemble, collect, put together

❷ *We felt the tension **building up** in the crowd.*
• **increase, intensify, rise, grow, mount up, escalate**

build *NOUN*
*Charlotte was a girl of slender **build**.*
• **body, form, frame, figure, physique**
see also **body**

building *NOUN*
*The new **building** will have seven storeys.*
• **construction, structure, dwelling**

WORD WEB

A person who designs buildings is an **architect**.

BUILDINGS WHERE PEOPLE LIVE:

• **apartment, barracks, bungalow, castle, cottage, farmhouse, flat, fort, fortress, house, mansion, palace, skyscraper, tenement, terrace, tower, villa**
see also **house**

BUILDINGS WHERE PEOPLE WORK:

• **factory, garage, lighthouse, mill, shop, store, warehouse**

BUILDINGS WHERE PEOPLE WORSHIP:

• **abbey, cathedral, chapel, church, monastery, mosque, pagoda, shrine, synagogue, temple**
see also **church**

OTHER TYPES OF BUILDING:

• **cabin, cafe, cinema, college, gallery, hotel, inn, library, museum, observatory, police station, post office, power station, prison, restaurant, school, shed, theatre**

PARTS YOU MIGHT FIND INSIDE A BUILDING:

• **balcony, basement, cellar, conservatory, corridor, courtyard, crypt, dungeon, foyer, gallery, lobby, porch, room, staircase, veranda**
see also **room**

PARTS YOU MIGHT FIND OUTSIDE A BUILDING:

• **arch, balustrade, bay window, bow window, buttress, chimney, colonnade, column, dome, dormer window, drainpipe, eaves, foundations, gable, gutter, masonry, parapet, pediment, pillar, pipes, quadrangle, roof, tower, turret, vault, wall, window, window sill**
for parts of a castle see **castle**

WRITING TIPS

You can use these words to describe a building:
• **airy, compact, cramped, crumbling, forbidding, grand, imposing, ramshackle, ruined, run-down, spacious, sprawling, squalid, stark, stately**
They lived—Aunt Sponge, Aunt Spiker, and now James as well—in a queer ramshackle house on the top of a high hill in the south of England.—JAMES AND THE GIANT PEACH, Roald Dahl

bulge *NOUN*
*There was a large **bulge** in the robber's sack.*
• **bump, hump, lump, swelling, protuberance**

bulge *VERB*
*The creature had eyes which **bulged** out of its head.*
• **stick out, swell, puff out, protrude**

bulk *NOUN*
❶ *The sheer **bulk** of the iceberg was staggering.*
• **size, dimensions, magnitude, mass, largeness, immensity**
❷ *We spent the **bulk** of our holiday lazing on the beach.*
• **most, most part, greater part, majority**

bulky *ADJECTIVE*
*The parcel is too **bulky** to go through the letterbox.*
• **big, large, hefty, substantial, sizeable, cumbersome, unwieldy**
OPPOSITES **small, compact**

bully *VERB*
*Some of the children were afraid of being **bullied**.*
• **persecute, torment, intimidate, terrorise, push around**

bump *VERB*
❶ *The baby **bumped** his head on the table.*
• **hit, strike, knock, bang**
❷ *My bicycle **bumped** up and down over the cobbles.*
• **bounce, shake, jerk, jolt**
➤ **to bump into**
❶ *The taxi **bumped into** the car in front of it.*
• **collide with, bang into, run into, crash into**
❷ *I **bumped into** one of my friends in the bookshop.*
• **meet, come across, run into**

bump *NOUN*
❶ *We felt a **bump** as the plane landed.*
• **thud, thump, bang, blow, knock**
❷ *How did you get that **bump** on your head?*
• **lump, swelling, bulge**

bumpy *ADJECTIVE*
❶ *The car jolted up and down on the **bumpy** road.*
• **rough, uneven, irregular, lumpy**
OPPOSITES **smooth, even**
❷ *We had a **bumpy** ride in a jeep over muddy tracks.*
• **bouncy, jerky, jolting, lurching, choppy**

bunch *NOUN*
❶ *The jailer jangled a **bunch** of keys.*
• **bundle, cluster, collection, set**
❷ *She picked a **bunch** of flowers.*
• **bouquet, posy, spray**
❸ *(informal) They're a friendly **bunch** of people.*
• **group, set, circle, band, gang, crowd**

bundle *NOUN*
*I found a **bundle** of old newspapers.*
• **bunch, batch, pile, stack, collection, pack, bale**

bundle *VERB*
❶ *We **bundled** up the papers that were on the desk.*
• **pack, tie, fasten, bind**
❷ *The police **bundled** him into the back of their car.*
• **move hurriedly, push, jostle**

burden *NOUN*
❶ *Each mule was carrying a heavy **burden**.*
• **load, weight, cargo**
❷ *The captain has the **burden** of organising the players.*
• **responsibility, obligation, duty, pressure, stress, trouble, worry**

burden *VERB*
*I won't **burden** you with my own problems.*
• **bother, worry, trouble, distress, encumber, lumber**
(informal) **saddle**

burglar *NOUN*
*The **burglars** must have got in through the window.*
• **robber, thief, intruder**

burglary *NOUN*
see **stealing**

burn *VERB* **burns, burning, burnt** or **burned**
❶ *We could see the campfire **burning** in the distance.*
• **be alight, be on fire, blaze, flame, flare, flicker**
To burn without flames is to **glow** or **smoulder**.
❷ *The captain ordered them to **burn** the enemy ship.*
• **set fire to, incinerate, reduce to ashes**
To start something burning is to **ignite, kindle** or **light** it.
To burn something slightly is to **char, scorch** or **singe** it.
To hurt someone with boiling liquid or steam is to **scald** them.
To burn a dead body is to **cremate** it.
To burn a mark on an animal is to **brand** it.

burrow *NOUN*
The field was full of rabbit ***burrows.***
• **hole, tunnel**
A piece of ground with many burrows is a **warren.**
A fox's burrow is called an **earth.**
A badger's burrow is called an **earth** or **sett.**
for other animal homes see **animal**

burrow *VERB*
Rabbits have been ***burrowing*** *under the fence.*
• **tunnel, dig, excavate, mine**

burst *VERB*
The balloon ***burst*** *when my brother sat on it.*
• **puncture, rupture, break, give way, split, tear**

bury *VERB*
❶ *The document was* ***buried*** *under a pile of old letters.*
• **cover, conceal, hide, secrete**
❷ *They say the old witch was* ***buried*** *in that graveyard.*
• **inter, entomb**

bush *NOUN*
Birds often build their nests in ***bushes.***
• **shrub**

bushy *ADJECTIVE*
The troll had ***bushy*** *green eyebrows.*
• **hairy, thick, dense, shaggy, bristly**

business *NOUN*
❶ *My uncle runs a restaurant* ***business.***
• **company, firm, organisation**
❷ *The new bookshop does a lot of* ***business.***
• **trade, trading, buying and selling, commerce**
❸ *What sort of* ***business*** *do you want to go into?*
• **work, job, career, employment, industry, occupation, profession, trade**
❹ *He left early to attend to some urgent* ***business.***
• **matter, issue, affair, problem, point, concern, question**

bustle *VERB*
Miss Flyte ***bustled*** *about the kitchen making tea.*
• **rush, dash, hurry, scurry, scuttle, fuss**

busy *ADJECTIVE*
❶ *Mum is* ***busy*** *making my birthday cake just now.*
• **occupied, engaged, employed, working, slaving away**
(informal) **hard at it, up to your eyes, beavering away**
A common simile is **as busy as a bee.**
OPPOSITE **idle**
❷ *Christmas is a very* ***busy*** *time for shops.*
• **active, hectic, frantic, lively**
OPPOSITES **quiet, restful**
❸ *Is the town always this* ***busy*** *on Saturdays?*
• **crowded, bustling, hectic, lively, teeming**
OPPOSITES **quiet, peaceful**

butt *VERB*
The Minotaur ***butted*** *Theseus against the wall.*
• **hit, bump, knock, push, ram, shove**
➤ **to butt in**
Please don't ***butt in*** *when I'm talking.*
• **interrupt, cut in**

buy *VERB* **buys, buying, bought**
I'm saving up to ***buy*** *a skateboard.*
• **get, pay for, purchase, acquire**
OPPOSITE **sell**

buzz *NOUN, VERB*
for various sounds see **sound**

a b c d e f g h i j k l m n o p q r s t u v w x y z

Cc

cabin *NOUN*

❶ *The outlaws hid in a* ***cabin*** *in the woods.*
• **hut, shack, shed, lodge, chalet, shelter**
❷ *The crew assembled in the captain's* ***cabin.***
• **berth, quarters, compartment**

cable *NOUN*

❶ *The tent was held down with strong* ***cables.***
• **rope, cord, line, chain**
❷ *Don't trip over the computer* ***cable.***
• **flex, lead, wire, cord**

cafe *NOUN*

We had lunch in a ***cafe*** *overlooking the river.*
• **cafeteria, coffee shop, tea room, snack bar, buffet, canteen, bistro, brasserie**
for other places to eat see **restaurant**

cage *NOUN*

A large cage or enclosure for birds is an **aviary.**
A cage or enclosure for poultry is a **coop.**
A cage or enclosure for animals is a **pen.**
A cage or box for a pet rabbit is a **hutch.**

cake *NOUN*

Do you prefer carrot ***cake*** *or chocolate cake?*
• **sponge, flan**
A small individual cake is a **cupcake** or **fairy cake.**
for puddings and other sweet foods see **food**

calamity *NOUN*

The fire in the warehouse was a ***calamity.***
• **disaster, catastrophe, tragedy, misfortune, mishap, blow**

calculate *VERB*

I ***calculated*** *that it would take an hour to walk home.*
• **work out, compute, figure out, reckon, add up, count, total**
To calculate something roughly is to **estimate.**

call *NOUN*

❶ *We heard a* ***call*** *for help from inside the cave.*
• **cry, exclamation, scream, shout, yell**
❷ *Grandad made an unexpected* ***call.***
• **visit, stop, stay**
❸ *There's not much* ***call*** *for suncream in winter.*
• **demand, need**

call *VERB*

❶ *'Stop that racket!'* ***called*** *the janitor.*
• **cry out, exclaim, shout, yell**
for other ways to say something see **say**
❷ *It was too late at night to* ***call*** *my friends.*
• **phone, ring, telephone**
❸ *The head teacher* ***called*** *me to her office.*
• **summon, invite, send for, order**
❹ *The doctor* ***called*** *to see if I was feeling better.*
• **visit, pay a visit, drop in, drop by**
❺ *They* ***called*** *the baby Jessica.*
• **name, baptise, christen, dub**
❻ *What is your new book going to be* ***called?***
• **name, title, entitle**

➤ to call something off

It was so rainy that we ***called off*** *the barbecue.*
• **cancel, abandon, postpone**

➤ to call someone names

It's not funny to ***call*** *people* ***names.***
• **insult, be rude to, make fun of, mock**

calm *ADJECTIVE*

❶ *The weather was too* ***calm*** *to fly our kites.*
• **still, quiet, peaceful, tranquil, serene, windless**
OPPOSITE **stormy, windy**
❷ *The sea was* ***calm,*** *and we had a pleasant voyage.*
• **smooth, still, flat, motionless, tranquil**
OPPOSITE **rough, choppy**
❸ *I tried to stay* ***calm*** *before my judo exam.*
• **cool, level-headed, patient, relaxed, sedate, unemotional, unexcitable, untroubled**
OPPOSITE **anxious, nervous**

came *past tense see* **come**

camel *NOUN*
A camel with a single hump is a **dromedary.**
A camel with two humps is a **Bactrian.**

camp *NOUN*
From the hill we saw a ***camp*** *in the field below us.*
• **campsite, camping ground, base**
A military camp is an **encampment.**

campaign *NOUN*
❶ *Will you join our* ***campaign*** *to save the whale?*
• **movement, crusade, drive, fight, effort, struggle**
❷ *The army launched a* ***campaign*** *to recapture the city.*
• **operation, offensive, action, war**

cancel *VERB*
We had to ***cancel*** *the race because of the weather.*
• **abandon, call off, scrap, drop, axe**
(informal) **scrub, ditch**
To cancel something after it has already begun is to **abort** it.
To cancel something, but rearrange it for later, is to **postpone** it or **put it off.**
To cancel items on a list is to **cross out, delete** or **erase** them.

candidate *NOUN*
A candidate for a job is an **applicant.**
A candidate in an examination is an **entrant.**
A person competing with others in a contest is a **competitor, contender** or **contestant.**

canopy *NOUN*
We sheltered from the rain under a ***canopy.***
• **awning, cover, shade**

cap *NOUN*
❶ *The tennis players wore* ***caps*** *because it was sunny.*
for various kinds of hat see **hat**
❷ *Who left the* ***cap*** *off the toothpaste?*
• **cover, lid, top**

cap *VERB*
Mount Everest is always ***capped*** *with snow.*
• **cover, top, crown**

capable *ADJECTIVE*
She is a ***capable*** *ballet dancer.*
• **competent, able, accomplished, proficient, skilful, skilled, gifted, talented**
OPPOSITE **incompetent**
➤ **to be capable of**
Do you think the professor is ***capable of*** *murder?*
• **be able to do, be equal to, be up to**
OPPOSITE **be incapable of**

capacity *NOUN*
❶ *Alice has a great* ***capacity*** *for making friends.*
• **ability, power, potential, capability, competence, talent**
(informal) **knack**
❷ *What is the* ***capacity*** *of this glass?*
• **size, volume, space, extent, room**
❸ *She spoke in her* ***capacity*** *as team leader.*
• **position, function, role, office**

cape *NOUN*
❶ *We could see the island from the* ***cape.***
• **headland, promontory, point, head**
❷ *The lady wore a* ***cape*** *of black velvet.*
• **cloak, shawl, wrap, robe**
(old use) **mantle**

capital *NOUN*
❶ *Paris is the* ***capital*** *of France.*
• **capital city, centre of government**
❷ *We have enough* ***capital*** *to start a new business.*
• **funds, money, finance, cash, assets, savings, means, resources**
➤ **capital letter**
Start a new sentence with a ***capital letter.***
• **block capital, block letter**

capsize *VERB*
The canoe ***capsized*** *when it hit a rock.*
• **overturn, tip over, turn over, keel over**
(informal) **turn turtle**

capsule *NOUN*
❶ *This **capsule** contains poison.*
• **pill, tablet, lozenge**
❷ *The space **capsule** is designed to orbit Mars.*
• **module, craft, pod**
for other words to do with space travel see **space**

captain *NOUN*
*The **captain** brought his ship safely into harbour.*
• **commander, commanding officer, master, skipper**

captive *NOUN*
*The **captives** were thrown into the dungeon.*
• **prisoner, convict**
A person who is held captive until demand is met is a **hostage**.

captive *ADJECTIVE*
*The pirates held the crew **captive** for ten days.*
• **imprisoned, captured, arrested, detained, jailed**
OPPOSITES **free, released**

captivity *NOUN*
*The hostages have been released from **captivity**.*
• **imprisonment, confinement, detention, incarceration**
OPPOSITE **freedom**

capture *VERB*
❶ *The bank robbers were **captured** by police this morning.*
• **catch, arrest, apprehend, seize, take prisoner**
(informal) **nab, nick**
❷ *The castle has never been **captured** by enemy forces.*
• **occupy, seize, take, take over, win**

car *NOUN*
*Our **car** is getting repaired in the garage.*
• **motor car, motor, vehicle**
(North American) **automobile**

WORD WEB

An informal name for an old, noisy car is a **banger**.

SOME TYPES OF CAR:

• **convertible, coupé, electric car, estate, four-wheel drive, hatchback,** *(trademark)* **Jeep,** *(trademark)* **Land Rover, limousine** or *(informal)* **limo,** *(trademark)* **Mini, patrol car** or **police car, people carrier, racing car, saloon, sports car**
Very early cars are **veteran** or **vintage** cars.

THE MAIN PARTS OF A CAR ARE:

• **body, bonnet, boot, bumper, chassis, doors, engine, exhaust pipe, fuel tank, gearbox, headlamps, lights, mirrors, roof, tyres, undercarriage, wheels, windscreen, wings**

THE MAIN CONTROLS IN A CAR ARE:

• **accelerator, brake, choke, clutch, gear lever, handbrake, ignition key, indicators, speedometer, steering wheel, windscreen wipers**
Now Commander Pott really trod hard down on the accelerator and the speedometer climbed up and hung around a hundred miles an hour.—CHITTY CHITTY BANG BANG, Ian Fleming
for other vehicles see **vehicle**

carcass *NOUN*
*The lions fed on the **carcass** of the antelope.*
• **body, corpse, cadaver, remains**

card *NOUN*

WORD WEB

CARDS TO SEND ON SPECIAL OCCASIONS:

❶ *Did you send her a birthday **card**?*
• **birthday card, Christmas card, Diwali card, Easter card, get well card, greetings card, Hanukkah card, invitation, notelet, picture postcard, sympathy card, thank-you card, Valentine**

SOME CARD GAMES:

❷ *The magician shuffled the pack of **cards**.*
• **beggar-my-neighbour, blackjack, bridge, canasta, cribbage, happy families, old maid, patience, poker, pontoon, rummy, snap, solitaire, whist**
A complete set of playing cards is a **pack**.
All the cards with the same sign on them are a **suit**.
The suits in a pack of cards are **clubs, diamonds, hearts** and **spades**.
Names for special cards are **king, queen. jack** or **knave, ace** and **joker**.
The king, queen and jack are called **court cards**.

care *NOUN*
❶ *The old wizard's face was full of **care**.*
• **worry, anxiety, trouble, concern, burden, responsibility, sorrow, stress**
❷ *I took great **care** with my handwriting.*
• **attention, concentration, thoroughness, thought, meticulousness**
OPPOSITE **carelessness**
❸ *Jake left his pet hamster in my **care**.*
• **charge, keeping, protection, safe keeping, supervision**
➤ **to take care**
*Please **take care** crossing the road.*
• **be careful, be on your guard, look out, watch out**
➤ **to take care of someone** or **something**
*My granny **takes care of** me after school.*
• **care for, look after, mind, watch over, attend to, tend**

care *VERB*
*Do you **care** which team wins the World Cup?*
• **mind, bother, worry, be interested, be troubled, be bothered, be worried**
➤ **to care for someone** or **something**
❶ *The veterinary hospital **cares for** sick animals.*
• **take care of, look after, attend to, tend, nurse**
❷ *I don't really **care for** broccoli.*
• **like, be fond of, be keen on, love**

career *NOUN*
*Max had a successful **career** as a racing driver.*
• **job, occupation, profession, trade, business, employment, calling**
for various careers see **job**

careful *ADJECTIVE*
❶ *You must be more **careful** with your spelling.*
• **accurate, conscientious, thorough, thoughtful, meticulous, painstaking, precise**
OPPOSITES **careless, inaccurate**
❷ *Dad kept a **careful** watch on the bonfire.*
• **attentive, cautious, watchful, alert, wary, vigilant**
OPPOSITES **careless, inattentive**
➤ **to be careful**
*Please **be careful** with those scissors.*
• **take care, be on your guard, look out, watch out**

careless *ADJECTIVE*
❶ *This is a very **careless** piece of work.*
• **messy, untidy, thoughtless, inaccurate, slapdash, shoddy, scrappy, sloppy, slovenly**
OPPOSITES **careful, accurate**
❷ *I was **careless** and cut my finger.*
• **inattentive, thoughtless, absent-minded, heedless, irresponsible, negligent, reckless**
OPPOSITES **careful, attentive**

caress *NOUN*
*The mother bear gave each cub a **caress**.*
• **hug, kiss, embrace, pat, stroke, touch**

caress *VERB*
*The woman gently **caressed** her child's hair.*
• **stroke, touch, smooth**

cargo *NOUN*
*Some planes carry **cargo** instead of passengers.*
• **goods, freight, merchandise**

carnival *NOUN*
*The whole village comes out for the annual **carnival**.*
• **fair, festival, fête, gala, parade, procession, show, celebration, pageant**

carriage *NOUN*
for types of vehicle see **vehicle**

carry *VERB*
❶ *I helped Mum to* ***carry*** *the shopping to the car.*
• **take, transfer, lift, fetch, bring, lug**
❷ *Aircraft* ***carry*** *passengers and goods.*
• **transport, convey**
❸ *The rear axle* ***carries*** *the greatest weight.*
• **bear, support, hold up**
➤ **to carry on**
We ***carried on*** *in spite of the rain.*
• **continue, go on, persevere, persist, keep on, remain, stay, survive**
➤ **to carry something out**
The soldiers ***carried out*** *the captain's orders.*
• **perform, do, execute, accomplish, achieve, complete, finish**

cart *NOUN*
for types of vehicle see **vehicle**

carton *NOUN*
I put a ***carton*** *of juice in my lunchbox.*
• **box, pack, package, packet**

carve *VERB*
❶ *The statue was* ***carved*** *out of stone.*
• **sculpt, chisel, hew**
❷ *Mum* ***carved*** *the chicken for Sunday dinner.*
• **cut, slice**

case *NOUN*
❶ *I loaded my* ***case*** *into the boot of the car.*
• **suitcase, trunk, bag**
A number of suitcases that you take on a trip is your **baggage** or **luggage**.
❷ *What's in those* ***cases*** *in the attic?*
• **box, chest, crate, carton, casket**
❸ *This has been a clear* ***case*** *of mistaken identity.*
• **instance, occurrence, example, illustration**
❹ *It was one of Sherlock Holmes's most famous* ***cases****.*
• **inquiry, investigation**
❺ *They presented a good* ***case*** *against fox hunting.*
• **argument, line of reasoning**

cash *NOUN*
How much ***cash*** *do you have?*
• **money, change, loose change, ready money, coins, notes, currency**

cast *VERB* **casts, casting, cast**
❶ *The child* ***cast*** *a penny into the wishing-well.*
• **throw, toss, drop, fling, lob, sling**
❷ *The statue was* ***cast*** *in bronze.*
• **form, mould, shape**

castle *NOUN*

WORD WEB

CASTLES AND OTHER FORTIFIED BUILDINGS:
• **château, citadel, fort, fortress, motte and bailey, palace, stronghold, tower**

PARTS OF A CASTLE:
• **bailey, barbican, battlement, buttress, courtyard, donjon, drawbridge, dungeon, gate, gateway, keep, magazine, moat, motte, parapet, portcullis, postern, rampart, tower, turret, wall, watchtower**
Tiuri stood in the rain, looking at the river and the castle. An open drawbridge led to the gate, which was positioned between two large towers.—THE LETTER FOR THE KING, Tonke Dragt

casual *ADJECTIVE*
❶ *It was just a* ***casual*** *remark, so don't take it too seriously.*
• **accidental, chance, unexpected, unintentional, unplanned**
OPPOSITE **deliberate**
❷ *The restaurant had a* ***casual*** *atmosphere.*
• **easy-going, informal, relaxed**
OPPOSITE **formal**
❸ *The teacher complained about our* ***casual*** *attitude.*
• **apathetic, careless, slack, unenthusiastic**
OPPOSITE **enthusiastic**

casualty *NOUN*
*Police are reporting heavy **casualties** from the fire.*
• death, fatality, injury, loss, victim

cat *NOUN*

WORD WEB

A male cat is a **tom**.
A young cat is a **kitten**.
A cat with streaks in its fur is a **tabby**.
An informal word for a cat is **puss** or **pussy cat**.
A word meaning 'to do with cats' is **feline**.
I have a Gumbie Cat in mind, her name is Jennyanydots; Her coat is of the tabby kind, with tiger stripes and leopard spots.—OLD POSSUM'S BOOK OF PRACTICAL CATS, T. S. Eliot

SOME BREEDS OF CAT:
• Abyssinian, Burmese, chinchilla, Manx, Persian, Siamese

SOUNDS MADE BY CATS:
• mew, miaow, purr

SOME WILD ANIMALS OF THE CAT FAMILY:
• bobcat, cheetah, jaguar, leopard, lion, lynx, ocelot, puma, tiger, wild cat
see also **animal**

catastrophe *NOUN*
*The drought is a **catastrophe** for the farmers.*
• disaster, calamity, misfortune, mishap, tragedy

catch *VERB* **catches, catching, caught**
❶ *My friends yelled at me to **catch** the ball.*
• clutch, grab, grasp, grip, hang on to, hold, seize, snatch, take
❷ *One of the anglers **caught** a fish.*
• hook, net, trap
❸ *The police hoped to **catch** the thief red-handed.*
• arrest, capture, corner
(informal) nab
❹ *I hope you don't **catch** my cold.*
• become infected by, contract, get
(informal) go down with
❺ *You must hurry if you want to **catch** the bus.*
• be in time for, get on
➤ **to catch on**
*Their latest record didn't **catch on**.*
• become popular, do well, succeed
(informal) make it
➤ **to catch up with someone**
*If we run we'll **catch up with** them.*
• gain on, overtake

catch *NOUN*
❶ *The angler got a large **catch** of salmon.*
• haul
❷ *The car is so cheap that there must be a **catch**.*
• problem, obstacle, snag, difficulty, disadvantage, drawback, trap, trick
❸ *All the windows are fitted with safety **catches**.*
• fastening, latch, lock, bolt, hook

catching *ADJECTIVE*
*Chickenpox is **catching**.*
• contagious, infectious

category *NOUN*
*I won first prize in the under-10s **category**.*
• group, section, class, division, set

cater *VERB*
➤ **to cater for**
*The hotel can **cater for** a hundred guests.*
• cook for, provide food for, serve, supply

cattle *PLURAL NOUN*
Male cattle are **bulls, steers** or **oxen**.
Female cattle are **cows**.
Young male cattle are **calves** or **bullocks**.
Young female cattle are **calves** or **heifers**.
A word meaning 'to do with cattle' is **bovine**.
Farm animals in general are **livestock**.

caught *past tense see* **catch**

cause *NOUN*
❶ *What was the **cause** of the trouble?*
• origin, source, start
You can also talk about the **reasons** for the trouble.
❷ *You've got no **cause** to complain.*
• grounds, basis, motive, reason

❸ *The sponsored walk is for a good **cause**.*
• purpose, object

cause *VERB*
*A single spark from the fire could **cause** an explosion.*
• bring about, create, generate, lead to, give rise to, result in, provoke, arouse

caution *NOUN*
❶ *We decided to proceed with **caution**.*
• care, attention, watchfulness, wariness, vigilance
❷ *The traffic warden let him off with a **caution**.*
• warning, reprimand, telling-off *(informal)* ticking-off

cautious *ADJECTIVE*
*My grandad is a **cautious** driver.*
• careful, attentive, watchful, wary, vigilant, hesitant
OPPOSITE reckless

cave *NOUN*
*The **cave** walls were covered with prehistoric paintings.*
• cavern, pothole, underground chamber

WORD WEB

A man-made cave with decorative walls is a **grotto**.

THINGS YOU MIGHT SEE IN A CAVE:

• cave painting, stalactite, stalagmite

The entrance to a cave is the **mouth**.

The top of a cave is the **roof** and the bottom is the **floor**.

Prehistoric people who lived in caves were **cavemen** and **cavewomen**, or **troglodytes**.

Someone who enjoys exploring caves is a **potholer**.

cave *VERB*
➤ **to cave in**
*The miners had a lucky escape when the roof **caved in**.*
• collapse, fall in

cavity *NOUN*
*The map was lodged in a secret **cavity** in the wall.*
• hole, hollow, space, chamber

cease *VERB*
*The fighting **ceased** at midnight.*
• come to an end, end, finish, stop, halt
OPPOSITE begin

ceaseless *ADJECTIVE*
*The **ceaseless** noise of traffic kept me awake all night.*
• constant, continual, continuous, never-ending, non-stop, incessant, interminable, endless, everlasting, permanent, perpetual, unending, persistent, relentless
OPPOSITE brief

celebrate *VERB*
❶ *Let's **celebrate**!*
• enjoy yourself, have a good time, be happy, rejoice
❷ *What shall we do to **celebrate** Granny's birthday?*
• commemorate, observe, keep

celebrated *ADJECTIVE*
*Beatrix Potter is a **celebrated** author of children's books.*
• famous, well-known, respected, renowned, eminent, distinguished, notable, outstanding, popular, prominent
OPPOSITE unknown

celebration *NOUN*
*We had a big **celebration** for my cousin's wedding.*
• festivity, party, feast, festival, banquet, jamboree

celebrity *NOUN*
*The awards were handed out by a TV **celebrity**.*
• famous person, personality, public figure, VIP, star, idol

cellar *NOUN*
We keep our bikes and sports gear in the ***cellar.***
• **basement, vault**
see also **basement**

cemetery *NOUN*
A famous author is buried in the local ***cemetery.***
• **graveyard, burial ground, churchyard**
A place where dead people are cremated is a **crematorium.**

central *ADJECTIVE*
❶ *We are now in the* ***central*** *part of the building.*
• **middle, core, inner, interior**
OPPOSITE **outer**
❷ *Who are the* ***central*** *characters in the story?*
• **chief, crucial, essential, fundamental, important, main, major, principal, vital**
OPPOSITE **unimportant**

centre *NOUN*
The library is in the ***centre*** *of the town.*
The burial chamber is in the ***centre*** *of the pyramid.*
• **middle, heart, core, inside, interior**
The centre of a planet or a piece of fruit is the **core.**
The centre of an atom or living cell is the **nucleus.**
The centre of a wheel is the **hub.**
The point at the centre of a see-saw is the **pivot.**
The edible part in the centre of a nut is the **kernel.**
OPPOSITES **edge, outside, surface**

ceremony *NOUN*
❶ *We watched the* ***ceremony*** *of the opening of parliament.*
• **rite, ritual, formalities**
A ceremony where someone is given a prize is a **presentation.**
A ceremony where someone is given a special honour is an **investiture.**
A ceremony to celebrate something new is an **inauguration** or **opening.**
A ceremony where someone becomes a member of a society is an **initiation.**
A ceremony to make a church or other building sacred is a **dedication.**
A ceremony to remember a dead person or a past event is a **commemoration.**
A ceremony held in a church is a **service.**
for ceremonies which can be held in a church see **church**
❷ *They had a quiet wedding without a lot of* ***ceremony.***
• **formality, pomp, pageantry, spectacle**

certain *ADJECTIVE*
❶ *My mum was* ***certain*** *she would win the cookery competition.*
• **confident, convinced, positive, sure, determined**
OPPOSITE **uncertain**
❷ *We have* ***certain*** *proof that the painting is a forgery.*
• **definite, clear, convincing, absolute, unquestionable, reliable, trustworthy, undeniable, infallible, genuine, valid**
OPPOSITE **unreliable**
❸ *The damaged plane faced* ***certain*** *disaster.*
• **inevitable, unavoidable**
OPPOSITE **possible**
❹ *Her new book is* ***certain*** *to be a bestseller.*
• **bound, sure**
➤ **for certain**
I'll give you the money tomorrow ***for certain.***
• **certainly, definitely, for sure, without doubt, sure**
➤ **to make certain**
Please ***make certain*** *that you switch off the lights.*
• **make sure, ensure**

certainly *ADVERB*
Baby dragons are ***certainly*** *not timid.*
• **definitely, undoubtedly, unquestionably, assuredly, without a doubt**

certificate *NOUN*
At the end of the course, you will receive a ***certificate.***
• **diploma, document, licence**

chain *NOUN*
❶ *The anchor was attached to a **chain**.*
One ring in a chain is a **link**.
A chain used to link railway wagons together is a **coupling**.
❷ *The police formed a **chain** to keep the crowd back.*
• **line, row, cordon**
❸ *Holmes described the **chain** of events that led to the murder.*
• **series, sequence, succession, string**

chair *NOUN*
for furniture to sit on see **seat**

challenge *VERB*
*I **challenged** Jo not to eat sweets for a week.*
• **dare, defy**

champion *NOUN*
❶ *She is the current world **champion** at ice-skating.*
• **title-holder, prizewinner, victor, winner, conqueror**
❷ *Martin Luther King was a **champion** of civil rights.*
• **supporter, advocate, defender, upholder, patron, backer**

championship *NOUN*
*Fifteen schools took part in the karate **championship**.*
• **competition, contest, tournament**

chance *NOUN*
❶ *They say there's a **chance** of rain later.*
• **possibility, likelihood, probability, prospect, danger, risk**
❷ *I haven't had a **chance** to reply yet.*
• **opportunity, time, occasion**
❸ *The director took a **chance** in hiring an unknown actor.*
• **gamble, risk**
➤ **by chance**
*I found the house quite **by chance**.*
• **by accident, accidentally, by coincidence**
An unfortunate chance is **bad luck** or a **misfortune**.
A fortunate chance is **good luck** or a **fluke**.

change *VERB*
❶ *They've **changed** the programme for the concert.*
• **alter, modify, rearrange, reorganise, adjust, adapt, vary**
❷ *The town has **changed** a lot since Victorian times.*
• **alter, become different, develop, grow, move on**
❸ *Can I **change** these jeans for a bigger size, please?*
• **exchange, replace, switch, substitute** *(informal)* **swap**
➤ **to change into**
*Tadpoles **change into** frogs.*
• **become, turn into, metamorphose into**

change *NOUN*
*There has been a slight **change** of plan.*
• **alteration, modification, variation, difference, break**
A change to something worse is a **deterioration**.
A change to something better is an **improvement** or a **reform**.
A very big change is a **revolution**, **transformation** or **U-turn**.
A change in which one person or thing is replaced by another is a **substitution**.
A complete change made by some living things is a **metamorphosis**.

changeable *ADJECTIVE*
*The weather has been **changeable** today.*
• **variable, unsettled, unpredictable, unreliable, inconsistent, erratic, unstable**
If your loyalty is changeable you are **fickle**.
OPPOSITE **steady**

channel *NOUN*
❶ *The rainwater runs along this **channel**.*
• **ditch, duct, gully, gutter, furrow, trough**
❷ *How many TV **channels** do you get?*
• **station**

chaos *NOUN*
*After the earthquake, the city was in **chaos**.*
• **confusion, disorder, mayhem, uproar, tumult, pandemonium, anarchy, bedlam, muddle, shambles**
OPPOSITE **order**

chaotic *ADJECTIVE*
*Alice finds that life in Wonderland is **chaotic**.*
• **confused, disorderly, disorganised, muddled, topsy-turvy, untidy, unruly, riotous**
OPPOSITES **orderly, organised**

chapter *NOUN*
*I read a **chapter** of my book last night.*
• **part, section, division**
One section of a play is an **act** or **scene**.
One part of a serial is an **episode** or **instalment**.

character *NOUN*
❶ *Her **character** is quite different from her sister's.*
• **personality, temperament, nature, disposition, make-up, manner**
❷ *Our neighbour is a well-known **character** in our street.*
• **figure, personality, individual, person**
❸ *Who is your favourite **character** in 'Harry Potter'?*
• **part, role**
for ways to describe the characters in a story see **writing**

characteristic *NOUN*
*The Martians had some odd physical **characteristics**.*
• **feature, peculiarity, attribute, trait, distinguishing feature**

characteristic *ADJECTIVE*
*Windmills are a **characteristic** feature of this area.*
• **typical, distinctive, recognisable, particular, special, unique, singular**

charge *NOUN*
❶ *The admission **charge** is five euros.*
• **price, rate**
The charge made for a ride on public transport is the **fare**.
The charge made to post a letter or parcel is the **postage**.
A charge made to join a club is a **fee** or **subscription**.
A charge made for certain things by the government is a **duty** or a **tax**.
A charge made to use a private road, bridge or tunnel is a **toll**.
❷ *The robbers face several criminal **charges**.*
• **accusation, allegation**
❸ *Many soldiers were killed in the **charge**.*
• **assault, attack, onslaught, raid**
❹ *My best friend left her hamster in my **charge**.*
• **care, keeping, protection, custody, trust**
➤ **to be in charge of something**
*An experienced sailor was **in charge of** the crew.*
• **manage, lead, command, direct, supervise, run**

charge *VERB*
❶ *The library **charges** ten pence for a photocopy.*
• **ask for, make you pay**
❷ *A man has been **charged** with attempted robbery*
• **accuse (of)**
❸ *The cavalry **charged** the enemy line.*
• **attack, assault, storm, rush**

charm *NOUN*
❶ *In the painting, the girl's face is full of youthful **charm**.*
• **attractiveness, appeal, charisma**
❷ *The sorcerer recited a magic **charm**.*
• **spell, incantation**
for other words to do with magic see **magic**
❸ *The boy carried a crystal as a lucky **charm**.*
• **talisman, mascot, amulet, trinket**

charm *VERB*
*Winnie the Pooh has **charmed** readers all over the world.*
• **bewitch, captivate, delight, enchant, entrance, fascinate, please**

charming *ADJECTIVE*
*We drove through some **charming** scenery.*
• **delightful, attractive, pleasant, pleasing, likeable, appealing**

chart *NOUN*
❶ *The explorer stopped to consult his* ***chart****.*
• map
❷ *This* ***chart*** *shows the average monthly rainfall.*
• diagram, graph, table

charter *VERB*
We ***chartered*** *a minibus for our trip.*
• hire, lease, rent

chase *VERB*
The wolves ***chased*** *a deer through the forest.*
• pursue, run after, follow, track, trail, hunt

chasm *NOUN*
From the bridge, we looked down at a deep ***chasm****.*
• hole, ravine, crevasse, canyon, gorge, abyss, gulf, fissure, pit, rift

chat or **chatter** *VERB*
see talk

chatty *ADJECTIVE*
Frank is usually shy, but today he's quite ***chatty****.*
• talkative, communicative
OPPOSITE silent

cheap *ADJECTIVE*
❶ *We got a* ***cheap*** *flight to London.*
• inexpensive, affordable, bargain, cut-price, discount, reasonable
❷ *These tyres are made from* ***cheap*** *rubber.*
• inferior, shoddy, second-rate, worthless, trashy
(informal) tacky, tatty
OPPOSITES superior, good-quality

cheat *VERB*
❶ *She was* ***cheated*** *into buying a fake diamond ring.*
• deceive, trick, swindle, double-cross, hoax, fool
(informal) con, diddle, fleece, rip-off
❷ *Anyone who* ***cheats*** *in the quiz will be disqualified.*
• copy, crib

cheat *NOUN*
Don't trust him—he's a ***cheat****.*
• cheater, deceiver, swindler, fraud, impostor, hoaxer, charlatan

check *VERB*
❶ *Have you* ***checked*** *your work carefully?*
• examine, inspect, look over, scrutinise
❷ *The heavy snow* ***checked*** *their progress towards the Pole.*
• hamper, hinder, block, obstruct, delay, hold back, slow, slow down, halt, stop

check *NOUN*
I need to run some ***checks*** *on your computer.*
• test, examination, inspection, check-up

cheeky *ADJECTIVE*
Don't be so ***cheeky****!*
• disrespectful, facetious, flippant, impertinent, impolite, impudent, insolent, insulting, irreverent, mocking, rude, saucy, shameless
OPPOSITE respectful

cheer *VERB*
❶ *We* ***cheered*** *when our team scored a goal.*
• clap, applaud, shout, yell
OPPOSITE jeer
❷ *The good news* ***cheered*** *us.*
• comfort, console, gladden, delight, please, encourage, uplift
OPPOSITE sadden
➤ **to cheer up**
The weather had ***cheered up*** *by the afternoon.*
• become more cheerful, brighten

cheerful *ADJECTIVE*
The sun was shining, and we set out in a ***cheerful*** *mood.*
• happy, good-humoured, light-hearted, merry, jolly, joyful, joyous, glad, pleased, optimistic, lively, elated, animated, bright, buoyant, jovial, gleeful, chirpy
OPPOSITE sad

cheese *NOUN*

WORD WEB

SOME TYPES OF CHEESE:

• **blue cheese, Brie, cottage cheese, cream cheese, Cheddar, crowdie, mozzarella, parmesan, ricotta, Stilton**
for other kinds of food see **food**

chemist *NOUN*
• **pharmacist**
(historical) **apothecary, alchemist**
A chemist's shop is a **dispensary** or **pharmacy.**

chess *NOUN*

WORD WEB

THE PIECES USED IN PLAYING CHESS ARE:

• **bishop, castle** or **rook, king, knight, pawn, queen**

SOME TERMS USED IN PLAYING CHESS:

• **castle, check, checkmate, mate, move, stalemate, take**
for other board games see **game**

chest *NOUN*
I found some old books in a ***chest*** *in the attic.*
• **box, crate, case, trunk**

chew *VERB*
Are you still ***chewing*** *that toffee?*
• **eat, gnaw, munch**
for other ways to eat see **eat**

chicken *NOUN*
A female chicken is a **hen.**
A male chicken is a **rooster.**
A young chicken is a **chick.**
A group of chickens is a **brood.**
A farm which keeps chickens is a **poultry farm.**

chief *NOUN*
The pirates chose Redbeard as their ***chief.***
• **leader, ruler, head, commander, captain, chieftain, master, governor, president, principal**
(informal) **boss**

chief *ADJECTIVE*
❶ *The* ***chief*** *ingredients in a trifle are jelly, custard and cream.*
• **main, central, key, principal, crucial, basic, essential, important, vital, major, primary, foremost, fundamental, indispensable, necessary, significant, predominant, prominent**
OPPOSITES **unimportant, minor, trivial**
❷ *Albert was Queen Victoria's* ***chief*** *advisor.*
• **head, senior**

chiefly *ADVERB*
Kangaroos are found ***chiefly*** *in Australia.*
• **mainly, mostly, predominantly, primarily, principally, especially**

child *NOUN*
❶ *The book festival is aimed especially at* ***children.***
• **boy** or **girl, infant, juvenile, youngster, youth, lad** or **lass**
(informal) **kid, tot, nipper**
❷ *How many* ***children*** *do you have?*
• **son** or **daughter, descendant, offspring**
A child who expects to inherit a title or fortune from parents is an **heir** or **heiress.**
A child whose parents are dead is an **orphan.**
A child looked after by a guardian is a **ward.**
see also **baby**

childhood *NOUN*
Neil spent much of his ***childhood*** *by the sea.*
• **infancy, youth, boyhood** or **girlhood**
The time when someone is a baby is their **babyhood.**
The time when someone is a teenager is their **adolescence** or **teens.**
OPPOSITE **adulthood**

A B C D E F G H I J K L M N O P Q R S T U V W X Y Z

childish *ADJECTIVE*
It's ***childish*** *to make rude noises.*
• **babyish, immature, juvenile, infantile**
OPPOSITE **mature**

chill *VERB*
Chill *the pudding before serving it.*
• **freeze, cool, make cold, refrigerate**
OPPOSITE **warm**

chilly *ADJECTIVE*
❶ *It's a* ***chilly*** *evening, so wrap up well.*
• **cold, cool, frosty, icy, crisp, fresh, raw, wintry** *(informal)* **nippy**
OPPOSITE **warm**
❷ *The librarian gave me a very* ***chilly*** *look.*
• **unfriendly, hostile, unwelcoming, unsympathetic**
OPPOSITE **friendly**

chime *VERB*
The church clock ***chimed*** *at midnight.*
• **ring, sound, strike, peal, toll**
for sounds made by a bell see **bell**

chimney *NOUN*
A chimney on a ship or steam engine is a **funnel.**
A pipe to take away smoke and fumes is a **flue.**

chip *NOUN*
❶ *There were* ***chips*** *of broken glass on the pavement.*
• **bit, piece, fragment, scrap, sliver, splinter, flake, shaving**
❷ *This mug's got a* ***chip*** *in it.*
• **crack, nick, notch, flaw**

chip *VERB*
I ***chipped*** *a cup while I was washing up.*
• **crack, nick, notch, damage**

choice *NOUN*
❶ *My bike had a flat tyre, so I had no* ***choice*** *but to walk.*
• **alternative, option**
❷ *She wouldn't be my* ***choice*** *as team captain.*
• **preference, selection, pick, vote**
❸ *The greengrocer has a good* ***choice*** *of vegetables.*
• **range, selection, assortment, array, mixture, variety, diversity**

choke *VERB*
❶ *This tie is so tight it's* ***choking*** *me.*
• **strangle, suffocate, stifle, throttle**
❷ *Thick fumes made the firefighters* ***choke.***
• **cough, gasp**

choose *VERB* **chooses, choosing, chose, chosen**
❶ *We had a show of hands to* ***choose*** *a winner.*
• **select, appoint, elect, vote for**
❷ *I* ***chose*** *the blue shoes to go with my dress.*
• **decide on, select, pick out, opt for, plump for, settle on, single out**
❸ *Lola* ***chose*** *to stay at home.*
• **decide, make a decision, determine, prefer, resolve**

chop *VERB*
❶ ***Chop*** *the celery into large chunks.*
• **cut, split**
❷ *They* ***chopped*** *down the undergrowth to make a path.*
• **hack, slash**
To chop down a tree is to **fell** it.
To chop a branch off a tree is to **lop** it.
To chop off an arm or leg is to **amputate** it.
To chop food into small pieces is to **dice** or **mince** it.

chorus *NOUN*
❶ *I'm singing in the* ***chorus*** *in the school musical.*
• **choir**
❷ *I forgot the words to the song, so I just sang the* ***chorus.***
• **refrain**

chubby *ADJECTIVE*
The baby chicks are fluffy and ***chubby.***
• **plump, tubby, podgy, dumpy**

chunk *NOUN*
*I bit a **chunk** out of my apple.*
• piece, portion, lump, block, hunk, slab, wedge

church *NOUN*

WORD WEB

PLACES WHERE CHRISTIANS WORSHIP:
• abbey, cathedral, chapel, meeting house, parish church
for places where people of other religions worship see **building**

PARTS OF A CHURCH:
• aisle, belfry, chancel, cloister, crypt, nave, spire, steeple, transept, vestry

THINGS YOU MIGHT SEE IN A CHURCH:
• altar, crucifix, font, lectern, pews, pulpit

SERVICES WHICH MAY BE HELD IN A CHURCH:
• baptism or christening, communion, confirmation, funeral, mass, wedding

circle *NOUN*
❶ *We arranged the chairs in a **circle**.*
• ring, round, hoop, loop, band
A flat solid circle is a **disc**.
A three-dimensional round shape is a **sphere**.
An egg shape is an **oval** or **ellipse**.
for other shapes see **shape**
The distance round a circle is the **circumference**.
The distance across a circle is the **diameter**.
The distance from the centre to the circumference is the **radius**.
A circular movement is a **revolution** or **rotation**.
A circular trip round the world is a **circumnavigation**.
A circular trip round a planet is an **orbit**.
❷ *She has a wide **circle** of friends.*
• group, set, crowd

circle *VERB*
*The vultures **circled** overhead.*
• turn, go round, revolve, rotate, wheel

circular *ADJECTIVE*
*The flying saucer was **circular** in shape.*
• round, ring-shaped, disc-shaped

circulate *VERB*
❶ *Blood **circulates** in the body.*
• go round, move round
❷ *I asked friends to **circulate** our newsletter.*
• distribute, send round, issue

circumference *NOUN*
*There is a fence around the **circumference** of the field.*
• perimeter, border, boundary, edge, fringe

circumstances *PLURAL NOUN*
*He described the **circumstances** which led to the accident.*
• situation, conditions, background, causes, context, details, facts, particulars

citizen *NOUN*
*The **citizens** of New York are proud of their city.*
• resident, inhabitant

city *NOUN*
The main city of a country or region is the **metropolis**.
An area of houses outside the central part of a city is the **suburbs**.
A word meaning 'to do with a town or city' is **urban**.
A word meaning 'to do with a city and its suburbs' is **metropolitan**.
see also **town**

civilisation *NOUN*
*We are studying the **civilisation** of ancient Egypt.*
• culture, society, achievements, attainments

civilised *ADJECTIVE*
*Trolls seldom behave in a **civilised** manner.*
• polite, well-behaved, well-mannered, orderly, cultured, sophisticated, refined
OPPOSITE **uncivilised**

A B C D E F G H I J K L M N O P Q R S T U V W X Y Z

claim *VERB*
❶ *You can **claim** your prize for the raffle here.*
• ask for, request, collect, demand, insist on
❷ *The professor **claims** to be an expert on dinosaurs.*
• declare, assert, allege, maintain, argue, insist

clamber *VERB*
*We **clambered** over the rocks towards the sea.*
• climb, scramble, crawl, move awkwardly

clang and **clank** *NOUN, VERB*
see **sound**

clap *VERB*
❶ *The audience **clapped** loudly at the end of the concert.*
• applaud, cheer
❷ *Suddenly, a hand **clapped** me on the shoulder.*
• slap, hit, pat, smack

clash *NOUN*
❶ *The **clash** of cymbals made me jump.*
• crash, bang, ringing
❷ *There was a **clash** between rival supporters at the match.*
• argument, confrontation, conflict, fight, scuffle
(informal) scrap

clash *VERB*
❶ *The cymbals **clashed**.*
• crash, resound
❷ *Two good films **clash** on TV tonight.*
• coincide, happen at the same time
❸ *Demonstrators **clashed** with the police.*
• argue, fight, get into conflict, squabble

clasp *VERB*
❶ *My little brother **clasped** my hand.*
• grasp, grip, hold, squeeze, cling to
❷ *She **clasped** him in her arms.*
• embrace, hug

clasp *NOUN*
*The cloak was held in place by a gold **clasp**.*
• fastener, fastening, brooch, clip, pin, buckle, hook

class *NOUN*
❶ *There are 26 children in our **class**.*
• form, set, stream
The other pupils in your class are your classmates.
❷ *There are many different **classes** of plants.*
• category, group, classification, division, set, sort, type, kind, species
❸ *The ancient Romans divided people into social **classes**.*
• level, rank, status

classic *ADJECTIVE*
*That was a **classic** tennis final this year.*
• excellent, first-class, first-rate, top-notch, exceptional, fine, great, admirable, masterly, model, perfect
OPPOSITE ordinary
WHICH WORD? Note that **classic** is not the same as **classical**, which means either 'to do with the ancient Greeks and Romans' or 'to do with serious music written in the past'.

claw *VERB*
*We could hear the monster **clawing** at the door.*
• scratch, scrape, tear, savage

clean *ADJECTIVE*
❶ *Can you bring me a **clean** cup, please?*
• spotless, washed, scrubbed, swept, tidy, immaculate, hygienic, sanitary
An informal word meaning 'very clean' is **squeaky-clean**.
A common simile is **as clean as a whistle**.
OPPOSITE dirty
❷ *I began my diary on a **clean** piece of paper.*
• blank, unused, unmarked, empty, bare, fresh, new
OPPOSITE used
❸ *This plaster will keep the wound **clean**.*
• sterile, sterilised, uninfected
❹ *You can get **clean** water from this tap.*
• pure, clear, fresh, unpolluted, uncontaminated
❺ *The referee said he wanted a **clean** fight.*
• fair, honest, honourable, sporting, sportsmanlike
OPPOSITE dishonourable

clean *VERB*

❶ *We **cleaned** the house from top to bottom. I tried to **clean** the mud off my boots.*
• **wash, wipe, mop, scour, scrub, polish, dust, sweep, vacuum, rinse, wring out, hose down, sponge, shampoo, swill**
To clean clothes is to **launder** them.
OPPOSITE **dirty, mess up**
❷ *The nurse **cleaned** the wound with an antiseptic wipe.*
• **cleanse, bathe, disinfect, sanitise, sterilise**
OPPOSITES **infect, contaminate**

clear *ADJECTIVE*

❶ *We saw fish swimming in the **clear** pool.*
• **clean, pure, colourless, transparent**
A common simile is **as clear as crystal**.
OPPOSITE **opaque**
❷ *It was a beautiful **clear** day.*
• **bright, sunny, cloudless, unclouded**
A clear night is a **moonlit** or **starlit** night.
OPPOSITES **cloudy, overcast**
❸ *The instructions on the map were quite **clear**.*
• **plain, understandable, intelligible, lucid, unambiguous**
OPPOSITES **ambiguous, confusing**
❹ *The actor spoke his words with a **clear** voice.*
• **distinct, audible**
A common simile is **as clear as a bell**.
OPPOSITE **muffled**
❺ *The signature on this letter is not **clear**.*
• **legible, recognisable, visible**
OPPOSITE **illegible**
❻ *My camera takes nice **clear** pictures.*
• **sharp, well defined, focused**
OPPOSITE **unfocused**
❼ *Are you sure that your conscience is **clear**?*
• **innocent, untroubled, blameless**
OPPOSITE **guilty**
❽ *There's a **clear** difference between a male blackbird and a female.*
• **obvious, definite, noticeable, conspicuous, perceptible, pronounced**
OPPOSITE **imperceptible**
❾ *They made sure the road was **clear** for the ambulance.*
• **open, empty, free, passable, uncrowded, unobstructed**
OPPOSITE **congested**

clear *VERB*

❶ *I **cleared** the weeds from the flower bed.*
• **get rid of, remove, eliminate, strip**
❷ *The plumber **cleared** the blocked drain.*
• **unblock, unclog, clean out, open up**
To clear a channel is to **dredge** it.
❸ *I **cleared** the misty windows.*
• **clean, wipe, polish**
❹ *If the fire alarm goes, **clear** the building.*
• **empty, evacuate**
❺ *The fog **cleared** slowly.*
• **disappear, vanish, disperse, evaporate, melt away**
❻ *The forecast said that the weather will **clear**.*
• **become clear, brighten, brighten up**
❼ *He was **cleared** of all the charges against him.*
• **acquit, free, release**
❽ *The runners **cleared** the first hurdle.*
• **go over, get over, jump over, pass over, vault**

➤ **to clear up**
*Please **clear up** this mess before you go.*
• **clean up, tidy up, put right, put straight**

clench *VERB*

❶ *The warrior **clenched** his teeth and gripped his sword.*
• **close tightly, squeeze together, grit**
❷ *She **clenched** the coin tightly in her hand.*
• **clasp, hold, grasp, grip**

clever *ADJECTIVE*

❶ *Dr Hafiz is very **clever** and can read hieroglyphics.*
• **intelligent, bright, gifted, able, knowledgeable**
(informal) **brainy, smart**
OPPOSITE **unintelligent**
An informal name for a clever person is a **brainbox**.
An uncomplimentary synonym is **clever clogs** or **smarty pants**.
❷ *The elves were very **clever** with their fingers.*
• **accomplished, capable, gifted, skilful, talented**
If you are clever at a lot of things you are **versatile**.
OPPOSITE **unskilful**

A B C D E F G H I J K L M N O P Q R S T U V W X Y Z

❸ *They are **clever** enough to get away with it.*
• **quick, sharp, shrewd, smart**
Uncomplimentary synonyms are **artful, crafty, cunning, wily.**
OPPOSITE **stupid**

client *NOUN*
*The shop has a growing number of overseas **clients.***
• **customer, user, buyer, consumer**

cliff *NOUN*
*The car rolled over the edge of a **cliff.***
• **crag, precipice, rock face**

climate *NOUN*
see **weather**

climax *NOUN*
*The **climax** of the film is a stunning car chase.*
• **high point, highlight, peak**
OPPOSITE **anticlimax**

climb *VERB*
❶ *It took us several hours to **climb** the mountain.*
• **ascend, clamber up, go up, scale**
❷ *The plane **climbed** into the clouds.*
• **lift off, soar, take off**
❸ *The road **climbs** steeply up to the castle.*
• **rise, slope**
➤ **to climb down**
❶ *It's harder to **climb down** the rock than to get up it.*
• **descend, get down from**
❷ *We all told him he was wrong, so he had to **climb down.***
• **admit defeat, give in, surrender**

climb *NOUN*
*It's a steep **climb** up to the castle.*
• **ascent, hill, gradient, rise, slope, incline**

cling *VERB* **clings, clinging, clung**
➤ **to cling to someone** or **something**
❶ *The baby koala **clung to** its mother.*
• **clasp, grasp, clutch, embrace, hug**
❷ *Ivy **clings** to the wall.*
• **adhere to, fasten on to, stick to**

clip *VERB*
❶ *The sheets of paper were **clipped** together.*
• **pin, staple**
❷ *Dad **clipped** the hedges in the back garden.*
• **cut, trim**
To cut unwanted parts off a tree or bush is to **prune** it.

cloak *NOUN*
*The girl wrapped her **cloak** tightly around herself.*
• **cape, coat, wrap**
(old use) **mantle**

clock *NOUN*
for instruments used to measure time see **time**

clog *VERB*
*The dead leaves are **clogging** the drain.*
• **block, choke, congest, obstruct, bung up, jam, stop up**

close *ADJECTIVE (say* **klohss***)*
❶ *Our house is **close** to the shops.*
• **near, nearby, not far**
To be actually by the side of something is to be **adjacent.**
OPPOSITES **far, distant**
❷ *Anisha and I are **close** friends.*
• **intimate, dear, devoted, fond, affectionate**
❸ *The police made a **close** examination of the stolen car.*
• **careful, detailed, painstaking, minute, thorough**
OPPOSITE **casual**
❹ *It was an exciting race because it was so **close.***
• **equal, even, level, well-matched**
❺ *Open the window—it's very **close** in here.*
• **humid, muggy, stuffy, clammy, airless, stifling, suffocating**
OPPOSITE **airy**

close *VERB (say* **klohz***)*
❶ *Don't forget to **close** the lid.*
• **shut, fasten, seal, secure**
❷ *The road has been **closed** to traffic for the parade.*
• **barricade, block, obstruct, stop up**

❸ *The band **closed** the concert with my favourite song.*
• finish, end, complete, conclude, stop, terminate
(informal) wind up

clot *VERB*

*If you cut yourself, the blood will **clot** and form a scab.*
• thicken, solidify

cloth *NOUN*

*The curtains were made of striped cotton **cloth**.*
• fabric, material
A word for cloth in general is **textiles**.
for types of cloth see **fabric**

clothe *VERB*

➤ **to be clothed in**
*The bridesmaids were **clothed in** white.*
• be dressed in, be wearing

clothes *PLURAL NOUN*

*What **clothes** are you taking on holiday?*
• clothing, garments, outfits, dress, attire, garb, finery
(informal) gear, togs, get-up
A set of clothes to wear is a **costume**, **outfit** or **suit**.
An official set of clothes worn for school or work is a **uniform**.

WORD WEB

SOME ITEMS OF CLOTHING:

• blouse, caftan, camisole, dress, dungarees, frock, gown, hijab, jeans, jersey, jodhpurs, jumper, kaftan, kilt, kimono, leggings, miniskirt, pinafore, polo shirt, pullover, robe, sari, sarong, shirt, shorts, skirt, slacks, smock, suit, sweater, sweatshirt, trousers, trunks, T-shirt, tunic, waistcoat

OUTER CLOTHES:

• anorak, apron, blazer, cagoule, cape, cardigan, cloak, coat, dressing gown, duffel coat, fleece, gilet, hoody, greatcoat, jacket, mackintosh, oilskins, overalls, overcoat, parka, poncho, raincoat, shawl, shrug, stole, tracksuit

UNDERWEAR:

• boxer shorts, bra, briefs, crop top, drawers, knickers, pants, petticoat, slip, socks, stockings, tights, underpants, vest

CLOTHES FOR SLEEPING IN:

• nightdress or *(informal)* nightie, nightshirt, onesie, pyjamas or *(informal)* PJs

CLOTHES WORN IN THE PAST:

• corset, doublet, frock coat, gauntlet, ruff, toga

ACCESSORIES WORN WITH CLOTHES:

• belt, braces, cravat, earmuffs, gloves, sash, scarf, shawl, tie
see also **hat**, **shoe**

PARTS OF A GARMENT:

• bodice, button, buttonhole, collar, cuff, hem, lapel, pocket, seam, sleeve, waistband, zip

THINGS USED TO DECORATE CLOTHES:

• beads, frills, fringes, lace, ruffles, sequins, tassels

WRITING TIPS

You can use these words to describe **clothes**:
• baggy, casual, chic, dowdy, drab, fashionable, fine, flashy, flattering, frilly, frumpy, glamorous, ill-fitting, loose, luxurious, old-fashioned, ornate, ragged, roomy, shabby, skimpy, smart, sporty, stylish, tattered or in tatters, threadbare, tight-fitting, trendy, worn

The stranger was wearing an extremely shabby set of wizard's robes which had been darned in several places.—HARRY POTTER AND THE PRISONER OF AZKABAN, J. K. Rowling

cloud *NOUN*
A ***cloud*** *of steam billowed from the kettle.*
• billow, puff, haze, mist

cloudy *ADJECTIVE*
❶ *The day was cold and* ***cloudy.***
• dull, overcast, grey, dark, dismal, gloomy, sunless
OPPOSITE **cloudless**
see also **weather**
❷ *We couldn't see any fish in the* ***cloudy*** *water.*
• muddy, murky, hazy, milky
OPPOSITES **clear, transparent**

club *NOUN*
❶ *The warrior brandished a wooden* ***club.***
• stick, baton, truncheon
❷ *Would you like to join our book* ***club?***
• group, society, association, organisation, circle, union

club *VERB*
The giant ***clubbed*** *Jack on the head.*
• hit, strike, thump, whack, batter
(informal) **bash**
for other ways of hitting see **hit**

clue *NOUN*
❶ *I don't know the answer. Can you give me a* ***clue?***
• hint, suggestion, indication, pointer, tip, idea
❷ *'This footprint is an important* ***clue,'*** *said the detective.*
• piece of evidence, lead
see also **detective**

clump *NOUN*
The owl flew into a ***clump*** *of trees on the hill.*
• group, thicket, cluster, collection
A clump of grass or hair is a **tuft.**

clumsy *ADJECTIVE*
The ***clumsy*** *gnome was always breaking things.*
• careless, awkward, ungainly, inept
An informal name for a clumsy person is **butterfingers.**
OPPOSITE **graceful**

cluster *NOUN*
A ***cluster*** *of people waited outside the cinema.*
• crowd, bunch, collection, assembly, gathering, knot
see also **group**

clutch *VERB*
The mountaineer ***clutched*** *his rope.*
• catch, clasp, cling to, grab, grasp, grip, hang on to, hold on to, seize, snatch

clutches *PLURAL NOUN*
The evil wizard had us in his ***clutches.***
• grasp, power, control

clutter *NOUN*
We'll have to clear up all this ***clutter.***
• mess, muddle, junk, litter, rubbish, odds and ends

coach *NOUN*
❶ *We went to Cardiff by* ***coach.***
• bus
for other vehicles see **vehicle**
❷ *Their football team has a new* ***coach.***
• trainer, instructor

coach *VERB*
He was ***coached*** *by a former champion.*
• train, teach, instruct

coarse *ADJECTIVE*
❶ *The blanket was made of* ***coarse*** *woollen material.*
• rough, harsh, scratchy, bristly, hairy
OPPOSITE **soft**
❷ *We were shocked by their* ***coarse*** *table manners.*
• rude, offensive, impolite, improper, indecent, crude, vulgar
OPPOSITES **polite, refined**

coast *NOUN*
After the disaster, oil was washed up along the ***coast****.*
• **coastline, shore**
see also **seashore**

coast *VERB*
I ***coasted*** *down the hill on my bike.*
• **cruise, freewheel, glide**

coat *NOUN*
❶ *The detective was wearing a thick winter* ***coat****.*
for coats and other garments see **clothes**
❷ *The fox had a reddish-brown* ***coat****.*
• **hide, pelt, skin, fur, hair**
A sheep's coat is a **fleece**.
❸ *The front door needs a* ***coat*** *of paint.*
• **layer, coating, covering**
(informal) **lick**

coat *VERB*
We ate marshmallows ***coated*** *with chocolate.*
• **cover, spread, smear, glaze**

coax *VERB*
Sam ***coaxed*** *the hamster back into its cage.*
• **persuade, tempt, entice**

code *NOUN*
❶ *There is a strict* ***code*** *of conduct for using the pool.*
• **rules, regulations, laws**
❷ *The message was written in a secret* ***code****.*
To put a message in code is to **encode** or **encrypt** it.
To understand a message in code is to **decode**, **decipher** or *(informal)* **crack** it.
A person who studies how to make and decipher codes is a **cryptographer**.

coil *NOUN*
The snake twisted itself into a ***coil****.*
• **spiral, twist, curl, twirl, screw, corkscrew, whirl, whorl, roll, scroll**
A coil of wool or thread is a **skein**.

coil *VERB*
The snake ***coiled*** *itself round a branch.*
• **curl, loop, roll, spiral, turn, twist, twirl, wind, writhe**

coin *NOUN*
Do you have a 50 pence ***coin****?*
• **piece, bit**

WORD WEB

SOME TYPES OF COIN USED IN THE PAST:
• **doubloon, ducat, farthing, florin, guinea, shilling, sovereign**
A person who studies or collects coins is a **numismatist**.

coin *VERB*
We ***coined*** *a new name for our group.*
• **invent, make up, think up, create, devise, produce**

coincide *VERB*
My birthday ***coincides*** *with the school holidays.*
• **clash, fall together, happen together**

coincidence *NOUN*
➤ **by coincidence**
We met in town ***by coincidence****.*
• **by accident, by chance, accidentally, unintentionally, by a fluke**

cold *ADJECTIVE*
❶ *Wrap up warm in this* ***cold*** *weather.*
• **freezing, chilly, frosty, icy, raw, arctic, bitter, cool, crisp, snowy, wintry**
(informal) **perishing**
A common simile is **as cold as ice**.
OPPOSITES **hot, warm**
❷ *I tried to shelter from the* ***cold*** *wind.*
• **biting, bitter, keen, penetrating, piercing**
❸ *I was* ***cold*** *in spite of my woolly hat.*
• **freezing, frozen, chilly, chilled, shivering, shivery**
To be so cold that you become ill is to suffer from **hypothermia**.
OPPOSITES **hot, warm**
❹ *The cyclops gave us a* ***cold*** *stare from his one eye.*
• **unfriendly, unkind, unfeeling, distant, cool, heartless, indifferent, reserved, stony, uncaring, unemotional, unsympathetic**
OPPOSITES **warm, friendly**

A B C D E F G H I J K L M N O P Q R S T U V W X Y Z

collaborate *VERB*
*Several zoos **collaborated** on the rhino project.*
• cooperate, work together

collapse *VERB*
❶ *Many buildings **collapsed** in the earthquake.*
• fall down, fall in, cave in, give way, crumble, crumple, buckle, disintegrate, tumble down
❷ *Some of the runners **collapsed** in the heat.*
• faint, pass out, fall over, keel over

colleague *NOUN*
*The police officer discussed the plan with her **colleagues**.*
• associate, partner, teammate, co-worker, workmate

collect *VERB*
❶ *Squirrels **collect** nuts for the winter.*
• gather, accumulate, hoard, heap, pile up, store up, stockpile, amass
❷ *A crowd **collected** to watch the fire.*
• assemble, gather, come together, converge
OPPOSITE scatter, disperse
❸ *We **collected** a large sum for charity.*
• raise, take in
❹ *She **collected** the car from the garage.*
• fetch, get, obtain, bring
OPPOSITE drop off, hand in

collection *NOUN*
*Would you like to see my fossil **collection**?*
• assortment, set, accumulation, array, hoard, pile
A collection of books is a **library**.
A collection of poems or short stories is an **anthology**.

collective noun *NOUN*
for collective nouns see **group**

college *NOUN*
for places where people study
see **education**

collide *VERB*
➤ **to collide with**
*The runaway trolley **collided with** a wall.*
• bump into, crash into, run into, smash into, hit, strike

collision *NOUN*
*The **collision** dented the front wheel of my bike.*
• bump, crash, smash, knock, accident
A collision involving a lot of vehicles is a **pile-up**.

colloquial *ADJECTIVE*
*The book is written in a **colloquial** style.*
• everyday, informal, conversational, slangy
OPPOSITE formal

colossal *ADJECTIVE*
*A **colossal** statue towered above us.*
• huge, enormous, gigantic, immense, massive, giant, mammoth, monumental, towering, vast
OPPOSITE small, tiny

colour *NOUN*
*What do you call that **colour**?*
• hue, shade, tint, tone, tinge

WORD WEB

NAMES OF VARIOUS COLOURS:

• black, blue, brown, cream, gold, golden, green, grey, lavender, orange, pink, purple, red, silver, turquoise, violet, white, yellow
The colours red, yellow and blue are known as **primary colours**.
for shades of colours see **black, blue, brown, green, red, white, yellow**

WRITING TIPS

You can use these words to describe a colour:

TO DESCRIBE A PALE COLOUR:

• **delicate, dull, faded, faint, light, muted, neutral, pallid, pastel, soft, washed-out**
The west was a glory of soft, mingled hues, and the pond reflected them all in still softer shadings.—ANNE OF GREEN GABLES, L. M. Montgomery

TO DESCRIBE A STRONG COLOUR:

• **bright, brilliant, deep, fluorescent, garish, loud, lurid, neon, rich, vibrant, zingy**
My bike helmet is fluorescent orange.

colour *VERB*
*I **coloured** the icing deep pink.*
• **paint, dye, tint**

colourful *ADJECTIVE*
❶ *The rose garden is **colourful** in the summer.*
• **multicoloured, showy, vibrant, bright, brilliant, gaudy**
OPPOSITE **colourless**
❷ *The book gives a **colourful** account of life on an island.*
• **exciting, interesting, lively, vivid, striking, rich, picturesque**
OPPOSITE **dull**

colourless *ADJECTIVE*
❶ *The flask contained a **colourless** liquid.*
• **uncoloured, clear, transparent, neutral, pale**
Something which has lost its colour is **bleached** or **faded**.
❷ *All the characters in the book are **colourless**.*
• **dull, boring, uninteresting, unexciting, drab, dreary, lacklustre**
OPPOSITES **colourful, interesting**

column *NOUN*
❶ *The roof of the temple was supported by stone **columns**.*
• **pillar, post, support, shaft**
❷ *A **column** of soldiers wound its way across the desert.*
• **line, file, procession, row, string**
❸ *I sometimes read the sports **column** in the newspaper.*
• **article, piece, report, feature**

comb *VERB*
❶ *I **combed** my hair and put it in a ponytail.*
• **arrange, groom, tidy, untangle**
❷ *The police **combed** the house in search of clues.*
• **search thoroughly, hunt through, scour, ransack, rummage through**

combat *NOUN*
*Two hundred warriors were killed in **combat**.*
• **battle, war, warfare, fighting**
see also **fight**

combat *VERB*
*There's a new campaign to **combat** crime in the city.*
• **fight, oppose, resist, stand up to, tackle, battle against, grapple with**

combine *VERB*
❶ *We **combined** our pocket money to buy a kite.*
• **put together, add together, join, merge, unite, amalgamate**
OPPOSITE **divide**
❷ ***Combine** the mixture with water to make a paste.*
• **mix, stir together, blend, mingle, bind**
OPPOSITE **separate**

come *VERB* **comes, coming, came, come**
❶ *We expect our guests to **come** in the afternoon.*
• **arrive, appear, visit**
OPPOSITE **go**
❷ *When you hear a cuckoo, you know that summer is **coming**.*
• **advance, draw near**
➤ **to come about**
*Can you tell me how the accident **came about**?*
• **happen, occur, take place, result**

A B C D E F G H I J K L M N O P Q R S T U V W X Y Z

➤ **to come across**
*I **came across** an old friend of mine.*
• **find, discover, chance upon, meet, bump into**
➤ **to come round** or **to come to**
*How long did it take me to **come round** after the operation?*
• **become conscious, revive, wake up**
➤ **to come to**
❶ *Tell me when you **come to** the last chapter.*
• **reach, get to, arrive at**
❷ *What did the repair bill **come to?***
• **add up to, amount to, total**

comfort *NOUN*
❶ *My teddy bear was a **comfort** to me when I was ill.*
• **reassurance, consolation, encouragement, support, relief**
❷ *If I had a million pounds, I could live in **comfort**.*
• **ease, luxury, contentment, well-being, prosperity, affluence**

comfort *VERB*
*The coach tried to **comfort** the team after they lost.*
• **cheer up, console, reassure, encourage, hearten, sympathise with, soothe**

comfortable *ADJECTIVE*
❶ *The bed was so **comfortable** I fell fast asleep.*
• **cosy, snug, relaxing, easy, soft, warm, roomy, padded, plush**
(informal) **comfy**
OPPOSITE **uncomfortable**
❷ *We'll need **comfortable** clothes for travelling.*
• **casual, informal, loose-fitting**
❸ *Our cat leads a **comfortable** life.*
• **contented, happy, pleasant, agreeable, well-off, prosperous, luxurious, affluent**

comic or comical *ADJECTIVE*
*We laughed at his **comic** remarks.*
• **amusing, humorous, funny, hilarious, witty, diverting**
(informal) **hysterical**
To be comical in a cheeky way is to be **facetious**.
To be comical in a silly way is to be **absurd, farcical, ludicrous** or **ridiculous.**
To be comical in a hurtful way is to be **sarcastic.**

command *NOUN*
❶ *The general gave the **command** to attack.*
• **order, instruction, commandment, edict**
❷ *Captain Nemo has **command** of the whole crew.*
• **charge, control, authority (over), power (over), management, supervision**
❸ *My sister has a good **command** of Spanish.*
• **knowledge, mastery, grasp, understanding, ability (in), skill (in)**

command *VERB*
❶ *The officer **commanded** his troops to fire.*
• **order, instruct, direct, tell, bid**
❷ *The captain **commands** the ship.*
• **control, direct, be in charge of, govern, head, lead, manage, administer, supervise**

commander *NOUN*
*The **commander** decided to abandon the expedition.*
• **leader, chief, head, officer-in-charge**

commence *VERB*
*The flag is a signal for the race to **commence**.*
• **begin, start, embark (on)**

commend *VERB*
*The head **commended** us on our work.*
• **congratulate, compliment, praise, applaud**
OPPOSITE **criticise**

comment *NOUN*
*He made some nasty **comments** about his boss.*
• **remark, statement, observation, opinion, mention, reference**
A hostile comment is a **criticism.**

commit *VERB*
*The thieves were planning to **commit** another robbery.*
• **carry out, do, perform, execute**

commitment *NOUN*
❶ *Our team certainly has the* ***commitment*** *to win.*
• determination, dedication, enthusiasm, keenness, passion, resolution
❷ *I've made a* ***commitment*** *to join the choir.*
• promise, pledge, vow, undertaking, guarantee

committee *NOUN*
The tennis club is run by a ***committee*** *of volunteers.*
• board, panel, council, body, cabinet

common *ADJECTIVE*
❶ *Colds are a* ***common*** *complaint in winter.*
• commonplace, everyday, frequent, normal, ordinary, familiar, well-known, widespread
OPPOSITE rare
❷ *'Good morning' is a* ***common*** *way to greet people.*
• typical, usual, regular, routine, standard, customary, conventional, habitual, traditional
OPPOSITE uncommon
❸ *My friends and I have a* ***common*** *interest in music.*
• shared, mutual, joint

commonplace *ADJECTIVE*
Computers are now ***commonplace*** *in schools.*
• common, everyday, frequent, usual, normal, ordinary, routine, familiar

commotion *NOUN*
Football supporters were causing a ***commotion*** *outside.*
• disturbance, row, fuss, trouble, disorder, unrest, agitation, turmoil, uproar, racket, rumpus, upheaval, riot, fracas, furore, hullabaloo, brouhaha, pandemonium, bedlam

communal *ADJECTIVE*
The swimming pool has ***communal*** *showers.*
• shared, public, common
OPPOSITE private

communicate *VERB*
❶ *Steve* ***communicated*** *his boredom with a yawn.*
• express, make known, indicate, convey, disclose, announce, pass on, proclaim, publish, report
❷ *Nowadays, we* ***communicate*** *by email.*
• contact each other, correspond, be in touch

communication *NOUN*
❶ *Dolphins use sound for* ***communication****.*
• communicating, contact, understanding each other
❷ *I've received an urgent* ***communication****.*
• message, dispatch, letter, statement, announcement

WORD WEB

SOME FORMS OF SPOKEN COMMUNICATION:
• chat, conversation, dialogue, gossip, lecture, message, phone call, rumour, speech, voicemail

SOME FORMS OF WRITTEN COMMUNICATION:
• blog, correspondence, email, greetings card, letter, memo or memorandum, note, notice, postcard, text, tweet

OTHER FORMS OF COMMUNICATION:
• body language, Braille, hand gesture, the Internet, Morse code, podcast, radio, semaphore, sign language or signing, social media, telepathy, television, vlog, website

community *NOUN*
My uncle grew up in a farming ***community****.*
• area, district, neighbourhood, locality

compact *ADJECTIVE*
This camera is light and ***compact****.*
• small, portable, petite
OPPOSITE large

A B C D E F G H I J K L M N O P Q R S T U V W X Y Z

companion *NOUN*
Zak's pony was his favourite ***companion.***
• friend, partner, comrade
(informal) mate, buddy, pal, chum

company *NOUN*
❶ *My cousin works for a computer* ***company.***
• business, firm, corporation, organisation, establishment
❷ *Shrek shunned the* ***company*** *of other ogres.*
• fellowship, companionship, friendship, society

compare *VERB*
Can you ***compare*** *these sets of figures?*
• contrast, juxtapose, relate, set side by side
➤ **to compare with**
This copy can't ***compare with*** *the original painting.*
• compete with, rival, emulate, equal, match

comparison *NOUN*
❶ *I put the two dresses side by side for* ***comparison.***
• comparing, contrast, juxtaposition
❷ *There's no* ***comparison*** *between their team and ours.*
• similarity, resemblance, likeness, match

compartment *NOUN*
The sewing box has ***compartments*** *for needles and pins.*
• section, division, area, space

compatible *ADJECTIVE*
Miss Scott and her mother were not at all ***compatible.***
• well-suited, well-matched
OPPOSITE incompatible

compel *VERB*
You can't ***compel*** *me to come with you.*
• force, make

compete *VERB*
Five schools will be ***competing*** *in the hockey tournament.*
• participate, perform, take part, enter
➤ **to compete against**
We are ***competing against*** *a strong team this week.*
• oppose, play against, contend with

competent *ADJECTIVE*
You have to be a ***competent*** *swimmer to join the club.*
• able, capable, skilful, skilled, accomplished, proficient, experienced, expert, qualified, trained
OPPOSITE incompetent

competition *NOUN*

WORD WEB

SOME KINDS OF COMPETITION:

• championship, contest, game, knockout competition, match, quiz, race, rally, series, tournament, trial
see also **sport**

competitor *NOUN*
The ***competitors*** *lined up for the start of the race.*
• contestant, contender, challenger, participant, opponent, rival
People who take an exam are **candidates** or **entrants.**

complain *VERB*
Miss Grouch spent most of her life ***complaining.***
• moan, protest, grumble, grouse, gripe, whinge, make a fuss
➤ **to complain about**
I wrote a letter ***complaining about*** *the noise.*
• protest about, object to, criticise, find fault with
OPPOSITE praise

complaint *NOUN*
❶ *They received hundreds of* ***complaints*** *about the film.*
• criticism, objection, protest, moan, grumble

❷ *You have a nasty stomach **complaint**.*
• disease, illness, ailment, sickness, infection

complement *VERB*
*That shade of green **complements** your eyes.*
• accompany, go with

complete *ADJECTIVE*
❶ *Your training as a witch is not yet **complete**.*
• completed, ended, finished, accomplished, concluded
OPPOSITE unfinished
❷ *Have you got a **complete** set of cards?*
• whole, entire, full, intact
OPPOSITE incomplete
❸ *My birthday party was a **complete** disaster.*
• total, utter, sheer, absolute, thorough, downright, perfect, pure

complete *VERB*
*We have **completed** all the tasks on the sheet.*
• finish, end, conclude, carry out, perform

complex *ADJECTIVE*
*Defusing a bomb is a **complex** task.*
• complicated, difficult, elaborate, detailed, intricate, involved
(informal) fiddly
OPPOSITE simple

complexion *NOUN*
*The elf had a greenish tinge to his **complexion**.*
• skin, colour, colouring
for ways to describe complexion see **face**

complicated *ADJECTIVE*
*The plot of the film is very **complicated**.*
• complex, intricate, involved, difficult, elaborate, convoluted
OPPOSITES simple, straightforward

complimentary *ADJECTIVE*
❶ *My teacher made **complimentary** remarks on my playing.*
• appreciative, approving, admiring, positive, favourable, flattering
OPPOSITES critical, insulting, negative
❷ *We were given **complimentary** tickets for the game.*
• free, gratis

compliments *PLURAL NOUN*
*It was nice to get **compliments** about my cooking.*
• praise, appreciation, approval, congratulations, tribute
Compliments which you don't deserve are flattery.
OPPOSITE insults

component *NOUN*
*The factory makes **components** for cars.*
• part, bit, piece, element, spare part

compose *VERB*
*Beethoven **composed** nine symphonies.*
• create, devise, produce, make up, think up, write
➤ **to be composed of**
*This quilt is **composed of** pieces of patchwork.*
• be made of, consist of, comprise

composition *NOUN*
*Is the song your own **composition**?*
• piece, work, creation
(formal) opus
for types of musical composition see **music**

comprehend *VERB*
*The crowd couldn't **comprehend** what was happening.*
• understand, realise, appreciate, figure out, grasp, perceive, follow

A B C D E F G H I J K L M N O P Q R S T U V W X Y Z

comprehensive *ADJECTIVE*
She gave us a ***comprehensive*** *account of her travels.*
• complete, full, thorough, detailed, extensive, inclusive, exhaustive, wide-ranging, encyclopedic
OPPOSITE selective

compress *VERB*
I tried to ***compress*** *all my clothes into one bag.*
• press, squeeze, cram, crush, jam, squash, stuff, flatten

comprise *VERB*
The team ***comprised*** *athletes from several countries.*
• be composed of, consist of, include, contain

compulsive *ADJECTIVE*
❶ *Suddenly, I felt a* ***compulsive*** *urge to laugh.*
• compelling, overwhelming, overpowering, irresistible, uncontrollable
❷ *We knew he was a* ***compulsive*** *liar.*
• habitual, obsessive, incurable

compulsory *ADJECTIVE*
The wearing of seat belts is ***compulsory.***
• required, obligatory, necessary
OPPOSITE optional

computer *NOUN*

WORD WEB

SOME KINDS OF COMPUTER:

• desktop, laptop, notebook, PC, server, tablet

SOME PARTS OF A COMPUTER SYSTEM:

• DVD drive, flash drive, games console, hard disk, keyboard, keypad, memory stick, microchip, microprocessor, monitor, motherboard, mouse, processor, screen, touchpad, touchscreen, USB port, webcam

OTHER TERMS USED IN COMPUTING:

• app, attachment, back-up, broadband, browser, byte, cursor, data, database, directory, download, digital, email, file, folder, games console, gaming, gigabyte, hardware, Internet, megabyte, memory, menu, MP3, network, offline, online, printout, program, RAM, screenshot, software, spam, streaming, upload, virus, web, window, wifi, wireless, word processor

concave *ADJECTIVE*
see **curved**
OPPOSITE convex

conceal *VERB*
❶ *The dog tried to* ***conceal*** *its bone.*
• hide, cover up, bury
❷ *We tried to* ***conceal*** *our hiding place.*
• disguise, mask, screen, camouflage, make invisible
❸ *Don't* ***conceal*** *the truth.*
• keep quiet about, keep secret, hush up, suppress

conceited *ADJECTIVE*
He was so ***conceited*** *when he won first prize!*
• boastful, arrogant, proud, vain, self-satisfied
(informal) big-headed, cocky
OPPOSITE modest

conceive *VERB*
❶ *Who* ***conceived*** *this silly plan?*
• think up, devise, invent, make up, originate, plan, produce, work out
(informal) dream up
❷ *I could not* ***conceive*** *how the plan would work.*
• imagine, see

concentrate *VERB*
❶ *I had to* ***concentrate*** *to hear what she was saying.*
• be attentive, think hard, focus

❷ *The crowds **concentrated** in the middle of town.*
• collect, gather, converge

concept *NOUN*
*I find the **concept** of time travel fascinating.*
• idea, thought, notion

concern *VERB*
❶ *This conversation doesn't **concern** you.*
• affect, involve, be important to, matter to, be relevant to, relate to
❷ *It **concerns** me that we are destroying the rainforests.*
• bother, distress, trouble, upset, worry

concern *NOUN*
❶ *My private life is no **concern** of theirs.*
• affair, business
❷ *Global warming is a great **concern** to us all.*
• worry, anxiety, fear
❸ *She's the head of a business **concern**.*
• company, firm, enterprise, establishment

concerned *ADJECTIVE*
❶ *After waiting an hour, Julia began to feel **concerned**.*
• worried, bothered, troubled, anxious, upset, distressed
❷ *We're writing a letter to all those **concerned**.*
• involved, connected, related, affected

concerning *PREPOSITION*
*The head spoke to me **concerning** my future.*
• about, regarding, relating to, with reference to, relevant to

concert *NOUN*
*The jazz band is giving a **concert** tonight.*
• recital, performance, show

concise *ADJECTIVE*
*He gave the police a **concise** account of what happened.*
• brief, short, condensed, succinct
A concise account of something is a **precis** or **summary**.
OPPOSITE long

conclude *VERB*
❶ *We **concluded** the Christmas concert with carols.*
• end, finish, complete, round off, wind up
❷ *The concert **concluded** with some carols.*
• close, terminate, culminate
❸ *They **concluded** that he was guilty.*
• decide, deduce, infer, suppose, assume, gather

conclusion *NOUN*
❶ *The **conclusion** of the film was a bit puzzling.*
• close, end, finale, finish, completion, culmination
❷ *'What is your **conclusion**, Inspector?'*
• decision, judgement, opinion, verdict, deduction

concrete *ADJECTIVE*
*The police are looking for **concrete** evidence.*
• real, actual, definite, firm, solid, substantial, physical, factual, objective
OPPOSITE abstract

condemn *VERB*
❶ *The manager **condemned** the behaviour of the players.*
• criticise, disapprove of, denounce, deplore, reproach
OPPOSITE praise
❷ *The judge **condemned** the men to death.*
• sentence
OPPOSITE acquit

condense *VERB*
❶ *I **condensed** my poem so that it fitted on one page.*
• reduce, shorten, compress, summarise
OPPOSITE expand
❷ *Steam **condenses** on a cold window.*
• become liquid, form condensation
OPPOSITE evaporate

A B C D E F G H I J K L M N O P Q R S T U V W X Y Z

condition *NOUN*
❶ *Is your bike in good **condition**?*
• state, order, repair
❷ *A dog needs exercise to stay in good **condition**.*
• fitness, health, shape
❸ *It's a **condition** of membership that you pay a subscription.*
• requirement, obligation, term
➤ **on condition that**
*You can come **on condition that** you pay your own fare.*
• provided, providing that, only if

conduct *VERB*
❶ *A guide **conducted** us round the museum.*
• guide, lead, take, accompany, escort
❷ *We asked the eldest girl to **conduct** our meeting.*
• lead, manage, control, run, administer, supervise, preside over, organise, handle
➤ **to conduct yourself**
*The grown-ups did not **conduct themselves** well.*
• behave, act, carry on

conduct *NOUN*
*Our teacher congratulated us on our good **conduct**.*
• behaviour, manners, attitude

confer *VERB*
❶ *They **conferred** the freedom of the city on the victorious team.*
• give (to), grant (to), present (to), award (to)
❷ *The king **conferred** with his advisors before making a decision.*
• consult, have a discussion, talk things over, converse

conference *NOUN*
*All the witches were invited to a grand **conference**.*
• meeting, consultation, discussion

confess *VERB*
*The goblin **confessed** that he had stolen the gold.*
• admit, own up to, acknowledge, reveal

confidence *NOUN*
❶ *We can face the future with **confidence**.*
• hope, optimism, faith
OPPOSITE doubt
❷ *I wish I had her **confidence**.*
• self-confidence, assurance, boldness, conviction

confident *ADJECTIVE*
❶ *I am **confident** that we will win.*
• certain, sure, positive, optimistic
OPPOSITE doubtful
❷ *She is a **confident** sort of person.*
• self-confident, assertive, bold, fearless, unafraid

confidential *ADJECTIVE*
*The details of the plan are **confidential**.*
• secret, private
OPPOSITE public

confine *VERB*
❶ *They **confined** their discussion to the weather.*
• limit, restrict
❷ *Our farm animals are not **confined** indoors.*
• enclose, surround, fence in, shut in, coop up, hem in

confirm *VERB*
❶ *The strange events **confirmed** his belief in ghosts.*
• prove, justify, support, back up, reinforce
OPPOSITE disprove
❷ *I phoned to **confirm** my appointment at the dentist.*
• verify, make official
OPPOSITE cancel

confiscate *VERB*
*The janitor **confiscated** our ball.*
• take away, take possession of, seize

conflict *NOUN*
There's a lot of ***conflict*** *in their family.*
• disagreement, quarrelling, fighting, hostility, friction, antagonism, opposition, strife, unrest

conflict *VERB*
➤ **to conflict with**
Her account of what happened ***conflicts with*** *mine.*
• disagree with, differ from, contradict, contrast with, clash with

conflicting *ADJECTIVE*
My brother and I have ***conflicting*** *tastes in music.*
• different, contrasting, contradictory, opposite, incompatible

conform *VERB*
➤ **to conform to** or **with**
The club expels anyone who doesn't ***conform with*** *the rules.*
• follow, keep to, obey, abide by, agree with, fit in with, submit to
OPPOSITE disobey

confront *VERB*
I decided to ***confront*** *her and demand an apology.*
• challenge, stand up to, face up to

confuse *VERB*
❶ *I was* ***confused*** *by the directions on the map.*
• puzzle, bewilder, mystify, baffle, perplex
❷ *You must be* ***confusing*** *me with someone else.*
• mix up, muddle

confusion *NOUN*
❶ *There was great* ***confusion*** *when the lights went out.*
• chaos, commotion, fuss, uproar, turmoil, pandemonium, bedlam, hullabaloo
❷ *There was a look of* ***confusion*** *on her face.*
• bewilderment, puzzlement, perplexity

congratulate *VERB*
We ***congratulated*** *the winners.*
• praise, applaud, compliment
OPPOSITE criticise

congregate *VERB*
The party guests ***congregated*** *in the hall.*
• gather, assemble, collect, come together
OPPOSITE disperse

connect *VERB*
1 *What's the best way to* ***connect*** *these wires?*
• join, attach, fasten, link, couple, fix together, tie together
OPPOSITE separate
❷ *The fingerprints* ***connected*** *him with the crime.*
• make a connection between, associate, relate

connection *NOUN*
There is a close ***connection*** *between our two families.*
• association, relationship, link

conquer *VERB*
❶ *Extra troops were sent to* ***conquer*** *the enemy forces.*
• beat, defeat, overcome, vanquish, get the better of, overwhelm, crush, rout, thrash
❷ *Gaul was* ***conquered*** *by Julius Caesar.*
• seize, capture, take, win, occupy, possess
❸ *Several climbers have* ***conquered*** *Mount Everest.*
• climb, reach the top of

conqueror *NOUN*
Cheering crowds greeted the ***conquerors.***
• victor, winner

conquest *NOUN*
The book gave an account of the Norman ***conquest.***
• invasion, occupation, capture, possession

a b c d e f g h i j k l m n o p q r s t u v w x y z

A B C D E F G H I J K L M N O P Q R S T U V W X Y Z

conscientious *ADJECTIVE*
*Elves are very **conscientious** workers.*
• hard-working, careful, dependable, reliable, responsible, dutiful, meticulous, painstaking, thorough
OPPOSITE careless

conscious *ADJECTIVE*
❶ *The patient was **conscious** throughout the operation.*
• awake, alert, aware
OPPOSITE unconscious
❷ *She made a **conscious** effort to improve her work.*
• deliberate, intentional, planned
OPPOSITE accidental

consent *VERB*
➤ **to consent to**
*The head has **consented to** our request.*
• agree to, grant, approve of, authorise
OPPOSITE refuse

consequence *NOUN*
❶ *He drank the potion without thinking of the **consequences**.*
• effect, result, outcome, upshot, sequel
❷ *The loss of a few pence is of no **consequence**.*
• importance, significance

conservation *NOUN*
*Our group supports the **conservation** of wildlife.*
• preservation, protection, maintenance, upkeep
OPPOSITE destruction

conservative *ADJECTIVE*
❶ *Miss Frump has a very **conservative** taste in clothes.*
• old-fashioned, conventional, unadventurous, traditional
OPPOSITES progressive, up-to-date
❷ *At a **conservative** estimate, the work will take six months.*
• cautious, moderate, reasonable
OPPOSITE extreme

conserve *VERB*
*The explorers had to **conserve** their water supply.*
• save, preserve, be sparing with, use wisely, look after, protect
OPPOSITE waste

consider *VERB*
❶ *The detective **considered** the problem carefully.*
• think about, examine, contemplate, ponder on, reflect on, study, weigh up, meditate about
❷ *I **consider** this to be my best work.*
• believe, judge, reckon

considerable *ADJECTIVE*
*1000 dollars is a **considerable** sum of money.*
• big, large, significant, substantial, sizeable
OPPOSITES negligible, insignificant

considerate *ADJECTIVE*
*It was **considerate** of you to lend me your umbrella.*
• kind, kind-hearted, helpful, obliging, sympathetic, thoughtful, unselfish, caring, charitable, neighbourly
OPPOSITE selfish

consist *VERB*
➤ **to consist of**
❶ *The planet **consists** largely **of** craters.*
• be made of, be composed of, comprise, contain, include, incorporate
❷ *His job **consists** mostly **of** answering the phone.*
• involve

consistency *NOUN*
*The mixture had the **consistency** of porridge.*
• texture, thickness, density

consistent *ADJECTIVE*
❶ *These plants need to be kept at a **consistent** temperature.*
• steady, constant, regular, stable, unchanging
❷ *Fortunately, our goalkeeper is a **consistent** player.*
• predictable, dependable, reliable
OPPOSITE inconsistent

console *VERB*
*He did his best to **console** me when my dog died.*
• **comfort, soothe, sympathise with, support**

conspicuous *ADJECTIVE*
❶ *The clock tower is a **conspicuous** landmark.*
• **prominent, notable, obvious, eye-catching, unmistakable, visible**
❷ *I had made some **conspicuous** mistakes.*
• **clear, noticeable, obvious, evident, glaring**
OPPOSITE **inconspicuous**

constant *ADJECTIVE*
❶ *There is a **constant** noise of traffic on the motorway.*
• **continual, continuous, never-ending, non-stop, ceaseless, incessant, interminable, endless, everlasting, permanent, perpetual, unending, persistent, relentless**
OPPOSITE **changeable**
❷ *My dog has been my **constant** friend for many years.*
• **faithful, loyal, dependable, reliable, firm, true, trustworthy, devoted**
OPPOSITE **unreliable**

constitute *VERB*
*In rugby, fifteen players **constitute** a team.*
• **make up, compose, comprise, form**

construct *VERB*
*We **constructed** a tree house in the back garden.*
• **build, erect, assemble, make, put together, put up, set up**
OPPOSITE **demolish**

construction *NOUN*
❶ *The **construction** of the tree house took all afternoon.*
• **building, erecting, erection, assembly, setting-up**
❷ *The hut was a flimsy **construction**.*
• **building, structure**

consult *VERB*
❶ *You should **consult** the dentist about your sore tooth.*
• **ask, get advice from, speak to**
❷ *If you don't know how to spell a word, **consult** your dictionary.*
• **refer to**

consume *VERB*
❶ *The birds **consumed** all the bread in ten minutes!*
• **eat, devour, gobble up, guzzle**
❷ *The truck **consumed** a great deal of fuel.*
• **use up**
❸ *The building was **consumed** by fire.*
• **destroy**

contact *VERB*
*I'll **contact** you when I have some news.*
• **call, call on, get in touch with, speak to, communicate with, notify, talk to, correspond with, phone, ring, write to**

contagious *ADJECTIVE*
*Mumps is a very **contagious** disease.*
• **catching, infectious**

contain *VERB*
❶ *This box **contains** various odds and ends.*
• **hold**
❷ *A dictionary **contains** words and definitions.*
• **include, incorporate, comprise, consist of**

container *NOUN*
*Put the leftover sauce in a **container**.*
• **vessel, receptacle, holder, box, case, canister, carton, pot, tub, tin**

contaminate *VERB*
*The river had been **contaminated** with chemicals.*
• **pollute, poison, infect**
OPPOSITE **purify**

contemplate *VERB*
❶ *The princess* ***contemplated*** *herself in the mirror.*
• look at, view, observe, survey, watch, stare at, gaze at
❷ *The robbers* ***contemplated*** *what to do next.*
• think about, consider, ponder, study, reflect on, weigh up, meditate about

contemporary *ADJECTIVE*
Do you like ***contemporary*** *music?*
• current, fashionable, modern, up-to-date, the latest
(informal) trendy
OPPOSITE old-fashioned, out-of-date

contempt *NOUN*
The knight stared at his enemy with a look of ***contempt****.*
• hatred, scorn, loathing, disgust, dislike, distaste
OPPOSITE admiration

contend *VERB*
I ***contend*** *that I was right.*
• declare, claim, argue, assert, maintain
➤ **to contend with**
❶ *The team had to* ***contend with*** *strong opposition.*
• compete with, fight against, oppose, grapple with, struggle against, strive against
❷ *We had to* ***contend with*** *bad weather and midges!*
• cope with, deal with, face, put up with

content *ADJECTIVE*
Fergus was perfectly ***content*** *to sit reading a book.*
• happy, contented, satisfied, pleased, willing
OPPOSITE unwilling

contented *ADJECTIVE*
After her meal, the cat looked very ***contented****.*
• happy, pleased, content, satisfied, fulfilled, serene, peaceful, relaxed, comfortable, tranquil, untroubled
OPPOSITE discontented

contents *PLURAL NOUN*
We all tried to guess the ***contents*** *of the mystery parcel.*
• elements, ingredients, parts

contest *NOUN*
The tennis final was an exciting ***contest****.*
• competition, challenge, fight, bout, encounter, struggle, game, match, tournament

contest *VERB*
Several players ***contested*** *the referee's decision.*
• challenge, disagree with, question, oppose, argue against, quarrel with

contestant *NOUN*
There are twenty ***contestants*** *in the spelling competition.*
• competitor, participant, player, contender

continual *ADJECTIVE*
I get sick of their ***continual*** *arguing.*
• constant, persistent, perpetual, repeated, frequent, recurrent, eternal, unending
see also **continuous**
OPPOSITE occasional

continue *VERB*
❶ *We* ***continued*** *our search until it got dark.*
• keep up, prolong, sustain, persevere with, pursue
(informal) stick at
❷ *This rain can't* ***continue*** *for long.*
• carry on, last, persist, endure, keep on, go on, linger
❸ *We'll* ***continue*** *our meeting after lunch.*
• resume, proceed with, pick up

continuous *ADJECTIVE*
We had ***continuous*** *rain all through our holiday.*
• never-ending, non-stop, ceaseless, everlasting, incessant, unbroken, unceasing, uninterrupted
An illness which continues for a long time is a chronic illness.
see also **continual**
OPPOSITE intermittent

contract *NOUN*
*The actress has signed a **contract** for a new film.*
• agreement, deal, undertaking
A contract between two countries is an **alliance** or **treaty**.
A contract to end a dispute about money is a **settlement**.

contract *VERB*
❶ *Metal **contracts** when it gets colder.*
• reduce, lessen, shrink, tighten
OPPOSITE expand
❷ *The crew **contracted** a mysterious illness.*
• catch, develop, get

contradict *VERB*
*I didn't dare to **contradict** the witch.*
• challenge, disagree with, speak against

contraption *NOUN*
*The inventor's house was full of weird **contraptions**.*
• machine, device, gadget, invention, apparatus, contrivance, mechanism
(informal) gizmo

contrary *ADJECTIVE*
*Griselda had always been a sulky, **contrary** child.*
• awkward, difficult, stubborn, disobedient, obstinate, uncooperative, unhelpful, wilful, perverse
OPPOSITE cooperative
➤ **contrary to**
***Contrary to** popular belief, snakes are not slimy.*
• differing from, against, opposing, in the face of, unlike

contrast *VERB*
❶ *We were asked to **contrast** two of our favourite poems.*
• compare, juxtapose, distinguish between
❷ *Her handwriting **contrasts** with mine.*
• differ (from), clash

contrast *NOUN*
*There is a sharp **contrast** between the two paintings.*
• difference, distinction, opposition
OPPOSITE similarity

contribute *VERB*
*Will you **contribute** something to our charity collection?*
• donate, give, provide
(informal) chip in
➤ **to contribute to**
*The sunny weather **contributed to** our enjoyment.*
• add to, help, aid, encourage, enhance

contrive *VERB*
*They **contrived** a way to escape from the dungeon.*
• think up, plan, make up, create, invent

control *NOUN*
*The captain had complete **control** over the crew.*
• authority, power, command, government, management, direction, leadership, guidance

control *VERB*
❶ *The government **controls** the country's affairs.*
• be in control of, be in charge of, manage, run, command, direct, lead, guide, govern, administer, regulate, rule, superintend, supervise
❷ *Can't you **control** that dog?*
• manage, handle, restrain
❸ *They built a dam to **control** the floods.*
• check, curb, hold back, contain

controversial *ADJECTIVE*
*The decision to award a penalty was **controversial**.*
• debatable, questionable, arguable

A B C D E F G H I J K L M N O P Q R S T U V W X Y Z

controversy *NOUN*
There is much ***controversy*** *about the election results.*
• **disagreement, debate, argument, dispute, quarrelling**

convenient *ADJECTIVE*
❶ *Is there a* ***convenient*** *place to put my umbrella?*
• **suitable, appropriate, available, nearby, accessible**
OPPOSITE **inconvenient**
❷ *Mum has a* ***convenient*** *tool for opening jars.*
• **handy, helpful, useful, labour-saving, neat**

conventional *ADJECTIVE*
The ***conventional*** *way to greet someone is to shake hands.*
• **customary, traditional, usual, accepted, common, normal, ordinary, everyday, routine, standard, regular, habitual, orthodox**
OPPOSITE **unconventional**

converge *VERB*
The two rivers ***converge*** *at this point.*
• **come together, join, meet, merge, combine, coincide**
OPPOSITE **divide**

conversation *NOUN*
An informal conversation is a **chat** or **gossip**.
A more formal conversation is a **discussion**.
A very formal conversation is a **conference**.
Conversation in a play or novel is **dialogue**.

converse *VERB*
The travellers ***conversed*** *happily for several minutes.*
• **chat, talk, have a conversation, engage in conversation**
see also **talk**

convert *VERB*
❶ *We have* ***converted*** *our attic into a games room.*
• **change, adapt, alter, transform**
❷ *I never used to like football, but my cousin* ***converted*** *me.*
• **change someone's mind, persuade, convince, win over**

convex *ADJECTIVE*
see **curved**
OPPOSITE **concave**

convey *VERB*
❶ *The breakdown truck* ***conveyed*** *our car to a garage.*
• **bring, carry, deliver, take, move, bear, transfer, transport**
To convey something by sea is to **ferry** or **ship** it.
❷ *What does his message* ***convey*** *to you?*
• **communicate, tell, reveal, indicate, signify, mean**

convict *NOUN*
Four ***convicts*** *have escaped from the prison.*
• **prisoner, criminal**

convict *VERB*
The thieves were ***convicted*** *and sent to prison.*
• **condemn, declare guilty, sentence**
OPPOSITE **acquit**

convince *VERB*
The prisoner ***convinced*** *them that he was innocent.*
• **persuade, assure, satisfy, make believe, win round**

convincing *ADJECTIVE*
I tried to think of a ***convincing*** *excuse.*
• **persuasive, believable, credible, plausible**

cook *VERB*

WORD WEB

To cook food for guests or customers is to **cater** for them.
Cooking as a business is **catering**.
The art or skill of cooking is **cookery**.

SOME WAYS TO COOK FOOD:

• bake, barbecue, boil, braise, brew, broil, casserole, deep-fry, fry, grill, poach, roast, sauté, simmer, steam, stew, toast

OTHER WAYS TO PREPARE FOOD:

• baste, blend, chop, dice, grate, grind, infuse, knead, liquidise, marinade, mince, mix, peel, purée, sieve, sift, stir, whisk

SOME ITEMS THAT ARE USED FOR COOKING:

• baking tin or tray, barbecue, blender, bowl, carving knife, casserole, cauldron, chopping board, colander, cooker, dish, food processor, frying pan, grill, ladle, liquidiser, microwave, mincer, oven, pan, pot, rolling pin, saucepan, skewer, spatula, spit, strainer, toaster, whisk, wok, wooden spoon

see also **crockery, cutlery, kitchen**

cook *NOUN*

The chief cook in a restaurant or hotel is the **chef**.
A person who cooks food as a business is a **caterer**.

cool *ADJECTIVE*

❶ *The weather is* ***cool*** *for the time of year.*
• chilly, coldish
OPPOSITES hot, warm

❷ *Would you like a* ***cool*** *glass of lemonade?*
• chilled, iced, refreshing
OPPOSITE hot

❸ *Clifford remained* ***cool*** *when everyone else panicked.*
• calm, level-headed, relaxed, unexcitable, unflustered
(informal) laid-back
A common simile is **as cool as a cucumber**.
OPPOSITE frantic

❹ *(informal) Those roller skates are really* ***cool****!*
• chic, fashionable, smart
(informal) trendy

cooperate *VERB*

➤ to cooperate with
The scouts ***cooperated with*** *each other to build a fire.*
• work with, work together with, collaborate with, aid, assist, support

cope *VERB*

Shall I help you, or can you ***cope*** *on your own?*
• manage, carry on, get by, make do, survive

➤ to cope with
I can't ***cope with*** *all this homework!*
• deal with, handle, manage, get through

copy *NOUN*

That isn't the original painting—it's a ***copy****.*
• replica, reproduction, duplicate, imitation, likeness
A copy made to deceive someone is a **fake** or a **forgery**.
A living organism which is identical to another is a **clone**.

copy *VERB*

❶ *I* ***copied*** *the poem into my planner.*
• duplicate, reproduce, write out
To copy something in order to deceive is to **fake** or **forge** it.

❷ *My parrot can* ***copy*** *my voice.*
• imitate, impersonate, mimic

cord *NOUN*

The pilot pulled the ***cord*** *to open his parachute.*
• string, rope, tape, strap, line, cable, flex

core *NOUN*

It is very hot at the earth's ***core****.*
• centre, middle, inside, heart, nucleus

A B C D E F G H I J K L M N O P Q R S T U V W X Y Z

corn *NOUN*
The farmer was growing ***corn*** *in the field.*
• **grain, cereal, wheat**

corner *NOUN*
❶ *I'll meet you at the* ***corner*** *of the road.*
• **turn, turning, junction, crossroads, intersection**
The place where two lines meet is an **angle**.
❷ *I sat in a quiet* ***corner*** *and read her letter.*
• **alcove, recess, nook**

correct *ADJECTIVE*
❶ *Your answers are all* ***correct****.*
• **right, accurate, exact, faultless**
❷ *I hope he has given us* ***correct*** *information.*
• **true, genuine, authentic, precise, reliable, factual**
❸ *What is the* ***correct*** *way to address this letter?*
• **proper, acceptable, regular, appropriate, suitable**
OPPOSITE **wrong**

correct *VERB*
❶ *I have to* ***correct*** *my spelling mistakes.*
• **alter, put right, make better, improve**
❷ *Miss Nicol spent the day* ***correcting*** *exam papers.*
• **mark**

correspond *VERB*
➤ **to correspond with**
❶ *Her version of the story doesn't* ***correspond with*** *mine.*
• **agree with, match, be similar to, be consistent with, tally with**
❷ *Carol* ***corresponds with*** *a friend in Paris.*
• **write to, communicate with, send letters to**

corrode *VERB*
This acid will ***corrode*** *metal.*
• **eat away, erode, rot, rust**

corrupt *ADJECTIVE*
Corrupt *officials had accepted millions of pounds in bribes.*
• **dishonest, criminal, untrustworthy**
(informal) **bent, crooked**
OPPOSITE **honest**

cost *VERB* **costs, costing, cost**
How much do these shoes ***cost****?*
• **be worth, go for, sell for**

cost *NOUN*
The bill shows the total ***cost****.*
• **price, charge, amount, payment, fee, figure, expense, expenditure, tariff**
The cost of travelling on public transport is the **fare**.

costly *ADJECTIVE*
It would be too ***costly*** *to repair the car.*
• **dear, expensive**
OPPOSITE **cheap**

costume *NOUN*
The Irish dancers were wearing national ***costumes****.*
• **outfit, dress, clothing, suit, attire, garment, garb**
(informal) **get-up**
A costume you dress up in for a party is **fancy dress**.
A set of clothes worn by soldiers or members of an organisation is a **uniform**.
see also **clothes**

cosy *ADJECTIVE*
It's good to feel ***cosy*** *in bed when it's cold outside.*
• **comfortable, snug, soft, warm, secure**
OPPOSITE **uncomfortable**

couch *NOUN*
My brother sat on the ***couch*** *watching TV all weekend.*
• **settee, sofa**
for other types of seat see **seat**

counsel *VERB*
His advisors ***counselled*** *him to surrender.*
• **advise, guide, direct, encourage, recommend, urge**

count *VERB*
❶ *I'm* ***counting*** *the days until my birthday.*
• **add up, calculate, compute, estimate, reckon, figure out, work out, total**
❷ *It's playing well that* ***counts,*** *not winning.*
• **be important, be significant, matter**
➤ **to count on**
You can ***count on*** *me to support you.*
• **depend on, rely on, trust, bank on**

countless *ADJECTIVE*
I've seen that film ***countless*** *times.*
• **a great many, numerous, innumerable, myriad, untold**
OPPOSITE **finite**

country *NOUN*
❶ *England and Wales are separate* ***countries.***
• **nation, state, land, territory**
A country ruled by a king or queen is a **kingdom, monarchy** or **realm.**
A country governed by leaders elected by the people is a **democracy.**
A democratic country with a president is a **republic.**
❷ *We went for a picnic in the* ***country.***
• **countryside, landscape, outdoors**
OPPOSITES **town, city**
A word meaning 'to do with the country' is **rural** and its opposite is **urban.**

coupon *NOUN*
You can exchange these ***coupons*** *for a free mug.*
• **token, voucher, ticket**

courage *NOUN*
The rescue dogs showed great ***courage.***
• **bravery, boldness, daring, fearlessness, nerve, pluck, valour, heroism, grit**
(informal) **guts**
OPPOSITE **cowardice**

courageous *ADJECTIVE*
The warriors were always ***courageous*** *in battle.*
• **brave, bold, daring, fearless, heroic, intrepid, plucky, gallant, valiant**
OPPOSITE **cowardly**

course *NOUN*
❶ *The hot-air balloon was drifting off its* ***course.***
• **direction, path, route, way, progress, passage**
❷ *The war changed the* ***course*** *of history.*
• **development, progression, sequence, succession**
➤ **of course**
Of course *you can come to my party.*
• **naturally, certainly, definitely, undoubtedly**

courteous *ADJECTIVE*
I received a ***courteous*** *reply to my letter.*
• **polite, respectful, well-mannered, civil, considerate, friendly, helpful**
OPPOSITE **rude**

cover *VERB*
❶ *A coat of paint will* ***cover*** *the graffiti.*
• **conceal, disguise, hide, obscure, mask, blot out**
❷ *She* ***covered*** *her face with her hands.*
• **shield, screen, protect, shade, veil**
❸ *The hikers are hoping to* ***cover*** *twenty-five miles a day.*
• **progress, travel**
❹ *An encyclopedia* ***covers*** *many subjects.*
• **deal with, include, contain, incorporate**
❺ *Will £50* ***cover*** *your expenses?*
• **be enough for, pay for**

cover *NOUN*
❶ *The* ***cover*** *of the book was torn.*
• **wrapper**
A cover for a letter is an **envelope.**
A cover for a book is a **jacket.**
A cover to keep papers in is a **file** or **folder.**
❷ *On the bare hillside, there was no* ***cover*** *from the storm.*
• **shelter, protection, defence, shield, refuge, sanctuary**

A B C D E F G H I J K L M N O P Q R S T U V W X Y Z

covering *NOUN*
*There was a light **covering** of snow on the hills.*
• **coating, coat, layer, blanket, carpet, film, sheet, skin, veil**

cowardly *ADJECTIVE*
*It was **cowardly** to run away.*
• **timid, faint-hearted, spineless, gutless**
(informal) **yellow, chicken**
OPPOSITE **brave**

cower *VERB*
*A frightened creature was **cowering** in the corner.*
• **cringe, shrink, crouch, flinch, quail**

crack *NOUN*
❶ *There's a **crack** in this cup.*
• **break, chip, fracture, flaw, chink, split**
❷ *The outlaw hid in a **crack** between two rocks.*
• **gap, opening, crevice, rift, cranny**
❸ *The detective heard the **crack** of a pistol shot.*
• **bang, fire, explosion, snap, pop**
❹ *She gave the robber a **crack** on the head.*
• **blow, bang, knock, smack, whack**
❺ *I had a **crack** at writing a poem.*
• **try, attempt, shot, go**

crack *VERB*
*A brick fell down and **cracked** the pavement.*
• **break, fracture, chip, split, shatter, splinter**

craft *NOUN*
❶ *I'd like to learn the **craft** of weaving.*
• **art, skill, technique, expertise, handicraft**
for names of arts and crafts see **art**
❷ *All sorts of **craft** were in the harbour.*
• **boats, ships, vessels**
for types of boat or ship see **boat**

crafty *ADJECTIVE*
*The evil sorceress had a **crafty** plan.*
• **cunning, clever, shrewd, scheming, sneaky, sly, tricky, wily, artful**

cram *VERB*
❶ *We can't **cram** any more people in—the car is full.*
• **pack, squeeze, crush, force, jam, compress**
❷ *My sister is **cramming** for her maths exam.*
• **revise, study**
(informal) **swot**

cramped *ADJECTIVE*
*The seating on the train was a bit **cramped**.*
• **confined, narrow, restricted, tight, uncomfortable, crowded**
(informal) **poky**
OPPOSITE **roomy**

crash *NOUN*
❶ *I heard a loud **crash** from the kitchen.*
• **bang, smash**
for other kinds of sound see **sound**
❷ *We saw a nasty **crash** on the motorway.*
• **accident, collision, smash, bump**
A crash involving a lot of vehicles is a **pile-up**.
A train crash may involve a **derailment**.

crash *VERB*
*The car **crashed** into a lamp post.*
• **bump, smash, collide, knock**

crate *NOUN*
*We packed our belongings into **crates**.*
• **box, case, chest, packing case**

crater *NOUN*
*The surface of the moon is full of **craters**.*
• **pit, hole, hollow, cavity, chasm, opening, abyss**

crawl *VERB*
*I saw a caterpillar **crawling** along a leaf.*
• **creep, edge, inch, slither, clamber**

craze *NOUN*
*This game is the latest **craze** in the playground.*
• **fad, trend, vogue, fashion, enthusiasm, obsession, passion**

crazy *ADJECTIVE*
❶ *The dog went **crazy** when it was stung by a wasp.*
• **mad, insane, frenzied, hysterical, frantic, berserk, delirious, wild**
(informal) **loopy, nuts**
❷ *It was a **crazy** idea to try to build a space rocket!*
• **absurd, ridiculous, ludicrous, daft, idiotic, senseless, silly, stupid, foolhardy, preposterous**
(informal) **bonkers, barmy, wacky**
OPPOSITE **sensible**

creamy *ADJECTIVE*
*That ice cream is really **creamy**!*
• **rich, smooth, thick, velvety**

crease *NOUN*
*Can you iron the **creases** out of this shirt?*
• **wrinkle, crinkle, pucker, fold, furrow, groove, line**
A crease made deliberately in a skirt or other garment is a **pleat**.

crease *VERB*
*Pack the clothes carefully, so you don't **crease** them.*
• **wrinkle, crinkle, crumple, crush, pucker**

create *VERB*
❶ *The cats were **creating** a racket outside.*
• **make, cause, produce**
❷ *We have **created** a website for our chess club.*
• **set up, start up, bring about, bring into existence, originate**
You **write** a poem or story.
You **compose** music.
You **draw** or **paint** a picture.
You **carve** a statue.
You **invent** or **think up** a new idea.
You **design** a new product.
You **devise** a plan.
You **found** a new club or organisation.
You **manufacture** goods.
You **generate** electricity.
You **build** or **construct** a model or a building.
OPPOSITE **destroy**

creation *NOUN*
❶ *The TV programme is about the **creation** of life on earth.*
• **beginning, origin, birth, generation, initiation**
❷ *They raised money for the **creation** of a sports centre.*
• **building, construction, establishing, foundation**
❸ *This pizza recipe is my own **creation**.*
• **concept, invention**

creative *ADJECTIVE*
*My aunt is a very **creative** person.*
• **artistic, imaginative, inventive, original, inspired**
OPPOSITE **unimaginative**

creator *NOUN*
*Walt Disney was the **creator** of Mickey Mouse.*
• **inventor, maker, originator, producer, deviser**
The creator of a design is an **architect** or **designer**.
The creator of goods for sale is a **manufacturer**.

creature *NOUN*
*A wild-looking **creature** emerged from the swamp.*
• **animal, beast, being**
see also **animal**
for creatures found in myths and legends see **myth**

credible *ADJECTIVE*
*The detective did not find the woman's story **credible**.*
• **believable, convincing, persuasive, trustworthy, likely, possible, reasonable**
OPPOSITE **incredible**

credit *NOUN*
*The author is finally getting the **credit** she deserves.*
• **recognition, honour, praise, distinction, fame, glory, reputation**
OPPOSITE **dishonour**

credit *VERB*
*It's hard to **credit** that they are brother and sister.*
• **believe, accept, have faith in, trust**
OPPOSITE **doubt**

creed *NOUN*
*Pupils of all races and **creeds** attend the school.*
• **religion, doctrine, faith, set of beliefs**

creep *VERB* **creeps, creeping, crept**
❶ *I watched the lizard **creep** back into its hiding place.*
• **crawl, edge, inch, slither, wriggle**
❷ *I **crept** out of bed without waking the others.*
• **move quietly, sneak, tiptoe, slip, slink, steal**

creepy *ADJECTIVE*
*There were **creepy** noises coming from the cellar.*
• **scary, frightening, eerie, ghostly, weird, sinister, uncanny, unearthly**
(informal) **spooky**
see also **ghost**

crest *NOUN*
❶ *The bird had a large red **crest** on its head.*
• **comb, plume, tuft**
❷ *There was a wonderful view from the **crest** of the hill.*
• **top, peak, summit, crown, head, brow**

crevice *NOUN*
*Moss was growing in the **crevices** in the rock.*
• **crack, cranny, gap, opening, rift, split**
A deep crack in a glacier is a **crevasse**.

crew *NOUN*
for words for groups of people see **group**

cricket *NOUN*

WORD WEB

PEOPLE WHO PLAY CRICKET:

• **batsman, bowler, cricketer, fielder or fieldsman, wicketkeeper**
The official who makes sure players keep to the rules is the **umpire**.

SOME OTHER TERMS USED IN CRICKET:

• **boundary, crease, innings, maiden over, over, pitch, run, stump, wicket**

crime *NOUN*
*Robbing a bank is a serious **crime**.*
• **offence, lawbreaking, wrongdoing**

criminal *NOUN*
*These men are dangerous **criminals**.*
• **lawbreaker, offender, wrongdoer**
(informal) **crook**
A criminal who has been sent to prison is a **convict**.

WORD WEB

SOME TYPES OF CRIMINAL:

• **assassin, bandit, blackmailer, brigand, burglar, cat burglar, con man, gangster, highwayman, hijacker, kidnapper, mugger, murderer, outlaw, pickpocket, pirate, poacher, robber, shoplifter, smuggler, terrorist, thief, thug, vandal**

criminal *ADJECTIVE*
*The gang were involved in many **criminal** schemes.*
• **illegal, unlawful, corrupt, dishonest, wrong**
(informal) **bent, crooked**
OPPOSITE **honest**

cringe *VERB*
*I **cringed** with embarrassment when my name was called.*
• shrink, flinch, wince, cower

cripple *VERB*
❶ *The fall may have **crippled** the horse.*
• maim, lame
❷ *The country was nearly **crippled** by the war.*
• ruin, destroy, crush, wreck, damage, weaken

crisis *NOUN*
*The election result caused a **crisis** in the country.*
• emergency, problem, difficulty, predicament

crisp *ADJECTIVE*
❶ *Fry the bacon until it's **crisp**.*
• crispy, crunchy, brittle
OPPOSITES soft, soggy, limp
❷ *It was a **crisp** winter morning.*
• cold, fresh, frosty

critical *ADJECTIVE*
❶ *Some people made **critical** comments about my hairstyle.*
• negative, disapproving, derogatory, uncomplimentary, unfavourable
OPPOSITE complimentary
❷ *This match is **critical** for our team's chances of success.*
• crucial, important, vital, serious, decisive
OPPOSITE unimportant

criticise *VERB*
*She **criticised** us for being so careless.*
• blame, condemn, disapprove of, find fault with, reprimand, reproach, scold, berate
OPPOSITE praise

criticism *NOUN*
*I think his **criticism** of my singing was unfair.*
• attack, disapproval, reprimand, reproach

crockery *NOUN*
*Please put the **crockery** away.*
• china, dishes, plates

WORD WEB

SOME ITEMS OF CROCKERY:

• bowl, butter dish, cup, dinner plate, gravy boat, milk jug, mug, plate, saucer, side plate, sugar bowl, teacup, teapot, tureen

crooked *ADJECTIVE*
❶ *The wizard bent his wand into a **crooked** shape.*
• bent, twisted, warped, gnarled
OPPOSITE straight
❷ *(informal) The **crooked** salesman was selling fake diamonds.*
• criminal, dishonest, corrupt
(informal) bent
OPPOSITE honest

crop *NOUN*
*We had a good **crop** of apples this year.*
• harvest, yield, produce

crop *VERB*
*Miss Marshall was **cropping** her garden hedge.*
• cut, trim, clip, snip, shear
➤ **to crop up**
*Several problems have **cropped up**.*
• arise, appear, occur, emerge, come up, turn up

cross *VERB*
❶ *There is a bus stop where the two roads **cross**.*
• criss-cross, intersect
❷ *You can **cross** the river at the footbridge.*
• go across, pass over, traverse, ford, span

cross *ADJECTIVE*
*My mum will be **cross** if we're late.*
• angry, annoyed, upset, vexed, bad-tempered, ill-tempered, irritable, grumpy, testy, irate
see also **angry**
OPPOSITE pleased

A B C D E F G H I J K L M N O P Q R S T U V W X Y Z

crouch *VERB*
The outlaws ***crouched*** *silently in the bushes.*
• **squat, kneel, stoop, bend, duck, bob down, hunch, huddle**

crowd *NOUN*
❶ *A* ***crowd*** *of people waited outside the theatre.*
• **gathering, group, assembly, bunch, cluster, throng, mob, multitude, crush, horde, swarm**
❷ *There was a huge* ***crowd*** *for the tennis final.*
• **audience, spectators, gate, attendance**

crowd *VERB*
❶ *People* ***crowded*** *on the pavement to watch the parade.*
• **gather, collect, assemble, congregate, mass, flock, muster**
❷ *Hundreds of people* ***crowded*** *into the hall.*
• **push, pile, squeeze, pack, cram, crush, jam, bundle, herd**

crowded *ADJECTIVE*
The shops are always ***crowded*** *at Christmas time.*
• **full, packed, teeming, swarming, overflowing, jammed, congested**
OPPOSITE **empty**

crown *NOUN*
The royal ***crown*** *was made of solid gold.*
• **coronet, diadem, tiara**

crown *VERB*
Mary was ***crowned*** *Queen of Scots when she was a baby.*
• **enthrone, anoint**
A ceremony at which a king or queen is crowned is a **coronation**.

crucial *ADJECTIVE*
We are at a ***crucial*** *point in our chess game.*
• **important, critical, decisive, vital, serious, momentous**
OPPOSITE **unimportant**

crude *ADJECTIVE*
❶ *The refinery processes* ***crude*** *oil.*
• **raw, natural, unprocessed, unrefined**
OPPOSITE **refined**
❷ *We made a* ***crude*** *shelter out of twigs.*
• **rough, clumsy, makeshift, primitive**
OPPOSITE **skilful**
❸ *The teacher told them to stop using* ***crude*** *language.*
• **rude, coarse, dirty, foul, impolite, indecent, vulgar**
OPPOSITE **polite**

cruel *ADJECTIVE*
I think hunting is a ***cruel*** *way to kill animals.*
• **brutal, savage, vicious, fierce, barbaric, bloodthirsty, barbarous, heartless, ruthless, merciless, inhuman, sadistic, uncivilised, beastly**
OPPOSITES **kind, humane, gentle**

crumb *NOUN*
We put out some ***crumbs*** *of bread for the birds.*
• **bit, fragment, scrap, morsel**
see also **bit**

crumble *VERB*
❶ *The walls of the castle were beginning to* ***crumble****.*
• **disintegrate, break up, collapse, fall apart, decay, decompose**
❷ *The farmer* ***crumbled*** *some bread into his soup.*
• **crush, grind, pound, pulverise**

crumpled *ADJECTIVE*
Your shirt is ***crumpled****.*
• **creased, wrinkled, crinkled, crushed**

crunch *VERB*
❶ *The dog was* ***crunching*** *on a bone.*
• **chew, munch, chomp, grind**
see also **eat**
❷ *I heard heavy footsteps* ***crunching*** *up the path.*
• **crush, grind, pound, smash**

crush *VERB*
❶ *He **crushed** his anorak into his school bag.*
• **squash, squeeze, mangle, pound, press, bruise, crunch, scrunch**
To crush something into a soft mess is to **mash** or **pulp** it.
To crush something into a powder is to **grind** or **pulverise** it.
To crush something out of shape is to **crumple** or **smash** it.
❷ *Our soldiers **crushed** the attacking army.*
• **defeat, conquer, vanquish, overcome, overwhelm, quash, trounce, rout**

crush *NOUN*
*There was a **crush** of people at the front gates.*
• **crowd, press, mob, throng, jam, congestion**

cry *VERB*
❶ *Someone was **crying** for help from the burning house.*
• **call, shout, yell, exclaim, roar, bawl, bellow, scream, screech, shriek**
❷ *The baby started to **cry** when she dropped her toy.*
• **sob, weep, bawl, blubber, wail, shed tears, snivel**
When someone starts to cry, their eyes **well up with tears**.

cry *NOUN*
*The wounded man let out a **cry** of pain.*
• **call, shout, yell, roar, howl, exclamation, bellow, scream, screech, shriek, yelp**

cuddle *VERB*
*My baby brother **cuddles** a teddy bear in bed.*
• **hug, hold closely, clasp, embrace, caress, nestle against, snuggle against**

cue *NOUN*
*When I nod, that is your **cue** to speak.*
• **sign, signal, reminder**

culprit *NOUN*
*Police are searching for the **culprits**.*
• **criminal, offender, wrongdoer**

cultivate *VERB*
❶ *Farmers have **cultivated** this land for centuries.*
• **farm, work, till, plough, grow crops on**
❷ *We want to **cultivate** good relations with our neighbours.*
• **develop, encourage, promote, try to achieve, further, improve**

cunning *ADJECTIVE*
*The pirates had a **cunning** plan to seize the ship.*
• **clever, crafty, devious, wily, ingenious, shrewd, artful, scheming, sly, tricky**

cup *NOUN*
A tall cup with straight sides is a **mug**.
A tall cup without a handle is a **beaker** or **tumbler**.
A decorative drinking cup is a **goblet**.
for other containers for drinks see **drink**

cupboard *NOUN*
*There are some spare pillows in the **cupboard**.*
• **cabinet, dresser, sideboard**
A cupboard for food is a **larder**.
for other items of furniture see **furniture**

curb *VERB*
*You must try to **curb** your anger.*
• **control, restrain, suppress, check, hold back, limit, moderate, repress, restrict**
OPPOSITE **encourage**

cure *VERB*
❶ *These pills will **cure** your headache.*
• **ease, heal, help, improve, make better, relieve**
OPPOSITE **aggravate**
❷ *No-one can **cure** the problem with my computer.*
• **correct, mend, sort, repair, fix, put an end to, put right**

cure *NOUN*
*I wish they could find a **cure** for colds.*
• **remedy, treatment, antidote, medicine, therapy**

curiosity *NOUN*
*Babies are full of **curiosity** about the world.*
• **inquisitiveness, interest**
Uncomplimentary words are **nosiness, prying** and **snooping.**

curious *ADJECTIVE*
❶ *We were all very **curious** about the secret chamber.*
• **inquisitive, inquiring, interested, intrigued, agog**
An uncomplimentary word is **nosy.**
OPPOSITE **uninterested, indifferent**
❷ *What is that **curious** smell?*
• **odd, strange, peculiar, abnormal, queer, unusual, extraordinary, funny, mysterious, puzzling, weird**

curl *VERB*
❶ *The snake **curled** itself around a branch.*
• **wind, twist, loop, coil, wrap, curve, turn, twine**
❷ *Steam **curled** upwards from the cauldron.*
• **coil, spiral, twirl, swirl, furl, snake, writhe, ripple**

curl *NOUN*
*The girl's hair was a mass of golden **curls**.*
• **wave, ringlet, coil, loop, twist, roll, scroll, spiral**

curly *ADJECTIVE*
*My new doll has **curly** black hair.*
• **curled, curling, wavy, frizzy, crinkly, ringletted**
OPPOSITE **straight**

current *NOUN*
*The wooden raft drifted along with the **current**.*
• **flow, tide, stream**
A current of air is a **draught.**

current *ADJECTIVE*
❶ *The shop sells all the **current** teenage fashions.*
• **modern, contemporary, present-day, up to date, topical, prevailing, prevalent**
OPPOSITES **past, old-fashioned**
❷ *Have you got a **current** passport?*
• **valid, usable, up to date**
OPPOSITE **out of date**
❸ *Who is the **current** prime minister?*
• **present, existing**
OPPOSITES **past, former**

curse *NOUN*
❶ *Long ago, a wizard put a **curse** on the family.*
• **jinx, hex**
❷ *When the gardener hit his finger, he let out a **curse**.*
• **swear word, oath**

curve *NOUN*
*Try to draw a straight line without any **curves**.*
• **bend, curl, loop, turn, twist, arch, arc, bow, bulge, wave**
A curve in the shape of a new moon is a **crescent.**
A curve on a road surface is a **camber.**

curve *VERB*
*The road ahead **curves** round to the right.*
• **bend, wind, turn, twist, curl, loop, swerve, veer, snake, meander**

curved *ADJECTIVE*
*The wall was painted with a series of **curved** lines.*
• **curving, curvy, curled, looped, coiled, rounded, bulging, bent, arched, bowed, twisted, crooked, spiral, winding, meandering, serpentine, snaking, undulating**
A surface which is curved like the inside of a circle is **concave.**
A surface which is curved like the outside of a circle is **convex.**

cushion *VERB*
*If you fall off the swing, the mat will **cushion** your fall.*
• **soften, reduce the effect of, absorb, muffle**

custom *NOUN*

❶ *It's our **custom** to give presents at Christmas.*

• **tradition, practice, habit, convention, fashion, routine, way**

❷ *The shop is having a sale to attract more **custom**.*

• **customers, buyers, trade, business**

customary *ADJECTIVE*

*It is **customary** to leave the waiter a tip.*

• **traditional, conventional, usual, normal, common, typical, expected, habitual, routine, regular, everyday, ordinary, prevailing, prevalent**

OPPOSITE **unusual**

customer *NOUN*

*There was a queue of **customers** at the checkout.*

• **buyer, shopper, client**

cut *VERB* **cuts, cutting, cut**

❶ *The woodcutter **cut** the tree trunk to make logs.*

• **chop, slit, split, chip, notch, axe, hack, hew, cleave**

To cut off a limb is to **amputate** or **sever** it.
To cut down a tree is to **fell** it.
To cut branches off a tree is to **lop** them.
To cut twigs off a growing plant is to **prune** it.
To cut something up to examine it is to **dissect** it.
To cut stone to make a statue is to **carve** it.
To cut an inscription in stone is to **engrave** it.

❷ *The cook **cut** the apples into small pieces.*

• **chop, slice, dice, grate, mince, shred**

❸ *I'm going to get my hair **cut** in the holidays.*

• **trim, clip, crop, snip, shave**

To cut wool off a sheep is to **shear** it.
To cut grass is to **mow** it.
To cut corn is to **harvest** or **reap** it.

❹ *Josh **cut** his foot on a sharp stone.*

• **gash, slash, nick, stab, pierce, wound**

❺ *This letter is too long—I'll need to **cut** it.*

• **shorten, condense, edit**

❻ *The shop has **cut** its prices by 10%.*

• **lower, reduce, decrease**

If you cut something by half, you **halve** it.

cut *NOUN*

❶ *I got a nasty **cut** when I was slicing bread.*

• **gash, wound, injury, nick, slash, scratch, slit, snip**

❷ *There has been a **cut** in the price of petrol.*

• **fall, reduction, decrease**

cutlery *NOUN*

WORD WEB

SOME ITEMS OF CUTLERY:

• **bread knife, butter knife, carving knife, cheese knife, chopsticks, dessert spoon, fish knife, fork, knife, ladle, spoon, steak knife, tablespoon, teaspoon**

cutting *ADJECTIVE*

*She made a **cutting** remark about my dress.*

• **sharp, hurtful, biting, stinging, vicious**

cycle *NOUN*

see **bicycle**

Dd

daily *ADJECTIVE*
*Walking to school is part of my **daily** exercise routine.*
• everyday, regular
OPPOSITES infrequent, irregular

dainty *ADJECTIVE*
*The doll's hair was tied with a **dainty** little ribbon.*
• delicate, neat, charming, fine, exquisite, bijou *(informal)* cute, dinky
OPPOSITE clumsy

dam *NOUN*
*Some beavers have built a **dam** in this river.*
• barrier, barrage, embankment, dyke, weir

dam *VERB*
*The river was **dammed** to make a reservoir.*
• block, check, hold back

damage *VERB*
*Many books were **damaged** in the fire.*
• harm, spoil, mar, break, impair, weaken, disfigure, deface, mutilate, scar
To damage something beyond repair is to **destroy**, **ruin** or **wreck** it.
To damage something deliberately is to **sabotage** or **vandalise** it.

damp *ADJECTIVE*
❶ *Don't wear those clothes if they are **damp**.*
• moist, soggy, clammy, dank
❷ *I don't like this **damp** weather.*
• drizzly, foggy, misty, rainy, wet
Weather which is both damp and warm is **humid** or **muggy** weather.
OPPOSITE dry

dampen *VERB*
❶ ***Dampen** the cloth with a little water.*
• moisten, wet
❷ *Nothing could **dampen** her enthusiasm.*
• make less, decrease, reduce

dance *NOUN*

WORD WEB

SOME KINDS OF DANCE OR DANCING:

• ballet, ballroom dancing, barn dance, belly-dancing, bolero, breakdancing, cancan, disco, flamenco, folk dance, Highland dancing, hornpipe, jazz dance, jig, jive dancing, limbo dancing, line-dancing, mazurka, morris dance, quadrille, reel, rumba, samba, Scottish country dancing, square dance, step dancing, street dance, tap-dancing, tarantella
A person who writes the steps for a dance is a **choreographer**.

SOME BALLROOM DANCES:

• foxtrot, minuet, polka, quickstep, tango, waltz

GATHERINGS WHERE PEOPLE DANCE:

• ball, ceilidh, disco

dance *VERB*
*I could have **danced** for joy.*
• caper, cavort, frisk, frolic, gambol, hop about, jig about, jump about, leap, prance, skip, whirl

danger *NOUN*
❶ *Who knows what **dangers** lie ahead?*
• peril, jeopardy, trouble, crisis, hazard, menace, pitfall, threat, trap
OPPOSITE safety
❷ *The forecast says there's a **danger** of frost.*
• chance, possibility, risk

dangerous *ADJECTIVE*
❶ *We were in a **dangerous** situation.*
• hazardous, perilous, risky, precarious, treacherous, unsafe, alarming, menacing *(informal)* hairy
❷ *The police arrested him for **dangerous** driving.*
• careless, reckless

❸ *A **dangerous** criminal had escaped from prison.*
• violent, desperate, ruthless, treacherous
❹ *It's wicked to empty **dangerous** chemicals into the river.*
• harmful, poisonous, deadly, toxic
OPPOSITES harmless, safe

dangle *VERB*
*There was a bunch of keys **dangling** from the chain.*
• hang, swing, sway, droop, wave about, flap, trail

dare *VERB*
❶ *I wouldn't **dare** to make a parachute jump.*
• have the courage, take the risk
❷ *They **dared** me to climb the tree.*
• challenge, defy

daring *ADJECTIVE*
*It was a very **daring** plan.*
• bold, brave, adventurous, courageous, fearless, intrepid, plucky, valiant
A daring person is a **daredevil.**
OPPOSITE timid

dark *ADJECTIVE*
❶ *It was a very **dark** night.*
• black, dim, murky, shadowy, gloomy, dingy
OPPOSITE bright
❷ *She wore a **dark** green coat.*
OPPOSITES pale, light

darken *VERB*
*The sky **darkened**.*
• become overcast, blacken, cloud over
OPPOSITE brighten

dash *NOUN*
❶ *When the storm broke, we made a **dash** for shelter.*
• run, rush, race, sprint
❷ *I like just a **dash** of milk in my tea.*
• drop, small amount, splash, spot

dash *VERB*
❶ *We **dashed** home because it was raining.*
• hurry, run, rush, race, hasten, sprint, speed, tear, zoom
❷ *She **dashed** her cup against the wall.*
• throw, hurl, knock, smash

data *NOUN*
*I entered all the **data** into the computer.*
• information, details, facts
Data can be in the form of **figures, numbers** or **statistics.**

date *NOUN*
*I have a **date** with some friends this evening.*
• meeting, appointment, engagement

dawn *NOUN*
❶ *I was woken at **dawn** by the birds singing outside.*
• daybreak, sunrise, first light
OPPOSITES dusk, sunset
❷ *It was the **dawn** of the modern age.*
• beginning, start, birth, origin

day *NOUN*
❶ *Badgers sleep during the **day**.*
• daytime
OPPOSITE night
❷ *Things were different in my grandfather's **day**.*
• age, time, era, epoch, period

WORD WEB

VARIOUS TIMES OF THE DAY:

• dawn or daybreak or sunrise, morning, noon or midday, afternoon, evening, nightfall or sunset, dusk or twilight, night, midnight

dazed *ADJECTIVE*
*He had a **dazed** expression on his face.*
• confused, bewildered, muddled, perplexed

A B C D E F G H I J K L M N O P Q R S T U V W X Y Z

dazzle *VERB*
❶ *My eyes were **dazzled** by the bright lights.*
• **daze, blind**
❷ *The acrobats **dazzled** the audience with their skill.*
• **amaze, astonish, impress, fascinate, awe**

dead *ADJECTIVE*
❶ *A **dead** fish floated near the river's edge.*
• **deceased, lifeless**
Instead of 'the king who has just died', you can say 'the **late** king'.
A dead body is a **carcass** or **corpse**.
A common simile is **as dead as a doornail**.
OPPOSITE **alive**
❷ *Latin is a **dead** language.*
• **extinct, obsolete**
OPPOSITE **living**
❸ *This battery is **dead**.*
• **flat, not working, worn out**
❹ *The town centre is **dead** at this time of night.*
• **dull, boring, uninteresting, slow**
OPPOSITE **lively**

deaden *VERB*
❶ *The dentist gave me an injection to **deaden** the pain.*
• **anaesthetise, lessen, reduce, suppress**
OPPOSITE **increase**
❷ *Double glazing **deadens** the noise of the traffic.*
• **dampen, muffle, quieten**
OPPOSITE **amplify**

deadly *ADJECTIVE*
*The witch gave her a **deadly** dose of poison.*
• **lethal, fatal, harmful, dangerous, destructive**
OPPOSITE **harmless**

deafening *ADJECTIVE*
*We complained about the **deafening** noise.*
• **loud, blaring, booming, thunderous, penetrating**

deal *VERB* **deals, dealing, dealt**
❶ *Who is going to **deal** the cards?*
• **give out, distribute, share out**
❷ *My uncle used to **deal** in second-hand cars.*
• **do business, trade**
➤ **to deal with something**
❶ *I can **deal with** this problem.*
• **cope with, sort out, attend to, see to, handle, manage, control, grapple with, look after, solve**
❷ *The book **deals with** the history of Rome.*
• **be concerned with, cover, explain about**

deal *NOUN*
*She made a **deal** with the garage for her new car.*
• **arrangement, agreement, contract, bargain**
➤ **a good deal** or **a great deal**
*We went to **a great deal of** trouble to do things properly.*
• **a lot, a large amount**

dear *ADJECTIVE*
❶ *She is a very **dear** friend.*
• **close, loved, valued, beloved**
OPPOSITE **distant**
❷ *I didn't buy the watch because it was too **dear**.*
• **expensive, costly**
(informal) **pricey**
OPPOSITE **cheap**

death *NOUN*
❶ *The Vikings mourned the **death** of their chief.*
• **dying, end, passing**
❷ *The accident resulted in several **deaths**.*
• **fatality**

debate *NOUN*
*We had a **debate** about animal rights.*
• **discussion, argument, dispute**
Something which people argue about a lot is a **controversy**.

debate *VERB*
❶ *We **debated** whether it is right to kill animals for food.*
• **discuss, argue**
❷ *I **debated** what to do next.*
• **consider, ponder, deliberate, weigh up, reflect on**

debris *NOUN*
Debris from the crashed aircraft was scattered over a large area.
• **remains, wreckage, fragments, pieces**

decay *VERB*
*Dead leaves fall to the ground and **decay**.*
• **decompose, rot, disintegrate, break down**

deceit *NOUN*
*I saw through his **deceit**.*
• **deception, trickery, dishonesty, fraud, duplicity, double-dealing, pretence, bluff, cheating, deceitfulness, lying**
OPPOSITE **honesty**

deceitful *ADJECTIVE*
*Don't trust him—he's a **deceitful** person.*
• **dishonest, underhand, insincere, duplicitous, false, cheating, hypocritical, lying, treacherous, two-faced, sneaky**
OPPOSITE **honest**

deceive *VERB*
*The spy had been **deceiving** them for years.*
• **fool, trick, delude, dupe, hoodwink, cheat, double-cross, mislead, swindle, take in**
(informal) **con, diddle**

decent *ADJECTIVE*
❶ *I did the **decent** thing and owned up.*
• **honest, honourable**
❷ *My friend's jokes were not **decent**.*
• **polite, proper, respectable, acceptable, appropriate, suitable, fitting**
OPPOSITE **indecent**
❸ *I haven't had a **decent** meal for ages!*
• **satisfactory, agreeable, good, nice**
OPPOSITE **bad**

deception *NOUN*
see **deceit**

deceptive *ADJECTIVE*
*Appearances can be **deceptive**.*
• **misleading, unreliable, false**

decide *VERB*
❶ *We **decided** to finish our work instead of going out to play.*
• **choose, make a decision, make up your mind, opt, elect, resolve**
❷ *The referee **decided** that the player was offside.*
• **conclude, judge, rule**
❸ *The last lap **decided** the result of the race.*
• **determine, settle**

decision *NOUN*
❶ *Can you tell me what your **decision** is?*
• **choice, preference**
❷ *The judge announced his **decision**.*
• **conclusion, judgement, verdict, findings**

decisive *ADJECTIVE*
❶ *A **decisive** piece of evidence proved that he was innocent.*
• **crucial, convincing, definite**
❷ *A referee needs to be **decisive**.*
• **firm, forceful, strong-minded, resolute, quick-thinking**
OPPOSITE **hesitant**

declare *VERB*
*He **declared** that he was innocent.*
• **announce, state, assert, make known, pronounce, proclaim, swear**

decline *VERB*
❶ *Our enthusiasm **declined** as the day went on.*
• **become less, decrease, diminish, lessen, weaken, dwindle, flag, wane, tail off**
OPPOSITE **increase**
❷ *Why did you **decline** my invitation to lunch?*
• **refuse, reject, turn down**
OPPOSITE **accept**

decode *VERB*
see **code**

decorate *VERB*
❶ *We **decorated** the Christmas tree with tinsel.*
• **adorn, beautify, prettify, deck, festoon**
To decorate a dish of food is to **garnish** it.

a b c d e f g h i j k l m n o p q r s t u v w x y z

To decorate clothes with lace or ribbon is to **trim** them.

❷ *Dad is going to* ***decorate*** *my bedroom next weekend.*
- **paint, paper, wallpaper**

(informal) **do up, make over**

❸ *The firefighters were* ***decorated*** *for their bravery.*
- **award or give a medal to, honour, reward**

decorative *ADJECTIVE*

The book had a ***decorative*** *design on the cover.*
- **ornamental, elaborate, fancy, attractive, beautiful, colourful, pretty**

OPPOSITE **plain**

decrease *VERB*

❶ *We* ***decreased*** *speed.*
- **reduce, cut, lower, slacken**

❷ *Our enthusiasm* ***decreased*** *as the day went on.*
- **become less, decline, diminish, lessen, weaken, dwindle, flag, wane, tail off, shrink, subside**

OPPOSITE **increase**

decrease *NOUN*

There has been a ***decrease*** *in the number of sparrows this year.*
- **decline, drop, fall, cut, reduction**

OPPOSITE **increase**

decree *VERB*

The king ***decreed*** *that the day would be a holiday.*
- **order, command, declare, pronounce, proclaim**

dedicate *VERB*

He ***dedicates*** *himself entirely to his art.*
- **commit, devote**

dedicated *ADJECTIVE*

A group of ***dedicated*** *fans waited at the stage door.*
- **committed, devoted, keen, enthusiastic, faithful, zealous**

deduce *VERB*

The detective ***deduced*** *that the footprints were fresh.*
- **conclude, work out, infer, reason, gather**

deduct *VERB*

Tax is ***deducted*** *from your salary.*
- **subtract, take away, knock off**

OPPOSITE **add**

deed *NOUN*

They thanked the rescue team for their heroic ***deed****.*
- **act, action, feat, exploit, effort, achievement**

deep *ADJECTIVE*

❶ *The pond is quite* ***deep*** *in the middle.*

OPPOSITE **shallow**

❷ *The letter expressed his* ***deep*** *regret.*
- **intense, earnest, genuine, sincere**

OPPOSITE **insincere**

❸ *Veronica fell into a* ***deep*** *sleep.*
- **heavy, sound**

OPPOSITE **light**

❹ *The actor spoke in a* ***deep*** *and sombre voice.*
- **low, bass**

OPPOSITE **high**

deer *NOUN*

A male deer is a **buck, hart, roebuck** or **stag**.
A female deer is a **doe** or **hind**.
A young deer is a **fawn**.
Deer's flesh used as food is **venison**.

defeat *VERB*

The Greeks attacked and ***defeated*** *the Trojans.*
- **beat, conquer, vanquish, triumph over, win a victory over, overcome, overpower, crush, rout, trounce**

To defeat someone in chess is to **checkmate** them.
To be defeated is to **lose**.

defeat *NOUN*

The team suffered a humiliating ***defeat****.*
- **failure, humiliation, rout, trouncing**

OPPOSITE **victory**

defect *NOUN*
*Cars are tested for **defects** before they leave the factory.*
• **fault, flaw, imperfection, shortcoming, failure, weakness**
A defect in a computer program is a **bug**.

defence *NOUN*
❶ *What was the accused woman's **defence**?*
• **justification, excuse, explanation, argument, case**
❷ *The castle was built as a **defence** against enemy attack.*
• **protection, guard, safeguard, fortification, barricade, shield**

defend *VERB*
❶ *They tried to **defend** themselves against the enemy.*
• **protect, guard, keep safe**
OPPOSITE **attack**
❷ *He gave a speech **defending** his actions.*
• **justify, support, stand up for, make a case for**
OPPOSITE **accuse**

defer *VERB*
*They **deferred** their departure until the weekend.*
• **delay, put off, postpone**

defiant *ADJECTIVE*
*The prisoner cursed with a **defiant** look in his eye.*
• **rebellious, insolent, aggressive, challenging, disobedient, obstinate, quarrelsome, uncooperative, stubborn, mutinous**
OPPOSITES **submissive, compliant**

deficient *ADJECTIVE*
*Their diet is **deficient** in vitamins.*
• **lacking, wanting, short of, inadequate, insufficient, unsatisfactory**
OPPOSITE **adequate**

define *VERB*
*A dictionary **defines** lots of words.*
• **explain, give the meaning of, interpret, clarify**

definite *ADJECTIVE*
❶ *Is it **definite** that we're going to move?*
• **certain, sure, fixed, settled, decided**
❷ *The doctor saw **definite** signs of improvement.*
• **clear, distinct, noticeable, obvious, marked, positive, pronounced, unmistakable**
OPPOSITE **indefinite**

definitely *ADVERB*
*I'll **definitely** phone you tomorrow.*
• **certainly, for certain, positively, surely, unquestionably, without doubt, without fail**
OPPOSITE **perhaps**

deflect *VERB*
*The goalkeeper was able to **deflect** the shot.*
• **divert, turn aside, intercept, avert, fend off, ward off**

deft *ADJECTIVE*
*She applied the paint with a **deft** flick of her brush.*
• **skilful, agile, nimble, quick, clever, expert, proficient, adept**
(informal) **nifty**
OPPOSITE **clumsy**

defy *VERB*
❶ *The rebel army decided to **defy** the king.*
• **disobey, refuse to obey, resist, stand up to, confront**
OPPOSITE **obey**
❷ *I **defy** you to come up with a better idea.*
• **challenge, dare**
❸ *The jammed door **defied** our efforts to open it.*
• **resist, withstand, defeat, frustrate, beat**

degrading *ADJECTIVE*
*Losing by ten goals to nil was a **degrading** experience.*
• **shameful, humiliating, embarrassing, undignified**

degree *NOUN*
*The young gymnast showed a high **degree** of skill.*
• **standard, level, grade, measure, extent**

A B C D E F G H I J K L M N O P Q R S T U V W X Y Z

dejected *ADJECTIVE*
*I felt **dejected** when I failed the test.*
• **depressed, disheartened, downhearted, unhappy, sad, low, gloomy, glum, melancholy, miserable, downcast, despondent, woeful, wretched, forlorn**
(informal) **fed up, down**
OPPOSITES **happy, cheerful**

delay *VERB*
❶ *Don't let me **delay** you.*
• **detain, hold up, keep waiting, make late, hinder, slow down**
❷ *They **delayed** the race because of bad weather.*
• **postpone, put off, defer**
❸ *You'll miss the bus if you **delay**.*
• **hesitate, linger, pause, wait, dawdle, loiter**
(informal) **hang about** or **around, drag your feet**

delay *NOUN*
*There has been a **delay** with the building work.*
• **hold-up, wait, pause**

delete *VERB*
*I **deleted** your email by mistake.*
• **remove, erase, cancel, cross out**

deliberate *ADJECTIVE*
❶ *That remark was a **deliberate** insult.*
• **intentional, planned, calculated, conscious, premeditated**
OPPOSITES **accidental, unintentional**
❷ *He walked with **deliberate** steps across the room.*
• **careful, steady, cautious, slow, unhurried**
OPPOSITES **hasty, careless**

deliberately *VERB*
*Did you say that **deliberately** to hurt my feelings?*
• **on purpose, intentionally**
OPPOSITES **accidentally, unintentionally**

delicate *ADJECTIVE*
❶ *The blouse has **delicate** embroidery on the cuffs.*
• **dainty, exquisite, intricate, neat**
❷ *Take care not to damage the **delicate** material.*
• **fragile, fine, flimsy, thin**
❸ ***Delicate** plants should be protected from frost.*
• **sensitive, tender**
OPPOSITES **tough, hardy**
❹ *The child was born with a **delicate** constitution.*
• **frail, weak, feeble, sickly, unhealthy**
OPPOSITE **strong**
❺ *The pianist's fingers had a **delicate** touch.*
• **gentle, light, soft**
❻ *He discussed the matter in a **delicate** way.*
• **tactful, sensitive, considerate, diplomatic, careful, discreet**
OPPOSITE **insensitive**
❼ *Can you help me with a **delicate** problem?*
• **awkward, embarrassing**

delicious *ADJECTIVE*
*The food at the banquet was **delicious**.*
• **tasty, appetising, mouthwatering, delectable**
(informal) **yummy, scrumptious, scrumdiddlyumptious**
for other ways to describe food see **food**
OPPOSITES **horrible, disgusting**

delight *NOUN*
*Imagine my **delight** when I saw my friend again!*
• **happiness, joy, pleasure, enjoyment, bliss, ecstasy**

delight *VERB*
*The puppet show **delighted** the crowd.*
• **please, charm, entertain, amuse, divert, enchant, entrance, fascinate, thrill**
OPPOSITE **dismay**

delighted *ADJECTIVE*
*The **delighted** crowd cheered the winners.*
• **pleased, happy, joyful, thrilled, ecstatic, elated, exultant**

delightful *ADJECTIVE*
*The poem she wrote was **delightful**.*
• lovely, pleasant, pleasing, beautiful, attractive, charming

deliver *VERB*
❶ *Does anyone **deliver** mail to the island?*
• convey, bring, hand over, distribute, present, supply, take round
❷ *The head **delivered** a lecture on good behaviour.*
• give, make, read out

delude *VERB*
*He **deluded** us into thinking he was very rich.*
• deceive, fool, trick, mislead, hoax, bluff
(informal) con

delusion *NOUN*
*Your belief that you are a great writer is a **delusion**!*
• fantasy, dream, self-deception

demand *VERB*
❶ *I **demanded** a refund for my train fare.*
• insist on, claim, call for, require, want
❷ *'What do you want?' **demanded** a voice inside.*
• ask, enquire, inquire

demand *NOUN*
❶ *The king refused the **demands** of his people.*
• request, claim, requirement
❷ *There is not much **demand** for ice lollies in winter.*
• need, call

demanding *ADJECTIVE*
❶ *Toddlers can be very **demanding**.*
• difficult, trying, tiresome, insistent
❷ *The expedition leader had a very **demanding** job.*
• difficult, challenging, exhausting, hard, tough, testing, taxing, onerous
OPPOSITE easy

demolish *VERB*
*They **demolished** a building to make way for the road.*
• destroy, flatten, knock down, level, pull down, tear down, bulldoze
OPPOSITES build, construct

demonstrate *VERB*
❶ *The teacher **demonstrated** how warm air rises.*
• show, exhibit, illustrate
❷ *Animal rights campaigners were **demonstrating** in the street.*
• protest, march, parade

demonstration *NOUN*
❶ *I watched a **demonstration** of the new computer game.*
• show, display, presentation
❷ *Everyone joined the **demonstration** against world poverty.*
• protest, rally, march, parade
(informal) demo

demote *VERB*
*The team may be **demoted** to a lower division.*
• put down, relegate
OPPOSITE promote

den *NOUN*
*We built a **den** in the garden.*
• hideout, shelter, hiding place, secret place
The den of a wild animal is its lair.

denote *VERB*
*What does this symbol **denote**?*
• mean, indicate, signify, stand for, be a sign of, express

dense *ADJECTIVE*
❶ *The accident happened in **dense** fog.*
• thick, heavy
❷ *A **dense** crowd waited in the square.*
• compact, packed, solid
❸ *I'm being rather **dense** today!*
• stupid, slow

a b c d e f g h i j k l m n o p q r s t u v w x y z

A B C D E F G H I J K L M N O P Q R S T U V W X Y Z

dent *NOUN*
*There was a large **dent** in the car door.*
• indentation, depression, hollow, dip, dimple

dent *VERB*
*A football hit the car door and **dented** it.*
• make a dent in, knock in, push in

dentist *NOUN*
A dentist who specialises in straightening teeth is an **orthodontist**.
for other words to do with your teeth see **tooth**

deny *VERB*
❶ *The boy **denied** that he had stolen the money.*
• reject, dispute, disagree with, contradict, dismiss, oppose
OPPOSITES admit, accept
❷ *Her parents don't **deny** her anything.*
• refuse, deprive of, withhold
OPPOSITE give

depart *VERB*
❶ *What time is the train due to **depart**?*
• leave, set off, get going, set out, start, begin a journey
OPPOSITES arrive, get in
❷ *It looks as if the robbers **departed** in a hurry.*
• leave, exit, go away, retreat, withdraw, make off
(informal) clear off, scram, scarper
OPPOSITE arrive

department *NOUN*
*Mr Taylor works in the sales **department**.*
• section, branch, division, office

depend *VERB*
➤ **to depend on someone**
*I **depend on** you to help me.*
• rely on, count on, bank on, trust
➤ **to depend on something**
*My success will **depend on** good luck.*
• be decided by, rest on, hinge on

dependable *ADJECTIVE*
*Are these friends of yours **dependable**?*
• reliable, trustworthy, loyal, faithful, trusty, honest, sound, steady
OPPOSITE unreliable

dependent *ADJECTIVE*
➤ **dependent on**
*Everything is **dependent on** the weather.*
• determined by, subject to, controlled by, reliant on

depict *VERB*
❶ *She **depicted** the landscape in watercolours.*
• draw, paint, sketch
❷ *The film **depicts** the horror of war.*
• show, represent, portray, describe, illustrate, outline

deplorable *ADJECTIVE*
*Their rudeness was **deplorable**.*
• disgraceful, shameful, scandalous, shocking, unforgivable, lamentable, reprehensible, inexcusable
OPPOSITE praiseworthy

deplore *VERB*
*We all **deplore** cruelty to animals.*
• condemn, disapprove of, hate

deport *VERB*
*He was **deported** from Australia.*
• exile, banish, expel, send abroad

deposit *NOUN*
❶ *Dad paid the **deposit** on a new car.*
• down-payment, first instalment, initial payment
❷ *There was a **deposit** of mud at the bottom of the river.*
• layer, sediment

depress *VERB*
*The miserable weather was **depressing** us.*
• sadden, discourage, dishearten, dispirit
OPPOSITE cheer

depressed *ADJECTIVE*
*After his friends left, he began to feel **depressed**.*
• **disheartened, dejected, discouraged, downcast, downhearted, unhappy, sad, low, gloomy, glum, melancholy, miserable, despondent, desolate, in despair**
(informal) **down**
OPPOSITE **cheerful**

depressing *ADJECTIVE*
*It was a **depressing** situation to be in.*
• **discouraging, dispiriting, disheartening, gloomy, sad, dismal, dreary, sombre, bleak**
OPPOSITE **cheerful**

depression *NOUN*
❶ *She sank into a state of **depression**.*
• **despair, dejection, sadness, gloom, unhappiness, hopelessness, low spirits, melancholy, misery, desolation, pessimism, glumness**
OPPOSITE **cheerfulness**
❷ *Most businesses do badly during a **depression**.*
• **recession, slump**
OPPOSITE **boom**
❸ *The rain had collected in several **depressions** in the ground.*
• **hollow, indentation, dent, dip, hole, pit, rut**
OPPOSITE **bump**

deprived *ADJECTIVE*
*The charity tries to help **deprived** families.*
• **poor, needy, underprivileged**
OPPOSITES **wealthy, privileged**

deputy *NOUN*
*The sheriff appointed a new **deputy**.*
• **second-in-command, assistant, stand-in, substitute**
WHICH WORD? Note that words beginning vice- usually mean 'the deputy for a particular person', for example the **vice-captain** or the **vice-president**.

derelict *ADJECTIVE*
*They plan to pull down those **derelict** buildings.*
• **dilapidated, crumbling, decrepit, neglected, deserted, abandoned, ruined**

deride *VERB*
*The book was **derided** when it first came out.*
• **ridicule, mock, laugh at, dismiss**
(informal) **pooh-pooh**
OPPOSITE **praise**

derive *VERB*
❶ *Bill **derives** a lot of pleasure from his garden.*
• **get, obtain, receive, gain**
❷ *She **derived** many of her ideas from books.*
• **borrow, draw, pick up, take**
(informal) **lift**

descend *VERB*
❶ *After admiring the view, we began to **descend** the mountain.*
• **climb down, come down, go down, move down**
To descend through the air is to **drop** or **fall**.
To descend through water is to **sink**.
❷ *The road **descends** gradually into the valley.*
• **drop, fall, slope, dip, incline**
OPPOSITE **ascend**
➤ **to be descended from someone**
*She's **descended from** a French family.*
• **come from, originate from**

descendant *NOUN*
A person's descendants are their **heirs** or **successors**.
OPPOSITE **ancestor**

descent *NOUN*
*The path makes a steep **descent** into the valley.*
• **drop, fall, dip, incline**
OPPOSITE **ascent**

describe *VERB*
❶ *An eyewitness **described** how the accident happened.*
• **report, tell about, depict, explain, outline**
❷ *Friends **described** him as a quiet, shy man.*
• **portray, characterise, represent, present**

A B C D E F G H I J K L M N O P Q R S T U V W X Y Z

description *NOUN*

❶ *I wrote a **description** of our day at the seaside.*

• **report, account, story**

❷ *Write a **description** of your favourite character in the play.*

• **portrait, representation, sketch**

descriptive *ADJECTIVE*

*The author writes in a very **descriptive** style.*

• **expressive, colourful, detailed, graphic, vivid**

desert *NOUN*

WORD WEB

THINGS YOU MIGHT SEE OR EXPERIENCE IN A DESERT:

• **mirage, oasis, sand dune, sandstorm, whirlwind**

SOME ANIMALS WHICH LIVE IN DESERTS:

• **armadillo, camel, chameleon, coyote, desert rat, gerbil, lizard, locust, meerkat, rattlesnake, roadrunner, scorpion, tarantula, vulture**

SOME PLANTS WHICH ARE FOUND IN DESERTS:

• **cactus, date palm, grasses, prickly pear, sagebrush, tumbleweed**

A group of people travelling together across a desert is a **caravan**.

People who live in the desert are often **nomads**.

for desert islands see **island**

desert *VERB*

*He **deserted** his friends when they needed him most.*

• **abandon, leave, forsake, betray**

(informal) **walk out on**

To desert someone in a place they can't get away from is to **maroon** or **strand** them.

deserted *ADJECTIVE*

*By midnight, the streets of the town were **deserted**.*

• **empty, unoccupied, uninhabited, vacant**

OPPOSITE **crowded**

deserve *VERB*

*You **deserve** a break after all your hard work.*

• **be worthy of, be entitled to, have earned, merit, warrant**

design *NOUN*

❶ *This is the winning **design** for the new art gallery.*

• **plan, drawing, outline, blueprint, sketch**

A first example of something, used as a model for making others, is a **prototype**.

❷ *Do you like the **design** of this wallpaper?*

• **style, pattern, arrangement, composition**

for types of art and design see **art**

design *VERB*

*She **designs** all her own clothes.*

• **create, develop, invent, devise, conceive, think up**

desirable *ADJECTIVE*

❶ *The house has many **desirable** features.*

• **appealing, attractive, interesting, tempting**

OPPOSITE **worthless**

❷ *It is **desirable** to phone before you arrive.*

• **advisable, sensible, prudent, wise**

OPPOSITE **unwise**

desire *VERB*

*The magic mirror will show you what you most **desire**.*

• **wish for, long for, want, crave, fancy, hanker after, yearn for, pine for, set your heart on, have a yen for**

desire *NOUN*

*My greatest **desire** is to swim with dolphins.*

• **wish, want, longing, ambition, craving, fancy, hankering, urge, yearning**

A desire for food is **appetite** or **hunger**.

A desire for drink is **thirst**.

Excessive desire for money or other things is **greed**.

desolate *ADJECTIVE*
❶ *Jamie felt* ***desolate*** *when his goldfish died.*
• depressed, dejected, miserable, sad, melancholy, hopeless, wretched, forlorn
OPPOSITE cheerful
❷ *No-one wants to live in that* ***desolate*** *place.*
• bleak, depressing, dreary, gloomy, dismal, cheerless, inhospitable, deserted, uninhabited, abandoned, godforsaken
OPPOSITE pleasant

despair *NOUN*
The defeated knight was overcome by ***despair.***
• depression, desperation, gloom, hopelessness, misery, anguish, dejection, melancholy, pessimism, wretchedness
OPPOSITE hope

despatch *NOUN, VERB*
see **dispatch**

desperate *ADJECTIVE*
❶ *The shipwrecked crew were in a* ***desperate*** *situation.*
• difficult, critical, grave, serious, severe, drastic, dire, urgent, extreme
❷ *The hills were home to a band of* ***desperate*** *outlaws.*
• dangerous, violent, reckless

despicable *ADJECTIVE*
The pirates were known for ***despicable*** *acts of cruelty.*
• disgraceful, hateful, shameful, contemptible, loathsome, vile

despise *VERB*
I ***despise*** *people who cheat at cards.*
• hate, loathe, feel contempt for, deride, have a low opinion of, look down on, scorn, sneer at
OPPOSITE admire

despite *PREPOSITION*
We went for a walk ***despite*** *the rain.*
• in spite of, regardless of, notwithstanding
OPPOSITE because of

dessert *NOUN*
For ***dessert****, there's apple pie and ice cream.*
• pudding, sweet
(informal) afters

destination *NOUN*
The train arrived at its ***destination*** *five minutes early.*
• terminus, stop

destined *ADJECTIVE*
❶ *It was* ***destined*** *that he would become a famous actor.*
• fated, doomed, intended, meant, certain, inevitable, unavoidable, inescapable
❷ *This parcel is* ***destined*** *for Japan.*
• bound, directed, intended, headed

destiny *NOUN*
Was it ***destiny*** *that brought us together?*
• fate, fortune

destroy *VERB*
❶ *An avalanche* ***destroyed*** *the village.*
• demolish, devastate, crush, flatten, knock down, level, pull down, shatter, smash, sweep away
❷ *He tried to* ***destroy*** *the good work we had done.*
• ruin, wreck, sabotage, undo

destruction *NOUN*
❶ *The hurricane caused* ***destruction*** *all along the coast.*
• devastation, damage, demolition, ruin, wrecking
OPPOSITE creation
❷ *Global warming may cause the* ***destruction*** *of many animal species.*
• elimination, annihilation, obliteration, extermination, extinction
OPPOSITE conservation

destructive *ADJECTIVE*
Tornadoes have a great ***destructive*** *power.*
• damaging, devastating, catastrophic, disastrous, harmful, injurious, ruinous, violent

A B C D E F G H I J K L M N O P Q R S T U V W X Y Z

detach *VERB*

*The camera lens can be **detached** for cleaning.*

• **remove, separate, disconnect, take off, release, undo, unfasten, part**

To detach a caravan from a vehicle is to **unhitch** it.

To detach railway wagons from a locomotive is to **uncouple** them.

To detach something by cutting it off is to **sever** it.

OPPOSITE **attach**

detail *NOUN*

*Her account of what happened was accurate in every **detail**.*

• **fact, feature, particular, aspect, item, point, respect**

detailed *ADJECTIVE*

*This book gives a **detailed** description of Victorian London.*

• **precise, exact, specific, full, thorough, elaborate, comprehensive, exhaustive**

OPPOSITES **rough, vague**

detain *VERB*

❶ *The police **detained** the suspect.*

• **hold, arrest, capture, imprison, restrain**

OPPOSITE **release**

❷ *I'll try not to **detain** you for long.*

• **delay, hold up, hinder, keep waiting**

detect *VERB*

*I could **detect** the smell of burning in the air.*

• **identify, recognise, spot, find, discover, reveal, diagnose, track down**

detective *NOUN*

***Detective** Dewar solved the case of the stolen tiara.*

• **investigator, sleuth**

(informal) **private eye**

WORD WEB

THINGS A DETECTIVE MIGHT LOOK FOR:

• **bloodstains, clues, evidence, eyewitness, fingerprints, footprints, murder weapon, proof, tracks; criminal, crook, culprit, felon, suspect, mastermind**

That stain should have been the final proof that Sir Henry had bumped off his wife in one of the most gruesome murders any detective would have to solve.—MASTER DETECTIVE, Astrid Lindgren

THINGS A DETECTIVE MIGHT DO:

• **analyse, comb (an area), deduce, deduct, detect, dig up, ferret out, follow a hunch, follow a lead or a tip-off, interrogate or question (a witness), investigate, pursue, shadow, solve (a case), stake out (a hiding place), tail or track down (a suspect)**

An informal name for a story in which a detective solves a crime is a **whodunnit**.

deter *VERB*

*How can we **deter** birds from eating the pears?*

• **discourage, put off, dissuade, prevent, stop**

OPPOSITE **encourage**

deteriorate *VERB*

❶ *The queen's health had begun to **deteriorate**.*

• **worsen, decline, degenerate, get worse, go downhill**

❷ *The walls will **deteriorate** if we don't maintain them.*

• **decay, disintegrate, crumble**

OPPOSITE **improve**

determination *NOUN*

*Marathon runners show great **determination**.*

• **resolve, commitment, willpower, courage, dedication, drive, grit, perseverance, persistence, spirit**

(informal) **guts**

determine *VERB*

*Our task was to **determine** the depth of the loch.*

• **calculate, compute, figure out, work out, reckon, decide**

determined ADJECTIVE
❶ *Boudicca must have been a **determined** woman.*
• resolute, decisive, firm, strong-minded, assertive, persistent, tough
OPPOSITE weak-minded
❷ *I'm **determined** to finish the race.*
• committed, resolved

detest VERB
*I **detest** the smell of boiled cabbage.*
• dislike, hate, loathe
Informal expressions are **can't bear** and **can't stand**.
OPPOSITE love

detour NOUN
*I wasted time by taking a **detour**.*
• diversion, indirect route, roundabout route

detrimental ADJECTIVE
*Too much water can be **detrimental** to plants.*
• damaging, harmful, destructive, adverse
OPPOSITE beneficial

devastate VERB
*The earthquake **devastated** the island.*
• destroy, wreck, ruin, demolish, flatten, level

devastating ADJECTIVE
*The siege had a **devastating** effect on the town.*
• overwhelming, stunning, shocking, shattering

develop VERB
❶ *The zoo is **developing** its education programme.*
• expand, extend, enlarge, build up, diversify
❷ *Her piano playing has **developed** this year.*
• improve, progress, evolve, advance, get better
❸ *The plants will **develop** quickly in the spring.*
• grow, flourish
❹ *How did he **develop** that posh accent?*
• get, acquire, pick up, cultivate

development NOUN
❶ *Were there any **developments** while I was away?*
• event, happening, incident, occurrence, change
❷ *We are pleased with the **development** of our website.*
• growth, expansion, improvement, progress, spread

deviate VERB
*We were forced to **deviate** from our original plan.*
• depart, diverge, differ, stray

device NOUN
*The TV comes with a remote control **device**.*
• tool, implement, instrument, appliance, apparatus, gadget, contraption
(informal) gizmo

devious ADJECTIVE
❶ *The mad professor had a **devious** plan to take over the world.*
• cunning, deceitful, dishonest, furtive, scheming, sly, sneaky, treacherous, wily
❷ *Because of the roadworks, we took a **devious** route home.*
• indirect, roundabout, winding, meandering
OPPOSITE direct

devise VERB
*We need to **devise** a strategy for Saturday's game.*
• conceive, form, invent, contrive, formulate, come up with, make up, plan, prepare, map out, think out, think up

devote VERB
*My brother **devotes** all his free time to football.*
• set aside, dedicate, assign, commit

devoted ADJECTIVE
*She's a **devoted** supporter of our team.*
• loyal, faithful, dedicated, enthusiastic, committed
OPPOSITE apathetic

a b c d e f g h i j k l m n o p q r s t u v w x y z

A B C D E F G H I J K L M N O P Q R S T U V W X Y Z

devotion *NOUN*
*Penguins show great **devotion** to their offspring.*
• attachment, fondness, loyalty, dedication, commitment

devour *VERB*
*He **devoured** a whole plateful of sandwiches.*
• eat, consume, guzzle, gobble up, gulp down, swallow
(informal) scoff, wolf down
see also **eat**

diagram *NOUN*
*We drew a **diagram** of the life cycle of a frog.*
• chart, plan, sketch, outline

dial *VERB*
*I **dialled** 999 for an ambulance.*
• phone, call, ring, telephone

dialogue *NOUN*
*The play consists of a series of **dialogues**.*
• conversation, talk, discussion, exchange, debate, chat

diary *NOUN*
*I wrote all about my birthday party in my **diary**.*
• journal, daily record
A diary describing a voyage or mission is a **log** or **logbook**.
A diary in which you insert pictures and souvenirs is a **scrapbook**.
A diary published on a website is a **blog**.

dictate *VERB*
➤ **to dictate to someone**
*You've got no right to **dictate to** me!*
• order about, give orders to, command, bully
(informal) boss about, push around, lord it over

die *VERB*
❶ *My sister's hamster **died** last week.*
• expire, pass away, perish
(informal) snuff it, kick the bucket, croak
To die of hunger is to **starve**.
❷ *The flowers will **die** if they don't have water.*
• wither, wilt, droop, fade
➤ **to die down**
*The flames will **die down** eventually.*
• become less, decline, decrease, subside, weaken, dwindle, fizzle out, wane
➤ **to die out**
*When did the dinosaurs **die out**?*
• become extinct, cease to exist, come to an end, disappear, vanish

diet *NOUN*
*Koalas live on a **diet** of eucalyptus leaves.*
• food, nourishment, nutrition
If you choose what to eat in order to lose weight, you are on a **slimming** diet.
A **vegetarian** diet excludes meat.
A **vegan** diet excludes all animal products.
see also **food**
➤ **on a diet**
*We ate too much on holiday—now we're **on a diet**.*
• trying to lose weight

differ *VERB*
*The two men **differed** in their beliefs.*
• disagree, conflict, argue, clash, contradict each other, oppose each other, quarrel
OPPOSITE agree
➤ **to differ from**
*My style of painting **differs from** hers.*
• be different from, contrast with

difference *NOUN*
❶ *Can you see any **difference** between these two colours?*
• contrast, distinction
OPPOSITE similarity
❷ *This money will make a **difference** to their lives.*
• change, alteration, modification, variation

different *ADJECTIVE*
❶ *We have **different** views about global warming.*
• differing, contradictory, opposite, clashing, conflicting
❷ *It's important that the teams wear **different** colours.*
• contrasting, dissimilar, distinguishable

❸ *The packet contains sweets of **different** flavours.*
• various, assorted, mixed, several, diverse, numerous, miscellaneous
❹ *Let's go somewhere **different** on holiday this year.*
• new, original, fresh
❺ *Everyone's handwriting is **different**.*
• distinct, distinctive, individual, special, unique
OPPOSITES identical, similar

difficult *ADJECTIVE*
❶ *This crossword is really **difficult**.*
*We were faced with a **difficult** problem.*
• hard, complicated, complex, involved, intricate, baffling, perplexing, puzzling
(informal) tricky, thorny, knotty
OPPOSITE simple
❷ *It is a **difficult** climb to the top of the hill.*
• challenging, arduous, demanding, taxing, exhausting, formidable, gruelling, laborious, strenuous, tough
OPPOSITE easy
❸ *Mum says I was a **difficult** child when I was little.*
• troublesome, awkward, trying, tiresome, annoying, disruptive, obstinate, stubborn, uncooperative, unhelpful
OPPOSITE cooperative

difficulty *NOUN*
❶ *The explorers were used to facing **difficulty**.*
• trouble, adversity, challenges, hardship
❷ *There are some **difficulties** with your application.*
• problem, complication, hitch, obstacle, snag

dig *VERB* **digs, digging, dug**
❶ *We spent the afternoon **digging** the garden.*
• cultivate, fork over, turn over
❷ *Rabbits **dig** holes in the ground.*
• burrow, excavate, tunnel, gouge out, hollow out, scoop out
❸ *Did you **dig** me in the back?*
• poke, prod, jab

dignified *ADJECTIVE*
*Lady Snodgrass was a very **dignified** old lady.*
• refined, stately, distinguished, noble, sedate, solemn, proper, grave, grand, august
OPPOSITE undignified

dignity *NOUN*
❶ *Their laughter spoilt the **dignity** of the occasion.*
• formality, seriousness, solemnity
❷ *She handled the problem with **dignity**.*
• calmness, poise, self-control

dilute *VERB*
*You need to **dilute** orange squash with water.*
• thin, water down, weaken
OPPOSITE concentrate

dim *ADJECTIVE*
❶ *I could see the **dim** outline of a figure in the mist.*
• indistinct, faint, blurred, fuzzy, hazy, shadowy, vague
OPPOSITE clear
❷ *The light in the cave was rather **dim**.*
• dark, dull, dingy, murky, gloomy
OPPOSITE bright

dimensions *PLURAL NOUN*
*We measured the **dimensions** of the room.*
• measurements, size, extent, capacity
for words used in measuring see **measurement**

diminish *VERB*
❶ *Don't **diminish** his confidence by making fun of him.*
• lessen, reduce, make smaller, minimise
❷ *Our water supply was **diminishing** rapidly.*
• become less, decrease, decline, subside, dwindle, wane
OPPOSITE increase

din *NOUN*
*I can't hear you because of that awful **din**!*
• noise, racket, row, clatter, hullabaloo, cacophony

A B C D E F G H I J K L M N O P Q R S T U V W X Y Z

dine *VERB*
*We will be **dining** at eight o'clock.*
• eat, have dinner, sup

dingy *ADJECTIVE*
*How can we brighten up this **dingy** room?*
• dull, drab, dreary, dowdy, colourless, dismal, gloomy, murky
OPPOSITE bright

dinosaur *NOUN*

WORD WEB

SOME TYPES OF DINOSAUR:
• apatosaurus, archaeopteryx, brachiosaurus, diplodocus, gallimimus, ichthyosaur, iguanodon, megalosaurus, pterodactyl, stegosaur, triceratops, T-rex or tyrannosaurus rex, velociraptor
I could see at my very feet the glade of the iguanodons, and farther off was a round opening in the trees which marked the swamp of the pterodactyls.—THE LOST WORLD, Arthur Conan Doyle

BODY PARTS WHICH A DINOSAUR MAY HAVE:
• dorsal plates, bony frill, fleshy fin, horn, wings, crest
A person who studies dinosaurs and other fossils is a **palaeontologist**.
for other prehistoric animals see **prehistoric**

dip *VERB*
❶ *I **dipped** my hand in the water.*
• immerse, lower, plunge, submerge, dunk
❷ *The road **dips** down into the valley.*
• descend, go down, slope down

dip *NOUN*
❶ *There was a **dip** in the road ahead.*
• hollow, hole, depression, slope
❷ *It was so hot we decided to have a **dip** in the sea.*
• swim, bathe

dire *ADJECTIVE*
❶ *The survivors were in a **dire** situation.*
• dreadful, terrible, awful, appalling, severe, grave, drastic, extreme
❷ *After weeks of drought, the garden is in **dire** need of rain.*
• urgent, desperate, pressing, sore

direct *ADJECTIVE*
❶ *It would be quicker to take the **direct** route.*
• straight, shortest
OPPOSITE indirect
❷ *Please give me a **direct** answer.*
• straightforward, frank, honest, sincere, blunt, plain, outspoken, candid, unambiguous
OPPOSITE evasive

direct *VERB*
❶ *Can you **direct** me to the station?*
• guide, point, show the way, give directions to
❷ *A new manager has been appointed to **direct** the company.*
• manage, run, be in charge of, control, administer, superintend, supervise, take charge of
To direct an orchestra is to **conduct** it.
❸ *The teacher **directed** the students to begin.*
• instruct, command, order, tell

direction *NOUN*
*Which **direction** did they go in?*
• way, route, course, path
➤ **directions**
*I read the **directions** for building the model.*
• instructions, guidance, guidelines, plans

director *NOUN*
*Who is the **director** of the company?*
• manager, head, chief, leader, president
(informal) boss

dirt *NOUN*
❶ *The floor was covered in **dirt**.*
• filth, grime, mess, muck, mud, dust
❷ *Chickens scratched about in the **dirt**.*
• earth, soil, clay, loam, mud

dirty *ADJECTIVE*
❶ *Those **dirty** clothes need to be washed.*
• **unclean, filthy, grimy, grubby, soiled, stained, messy, mucky, muddy, sooty, foul** *(informal)* **manky, grotty**
OPPOSITE **clean**
❷ *We refused to drink the **dirty** water.*
• **impure, polluted, murky, cloudy**
OPPOSITE **pure**
❸ *The other team used **dirty** tactics.*
• **unfair, dishonest, illegal, mean, unsporting**
OPPOSITE **honest**
❹ *The comedian used a lot of **dirty** words.*
• **rude, offensive, coarse, crude, improper, indecent**
OPPOSITE **decent**

disability *NOUN*
*She leads a normal life in spite of her **disabilities**.*
• **incapacity, infirmity**

disabled *ADJECTIVE*
*He has been **disabled** since the accident.*
• **incapacitated, impaired**
OPPOSITE **able-bodied**
An animal which is injured and cannot walk is **lame**.
A person who cannot move part of their body is **paralysed**.

disadvantage *NOUN*
*It's a **disadvantage** to be small if you play basketball.*
• **drawback, handicap, hindrance, inconvenience, downside, snag**

disagree *VERB*
*My sister and I often **disagree** about music.*
• **argue, differ, clash, quarrel, squabble, bicker, fall out**
OPPOSITE **agree**
➤ **to disagree with**
❶ *He **disagrees with** everything I say.*
• **argue with, contradict, oppose, object to**
❷ *Broccoli **disagrees with** me.*
• **have a bad effect on, upset**

disagreeable *ADJECTIVE*
*There's no need to be so **disagreeable**.*
• **unpleasant, horrible, nasty, offensive, horrid, revolting**
OPPOSITE **pleasant**

disagreement *NOUN*
*We had a **disagreement** over who should pay for the meal.*
• **argument, dispute, difference of opinion, quarrel, row, clash, squabble, conflict**
OPPOSITE **agreement**

disappear *VERB*
❶ *The markings will **disappear** as the chicks grow older.*
• **become invisible, vanish, fade, clear, disperse, dissolve**
❷ *The thief **disappeared** around the corner.*
• **run away, escape, flee, go away, withdraw**
OPPOSITE **appear**

disappoint *VERB*
*She didn't want to **disappoint** her fans by cancelling the show.*
• **let down, fail, dissatisfy, displease, upset**
OPPOSITES **please, satisfy**

disappointed *ADJECTIVE*
*I'm **disappointed** that you can't come to my party.*
• **saddened, unhappy, upset, let down, unsatisfied, displeased**
OPPOSITES **pleased, satisfied**

disapprove *VERB*
➤ **to disapprove of**
*My aunt **disapproves of** watching television.*
• **object to, take exception to, dislike, deplore, condemn, criticise, denounce, frown on** *(informal)* **take a dim view of**
OPPOSITE **approve of**

A B C D E F G H I J K L M N O P Q R S T U V W X Y Z

disaster *NOUN*
*There was a near **disaster** when the engine caught fire.*
• catastrophe, calamity, tragedy

WORD WEB

SOME TYPES OF NATURAL DISASTER:

• avalanche, earthquake, epidemic, famine, fire, flood, hurricane, landslide, plague, tidal wave, tornado, tsunami, volcanic eruption

disastrous *ADJECTIVE*
*The **disastrous** fire cost millions of pounds.*
• catastrophic, devastating, calamitous, destructive, dire, dreadful, terrible, ruinous

disc *NOUN*
*The full moon appears as a **disc** in the sky.*
see **circle**

discard *VERB*
*I **discarded** some of my old toys.*
• get rid of, throw away, throw out, reject, cast off, dispose of, dump, scrap

discharge *VERB*
❶ *The accused man was found not guilty and **discharged**.*
• free, release, clear, acquit, let off, allow to leave, liberate
❷ *The chimney **discharged** thick smoke.*
• expel, emit, give out, pour out, eject, belch, produce

disciple *NOUN*
*The religious leader had many **disciples**.*
• follower, supporter, admirer, devotee
In Christianity, the disciples of Jesus are called the **apostles**.

discipline *NOUN*
***Discipline** is important in the army.*
• order, control

disclose *VERB*
*He never **disclosed** the truth.*
• reveal, tell, make known, confess, make public
OPPOSITE conceal

discomfort *NOUN*
*He still experiences a lot of **discomfort** from his injury.*
• pain, soreness, distress, unease

disconnect *VERB*
*We need to **disconnect** the cooker before we can move it.*
• detach, cut off, unplug, unhook

discontented *ADJECTIVE*
*She felt very **discontented** with her job.*
• dissatisfied, miserable, unhappy, upset
(informal) fed up
OPPOSITES happy, satisfied

discontinue *VERB*
*That style of shoe has been **discontinued**.*
• stop, end, terminate
OPPOSITES introduce, establish

discount *NOUN*
*I got a **discount** on the full price.*
• deduction, reduction, cut, concession, allowance

discourage *VERB*
❶ *Don't let her criticism **discourage** you.*
• demoralise, depress
(informal) put you off
❷ *The burglar alarm will **discourage** thieves.*
• deter, dissuade, prevent, restrain, stop, hinder
OPPOSITE encourage

discover *VERB*
*I **discovered** some old toys in the attic.*
• find, come across, spot, stumble across, uncover
To discover something that has been buried is to **unearth** it.
To discover something that has been under water is to **dredge it up**.
To discover something you have been pursuing is to **track it down**.
OPPOSITE hide

discovery *NOUN*
*Scientists have made an exciting new **discovery**.*
• find, breakthrough

discreet *ADJECTIVE*
*I asked a few **discreet** questions about her illness.*
• **tactful, sensitive, delicate, careful, cautious, diplomatic, wary**
OPPOSITE **tactless**

discriminate *VERB*
*It's sometimes hard to **discriminate** between poisonous mushrooms and edible ones.*
• **distinguish, tell the difference**
➤ **to discriminate against**
*It's wrong to **discriminate against** people because of their age.*
• **be biased against, be intolerant of, be prejudiced against**

discrimination *NOUN*
❶ *The school has a policy against racial **discrimination**.*
• **prejudice, bias, intolerance, unfairness**
Discrimination against people because of their sex is **sexism**.
Discrimination against people because of their race is **racism**.
❷ *She shows **discrimination** in her choice of music.*
• **good taste, good judgement**

discuss *VERB*
*I **discussed** the idea with my parents.*
• **talk about, confer about, debate**

discussion *NOUN*
*We had a lively **discussion** about pocket money.*
• **conversation, argument, exchange of views**
A formal discussion is a **conference** or **debate**.

disease *NOUN*
*He was suffering from a serious **disease**.*
• **illness, ailment, sickness, complaint, affliction**
(informal) **bug**
see also **illness**

diseased *ADJECTIVE*
*Gardeners throw away **diseased** plants.*
• **unhealthy, sickly, infected**
OPPOSITE **healthy**

disembark *VERB*
*The passengers **disembarked** from the ferry.*
• **go ashore**
OPPOSITE **embark**

disgrace *NOUN*
❶ *He never got over the **disgrace** of being caught cheating.*
• **humiliation, shame, embarrassment, dishonour**
❷ *The way he treats them is a **disgrace**!*
• **outrage, scandal**

disgraceful *ADJECTIVE*
*We were shocked by her **disgraceful** behaviour.*
• **shameful, shocking, appalling, outrageous, scandalous**
OPPOSITE **honourable**

disguise *VERB*
*I tried to **disguise** my feelings.*
• **conceal, hide, cover up, camouflage, mask**
➤ **to disguise yourself as**
*The spy **disguised himself as** a hotel porter.*
• **dress up as, pretend to be**

disguise *NOUN*
*I didn't recognise him in that **disguise**.*
• **costume, camouflage, make-up, mask**

disgust *NOUN*
*The sight of the carcass filled me with **disgust**.*
• **repulsion, repugnance, distaste, dislike, horror, loathing, detestation**
OPPOSITE **liking**

disgust *VERB*
*The smell of rotten eggs **disgusts** me.*
• **repel, revolt, sicken, appal, offend, distress, shock, horrify**
(informal) **put you off, turn your stomach**
OPPOSITE **please**

disgusting *ADJECTIVE*
*The brew in the cauldron looked **disgusting**.*
• **repulsive, revolting, horrible, nasty, loathsome, repellent, repugnant, offensive, appalling, sickening, nauseating**
(informal) **yucky, icky, gross**
OPPOSITES **delightful, pleasing**

A B C D E F G H I J K L M N O P Q R S T U V W X Y Z

dish *NOUN*
❶ *Mum served the trifle in a large glass* ***dish****.*
• **bowl, basin, plate, platter**
A dish to serve soup from is a **tureen.**
see also **crockery**
❷ *What's your favourite* ***dish****?*
• **food, recipe, meal**

dishevelled *ADJECTIVE*
His clothes were a mess and his hair was ***dishevelled****.*
• **messy, untidy, scruffy, unkempt, bedraggled, slovenly**
OPPOSITES **neat, tidy**

dishonest *ADJECTIVE*
❶ *They were taken in by a* ***dishonest*** *salesman.*
• **deceitful, cheating, corrupt, disreputable, untrustworthy, immoral, lying, swindling, thieving**
(informal) **bent, crooked, dodgy, shady**
❷ *The author makes some* ***dishonest*** *claims.*
• **false, misleading, untruthful, fraudulent, devious**
OPPOSITE **honest**

dishonesty *NOUN*
The MP was accused of ***dishonesty****.*
• **deceit, cheating, corruption, insincerity, lying, deviousness**
(informal) **crookedness**
OPPOSITE **honesty**

disinfect *VERB*
The nurse ***disinfected*** *my wound.*
• **cleanse, sterilise**
OPPOSITE **infect**
To disinfect an infected place is to **decontaminate** it.
To disinfect a room using fumes is to **fumigate** it.

disintegrate *VERB*
The cloth is so old that it's starting to ***disintegrate****.*
• **break up, fall apart, break into pieces, crumble, decay, decompose**

disinterested *ADJECTIVE*
A referee must be ***disinterested****.*
• **impartial, neutral, unbiased, unprejudiced, detached, fair**
OPPOSITE **biased**

disk *NOUN*
see **disc**

dislike *NOUN*
His colleagues regarded him with intense ***dislike****.*
• **hatred, loathing, detestation, disapproval, disgust, revulsion**
OPPOSITE **liking**

dislike *VERB*
I ***dislike*** *people who hunt wild animals.*
• **hate, loathe, detest, disapprove of**
OPPOSITE **like**

dislodge *VERB*
The wind ***dislodged*** *some tiles on the roof.*
• **displace, move, shift, disturb**

disloyal *ADJECTIVE*
The rebels were accused of being ***disloyal*** *to the king.*
• **unfaithful, treacherous, faithless, false, unreliable, untrustworthy**
OPPOSITE **loyal**

dismal *ADJECTIVE*
❶ *How can we brighten up this* ***dismal*** *room?*
• **dull, drab, dreary, dingy, colourless, cheerless, gloomy, murky**
OPPOSITES **bright, cheerful**
❷ *(informal) It was a* ***dismal*** *performance by the home team.*
• **dreadful, awful, terrible, feeble, useless, hopeless**
(informal) **pathetic**
OPPOSITES **brilliant, splendid**

dismantle *VERB*
After the school fair, we had to ***dismantle*** *all the stalls.*
• **take apart, take down**
To dismantle your group's tents is to **strike camp.**
OPPOSITE **assemble**

dismay *NOUN*
*We listened with **dismay** to the bad news.*
• distress, alarm, shock, concern, anxiety, gloom

dismayed *ADJECTIVE*
*I was **dismayed** by the failure of our plan.*
• distressed, discouraged, depressed, devastated, shocked, appalled
OPPOSITE encouraged

dismiss *VERB*
❶ *The teacher **dismissed** the class.*
• send away, discharge, free, let go, release
❷ *The firm **dismissed** ten workers.*
• sack, give the sack, give notice to, make redundant
(*informal*) fire
❸ *The weather was so bad that we **dismissed** the idea of having a picnic.*
• discard, drop, reject

dismount *VERB*
*The knight **dismounted** from his horse.*
• descend, get off

disobedient *ADJECTIVE*
*She said she had never known such a **disobedient** child.*
• naughty, badly behaved, undisciplined, uncontrollable, unmanageable, unruly, ungovernable, troublesome, defiant, disruptive, mutinous, rebellious, contrary
OPPOSITE obedient

disobey *VERB*
❶ *You will be penalised if you **disobey** the rules.*
• break, ignore, disregard, defy, violate
❷ *Soldiers are trained never to **disobey**.*
• be disobedient, rebel, revolt, mutiny
OPPOSITE obey

disorder *NOUN*
❶ *The public meeting broke up in **disorder**.*
• disturbance, uproar, commotion, quarrelling, rioting, brawling, fighting, lawlessness, anarchy
❷ *It's time I tidied up the **disorder** in my room.*
• mess, muddle, untidiness, chaos, confusion, clutter, jumble
OPPOSITE order

disorderly *ADJECTIVE*
*The class were behaving in a **disorderly** manner.*
• badly behaved, disobedient, unruly, uncontrollable, undisciplined, ungovernable, unmanageable
OPPOSITE orderly

dispatch *NOUN*
*The messenger brought a **dispatch** from headquarters.*
• message, communication, report, letter, bulletin

dispatch *VERB*
*The parcel has already been **dispatched**.*
• post, send, transmit

dispense *VERB*
➤ **to dispense with**
*Now that I have new trainers, I can **dispense** with the old ones.*
• get rid of, dispose of, do without, remove

disperse *VERB*
❶ *The police **dispersed** the crowd.*
• break up, send away, drive away, separate, send in different directions
❷ *The crowd **dispersed** quickly after the match.*
• scatter, spread out, disappear, dissolve, melt away, vanish
OPPOSITE gather

displace *VERB*
❶ *The gales have **displaced** some of the roof tiles.*
• dislodge, put out of place, shift, disturb
❷ *A brilliant new player **displaced** me in the team.*
• replace, take the place of, succeed

display *VERB*
*We planned the best way to **display** our work.*
• **demonstrate, exhibit, present, put on show, set out, show, show off**
To display something boastfully is to **flaunt** it.

display *NOUN*
*We set out a **display** of our art work.*
• **exhibition, show, presentation, demonstration**

displease *VERB*
*I must have done something to **displease** her.*
• **annoy, irritate, upset, anger, exasperate, vex**

dispose *VERB*
➤ **to dispose of something**
*Let's **dispose of** this old carpet.*
• **get rid of, discard, throw away, give away, scrap**
(informal) **dump**
➤ **to be disposed to do something**
*He didn't seem **disposed to** help us.*
• **be willing to, be inclined to, be ready to, be likely to**

disposition *NOUN*
*Our labrador has a very friendly **disposition**.*
• **character, nature, personality**

dispute *NOUN*
*We settled the **dispute** about who should wash the dishes.*
• **argument, disagreement, quarrel, debate, controversy, difference of opinion**

disqualify *VERB*
*Two athletes have been **disqualified** from the competition.*
• **bar, prohibit**

disregard *VERB*
*I **disregarded** the doctor's advice.*
• **ignore, pay no attention to, take no notice of, reject**
OPPOSITE **heed**

disrespectful *ADJECTIVE*
*She was very **disrespectful** towards her parents.*
• **rude, bad-mannered, insulting, impolite, insolent, cheeky**
OPPOSITE **respectful**

disrupt *VERB*
*Bad weather has **disrupted** the tennis tournament.*
• **interrupt, upset, interfere with, throw into confusion or disorder**

dissatisfied *ADJECTIVE*
*I was **dissatisfied** with my piano playing.*
• **displeased, disappointed, discontented, frustrated, annoyed**
OPPOSITE **satisfied**

dissolve *VERB*
*Stir your tea until the sugar **dissolves**.*
• **disperse, disintegrate, melt**

dissuade *VERB*
➤ **to dissuade someone from doing something**
*We tried to **dissuade** him **from** going out in the storm.*
• **discourage someone from, persuade someone not to, deter someone from, warn someone against**
OPPOSITE **persuade**

distance *NOUN*
*What is the **distance** from Earth to the Sun?*
• **measurement, space, extent, reach, mileage**
The distance across something is the **breadth** or **width**.
The distance along something is the **length**.
The distance between two points is a **gap** or **interval**.
for units for measuring distance
see **measurement**

distant *ADJECTIVE*
❶ *I'd love to travel to **distant** countries.*
• **faraway, remote, out of the way, inaccessible, exotic**
OPPOSITE **close**

❷ *His* **distant** *manner puts me off.*
• unfriendly, unapproachable, formal, reserved, withdrawn, cool, haughty, aloof
OPPOSITE friendly

distinct *ADJECTIVE*
❶ *There is a* **distinct** *improvement in your handwriting.*
• definite, evident, noticeable, obvious, perceptible
OPPOSITE imperceptible
❷ *It was a small photo, but the details were quite* **distinct**.
• clear, distinguishable, plain, recognisable, sharp, unmistakable, visible, well defined
OPPOSITE indistinct
❸ *Organise your essay into* **distinct** *sections.*
• individual, separate

distinction *NOUN*
❶ *There's a clear* **distinction** *between the real diamond and the fake.*
• difference, contrast, distinctiveness
❷ *He had the* **distinction** *of being the team captain.*
• honour, glory, merit, credit, prestige

distinctive *ADJECTIVE*
We spotted the **distinctive** *footprints of a yeti in the snow.*
• characteristic, recognisable, unmistakable, special, unique

distinguish *VERB*
❶ *It was impossible to* **distinguish** *one twin from the other.*
• tell apart, pick out, discriminate, differentiate, make a distinction, decide
❷ *In the dark we couldn't* **distinguish** *who was walking past.*
• identify, tell, make out, determine, perceive, recognise, single out

distinguished *ADJECTIVE*
❶ *The school has a* **distinguished** *academic record.*
• excellent, first-rate, outstanding, exceptional
OPPOSITE ordinary
❷ *He is a very* **distinguished** *actor.*
• famous, celebrated, well-known, eminent, notable, prominent, renowned
OPPOSITES unknown, obscure

distort *VERB*
❶ *When my bike hit the kerb, it* **distorted** *the wheel.*
• bend, buckle, twist, warp, contort
❷ *The newspaper* **distorted** *the facts of the story.*
• twist, slant, misrepresent

distract *VERB*
Don't **distract** *the bus driver.*
• divert the attention of, disturb, put off

distress *NOUN*
The trapped animal was clearly in **distress**.
• suffering, torment, anguish, dismay, anxiety, grief, misery, pain, sadness, sorrow, worry, wretchedness

distress *VERB*
We could see that the bad news **distressed** *her.*
• upset, disturb, trouble, worry, alarm, dismay, torment
OPPOSITE comfort

distribute *VERB*
❶ *The coach* **distributed** *water to the players at half-time.*
• give out, hand round, circulate, dispense, issue, share out, take round
(informal) dish out, dole out
❷ **Distribute** *the seeds evenly.*
• scatter, spread, disperse

district *NOUN*
Granny lives in a quiet **district**.
• area, neighbourhood, locality, region, vicinity

distrust *VERB*
I **distrusted** *the professor from the moment I met him.*
• doubt, mistrust, question, suspect, be suspicious or wary of, be sceptical about, feel uncertain or uneasy or unsure about
OPPOSITE trust

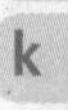
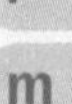

disturb *VERB*
❶ *Don't* ***disturb*** *the baby when she's asleep.*
• **bother, interrupt, annoy, pester**
❷ *They were* ***disturbed*** *by the bad news.*
• **distress, trouble, upset, worry, alarm, frighten**
❸ *Please don't* ***disturb*** *the papers on my desk.*
• **muddle, mix up, move around, mess about with**

disused *ADJECTIVE*
They made the ***disused*** *railway line into a cycle track.*
• **abandoned, unused, closed down**

ditch *NOUN*
We dug a ***ditch*** *to drain away the water.*
• **trench, channel, drain, gully**

dither *VERB*
Stop ***dithering*** *and make up your mind!*
• **hesitate, waver, be in two minds**
(informal) **shilly-shally**

dive *VERB*
❶ *The mermaid* ***dived*** *into the water.*
• **plunge, jump, leap**
A dive in which you land flat on your front is a **bellyflop**.
❷ *The eagle* ***dived*** *towards its prey.*
• **pounce, swoop**

diver *NOUN*
A diver who wears a rubber suit and flippers and breathes air from a portable tank is a **scuba diver** or **frogman**.

diverse *ADJECTIVE*
People from many ***diverse*** *cultures live in the area.*
• **different, differing, varied, various, contrasting**

diversion *NOUN*
❶ *The police had set up a traffic* ***diversion***.
• **detour, indirect route, roundabout route**
❷ *There were lots of* ***diversions*** *at the holiday camp.*
• **entertainment, amusement, recreation**

divert *VERB*
❶ *They* ***diverted*** *the plane to another airport.*
• **redirect, switch**
❷ *She* ***diverted*** *herself by practising handstands.*
• **entertain, amuse, occupy, interest, keep happy**

divide *VERB*
❶ *We* ***divided*** *the class into two groups.*
• **separate, split, break up, move apart, part**
OPPOSITE **combine**
❷ *I* ***divided*** *the cake between my friends.*
• **distribute, share out, give out, allot, deal out, dispense**
❸ *Which way do we go? The path* ***divides*** *here.*
• **branch, fork**
OPPOSITE **converge**

divine *ADJECTIVE*
❶ *The temple is used for* ***divine*** *worship.*
• **holy, religious, sacred, spiritual**
❷ *The Greeks believed* ***divine*** *beings lived on Mount Olympus.*
• **godlike, immortal, heavenly**
❸ *(informal) These fairy cakes taste* ***divine****!*
• **excellent, wonderful, superb**

division *NOUN*
❶ *The map shows the* ***division*** *of Europe after the war.*
• **dividing, splitting, separation, partition**
❷ *There was a* ***division*** *in the government.*
• **disagreement, split, feud**
❸ *There is a movable* ***division*** *between the two classrooms.*
• **partition, divider, dividing wall, screen**
❹ *They work in different* ***divisions*** *of the same company.*
• **branch, department, section, unit**

dizzy *ADJECTIVE*
Going on a roundabout makes me feel ***dizzy***.
• **dazed, giddy, faint, reeling, unsteady**

do *VERB* **does, doing, did, done**
❶ *My friend always knows what to* ***do*** *in a crisis.*
• **act, behave, conduct yourself**

❷ *The vet has a lot of work to **do** this morning.*
• attend to, cope with, deal with, handle, look after, perform, undertake
❸ *It took me half an hour to **do** the washing-up.*
• accomplish, achieve, carry out, complete, execute, finish
❹ *I need to **do** all of these sums.*
• answer, puzzle out, solve, work out
❺ *Staring at the sun can **do** damage to your eyes.*
• bring about, cause, produce, result in
❻ *If you don't have lemonade, water will **do**.*
• be acceptable, be enough, be satisfactory, be sufficient, serve

➤ to do away with
*I wish our school would **do away with** homework.*
• get rid of, abolish, eliminate, end, put an end to

➤ to do up
*These jeans are too tight to **do up**.*
• button up, fasten

docile *ADJECTIVE*
*Don't be afraid of the dog—he's quite **docile**.*
• tame, gentle, meek, obedient, manageable, safe, submissive
OPPOSITE fierce

dock *NOUN*
*A boat was waiting for us at the end of the **dock**.*
• harbour, quay, jetty, wharf, landing stage, dockyard, pier, port, marina

dock *VERB*
*We can't disembark until the ship **docks**.*
• moor, tie up

doctor *NOUN*
*for people who practise medicine see **medicine***

document *NOUN*
*The library contains many old **documents**.*
• paper, record, file, certificate, deed

dodge *VERB*
*I just managed to **dodge** the snowball.*
• avoid, evade, side-step

dog *NOUN*

WORD WEB

A female dog is a **bitch**.
A young dog is a **pup**, **puppy** or **whelp**.
Informal words for a dog are **mutt** and **pooch**.
An uncomplimentary word for a dog is **cur**.
A dog of pure breed with known ancestors has a **pedigree**.
A dog of mixed breeds is a **mongrel**.
A dog used for hunting is a **hound**.
A word meaning 'to do with dogs' is **canine**.

SOME BREEDS OF DOG:

• Afghan hound, Alsatian, basset hound, beagle, bloodhound, boxer, bulldog, bull terrier, cairn terrier, chihuahua, cocker spaniel, collie, corgi, dachshund, Dalmatian, Doberman, fox terrier, Great Dane, greyhound, husky, Irish Setter, Labrador, mastiff, Pekinese or Pekingese, Pomeranian, poodle, pug, golden retriever, Rottweiler, St Bernard, Schnauzer, setter, sheepdog, spaniel, terrier, West Highland terrier, whippet, wolfhound, Yorkshire terrier

SOUNDS MADE BY DOGS:

• bark, growl, snap, snarl, woof, yap, yelp
The Sheepdog barked a low, cautious bark. He was answered by a high, shrill bark. Then he heard a yelp, as if some dog had been cuffed.—THE HUNDRED AND ONE DALMATIANS, Dodie Smith
see also **animal**

domestic *ADJECTIVE*
❶ *At weekends I do various **domestic** chores.*
• household, family
❷ *Cats and dogs are popular **domestic** animals.*
• domesticated, tame

dominant *ADJECTIVE*
❶ *The captain plays a **dominant** role in the team.*
• **leading, main, chief, major, powerful, principal, important, influential**
OPPOSITE **minor**
❷ *The castle is a **dominant** feature in the landscape.*
• **conspicuous, prominent, obvious, large, imposing, eye-catching**
OPPOSITE **insignificant**

dominate *VERB*
*The visiting team **dominated** the game.*
• **control, direct, monopolise, govern, take control of, take over**

donate *VERB*
*Will you **donate** something to our collection?*
• **give, contribute**

donation *NOUN*
*The museum relies on **donations** from the public.*
• **contribution, gift, offering**

done *ADJECTIVE*
❶ *All my thank-you letters are **done** now.*
• **finished, complete, over**
❷ *The cake will be brown on top when it's **done**.*
• **cooked, ready**

donor *NOUN*
*A generous **donor** gave us money for new sports equipment.*
• **benefactor, contributor, sponsor**

doomed *ADJECTIVE*
*The expedition was **doomed** from the start.*
• **ill-fated, condemned, fated, cursed, jinxed, damned**

door *NOUN*
A door in a floor or ceiling is a **hatch** or **trapdoor**.
The plank or stone underneath a door is the **threshold**.
The beam or stone above a door is the **lintel**.
The opening into which a door fits is the **doorway**.
The device on which a door turns when it opens is the **hinge**.
To leave a door slightly open is to leave it **ajar**.

dose *NOUN*
*The nurse gave me a **dose** of the medicine.*
• **measure, correct amount, dosage, portion**

dot *NOUN*
*She was furious when she saw **dots** of paint on the carpet.*
• **spot, speck, fleck, point, mark**
The dot you always put at the end of a sentence is a **full stop**.
➤ **on the dot** *(informal)*
*We left the house at nine o'clock **on the dot**.*
• **exactly, precisely**

double *ADJECTIVE*
*You enter the room through a **double** set of doors.*
• **dual, twofold, paired, twin, matching, duplicate**

double *NOUN*
*She's so like you—she's almost your **double**.*
• **twin**
(informal) **lookalike, spitting image, dead ringer**
A living organism created as an exact copy of another living organism is a **clone**.

doubt *NOUN*
❶ *Have you any **doubt** about his honesty?*
• **distrust, suspicion, mistrust, hesitation, reservation, scepticism**
OPPOSITE **confidence**
❷ *There is no **doubt** that you will pass your exam.*
• **question, uncertainty, ambiguity, confusion**
OPPOSITE **certainty**

doubt *VERB*
*There is no reason to **doubt** her story.*

• distrust, feel uncertain or uneasy or unsure about, question, mistrust, suspect, be sceptical about, be suspicious or wary of
OPPOSITE trust

doubtful *ADJECTIVE*
❶ *He looked* ***doubtful****, but agreed to let us go.*
• unsure, uncertain, unconvinced, hesitant, distrustful, sceptical, suspicious
OPPOSITE certain
❷ *The referee made a* ***doubtful*** *decision there.*
• questionable, debatable, arguable

downfall *NOUN*
After the government's ***downfall****, there was a general election.*
• collapse, fall, ruin

downward *ADJECTIVE*
We took the ***downward*** *path into the valley.*
• downhill, descending
OPPOSITE upward

doze *VERB*
Dad often ***dozes*** *in the evening.*
• rest, sleep, nod off
(informal) drop off

drab *ADJECTIVE*
That dress is too ***drab*** *to wear to the party.*
• dull, dingy, dreary, cheerless, colourless, dismal, gloomy, grey
OPPOSITES bright, cheerful

draft *NOUN*
I jotted down a ***draft*** *of my story.*
• outline, plan, sketch, rough version

draft *VERB*
I began to ***draft*** *my story.*
• outline, plan, prepare, sketch, work out

drag *VERB*
The tractor ***dragged*** *the car out of the ditch.*
• pull, tow, tug, draw, haul, lug
OPPOSITE push

dragon *NOUN*
A fearsome ***dragon*** *once lived in these hills.*

WORD WEB

SOME WAYS TO DESCRIBE A DRAGON:

• ancient, fearsome, fiery, fire-breathing, legendary, mighty, monstrous, scaly, winged

And there was the Horntail ... crouched low over her clutch of eggs, her wings half furled, her evil, yellow eyes upon him, a monstrous, scaly black lizard, thrashing her spiked tail.
—HARRY POTTER AND THE GOBLET OF FIRE, J. K. Rowling

BODY PARTS A DRAGON MIGHT HAVE:

• barbed tail, bat-like wings, claws, crest, forked tail or tongue, pointed teeth, scales, spikes or spines, talons

A DRAGON'S SCALES MIGHT BE:

• dazzling, iridescent, patterned, shimmering

A DRAGON'S BREATH MIGHT BE:

• fiery, flaming, scorching, searing

THINGS A DRAGON MIGHT DO:

• breathe fire, change shape, curl its body, furl or unfurl its wings, puff smoke, roar, snort, soar, swoop, thrash its tail

PLACES WHERE A DRAGON MIGHT LIVE:

• cave, den, lair

for other creatures found in myths and legends see **myth**

drain *NOUN*
Surplus water runs away along a ***drain****.*
• ditch, channel, drainpipe, gutter, pipe, sewer

drain *VERB*
❶ *If they* ***drain*** *the marsh, lots of waterbirds will die.*
• dry out, remove water from
❷ *She* ***drained*** *the oil from the engine.*
• draw off, empty

a b c d e f g h i j k l m n o p q r s t u v w x y z

A
B
C
D
E
F
G
H
I
J
K
L
M
N
O
P
Q
R
S
T
U
V
W
X
Y
Z

❸ *The water slowly **drained** away.*
• **trickle, ooze, seep**
❹ *The tough climb **drained** my energy.*
• **use up, consume, exhaust**

drama NOUN
❶ ***Drama** is one of my favourite subjects.*
• **acting**
see also **theatre**
❷ *I witnessed the **drama** of a real robbery.*
• **action, excitement, suspense, spectacle**

dramatic ADJECTIVE
*We watched the **dramatic** rescue on TV.*
• **exciting, eventful, thrilling, sensational, spectacular, gripping**

drank *past tense see* **drink**

drastic ADJECTIVE
*After being without food for three days, the explorers needed to take **drastic** action.*
• **desperate, extreme, radical, harsh, severe**
OPPOSITE **moderate**

draught NOUN
*I felt a **draught** of air from the open window.*
• **breeze, current, movement, puff**

draw VERB **draws, drawing, drew, drawn**
❶ *I **drew** some pictures of the flowers in our garden.*
• **sketch, trace, doodle**
❷ *I'm not very good at **drawing** faces.*
• **depict, portray, represent**
❸ *The horse was **drawing** a cart.*
• **pull, tow, drag, haul, tug, lug**
❹ *We expect tomorrow's match to **draw** a big crowd.*
• **attract, bring in, pull in**
❺ *The two teams **drew** 1-1.*
• **finish equal, tie**
➤ **to draw near**
*As the spaceship **drew near**, I began to get nervous.*
• **approach, advance, come near**

draw NOUN
Kinds of prize draw are a **lottery** and a **raffle**.

drawback NOUN
*It's a **drawback** to be small if you play basketball.*
• **disadvantage, difficulty, handicap, obstacle, inconvenience, hindrance, downside, snag**

drawing NOUN

WORD WEB

SOME TYPES OF DRAWING:
• **caricature, cartoon, design, doodle, illustration, outline, sketch**

TOOLS USED FOR DRAWING:
• **chalk, charcoal, crayon, ink, pastel, pen, pencil**

dread NOUN
*Our teacher has a **dread** of spiders.*
• **fear, horror, terror, phobia (about), anxiety (about)**

dreadful ADJECTIVE
❶ *There has been a **dreadful** accident at sea.*
• **horrible, terrible, appalling, horrendous, distressing, shocking, upsetting, tragic, grim**
❷ *The weather at the weekend was **dreadful**.*
• **bad, awful, terrible, abysmal, abominable, dire, foul, nasty**
OPPOSITES **good, pleasant**

dream NOUN
A bad dream is a **nightmare**.
A dreamlike experience you have while awake is a **daydream, fantasy** or **reverie**.
Something you see in a dream or daydream is a **vision**.
The dreamlike state when you are hypnotised is a **trance**.
Something you think you see that is not real is a **hallucination** or **illusion**.

dream VERB **dreams, dreaming, dreamt** or **dreamed**
*I **dreamed** that I was a mermaid.*
• **daydream, imagine, fancy, fantasise**

dreary *ADJECTIVE*
❶ *The newsreader had a very **dreary** voice.*
• dull, boring, flat, tedious, unexciting, uninteresting
OPPOSITE lively
❷ *When will this **dreary** weather end?*
• depressing, dismal, dull, gloomy, cheerless, murky, overcast
OPPOSITES bright, sunny

drench *VERB*
*The rain **drenched** me to the skin.*
• soak, wet thoroughly

dress *NOUN*
❶ *What kind of **dress** are you wearing to the party?*
• frock, gown
❷ *The invitation said to wear casual **dress**.*
• clothes, clothing, outfit, costume, garments
see also **clothes**

dress *VERB*
❶ *I helped to **dress** my little brother.*
• clothe, put clothes on
OPPOSITE undress
❷ *A nurse **dressed** my wound.*
• bandage, put a dressing on, bind up

dressing *NOUN*
*The nurse put a **dressing** on the wound.*
• bandage, plaster

drew *past tense see* **draw**

dribble *VERB*
❶ *Careful, the baby's **dribbling** on your jumper.*
• drool
❷ *Water **dribbled** out of the hole in the tank.*
• drip, trickle, leak, ooze, seep

drift *VERB*
❶ *The boat **drifted** downstream.*
• float, be carried, move slowly
❷ *The crowd lost interest and **drifted** away.*
• stray, wander, meander, ramble, walk aimlessly
❸ *The snow will **drift** in this wind.*
• pile up, accumulate, make drifts

drift *NOUN*
❶ *The car was stuck in a snow **drift**.*
• bank, heap, mound, pile, ridge
❷ *Did you understand the **drift** of the speech?*
• gist, main idea, point

drill *NOUN*
❶ *There will be a fire **drill** at school next week.*
• practice, training
❷ *Do you all know the **drill** for erecting a tent?*
• procedure, routine, system

drill *VERB*
*It took a long time to **drill** through the wall.*
• bore, penetrate, pierce

drink *NOUN*

WORD WEB

SOME HOT DRINKS:
• chocolate, cocoa, coffee, tea

SOME NON-ALCOHOLIC COLD DRINKS:
• barley water, cola, cordial, fruit juice, ginger beer, iced tea, lemonade, milk, milkshake, mineral water, smoothie, soda water, squash, water

SOME ALCOHOLIC DRINKS:
• beer, brandy, champagne, cider, gin, port, punch, rum, sherry, vodka, whisky, wine
Very strong alcoholic drinks are **spirits**.

CONTAINERS FOR DRINKS:
• beaker, bottle, can, cup, glass, goblet, mug, tankard, tumbler, wine glass
bottle, cup

a b c d e f g h i j k l m n o p q r s t u v w x y z

A B C D E F G H I J K L M N O P Q R S T U V W X Y Z

drink *VERB* **drinks, drinking, drank, drunk**
To drink greedily is to **gulp, guzzle** or **swig**.
To drink noisily is to **slurp**.
To drink a small amount at a time is to **sip**.
To drink with the tongue as a cat does is to **lap**.

drip *NOUN*
Dad was worried by the ***drips*** *of oil underneath the car.*
• **spot, dribble, splash, trickle**

drip *VERB*
The oil ***dripped*** *on to the garage floor.*
• **drop, leak, dribble, splash, trickle**

drive *VERB* **drives, driving, drove, driven**
❶ *The dog* ***drove*** *the sheep through the gate.*
• **direct, guide, herd**
❷ *I couldn't* ***drive*** *the spade into the hard ground.*
• **push, thrust, hammer, plunge, ram**
❸ *When can I learn to* ***drive*** *a car?*
• **control, handle, manage**
❹ *Lack of money* ***drove*** *him to steal.*
• **force, compel, oblige**
➤ **to drive someone out**
The invading soldiers ***drove*** *the people* ***out****.*
• **eject, expel, throw out**
To drive people out of their homes is to **evict** them.
To drive people out of their country is to **banish** or **exile** them.

drive *NOUN*
❶ *We went for a* ***drive*** *in the country.*
• **ride, trip, journey, outing, excursion, jaunt**
❷ *Have you got the* ***drive*** *to succeed?*
• **ambition, determination, keenness, motivation, energy, zeal**

driver *NOUN*
Many ***drivers*** *go too fast.*
• **motorist**
A person who drives someone's car as a job is a **chauffeur**.

droop *VERB*
Plants tend to ***droop*** *in dry weather.*
• **sag, wilt, bend, flop, be limp**

drop *NOUN*
❶ *Large* ***drops*** *of rain began to fall.*
• **drip, droplet, spot, bead, blob**
❷ *Could I have another* ***drop*** *of milk in my tea?*
• **dash, small quantity**
❸ *We expect a* ***drop*** *in the price of fruit in the summer.*
• **decrease, reduction, cut**
❹ *There's a* ***drop*** *of two metres on the other side of the wall.*
• **fall, descent, plunge**

drop *VERB*
❶ *The hawk* ***dropped*** *on to its prey.*
• **descend, dive, plunge, swoop**
❷ *I* ***dropped*** *to the ground exhausted.*
• **collapse, fall, sink, subside, slump, tumble**
❸ *Why did you* ***drop*** *me from the team?*
• **omit, eliminate, exclude, leave out**
❹ *They* ***dropped*** *the plan for a new bypass.*
• **abandon, discard, reject, give up, scrap**
➤ **to drop in**
Drop in *on your way home.*
• **visit, call, pay a call**
➤ **to drop out**
Why did you ***drop out*** *of the race at the last minute?*
• **withdraw, back out, pull out**
(informal) **quit**

drove *past tense see* **drive**

drown *VERB*
The music from upstairs ***drowned*** *our conversation.*
• **overwhelm, overpower, drown out**

drowsy *ADJECTIVE*
If you feel ***drowsy****, why not go to bed?*
• **sleepy, tired, weary**

drug *NOUN*
A new ***drug*** *has been discovered for back pain.*
• **medicine, remedy, treatment**
A drug which relieves pain is an **analgesic** or **painkiller**.
A drug which calms you down is a **sedative** or **tranquilliser**.
Drugs which make you more active are **stimulants**.

drum *NOUN*

WORD WEB

SOME TYPES OF DRUM:

• **bass drum, bongo drum, kettledrum or timpani, snare drum, tabor, tambour, timpani, tom-tom**
for other musical instruments see **music**

dry *ADJECTIVE*
❶ *Nothing will grow in this* ***dry*** *soil.*
• **arid, parched, moistureless, waterless, dehydrated, desiccated, barren**
OPPOSITE **wet**
A common simile is **as dry as a bone.**
When your throat feels very dry, you are **parched.**
❷ *He gave rather a* ***dry*** *speech.*
• **dull, boring, dreary, tedious, uninteresting**
OPPOSITE **interesting**
❸ *I can't understand his* ***dry*** *sense of humour.*
• **ironic, wry, witty, subtle**

dry *VERB*
❶ *If it's sunny, I'll hang the clothes out to* ***dry.***
• **get dry, dry out**
❷ *Will you please* ***dry*** *the dishes?*
• **wipe dry**
When you dry food to preserve it, you **dehydrate** it.

dual *ADJECTIVE*
The building has a ***dual*** *purpose: it can be either a cinema or a theatre.*
• **double, twofold, twin, combined**

dubious *ADJECTIVE*
I'm a bit ***dubious*** *about getting a snake for a pet.*
• **doubtful, uncertain, unsure, hesitant**
OPPOSITES **certain, sure**

duck *NOUN*
A male duck is a **drake.**
A young duck is a **duckling.**

duck *VERB*
❶ *Oliver* ***ducked*** *to avoid the snowball.*
• **bend down, bob down, crouch, stoop**
❷ *My friends threatened to* ***duck*** *me in the pool.*
• **dip, immerse, plunge, submerge**

due *ADJECTIVE*
❶ *The train is* ***due*** *in five minutes.*
• **expected, anticipated**
❷ *Subscriptions are now* ***due.***
• **owed, owing, payable**
❸ *I give her* ***due*** *credit for what she did.*
• **fitting, proper, appropriate, suitable, deserved, well-earned**

dug *past tense see* **dig**

dull *ADJECTIVE*
❶ *I don't like the* ***dull*** *colours in this room.*
• **dim, dingy, drab, dreary, dismal, faded, gloomy, sombre, subdued**
OPPOSITES **bright, colourful**
❷ *The sky was* ***dull*** *that day.*
• **cloudy, overcast, grey, sunless, murky**
OPPOSITE **clear**
❸ *I heard a* ***dull*** *thud from upstairs.*
• **indistinct, muffled, muted**
OPPOSITE **distinct**
❹ *He's rather a* ***dull*** *student.*
• **stupid, slow, unintelligent, dim, unimaginative, dense, obtuse** *(informal)* **thick**
OPPOSITE **clever**
❺ *The play was so* ***dull*** *that I fell asleep.*
• **boring, dry, monotonous, tedious, uninteresting, unexciting, lacklustre**
OPPOSITE **interesting**
A common simile is **as dull as ditchwater.**

dumb *ADJECTIVE*
❶ *The spectators were struck* ***dumb*** *with amazement.*
If you do not speak, you are **mute** or **silent.**
If you cannot speak because you are surprised, confused or embarrassed, you are **speechless** or **tongue-tied.**
If you find it hard to express yourself, you are **inarticulate.**

a b c d e f g h i j k l m n o p q r s t u v w x y z

A B C D E F G H I J K L M N O P Q R S T U V W X Y Z

❷ *(informal) He's too **dumb** to understand.*
• **stupid, unintelligent, dim, slow, dense, obtuse**
(informal) **thick**

dummy *ADJECTIVE*
*There was a **dummy** door at the side of the stage.*
• **imitation, fake, copy, toy**

dump *VERB*
❶ *I decided to **dump** some of my old toys.*
• **get rid of, throw away, throw out, discard, dispose of, scrap**
❷ *Just **dump** your things in the bedroom.*
• **put down, set down, deposit, place, drop, throw down, tip**

duplicate *NOUN*
*We made a **duplicate** of the original document.*
• **copy, photocopy, reproduction, replica**
An exact copy of a historic document or manuscript is a **facsimile**.
A person who looks like you is your **double** or **twin**.
A living organism which is a duplicate of another living organism is a **clone**.

duration *NOUN*
*We slept in a tent for the **duration** of the holiday.*
• **length, period, extent**

dusk *NOUN*
*Bats begin to emerge at **dusk**.*
• **twilight, nightfall, sunset, sundown**
OPPOSITE **dawn**

dust *NOUN*
*There was a lot of **dust** on the furniture.*
• **dirt, grime, particles, powder, grit**

dust *VERB*
❶ *I **dusted** the bookshelves.*
• **wipe over, clean, polish**
❷ *Mum **dusted** the top of the cake with icing sugar.*
• **powder, sprinkle**

dusty *ADJECTIVE*
*The books we found in the attic were very **dusty**.*
• **dirty, grimy**
OPPOSITE **clean**

duty *NOUN*
❶ *I have a **duty** to help my parents.*
• **responsibility, obligation**
❷ *I carried out my **duties** conscientiously.*
• **job, task, assignment, chore**
❸ *The government has increased the **duty** on petrol.*
• **charge, tax**

dwell *VERB* **dwells, dwelling, dwelt**
➤ **to dwell in**
*It is said that bandits **dwell in** these caves.*
• **live in, inhabit, occupy, reside in**
➤ **to dwell on**
*Try not to **dwell on** things that happened in the past.*
• **keep thinking about, worry about, brood over**

dwelling *NOUN*
see **house**

dwindle *VERB*
*Our enthusiasm **dwindled** as the day went on.*
• **become less, diminish, decline, decrease, lessen, subside, wane, weaken**
OPPOSITE **increase**

dynamic *ADJECTIVE*
*The team has a new, **dynamic** captain.*
• **energetic, lively, enthusiastic, vigorous, active, forceful, powerful**
OPPOSITE **apathetic**

Ee

eager *ADJECTIVE*
*He is always **eager** to help.*
• keen, enthusiastic, desperate, anxious
OPPOSITE unenthusiastic

early *ADJECTIVE*
❶ *The bus was **early** today.*
• ahead of time, ahead of schedule
OPPOSITE late
❷ *The **early** computers were huge machines.*
• first, old, primitive, ancient
OPPOSITES recent, new

earn *VERB*
❶ *Bob **earns** extra pocket money washing cars.*
• work for, receive, get, make, obtain, bring in
❷ *She trained hard and **earned** her success.*
• deserve, merit

earnest *ADJECTIVE*
*He's a terribly **earnest** young man.*
• serious, sincere, solemn, thoughtful, grave
OPPOSITES casual, flippant

earth *NOUN*
*The **earth** was so dry that many plants died.*
• ground, land, soil
Rich, fertile earth is **loam**.
The top layer of fertile earth is **topsoil**.
Rich earth consisting of decayed plants is **humus**.
A heavy, sticky kind of earth is **clay**.

earthquake *NOUN*
When there is an earthquake, you feel a **shock** or **tremor**.
An instrument which detects and measures earthquakes is a **seismograph**.

ease *NOUN*
❶ *She swam ten lengths of the pool with **ease**.*
• facility, skill, speed
OPPOSITE difficulty
❷ *Lady Deadwood leads a life of **ease**.*
• comfort, contentment, leisure, peace, quiet, relaxation, rest, tranquillity
OPPOSITE stress

ease *VERB*
❶ *The doctor gave her some pills to **ease** her pain.*
• relieve, lessen, soothe, moderate
OPPOSITE aggravate
❷ *After taking the pills, the pain began to **ease**.*
• decrease, reduce, slacken
OPPOSITE increase
❸ *We **eased** the piano into position.*
• edge, guide, manoeuvre, inch, slide, slip

east *NOUN, ADJECTIVE, ADVERB*
The parts of a country or continent in the east are the **eastern** parts.
In the past, the countries of east Asia, east of the Mediterranean, were called **oriental** countries.
To travel towards the east is to travel **eastward** or **eastwards** or **in an easterly direction**.
A wind from the east is an **easterly** wind.

easy *ADJECTIVE*
❶ *Tonight's homework is really **easy**.*
• undemanding, effortless, light
An informal word for an easy task is a **doddle**.
❷ *The instructions were **easy** to understand.*
• simple, straightforward, clear, plain, elementary
A common simile is **as easy as ABC**.
❸ *Our cat has an **easy** life.*
• carefree, comfortable, peaceful, relaxed, leisurely, restful, tranquil, untroubled
OPPOSITE difficult

A B C D E F G H I J K L M N O P Q R S T U V W X Y Z

eat *VERB* **eats, eating, ate, eaten**
*Hannah was **eating** a cheese sandwich.*
• **consume, devour**
(informal) **scoff**
When cattle eat grass they are **grazing.**
A person who eats a large amount is said to **eat like a horse.**
for various things to eat see **food**

OVERUSED WORD

Try to vary the words you use for **eat.** Here are some other words you could use.

TO EAT GREEDILY OR QUICKLY:

• **guzzle, gobble, gulp, gorge, bolt down, polish off, wolf down**
Because I is refusing to gobble up human beans like the other giants, I must spend my life guzzling up icky-poo snozzcumbers instead.—THE BFG, Roald Dahl

TO EAT NOISILY:

• **munch, chomp, crunch, gnash, gnaw, slurp**
*Rabbits like to **chomp** raw carrots.*

TO EAT IN SMALL AMOUNTS:

• **nibble, peck, pick at** or **pick away at, taste**
*Do you have any biscuits we could **nibble?***

TO EAT WITH ENJOYMENT:

• **relish, savour, tuck into**
*Mr Hogg was **savouring** a sausage roll.*

TO EAT A FORMAL MEAL:

• **dine, feast, banquet**
*The guests will be **dining** in the great hall.*

ebb *VERB*
❶ *The fishermen waited for the tide to **ebb.***
• **recede, retreat, flow back, fall, go down**
❷ *She fell ill and her strength began to **ebb.***
• **decline, weaken, lessen, fade, wane**

eccentric *ADJECTIVE*
*Uncle Otto had always been a little **eccentric.***
• **odd, peculiar, strange, weird, abnormal, unusual, curious, unconventional, unorthodox, quirky**
(informal) **way-out, dotty, crackpot**
OPPOSITES **conventional, orthodox**

echo *VERB*
❶ *The sound **echoed** across the valley.*
• **resound, reverberate**
❷ *'He's gone home.' 'Gone home?' she **echoed.***
• **repeat, imitate, mimic**

edge *NOUN*
The edge of a cliff or other steep place is the **brink.**
The edge of a cup or other container is the **brim** or **rim.**
The line round the edge of a circle is the **circumference.**
The line round the edge of any other shape is its **outline.**
The distance round the edge of an area is the **perimeter.**
The stones along the edge of a road are the **kerb.**
Grass along the edge of a road is the **verge.**
The space down the edge of a page is the **margin.**
The space round the edge of a picture is a **border.**
Something that fits round the edge of a picture is a **frame.**
The edge of a garment is the **hem.**
An edge with threads or hair hanging loosely down is a **fringe.**
The edge of a crowd is the **fringe** of the crowd.
The area round the edge of a city is the **outskirts** or **suburbs.**
The edge of a cricket field is the **boundary.**
The edge of a football pitch is the **touchline.**

edge *VERB*
❶ *We **edged** away from the lion's den.*
• **creep, inch, move stealthily, steal, slink**
❷ *Her bonnet was **edged** with black lace.*
• **trim, hem**

edgy *ADJECTIVE*
*Horses become **edgy** during thunderstorms.*
• **nervous, restless, anxious, agitated, excitable, tense, jumpy, fidgety**
(informal) **uptight, jittery**
OPPOSITE **calm**

edible *ADJECTIVE*
*Are these toadstools **edible**?*
• **eatable, fit to eat, good to eat, safe to eat**
OPPOSITES **poisonous, uneatable**

edit *VERB*
*The letters were **edited** before they were published.*
• **revise, correct, adapt, rework, rewrite, rephrase**

edition *NOUN*
*We're preparing a Christmas **edition** of our magazine.*
• **copy, issue, number, version**

educate *VERB*
*The job of a school is to **educate** young people.*
• **teach, train, inform, instruct, tutor**

educated *ADJECTIVE*
*She is an **educated** woman.*
• **knowledgeable, learned, literate, well read, well-informed, cultivated, cultured**

education *NOUN*
*This school is for the **education** of young witches and wizards.*
• **schooling, teaching, training, instruction, tuition, tutoring, coaching**
A programme of education is the **curriculum** or **syllabus**.

WORD WEB

PEOPLE WHO PROVIDE EDUCATION:
• **coach, counsellor, governess, head teacher, instructor, lecturer, professor, teacher, trainer, tutor**

PLACES TO RECEIVE EDUCATION:
• **academy, college, kindergarten, nursery, playgroup, primary school, secondary school, sixth-form college, university**

eerie *ADJECTIVE*
*I heard some **eerie** sounds in the night.*
• **strange, weird, uncanny, mysterious, frightening, creepy, ghostly, sinister, unearthly, unnatural**
(informal) **scary, spooky**

effect *NOUN*
❶ *One **effect** of global warming is that the ice caps are melting.*
• **result, consequence, outcome, sequel, upshot**
❷ *The magic potion was beginning to have an **effect**.*
• **impact, influence**
❸ *The lighting gives an **effect** of warmth.*
• **feeling, impression, sense, illusion**

effective *ADJECTIVE*
❶ *I wish they could find an **effective** cure for colds.*
• **successful**
❷ *Our team needs an **effective** goalkeeper.*
• **competent, able, capable, proficient, skilled**
❸ *He presented an **effective** argument against hunting.*
• **convincing, persuasive, compelling, impressive, telling**
OPPOSITE **useless**

efficient *ADJECTIVE*
❶ *An **efficient** worker can do the job in an hour.*
• **effective, competent, able, capable, proficient**
❷ *Dad tried to work out an **efficient** way of heating our house.*
• **economic, productive**
OPPOSITE **inefficient**

A B C D E F G H I J K L M N O P Q R S T U V W X Y Z

effort *NOUN*
❶ *A lot of **effort** went into making the film.*
• work, trouble, exertion, industry, labour, toil
❷ *She congratulated us on a good **effort**.*
• attempt, try, endeavour, go, shot

eject *VERB*
❶ *Lava was **ejected** from the volcano when it erupted.*
• discharge, emit
❷ *The caretaker **ejected** an intruder from the building.*
• remove, expel, evict, banish, kick out, throw out, turn out

elaborate *ADJECTIVE*
*The plot of the book is so **elaborate** that I got lost halfway through.*
• complicated, complex, detailed, intricate, involved, convoluted
OPPOSITE simple

elated *ADJECTIVE*
*We were **elated** when we won the match.*
• delighted, pleased, thrilled, joyful, ecstatic, gleeful, exultant, delirious
(informal) over the moon

elbow *VERB*
*Miss Crook **elbowed** her way to the front of the queue.*
• push, shove, nudge, jostle

elder *ADJECTIVE*
*My **elder** brother is in the football team.*
• older

elderly *ADJECTIVE*
*I helped the **elderly** couple to get on the bus.*
• aged, aging, old, senior
OPPOSITE young

eldest *ADJECTIVE*
*Jane is my **eldest** sister.*
• oldest

elect *VERB*
*We **elected** a new captain.*
• vote for, appoint

election *NOUN*
*We had an **election** to choose a new captain.*
• vote, ballot, poll

elegant *ADJECTIVE*
*She always wears **elegant** clothes.*
• graceful, stylish, fashionable, chic, smart, tasteful, sophisticated
OPPOSITE inelegant

element *NOUN*
*They discussed various **elements** of the book.*
• part, component, feature, constituent
➤ **to be in your element**
*Doug was **in his element** at a computer.*
• be at home, be comfortable, be happy, enjoy yourself

eligible *ADJECTIVE*
*Children over twelve are not **eligible** to enter this race.*
• qualified, allowed, authorised, suitable
OPPOSITE ineligible

eliminate *VERB*
*The government wants to **eliminate** crime.*
• get rid of, put an end to
To be eliminated from a competition is to be knocked out.

elude *VERB*
*The police chased him, but he managed to **elude** them.*
• avoid, evade, escape from, get away from

embark *VERB*
*The passengers **embarked** in time for the ship to sail at high tide.*
• board, go aboard
OPPOSITE disembark
➤ **to embark on something**
*Today we **embarked** on a big project.*
• begin, start, commence, undertake

embarrass *VERB*
Will it ***embarrass*** *you if I tell people our secret?*
• **humiliate, distress, mortify, make you blush**

embarrassed *ADJECTIVE*
Don't feel ***embarrassed***—*it happens to everyone!*
• **humiliated, ashamed, awkward, uncomfortable, bashful, distressed, flustered, mortified, self-conscious**

emblem *NOUN*
The dove is an ***emblem*** *of peace.*
• **sign, symbol, motif**

embrace *VERB*
❶ *The mother gorilla* ***embraced*** *her baby.*
• **hug, clasp, cuddle, hold**
❷ *She's always ready to* ***embrace*** *new ideas.*
• **welcome, accept, adopt, take on**
❸ *The syllabus* ***embraces*** *all aspects of the subject.*
• **include, incorporate, take in**

emerge *VERB*
He didn't ***emerge*** *from his bedroom until ten o'clock.*
• **appear, come out**

emergency *NOUN*
Try to keep calm in an ***emergency****.*
• **crisis, serious situation, danger, difficulty**

emigrant *NOUN*
Millions of ***emigrants*** *crossed the Atlantic for a new life.*
Someone who has had to leave their country because of war or disaster is a **refugee**.
OPPOSITE **immigrant**

emigrate *VERB*
During the famine, many Irish people were forced to ***emigrate*** *to America.*
• **leave the country, move abroad**
OPPOSITE **immigrate**

emit *VERB*
❶ *The exhaust pipe* ***emitted*** *clouds of smoke.*
• **discharge, expel, belch, blow out, give off**
❷ *The satellite was* ***emitting*** *radio signals.*
• **transmit, give out, send out**

emotion *NOUN*
His voice was full of ***emotion****.*
• **feeling, passion, sentiment, fervour**

emotional *ADJECTIVE*
❶ *He made an* ***emotional*** *farewell speech.*
• **moving, touching**
❷ *The music for the love scenes was very* ***emotional****.*
• **romantic, sentimental**
❸ *She's a very* ***emotional*** *woman.*
• **passionate, intense**
OPPOSITES **unemotional, cold**

emphasis *NOUN*
In the word 'aardvark' the ***emphasis*** *is on the first syllable.*
• **stress, accent, weight**

emphasise *VERB*
She ***emphasised*** *the important points.*
• **highlight, stress, focus on, dwell on, underline**

employ *VERB*
❶ *The new factory plans to* ***employ*** *100 workers.*
• **hire, engage, give work to, take on**
❷ *The factory will* ***employ*** *the latest methods.*
• **use, utilise**

employee *NOUN*
100 ***employees*** *will work at the new factory.*
• **worker**
A word for all the employees of an organisation is **staff** or **workforce**.

employment *NOUN*
He's still looking for suitable ***employment****.*
• **work, a job, an occupation, a profession, a trade**
for various kinds of employment see **job**

A B C D E F G H I J K L M N O P Q R S T U V W X Y Z

empty *ADJECTIVE*

❶ *Please put the **empty** milk bottles outside the door.*

OPPOSITE full

❷ *The house next to ours has been **empty** for weeks.*

• unoccupied, uninhabited, vacant, deserted

OPPOSITE occupied

❸ *There is still some **empty** space on the wall.*

• blank, bare, clear, unused

empty *VERB*

❶ ***Empty** the dirty water into the sink.*

• drain, pour out

OPPOSITE fill

❷ *Did you **empty** all the shopping from the trolley?*

• remove, unload

❸ *The room slowly began to **empty**.*

• clear, be vacated

enable *VERB*

❶ *The fine weather **enabled** us to do the job quickly.*

• allow, make it possible for, help, aid, assist

❷ *A passport **enables** you to travel abroad.*

• allow, entitle, permit, authorise

OPPOSITE prevent

enchanting *ADJECTIVE*

*The ballet dancers were **enchanting**.*

• delightful, charming, appealing, attractive, bewitching, spellbinding

enchantment *NOUN*

❶ *The forest had an air of **enchantment**.*

• magic, wonder, delight, pleasure

❷ *The witch recited an **enchantment**.*

• spell, incantation

see also **magic**

enclose *VERB*

❶ *The documents were **enclosed** in a brown paper envelope.*

• contain, insert, wrap, bind, sheathe

❷ *The animals were **enclosed** within a wire fence.*

• confine, restrict, fence in, shut in, imprison

enclosure *NOUN*

An animal's enclosure with bars is a **cage**.
An enclosure for chickens is a **coop** or **run**.
An enclosure for cattle and other animals is a **pen** or **corral**.
An enclosure for horses is a **paddock**.
An enclosure for sheep is a **fold**.

encounter *VERB*

❶ *He **encountered** her outside the station.*

• meet, come across, run into, bump into, come face to face with

❷ *We **encountered** some problems.*

• experience, come upon, confront, be faced with

encourage *VERB*

❶ *We went to the match to **encourage** our team.*

• inspire, support, motivate, cheer, spur on, egg on

❷ *The poster **encourages** people to eat healthily.*

• persuade, urge

❸ *Is advertising likely to **encourage** sales?*

• increase, boost, stimulate, further, promote, help, aid

OPPOSITE discourage

encouragement *NOUN*

*Our team needs some **encouragement**.*

• reassurance, inspiration, incitement, stimulation, urging, incentive, stimulus, support

encouraging *ADJECTIVE*

*The results of the tests were **encouraging**.*

• hopeful, positive, promising, reassuring, optimistic, cheering, favourable

end *NOUN*

❶ *The fence marks the **end** of the garden.*

• boundary, limit

❷ *The **end** of the film was the most exciting part.*

• ending, finish, close, conclusion, culmination

The last part of a show or piece of music is the **finale**.
A section added at the end of a letter is a **postscript**.
A section added at the end of a story is an **epilogue**.
❸ *I was tired by the time we got to the* ***end*** *of the journey.*
• **termination, destination**
❹ *We arrived late and found ourselves at the* ***end*** *of the queue.*
• **back, rear, tail**
❺ *What* ***end*** *did you have in view when you started?*
• **aim, purpose, intention, objective, plan, outcome, result**

end *VERB*
❶ *The meeting should* ***end*** *in time for lunch.*
• **finish, complete, conclude, break off, halt** *(informal)* **round off**
❷ *When did they* ***end*** *public executions?*
• **abolish, do away with, get rid of, put an end to, discontinue, eliminate**
❸ *The festival* ***ended*** *with a show of fireworks.*
• **close, come to an end, stop, cease, terminate, culminate, wind up**

endanger *VERB*
Bad driving ***endangers*** *other people.*
• **put at risk, threaten**
OPPOSITE **protect**

endeavour *VERB*
Please ***endeavour*** *to behave well.*
• **try, attempt, aim, strive, make an effort**

ending *NOUN*
The ***ending*** *of the film was the most exciting part.*
• **end, finish, close, conclusion, culmination, last part**
The ending of a show or piece of music is the **finale**.

endless *ADJECTIVE*
❶ *Teachers need* ***endless*** *patience.*
• **unending, limitless, infinite, inexhaustible, unlimited**
❷ *There's an* ***endless*** *procession of cars along the main road.*
• **continual, continuous, constant, incessant, interminable, perpetual, unbroken, uninterrupted, everlasting, ceaseless**

endurance *NOUN*
The climb was a test of their ***endurance****.*
• **perseverance, persistence, determination, resolution, stamina**

endure *VERB*
❶ *She had to* ***endure*** *a lot of pain.*
• **bear, stand, suffer, cope with, experience, go through, put up with, tolerate, undergo**
❷ *These traditions have* ***endured*** *for centuries.*
• **survive, continue, last, persist, carry on, keep going**

enemy *NOUN*
They used to be friends but now they are bitter ***enemies****.*
• **opponent, adversary, foe, rival**
OPPOSITES **friend, ally**

energetic *ADJECTIVE*
❶ *She's a very* ***energetic*** *person.*
• **dynamic, spirited, enthusiastic, animated, active, zestful**
OPPOSITES **inactive, lethargic**
❷ *It was a very* ***energetic*** *exercise routine.*
• **lively, vigorous, brisk, fast, quick moving, strenuous**
OPPOSITES **slow-paced, sluggish**

energy *NOUN*
❶ *The dancers had tremendous* ***energy****.*
• **liveliness, spirit, vitality, vigour, life, drive, zest, verve, enthusiasm, dynamism** *(informal)* **get-up-and-go, zip**
OPPOSITE **lethargy**
❷ *Wind power is a renewable source of* ***energy****.*
• **power, fuel**

A B C D E F G H I J K L M N O P Q R S T U V W X Y Z

enforce *VERB*
*The umpire's job is to **enforce** the rules.*
• carry out, administer, apply, implement, put into effect, impose, insist on

engage *VERB*
❶ *The builder **engaged** extra workers in order to complete the job on time.*
• employ, hire, take on
❷ *The general decided to **engage** the enemy at dawn.*
• attack, start fighting

engaged *ADJECTIVE*
❶ *The painter was **engaged** in his work.*
• busy, occupied, employed, tied up, immersed, absorbed, engrossed
❷ *I tried to phone but the line was **engaged**.*
• busy, being used, unavailable
OPPOSITES free, available

engagement *NOUN*
*She has a business **engagement** this afternoon.*
• meeting, appointment, commitment, date

engine *NOUN*
*The lawnmower needs a new **engine**.*
• motor, mechanism, turbine
A railway engine is a **locomotive**.

engrossed *ADJECTIVE*
*Aunt Peggy was **engrossed** in her knitting.*
• absorbed, busy, occupied, preoccupied, engaged, immersed

engulf *VERB*
*The floods **engulfed** several villages.*
• flood, drown, immerse, inundate, overwhelm, submerge, swallow up, swamp

enhance *VERB*
*The team's victory **enhanced** their reputation.*
• improve, strengthen

enjoy *VERB*
*I really **enjoyed** the film.*
• like, love, get pleasure from, be pleased by, admire, appreciate

enjoyable *ADJECTIVE*
*It was an **enjoyable** party.*
• pleasant, agreeable, delightful, entertaining, amusing
OPPOSITE unpleasant

enlarge *VERB*
*The zoo is going to **enlarge** the lion enclosure.*
• expand, extend, develop, make bigger
To make something wider is to **broaden** or **widen** it.
To make something longer is to **extend**, **lengthen** or **stretch** it.
To make something seem larger is to **magnify** it.
OPPOSITE reduce

enormous *ADJECTIVE*
***Enormous** waves battered the ship.*
• huge, gigantic, immense, colossal, massive, monstrous, monumental, mountainous, towering, tremendous, vast
(informal) ginormous, humungous
OPPOSITE small

enough *DETERMINER*
*Is there **enough** food for ten people?*
• sufficient, adequate, ample

enquire *VERB*
➤ **to enquire about**
*I **enquired about** train times to Bristol.*
• ask for, get information about, request, investigate

enquiry *NOUN*
*The librarian helped me with my **enquiry**.*
• question, query, request, investigation, research

enrage *VERB*
*I was **enraged** by their stupidity.*
• anger, infuriate, madden, incense, exasperate, provoke
OPPOSITE pacify

enrol *VERB*
I ***enrolled*** *as a member of the drama club.*
• join, sign up, put your name down, volunteer

ensure *VERB*
Please ***ensure*** *that you lock the door.*
• make certain, make sure, confirm, see

enter *VERB*
❶ *Silence fell as I* ***entered*** *the room.*
• come in, walk in
OPPOSITE leave
To enter a place without permission is to invade it.
❷ *The arrow* ***entered*** *his shoulder.*
• go into, penetrate, pierce
❸ *Can I* ***enter*** *my name on the list?*
• insert, record, register, put down, set down, sign, write, inscribe
OPPOSITE cancel
❹ *Our class decided to* ***enter*** *the competition.*
• take part in, enrol in, sign up for, go in for, join in, participate in, volunteer for
OPPOSITE withdraw from

enterprise *NOUN*
❶ *She showed* ***enterprise*** *in starting her own business.*
• drive, initiative
❷ *The expedition was a very rash* ***enterprise****.*
• adventure, operation, project, undertaking, venture, effort, mission

entertain *VERB*
❶ *The storyteller* ***entertained*** *us with scary ghost stories.*
• amuse, divert, keep amused, make you laugh, please, cheer up
OPPOSITE bore
❷ *You can* ***entertain*** *friends in the private dining room.*
• receive, welcome, cater for, give hospitality to

entertainer *NOUN*

WORD WEB

SOME KINDS OF ENTERTAINER:

• acrobat, actor, actress, ballerina, busker, clown, comedian or comic, conjuror, dancer, escape artist or escapologist, juggler, magician, mime artist, musician, singer, street entertainer, stuntman or stuntwoman, trapeze artist, TV presenter, ventriloquist, vlogger
A famous entertainer is a star or superstar.
for types of musician see **music**

ENTERTAINERS IN THE PAST:

• fool or jester, gladiator, minstrel

entertainment *NOUN*
Our hosts had arranged some ***entertainment*** *for us.*
• amusements, recreation, diversions, enjoyment, fun, pastimes

enthusiasm *NOUN*
❶ *The young athletes showed plenty of* ***enthusiasm****.*
• keenness, commitment, ambition, drive, zeal, zest
OPPOSITE apathy
❷ *Collecting fossils is one of my* ***enthusiasms****.*
• interest, passion, pastime, hobby, craze, diversion, fad

enthusiast *NOUN*
My brother is a football ***enthusiast****.*
• fan, fanatic, devotee, lover, supporter, addict *(informal)* freak, nut

enthusiastic *ADJECTIVE*
❶ *He's an* ***enthusiastic*** *supporter of our local team.*
• keen, passionate, avid, devoted, energetic, fervent, zealous

a b c d e f g h i j k l m n o p q r s t u v w x y z

❷ *The audience burst into **enthusiastic** applause.*
• eager, excited, lively, vigorous, exuberant, hearty
OPPOSITES unenthusiastic, apathetic

entire *ADJECTIVE*
*Donald spent the **entire** evening watching television.*
• complete, whole, total, full

entirely *ADVERB*
*I'm not **entirely** sure that I agree with you.*
• completely, absolutely, wholly, totally, utterly, fully, perfectly, quite

entitle *VERB*
*The voucher **entitles** you to claim a discount.*
• permit, allow, enable, authorise

entrance *NOUN (say* en-transs*)*
❶ *Please pay at the **entrance**.*
• entry, way in, access, door, gate
When you go through the entrance to a building, you cross the **threshold**.
❷ *I'll meet you in the **entrance**.*
• entrance hall, foyer, lobby, porch
❸ *Her sudden **entrance** took everyone by surprise.*
• entry, arrival, appearance
OPPOSITE exit

entrance *VERB (say* en-transs*)*
*The crowd were **entranced** by the fireworks display.*
• charm, delight, please, enchant

entrant *NOUN*
*A prize will be awarded to the winning **entrant**.*
• contestant, competitor, contender, candidate, participant

entry *NOUN*
❶ *A van was blocking the **entry** to the school.*
• way in, entrance, access, door, gate
❷ *Every evening I write an **entry** in my diary.*
• item, note

envelop *VERB*
*Mist **enveloped** the top of the mountain.*
• cover, hide, mask, conceal

envious *ADJECTIVE*
*He was **envious** of his brother's success.*
• jealous, resentful

environment *NOUN*
*Animals should live in their natural **environment**, not in cages.*
• habitat, surroundings, setting, conditions, situation
➤ **the environment**
*We must do all we can to protect **the environment**.*
• the natural world, nature, the earth, the world

envy *NOUN*
*I didn't feel any **envy**, even when I saw how rich she was.*
• jealousy, resentment, bitterness

envy *VERB*
*The evil queen **envied** Snow White's beauty.*
• be jealous of, begrudge, grudge, resent

episode *NOUN*
❶ *I paid for the broken window, and I want to forget the whole **episode**.*
• event, incident, experience
❷ *I missed last night's **episode** of 'Dr Who'.*
• instalment, part

equal *ADJECTIVE*
❶ *Give everyone an **equal** amount.*
• equivalent, identical, matching, similar, corresponding, fair
❷ *The scores were **equal** at half-time.*
• even, level, the same, square
To make the scores equal is to **equalise**.

equip *VERB*
*All the bedrooms are **equipped** with a colour television.*
• provide, supply
To equip soldiers with weapons is to **arm** them.
To equip a room with furniture is to **furnish** it.

equipment *NOUN*
The shed is full of gardening ***equipment****.*
• **apparatus, gear, kit, tackle, tools, implements, instruments, materials, machinery, paraphernalia, things**
Computing equipment is **hardware**.

equivalent *ADJECTIVE*
A metre is ***equivalent*** *to a hundred centimetres.*
• **matching, similar, corresponding, identical, the same as**

era *NOUN*
Shakespeare lived in the Elizabethan ***era****.*
• **age, period, time, epoch**

erase *VERB*
I ***erased*** *the writing on the blackboard.*
• **delete, remove, rub out, wipe out, get rid of**

erect *ADJECTIVE*
The dog stood with its ears ***erect****.*
• **upright, vertical, perpendicular**

erect *VERB*
The town hall was ***erected*** *in 1890.*
• **build, construct, raise, put up, set up**
To erect a tent is to **pitch** it.

erode *VERB*
The flood water ***eroded*** *the river bank.*
• **wear away, eat away, destroy**

errand *NOUN*
I went on an ***errand*** *to the corner shop.*
• **job, task, assignment, trip, journey**

erratic *ADJECTIVE*
The team's performance has been ***erratic*** *this season.*
• **inconsistent, irregular, uneven, variable, changeable, fluctuating, unpredictable**
OPPOSITE **consistent**

error *NOUN*
❶ *The accident was the result of an* ***error*** *by the driver.*
• **mistake, fault, lapse, blunder**
❷ *I think there is an* ***error*** *in your argument.*
• **flaw, inaccuracy, misunderstanding, inconsistency**
The error of leaving something out is an **omission** or **oversight**.

erupt *VERB*
Smoke began to ***erupt*** *from the volcano.*
• **be discharged, be emitted, pour out, issue, spout, gush, spurt, belch**

escape *VERB*
❶ *Why did you let him* ***escape****?*
• **get away, get out, run away, break free, break out**
(informal) **give you the slip**
A performer who escapes from chains, etc. is an **escape artist** or **escapologist**.
❷ *She always* ***escapes*** *the nasty jobs.*
• **avoid, get out of, evade, dodge, shirk**

escape *NOUN*
❶ *The prisoner's* ***escape*** *was filmed by security cameras.*
• **getaway, breakout, flight**
❷ *The explosion was caused by an* ***escape*** *of gas.*
• **leak, leakage, seepage**

escort *NOUN*
❶ *The president always has an* ***escort*** *to protect him.*
• **bodyguard, guard**
❷ *The actress arrived with her* ***escort****.*
• **companion, partner**

escort *VERB*
The queen was ***escorted*** *by a number of attendants.*
• **accompany, guard, protect, look after**

especially *ADVERB*
I like apple pie, ***especially*** *with ice cream.*
• **above all, chiefly, most of all**

espionage *NOUN*
see **spy**

A B C D E F G H I J K L M N O P Q R S T U V W X Y Z

essential *ADJECTIVE*
Fruit and vegetables are an ***essential*** *part of our diet.*
• **important, necessary, basic, vital, principal, fundamental, chief, crucial, indispensable**

establish *VERB*
❶ *He plans to* ***establish*** *a new business.*
• **set up, start, begin, create, found, initiate, institute, introduce, launch, originate**
❷ *The police have not managed to* ***establish*** *his guilt.*
• **prove, show to be true, confirm, verify**

estate *NOUN*
❶ *There's a new housing* ***estate*** *near our school.*
• **area, development, scheme**
❷ *The castle is sited on a large* ***estate****.*
• **land, grounds**
❸ *The millionaire left his* ***estate*** *to charity.*
• **property, fortune, wealth, possessions**

estimate *NOUN*
What is your ***estimate*** *of how much it will cost?*
• **assessment, calculation, evaluation, guess, judgement, opinion**
An official estimate of the value of something is a **valuation**.
An official estimate of what a job is going to cost is a **quotation** or **tender**.

estimate *VERB*
The builders ***estimate*** *that the work will take four months.*
• **calculate, assess, work out, compute, count up, evaluate, judge, reckon, think out**

eternal *ADJECTIVE*
❶ *The magic fountain was said to give* ***eternal*** *youth.*
• **everlasting, infinite, lasting, unending, timeless**
Beings with eternal life are said to be **immortal**.
❷ *I'm sick of your* ***eternal*** *quarrelling!*
• **constant, continual, never-ending, non-stop, persistent, perpetual, endless, ceaseless, incessant, unceasing**

evacuate *VERB*
❶ *The firefighters* ***evacuated*** *everyone from the building.*
• **remove, clear, send away, move out**
❷ *We were told to* ***evacuate*** *the building.*
• **leave, quit, abandon, withdraw from, empty, vacate**

evade *VERB*
Don't try to ***evade*** *your responsibilities.*
• **avoid, dodge, shirk, escape from, steer clear of, fend off**
OPPOSITE **confront**

even *ADJECTIVE*
❶ *You need an* ***even*** *surface for ice skating.*
• **level, flat, smooth, straight**
OPPOSITE **uneven**
❷ *The runners kept up an* ***even*** *pace.*
• **regular, steady, unvarying, rhythmical, monotonous**
OPPOSITE **irregular**
❸ *Mr Humphreys has an* ***even*** *temper.*
• **calm, cool, placid, unexcitable**
OPPOSITE **excitable**
❹ *The scores were* ***even*** *at half time.*
• **equal, level, matching, identical, the same, square**
OPPOSITE **different**
❺ *The numbers 2, 4 and 6 are* ***even*** *numbers.*
OPPOSITE **odd**

even *VERB*
➤ **to even something up**
If you join their team, that will ***even up*** *the numbers.*
• **equalise, level, balance, match, square**

evening *NOUN*
Towards ***evening*** *it clouded over and began to rain.*
• **dusk, nightfall, sundown, sunset, twilight**

event *NOUN*
❶ *Her autobiography describes the main* ***events*** *of her life.*
• **happening, incident, occurrence**

❷ *There was an* **event** *to mark the launch of the new film.*
• **function, occasion, ceremony, entertainment, party, reception**
❸ *The World Cup is an important* **event** *for football fans.*
• **competition, contest, fixture, engagement, meeting, game, match, tournament**

eventful *ADJECTIVE*
We had an **eventful** *journey.*
• **interesting, exciting, busy, lively, active**
OPPOSITES **uneventful, dull**

eventual *ADJECTIVE*
We were happy with our **eventual** *score.*
• **final, ultimate, resulting, overall, ensuing**

eventually *ADVERB*
The journey took ages, but **eventually** *we arrived safely.*
• **finally, at last, in the end, ultimately**

evergreen *ADJECTIVE*
Most pine trees are **evergreen**.
OPPOSITE **deciduous**

everyday *ADJECTIVE*
Don't dress up—just wear your **everyday** *clothes.*
• **normal, ordinary, usual, regular, customary**

evidence *NOUN*
This piece of paper is **evidence** *that he is lying.*
• **proof, confirmation**
Evidence that someone accused of a crime was not there when the crime was committed is an **alibi**.
Evidence given in a law court is a **testimony**.
To give evidence in court is to **testify**.

evident *ADJECTIVE*
It was **evident** *that someone had been in the room.*
• **clear, obvious, apparent, plain, certain, unmistakable, undeniable, noticeable, perceptible, visible**

evidently *ADVERB*
The woman was **evidently** *upset.*
• **clearly, obviously, apparently, plainly, undoubtedly**

evil *ADJECTIVE*
❶ *The charm was used to keep away* **evil** *spirits.*
• **malevolent, fiendish, diabolical**
❷ *Who would do such an* **evil** *deed?*
• **wicked, immoral, cruel, sinful, villainous, malicious, foul, hateful, vile**
OPPOSITE **good**

evil *NOUN*
❶ *The good witch tried to fight against* **evil**.
• **wickedness, badness, wrongdoing, sin, immorality, villainy, malevolence, malice**
❷ *They had to endure the* **evils** *of famine and drought.*
• **disaster, misfortune, suffering, pain, affliction, curse**

evolve *VERB*
Life **evolved** *on Earth over millions of years.*
• **develop, grow, progress, emerge, mature**

exact *ADJECTIVE*
❶ *I gave the police an* **exact** *account of what happened.*
• **accurate, precise, correct, true, faithful, detailed, meticulous, strict**
❷ *Is this an* **exact** *copy of the original document?*
• **identical, perfect, indistinguishable**
OPPOSITE **inaccurate**

exactly *ADVERB*
At what time **exactly** *did you leave the house?*
• **precisely, specifically, accurately, correctly, strictly**
OPPOSITES **roughly, inaccurately**
A phrase meaning 'exactly on time' is to be **on the dot**.

exaggerate *VERB*
He tends to **exaggerate** *his problems.*
• **magnify, inflate, overdo, make too much of**
OPPOSITE **minimise**

a b c d e f g h i j k l m n o p q r s t u v w x y z

A B C D E F G H I J K L M N O P Q R S T U V W X Y Z

examination *NOUN*
❶ *The results of the **examinations** will be announced next month.*
• **test, assessment**
(informal) **exam**
❷ *The judge made a thorough **examination** of the facts.*
• **investigation, inspection, study, analysis, survey, review, appraisal**
❸ *He was sent to hospital for an **examination**.*
• **check-up**
A medical examination of a dead person is a **post-mortem.**

examine *VERB*
❶ *The judge **examined** the evidence.*
• **inspect, study, investigate, analyse, look closely at, pore over, scrutinise, probe, survey, review, weigh up, sift**
❷ *They were **examined** on their knowledge of history.*
• **question, interrogate, quiz**
To examine someone rigorously is to **grill** them.

example *NOUN*
❶ *Give me an **example** of what you mean.*
• **instance, illustration, sample, specimen, case**
❷ *She's an **example** to us all.*
• **model, ideal**

exasperate *VERB*
*Her constant questions began to **exasperate** me.*
• **annoy, irritate, upset, frustrate, anger, madden, vex**

exceed *VERB*
*She **exceeded** the previous race record by two seconds.*
• **beat, better, outdo, pass, surpass, go over**

excel *VERB*
*She's a good all-round athlete, but she **excels** at sprinting.*
• **do best, stand out, shine**

excellent *ADJECTIVE*
*That's an **excellent** idea!*
• **first-class, first-rate, outstanding, exceptional, remarkable, tremendous, wonderful, superb, great, fine, marvellous, superior, superlative, top-notch**
(informal) **brilliant, fantastic, terrific, fabulous, sensational, super**
for other ways to describe something good see **good**
OPPOSITES **bad, awful, second-rate**

except *PREPOSITION*
*Everyone got a prize **except** me.*
• **apart from, but, with the exception of, excluding**

exception *NOUN*
➤ **to take exception to something**
*She **took exception to** what he said about her clothes.*
• **dislike, object to, complain about, disapprove of, be upset by**

exceptional *ADJECTIVE*
*It is **exceptional** to have such cold weather in June.*
• **unusual, extraordinary, uncommon, unexpected, amazing, rare, odd, peculiar, strange, surprising, special, abnormal, phenomenal, unheard-of, bizarre**
OPPOSITES **normal, usual**

excerpt *NOUN*
*She recited an **excerpt** from the poem.*
• **extract, passage, part, section**
A short excerpt is a **quotation.**
The most interesting excerpts from something are the **highlights.**
Excerpts from a film are **clips.**

excess *NOUN*
If there is an excess of something, so that it is hard to sell it, there is a **glut.**
When a business has an excess of income over its expenses, it has a **profit** or a **surplus.**

excessive *ADJECTIVE*
❶ *I think his enthusiasm for football is **excessive**.*
• **extreme, exaggerated, fanatical**
❷ *Mum prepared **excessive** amounts of food for the party.*
• **unnecessary, needless, superfluous, extravagant, wasteful, unreasonable**

exchange *VERB*
*The shop will **exchange** faulty goods.*
• **change, replace**
To exchange goods for other goods without using money is to **barter**.
To exchange an old thing for part of the cost of a new one is to **trade it in**.
To exchange things with your friends is to **swap** them.
To exchange players for other players in a football match, etc., is to **substitute** them.

excite *VERB*
*The prospect of going to Italy **excited** Miss MacKillop.*
• **thrill, enthuse, stimulate, electrify, rouse, stir up**
OPPOSITE **calm**

excited *ADJECTIVE*
*On Christmas Eve, my little brother was too **excited** to sleep.*
• **agitated, lively, enthusiastic, exuberant, thrilled, elated, eager, animated**
OPPOSITE **calm**

excitement *NOUN*
*I could hardly bear the **excitement**!*
• **suspense, tension, drama, thrill**

exciting *ADJECTIVE*
*The last minutes of the match were the most **exciting** of all!*
• **dramatic, eventful, thrilling, gripping, sensational, stirring, rousing, stimulating, electrifying**
OPPOSITES **dull, boring**

exclaim *VERB*
*'Get out of my house!' she **exclaimed**.*
• **call, shout, cry out, yell**
for other ways to say something see **say**

exclamation *NOUN*
*Holmes gave an **exclamation** of surprise.*
• **cry, shout, yell**
An impolite exclamation is an **oath** or **swear word**.

WRITING TIPS

SOMEONE WHO IS ANGRY OR ANNOYED MIGHT SAY:

• **blast, bother, drat, fiddlesticks**
*'**Fiddlesticks!**' said Merlin. 'I've forgotten the spell!'*

SOMEONE WHO IS SURPRISED OR ALARMED MIGHT SAY:

• **blimey, crikey, crumbs, golly, goodness me, good gracious, good heavens, gosh, my goodness, my word, yikes**
My goodness!' said Commander Pott anxiously. 'Now we've had it!'—CHITTY CHITTY BANG BANG, Ian Fleming

exclude *VERB*
❶ *Adults are **excluded** from joining our club.*
• **ban, bar, prohibit, keep out, banish, reject**
❷ *She had to **exclude** dairy products from her diet.*
• **leave out, omit**
OPPOSITE **include**

excluding *PREPOSITION*
*The gardens are open every day **excluding** Christmas.*
• **except, except for, with the exception of, apart from, bar**

exclusive *ADJECTIVE*
*They stayed at a very **exclusive** hotel.*
• **select, private, snobbish, upmarket** *(informal)* **posh, fancy**

excursion *NOUN*
*We went on an **excursion** to the seaside.*
• trip, journey, outing, expedition, jaunt

excuse *NOUN*
*What is your **excuse** for being so late?*
• reason, explanation, defence, justification

excuse *VERB*
*I can't **excuse** his bad behaviour.*
• forgive, overlook, pardon
OPPOSITE punish
➤ **to be excused something**
*May I **be excused** swimming?*
• be exempt from, be let off, be released from

execute *VERB*
❶ *In some countries, criminals may still be **executed**.*
• put to death
Someone who executes people is an **executioner**.
To execute someone unofficially without a proper trial is to **lynch** them.
❷ *She **executed** a perfect somersault.*
• perform, carry out, produce, complete, accomplish

exercise *NOUN*
❶ ***Exercise** helps to keep you fit.*
• physical activity, working out, keep-fit, training
❷ *Doing **exercises** will improve your guitar playing.*
• practice, training, drill

exercise *VERB*
❶ *If you **exercise** regularly, you will keep fit.*
• keep fit, train, exert yourself
❷ *I sometimes **exercise** our neighbour's dog.*
• take for a walk, take out, walk
❸ *We must **exercise** patience.*
• show, use, apply, display, employ

exert *VERB*
*He **exerted** all his strength to lift the box.*
• use, apply, employ

exertion *NOUN*
*The **exertion** of climbing the stairs made him sweat.*
• effort, hard work, labour, toil

exhale *VERB*
*The doctor asked me to **exhale** slowly.*
• breathe out
OPPOSITE inhale

exhaust *NOUN*
*The **exhaust** from cars damages the environment.*
• fumes, smoke, emissions, gases

exhaust *VERB*
❶ *The steep climb up the hill **exhausted** me.*
• tire, wear out
❷ *We had **exhausted** our food supply by midday.*
• finish, go through, use up, consume
(informal) polish off

exhausted *ADJECTIVE*
*After a hard race, we lay **exhausted** on the grass.*
• tired, weary, worn out, fatigued, breathless, gasping, panting
(informal) all in, done in, bushed, zonked

exhausting *ADJECTIVE*
*Digging the garden is **exhausting** work.*
• tiring, demanding, hard, laborious, strenuous, difficult, gruelling, wearisome
OPPOSITE easy

exhaustion *NOUN*
*He was overcome by sheer **exhaustion**.*
• tiredness, fatigue, weariness, weakness

exhibit *VERB*

❶ *Her paintings were **exhibited** in galleries all over Europe and America.*

• display, show, present, put up, set up, arrange

❷ *He was **exhibiting** signs of anxiety.*

• show, demonstrate, reveal

OPPOSITE hide

exhibition *NOUN*

*We went to see an **exhibition** of paintings by Picasso.*

• display, show

exile *VERB*

*As a result of the war, many people were **exiled** from their own country.*

• banish, expel, drive out, deport, eject, send away

exile *NOUN*

*He returned to his country after 24 years of **exile**.*

• banishment, expulsion, deportation

A person who has been exiled is an **exile** or a **refugee**.

exist *VERB*

❶ *Some people claim that ghosts actually **exist**.*

• be real, occur

❷ *We can't **exist** without food.*

• live, remain alive, survive, keep going, last, continue, endure

existence *NOUN*

❶ *Do you believe in the **existence** of ghosts?*

• reality

❷ *Most plants depend on sunlight for their **existence**.*

• life, survival

existing *ADJECTIVE*

❶ *There are only two **existing** species of elephants.*

• surviving, living, remaining

❷ *Next year, the **existing** rules will be replaced by new ones.*

• present, current

exit *NOUN*

❶ *I'll wait for you by the **exit**.*

• door, way out, doorway, gate, barrier

OPPOSITE entrance

❷ *The robbers made a hurried **exit**.*

• departure

OPPOSITE entrance

exit *VERB*

*The actors **exited** from the left of the stage.*

• go out, leave, depart, withdraw

OPPOSITE enter

exotic *ADJECTIVE*

*My aunt has travelled to many **exotic** places.*

• remote, foreign, alien, different, exciting, romantic, strange, unfamiliar, wonderful

OPPOSITE familiar

expand *VERB*

*Their computer business is **expanding** rapidly.*

• increase, enlarge, extend, build up, develop, make bigger

To become larger is to **grow** or **swell**.

To become wider is to **broaden**, **thicken** or **widen**.

To become longer is to **extend**, **lengthen** or **stretch**.

OPPOSITES contract, reduce

expanse *NOUN*

*The explorers crossed a large **expanse** of desert.*

• area, stretch, tract

An expanse of water or ice is a **sheet**.

expect *VERB*

❶ *I **expect** that it will rain today.*

• anticipate, imagine, forecast, predict, foresee, prophesy

❷ *She **expects** me to do everything for her!*

• require, want, count on, insist on, demand

❸ *I **expect** they missed the bus.*

• believe, imagine, guess, suppose, presume, assume, think

A B C D E F G H I J K L M N O P Q R S T U V W X Y Z

expedition *NOUN*
An expedition into unknown territory is an **exploration**.
An expedition to carry out a special task is a **mission**.
An expedition to find something is a **quest**.
An expedition to worship at a holy place is a **pilgrimage**.
An expedition to see or hunt wild animals is a **safari**.
see also **explorer**

expel *VERB*
❶ *A fan **expels** the stale air and fumes.*
• **send out, force out**
❷ *He was **expelled** from school.*
• **dismiss, ban, remove, throw out, send away**
To expel someone from their home is to **eject** or **evict** them.
To expel someone from their country is to **banish** or **exile** them.
To expel evil spirits is to **exorcise** them.

expense *NOUN*
*She was worried about the **expense** of the holiday.*
• **cost, charges, expenditure**

expensive *ADJECTIVE*
*Houses are very **expensive** in this area.*
• **dear, costly**
OPPOSITE **cheap**

experience *NOUN*
❶ *Have you had any **experience** of singing in a choir?*
• **practice, involvement, participation**
❷ *I had an unusual **experience** today.*
• **happening, event, occurrence, incident**
An exciting experience is an **adventure**.
An unpleasant experience is an **ordeal**.

experienced *ADJECTIVE*
*He's an **experienced** actor who has been in many films.*
• **skilled, qualified, expert, knowledgeable, trained, professional**
OPPOSITE **inexperienced**

experiment *NOUN*
*We carried out a scientific **experiment**.*
• **test, trial**
A series of experiments is **research** or an **investigation**.

experiment *VERB*
*They **experimented** to see if their robot would work.*
• **do tests**
To experiment on or with something is to **test** it or **try it out**.

expert *NOUN*
*He's an **expert** at chess.*
• **specialist, authority, genius, wizard**
(informal) **dab hand, geek, whizz**

expert *ADJECTIVE*
*Only an **expert** sailor could cross the ocean.*
• **brilliant, capable, clever, competent, experienced, knowledgeable, professional, proficient, qualified, skilful, skilled, specialised, trained**
OPPOSITES **amateur, unskilful**

expertise *NOUN*
*Do you have the **expertise** to restore the painting?*
• **skill, ability, competence, knowledge, know-how, training**

expire *VERB*
❶ *The television licence **expires** next month.*
• **finish, run out, come to an end, become invalid**
❷ *The animal **expired** before the vet arrived.*
• **die, pass away**

explain *VERB*
❶ *The doctor **explained** the procedure carefully.*
• **make clear, give an explanation of, clarify, describe**
❷ *Can you **explain** your strange behaviour?*
• **give reasons for, account for, excuse, make excuses for, justify**

explanation *NOUN*

❶ *They could find no **explanation** for the accident.*
• **reason, excuse, justification**
❷ *He gave a brief **explanation** of how his invention worked.*
• **account, description, demonstration**

explode *VERB*

❶ *The firework **exploded** with a bang.*
• **blow up, make an explosion, go off, burst, shatter**
❷ *The slightest movement might **explode** the bomb.*
• **detonate, set off**

exploit *NOUN*

*The book describes her **exploits** as a secret agent.*
• **adventure, deed, feat, venture, escapade**

exploit *VERB*

*They plan to **exploit** the area as a tourist attraction.*
• **make use of, take advantage of, use, develop, profit from**
(informal) **cash in on**

explore *VERB*

❶ *The spacecraft will **explore** the solar system.*
• **search, survey, travel through, probe**
❷ *We must **explore** all the possibilities.*
• **examine, inspect, investigate, look into, research, analyse, scrutinise**

explorer *NOUN*

*The **explorers** were looking for the legendary Lost City.*
• **traveller, voyager, discoverer, wanderer**

WORD WEB

THINGS AN EXPLORER MIGHT FIND:

• **catacombs, cave, cavern, chest, hieroglyphics, inscription, labyrinth, maze, mummy, parchment, pyramid, riddle, sarcophagus, seal, secret passage, skeleton, stone tablet, temple, tomb, treasure, tunnel, underground chamber**

THINGS AN EXPLORER MIGHT USE OR CARRY:

• **binoculars, chart, compass, machete, map, penknife, rope, rucksack, telescope, tent, torch, water bottle**

Stella checked and re-checked her pockets and her explorer's bag ... to make sure she had her telescope, compass, magnifying glass, pocket map, emergency mint cake, matches and ball of string.—THE POLAR BEAR EXPLORERS' CLUB, Alex Bell

for explorers in polar regions see **polar**
for explorers in space see **astronaut**

explosion *NOUN*

*The **explosion** rattled the windows.*
• **blast, bang**

An explosion from a volcano is an **eruption**.
An explosion of laughter is an **outburst**.
The sound of a gun going off is a **report**.

export *VERB*

*The factory **exports** most of the cars it makes.*
• **sell abroad, send abroad, ship overseas**
OPPOSITE **import**

expose *VERB*

❶ *He yawned, **exposing** a set of white teeth.*
• **uncover**
❷ *The truth about his past was **exposed** in the newspaper.*
• **make known, publish, reveal, disclose**

express *VERB*

*He's always quick to **express** his opinions.*
• **voice, communicate, convey, put into words, phrase**

To express yourself by word of mouth is to **speak**.
To express yourself on paper is to **write**.
To express your feelings forcefully is to **give vent** to them.

a b c d e f g h i j k l m n o p q r s t u v w x y z

A B C D E F G H I J K L M N O P Q R S T U V W X Y Z

expression *NOUN*

❶ *'Tickled pink' is a colloquial* ***expression****.*

• **phrase, saying, term, wording**

An expression that people use too much is a **cliché**.

❷ *Did you see her* ***expression*** *when I told her the news?*

• **look, appearance, countenance, face**

❸ *Rhona plays the piano with great* ***expression****.*

• **feeling, emotion, sympathy, understanding**

WORD WEB

EXPRESSIONS YOU MIGHT SEE ON A FACE:

• **beam, frown, glare, glower, grimace, grin, leer, long face, pout, scowl, smile, smirk, sneer, wide-eyed look, wince, yawn**

see also **face**

Mr Coombes was looking grim. His hammy pink face had taken on that dangerous scowl which only appeared when he was extremely cross and somebody was for the high-jump.

—BOY, Roald Dahl

expressive *ADJECTIVE*

❶ *The old wizard gave me an* ***expressive*** *look.*

• **meaningful, significant, revealing, telling**

❷ *An actor needs to have an* ***expressive*** *voice.*

• **lively, varied, eloquent**

OPPOSITES **expressionless, flat**

exquisite *ADJECTIVE*

There was some ***exquisite*** *lace on the collar.*

• **beautiful, fine, delicate, intricate, dainty**

extend *VERB*

❶ *Stopping for lunch will* ***extend*** *our journey by an hour.*

• **lengthen, make longer, prolong, delay, draw out**

OPPOSITE **shorten**

❷ *They have recently* ***extended*** *their website.*

• **enlarge, expand, increase, build up, develop, add to, widen the scope of**

OPPOSITE **reduce**

❸ *He sat back and* ***extended*** *his legs.*

• **stretch out, hold out, put out, reach out, stick out**

❹ *We* ***extended*** *a warm welcome to the visitors.*

• **give, offer**

extension *NOUN*

They are building an ***extension*** *to the runway.*

• **continuation, addition**

extensive *ADJECTIVE*

The palace gardens cover an ***extensive*** *area.*

• **big, large, broad, wide, spread out**

OPPOSITE **small**

extent *NOUN*

❶ *The map shows the* ***extent*** *of the island.*

• **area, dimensions, expanse, spread, breadth, length, limits, measurement**

❷ *After the storm we went out to see the* ***extent*** *of the damage.*

• **amount, degree, level, size, scope, magnitude, range**

exterior *NOUN*

He painted the ***exterior*** *of his house.*

• **outside**

OPPOSITE **interior**

exterminate *VERB*

They used poison to ***exterminate*** *the rats.*

• **destroy, kill, get rid of, annihilate, wipe out**

external *ADJECTIVE*

In ***external*** *appearance, the house was rather gloomy.*

• **exterior, outside, outer**

OPPOSITE **internal**

extinct *ADJECTIVE*

An extinct species is one that has **died out** or **vanished**.

An extinct volcano is an **inactive** volcano.

extinguish *VERB*
*We **extinguished** the campfire before we went to bed.*
• **put out, quench, smother**
OPPOSITE **ignite**

extra *ADJECTIVE*
❶ *There is an **extra** charge for taking your bike on the train.*
• **additional, further, added, supplementary, excess**
❷ *There is **extra** food in the kitchen if you need it.*
• **more, spare, surplus, reserve**

extract *NOUN*
*There's an **extract** from the new Jacqueline Wilson book in the magazine.*
• **excerpt, passage, part, section**
A short extract is a **quotation.**
Especially interesting extracts from something are the **highlights.**
An extract from a newspaper is a **cutting.**
An extract from a film is a **clip.**

extract *VERB*
❶ *The dentist decided to **extract** my tooth.*
• **pull out, remove, take out, draw out, withdraw** *(informal)* **whip out**
❷ *The following passages are **extracted** from the book.*
• **derive, get, gather, obtain, quote, select**

extraordinary *ADJECTIVE*
*The astronauts saw many **extraordinary** sights.*
• **amazing, astonishing, remarkable, outstanding, exceptional, incredible, fantastic, marvellous, miraculous, phenomenal, rare, special, strange, surprising, unheard of, unusual, weird, wonderful, abnormal, curious**
OPPOSITE **ordinary**

extravagant *ADJECTIVE*
*He held a large, **extravagant** party for all his friends.*
• **expensive, lavish, wasteful**
Someone who spends money in an extravagant way is a **spendthrift.**
OPPOSITE **modest**

extreme *ADJECTIVE*
❶ *Polar bears can withstand **extreme** cold.*
• **great, intense, severe, acute, excessive**
❷ *She lives on the **extreme** edge of the town.*
• **farthest, furthest**

eye *NOUN*

WORD WEB

PARTS OF YOUR EYE:

• **cornea, eyeball, eyebrow, eyelash, eyelid, iris, lens, pupil, retina**
A person who tests your eyesight is an **optician.**
A word meaning 'to do with eyes' is **optical.**
A person with good eyesight is said to have **eyes like a hawk** or to be **eagle-eyed.**

WRITING TIPS

You can use these words to describe eyes:

• **beady, bulbous, bulging, deep-set, glassy, heavy-lidded, hooded, protuberant, saucer-like, sunken; cloudy, misty, moist, piercing, steely, tearful, watery**
Bod did not look up. If he had, he would have seen a pair of watery blue eyes watching him intently from a bedroom window.
—THE GRAVEYARD BOOK, Neil Gaiman

eye *VERB*
*The dog **eyed** the sausages hungrily.*
• **look at, regard, stare at, watch, gaze at, contemplate**

a b c d e f g h i j k l m n o p q r s t u v w x y z

A B C D E F G H I J K L M N O P Q R S T U V W X Y Z

Ff

fabric *NOUN*
*This **fabric** will make a lovely dress for my doll.*
• cloth, material, stuff
A plural word for different kinds of fabric is **textiles**.

WORD WEB

SOME TYPES OF FABRIC:

• canvas, chiffon, corduroy, cotton, damask, denim, felt, flannel, gingham, jersey, linen, *(trademark)* Lycra, muslin, nylon, polyester, rayon, satin, silk, taffeta, tweed, velvet, wool

fabulous *ADJECTIVE*
❶ *(informal) We had a **fabulous** time at the party.*
• excellent, first-class, marvellous, outstanding, superb, tremendous, wonderful *(informal)* brilliant, fantastic, smashing
❷ *Dragons are **fabulous** creatures.*
• fictitious, imaginary, legendary, mythical

face *NOUN*
❶ *We saw the anger in the witch's **face**.*
• expression, features, look, countenance
❷ *The **face** of the clock had been smashed.*
• front
❸ *A cube has six **faces**.*
• side, surface

WRITING TIPS

You can use these words to describe a face:

TO DESCRIBE ITS SHAPE:

• flat, long, oval, round, rounded; lantern-jawed, square-jawed

TO DESCRIBE ITS FEATURES:

• chiselled, chubby, craggy, delicate, fine, gaunt, haggard, hollow, pinched, prominent, puffy, skeletal, sunken, thin
*Their faces were **gaunt** and **pinched** from hunger.*

TO DESCRIBE ITS SKIN OR COLOUR:

• clear, dark, fair, flushed, freckled, fresh, glowing, healthy, rosy, ruddy, tanned; ashen, grey, leaden, pale, pallid, pasty, sallow, sickly, unhealthy, wan; flabby, saggy, shrivelled, weather-beaten, wizened, wrinkled, wrinkly; disfigured, pimply, pock-marked, scarred, spotty, unshaven
Doc Spencer ... was a tiny man with tiny hands and feet and a tiny round face. The face was as brown and wrinkled as a shrivelled apple.– DANNY THE CHAMPION OF THE WORLD, Roald Dahl

TO DESCRIBE THE LOOK ON A FACE:

• cheeky, cheerful, radiant, sunny; grave, grim, serious; sulky, sullen, surly; blank, deadpan, faceless, impassive, unmoving, vacant
*The guard stared ahead, his face **unmoving**.*
see also **expression**
for parts of a face see **eye** *and* **nose**

face *VERB*
❶ *Stand and **face** your partner.*
• be opposite to, look towards
❷ *The astronauts had to **face** many dangers.*
• cope with, deal with, face up to, stand up to, tackle, meet, encounter, confront
OPPOSITE avoid

fact *NOUN*
*It is a **fact** that dodos are now extinct.*
• reality, truth, certainty
OPPOSITE fiction
➤ **the facts**
*The detective considered **the facts** in the case.*
• details, particulars, information, data
Facts which are useful in trying to prove something are **evidence**.
Facts expressed as numbers are **statistics**.

factual *ADJECTIVE*
*Anne Frank wrote a **factual** account of her life during the war*
• **real, true, truthful, accurate, authentic, faithful, genuine, objective, reliable**
A film or story based on a person's life is **biographical.**
A film or story based on history is **historical.**
A film telling you about real events is a **documentary.**
OPPOSITES **made-up, fictional**

fade *VERB*
❶ *Sunlight has **faded** the curtains.*
• **make paler, bleach, blanch, whiten, dim**
OPPOSITE **brighten**
❷ *Those flowers will **fade** in a few days.*
• **wither, wilt, droop, flag, shrivel**
OPPOSITE **flourish**
❸ *Gradually, the light began to **fade**.*
• **weaken, decline, diminish, dwindle, fail, wane, disappear, melt away, vanish**
OPPOSITE **increase**

fail *VERB*
❶ *Their plan to steal the crown jewels **failed** miserably.*
• **be unsuccessful, go wrong, fall through, founder, come to grief, miscarry**
(informal) **flop, bomb**
OPPOSITE **succeed**
❷ *The rocket engine **failed** before take-off.*
• **break down, cut out, give up, stop working**
❸ *By late afternoon, the light had begun to **fail**.*
• **weaken, decline, diminish, dwindle, fade, get worse, deteriorate**
OPPOSITE **improve**
❹ *The professor **failed** to warn us of the danger.*
• **neglect, forget, omit**
OPPOSITE **remember**
❺ *I hope I don't **fail** my violin exam.*
(informal) **flunk**
OPPOSITE **pass**

failure *NOUN*
❶ *The storm caused a power **failure**.*
• **breakdown, fault, malfunction, crash, loss, collapse, stoppage**
❷ *Their attempt to reach the North Pole was a **failure**.*
• **defeat, disappointment, disaster, fiasco**
(informal) **flop, washout**
OPPOSITE **success**

faint *ADJECTIVE*
❶ *The details in the photograph are very **faint**.*
• **faded, dim, unclear, indistinct, vague, blurred, hazy, pale, shadowy, misty**
OPPOSITES **clear, distinct**
❷ *There was a **faint** smell of burning in the air.*
• **delicate, slight**
OPPOSITE **strong**
❸ *We heard a **faint** cry for help.*
• **weak, low, muffled, distant, hushed, muted, soft, thin**
OPPOSITE **loud**
❹ *Gordon was so hungry that he felt **faint**.*
• **dizzy, giddy, light-headed, unsteady, weak, exhausted, feeble**
(informal) **woozy**

faint *VERB*
*The explorers nearly **fainted** from exhaustion.*
• **become unconscious, collapse, pass out, black out**
(old use) **swoon**

fair *ADJECTIVE*
❶ *I think the referee made a **fair** decision.*
• **just, proper, right, fair-minded, honest, honourable, impartial, unbiased, unprejudiced, disinterested**
OPPOSITE **unfair**
❷ *The twins both have **fair** hair.*
• **blond or blonde, light, golden, yellow**
OPPOSITE **dark**
❸ *Our team has a **fair** chance of winning the cup.*
• **reasonable, moderate, average, acceptable, adequate, satisfactory, passable, respectable, tolerable**
❹ *The weather should be **fair** today.*
• **dry, fine, sunny, bright, clear, cloudless, pleasant, favourable**

A B C D E F G H I J K L M N O P Q R S T U V W X Y Z

fair *NOUN*
❶ *My sister won a teddy bear at the **fair**.*
• **fairground, funfair, carnival, fete, gala**
❷ *Our school is holding a book **fair** next week.*
• **show, exhibition, display, market, bazaar**

fairly *ADVERB*
❶ *The competition will be judged **fairly**.*
• **honestly, properly, justly, impartially**
❷ *The ground is still **fairly** wet.*
*I'm **fairly** certain that we are heading north.*
• **quite, rather, somewhat, slightly, moderately, up to a point, reasonably, tolerably**
(informal) **pretty**

fairy *NOUN*

WORD WEB

THINGS A FAIRY MIGHT HAVE OR USE:
• **fairy dust, lantern, wand, wings**

A FAIRY'S WINGS OR CLOTHES MIGHT BE:
• **diaphanous, feathery, glittering, glowing, gossamer, lustrous, sheer, sparkling, translucent, transparent**

PLACES WHERE A FAIRY MIGHT LIVE:
• **dell, glen, magic forest, magic tree, glade, mound, toadstool**
Fairies, as envisaged by the Muggle, inhabit tiny dwellings fashioned out of flower petals, hollowed-out toadstools and similar.
—FANTASTIC BEASTS AND WHERE TO FIND THEM, J. K. Rowling

SOME CREATURES SIMILAR TO FAIRIES:
• **brownie, elf, imp, leprechaun, nymph, pixie, sprite**
for other creatures found in myths and legends see **myth**

faith *NOUN*
❶ *The acrobat had complete **faith** in his assistant.*
• **belief, trust, confidence**
OPPOSITE **doubt**
❷ *In our school, we have pupils of many different **faiths**.*
• **religion, creed, doctrine, belief**

faithful *ADJECTIVE*
❶ *My dog, Scruffy, is my **faithful** friend.*
• **loyal, devoted, reliable, trustworthy, dependable, firm, constant, close**
OPPOSITE **unfaithful**
❷ *Is this a **faithful** copy of the map?*
• **accurate, exact, precise, true**

fake *NOUN*
*That's not a real Roman coin—it's a **fake**.*
• **copy, imitation, reproduction, replica, forgery**
(informal) **phoney**
An event that is a fake is a **hoax, sham** or **simulation.**
A person who pretends to be another person is an **impostor.**

fake *VERB*
*The spy tried to **fake** a foreign accent.*
• **imitate, copy, pretend, put on, reproduce, simulate**
To fake someone's signature is to **forge** it.

fall *VERB* **falls, falling, fell, fallen**
❶ *The acrobat **fell** off a ladder and broke his leg.*
• **tumble, topple, crash down, pitch, plunge**
❷ *Snow was beginning to **fall** quite thickly.*
• **drop, come down, descend, rain down, plummet**
❸ *The level of the river had **fallen** since March.*
• **go down, subside, recede, sink, ebb**
❹ *The temperature in the cave **fell** to below freezing.*
• **go down, become lower, decrease, decline, lessen, diminish, dwindle**
❺ *After a long siege, the town **fell** to the enemy.*
• **give in, surrender**
❻ *Millions of soldiers **fell** in the war.*
• **die, be killed, perish**
(old use) **be slain**
❼ *We arrived at the camp as night was **falling**.*
• **happen, occur, come, take place**

➤ to fall in
*The roof of the cabin **fell in** during the storm.*
• **cave in, collapse, give way**

➤ to fall out
*The twins are always **falling out** with each other.*
• **argue, disagree, quarrel, squabble, bicker**

➤ to fall through
*Our holiday plans have **fallen through** again.*
• **come to nothing, fail, collapse, founder**

fall NOUN

❶ *Ellen had a **fall** and cut her knee.*
• **tumble**
❷ *We noticed a sharp **fall** in the temperature.*
• **drop, lowering**
OPPOSITE **rise**
❸ *There has been a **fall** in the price of coffee.*
• **decrease, reduction, decline**
OPPOSITE **increase**
❹ *This is a story about the **fall** of Troy.*
• **defeat, surrender**

false ADJECTIVE

❶ *They gave us **false** information about the treasure.*
• **wrong, incorrect, untrue, inaccurate, mistaken, erroneous, faulty, invalid, misleading, deceptive**
OPPOSITE **correct**
❷ *The spy was travelling with a **false** passport.*
• **fake, bogus, sham, counterfeit, forged**
OPPOSITES **genuine, authentic**
❸ *Mrs Gummidge put in her **false** teeth.*
• **artificial, imitation**
OPPOSITES **real, natural**
❹ *The Black Knight turned out to be a **false** ally.*
• **unfaithful, disloyal, unreliable, untrustworthy, deceitful, dishonest, treacherous**
OPPOSITES **faithful, loyal**

falter VERB

❶ *The horse **faltered** as it approached the jump.*
• **hesitate, flinch, hold back, pause, stumble, waver, get cold feet**
To falter in your speech is to **stammer** or **stutter**.
❷ *The knight's courage began to **falter**.*
• **weaken, diminish, flag, wane**

fame NOUN

*Her Olympic medal brought her international **fame**.*
• **celebrity, stardom, renown, glory, reputation, name, standing, stature, prominence**
Fame that you get for doing something bad is **notoriety**.

familiar ADJECTIVE

❶ *Seagulls are a **familiar** sight on the beach.*
• **common, everyday, normal, ordinary, usual, regular, customary, frequent, mundane, routine**
OPPOSITE **rare**
❷ *It seems a bit **familiar** to call her by her first name.*
• **informal, friendly, intimate, relaxed, close**
OPPOSITES **formal, unfriendly**

➤ to be familiar with something
*Are you **familiar with** the rules of chess?*
• **be acquainted with, be aware of, know**

family NOUN

*Some members of my **family** live in New Zealand.*
• **relations, relatives**

WORD WEB

An old-fashioned term for your family is your **kin**.
The official term for your closest relative is **next of kin**.
A group of related Scottish families is a **clan**.
A succession of people from the same powerful family is a **dynasty**.
In certain societies, a group of families living together is a **tribe**.
A single stage in a family is a **generation**.
The line of ancestors from which a family is descended is its **ancestry**.
A diagram showing how people in your family are related is a **family tree**.
The study of family history is **genealogy**.
A family of young birds is a **brood**.
A family of kittens or puppies is a **litter**.

A B C D E F G H I J K L M N O P Q R S T U V W X Y Z

MEMBERS OF A FAMILY MAY INCLUDE:

- **adopted child, aunt, brother, child, cousin, daughter, father, foster child, foster parent, grandchild, grandparent, guardian, husband, mother, nephew, niece, parent, partner, sister, son, spouse, stepbrother, stepchild, stepfather, stepmother, stepsister, uncle, ward, wife**

famished *ADJECTIVE*
What's for dinner? I'm ***famished****!*
- **hungry, ravenous, starving**

If you are slightly hungry, you are **peckish**.

famous *ADJECTIVE*
Pele is a very ***famous*** *football player.*
- **well-known, celebrated, renowned, acclaimed, notable, prominent, distinguished, eminent**

To be famous for doing something bad is to be **notorious**.

OPPOSITES **unknown, obscure**

fan *NOUN*
❶ *Can you switch on the* ***fan****, please?*
- **ventilator, blower, extractor, air-conditioner**

❷ *I'm a big* ***fan*** *of science fiction.*
- **enthusiast, admirer, devotee, follower, supporter**

fanatic *NOUN*
My brother is a rugby ***fanatic****.*
- **enthusiast, addict, devotee**

(informal) **freak, nut**

fanatical *ADJECTIVE*
Wayne is ***fanatical*** *about football.*
- **enthusiastic, extreme, fervent, over-enthusiastic, passionate, rabid, zealous**

OPPOSITE **moderate**

fanciful *ADJECTIVE*
I like reading ***fanciful*** *stories about dragons.*
- **fantastic, unrealistic, whimsical, imaginary, fictitious, made-up**

OPPOSITE **realistic**

fancy *ADJECTIVE*
Alice bought a ***fancy*** *hat for her friend's wedding.*
- **elaborate, decorative, ornamental, ornate**

OPPOSITE **plain**

fancy *VERB*
❶ *What do you* ***fancy*** *to eat?*
- **feel like, want, wish for, desire, prefer**

❷ *I* ***fancied*** *I heard a noise downstairs.*
- **imagine, think, believe, suppose**

fantastic *ADJECTIVE*
❶ *The story is full of* ***fantastic*** *creatures.*
- **fanciful, extraordinary, strange, odd, weird, outlandish, far-fetched, incredible, imaginative**

OPPOSITE **realistic**

❷ *(informal) We had a* ***fantastic*** *time at camp.*
- **excellent, first-class, outstanding, superb, wonderful, tremendous, marvellous**

(informal) **brilliant, fabulous, smashing**

fantasy *NOUN*
Rosie had a ***fantasy*** *about being a mermaid.*
- **dream, daydream, delusion, fancy**

far *ADJECTIVE*
❶ *The castle stood in the* ***far*** *north of the country.*
- **distant, faraway, remote**

OPPOSITE **nearby**

❷ *The ferry took us to the* ***far*** *side of the river.*
- **opposite, other**

OPPOSITE **near**

fare *NOUN*
Do you have enough money for the bus ***fare****?*
- **price, charge, cost, payment, fee**

farm *NOUN*

WORD WEB

The formal word for farming is **agriculture**.
A farm which uses no artificial fertilisers or chemicals is an **organic farm**.
A very small farm is a **smallholding**.

A small farm growing fruit and vegetables is a **market garden**.
A small farm in Scotland is a **croft**.
A large cattle farm in America is a **ranch**.

FARM BUILDINGS:

• **barn, byre** or **cowshed, dairy, farmhouse, granary, outhouse, pigsty, stable**

OTHER PARTS OF A FARM:

• **barnyard** or **farmyard, cattle pen, fields, haystack, meadow, paddock, pasture, rick, sheep fold, silo**

ITEMS OF FARM EQUIPMENT:

• **baler, combine harvester, cultivator, drill, harrow, harvester, mower, planter, plough, tractor, trailer**

PEOPLE WHO WORK ON A FARM:

• **agricultural worker,** *(old use)* **dairymaid, farmer, farm labourer, ploughman, shepherd, stockbreeder, tractor driver**

SOME FARM ANIMALS:

• **bull, bullock, chicken** or **hen, cow, duck, goat, goose, horse, pig, sheep, turkey**
Birds kept on a farm are **poultry**.
Cows kept for milk or beef are **cattle**.
Farm animals in general are **livestock**.

farm *VERB*
The MacDonalds had ***farmed*** *the land for centuries.*
• **cultivate, work, till, plough**

fascinate *VERB*
We were ***fascinated*** *by the inventor's workshop.*
• **interest, engross, captivate, enthrall, absorb, beguile, entrance, attract, charm, enchant, delight**
OPPOSITE **bore**

fashion *NOUN*
❶ *The Martians behaved in a peculiar* ***fashion.***
• **way, manner**
❷ *Zoe dresses according to the latest* ***fashion.***
• **trend, vogue, craze, fad, style, look**

fashionable *ADJECTIVE*
Megan has a ***fashionable*** *new hairstyle.*
• **stylish, chic, up-to-date, popular, elegant, smart**
(informal) **trendy, hip, in**
OPPOSITE **unfashionable, out-of-date**

fast *ADJECTIVE*
The robber made a ***fast*** *exit when he heard us coming.*
• **quick, rapid, speedy, swift, brisk, hurried, hasty, high-speed, headlong, breakneck**
(informal) **nippy**
OPPOSITE **slow, unhurried**
Something which goes faster than sound is **supersonic**.
A common simile is **as fast as lightning**.

fast *ADVERB*
❶ *Mr Toad was driving too* ***fast*** *in his motor car.*
• **quickly, speedily, swiftly, rapidly, briskly**
❷ *The boat was stuck* ***fast*** *on the rocks.*
• **firmly, securely, tightly**
❸ *Be quiet! The baby is* ***fast*** *asleep.*
• **deeply, sound, soundly, completely**

fasten *VERB*
❶ *They* ***fastened*** *their ropes to the rock face.*
• **tie, fix, attach, connect, join, link, bind, hitch, clamp, pin, clip, tack, stick**
To fasten a boat is to **anchor** or **moor** it.
To fasten an animal is to **tether** it.
❷ *They* ***fastened*** *the gate with a heavy chain.*
• **secure, seal, lock, bolt, make fast**

fat *ADJECTIVE*
❶ *Your cat will get* ***fat*** *if you overfeed her.*
• **overweight, obese, chubby, plump, podgy, dumpy, flabby, portly, stout, round, rotund**
❷ *The witch opened a big,* ***fat*** *book of spells.*
• **thick, bulky, chunky, weighty, substantial**
OPPOSITE **thin**

fatal *ADJECTIVE*
❶ *The knight delivered a **fatal** wound to his enemy.*
• **deadly, lethal, mortal**
A fatal illness is an **incurable** or **terminal** illness.
❷ *Leaving the door unlocked was a **fatal** mistake.*
• **disastrous, catastrophic, dreadful, calamitous**

fate *NOUN*
❶ *The shipwrecked crew were in the hands of **fate**.*
• **fortune, destiny, providence, chance, luck**
❷ *The prisoner met with a terrible **fate**.*
• **death, end**

fatigue *NOUN*
*Some of the runners were overcome with **fatigue**.*
• **exhaustion, tiredness, weariness, weakness**

fatigued *ADJECTIVE*
*We were all **fatigued** by the time we got home.*
• **exhausted, tired, worn out, weary**
(informal) **all in**

fault *NOUN*
❶ *This DVD has a **fault** in it.*
• **defect, flaw, malfunction, snag, problem, weakness**
❷ *It was my **fault** that we missed our bus.*
• **responsibility, liability**

faultless *ADJECTIVE*
*The dancer's movements were **faultless**.*
• **perfect, flawless, ideal, impeccable**
OPPOSITE **imperfect**

faulty *ADJECTIVE*
*The TV was **faulty**, so we took it back to the shop.*
• **broken, not working, defective, out of order, unusable, damaged**
OPPOSITE **perfect**

favour *NOUN*
❶ *I asked my friend to do me a **favour**.*
• **good deed, good turn, kindness, service, courtesy**
❷ *The captain's plan found **favour** with most of the crew.*
• **approval, support, liking, goodwill**
➤ **to be in favour of something**
*We're all **in favour of** longer holidays.*
• **agree to, approve of, support, like the idea of**

favour *VERB*
*Do you **favour** the idea of free school meals?*
• **approve of, support, back, advocate, choose, like, opt for, prefer**
(informal) **fancy, go for**
OPPOSITE **oppose**

favourable *ADJECTIVE*
❶ *The weather conditions are **favourable** for sailing.*
• **advantageous, helpful, beneficial**
OPPOSITE **unfavourable**
❷ *The film has received **favourable** reviews.*
• **good, positive, complimentary, encouraging, enthusiastic, sympathetic, approving, agreeable**
OPPOSITE **critical, hostile, negative**

favourite *ADJECTIVE*
*What is your **favourite** book?*
• **best-loved, preferred, treasured, dearest, special, top**

fear *NOUN*
*When Garth heard the monster, he trembled with **fear**.*
• **fright, terror, horror, alarm, panic, dread, anxiety, apprehension, trepidation**
OPPOSITE **courage**
A formal word for a special type of fear is **phobia**.
A fear of open spaces is **agoraphobia**.
A fear of spiders is **arachnophobia**.
A fear of enclosed spaces is **claustrophobia**.
A fear or dislike of foreigners is **xenophobia**.

fear *VERB*
❶ *My sister **fears** snakes and spiders.*
• be frightened of, be afraid of, be scared of, dread
❷ *I **fear** we may be too late.*
• suspect, expect, anticipate

fearful *ADJECTIVE*
❶ *The young warrior had a **fearful** look in his eyes.*
• frightened, scared, terrified, afraid, panicky, nervous, anxious, timid
OPPOSITE brave
❷ *The erupting volcano was a **fearful** sight.*
• frightening, terrifying, shocking, fearsome, ghastly, dreadful, appalling, terrible

fearless *ADJECTIVE*
*The **fearless** explorers entered the dark cave.*
• brave, courageous, daring, heroic, valiant, intrepid, plucky
OPPOSITE cowardly

fearsome *ADJECTIVE*
*The dragon yawned, revealing a **fearsome** set of teeth.*
• frightening, fearful, horrifying, terrifying, dreadful, awesome
(informal) scary

feasible *ADJECTIVE*
*Is it **feasible** to fly to Paris and back in a day?*
• possible, practicable, practical, achievable, realistic, workable
OPPOSITES impractical, impossible

feast *NOUN*
*The king held a great **feast** to celebrate his birthday.*
• banquet, dinner
(informal) spread

feat *NOUN*
*The trapeze artists performed many daring **feats**.*
• act, action, deed, exploit, achievement, performance

feather *NOUN*
A large feather is a **plume**.
All the feathers on a bird are its **plumage**.
Soft, fluffy feathers are **down**.
A feather used as a pen is a **quill**.
for ways to describe a bird's feathers see **bird**

feature *NOUN*
❶ *The room has several unusual **features**.*
• characteristic, detail, point, aspect, quality, peculiarity, trait, facet
A person's features are their **face**.
for ways to describe facial features see **face**
❷ *There was a **feature** about our school in the newspaper.*
• article, report, story, item, piece

feature *VERB*
❶ *The film **features** some thrilling car chases.*
• give prominence to, highlight, spotlight, show off
❷ *A new cartoon character **features** in this film.*
• appear, take part, figure, star

fee *NOUN*
*The club charges an annual membership **fee**.*
• charge, cost, payment, price
A fee to use a private road or bridge is a **toll**.

feeble *ADJECTIVE*
❶ *The elderly knight looked tired and **feeble**.*
• weak, frail, infirm, delicate, poorly, sickly, puny, weary, weedy
OPPOSITES strong, powerful
❷ *I made a **feeble** attempt to stop the ball.*
*Do you expect me to believe that **feeble** excuse?*
• weak, poor, ineffective, inadequate, unconvincing, tame, flimsy, lame

feed *VERB* **feeds, feeding, fed**
*We have enough sandwiches to **feed** six people.*
• provide for, cater for, give food to, nourish
➤ **to feed on**
*The leopard was **feeding on** its prey.*
• eat, consume, devour

A B C D E F G H I J K L M N O P Q R S T U V W X Y Z

feel *VERB* **feels, feeling, felt**
❶ *I **felt** the llama's soft, woolly fur.*
• **touch, caress, stroke, fondle**
❷ *When the candle went out, we had to **feel** our way out of the cave.*
• **grope, fumble**
❸ *It **feels** colder today.*
• **appear, seem, strike you as**
❹ *Older people tend to **feel** the cold.*
• **notice, be aware of, be conscious of, experience, suffer from**
❺ *I **feel** that it's time we made a start.*
• **think, believe, consider**
➤ **to feel like**
*Do you **feel like** going for a walk?*
• **want, wish for, desire**
(informal) **fancy**

WRITING TIPS

You can use these words to describe how something feels:
• **bristly, coarse, creamy, crinkly, crunchy, dry, feathery, fibrous, fine, fluffy, grainy, hairy, knobbly, lumpy, moist, mushy, papery, rough, rubbery, runny, silky, smooth, soft, spongy, springy, squashy, sticky, stiff, stringy, velvety, watery, woolly**
(informal) **gooey, squishy**
The ground felt spongy under their feet, sucking at them gently at every step that seemed taken only just in time to keep from sinking.—THE EAGLE OF THE NINTH, Rosemary Sutcliff

feel *NOUN*
*I love the **feel** of warm sand between my toes.*
• **feeling, sensation, touch**

feeling *NOUN*
❶ *The cat had lost all **feeling** in its paw.*
• **sense of touch, sensation, sensitivity**
❷ *I didn't mean to hurt your **feelings**.*
• **emotion, passion, sentiment**
❸ *I have a **feeling** that something is wrong.*
• **suspicion, notion, inkling, hunch, idea, impression, fancy, intuition**
❹ *There was a good **feeling** at the party.*
• **atmosphere, mood, air, aura**

fell *past tense see* **fall**

female *ADJECTIVE*
for female human beings see **woman**
for female animals see **animal**
OPPOSITE **male**

feminine *ADJECTIVE*
*Lisa likes to dress in a **feminine** style.*
• **womanly, ladylike, girlish**
(informal) **girly**
OPPOSITE **masculine**

fence *NOUN*
*The mansion was surrounded by a tall **fence**.*
• **railing, barrier, wall, paling, stockade, hedge**

fence *VERB*
*The field was **fenced** with a thorn hedge.*
• **enclose, surround, bound, encircle**

fend *VERB*
➤ **to fend for yourself**
*The lion cubs will soon have to **fend for** themselves.*
• **look after, take care of, care for**
➤ **to fend someone** or **something off**
*The knight raised his shield to **fend off** the blow.*
• **repel, resist, ward off, fight off, hold off, thwart**

ferocious *ADJECTIVE*
*The mansion was guarded by a **ferocious** dog.*
• **fierce, fearsome, savage, wild, vicious, violent, bloodthirsty, brutal**
OPPOSITE **tame**

fertile *ADJECTIVE*
*The surrounding countryside was green and **fertile**.*
• **fruitful, productive, rich, fecund**
OPPOSITES **barren, sterile**

fertilise *VERB*
If you want good crops, you must ***fertilise*** *the soil.*
• **enrich, feed, manure**

fervent *ADJECTIVE*
My gran is a ***fervent*** *supporter of the local team.*
• **eager, keen, avid, ardent, committed, enthusiastic, fanatical, passionate, zealous**
OPPOSITES **apathetic, lukewarm**

festival *NOUN*
The town holds a ***festival*** *every summer.*
• **carnival, fiesta, fête, gala, fair, celebration, jamboree**
A celebration of a special anniversary is a **jubilee.**
for religious festivals see **religion**

festive *ADJECTIVE*
Chinese New Year is a ***festive*** *occasion.*
• **cheerful, happy, merry, jolly, cheery, joyful, joyous, jovial, light-hearted, celebratory**
OPPOSITES **gloomy, sombre**

fetch *VERB*
❶ *I* ***fetched*** *the shopping from the car.*
• **get, bring, carry, collect, transfer, transport, convey, pick up, retrieve, obtain**
❷ *If we sell our car, how much will it* ***fetch****?*
• **make, raise, sell for, go for, bring in, earn**

feud *NOUN*
There has been a ***feud*** *between our families for years.*
• **quarrel, dispute, conflict, hostility, enmity, rivalry, strife, antagonism**
A feud that lasts a long time is a **vendetta.**

feverish *ADJECTIVE*
❶ *I felt* ***feverish*** *with the cold.*
When you are feverish you are **hot** and **shivery.**
With a bad fever you may become **delirious.**
❷ *There was* ***feverish*** *activity in the kitchen.*
• **frenzied, frantic, frenetic, excited, agitated, hectic, busy, hurried, impatient, restless**

few *DETERMINER*
I've only been abroad a ***few*** *times.*
Few *astronauts have walked on the moon.*
• **not many, hardly any, a small number of, a handful of**
OPPOSITE **many**

fibre *NOUN*
Rope is made by twisting ***fibres*** *together.*
• **thread, strand, hair, filament**

fickle *ADJECTIVE*
Some ***fickle*** *supporters deserted the team when they lost.*
• **changeable, disloyal, unfaithful, unreliable, erratic, inconsistent, unpredictable, inconstant**
OPPOSITE **loyal**

fiction *NOUN*
❶ *Roald Dahl wrote* ***fiction*** *for both children and adults.*
for various kinds of literature see **writing**
❷ *Her account of what happened was pure* ***fiction****.*
• **fantasy, invention, fabrication, lies**
OPPOSITE **fact**

fictional *ADJECTIVE*
Harry Potter is a ***fictional*** *character.*
• **imaginary, made-up, invented, fanciful**
OPPOSITES **factual, real**

fictitious *ADJECTIVE*
The spy was using a ***fictitious*** *name.*
• **false, fake, fabricated, fraudulent, bogus, assumed, spurious, unreal**
OPPOSITES **genuine, real**

fiddle *VERB*
❶ *Who's been* ***fiddling*** *with the DVD player?*
• **tinker, meddle, tamper, play about, mess about, twiddle**
❷ *(informal) Mr Filch had been* ***fiddling*** *the bank account for years.*
• **falsify, alter, rig**
(informal) **cook the books**

fiddly *ADJECTIVE*
*Icing a cake can be a **fiddly** job.*
• **intricate, complicated, awkward, involved**
OPPOSITE **simple**

fidget *VERB*
*I begin to **fidget** when I'm bored.*
• **be restless, fiddle about, play about, mess about**

fidgety *ADJECTIVE*
*After waiting an hour, we began to get **fidgety**.*
• **restless, unsettled, impatient, agitated, jumpy, nervy**
OPPOSITE **calm**

field *NOUN*
❶ *Cattle were grazing in the **field**.*
• **meadow, pasture**
A small field for horses is a **paddock**.
An area of grass in a village is a **green**.
❷ *The **field** is too wet to play football.*
• **ground, pitch, playing field**
❸ *Electronics is not my **field**.*
• **special interest, speciality, area of study**

fierce *ADJECTIVE*
❶ *The travellers were killed in a **fierce** attack by armed bandits.*
• **vicious, ferocious, savage, brutal, violent, wild, cruel, merciless, ruthless, pitiless**
❷ *Our team will face **fierce** opposition in the final.*
• **strong, keen, eager, aggressive, competitive, passionate, relentless**
❸ *The explorers braved the **fierce** heat of the desert sun.*
• **blazing, intense, raging**

fiery *ADJECTIVE*
❶ *It's best to avoid the **fiery** heat of the midday sun.*
• **blazing, burning, hot, intense, fierce, raging, flaming, red-hot, glowing**
❷ *My great aunt has always had a **fiery** temper.*
• **violent, passionate, excitable, angry, furious**

fight *NOUN*
❶ *The warriors faced each other for a **fight** to the death.*
Fighting is **combat** or **hostilities**.
A fight between armies is a **battle**.
A minor unplanned battle is a **skirmish**.
A series of battles is a **campaign** or **war**.
A minor fight is a **brawl, scrap, scuffle** or **tussle**.
A fight arranged between two people is a **duel**.
❷ *We support the **fight** to save the rainforest.*
• **campaign, crusade, struggle**

fight *VERB* **fights, fighting, fought**
❶ *Two seagulls were **fighting** over a scrap of bread.*
• **have a fight, scrap, scuffle, exchange blows, come to blows**
❷ *The two countries **fought** each other in the war.*
• **do battle with, wage war with, attack**
Fighting with swords is **fencing**.
Fighting with fists is **boxing**.
Fighting in which you try to throw your opponent to the ground is **wrestling**.
Fighting sports such as karate and judo are **martial arts**.
❸ *We will **fight** the decision to close our local library.*
• **protest against, oppose, resist, make a stand, take a stand against, campaign against**

fighter *NOUN*

WORD WEB

PEOPLE WHO FIGHT IN A WAR OR CONFLICT:
• **guerrilla, soldier, warrior**
see also **soldier**

PEOPLE WHO FOUGHT IN PAST TIMES:
• **archer, gladiator, knight, ninja, samurai**

PEOPLE WHO FIGHT AS A SPORT:
• **boxer, fencer, kick-boxer, wrestler**

figure *NOUN*

❶ *Please write the **figure** '8' on the board.*
• **number, numeral, digit, integer**
❷ *What **figure** would you put on your old bike?*
• **price, value, amount, sum, cost**
❸ *Ballet dancers need to have a good **figure**.*
• **body, build, form, shape**
❹ *Inside the temple were several clay **figures**.*
• **statue, carving, sculpture**
❺ *The **figure** on page 22 shows the annual rainfall for Wales.*
• **diagram, graph, illustration, drawing**

figure *VERB*

*Donald Duck **figures** in many cartoons.*
• **appear, feature, take part**

➤ **to figure out**
*We couldn't **figure out** what the riddle meant.*
• **work out, make out, understand, see**

figure of speech *NOUN*

WORD WEB

SOME COMMON FIGURES OF SPEECH:
• **alliteration, metaphor, onomatopoeia, personification, simile**

file *NOUN*

❶ *I keep all my award certificates in a **file**.*
• **folder, binder, cover**
A file containing information, especially secret information, is a **dossier**.
❷ *Please walk in a single **file**.*
• **line, row, column, rank, queue, procession**

file *VERB*

❶ *I **file** all my letters in a pink folder.*
• **organise, put away, store**
❷ *We **filed** into the hall for assembly.*
• **walk in a line, march, troop, parade**

fill *VERB*

❶ *Dad **filled** the trolley with shopping.*
• **load, pack, stuff, cram, top up**
To fill a tyre with air is to **inflate** it.
OPPOSITE **empty**
❷ *What can I use to **fill** this hole?*
• **close up, plug, seal, block up, stop up**
❸ *Sightseers **filled** the streets.*
• **crowd, jam, block, obstruct**
(informal) **bung up**

filling *NOUN*

*The **filling** started to ooze out of my sandwich.*
• **stuffing, insides, innards, padding**

film *NOUN*

❶ *There is a good **film** on TV tonight.*
• **picture, video, DVD**
(North American) **movie**
A long film is a **feature film**.
A short excerpt from a film is a **clip**.
A script for a film is a **screenplay** and a writer of screenplays is a **screenwriter**.
A well-known film actor is a **film star**.
A theatre where films are shown is a **cinema**, **picture house** or *(North American)* **movie theatre**.
❷ *There was a **film** of oil on the water.*
• **coat, coating, layer, covering, sheet, skin**
A large patch of oil floating on water is a **slick**.

filth *NOUN*

*The walls of the dungeon were covered with **filth**.*
• **dirt, grime, muck, mess, mud, sludge, scum, slime**

filthy *ADJECTIVE*

❶ *Those trainers are **filthy**!*
• **dirty, mucky, messy, grimy, grubby, muddy, soiled, stained**
OPPOSITE **clean**
❷ *Don't drink the **filthy** water from the well.*
• **cloudy, contaminated, foul, impure, polluted, slimy, smelly, stinking**
OPPOSITE **pure**

A B C D E F G H I J K L M N O P Q R S T U V W X Y Z

final *ADJECTIVE*
❶ *The **final** moments of the match were very tense.*
• **last, closing, concluding**
OPPOSITE **opening**
❷ *What was the **final** result?*
• **eventual, ultimate**

finally *ADVERB*
*I've **finally** managed to finish my book.*
• **eventually, at last, in the end**

finances *PLURAL NOUN*
*Are your **finances** doing well?*
• **money, bank account, funds, resources, assets, wealth**

find *VERB* **finds, finding, found**
❶ *Did you **find** any fossils on the beach?*
• **come across, discover, see, spot, locate, encounter, stumble across, unearth**
❷ *The children never **found** the secret door again.*
• **trace, track down, recover, retrieve**
OPPOSITE **lose**
❸ *Did the doctor **find** what was wrong?*
• **find out, detect, identify, diagnose, ascertain**
❹ *You will **find** that building a tree house is hard work.*
• **find out, become aware, realise, learn, recognise, notice, observe**

findings *PLURAL NOUN*
*The detective told us of his **findings**.*
• **judgement, conclusion, verdict, decision**

fine *ADJECTIVE*
❶ *The young musicians gave a **fine** performance.*
• **excellent, first-class, superb, splendid, admirable, commendable, good**
OPPOSITE **bad**
❷ *As the weather was **fine**, we took a picnic.*
• **sunny, fair, bright, clear, cloudless, pleasant**
OPPOSITE **dull**
❸ *Spiders spin very **fine** thread for their webs.*
• **delicate, fragile, thin, flimsy, slender, slim**
OPPOSITE **thick**
❹ *The desert dunes were made of **fine** sand.*
• **dusty, powdery**
OPPOSITE **coarse**

fine *NOUN*
*The boy had to pay a **fine** for dropping litter.*
• **penalty, charge, damages**

finger *NOUN*
Your short fat finger is your **thumb**.
The finger next to your thumb is your **index finger**, because it is the finger you point with or indicate things with.
The next finger is your **middle finger**.
The next finger is your **ring finger**, because you can wear a wedding or engagement ring on that finger of your left hand.
Your small thin finger is your **little finger** or *(Scottish & North American)* **pinkie**.
The joints in your fingers are your **knuckles**.

finger *VERB*
*Please don't **finger** the food on the table.*
• **touch, feel, poke, fondle**

finish *VERB*
❶ *When are you likely to **finish** your homework?*
• **complete, reach the end of, cease, round off**
❷ *The film should **finish** around nine o'clock.*
• **end, stop, conclude, terminate**
(informal) **wind up**
❸ *I've already **finished** my bag of crisps.*
• **consume, use up, get through, exhaust**
(informal) **polish off**
OPPOSITE **start**

finish *NOUN*
*We stayed to watch the parade until the **finish**.*
• **end, close, conclusion, completion, result, termination**
OPPOSITE **start**

fire *NOUN*
*The campers toasted marshmallows in the **fire**.*
• **blaze, flames, burning, combustion**
A very big hot fire is an **inferno**.

An open fire out of doors is a **bonfire**.
An enclosed fire which produces great heat is a **furnace**.
An enclosed fire for cooking food is an **oven**.
An enclosed fire for making pottery is a **kiln**.
A team of people whose job is to put out fires is a **fire brigade**.
A member of a fire brigade is a **firefighter**.

fire *VERB*

❶ *The clay will harden if you **fire** it in a kiln.*
• **bake, harden, heat**

❷ *The soldier aimed his rifle and **fired** two shots.*
• **shoot, discharge, let off, set off**
To fire a missile is to **launch** it.

❸ *(informal) Miss Stark **fired** her assistant for being late for work.*
• **dismiss, sack**

firm *NOUN*

*Mr Perkins owns a **firm** that makes biscuits.*
• **company, business, organisation, enterprise**

firm *ADJECTIVE*

❶ *The surface of the planet was dry and **firm**.*
• **hard, solid, dense, compact, rigid, set**
OPPOSITE **soft**

❷ *Make sure the knots in the rope are **firm**.*
• **secure, tight, strong, stable, fixed, sturdy, steady**

❸ *Zelda had a **firm** belief in the power of magic.*
• **definite, certain, sure, decided, determined, resolute, unshakeable, unwavering**
OPPOSITE **unsure**

❹ *The two girls have become **firm** friends.*
• **close, devoted, faithful, loyal, constant, dependable, reliable**

first *ADJECTIVE*

❶ *The **first** inhabitants of the area were Picts.*
• **earliest, original**

❷ *The **first** thing to do in an emergency is to keep calm.*
• **principal, key, main, fundamental, basic, chief**

➤ **at first**
*At **first**, we thought the dog was asleep.*
• **at the beginning, to start with, initially, originally**

first-class or **first-rate** *ADJECTIVE*

*That was a **first-class** game of chess.*
• **excellent, first rate, outstanding, superb, exceptional, superior, superlative, top-notch**
OPPOSITES **second-rate, mediocre**

fish *NOUN*

WORD WEB

SOME TYPES OF FISH:

• **brill, carp, catfish, chub, cod, conger eel, dace, eel, flounder, goldfish, grayling, gudgeon, haddock, hake, halibut, herring, lamprey, ling, mackerel, minnow, mullet, perch, pike, pilchard, piranha, plaice, roach, salmon, sardine, sawfish, shark, skate, sole, sprat, squid, stickleback, sturgeon, swordfish, trout, tuna, turbot, whitebait, whiting**

for types of shellfish see **shellfish**

Young fish are **fry**.
An informal word for a very small fish is a **tiddler**.
A large number of fish swimming together is a **shoal**.
A person who sells fish is a **fishmonger**.
The sport or job of catching fish is **fishing**.
Fishing with a rod and a line is **angling** and a person who does this is an **angler**.
Fishing with nets from a boat is **trawling**.
Fishing equipment is **tackle**.

fit *ADJECTIVE*

❶ *Her wedding dress was **fit** for a princess.*
• **suitable, appropriate, fitting, right, good enough, worthy**
OPPOSITE **unsuitable**

❷ *I walk to school every day to keep **fit**.*
• **healthy, well, strong, robust**
(old use) **hale and hearty**
OPPOSITE **unhealthy**
A common simile is **as fit as a fiddle**.

❸ *After a long ride, the horses were **fit** to collapse.*
• **ready, liable, likely, about**

A B C D E F G H I J K L M N O P Q R S T U V W X Y Z

fit *VERB*
❶ *We need to **fit** a new lock on the door.*
• install, put in place, position
❷ *This key doesn't **fit** the lock.*
*He **fits** the description of the wanted criminal.*
• match, correspond to, go together with, tally with
❸ *Her speech perfectly **fitted** the occasion.*
• be suitable for, be appropriate to, suit

fit *NOUN*
*My friend and I had a **fit** of the giggles.*
• attack, bout, outburst, spell

fitting *ADJECTIVE*
*Scoring the winning goal was a **fitting** end to his career.*
• suitable, appropriate, apt, proper
OPPOSITE inappropriate

fix *VERB*
❶ *The soldier **fixed** a bayonet to the end of his rifle.*
• fasten, attach, connect, join, link
❷ *We **fixed** the tent poles in the ground.*
• set, secure, make firm, stabilise
❸ *Let's **fix** a time for the party.*
• decide on, agree on, set, arrange, settle, determine, specify, finalise
❹ *(informal) Dad says he can **fix** my bike.*
• repair, mend
(informal) sort, put right

fix *NOUN*
*(informal) Can you help me? I'm in a **fix**.*
• difficulty, mess, predicament, plight
(informal) jam, hole

fizz *VERB*
*The lemonade **fizzed** when I opened the bottle.*
• hiss, bubble, foam, froth

fizzy *ADJECTIVE*
*Could I have a bottle of **fizzy** water, please?*
• sparkling, bubbly, effervescent, gassy, foaming
OPPOSITE still

flabby *ADJECTIVE*
*This exercise is good for **flabby** thighs.*
• fat, fleshy, sagging, slack, loose, floppy, limp
OPPOSITE firm

flag *NOUN*
*The street was decorated with **flags** for the carnival.*
• banner, pennant, streamer
The flag of a regiment is its **colours** or **standard**.
A flag flown on a ship is an **ensign**.
Decorative strips of small flags are **bunting**.

flag *VERB*
*By evening, our energy was starting to **flag**.*
• diminish, lessen, decrease, decline, weaken, slump, fade, dwindle, wane

flap *VERB*
*The sail **flapped** in the wind.*
• flutter, sway, swing, wave about, thrash about

flare *VERB*
➤ **to flare up**
❶ *The fire **flared up** when we blew on it.*
• blaze, burn brightly, flame
❷ *My sister **flares up** at the slightest thing.*
• become angry, lose your temper

flash *VERB*
*We saw a light **flash** from an upstairs window.*
• shine, beam, blaze, flare, glare, gleam, glint, flicker, glimmer, sparkle

flash *NOUN*
*There were **flashes** of lightning in the sky.*
• blaze, flare, beam, ray, shaft, burst, gleam, glint, flicker, glimmer, sparkle
for other ways to describe light see **light**

flat *ADJECTIVE*
❶ *You need a **flat** surface to write on.*
• even, level, smooth, plane
A common simile is **as flat as a pancake**.
OPPOSITE uneven
❷ *I lay **flat** on the ground.*
• horizontal, outstretched, spread out

To be lying face downwards is to be **prone**.
To be lying face upwards is to be **supine**.
OPPOSITE upright
❸ *The robot spoke in a **flat**, electronic voice.*
• dull, boring, lifeless, uninteresting, monotonous, tedious
OPPOSITE lively
❹ *The front tyre of my bike was **flat**.*
• deflated, punctured
OPPOSITE inflated
❺ *Our request met with a **flat** refusal.*
• outright, straight, positive, absolute, total, utter, point-blank

flat *NOUN*
for places where people live see **building**

flatten *VERB*
❶ *We **flattened** the crumpled map on the desk.*
• smooth, press, roll out, iron out
❷ *The earthquake **flattened** several buildings.*
• demolish, destroy, knock down, pull down, level
❸ *The young plants were **flattened** by the rain.*
• squash, crush, trample,
(informal) squish

flaunt *VERB*
*She's always **flaunting** her expensive jewellery.*
• show off, display, parade, exhibit

flavour *NOUN*
❶ *I don't like the **flavour** of raw onions.*
• taste, tang
for ways to describe flavour see **food**
❷ *Which **flavour** of ice cream do you like best?*
• kind, sort, variety

flavour *VERB*
*The sauce was **flavoured** with garlic and herbs.*
• season, spice

flaw *NOUN*
❶ *Pride was the only **flaw** in his character.*
• weakness, fault, shortcoming, failing, lapse
❷ *I can see a **flaw** in your argument.*
• error, inaccuracy, mistake, slip
❸ *There is a tiny **flaw** in this glass.*
• imperfection, defect, blemish, break, chip, crack

fleck *NOUN*
*There were a few **flecks** of paint on the carpet.*
• spot, speck, flake, dot, dab
see also **bit**

flee *VERB* **flees, fleeing, fled**
*When they heard the alarm, the robbers **fled**.*
• run away, bolt, fly, escape, get away, take off, hurry off
(informal) clear off, make off, scarper

fleet *NOUN*
A fleet of boats or small ships is a **flotilla**.
A fleet of warships is an **armada**.
A military fleet belonging to a country is its **navy**.

fleeting *ADJECTIVE*
*I only caught a **fleeting** glimpse of the badger.*
• brief, momentary, quick, short, passing
OPPOSITES lengthy, lasting

flesh *NOUN*
• tissue, muscle, fat
An animal's flesh used for food is **meat**.
The decaying flesh of a dead animal is **carrion**.

flew *past tense see* **fly**

flex *NOUN*
*Don't trip over the **flex** of the iron!*
• cable, lead, wire

flexible *ADJECTIVE*
❶ *I need a pair of trainers with **flexible** soles.*
• bendable, supple, pliable, bendy, elastic, springy
OPPOSITES rigid, inflexible
❷ *My working hours are very **flexible**.*
• adjustable, adaptable, variable, open
OPPOSITE fixed

flicker *VERB*
*The candlelight **flickered** in the draught.*
• twinkle, glimmer, waver, flutter, blink, shimmer

A B C D E F G H I J K L M N O P Q R S T U V W X Y Z

flight *NOUN*
❶ *He is an expert on the history of **flight**.*
• flying, aviation, aeronautics
for other words to do with flying see **aircraft**
❷ *No-one saw the king's **flight** from the battlefield.*
• escape, getaway, retreat

flimsy *ADJECTIVE*
❶ *The kite was so **flimsy** that it broke apart.*
• fragile, delicate, frail, brittle, weak, wobbly, shaky, rickety,
OPPOSITE sturdy, robust
❷ *The fairy wore a dress of the **flimsiest** silk.*
• thin, fine, light, lightweight, floaty

flinch *VERB*
*He **flinched** as an arrow flew past his head.*
• back off, draw back, falter, recoil, shrink back, start, wince

fling *VERB* **flings, flinging, flung**
*I **flung** a stone into the pond.*
• throw, cast, sling, toss, hurl, pitch
(informal) chuck, bung

flip *VERB*
*We **flipped** a coin to decide who should go first.*
• toss, flick, spin

float *VERB*
*We watched the twigs **float** gently down the river.*
• sail, drift, glide, slip, slide, waft

flock *NOUN*
for groups of animals see **group**

flock *VERB*
*People **flocked** round to see what was happening.*
• crowd, gather, collect, herd, jostle

flood *NOUN*
❶ *The **flood** of water swept away the bridge.*
• deluge, inundation, rush, torrent, spate
❷ *The restaurant has received a **flood** of complaints.*
• succession, barrage, storm, volley

flood *VERB*
❶ *The river burst its banks and **flooded** the valley.*
• drown, swamp, inundate, submerge, immerse, engulf
❷ *We have been **flooded** with entries for our competition.*
• overwhelm, swamp, besiege

floor *NOUN*
❶ *The children in the audience sat on the **floor**.*
• ground, flooring, base
A floor on a ship is a **deck**.
❷ *Doreen's flat is on the top **floor**.*
• storey, level, tier, stage

flop *VERB*
❶ *I was so tired that I just **flopped** on to my bed.*
• collapse, drop, fall, slump
❷ *The plants will **flop** if you don't water them.*
• dangle, droop, hang down, sag, wilt
❸ *(informal) The first film **flopped**, but the sequel was a big hit.*
• be unsuccessful, fail, founder, fall flat

floppy *ADJECTIVE*
*The dog had long, **floppy** ears.*
• droopy, limp, saggy, soft
OPPOSITES stiff, rigid

flounder *VERB*
*The soldiers **floundered** through the mud.*
• struggle, stumble, stagger, fumble, wallow, blunder, falter

flourish *VERB*
❶ *My tomato plants are **flourishing** this year.*
• grow well, thrive, bloom, blossom, flower
OPPOSITE die
❷ *Sales on our website have continued to **flourish**.*
• be successful, do well, prosper, thrive, boom, succeed, progress, develop, increase
OPPOSITE fail
❸ *Ted **flourished** a newspaper to attract my attention.*
• wave, brandish, wield, shake

flow *VERB*
*The rainwater **flowed** along the gutter.*
• **run, stream, pour, glide**
To flow slowly is to **dribble, drip, ooze, seep** or **trickle.**
To flow fast is to **cascade, gush** or **sweep.**
To flow with sudden force is to **spurt** or **squirt.**
To flow over the edge of something is to **overflow** or **spill.**
When blood flows from someone, they **bleed.**
When the tide flows out, it **ebbs.**

flow *NOUN*
❶ *It's hard work rowing against the **flow**.*
• **current, tide, drift**
❷ *There was a steady **flow** of water into the pond.*
• **stream, flood, cascade, gush, rush, spate**

flower *NOUN*

WORD WEB

A single flower is a **bloom.**
A mass of small flowers growing together is **blossom.**
Flowers in a vase are an **arrangement.**
A bunch of flowers arranged for a special occasion is a **bouquet, posy** or **spray.**
Flowers arranged in a circle are a **garland** or **wreath.**
A person who sells and arranges flowers is a **florist.**

SOME WILD FLOWERS:
• **bluebell, buttercup, catkin, clover, cornflower, cowslip, daisy, dandelion, foxglove, harebell, heather, orchid, poppy, primrose**

SOME POPULAR CULTIVATED FLOWERS:
• **azalea, begonia, carnation, chrysanthemum, crocus, cyclamen, daffodil, dahlia, forget-me-not, freesia, fuchsia, geranium, gladiolus, hollyhock, hyacinth, iris, lilac, lily, lupin, marigold, nasturtium, pansy, peony, petunia, phlox, rose, snowdrop, sunflower, tulip, violet, water lily**

THE MAIN PARTS OF A FLOWER ARE:
• **anther, filament, ovary, petal, pistil, pollen, sepal, stamen, stigma, style**
The sweet liquid collected by bees from flowers is **nectar.**

flower *VERB*
*Most plants **flower** in the summer.*
• **bloom, blossom, bud**

fluffy *ADJECTIVE*
*Four **fluffy** ducklings were swimming in the pond.*
• **feathery, downy, furry, fuzzy, hairy, woolly, shaggy, soft**

fluid *NOUN*
*An oily **fluid** oozed from the pipe.*
• **liquid, solution, juice**
OPPOSITE **solid**

fluke *NOUN*
*It was a **fluke** that the ball went into the net.*
• **chance, accident, stroke of good luck**

flush *VERB*
*Rory **flushed** with embarrassment.*
• **blush, go red, colour, redden, burn**

flustered *ADJECTIVE*
*I get **flustered** when I have to read in assembly.*
• **confused, upset, bothered, agitated, unsettled, ruffled**
(informal) **rattled**
OPPOSITE **calm**

flutter *VERB*
*A moth **fluttered** about the light bulb.*
• **flap, beat, flicker, quiver, tremble, vibrate**

fly *NOUN*
for various insects see **insect**

A B C D E F G H I J K L M N O P Q R S T U V W X Y Z

fly *VERB* **flies, flying, flew, flown**

❶ *Two swallows were **flying** high in the sky.*
• **glide, swoop, flit, hover, float**
for ways to describe how birds move see **bird**

❷ *Suddenly the eagle **flew** into the air.*
• **rise, soar, mount, take off**

❸ *The ship was **flying** the British flag.*
• **display, show, hoist, raise**

❹ *Doesn't time **fly**!*
• **go quickly, pass quickly, rush by**

foam *NOUN*

*The bath water was covered with pinkish **foam**.*
• **bubbles, froth, suds, lather**
Foam made by seawater is **surf** or **spume**.

foam *VERB*

*The mixture in the cauldron **foamed** and gurgled.*
• **froth, bubble, fizz, boil, seethe, lather**

focus *NOUN*

❶ *Can you adjust the **focus** on your camera?*
• **clarity, sharpness**

❷ *The new lion cubs were the **focus** of everyone's attention.*
• **centre, focal point, target, core, pivot**

focus *VERB*

➤ **to focus on**
*Our teacher wants us to **focus on** our spelling.*
• **concentrate on, think about, examine, look at**

fog *NOUN*

*The top of the mountain was covered with **fog**.*
Thin fog is **haze** or **mist**.
A thick mixture of fog and smoke is **smog**.

foggy *ADJECTIVE*

❶ *It was too **foggy** to see through the windows.*
• **misty, hazy, murky, cloudy, smoggy**

❷ *My photo of the horses came out **foggy**.*
• **blurred, fuzzy, indistinct, out of focus**
OPPOSITES **clear, in focus**

foil *VERB*

*The guard-dog **foiled** their plan to break into the house.*
• **frustrate, thwart, block, prevent, obstruct, stop, check, halt**

fold *VERB*

***Fold** the paper along the dotted line.*
• **bend, double over, crease, pleat**

fold *NOUN*

❶ *She smoothed the soft **folds** of her dress.*
• **crease, furrow, layer**
A fold which is pressed into a garment is a **pleat**.

❷ *The dog drove the sheep into the **fold**.*
• **enclosure, pen**

folder *NOUN*

*I keep all my art work in a **folder**.*
• **file, binder, wallet, portfolio**

follow *VERB*

❶ *Why does thunder always **follow** lightning?*
• **come after, succeed, replace**
OPPOSITE **precede**

❷ *I think that car is **following** us!*
• **go after, chase, pursue, track, trail, tail, stalk, hunt, shadow**

❸ ***Follow** this path until you reach the river.*
• **go along, keep to**

❹ *I **followed** the instructions on the packet.*
• **carry out, comply with, heed, obey, observe**

❺ *Which football team do you **follow**?*
• **be a fan of, support**

❻ *We found it hard to **follow** what the creature was saying.*
• **understand, comprehend, grasp, take in, catch**

❼ *Although we are the same age, it doesn't **follow** that we are friends.*
• **mean, happen, result, ensue, arise, come about**

follower *NOUN*

Someone who follows you in a job is your **successor**.
Someone who follows a person or animal to try to catch them is a **hunter** or **pursuer**.

Someone who continually follows a person about is a **stalker**.
Someone who follows a person's teaching is a **disciple**.
Someone who follows a football team, etc. is a **fan** or **supporter**.

fond *ADJECTIVE*
❶ *Mrs Walker gave her pet poodle a* ***fond*** *kiss.*
• **loving, tender, affectionate**
❷ *Anna had a* ***fond*** *hope that she would become a film star.*
• **foolish, silly, unrealistic, fanciful**
➤ **to be fond of**
I'm very ***fond of*** *chocolate cake.*
• **be keen on, be partial to, like, love**

food *NOUN*
The banquet table was laid out with all kinds of ***food****.*
• **foodstuffs, rations, provisions, refreshments, eatables, nourishment, nutrition**
(informal) **grub, nosh**
for meat and foods made from meat see **meat**
The food that you normally eat or choose to eat is your **diet**.
A diet which includes no meat is a **vegetarian** diet.
A diet which includes no animal products is a **vegan** diet.
Food which includes fish or shellfish is **seafood**.
Foods made from milk, butter or cheese are **dairy foods**.
Food for farm animals is **fodder**.

WORD WEB

SOME TYPES OF SEAFOOD:

• **bloater, bream, caviare, cod, crab, eel, haddock, halibut, herring, kipper, lobster, mackerel, monkfish, mussels, oysters, pilchard, plaice, prawn, salmon, sardine, scampi, sea bass, shrimp, sole, sprat, trout, tuna, whelks, whitebait, whiting**

SOME DAIRY FOODS:

• **butter, cheese, cream, curds, ice cream, milk, yoghurt**
for types of cheese see **cheese**

FOODS MADE FROM FLOUR OR CEREALS:

• **bagel, batter, biscuits** or *(North American)* **cookies, bread, bun, chapatti, cornflakes, cracker, crispbread, dumpling, flatbread, muesli, nan, oatcake, pancake, pastry, pitta bread, poppadom, popcorn, porridge, rice cake, roll, scone, toast, tortilla, waffle**

SOME PREPARED DISHES OF FOOD:

• **balti, barbecue, broth, burger, casserole, chilli, chips** or *(North American)* **French fries, couscous, crisps, curry, dhal, falafel, fritter, goulash, hummus, kebab, lasagne, meatball, nachos, noodles, omelette, pakora, panini, pasta, pie, pizza, quiche, risotto, samosa, sandwich, soufflé, soup, stew, stir-fry, sushi, teriyaki**
for types of pasta see **pasta**

SOME PUDDINGS AND OTHER SWEET FOODS:

• **brownie, cake, chocolate, crumble, cupcake, custard, gateau, honey, jam, jelly, marmalade, marzipan, meringue, mousse, muffin, sponge, steamed pudding, sugar, tart, treacle, trifle**
For fruits and vegetables see **fruit, vegetable**

SOME FLAVOURINGS AND SAUCES FOR FOOD:

• **chilli, chutney, French dressing, garlic, gravy, herbs, ketchup, mayonnaise, mustard, pepper, pesto, pickle, salsa, salt, soy sauce, spices, vinegar**
Things like salt and pepper which you add to food are **condiments** or **seasoning**.

WRITING TIPS

You can use these words to describe food:

TO DESCRIBE HOW IT LOOKS OR FEELS:

• **chewy, creamy, crispy, crumbly, crunchy, doughy, dry, flaky, greasy, juicy, leathery, lumpy, milky, mushy, rubbery, runny, slimy, sloppy, smooth, soggy, soupy, spongy, sticky, stodgy, stringy, syrupy, velvety, watery**
(informal) **gooey**
Stella was delighted to see that they were having ice cream, complete with sprinkles, fudge sticks and gooey chocolate toffee sauce.—THE POLAR BEAR EXPLORERS' CLUB, Alex Bell

TO DESCRIBE HOW IT TASTES:

• **bitter, bland, fiery, flavoursome, fresh, fruity, hot, mellow, mild, peppery, piquant, pungent, refreshing, salty, savoury, sharp, sour, spicy, strong, sugary, sweet, syrupy, tangy, tart, vinegary**
The sauce was ***hot****, but not too* ***spicy****.*
for ways to describe how food smells see **smell**

TO DESCRIBE FOOD YOU LIKE:

• **appetising, delicious, luscious, mouthwatering, tasty, tempting, well-cooked**
(informal) **scrummy, scrumptious, scrumdiddlyumptious, yummy**
Something especially tasty to eat is a **delicacy** or **titbit**.
'Fleshlumpeater says he is never eating queen and he thinks perhaps she has an especially scrumdiddlyumptious flavour.' 'How dare he!' Sophie cried.—THE BFG, Roald Dahl

TO DESCRIBE FOOD YOU DON'T LIKE:

• **disgusting, flavourless, indigestible, inedible, nauseating, stomach-turning, tasteless, unappetising, uneatable; charred, mouldy, overcooked, stale, undercooked**
(informal) **yucky**
Measle didn't think the food was very good. The stew was watery and tasteless and the vegetables were soggy and overcooked.
—MEASLE AND THE DOOMPIT, Ian Ogilvy

fool *NOUN*

❶ *Only a* ***fool*** *would believe that ridiculous story.*
• **idiot, buffoon, clown, halfwit, dimwit, dunce, simpleton, blockhead, clot, dunderhead, imbecile, moron, ass**
(informal) **twit, chump, nitwit, nincompoop**
❷ *(historical) The king's* ***fool*** *entertained the court.*
• **jester, clown**

fool *VERB*

The spy ***fooled*** *everyone with his disguises.*
• **deceive, trick, mislead, hoax, dupe, hoodwink**
(informal) **con, kid, have you on, take you in, pull the wool over your eyes**
➤ **to fool about** or **around**
We were told not to ***fool about*** *in the swimming pool.*
• **play about, mess about, misbehave**

foolish *ADJECTIVE*

It would be ***foolish*** *to stand too close to the lions.*
• **stupid, silly, idiotic, senseless, ridiculous, nonsensical, unwise, ill-advised, half-witted, unintelligent, absurd, crazy, mad, hare-brained**
(informal) **daft**
OPPOSITE **sensible**

foot *NOUN*

❶ *Rhona walked on the sand in her bare* ***feet****.*
The foot of an animal that has claws is a **paw**.
The foot of a cow, deer or horse is a **hoof**.
A pig's foot is a **trotter**.
A bird's feet are its **claws**.
The feet of a bird of prey are its **talons**.
❷ *We set up camp at the* ***foot*** *of the mountain.*
• **base, bottom**

football *NOUN*

WORD WEB

Football is also known as **soccer**.
Someone who plays football is a **footballer**.
Football is played on a **field** or **pitch** in a **ground, park** or **stadium**.

MEMBERS OF A FOOTBALL TEAM:

• captain, defender, full back, forward, goalkeeper or *(informal)* goalie, midfielder, striker, substitute, sweeper, winger

OTHER PEOPLE INVOLVED IN FOOTBALL:

• ballboy or ballgirl, coach, linesman, manager, referee

SOME MOVES A FOOTBALLER MIGHT MAKE:

• chip, dribble, dummy, header, kick, mazy run, miss, pass, score, shot, tackle, volley
for ways to hit or kick a ball see **ball**

SOME OTHER TERMS USED IN FOOTBALL:

• corner, crossbar, deflection, dugout, equaliser, extra time, final whistle, foul, free kick, goal, goalposts, half-time, kick-off, net, offside, penalty, penalty shoot-out, red or yellow card, sending off, throw-in

footprint *NOUN*
We followed the ***footprints*** *in the snow.*
• footmark, track, print
The tracks left by an animal are also called a **spoor**.

footstep *NOUN*
I heard ***footsteps*** *crunching up the garden path.*
• step, footfall, tread

forbidden *ADJECTIVE*
Skateboarding is ***forbidden*** *in the playground.*
• banned, barred, prohibited, disallowed, outlawed
OPPOSITE allowed

forbidding *ADJECTIVE*
The haunted tower had a dark, ***forbidding*** *look.*
• gloomy, grim, menacing, ominous, stern, threatening, unfriendly, unwelcoming
OPPOSITE friendly

force *NOUN*
❶ *The firefighters had to use* ***force*** *to open the door.*
• strength, power, might, muscle, vigour, effort, energy
❷ *The* ***force*** *of the explosion broke all the windows.*
• impact, effect, shock, intensity
❸ *The soldiers are part of a peace-keeping* ***force****.*
• group, unit, team, corps, army, troops

force *VERB*
❶ *The slaves were* ***forced*** *to work in the mines.*
• compel, make, order, require, oblige, pressurise, coerce
❷ *The king* ***forced*** *a new law upon the country.*
• impose, inflict
❸ *The firefighters had to* ***force*** *the door.*
• break open, burst open, prise open, smash, wrench
(informal) yank

forceful *ADJECTIVE*
My great aunt has a very ***forceful*** *personality.*
• strong, powerful, dynamic, commanding, assertive, overbearing
OPPOSITE weak

forecast *NOUN*
The weather ***forecast*** *is for snow tomorrow.*
• outlook, prediction

forecast *VERB* **forecasts, forecasting, forecast** or **forecasted**
Snow has been ***forecast*** *for Tuesday.*
• foresee, foretell, predict

foreground *NOUN*
I took a photo of our house with my mum in the ***foreground****.*
• front
OPPOSITE background

foreign *ADJECTIVE*
❶ *Lots of* ***foreign*** *tourists visit Edinburgh in the summer.*
• overseas, international
OPPOSITES native, domestic

A B C D E F G H I J K L M N O P Q R S T U V W X Y Z

❷ *I like travelling to **foreign** countries.*
• overseas, distant, faraway, exotic, remote, far-flung
❸ *The idea of work was completely **foreign** to the princess.*
• unnatural, unfamiliar, strange, alien

foreigner *NOUN*
*Many **foreigners** have come to live in the city.*
• overseas visitor, stranger, outsider, newcomer
A formal word is **alien.**
A word describing people who come from abroad to live in a country is **immigrant.**

foremost *ADJECTIVE*
*Hans Christian Andersen was one of the **foremost** writers of fairy tales.*
• best known, leading, most important, greatest, principal, chief, major

foresee *VERB* **foresees, foreseeing, foresaw, foreseen**
*Do you **foresee** any problems with our plan?*
• anticipate, expect, predict, forecast, prophesy, foretell

forest *NOUN*
for places where trees grow see **tree**

foretell *VERB* **foretells, foretelling, foretold**
❶ *The fortune-teller **foretold** that I would go on a voyage.*
• predict, prophesy, forecast, foresee
❷ *The cold wind **foretold** a change in the weather.*
• herald, signify

forever *ADVERB*
*Timmy is **forever** complaining about something.*
• constantly, continually, always, perpetually

forge *VERB*
❶ *The blacksmith **forged** a new horseshoe.*
• cast, hammer out, beat into shape
❷ *That signature has been **forged**.*
• fake, copy, counterfeit

➤ **to forge ahead**
*After a slow start, the rowing team was **forging ahead**.*
• advance, make progress, make headway

forgery *NOUN*
*One of these paintings is a **forgery**.*
• fake, copy, imitation, reproduction, replica
(informal) phoney

forget *VERB* **forgets, forgetting, forgot, forgotten**
❶ *I **forgot** my toothbrush when I packed my suitcase.*
• leave out, leave behind, overlook
❷ *I **forgot** to switch off the computer.*
• omit, neglect, fail
OPPOSITE remember

forgetful *ADJECTIVE*
*As the professor grew older, he became more **forgetful**.*
• absent-minded, careless, inattentive, oblivious, vague, dreamy, lax

forgive *VERB* **forgives, forgiving, forgave, forgiven**
*Please **forgive** me for being so rude.*
• excuse, pardon, let off, overlook, spare

fork *VERB*
*The path ahead widened and then **forked** into two.*
• split, branch, divide

forlorn *ADJECTIVE*
*Aisha felt **forlorn** after her friends had left.*
• sad, unhappy, lonely, dejected, miserable, sorrowful
OPPOSITE cheerful

form *NOUN*
❶ *I made out the **form** of a man through the mist.*
• shape, figure, outline, silhouette
❷ *Ice is a **form** of water.*
• kind, sort, type, variety

❸ *My brother moves up into a higher* ***form*** *next term.*
• **class, year, grade, set**
❹ *If you want to join the club, sign this* ***form.***
• **document, paper, sheet, questionnaire**

form *VERB*
❶ *The sculptor* ***formed*** *the clay into the shape of a bird.*
• **shape, mould, model, fashion, work, cast**
❷ *My friends and I have* ***formed*** *a chess club.*
• **set up, establish, found, create, start**
❸ *Icicles had* ***formed*** *on the roof of the cave.*
• **appear, develop, grow, emerge, take shape**

formal *ADJECTIVE*
❶ *I was invited to the* ***formal*** *opening of the museum.*
• **official, ceremonial**
❷ *The letter was written in a very* ***formal*** *style.*
• **correct, proper, conventional, dignified, solemn**
OPPOSITES **informal, casual**

former *ADJECTIVE*
In ***former*** *times, the castle was surrounded by a moat.*
• **earlier, previous, past, bygone**

formula *NOUN*
The inventor was working on a new ***formula*** *for toothpaste.*
• **recipe, prescription**

forsake *VERB* **forsakes, forsaking, forsook, forsaken**
Ben knew that his old sheepdog would never ***forsake*** *him.*
• **abandon, desert, leave**

fort *NOUN*
A few soldiers were left to defend the ***fort.***
• **fortress, fortification, stronghold, castle, citadel, tower**
see also **castle**

fortify *VERB*
❶ *The townspeople built fences to* ***fortify*** *the town.*
• **defend, protect, secure, reinforce**
❷ *A good breakfast will* ***fortify*** *you for the morning.*
• **strengthen, support, sustain, bolster, boost, invigorate**
OPPOSITE **weaken**

fortunate *ADJECTIVE*
We were ***fortunate*** *to have good weather.*
• **lucky, in luck**
OPPOSITES **unfortunate, unlucky**

fortune *NOUN*
❶ *By good* ***fortune****, I stumbled across a secret doorway.*
• **chance, luck, accident, fate**
❷ *The millionairess left her* ***fortune*** *to charity.*
• **wealth, riches, possessions, property, assets, estate**
(informal) **millions**

fortune-teller *NOUN*
The ***fortune-teller*** *gazed into her crystal ball.*
• **clairvoyant, soothsayer, seer**

forward *ADJECTIVE*
❶ *We need to do some* ***forward*** *planning for the camping trip.*
• **advance, early, future**
❷ *Would it be too* ***forward*** *to send him an email?*
• **bold, cheeky, brash, familiar, impudent, presumptuous**

forwards *ADVERB*
❶ *The queue moved* ***forwards*** *very slowly.*
• **on, onwards, along**
❷ *All the seats face* ***forwards.***
• **to or toward the front, ahead**
OPPOSITE **backwards**

fossil *NOUN*
*Isla found a **fossil** on the beach.*

WORD WEB

SOME TYPES OF FOSSIL:

- **ammonite, dinosaur bone, petrified wood, trilobite**

A person who looks for fossils is a **fossil hunter.**
A person who studies fossils is a **palaeontologist.**

foster *VERB*
*My aunt has decided to **foster** a child.*
- **bring up, rear, raise, care for, look after, take care of**

To **adopt** a child is to make the child legally a full member of your family.

fought *past tense see* **fight**

foul *ADJECTIVE*
❶ *The knight fainted at the **foul** smell of the dragon's breath.*
- **disgusting, revolting, repulsive, rotten, stinking, offensive, unpleasant, loathsome, nasty, horrible, vile**

OPPOSITE **pleasant**
❷ *The walls and floor of the dungeon were **foul**.*
- **dirty, unclean, filthy, mucky, messy**

OPPOSITE **clean, pure**
❸ *The player was sent off for using **foul** language.*
- **rude, offensive, insulting, abusive, improper, indecent**

❹ *The referee blew her whistle for a **foul** tackle.*
- **illegal, prohibited, unfair**

OPPOSITE **fair**

found *past tense see* **find**

found *VERB*
*The school was **founded** a hundred years ago.*
- **establish, set up, start, begin, create, originate, initiate, institute**

foundation *NOUN*
❶ *There's no **foundation** for the rumour they are spreading.*
- **basis, grounds**

❷ *It's a hundred years since the **foundation** of the museum.*
- **founding, beginning, establishment, setting up**

founder *VERB*
❶ *The ship struck a rock and **foundered**.*
- **go under, sink, submerge**

❷ *The project **foundered** because of lack of money.*
- **fail, fall through, collapse, come to nothing** *(informal)* **fold, flop, bomb**

fountain *NOUN*
*A **fountain** of water shot into the air.*
- **jet, spout, spray, spring**

fox *NOUN*
A male fox is a **dog.**
A female fox is a **vixen.**
A young fox is a **cub.**
A fox lives in an **earth.**
A word meaning 'to do with foxes' is **vulpine.**

fox *VERB*
*The last clue in the crossword **foxed** me completely.*
- **puzzle, baffle, bewilder, mystify, perplex** *(informal)* **flummox, floor**

fraction *NOUN*
*Only a **fraction** of an iceberg shows above the water.*
- **bit, part, portion**

fracture *VERB*
*Steve fell off his bike and **fractured** his wrist.*
- **break, crack, split, splinter**

fracture *NOUN*
*The X-ray showed a **fracture** in the bone.*
- **break, breakage, crack, split, fissure**

fragile *ADJECTIVE*
*Fossil dinosaur bones are very **fragile**.*
• breakable, delicate, frail, brittle, easily damaged, weak
OPPOSITE strong

fragment *NOUN*
❶ *I dug up a **fragment** of broken pottery.*
• bit, piece, chip, sliver, shard
❷ *She overheard **fragments** of their conversation.*
• part, portion, scrap, snippet

fragrant *ADJECTIVE*
*The room was **fragrant** with the smell of roses.*
• sweet-smelling, perfumed, scented, aromatic

frail *ADJECTIVE*
❶ *My grandad felt **frail** after his illness.*
• weak, infirm, feeble
❷ *That step-ladder looks a bit **frail**.*
• flimsy, fragile, delicate, rickety, unsound
OPPOSITES strong, robust

frame *NOUN*
❶ *The **frame** of the house is made of timber.*
• framework, structure, shell, skeleton
❷ *I put the photo of my friend in a **frame**.*
• mount, mounting, surround, border, setting, edging

frank *ADJECTIVE*
*We had a very **frank** discussion about money.*
• honest, direct, sincere, genuine, candid, outspoken, plain, blunt, straightforward, truthful
OPPOSITE insincere

frantic *ADJECTIVE*
❶ *I was **frantic** with worry when our kitten got lost.*
• beside yourself, fraught, desperate, distraught, hysterical, worked up, berserk
❷ *There was **frantic** activity on the day of the wedding.*
• excited, hectic, frenzied, feverish, wild, mad
OPPOSITE calm

fraud *NOUN*
❶ *The bank manager was found guilty of **fraud**.*
• deceit, deception, dishonesty, swindling, cheating
❷ *The prize draw was just a **fraud**—nobody won anything.*
• swindle, trick, hoax, pretence, sham
(informal) con, scam
❸ *The salesman turned out to be a **fraud**.*
• cheat, swindler, trickster, hoaxer
(informal) con man, phoney

fraudulent *ADJECTIVE*
*Beware of **fraudulent** email messages.*
• dishonest, illegal, criminal, corrupt, swindling, bogus, sham
(informal) crooked, phoney
OPPOSITE honest

frayed *ADJECTIVE*
*The old woman wore a cloak of **frayed** tartan cloth.*
• tattered, ragged, worn, threadbare

free *ADJECTIVE*
❶ *You are **free** to wander anywhere in the building.*
• able, allowed, permitted, at liberty
OPPOSITE restricted
❷ *After ten years in jail, the prisoners were **free** at last.*
• freed, liberated, released, emancipated, at large, on the loose
A common simile is **as free as a bird**.
OPPOSITES imprisoned, enslaved
❸ *I got a **free** drink with my sandwich.*
• complimentary, free of charge, gratis, on the house
❹ *Are you **free** this weekend?*
• available, unoccupied
OPPOSITE busy, occupied
❺ *The bathroom is **free** now.*
• available, unoccupied, vacant, empty
OPPOSITE engaged
❻ *Uncle Jack is very **free** with his money.*
• generous, lavish, liberal
OPPOSITE mean

A B C D E F G H I J K L M N O P Q R S T U V W X Y Z

free *VERB*
❶ *The soldiers **freed** the prisoners of war.*
• **release, liberate, set free, deliver**
To free slaves is to **emancipate** them.
To free prisoners by paying money to their captors is to **ransom** them.
OPPOSITE **imprison**
❷ *We **freed** the dogs and let them run about.*
• **loose, turn loose, let go, untie, unchain**
OPPOSITE **confine**
❸ *The escapologist tried to **free** his arms from the chains.*
• **undo, untangle, work loose**

freedom *NOUN*
*The animals have a lot of **freedom** in the safari park.*
• **liberty, independence**

freeze *VERB* **freezes, freezing, froze, frozen**
❶ *Water begins to **freeze** at 0°C.*
• **become ice, ice over, harden, solidify**
❷ *If you **freeze** food, you can store it for a long time.*
• **deep-freeze, chill, refrigerate**
❸ *Season-ticket prices have been **frozen** for another year.*
• **fix, hold, peg, keep as they are**

freezing *ADJECTIVE*
*It's **freezing** outside in winter.*
• **chilly, frosty, icy, wintry, raw, bitter**

frequent *ADJECTIVE*
❶ *I send **frequent** email messages to my friends.*
• **numerous, constant, continual, recurring, recurrent, repeated, countless**
OPPOSITE **infrequent**
❷ *Badgers are **frequent** visitors to the garden.*
• **regular, habitual, common, familiar, persistent**
OPPOSITE **rare**

frequent *VERB*
*Office workers **frequent** the park at lunchtime.*
• **visit, attend, haunt**

fresh *ADJECTIVE*
❶ *This pudding is made with **fresh** fruit.*
• **natural, raw, unprocessed**
❷ *The shop bakes **fresh** bread every day.*
• **new**
OPPOSITES **old, stale**
❸ *Sally went outside to get some **fresh** air.*
• **clean, cool, crisp, refreshing**
OPPOSITE **stuffy**
❹ *Have you put **fresh** sheets on the bed?*
• **new, clean, laundered, washed**
OPPOSITE **dirty**
❺ *Having a shower makes me feel nice and **fresh**.*
• **refreshed, revived, restored, invigorated**
❻ *We need some **fresh** ideas for our magazine.*
• **new, original, different, novel, innovative**
OPPOSITE **old**

fret *VERB*
*My sister is **fretting** about her piano exam.*
• **worry, fuss, agonise, become stressed, get worked up**

friction *NOUN*
❶ *You can make fire from the **friction** of rubbing sticks together.*
• **rubbing, chafing, abrasion**
❷ *There was some **friction** between the two teams.*
• **conflict, disagreement, hostility, rivalry, antagonism, discord, quarrelling**

friend *NOUN*
*I am inviting four **friends** to my birthday party.*
• **companion, comrade**
(informal) **mate, pal, buddy, chum**
A friend you play games with is a **playmate**.
A friend you write to but don't normally meet is a **penfriend**.
A friend you know only slightly is an **acquaintance**.
OPPOSITE **enemy**

friendly *ADJECTIVE*
❶ *Our neighbour's pet dog is very **friendly**.*
• **affectionate, loving, good-natured, likeable, amiable, approachable, kind-hearted, kindly, amicable, genial, sociable, outgoing, sympathetic**

❷ *Those two are very **friendly** with each other.*
• close, familiar, intimate
(informal) pally, chummy
❸ *I like this cafe—it has a very **friendly** atmosphere.*
• warm, welcoming, hospitable, cordial, neighbourly
OPPOSITES unfriendly, hostile

friendship *NOUN*
*Their **friendship** has lasted for many years.*
• closeness, affection, fondness, familiarity, intimacy, attachment, comradeship, fellowship
OPPOSITE hostility
A formal friendship between countries or parties is an **alliance**.

fright *NOUN*
❶ *The girl jumped up in **fright** and began to scream.*
• fear, terror, alarm, horror, panic, dread
❷ *The explosion gave us an awful **fright**!*
• scare, shock, surprise, start, turn, jolt

frighten *VERB*
*Sorry—I didn't mean to **frighten** you.*
• scare, terrify, startle, alarm, shock, panic, petrify

frightened *ADJECTIVE*
*Mia always felt **frightened** in the dark.*
• afraid, scared, terrified, alarmed, fearful, panicky, petrified
see also **afraid**

frightening *ADJECTIVE*
*The ghost story she told was quite **frightening**.*
• terrifying, horrifying, alarming, nightmarish, chilling, spine-chilling, hair-raising, bloodcurdling, eerie, sinister, fearsome
(informal) scary, creepy, spooky

frill *NOUN*
❶ *My party dress has a **frill** round the hem.*
• ruffle, ruff, flounce, fringe
❷ *Our hotel was basic with no **frills**.*
• extra, luxury

fringe *NOUN*
❶ *My scarf has a beaded **fringe** at each end.*
• border, edging, frill, trimming
❷ *We live on the **fringe** of the town.*
• edge, border, margin, outskirts

frisky *ADJECTIVE*
*The new lion cubs in the zoo are very **frisky**.*
• playful, lively, high-spirited, sprightly

fritter *VERB*
➤ **to fritter away**
*Luke **frittered away** his pocket money on sweets.*
• waste, squander, spend unwisely, use up

frivolous *ADJECTIVE*
❶ *We were in a **frivolous** mood before we went on holiday.*
• playful, lively, high-spirited, jaunty
OPPOSITES serious, sombre
❷ *Don't waste my time asking **frivolous** questions.*
• foolish, silly, ridiculous, shallow, superficial, pointless, unimportant, trivial, petty
OPPOSITES serious, important

frock *NOUN*
for items of clothing see **clothes**

frog *NOUN*
A young frog is a **tadpole**.
Frogs' eggs are **frogspawn**.
The sound a frog makes is a **croak** or **ribbit**.

frolic *VERB*
*Lambs were **frolicking** in the field.*
• jump about, leap about, bound, caper, prance, gambol, romp, skip

front *NOUN*
❶ *We stood at the **front** of the queue.*
• head, start, beginning, lead, top
❷ *The **front** of the house was painted white.*
• face, facing, frontage, facade
OPPOSITE back, rear
The front of a ship is the **bow** or **prow**.
The front of a picture is the **foreground**.

A B C D E F G H I J K L M N O P Q R S T U V W X Y Z

front *ADJECTIVE*
❶ *The **front** runners came into sight round the corner.*
• first, leading, most advanced
OPPOSITE back
❷ *The horse had injured one of its **front** legs.*
• fore
OPPOSITES back, rear, hind

frontier *NOUN*
*We crossed the **frontier** between France and Belgium.*
• border, boundary

frosty *ADJECTIVE*
❶ *It was a clear, **frosty** night.*
• cold, crisp, icy, freezing, wintry
❷ *The shopkeeper gave us a **frosty** stare.*
• unfriendly, unwelcoming, cold, cool, stony
OPPOSITES warm, friendly

froth *NOUN*
*I like a lot of **froth** on my hot chocolate.*
• foam, bubbles, head
The froth on top of soapy water is **lather** or **suds**.
Dirty froth is **scum**.

frown *NOUN*
*On Christmas Eve, Scrooge had a **frown** on his face.*
• scowl, glare, grimace, glower, black look
for other facial expressions see **expression**

frown *VERB*
*The witch **frowned** when her spell didn't work.*
• scowl, glare, grimace, glower, knit your brow, look sullen

frugal *ADJECTIVE*
❶ *Mr Skinflint was always **frugal** with his money.*
• thrifty, sparing, economical, prudent
OPPOSITES wasteful, spendthrift
❷ *They ate a **frugal** meal of bread crusts.*
• meagre, paltry, plain, simple
OPPOSITE lavish

fruit *NOUN*

WORD WEB

SOME COMMON VARIETIES OF FRUIT:

• apple, apricot, avocado, banana, bilberry, blackberry, blackcurrant, blueberry, bramble, cherry, coconut, cranberry, damson, date, fig, gooseberry, grape, guava, kiwi fruit, loganberry, lychee, mango, melon, nectarine, pawpaw or papaya, peach, pear, pineapple, plum, pomegranate, quince, raspberry, redcurrant, rose hip, sloe, strawberry, tomato, watermelon

CITRUS FRUITS:

• clementine, grapefruit, kumquat, lemon, lime, mandarin, orange, satsuma, tangerine

DRIED FRUITS:

• currant, prune, raisin, sultana
Rhubarb is not a fruit, although it is cooked and eaten like one.
A person who sells fruit and vegetables is a greengrocer.

fruitful *ADJECTIVE*
*Did you have a **fruitful** shopping trip?*
• successful, productive, useful, worthwhile, profitable, rewarding
OPPOSITE fruitless

fruitless *ADJECTIVE*
*They spent a **fruitless** morning searching for clues.*
• unsuccessful, unprofitable, unproductive, futile, pointless, useless, vain
OPPOSITE successful

frustrate *VERB*
❶ *It **frustrated** us to have to wait in the long queue.*
• exasperate, discourage, dispirit, irritate

❷ *Our plan for the day was* ***frustrated*** *by the weather.*
• **block, foil, thwart, defeat, check, hinder, prevent**

fry *VERB*
for ways to cook things see **cook**

fugitive *NOUN*
Police searched everywhere for the ***fugitives****.*
• **runaway, escapee, outlaw, deserter**
Someone who is a fugitive from war or persecution is a **refugee**.

fulfil *VERB*
❶ *She* ***fulfilled*** *her ambition to play tennis at Wimbledon.*
• **achieve, realise, accomplish, attain, carry out, complete, succeed in**
❷ *To join the club, you must* ***fulfil*** *these conditions.*
• **meet, satisfy, conform to**

full *ADJECTIVE*
❶ *My suitcase is* ***full*** *to the brim.*
• **filled, loaded, topped up**
OPPOSITE **empty**
❷ *The shopping centre was* ***full*** *on Saturday.*
• **busy, crowded, jammed, packed, crammed, congested**
OPPOSITE **empty**
❸ *The detective gave a* ***full*** *account of his findings.*
• **complete, detailed, comprehensive, thorough, exhaustive**
OPPOSITE **incomplete**
❹ *The horses were galloping at* ***full*** *speed.*
• **top, maximum, greatest, highest**
OPPOSITE **minimum**
❺ *The wedding dress has a very* ***full*** *skirt.*
• **wide, broad, voluminous**
OPPOSITE **tight**

fun *NOUN*
We had great ***fun*** *at the beach on our holiday.*
• **amusement, diversion, enjoyment, entertainment, games, jokes, laughter, merriment, play, pleasure, recreation, sport**

➤ **to make fun of someone**
It was cruel to ***make fun of*** *her when she fell over.*
• **jeer at, laugh at, mock, ridicule, taunt, tease**

function *NOUN*
❶ *The* ***function*** *of a vet is to cure sick animals.*
• **duty, role, task, job, responsibility, purpose**
❷ *The hall is being used for an official* ***function****.*
• **event, occasion, party, reception**

function *VERB*
This camera doesn't ***function*** *properly.*
• **work, go, operate, run, perform**

fundamental *ADJECTIVE*
He taught me the ***fundamental*** *rules of chess.*
• **basic, elementary, essential, important, main, necessary, principal**

funds *PLURAL NOUN*
The school used some of its ***funds*** *to buy a minibus.*
• **money, cash, savings, capital, reserves**

funny *ADJECTIVE*
❶ *There are some very* ***funny*** *jokes in the film.*
• **amusing, humorous, comic, comical, hilarious, witty, entertaining, diverting**
(informal) **hysterical, priceless**
OPPOSITE **serious**
❷ *There's a* ***funny*** *smell in here.*
• **strange, odd, peculiar, curious, puzzling, weird, queer, bizarre**

fur *NOUN*
Arctic foxes have thick white ***fur*** *in the winter.*
• **hair, coat, hide, pelt**

furious *ADJECTIVE*
❶ *The manager was* ***furious*** *when his team lost.*
• **angry, mad, enraged, infuriated, incensed, livid, fuming, raging, seething**

❷ *The elves worked at a **furious** rate to finish their work.*
• **frantic, hectic, frenzied, extreme, intense**
OPPOSITE **calm**

furniture *NOUN*

WORD WEB

SOME ITEMS OF FURNITURE:

• **armchair, bed, bookcase, bureau, chair, chest of drawers, coffee table, couch, cupboard, desk, dresser, dressing table, filing cabinet, settee, sideboard, sofa, sofa bed, stool, table, wardrobe**
The soft covering on a chair or sofa is **upholstery**.
Old and valuable pieces of furniture are **antiques**.

furrow *NOUN*
*The tractor wheels had made deep **furrows** in the mud.*
• **groove, rut, ditch, channel, trench**

furry *ADJECTIVE*
*A small, **furry** creature was curled inside the box.*
• **hairy, fleecy, woolly, fuzzy, downy, feathery**

further *ADJECTIVE*
*Look on our website for **further** information.*
• **more, extra, additional, supplementary**

furtive *ADJECTIVE*
*The spy cast a **furtive** glance around the room.*
• **secretive, stealthy, surreptitious, underhand, crafty, sneaky, sly**

fury *NOUN*
❶ *The **fury** of the creature showed in its eyes.*
• **anger, rage, wrath, indignation**
❷ *There was no shelter from the **fury** of the storm.*
• **ferocity, fierceness, intensity, severity, violence, turbulence, savagery**

fuse *VERB*
*The metals had **fused** together into a solid mass.*
• **blend, combine, merge, unite, join, melt**
To fuse metals together when you are making or mending something is to **solder** or **weld** them.

fuss *NOUN*
*There was a lot of **fuss** when the queen arrived.*
• **bother, commotion, excitement, trouble, hullabaloo**

fuss *VERB*
*Please don't **fuss**!*
• **worry, fret, bother, get worked up**

fussy *ADJECTIVE*
❶ *Our cat is **fussy** about her food.*
• **finicky, hard to please, particular**
(informal) **choosy, picky**
An informal name for a fussy person is a **fusspot**.
❷ *I don't like clothes with **fussy** designs.*
• **fancy, elaborate, ornate, florid**

futile *ADJECTIVE*
*They made a **futile** attempt to put out the fire.*
• **fruitless, pointless, unsuccessful, useless, ineffectual, vain, wasted**
OPPOSITE **successful**

future *NOUN*
*She has a bright **future** as a tennis player.*
• **outlook, prospects**
OPPOSITE **past**

fuzzy *ADJECTIVE*
❶ *The TV picture has gone **fuzzy**.*
• **blurred, bleary, unfocused, unclear, indistinct, hazy, cloudy**
OPPOSITE **clear**
❷ *Mia was wearing a **fuzzy** cardigan.*
• **fluffy, frizzy, furry, woolly, fleecy**

Gg

gadget *NOUN*
My pocket torch is a handy little ***gadget.***
• **tool, instrument, implement, device, contraption**
(informal) **gizmo**

gain *VERB*
❶ *Martha* ***gained*** *a reputation as an excellent cook.*
• **get, acquire, obtain, earn, win**
OPPOSITE **lose**
❷ *We* ***gained*** *our target of raising £200.*
• **reach, get to, arrive at, achieve, attain**

game *NOUN*
❶ *My favourite* ***game*** *is hide-and-seek.*
• **amusement, pastime, sport, activity, recreation**
❷ *The big* ***game*** *is on this Saturday.*
• **match, contest, competition, tournament**

WORD WEB

INDOOR GAMES:

• **backgammon, bagatelle, battleships, billiards, bingo, board game, cards, chess, darts, dice, dominoes, draughts, go, hangman, ludo, mah-jong, pool, snakes and ladders, snooker, table tennis** or *(informal)* **ping-pong, tiddlywinks, video game**
for names of card games see **card**

PARTY GAMES:

• **charades, hide-and-seek, I-spy, musical chairs, pass the parcel**

PLAYGROUND AND OTHER OUTDOOR GAMES:

• **conkers, hopscotch, leapfrog, marbles, skipping, skittles, tag**
for more indoor and outdoor games see **sport**

gang *NOUN*
❶ *The sea was swarming with* ***gangs*** *of pirates.*
• **group, band, crowd, pack, set, mob**
❷ *A* ***gang*** *of workmen dug a hole in the road.*
• **team, unit, crew, squad, party**

gap *NOUN*
❶ *The animals escaped through a* ***gap*** *in the fence.*
• **opening, space, hole, breach, break, crack, rift**
❷ *She returned to work after a* ***gap*** *of two years.*
• **break, interval, interruption, pause, lull**

gaping *ADJECTIVE*
The meteor left a ***gaping*** *hole in the ground.*
• **wide, broad, yawning, vast, cavernous**

garden *NOUN*
A small area of garden is a **plot** or **patch.**
A rented garden for growing vegetables is an **allotment.**
A garden planted with trees is an **orchard.**
A formal word for gardening is **horticulture.**
A word meaning 'to do with gardens or gardening' is **horticultural.**
for tools used for gardening see **tool**

garment *NOUN*
see **clothes**

gas *NOUN*
The mixture gave off an evil-smelling ***gas.***
• **vapour, fumes**

gash *NOUN*
The broken glass made a nasty ***gash*** *in my foot.*
• **cut, slash, wound, slit**

gasp *VERB*
At the end of the race we lay ***gasping*** *for breath.*
• **gulp, pant**

A B C D E F G H I J K L M N O P Q R S T U V W X Y Z

gate *NOUN*
People waited at the ***gate*** *to be let in.*
• **gateway, doorway, entrance, portal**

gather *VERB*
❶ *A crowd* ***gathered*** *to watch the performers.*
• **assemble, collect, come together, congregate**
OPPOSITE **disperse**
❷ *The captain* ***gathered*** *her team to give them a talk.*
• **bring together, round up, muster**
❸ *We* ***gathered*** *daisies to make into chains.*
• **pick, pluck, collect, harvest**
❹ *I* ***gather*** *that you've been on holiday.*
• **understand, hear, learn, believe**

gathering *NOUN*
There was a family ***gathering*** *for granny's birthday.*
• **assembly, meeting, crowd, party, get-together**

gaudy *ADJECTIVE*
The newsreader wore a rather ***gaudy*** *tie.*
• **flashy, showy, loud, glaring, garish, lurid**

gauge *VERB*
They're trying to ***gauge*** *the size of the volcano.*
• **measure, calculate, judge, assess, estimate, reckon**

gaunt *ADJECTIVE*
The sorceress had a ***gaunt*** *face and stringy hair.*
• **haggard, drawn, thin, skinny, scraggy, scrawny, wasted, skeletal**

gave *past tense see* **give**

gaze *VERB*
The dog ***gazed*** *hungrily at the food.*
• **stare, look, gape**

gear *NOUN*
We put our fishing ***gear*** *in the back of the car.*
• **equipment, stuff, things, paraphernalia, tackle**

gem *NOUN*
The crown was made of solid gold, studded with ***gems****.*
• **jewel, precious stone**
for names of gem stones see **jewel**

general *ADJECTIVE*
❶ *There was a* ***general*** *air of gloom about the abbey.*
• **widespread, extensive, broad, sweeping, overall, prevalent**
❷ *I've only got a* ***general*** *idea of where we are.*
• **rough, approximate, indefinite, vague, loose**

generally *ADVERB*
I ***generally*** *travel to school by bus.*
• **usually, normally, as a rule, chiefly, mostly, mainly, commonly, on the whole**

generate *VERB*
Our website has ***generated*** *a lot of interest.*
• **create, produce, bring about, give rise to**

generous *ADJECTIVE*
❶ *It was* ***generous*** *of you to give me your seat.*
• **unselfish, charitable, kind-hearted**
OPPOSITE **selfish**
❷ *We each got a* ***generous*** *helping of ice cream.*
• **ample, large, lavish, plentiful**
OPPOSITE **meagre**

genial *ADJECTIVE*
The housekeeper greeted us with a ***genial*** *smile.*
• **friendly, kind, warm, warm-hearted, kindly, good-natured, pleasant, agreeable, cordial**
OPPOSITE **unfriendly**

genius *NOUN*
Nila is a ***genius*** *at maths.*
• **expert, master, mastermind, wizard, ace**

gentle *ADJECTIVE*
❶ *The vet is very* ***gentle*** *with sick animals.*
• **kind, tender, good-tempered, humane**
❷ *Grasses swayed in the* ***gentle*** *breeze.*
• **light, slight, mild, soft, faint**
OPPOSITE **strong**

❸ *There is a **gentle** slope to the top of the hill.*
• slight, gradual, easy
OPPOSITE steep

genuine *ADJECTIVE*
❶ *Is that a **genuine** diamond?*
• real, actual, true, authentic
OPPOSITE fake
❷ *Your friend seems like a very **genuine** person.*
• honest, sincere, frank, earnest
OPPOSITE false

gesture *NOUN*
*She opened her arms in a **gesture** of welcome.*
• sign, signal, motion, movement

get *VERB* **gets, getting, got**
❶ *We're **getting** a goldfish for our class.*
• acquire, obtain, buy, purchase
❷ *Can you **get** me another blanket, please?*
• bring, fetch, collect, pick up, retrieve
❸ *Cara **got** a medal for swimming.*
• receive, gain, earn, win, achieve
❹ *What time did you **get** home?*
• arrive at, reach, come to
OPPOSITE leave
❺ *It was starting to **get** dark outside.*
• become, grow, turn
❻ *I **got** a stomach bug on holiday last year.*
• catch, develop, pick up, come down with
❼ *You'll never **get** Oscar to eat celery.*
• persuade, urge, influence, coax
❽ *I don't **get** the point of that film.*
• understand, follow, comprehend, grasp
➢ **to get on** or **along**
*How are you **getting on** with playing the guitar?*
• manage, fare, cope, prosper, succeed
➢ **to get out of**
*My brother **got out of** doing the washing up.*
• avoid, evade, shirk
➢ **to get over**
*He hasn't **got over** the accident yet.*
• get better from, recover from, shake off, survive

ghastly *ADJECTIVE*
*The boy's face turned a **ghastly** shade of green.*
• appalling, awful, dreadful, frightful, grim, grisly, horrible, horrifying, shocking, monstrous, terrible

ghost *NOUN*
*Meldrop House was haunted by several **ghosts**.*
• spirit, spectre, phantom, ghoul, apparition, shade, wraith
(informal) spook
A ghost that makes a lot of noise is a **poltergeist**.

WORD WEB

A GHOST OR GHOSTLY EXPERIENCE MIGHT BE:
• bloodcurdling, chilling, grisly, gruesome, hair-raising, macabre, nightmarish, spine-chilling, spine-tingling

THINGS A GHOST MIGHT DO:
• flit, float, glide, glow, haunt a person or place, hover, lurk, materialise, pass through walls, rattle or drag chains, shimmer, vanish, waft, wander

NOISES A GHOST MIGHT MAKE:
• cackle, clang, clank, creak, groan, hoot, howl, moan, screech, sigh, sob, wail
The air was filled with phantoms, wandering hither and thither in restless haste, and moaning as they went. Every one of them wore chains like Marley's Ghost.–A CHRISTMAS CAROL, Charles Dickens

PLACES A GHOST MIGHT BE FOUND:
• catacombs, crypt, haunted house or mansion, graveyard, sepulchre, tomb, vault

OTHER THINGS THAT MIGHT BE IN A HAUNTED HOUSE:
• bats, candles, cellar, cobwebs, dungeon, gargoyle, mummy, owl, secret door or passage, skeleton, skull, trapdoor, turret

A B C D E F **G** H I J K L M N O P Q R S T U V W X Y Z

ghostly *ADJECTIVE*
The candlelight cast ***ghostly*** *shadows on the wall.*
• **spectral, phantom, ghoulish, unearthly, eerie, sinister, uncanny**
(informal) **spooky, creepy**

giant *NOUN*
The castle belonged to a fearsome ***giant.***
for creatures found in myths and legends
see **myth**

giant *ADJECTIVE*
A ***giant*** *tree towered above us.*
• **gigantic, huge, enormous, massive, immense, mammoth, colossal, monstrous**
see also **big**
OPPOSITE **tiny**

giddy *ADJECTIVE*
I felt ***giddy*** *when I stood at the edge of the cliff.*
• **dizzy, faint, unsteady**

gift *NOUN*
❶ *I received some nice* ***gifts*** *on my birthday.*
• **present**
❷ *Elsa has a* ***gift*** *for music.*
• **talent, ability, flair, knack, genius**

gifted *ADJECTIVE*
There are some ***gifted*** *players in the team.*
• **talented, able, accomplished, capable, skilful, expert**

gigantic *ADJECTIVE*
The dragon reared its ***gigantic*** *head.*
• **huge, giant, enormous, massive, colossal, immense, mammoth, monstrous**
(informal) **whopping, humungous**
OPPOSITE **tiny**

giggle *VERB*
Ailsa and I couldn't stop ***giggling.***
• **snigger, titter, chuckle, laugh**

girl *NOUN*
A synonym used in some parts of Britain is **lass.** Old-fashioned words are **damsel, maid** and **maiden.**

give *VERB* **gives, giving, gave, given**
❶ *Santa Claus* ***gave*** *each child a present.*
• **deal out, distribute, issue, supply, offer, present, hand over, pass, award**
❷ *Will you* ***give*** *something to our collection for charity?*
• **contribute, donate**
❸ *The giant* ***gave*** *a loud sneeze.*
• **utter, emit, let out**
❹ *We are* ***giving*** *a concert at the end of term.*
• **present, put on, lay on, organise, arrange**
❺ *Will this branch* ***give*** *if I sit on it?*
• **collapse, give way, bend, break, buckle**

➤ **to give in**
The boxer ***gave in*** *after a long fight.*
• **surrender, yield, submit, quit**

➤ **to give up**
He ***gave up*** *trying to start the car.*
• **abandon, stop, cease, quit**

glad *ADJECTIVE*
I'm ***glad*** *to hear that you're feeling better.*
• **pleased, happy, delighted, thrilled**
OPPOSITE **sad**

glamorous *ADJECTIVE*
She looked very ***glamorous*** *in a long black dress.*
• **beautiful, attractive, gorgeous, elegant, stylish, fashionable**

glance *VERB*
The bus driver ***glanced*** *quickly at his watch.*
• **look quickly, peek, peep, glimpse**

glare *VERB*
The troll ***glared*** *at us from under his bushy eyebrows.*
• **stare, frown, scowl, glower**

glare *NOUN*
❶ *The* ***glare*** *of the lights dazzled me.*
• **dazzle, blaze, brightness, brilliance**
❷ *Miss Frump silenced the children with an angry* ***glare.***
• **stare, scowl, glower, frown, nasty look**

glasses *PLURAL NOUN*
*She put on her **glasses** to read the letter.*
• spectacles
(informal) specs

WORD WEB

OTHER INSTRUMENTS WITH LENSES:

• binoculars, magnifying glass, microscope, telescope
An old word for a telescope is a **spyglass**.
A lens that you wear over one eye is a **monocle**.

gleam *NOUN*
*I saw a **gleam** of moonlight between the clouds.*
• glimmer, glint, flash, ray, shaft

gleam *VERB*
*The lights **gleamed** on the water.*
• glimmer, glint, glisten, shimmer, shine

glide *VERB*
*The boat **glided** gently across the lake.*
• move smoothly, slide, slip, drift, float, coast

glimmer *VERB*
*The city lights **glimmered** in the distance.*
• gleam, glint, glow, glisten, shimmer, flicker, blink

glimpse *VERB*
*I **glimpsed** a deer running through the forest.*
• catch sight of, spot, spy, sight

glimpse *NOUN*
*We caught a **glimpse** of a dolphin's tail.*
• peek, peep, glance, sighting, view

glint *VERB*
*Sunlight **glinted** on the windows.*
• flash, glitter, sparkle, twinkle

glisten *VERB*
*The pavement **glistened** with frost.*
• gleam, shine, glint, shimmer, glimmer

glitter *VERB*
*The jewels **glittered** under the bright lights.*
• sparkle, twinkle, shimmer, glimmer, glint, glisten, flash, shine

gloat *VERB*
*He was **gloating** about winning the poetry prize.*
• boast, brag, crow, show off

global *ADJECTIVE*
*The Internet is a **global** network of computers.*
• worldwide, international, universal

globe *NOUN*
❶ *I'd like to travel all round the **globe**.*
• world, planet, earth
❷ *The fortune teller used a crystal **globe**.*
• ball, sphere, orb

gloom *NOUN*
❶ *We could hardly see in the **gloom** of the cave.*
• darkness, dimness, shade, shadow, murk
The gloomy light late in the evening is **dusk** or **twilight**.
❷ *There was an air of **gloom** in the abandoned tower.*
• depression, sadness, unhappiness, melancholy, misery, despair

gloomy *ADJECTIVE*
❶ *It was cold and **gloomy** in the cellar.*
• dark, dingy, dim, dismal, dreary, sombre, cheerless, murky, shadowy
OPPOSITE bright
❷ *Eeyore was feeling **gloomy** again.*
• depressed, sad, unhappy, glum, miserable, melancholy, low, downcast, dejected
(informal) down in the dumps
OPPOSITE cheerful

glorious *ADJECTIVE*
*Look at that **glorious** sunset!*
• magnificent, splendid, stunning, spectacular, superb, magnificent, wonderful, marvellous

A B C D E F G H I J K L M N O P Q R S T U V W X Y Z

glossy *ADJECTIVE*
*The bear had a thick, **glossy** coat of black fur.*
• **shiny, sleek, silky, shining, gleaming, lustrous**
OPPOSITE **dull**

glove *NOUN*
for items of clothing see **clothes**

glow *NOUN*
*The soft **glow** of burning candles lit the room.*
• **brightness, shine, gleam, radiance**

glow *VERB*
*The embers of the bonfire were still **glowing**.*
• **shine, gleam, burn**
Something that glows in the dark is **luminous** or **phosphorescent**.

glower *VERB*
*The jailer **glowered** at the prisoners.*
• **glare, scowl, frown, stare angrily**

glue *NOUN*
*Put a blob of **glue** on each corner of the paper.*
• **adhesive, paste, gum**

glue *VERB*
***Glue** the edges of the box together.*
• **stick, paste, bond, seal**

glum *ADJECTIVE*
*Why are you looking so **glum**?*
• **depressed, sad, unhappy, gloomy, miserable, melancholy, low, downcast, dejected**
OPPOSITE **cheerful**

gnarled *ADJECTIVE*
*The branches of the tree were **gnarled** with age.*
• **bent, twisted, crooked, distorted, knobbly, knotty**

gnaw *VERB*
*The wolves **gnawed** at a pile of bones.*
• **chew, bite, nibble, munch**

go *VERB* **goes, going, went, gone**
❶ *A carriage was **going** slowly along the road.*
• **move, progress, proceed**
see also **move**
❷ *My granny has always wanted to **go** to China.*
• **travel, journey**
❸ *Some of the guests had already **gone**.*
• **leave, depart, get away, withdraw**
❹ *By morning, the ice had all **gone**.*
• **disappear, vanish**
❺ *The canal **goes** all the way from Inverness to Fort William.*
• **extend, lead, reach, stretch, run**
❻ *The mountaineer's face **went** blue with cold.*
• **become, turn, grow**
❼ *Is that old grandfather clock still **going**?*
• **function, operate, work, run**
❽ *Cups and saucers **go** on the bottom shelf.*
• **belong, be kept, be placed**
❾ *Time **goes** slowly when you're stuck indoors.*
• **pass, go by, elapse**

➤ **to go back**
*Sarah has **gone back** to the house.*
• **return, retreat, retrace your steps**

➤ **to go in for**
*I'm not **going in for** the race this year.*
• **enter, take part in, participate in**

➤ **to go off**
❶ *A bomb **went off** nearby.*
• **explode, blow up, detonate**
❷ *The milk will **go off** if it's not in the fridge.*
• **turn sour, go bad, rot**

➤ **to go on**
❶ *What's **going on** over there?*
• **happen, occur, take place**
❷ *Please **go on** with your story.*
• **carry on, continue, keep going, proceed**

➤ **to go with**
*Do these shoes **go with** my dress?*
• **match, suit, blend with**

go *NOUN*
*Would you like to have a **go** on my computer?*
• **try, turn, chance, opportunity**
(informal) **shot, bash, stab**

goal *NOUN*
❶ *The **goal** of the society is to protect wildlife.*
• **aim, ambition, intention, object, objective, purpose, target**
❷ *We managed to get a **goal** just before half-time.*
Three goals scored by the same player is known as a **hat-trick**.

gobble *VERB*
*Ladybirds love to **gobble** greenfly.*
• **guzzle, gulp, bolt, devour**

god or **goddess** *NOUN*
*Zeus was one of the **gods** of ancient Greece.*
• **deity**
A word meaning 'to do with a god or goddess' is **divine**.

gold *NOUN*
Something that is made of gold is **golden** or **gilded**.
A thin covering of gold is **gilt**.

good *ADJECTIVE*
*That is a really **good** idea!*
• **excellent, fine, lovely, nice, wonderful** *(informal)* **fantastic, great, super, cool, fantabulous, splendiferous**
OPPOSITE **bad**

OVERUSED WORD

Try to vary the words you use for **good**. Here are some other words you could use.

FOR A GOOD PERSON OR GOOD CREATURE:

• **honest, worthy, honourable, moral, decent, virtuous, noble, kind, kindly, humane, generous, charitable, merciful**
There was once a kindly old wizard who used his magic generously and wisely for the benefit of his neighbours.—THE TALES OF BEEDLE THE BARD, J. K. Rowling
OPPOSITES **evil, wicked**
A good character in a story or film is a **hero** or **heroine** or *(informal)* **goody**.

FOR GOOD BEHAVIOUR:

• **well-behaved, obedient, angelic, exemplary**
*The twins are surprisingly **well-behaved**.*
A common simile is **as good as gold**.
OPPOSITES **naughty, disobedient**

FOR A GOOD FRIEND:

• **true, loyal, loving, reliable, trusty, trustworthy**
*My dog, Rusty, is a **loyal** companion.*

FOR A GOOD FEELING OR GOOD MOOD:

• **happy, cheerful, light-hearted, positive, contented**
*Mr Fox was in a **cheerful** mood after his tea.*

FOR A GOOD EXPERIENCE OR GOOD NEWS:

• **pleasant, enjoyable, delightful, agreeable, pleasing**
OPPOSITES **unpleasant, disagreeable**
*The girls had an **enjoyable** time at the party.*
*The letter contained some **pleasing** news.*

FOR A GOOD PERFORMER OR GOOD WORK:

• **capable, skilful, clever, able, talented, competent, commendable, sound**
*My friend, Chris, is a **talented** dancer.*
OPPOSITES **poor, awful**

FOR GOOD FOOD OR A GOOD MEAL:

• **delicious, tasty, healthy, nourishing, nutritious, well-cooked, wholesome, substantial, hearty**
*The crew ate a **hearty** breakfast together.*

FOR A GOOD EXCUSE OR GOOD REASON:

• **acceptable, valid, proper, satisfactory, legitimate**
*I hope you have a **valid** excuse for being late.*
OPPOSITES **poor, unacceptable**

FOR GOOD TIMING:

• **convenient, suitable, fortunate, appropriate, opportune**
*Is this a **convenient** time for a chat?*
OPPOSITES **inconvenient, unsuitable**

FOR GOOD WEATHER:

• **fine, favourable**
*We are hoping for **fine** weather tomorrow.*
OPPOSITES **harsh, adverse**

goodbye *NOUN*
*The astronauts said **goodbye** to their families.*
• **farewell**
(informal) **cheerio**
A formal phrase meaning 'to say goodbye' is **to bid farewell**.

good-looking *ADJECTIVE*
*I think your cousin is quite **good-looking**.*
• **attractive, handsome, pretty**
OPPOSITES **ugly**

goods *PLURAL NOUN*
*The smugglers hid the stolen **goods** in a cave.*
• **property, merchandise, wares, cargo**

gorgeous *ADJECTIVE*
*The gardens look **gorgeous** in the summer.*
• **beautiful, glorious, dazzling, stunning, splendid, superb, glamorous, handsome**

gossip *VERB*
*Two neighbours were **gossiping** over the fence.*
• **chatter, tell tales**
(informal) **natter**

gossip *NOUN*
❶ *Don't believe all the **gossip** you hear.*
• **chatter, rumour, hearsay, scandal**
(informal) **tittle-tattle**
❷ *Our nextdoor neighbour is a dreadful **gossip**.*
• **busybody, chatterbox, telltale, scandalmonger**

gouge *VERB*
*The builders **gouged** a hole in the wall.*
• **dig, hollow out, scoop out, excavate**

govern *VERB*
*The ancient Romans **governed** a vast empire.*
• **rule, run, administer, direct, command, manage, be in charge of**

gown *NOUN*
*The mermaid wore a **gown** made of seaweed and pearls.*
• **dress, robe, frock**

grab *VERB*
*The cowboy **grabbed** the reins of the runaway horse.*
• **seize, grasp, catch, clutch, grip, get hold of, snatch**

graceful *ADJECTIVE*
*The gymnast made a **graceful** landing.*
• **elegant, beautiful, stylish, smooth, flowing, agile, nimble**
OPPOSITES **clumsy, graceless**

gracious *ADJECTIVE*
*The film star waved and gave a **gracious** smile.*
• **polite, courteous, good-natured, pleasant, agreeable, civil**

grade *NOUN*
*My sister has reached the top **grade** in judo.*
• **class, standard, level, stage, rank, degree**

grade *VERB*
*Eggs are **graded** according to size.*
• **group, sort, classify**

gradual *ADJECTIVE*
*There's been a **gradual** change in the weather.*
• **steady, slow, gentle, moderate, regular, even**
OPPOSITE **sudden**

grain *NOUN*
❶ *Some **grains** of sand stuck to my toes.*
• **bit, particle, speck, granule**
❷ *The **grain** will be made into bread.*
• **cereals, corn**

grand *ADJECTIVE*
❶ *The wedding was a **grand** occasion.*
• **magnificent, splendid, stately, impressive, big, great, important, imposing**
❷ *(informal) Keep going—you're doing a **grand** job!*
• **excellent, fine, good, first-class**

grant *VERB*
*The king **granted** the prisoners their freedom.*
• give, allow, permit, award

grapple *VERB*
*The guard **grappled** with the thief, but he got away.*
• struggle, wrestle, fight, tussle

grasp *VERB*
❶ *The climber **grasped** the end of the rope.*
• clutch, grab, grip, seize, catch, snatch, take hold of, hang on to
❷ *The ideas were quite difficult to **grasp**.*
• understand, comprehend, follow, take in

grasp *NOUN*
*Rita has a good **grasp** of mathematics.*
• understanding, comprehension, knowledge, mastery

grass *NOUN*
*People were told not to walk on the **grass**.*
• lawn, turf, green

grate *VERB*
❶ *I **grated** the cheese on to the pizza.*
• shred, grind
❷ *The chalk **grated** on the blackboard.*
• scrape, scratch

➤ **to grate on**
*That man's voice **grates on** my nerves.*
• annoy, irritate, jar on

grateful *ADJECTIVE*
*I'm **grateful** for your help.*
• thankful, appreciative, obliged, indebted
OPPOSITE ungrateful

gratitude *NOUN*
*We sent some flowers to show our **gratitude**.*
• thanks, appreciation

grave *NOUN*
see **tomb**

grave *ADJECTIVE*
❶ *They looked **grave** when they heard the news.*
• grim, sad, serious, thoughtful
OPPOSITE cheerful
❷ *She made a **grave** mistake.*
• crucial, important, serious, vital
OPPOSITE trivial

graveyard *NOUN*
*He was buried in the local **graveyard**.*
• burial ground, cemetery, churchyard

graze *VERB*
*I **grazed** my knee when I fell off my bike.*
• scrape, cut, scratch, scuff

greasy *ADJECTIVE*
*I don't like **greasy** food.*
• fatty, oily

great *ADJECTIVE*
❶ *The inventor had made a **great** discovery.*
• important, significant, major, leading, noteworthy
OPPOSITES insignificant, minor
❷ *Mozart was a **great** composer.*
• famous, notable, celebrated, eminent, distinguished, outstanding, brilliant
❸ *Their voices echoed round the **great** hall.*
• big, huge, large, enormous, vast, immense, gigantic, extensive, cavernous
OPPOSITE small
❹ *Beth took **great** care over her knitting.*
• considerable, extreme, exact
OPPOSITE little
❺ *(informal) That is a **great** idea!*
• very good, excellent, marvellous, outstanding, superb, tremendous, wonderful *(informal)* brilliant, fantastic, super, smashing, terrific
OPPOSITES bad, awful

greed *NOUN*
*The king wanted more gold to satisfy his **greed**.*
• avarice, selfishness, hunger, craving, gluttony

A B C D E F G H I J K L M N O P Q R S T U V W X Y Z

greedy *ADJECTIVE*
❶ *The boys were so* ***greedy*** *that they ate all the cakes.*
• **gluttonous**
(informal) **piggish**
A common simile is **as greedy as a pig.**
❷ *Mr Skimp is very* ***greedy*** *with his money.*
• **selfish, miserly, tight-fisted, grasping**

green *ADJECTIVE, NOUN*

WORD WEB

SOME SHADES OF GREEN:

• **bottle-green, emerald, jade, khaki, lime, olive, pea-green**

greens *PLURAL NOUN*
see **vegetable**

greet *VERB*
My aunt ***greeted*** *us with a friendly wave.*
• **welcome, hail, receive, salute**

grew *past tense see* **grow**

grey *ADJECTIVE*
❶ *The old wizard had a bushy* ***grey*** *beard.*
• **silver, silvery, grizzly, hoary, whitish**
❷ *The mother's face was* ***grey*** *with worry.*
• **ashen, pale, leaden, wan**
❸ *The day began cold and* ***grey.***
• **dull, cloudy, overcast**

grief *NOUN*
He couldn't hide his ***grief*** *at his friend's death.*
• **sorrow, sadness, mourning, unhappiness, distress, anguish, heartache**
OPPOSITE **joy**

grieve *VERB*
❶ *The family is still* ***grieving*** *over her death.*
• **mourn, lament, weep**
OPPOSITE **rejoice**
❷ *It* ***grieves*** *me to leave so soon.*
• **sadden, upset, distress, hurt**
OPPOSITE **please**

grim *ADJECTIVE*
❶ *The judge wore a* ***grim*** *expression on his face.*
• **stern, severe, harsh, bad-tempered, sullen**
OPPOSITE **cheerful**
❷ *The detective made the* ***grim*** *discovery of the body.*
• **unpleasant, horrible, dreadful, terrible, hideous, shocking, gruesome, grisly**
OPPOSITE **pleasant**

grime *NOUN*
There was a layer of ***grime*** *on the floor.*
• **dirt, filth, muck, mire, mess**

grimy *ADJECTIVE*
Don't wipe those ***grimy*** *feet on the carpet!*
• **dirty, filthy, grubby, mucky, soiled**
OPPOSITE **clean**

grin *NOUN, VERB*
Mark arrived with a silly ***grin*** *on his face.*
• **smile, beam, smirk**
A large grin is a **broad, wide** or **cheesy grin.**

grind *VERB* **grinds, grinding, ground**
❶ ***Grind*** *the spices into a fine powder.*
• **crush, pound, powder, pulverise, mill**
❷ *This tool is used for* ***grinding*** *knives.*
• **sharpen, file, hone, whet**

grip *VERB*
❶ ***Grip*** *the handle tightly.*
• **grasp, seize, clutch, clasp, hold**
❷ *The audience was* ***gripped*** *by the film.*
• **fascinate, engross, absorb, enthrall**

grisly *ADJECTIVE*
We found the ***grisly*** *remains of a dead sheep.*
• **gruesome, gory, ghastly, hideous, nasty, revolting, sickening**

grit *NOUN*
❶ *I've got some* ***grit*** *in my shoe.*
• **gravel, dust, sand**
❷ *The marathon runners showed real* ***grit.***
• **bravery, courage, toughness, spirit, pluck**
(informal) **guts**

groan *VERB*
The wounded soldier ***groaned*** *with pain.*
• cry out, moan, sigh, wail

groove *NOUN*
Thick ***grooves*** *had been carved in the stone wall.*
• channel, furrow, rut, cut, scratch, slot

grope *VERB*
I ***groped*** *in the dark for the light switch.*
• fumble, feel about, flounder

gross *ADJECTIVE*
❶ *That is a* ***gross*** *exaggeration!*
• extreme, glaring, obvious, sheer, blatant, outright
❷ *Most ogres have* ***gross*** *table manners.*
• offensive, rude, coarse, vulgar

ground *past tense see* **grind**

ground *NOUN*
❶ *I planted some seeds in the* ***ground.***
• earth, soil, land
❷ *The* ***ground*** *was too wet to play on.*
• field, pitch, park, stadium, arena

group *NOUN*
❶ *Japan consists of a* ***group*** *of islands.*
• collection, set, batch, cluster, clump
❷ *A* ***group*** *of children was waiting at the bus stop.*
• crowd, bunch, gathering, band, body, gang
❸ *The book* ***group*** *meets once a month.*
• club, society, association, circle
❹ *We sorted the fossils into different* ***groups.***
• category, class, type, kind, sort

WORD WEB

WORDS FOR GROUPS OF PEOPLE:

a **band** of musicians
a **class** of pupils
a **company** or **troupe** of actors
a **congregation** of worshippers in church
a **coven** of witches
a **crew** of sailors
a **gang** of workers
a **horde** of invaders
a **team** of players

WORDS FOR GROUPS OF ANIMALS:

an **army** or **colony** of ants
a **band** of gorillas
a **brood** of chicks
a **covey** of partridges
a **flock** of sheep or birds
a **gaggle** of geese
a **herd** of cattle or elephants
a **litter** of pigs or puppies
a **pack** of wolves
a **pride** of lions
a **school** or **pod** of dolphins or whales
a **shoal** of fish
a **swarm** of insects
a **troop** of monkeys

WORDS FOR GROUPS OF THINGS:

a **battery** of guns
a **bunch** of flowers
a **clump** of trees
a **clutch** of eggs in a nest
a **constellation** or **galaxy** of stars
a **convoy** or **fleet** of ships

grow *VERB* **grows, growing, grew, grown**
❶ *The puppies have* ***grown*** *since I last saw them.*
• get bigger, put on growth, spring up, sprout
❷ *The number of children in the school has* ***grown.***
• increase, develop, enlarge, expand, build up
OPPOSITE decrease
❸ *Our neighbour* ***grows*** *orchids in her greenhouse.*
• cultivate, produce, raise, farm
❹ *It is* ***growing*** *dark outside.*
• become, get, turn

grown-up *ADJECTIVE*
The female cheetah has two ***grown-up*** *cubs.*
• adult, mature, fully grown
OPPOSITE young

grown-up *NOUN*
Don't tell the ***grown-ups.***
• adult
OPPOSITES young person, child

A B C D E F G H I J K L M N O P Q R S T U V W X Y Z

growth *NOUN*
❶ *There's been a* ***growth*** *of interest in golf for kids.*
• increase, rise, spread, expansion, development, enlargement
❷ *The doctor examined the* ***growth*** *on my foot.*
• lump, swelling, tumour

grub *NOUN*
I found a ***grub*** *on the cabbage leaf.*
• larva, maggot, caterpillar

grubby *ADJECTIVE*
My hands were ***grubby*** *from working in the garden.*
• dirty, filthy, grimy, messy, mucky, soiled
OPPOSITE clean

grudge *NOUN*
Captain Hook bore a ***grudge*** *against Peter Pan.*
• grievance, bitterness, resentment, hard feelings, ill will, spite

gruelling *ADJECTIVE*
The marathon is a ***gruelling*** *race.*
• hard, tough, demanding, exhausting, challenging, difficult, laborious, strenuous, backbreaking, punishing
OPPOSITE easy

gruesome *ADJECTIVE*
The battlefield was a ***gruesome*** *sight.*
• grisly, gory, ghastly, hideous, monstrous, revolting, sickening, appalling, dreadful, frightful, shocking, abominable

gruff *ADJECTIVE*
The ogre spoke in a ***gruff*** *voice.*
• harsh, rough, hoarse, husky, throaty

grumble *VERB*
You're always ***grumbling*** *about the weather!*
• complain, moan, groan, protest, whine, gripe

grumpy *ADJECTIVE*
Marge was ***grumpy*** *because she had a headache.*
• bad-tempered, cross, irritable, testy, tetchy, cantankerous
(informal) grouchy
OPPOSITE good-humoured

guarantee *VERB*
I ***guarantee*** *that you will enjoy the show.*
• promise, assure, pledge, vow

guard *VERB*
The cave was ***guarded*** *by a one-eyed giant.*
• protect, defend, stand guard over, patrol, safeguard, shield, watch over

guard *NOUN*
A ***guard*** *was on duty at the gate.*
• sentry, sentinel, warder, lookout, watchman

guardian *NOUN*
The ***guardian*** *of the treasure was a fierce dragon.*
• defender, protector, keeper, minder, custodian

guess *NOUN*
My ***guess*** *is that it will rain tomorrow.*
• estimate, prediction, feeling, hunch

guess *VERB*
❶ *There was a prize for* ***guessing*** *the weight of the cake.*
• estimate, judge, work out, gauge, predict, reckon
❷ *I* ***guess*** *you must be tired after your journey.*
• suppose, imagine, expect, assume, think

guest *NOUN*
We are having ***guests*** *for tea on Sunday.*
• visitor, caller, company

guide *NOUN*
❶ *Our* ***guide*** *showed us around the zoo.*
• courier, escort, leader, chaperone
❷ *We bought a useful* ***guide*** *to the city.*
• guidebook, handbook, manual

guide *VERB*
The explorers used the stars to ***guide*** *them at night.*
• direct, lead, steer, conduct, escort, show the way

guilt *NOUN*
❶ *The prisoner admitted his* ***guilt****.*
• responsibility, liability, blame, wrongdoing
OPPOSITE innocence

❷ *You could see the look of **guilt** on her face.*
• **shame, remorse, regret, penitence, disgrace, dishonour**

guilty *ADJECTIVE*
❶ *The prisoner was found **guilty** of the crime.*
• **responsible, to blame, at fault, in the wrong, liable**
OPPOSITE **innocent**
❷ *You have a **guilty** look on your face!*
• **ashamed, guilt-ridden, remorseful, sorry, conscience-stricken, repentant, shamefaced, sheepish**
OPPOSITE **unrepentant**

gulp *VERB*
*Peter **gulped** down the cake in one go.*
• **swallow, bolt, gobble, guzzle, devour**
for other ways to eat see **eat**

gulp *NOUN*
*Amanda took a long **gulp** of lemonade.*
• **swallow, mouthful**
(informal) **swig**

gun *NOUN*
for various weapons see **weapon**

gurgle *VERB*
*The mountain stream **gurgled** over the rocks.*
• **burble, babble**

gush *NOUN*
*There was a **gush** of water from the pipe.*
• **rush, stream, torrent, cascade, flood, jet, spout, spurt**

gush *VERB*
*Water **gushed** from the broken pipe.*
• **rush, stream, flow, pour, flood, spout, spurt, squirt**

gust *NOUN*
*A **gust** of wind carried the kite into the sky.*
• **blast, rush, puff, squall, flurry**

guzzle *VERB*
*The seagulls **guzzled** all the bread.*
• **gobble, gulp, bolt, devour**
for other ways to eat see **eat**

habit *NOUN*
❶ *It's her **habit** to go for a walk each morning.*
• **custom, practice, routine, rule**
❷ *My dog has a **habit** of scratching his ear.*
• **mannerism, way, tendency, inclination, quirk**

hack *VERB*
*The explorers **hacked** their way through the jungle.*
• **chop, cut, hew, slash, lop**

had *past tense see* **have**

haggard *ADJECTIVE*
*The warriors looked **haggard** after the battle.*
• **drawn, gaunt, thin, pinched, wasted, shrunken, wan**
OPPOSITE **healthy**

haggle *VERB*
*The men **haggled** over the price of the gems.*
• **bargain, negotiate, argue, wrangle**

hair *NOUN*
*Rapunzel's **hair** reached down to the ground.*
• **locks, tresses**
(informal) **mop**

A single piece of hair is a **strand**.
A bunch of hair is a **hank, lock** or **tress**.
A mass of bushy hair is a **shock** of hair.
False hair is a **hairpiece, toupee** or **wig**.
An area without hair is a **bald patch**.
The way hair is cut is a **hairstyle** or *(informal)* **hairdo** or *(formal)* **coiffure**.
Hair is cut or styled by a **hairdresser** or **hairstylist**.
Men's hair is also cut by a **barber**.

a b c d e f g h i j k l m n o p q r s t u v w x y z

WORD WEB

SOME HAIRSTYLES:

• Afro, bob, braids, bun, bunches, chignon, cornrows, crew cut, curls, dreadlocks, fishtail, French braid or plait, fringe, Mohican, perm, pigtail, plaits, ponytail, quiff, ringlets, short back and sides, sideburns, skinhead, topknot

HAIR ON AN ANIMAL:

• bristles, coat, down, fleece, fur, mane, whiskers

WRITING TIPS

You can use these words to describe hair:

TO DESCRIBE ITS COLOUR:

• auburn, blond or blonde, brunette, *(informal)* carroty, dark, fair, flaxen, ginger, grey, grizzled, hoary, mousy, platinum blonde, raven, red, silver

He was a man of fifty, with a shock of grizzled hair, a broad but not unkindly face of regular features, bushy eyebrows, and the finest forehead that I ever saw.—MOONFLEET, J. Meade Faulkner

TO DESCRIBE HOW IT LOOKS OR FEELS:

• bristly, bushy, coarse, curly, dishevelled, fine, frizzy, glossy, greasy, lank, limp, matted, ringletted, shaggy, shiny, silky, spiky, straggly, straight, stringy, tangled, thick, tousled, tuggy, unkempt, wavy, windswept, wispy

The hair on Mr Twit's face didn't grow smooth and matted as it does on most hairy-faced men. It grew in spikes that stuck out straight like the bristles of a nailbrush.—THE TWITS, Roald Dahl

for ways to describe animal hair see **animal**

hairy *ADJECTIVE*
Mammoths were like elephants with thick ***hairy*** *coats.*
• shaggy, bushy, bristly, woolly, fleecy, furry, fuzzy, long-haired, hirsute

hall *NOUN*
❶ *The* ***hall*** *was full for the concert.*
• assembly hall, auditorium, concert hall, theatre
❷ *You can use the coat stand in the* ***hall***.
• entrance hall, hallway, lobby, foyer

halt *VERB*
❶ *The car* ***halted*** *at the red light.*
• stop, come to a halt, draw up, pull up, wait
❷ *A traffic jam* ***halted*** *the traffic.*
• stop, check, obstruct
❸ *Work* ***halted*** *when the whistle went.*
• end, cease, terminate, break off
OPPOSITES start, go

halve *VERB*
❶ ***Halve*** *the tomatoes and scoop out the seeds.*
• cut in half, divide into halves, split in two
❷ *The workforce has been* ***halved*** *in the last five years.*
• cut by half, reduce by half

hammer *VERB*
I ***hammered*** *on the door, but no one answered.*
• strike, beat, knock, batter, pummel, pound

hamper *VERB*
Bad weather ***hampered*** *the rescuers.*
• hinder, hold up, obstruct, impede, restrict, handicap, frustrate
OPPOSITE help

hand *NOUN*
When you clench your hand you make a fist.
The flat part of the inside of your hand is the **palm**.
Work that you do with your hands is **manual** work.

hand *VERB*
The postman ***handed*** *me several letters.*
• give, pass, present, offer, deliver
➤ **to hand something down**
This brooch has been ***handed down*** *from generation to generation.*
• pass down, pass on, bequeath

handicap *NOUN*
*Lack of experience can be a **handicap** in some jobs.*
• disadvantage, drawback, hindrance, obstacle, problem, difficulty, limitation
OPPOSITE advantage

handicap *VERB*
*The search was **handicapped** by bad weather.*
• hamper, hinder, hold up, restrict, impede
OPPOSITE help

handle *NOUN*
*The door **handle** is broken.*
• grip, handgrip, knob, shaft
The handle of a sword is the hilt.

handle *VERB*
❶ *Please don't **handle** the exhibits.*
• touch, feel, hold, stroke, fondle, finger, grasp
❷ *The referee **handled** the game well.*
• manage, control, conduct, deal with, cope with, tackle

handsome *ADJECTIVE*
❶ *Prince Charming was very **handsome**.*
• attractive, good-looking, nice-looking, gorgeous
(informal) dishy
OPPOSITES ugly, unattractive
❷ *They sold their house for a **handsome** profit.*
• big, large, substantial, sizeable
OPPOSITE slight

handy *ADJECTIVE*
❶ *This **handy** gadget is for peeling potatoes.*
• useful, helpful, convenient, practical
OPPOSITE awkward
❷ *I always keep my umbrella **handy**.*
• accessible, available, close at hand, nearby, ready
OPPOSITE inaccessible

hang *VERB* **hangs, hanging, hung**
❶ *A monkey was **hanging** from the tree branch.*
• dangle, be suspended, swing, sway
❷ *The dog had hair **hanging** down over his eyes.*
• droop, drape, flop, trail, cascade
❸ *I **hung** the picture on the wall.*
• fix, attach, fasten, stick, peg
❹ *Smoke **hung** in the air.*
• float, hover, drift, linger, cling
➤ **to hang about** or **around**
*Don't **hang about**; we'll miss the bus.*
• delay, dawdle, linger, loiter
➤ **to hang on** *(informal)*
*Try to **hang on** a bit longer.*
• carry on, continue, stay, remain, persist, keep going, persevere
➤ **to hang on to something**
❶ *Hang on to the rope.*
• hold, grip, grasp
❷ *Hang on to your bus ticket.*
• keep, retain, save

happen *VERB*
*Did anything interesting **happen** today?*
• take place, occur, arise, come about, crop up, emerge, result

happening *NOUN*
*There have been strange **happenings** here lately.*
• event, occurrence, incident, phenomenon

happiness *NOUN*
*The bride's face glowed with **happiness**.*
• joy, joyfulness, delight, jubilation, pleasure, contentment, gladness, cheerfulness, merriment, ecstasy, bliss
OPPOSITE sorrow

happy *ADJECTIVE*

OVERUSED WORD

Try to vary the words you use for **happy**. Here are some other words you could use.

FOR A HAPPY MOOD OR HAPPY PERSON:

• cheerful, cheery, joyful, jolly, merry, delighted, light-hearted, contented, gleeful
Dr Mead ... was a tall, broad-shouldered man with kind grey eyes, and a cheerful smile. Pollyanna liked him at once, and told him so.
—POLLYANNA, Eleanor H. Porter
*A common simile is **as happy as a lark**.*
OPPOSITES unhappy, sad

FOR A VERY HAPPY MOOD:

• **thrilled, ecstatic, elated, overjoyed**
(informal) **over the moon, thrilled to bits, tickled pink**
*Megan was **ecstatic** when she won first prize.*

FOR A HAPPY TIME OR HAPPY EXPERIENCE:

• **enjoyable, joyous, glorious, blissful, heavenly, idyllic**
*They spent a **glorious** summer on the island.*

FOR A HAPPY COINCIDENCE:

• **lucky, fortunate, favourable**
*By a **lucky** coincidence, we took the same train.*
OPPOSITE **unfortunate**

TO BE HAPPY TO DO SOMETHING:

• **pleased, glad, willing, delighted**
*I would be **glad** to help organise the party.*
OPPOSITE **unwilling**

harass *VERB*
*I keep being **harassed** with junk email.*
• **pester, trouble, bother, annoy, disturb, plague, torment, badger, hound, hassle**

harbour *NOUN*
*Several yachts were tied up in the **harbour**.*
• **port, dock, mooring, quay, pier, wharf**

hard *ADJECTIVE*

OVERUSED WORD

Try to vary the words you use for **hard**. Here are some other words you could use.

FOR HARD GROUND OR A HARD SURFACE:

• **solid, firm, dense, compact, rigid, stiff**
*The ground was **solid** and covered with frost.*
Common similes are **as hard as nails** and **as hard as a rock**.
OPPOSITE **soft**

FOR A HARD PULL OR HARD PUSH:

• **strong, forceful, heavy, powerful, violent**
*Try giving the door a **heavy** push.*
OPPOSITE **light**

FOR HARD WORK:

• **tough, gruelling, strenuous, tiring, exhausting, laborious, back-breaking**
*Digging the tunnel was **strenuous** work.*
OPPOSITE **easy**

FOR A HARD WORKER:

• **energetic, keen, diligent**
*At first, the apprentice was very **diligent**.*
OPPOSITE **lazy**

FOR A HARD PERSON OR HARD TREATMENT:

• **strict, stern, harsh, severe, cruel, hard-hearted, heartless, unfeeling, unkind**
'How dare you say I'm freckled and redheaded? You are a rude, impolite, unfeeling woman!'
—ANNE OF GREEN GABLES, L. M. Montgomery
OPPOSITE **mild**

FOR A HARD PROBLEM OR HARD QUESTION:

• **difficult, complicated, complex, intricate, perplexing, puzzling, baffling, knotty, thorny**
*None of us could solve the **complex** riddle.*
OPPOSITE **simple**

hard *ADVERB*
❶ *Ros is working **hard** at learning French.*
• **strenuously, energetically, diligently, keenly, intently**
❷ *It has been raining **hard** all afternoon.*
• **heavily, steadily**
(informal) **cats and dogs**

harden *VERB*
*We left the cement to **harden**.*
• **set, solidify, stiffen**
If you harden clay in a kiln, you **bake** or **fire** it.
OPPOSITE **soften**

hardly *ADVERB*
*I could **hardly** see in the fog.*
• barely, scarcely, only just, with difficulty

hardship *NOUN*
*They suffered years of **hardship** during the war.*
• suffering, trouble, difficulty, distress, misery, misfortune, need, want

hardy *ADJECTIVE*
*You must be **hardy** to go camping in winter.*
• tough, strong, robust, sturdy, hearty, rugged
OPPOSITE tender

harm *VERB*
❶ *His captors didn't **harm** him.*
• hurt, injure, ill-treat, wound
❷ *Too much direct sunlight may **harm** this plant.*
• damage, spoil, ruin

harm *NOUN*
*I didn't mean to cause him any **harm**.*
• damage, hurt, injury, pain
OPPOSITE benefit

harmful *ADJECTIVE*
*Junk food can be **harmful** to your health.*
• damaging, dangerous, destructive, injurious, unhealthy
OPPOSITES harmless, beneficial

harmless *ADJECTIVE*
❶ *You can drink the potion—it is quite **harmless**.*
• safe, non-toxic, innocuous
OPPOSITES harmful, dangerous
❷ *It was just a bit of **harmless** fun.*
• innocent, inoffensive

harsh *ADJECTIVE*
❶ *The trumpet sounded loud and **harsh**.*
• rough, rasping, grating, jarring, shrill, raucous
OPPOSITES soft, gentle
❷ *We blinked in the **harsh** light.*
• bright, brilliant, dazzling, glaring
OPPOSITES soft, subdued
❸ *The rescue team braved the **harsh** weather.*
• severe, strict, cruel, hard, tough, bleak
OPPOSITE mild
❹ *The coach had some **harsh** words to say.*
• strong, sharp, unkind, unfriendly

harvest *NOUN*
*There was a good **harvest** of apples this year.*
• crop, yield, return
Things grown on a farm are **produce**.
A plentiful harvest is a **bumper harvest**.

haste *NOUN*
*The elves worked with great **haste**.*
• hurry, rush, speed, urgency

hasty *ADJECTIVE*
❶ *The robbers made a **hasty** exit.*
• fast, hurried, quick, sudden, swift, rapid, speedy
OPPOSITE slow
❷ *The king regretted his **hasty** decision.*
• rash, reckless, impatient, foolhardy, thoughtless
OPPOSITES careful, measured

hat *NOUN*

WORD WEB

SOME KINDS OF HAT:

• balaclava, baseball cap, beanie, bearskin, beret, bicycle helmet, bonnet, bowler hat, cap, deerstalker, hard hat, helmet, mitre, mortar board, panama hat, skullcap, sombrero, sou'wester, Stetson, sun hat, tam o' shanter, top hat, trilby, turban, woolly hat

hatch *VERB*
*The gang **hatched** a plot to rob a bank.*
• plan, develop, conceive, think up, devise (*informal*) cook up, dream up

hate *VERB*
❶ *Eddie **hates** broccoli and peas.*
• dislike, detest, despise, loathe
❷ *I **hate** to bother you.*
• be sorry, be reluctant, regret
OPPOSITES like, love

hate *NOUN*
*Washing dishes is one of my pet **hates**.*
• dislike

hatred *NOUN*
The evil wizard stared with ***hatred*** *in his eyes.*
• hate, loathing, dislike, hostility, enmity, contempt, detestation
OPPOSITE love

haughty *ADJECTIVE*
Celia sniffed and gave us a ***haughty*** *look.*
• proud, arrogant, conceited, lofty, superior, pompous, disdainful
(informal) stuck-up
OPPOSITE modest

haul *VERB*
Eric ***hauled*** *his bike out of the shed.*
• drag, pull, tow, draw

haunt *VERB*
for things a ghost might do see **ghost**

have *VERB* **has, having, had**
❶ *I* ***have*** *my own phone now.*
• own, possess
❷ *Our house* ***has*** *three bedrooms.*
• consist of, comprise, include, incorporate
❸ *We are* ***having*** *a barbecue at the weekend.*
• hold, organise, provide, host, throw
❹ *Dad* ***had*** *trouble finding a place to park.*
• experience, go through, meet with, run into, face, suffer
❺ *Did you* ***have*** *a good time at the party?*
• experience, enjoy
❻ *The BBC has* ***had*** *lots of emails.*
• receive, get, be given, be sent
❼ *Sharon* ***had*** *the last slice of cake.*
• take, consume, eat
❽ *One of the giraffes has* ***had*** *a baby.*
• give birth to, bear, produce
❾ *I* ***have*** *to be home by six o'clock.*
• must, need, ought, should

haven *NOUN*
The lake is a ***haven*** *for wild birds.*
• refuge, shelter, retreat, sanctuary

havoc *NOUN*
The pixies were causing ***havoc*** *in the kitchen.*
• chaos, mayhem, disorder, disruption

hazard *NOUN*
The road through the mountains is full of ***hazards****.*
• danger, risk, threat, trap, pitfall, snag

hazardous *ADJECTIVE*
They made the ***hazardous*** *journey to the South Pole.*
• dangerous, risky, unsafe, perilous, precarious
OPPOSITE safe

haze *NOUN*
I could hardly see through the ***haze****.*
• fog, mist, cloud, steam, vapour

hazy *ADJECTIVE*
❶ *The face in the photograph was rather* ***hazy****.*
• blurred, misty, unclear, dim, faint
OPPOSITES clear, sharp
❷ *I have a* ***hazy*** *memory of that day.*
• uncertain, vague
OPPOSITE clear, strong

head *NOUN*
❶ *My dad hit his* ***head*** *on the attic ceiling.*
• skull, crown
(informal) nut
for other parts of your body see **body**
❷ *Can you add up these figures in your* ***head****?*
• brain, mind, intellect, intelligence
❸ *There is a new* ***head*** *of the music department.*
• chief, leader, manager, director, controller
(informal) boss
❹ *The girls waited at the* ***head*** *of the queue.*
• front, lead, top
OPPOSITES back, rear

head *VERB*
The professor was chosen to ***head*** *the expedition.*
• lead, be in charge of, direct, command, manage, oversee, supervise

➤ **to head for**
At the end of the day we ***headed for*** *home.*
• go towards, make for, aim for

heading *NOUN*
Each chapter had a different ***heading****.*
• title, caption, headline

headlong *ADJECTIVE*
We made a ***headlong*** *dash to get under cover.*
• quick, hurried, hasty, breakneck

headquarters *PLURAL NOUN*
The spy contacted ***headquarters*** *for instructions.*
• base, head office
(informal) HQ

head teacher *NOUN*
The ***head teacher*** *runs the school.*
• headmaster or headmistress, principal

heal *VERB*
❶ *It took two months for my leg to* ***heal*** *properly.*
• get better, mend, recover
❷ *Part of a vet's job is to* ***heal*** *sick animals.*
• cure, make better, treat, restore

health *NOUN*
The puppies are in excellent ***health****.*
• condition, fitness, shape, strength, vigour, well-being
for various medical treatments see **medicine**

healthy *ADJECTIVE*
❶ *Neil has always been a* ***healthy*** *child.*
• well, fit, strong, sturdy, vigorous, robust
(informal) in good shape
OPPOSITES ill, sickly
❷ *Porridge makes a very* ***healthy*** *breakfast.*
• health-giving, wholesome, invigorating
OPPOSITE unhealthy

heap *NOUN*
There was an untidy ***heap*** *of clothes on the floor.*
• mound, pile, stack, mountain, collection, mass

heap *VERB*
We ***heaped*** *up all the rubbish in the corner.*
• pile, stack, collect, bank, mass

hear *VERB* **hears, hearing, heard**
❶ *Did you* ***hear*** *what she said?*
• catch, listen to, make out, pick up, overhear, pay attention to
A sound that you can hear is **audible**.
A sound that you cannot hear is **inaudible**.
❷ *Have you* ***heard*** *the news?*
• be told, discover, find out, learn, gather

heart *NOUN*
❶ *Have you no* ***heart****?*
• compassion, feeling, sympathy, tenderness, affection, humanity, kindness, love
❷ *The hotel is located right in the* ***heart*** *of the city.*
• centre, middle, hub
❸ *They tried to get to the* ***heart*** *of the problem.*
• core, essence

heartless *ADJECTIVE*
How could she be so ***heartless****?*
• hard-hearted, callous, cruel, inhuman, unfeeling, unkind, pitiless, ruthless
OPPOSITE kind

hearty *ADJECTIVE*
❶ *He gave me a* ***hearty*** *slap on the back.*
• strong, forceful, vigorous
OPPOSITE feeble
❷ *The girls had a* ***hearty*** *appetite after their walk.*
• big, healthy
OPPOSITE poor
❸ *Our friends gave us a* ***hearty*** *welcome.*
• enthusiastic, sincere, warm
OPPOSITE unenthusiastic

heat *NOUN*
❶ *The cat basked in the* ***heat*** *of the fire.*
• warmth, glow
❷ *Last summer, the* ***heat*** *made me feel ill.*
• hot weather, high temperatures, closeness
A long period of hot weather is a **heatwave**.

heave *VERB*
The men ***heaved*** *the sacks onto a lorry.*
• haul, drag, pull, draw, tow, tug, hoist, lug, lift, raise, throw

A B C D E F G H I J K L M N O P Q R S T U V W X Y Z

heavy *ADJECTIVE*
❶ *The box was too* ***heavy*** *for me to lift.*
• **weighty, massive, dense, bulky**
❷ *Digging the garden is* ***heavy*** *work.*
• **hard, tough, gruelling, back-breaking, strenuous**
❸ *This book makes* ***heavy*** *reading.*
• **serious, intense, demanding**
❹ *The rain has caused* ***heavy*** *flooding.*
• **severe, extreme, torrential**
❺ *Both sides suffered* ***heavy*** *losses in the battle.*
• **large, substantial, considerable**
❻ *A* ***heavy*** *mist hung over the landscape.*
• **dense, thick**
OPPOSITE **light**
➤ **with a heavy heart**
She said goodbye ***with a heavy heart****.*
• **unhappily, sadly, sorrowfully, gloomily, in low spirits**

hectic *ADJECTIVE*
The days before the wedding were ***hectic****.*
• **busy, frantic, feverish, frenzied, chaotic**
(informal) **manic**
OPPOSITE **quiet, leisurely**

heed *VERB*
The sailors didn't ***heed*** *the captain's warning.*
• **listen to, pay attention to, take notice of, attend to, regard, obey, follow, mark, mind, note**
OPPOSITE **ignore**

hefty *ADJECTIVE*
❶ *The postman was carrying a* ***hefty*** *parcel.*
• **big, large, weighty, massive, bulky**
❷ *The wrestler was a* ***hefty*** *man.*
• **strong, sturdy, muscular, powerful, brawny, burly, hulking**
(informal) **beefy**
OPPOSITE **slight**

height *NOUN*
❶ *The plane was flying at its normal* ***height****.*
• **altitude, elevation**
❷ *His* ***height*** *wasn't a problem.*
• **tallness, size, stature**

held *past tense see* **hold**

help *NOUN*
❶ *Thank you for your* ***help****.*
• **aid, assistance, support, guidance, cooperation, advice**
OPPOSITE **hindrance**
❷ *Would a torch be of any* ***help*** *to you?*
• **use, benefit**

help *VERB*
❶ *Could you please* ***help*** *me with my luggage?*
• **aid, assist, cooperate with**
(informal) **give a hand to**
❷ *The Red Cross is an organisation that* ***helps*** *people in need.*
• **be helpful to, support, serve, stand by**
❸ *This medicine will* ***help*** *your cough.*
• **make better, cure, ease, relieve, improve**
OPPOSITES **aggravate, worsen**
❹ *I can't* ***help*** *coughing.*
• **stop, avoid, prevent, refrain from**

helpful *ADJECTIVE*
❶ *The staff were friendly and* ***helpful****.*
• **obliging, cooperative, kind, considerate, thoughtful, sympathetic**
OPPOSITE **unhelpful**
❷ *The shop assistant gave us some* ***helpful*** *advice.*
• **useful, valuable, worthwhile, beneficial, profitable**
OPPOSITE **worthless**

helping *NOUN*
I got a huge ***helping*** *of ice cream.*
• **serving, portion, plateful, amount, share, ration**

helpless *ADJECTIVE*
Kittens are born blind and ***helpless****.*
• **powerless, weak, feeble, dependent, defenceless, vulnerable**
OPPOSITE **independent, strong**

hem *VERB*
➤ **to hem someone in**
The bus was ***hemmed in*** *by some parked cars.*
• **shut in, box in, encircle, enclose, surround**

herb *NOUN*

WORD WEB

SOME COMMON HERBS:

• basil, chamomile, caraway, chervil, chicory, chive, coriander, cumin, dill, fennel, fenugreek, hyssop, lemon balm, liquorice, lovage, marjoram, mint, oregano, parsley, peppermint, rosemary, sage, tarragon, thyme

herd *NOUN*

for groups of animals see **group**

heroic *ADJECTIVE*

The firefighters made a ***heroic*** *effort to put out the blaze.*

• bold, brave, courageous, daring, fearless, noble, selfless, valiant

OPPOSITE cowardly

for words to describe superheroes see **superhero**

hesitant *ADJECTIVE*

The puppy was ***hesitant*** *about going outside.*

• uncertain, unsure, doubtful, cautious, tentative, timid, shy, wary

OPPOSITE confident

hesitate *VERB*

I ***hesitated*** *for a moment before ringing the doorbell.*

• pause, delay, wait, hold back, dither, falter, waver

(informal) think twice

hidden *ADJECTIVE*

❶ *The giant kept his gold* ***hidden*** *in a wooden chest.*

• concealed, out of sight, unseen, invisible, covered, disguised

OPPOSITE visible

❷ *There's a* ***hidden*** *message in the riddle.*

• secret, mysterious, obscure, coded, cryptic

OPPOSITE obvious

hide *VERB* **hides, hiding, hid, hidden**

❶ *Quick! Someone's coming—we'd better* ***hide****.*

• go into hiding, take cover, take refuge, keep out of sight, lie low, go to ground

❷ *They* ***hid*** *the jewels in a secret drawer.*

• conceal, secrete, bury

(informal) stash

OPPOSITE expose

❸ *The clouds* ***hid*** *the sun.*

• blot out, cover, screen, shroud, veil, mask

OPPOSITE uncover

❹ *I tried to* ***hide*** *my feelings.*

• disguise, keep secret, suppress, camouflage, cloak

OPPOSITE show

hideous *ADJECTIVE*

The troll had a ***hideous*** *grin on his face.*

• repulsive, revolting, ugly, grotesque, monstrous, ghastly, gruesome, horrible, appalling, dreadful, frightful

OPPOSITE beautiful

high *ADJECTIVE*

❶ *The castle was surrounded by a* ***high*** *wall.*

• tall, towering, elevated, lofty

OPPOSITE low

❷ *Sir Grinalot was a knight of* ***high*** *rank and status.*

• senior, top, leading, important, prominent, powerful

OPPOSITES low, junior

❸ *House prices are very* ***high*** *at the moment.*

• expensive, dear, costly, excessive

OPPOSITE low

❹ *A* ***high*** *wind was blowing.*

• strong, powerful, forceful, extreme

OPPOSITE gentle

❺ *The pixie spoke in a* ***high*** *squeaky voice.*

• high-pitched, sharp, shrill, piercing

OPPOSITE deep

A high singing voice is **soprano or treble**.

highlight *NOUN*

The ***highlight*** *of the holiday was spotting a wild dolphin.*

• high point, high spot, best moment, climax

A B C D E F G H I J K L M N O P Q R S T U V W X Y Z

highly *ADVERB*
*It is **highly** unusual to see badgers during the day.*
• **very, extremely, exceptionally, considerably, decidedly**

hike *VERB, NOUN*
*We often go **hiking** across the moors.*
• **trek, walk, ramble, tramp**

hilarious *ADJECTIVE*
*The boys thought the cartoon was **hilarious**.*
• **funny, amusing, comical**
(informal) **hysterical**

hill *NOUN*
❶ *From the top of this **hill** you can see for miles.*
• **mount, peak, ridge**
A small hill is a **hillock** or **mound**.
The top of a hill is the **summit**.
❷ *Jenny pushed her bike up the steep **hill**.*
• **slope, rise, incline, ascent, gradient**

hinder *VERB*
*The snowstorm **hindered** the rescue attempt.*
• **hamper, hold up, obstruct, impede, slow down, stand in the way of, restrict, handicap**
OPPOSITE **help**

hindrance *NOUN*
*The sharks were a **hindrance** to the divers.*
• **obstacle, obstruction, handicap, inconvenience, difficulty, disadvantage, drawback**
OPPOSITE **help**

hint *NOUN*
❶ *I don't know the answer—can you give me a **hint**?*
• **clue, indication, sign, suggestion, inkling**
❷ *The magazine offers handy **hints** for decorating.*
• **tip, pointer**

hint *VERB*
*Mum **hinted** that we might be getting a puppy.*
• **give a hint, suggest, imply, indicate**

hire *VERB*
If you hire a bus or aircraft you **charter** it.
If you hire someone to do a job you **engage** or **employ** them.
If you hire a building for a time you **lease** or **rent** it.

historic *ADJECTIVE*
*The first landing on the moon was a **historic** event.*
• **famous, notable, celebrated, important, renowned, momentous, significant, major**
OPPOSITE **unimportant**
WHICH WORD? Note that **historic** is not the same as **historical**. A **historic** event is important in history, whereas a **historical** event simply happened in the past.

historical *ADJECTIVE*
*Robin Hood may have been a **historical** character.*
• **real, real-life, true, actual, authentic**
OPPOSITE **fictitious**
WHICH WORD? Note that **historical** is not the same as **historic**. A **historical** event simply happened in the past, whereas a **historic** event is important in history.

history *NOUN*
❶ *Dr Rice is an expert on Egyptian **history**.*
• **heritage, past, antiquity, past times, olden days**
❷ *She wrote a **history** of the First World War.*
• **account, chronicle, record**
The history of a person's life is their **biography**.
The history of your own life is your **autobiography** or **memoirs**.

hit *NOUN*
❶ *Matt got a nasty **hit** on the head.*
• **bump, blow, bang, knock, whack**
A hit with your fist is a **punch**.
A hit with your open hand is a **slap** or **smack**.
A hit with a bat or club is a **drive, stroke** or **swipe**.
❷ *Their new CD was an instant **hit**.*
• **success, triumph**
(informal) **winner**

hit *VERB* **hits, hitting, hit**
❶ *Auntie Flo* ***hit*** *the burglar on the head with her umbrella.*
• **strike, knock, bang, bash, thump, bump, crack, rap, slam, swipe, slog, cuff**
(informal) **whack, wham, wallop, sock, clout, clobber, belt, biff**
(old use) **smite**
To hit with your fist is to **punch.**
To hit with the palm of your hand is to **slap** or **smack.**
To punish someone by hitting them is to **beat** them.
To hit someone with a stick is to **club** them.
To hit your toe on something is to **stub** it.
To kill an insect by hitting it is to **swat** it.
To hit something repeatedly is to **batter, buffet** or **pound** it.
To hit something gently is to **tap** it.
for ways to hit a ball see **ball**
❷ *The drought has* ***hit*** *many farms in the area.*
• **affect, damage, harm, hurt**

hoard *NOUN*
Hamish keeps a ***hoard*** *of sweets in his desk.*
• **cache, store, stock, supply, pile, stockpile**
A hoard of treasure is a **treasure trove.**

hoard *VERB*
Squirrels ***hoard*** *nuts for the winter.*
• **store, collect, gather, save, put by, pile up, stockpile**
(informal) **stash away**

hoarse *ADJECTIVE*
Mr Barker's voice was ***hoarse*** *from shouting.*
• **rough, harsh, husky, croaky, throaty, gruff, rasping, gravelly**

hoax *NOUN*
The telephone call was a ***hoax.***
• **joke, practical joke, prank, trick, spoof**
(informal) **con, scam**

hobby *NOUN*
My favourite ***hobby*** *is snorkelling.*
• **pastime, pursuit, interest, activity, recreation**

hoist *VERB*
The crane ***hoisted*** *the crates on to a ship.*
• **lift, pull up, raise, heave, winch up**

hold *NOUN*
The vet took a firm ***hold*** *of the dog's collar.*
• **grip, grasp, clutch, clasp**

hold *VERB* **holds, holding, held**
❶ *Please* ***hold*** *the dog's lead.*
• **clasp, grasp, grip, cling to, hang on to, clutch, seize**
❷ *Can I* ***hold*** *the baby?*
• **embrace, hug, cradle**
❸ *They* ***held*** *the suspect until the police arrived.*
• **confine, detain, keep**
❹ *Will the ladder* ***hold*** *my weight?*
• **bear, support, carry, take**
❺ *If our luck* ***holds,*** *we could reach the final.*
• **continue, last, carry on, persist, stay**
❻ *She* ***holds*** *strong opinions.*
• **believe in, maintain, stick to**

➤ **to hold out**
❶ *The robot* ***held out*** *one of his arms.*
• **extend, reach out, stick out, stretch out**
❷ *Our supplies won't* ***hold out*** *much longer.*
• **keep going, last, carry on, continue, endure**

➤ **to hold something up**
❶ *Please* ***hold up*** *your hand.*
• **lift, put up, raise**
❷ *The accident* ***held up*** *the traffic.*
• **delay, hinder, slow down**

hole *NOUN*
❶ *The meteor created a massive* ***hole*** *in the ground.*
• **pit, hollow, crater, dent, depression, cavity, chasm, abyss**
❷ *The rabbits escaped through a* ***hole*** *in the fence.*
• **gap, opening, breach, break, cut, slit, gash, split, tear, vent**

holiday *NOUN*
We spent our summer ***holiday*** *in Ireland.*
• **vacation, break, leave, time off**

hollow *ADJECTIVE*
Tennis balls are ***hollow.***
• **empty, unfilled**
OPPOSITE **solid**

hollow *NOUN*
The ball rolled into a ***hollow*** *in the ground.*
• **dip, dent, depression, hole, pit, crater**
A hollow between two hills is a **valley.**

hollow *VERB*
*We **hollowed** out a pumpkin to make a Halloween lantern.*
• dig, excavate, gouge, scoop

holy *ADJECTIVE*
❶ *The pilgrims knelt to pray in the **holy** shrine.*
• sacred, blessed, revered
❷ *The pilgrims were **holy** people.*
• religious, spiritual, devout, pious, godly, saintly

home *NOUN*
*The hurricane forced people to flee their **homes**.*
• house, residence, dwelling, abode, lodging
A home for the sick is a **convalescent home** or **nursing home**.
A place where a bird or animal lives is its **habitat**.
see also **house**
for homes of wild animals see **animal**

homely *ADJECTIVE*
*The hotel was small with a **homely** atmosphere.*
• friendly, informal, cosy, familiar, relaxed, easy-going, comfortable, simple

honest *ADJECTIVE*
❶ *He's an **honest** boy, so he gave the money back.*
• good, honourable, law-abiding, moral, trustworthy, upright, virtuous
OPPOSITE dishonest
❷ *Please give me your **honest** opinion.*
• sincere, genuine, truthful, direct, frank, candid, plain, straightforward, unbiased
OPPOSITE insincere

honour *NOUN*
❶ *Her success brought **honour** to the school.*
• credit, good reputation, good name, respect, praise, acclaim
❷ *It's an **honour** to meet you.*
• privilege, distinction

honour *VERB*
*The winners were **honoured** at a special ceremony.*
• praise, celebrate, salute, give credit to, pay tribute to, glorify

honourable *ADJECTIVE*
❶ *The knight was an **honourable** man.*
• good, honest, sincere, noble, principled, moral, righteous, trustworthy, upright, virtuous, worthy, decent, fair, trusty
❷ *It was an **honourable** thing to do.*
• noble, admirable, praiseworthy, decent
OPPOSITE unworthy

hook *VERB*
❶ *Dad **hooked** the trailer to the car.*
• attach, fasten, hitch, connect, couple
❷ *The angler **hooked** an enormous fish.*
• catch, land, take

hop *VERB*
*The goblins **hopped** about in excitement.*
• jump, leap, skip, spring, prance, caper, bound, dance

hope *VERB*
*I **hope** to see you again soon.*
• wish, trust, expect, look forward

hope *NOUN*
❶ *Her dearest **hope** was to see her family again.*
• ambition, dream, desire, wish
❷ *There's **hope** of better weather tomorrow.*
• prospect, expectation, likelihood

hopeful *ADJECTIVE*
❶ *I am feeling **hopeful** about tomorrow's match.*
• optimistic, confident, positive, expectant
OPPOSITE pessimistic
❷ *The future is beginning to look more **hopeful**.*
• promising, encouraging, favourable, reassuring
OPPOSITE discouraging

hopeless *ADJECTIVE*
❶ *The shipwrecked crew were in a **hopeless** situation.*
• desperate, wretched, beyond hope
OPPOSITE hopeful
❷ *I'm **hopeless** at ice-skating.*
• bad, poor, incompetent
(informal) useless, rubbish
OPPOSITES good, competent

horde *NOUN*
Hordes of people were queuing for tickets.
• crowd, throng, mob, swarm, gang, group

horizontal *ADJECTIVE*
*Lay the pole on the ground in a **horizontal** position.*
• flat, level
OPPOSITE vertical

horrible *ADJECTIVE*
*What a **horrible** smell!*
• awful, terrible, dreadful, appalling, unpleasant, disagreeable, offensive, objectionable, disgusting, repulsive, revolting, horrendous, horrid, nasty, hateful, odious, loathsome, beastly, ghastly
OPPOSITE pleasant

horrific *ADJECTIVE*
*The film has some **horrific** scenes of battle.*
• horrifying, terrifying, shocking, gruesome, dreadful, appalling, ghastly, hideous, atrocious, grisly, sickening

horrify *VERB*
*We were **horrified** by the sight of the monster.*
• appal, shock, terrify, frighten, alarm, scare, sicken, disgust

horror *NOUN*
❶ *Ingrid screamed in **horror** when she saw the snake.*
• terror, fear, fright, alarm, dread
❷ *The film depicts the full **horror** of war.*
• awfulness, hideousness, gruesomeness, ghastliness, frightfulness

horse *NOUN*

WORD WEB

A male horse is a **stallion** and a female is a **mare**.
A young horse is a **foal**, **colt** (male) or **filly** (female).
An uncomplimentary word for a horse is **nag**.
A poetic word for a horse is **steed**.
A word meaning 'to do with horses' is **equine**.
A cross between a donkey and a horse is a **mule**.

SOME TYPES OF HORSE:

• bronco, carthorse, Clydesdale, mustang, piebald, pony, racehorse, Shetland pony, shire horse, war horse

SOUNDS MADE BY HORSES:

• neigh, nicker, snort, whinny
In the eerie silence of no man's land all that could be heard was the jingle of the harness and the snorting of the horses.—WAR HORSE, Michael Morpurgo

WAYS A HORSE CAN MOVE:

• canter, gallop, trot, walk

PARTS OF A HORSE'S HARNESS:

• bit, blinker, bridle, girth, noseband, pommel, rein, saddle, stirrups

SPORTS AND ACTIVITIES INVOLVING HORSES:

• gymkhana, horse racing, jousting, rodeo, polo, showjumping, steeplechase
To get on a horse before riding is to **mount** and to get off a horse is to **dismount**.
A person who rides a horse in a race is a **jockey**.
A word meaning 'to do with horse riding' is **equestrian**.
Soldiers who fight on horseback are **cavalry**.
An old word for a cavalry horse was a **charger**.

hospital *NOUN*

WORD WEB

PLACES WHERE PEOPLE GO FOR MEDICAL TREATMENT:

• clinic, convalescent home, hospice, infirmary, nursing home, sanatorium

PARTS OF A HOSPITAL:

• accident and emergency, dispensary, intensive care unit, operating theatre, outpatients, pharmacy, X-ray department, ward
see also **medicine**

A B C D E F G H I J K L M N O P Q R S T U V W X Y Z

hostile *ADJECTIVE*
❶ *The warriors shook their weapons in a **hostile** manner.*
• aggressive, antagonistic, unfriendly, unwelcoming, warlike, malevolent
OPPOSITE friendly
❷ *The North Pole has a very **hostile** climate.*
• harsh, unfavourable, adverse, bad
OPPOSITE favourable

hostility *NOUN*
*The **hostility** between the two players was obvious.*
• dislike, enmity, hate, hatred, aggression, antagonism, bad feeling, detestation, ill will, unfriendliness, malice
OPPOSITE friendship

hot *ADJECTIVE*
❶ *The weather has been **hot** this summer.*
• warm, balmy, blazing, roasting, scorching, blistering, sweltering, stifling
OPPOSITES cold, cool
❷ *Careful—the soup's really **hot**.*
• burning, boiling, baking hot, piping hot, scalding, searing, sizzling, steaming
OPPOSITES cold, cool
❸ *I like curry, but only if it's not too **hot**.*
• spicy, peppery, fiery
OPPOSITE mild
❹ *My stepsister has a **hot** temper.*
• fierce, fiery, violent, passionate, raging, angry, intense
OPPOSITES calm, mild

house *NOUN*

WORD WEB

WORDS FOR THE PLACE YOU LIVE IN:

• abode, dwelling, home, lodging, quarters, residence

BUILDINGS WHERE PEOPLE LIVE:

• apartment, bungalow, chalet, cottage, council house, croft, detached house, farmhouse, flat, hovel, hut, igloo, lodge, manor, manse, mansion, rectory, semi-detached house, shack, shanty, tenement, terraced house, thatched house, vicarage, villa
for rooms in a house see **room**

house *VERB*
*The farm animals are **housed** indoors during the winter.*
• accommodate, lodge, shelter, take in, quarter, board

hover *VERB*
❶ *A flock of seagulls **hovered** overhead.*
• fly, flutter, float, hang, drift
❷ *He **hovered** outside the room, afraid to knock.*
• linger, pause, wait about, hesitate, dally, loiter, dither
(informal) hang about

however *ADVERB*
❶ *I couldn't lift the stone, **however** hard I tried.*
• no matter how
❷ *Spiders' silk is thin; **however**, it is also strong.*
• nevertheless, nonetheless, yet, still, even so

howl *VERB*
❶ *The injured boy **howled** in pain.*
• cry, yell, scream, yelp, shriek, wail
❷ *They heard wolves **howling** in the night.*
• bay, yowl

huddle *VERB*
*The penguins **huddled** together to get warm.*
• crowd, gather, flock, cluster, squeeze, pack, nestle, cuddle, snuggle
OPPOSITE scatter

hue *NOUN*
*Elliot's face turned a greenish **hue**.*
• colour, shade, tint, tone, tinge
for various colours see **colour**

hug *VERB*
*Ellie was **hugging** her favourite teddy bear.*
• cuddle, clasp, embrace, cling to, hold close, squeeze

huge *ADJECTIVE*
*Elephants are **huge** animals.*
• enormous, gigantic, massive, colossal, giant, immense, vast, mighty, mammoth, monumental, hulking, great, big, large
(informal) whopping, ginormous, humungous
OPPOSITES small, little, tiny

hum *VERB*
*We heard insects **humming** in the air.*
• buzz, drone, murmur, purr, whirr

humane *ADJECTIVE*
*A **humane** society should treat animals well.*
• kind, compassionate, sympathetic, civilised, benevolent, kind-hearted, charitable, loving, merciful
OPPOSITE cruel

humans *PLURAL NOUN*
***Humans** have smaller brains than whales.*
• human beings, the human race, humanity, mankind, people

humble *ADJECTIVE*
❶ *The gentle giant was both **humble** and kind.*
• modest, meek, unassuming, polite, respectful, submissive
OPPOSITE proud
❷ *Hansel and Gretel lived in a **humble** cottage.*
• simple, modest, plain, ordinary, commonplace, lowly
OPPOSITE grand

humid *ADJECTIVE*
*I don't like this **humid** weather.*
• muggy, clammy, close, sticky, steamy, sweaty
OPPOSITE fresh

humiliate *VERB*
*He **humiliated** her in front of her friends.*
• embarrass, disgrace, shame, make ashamed, humble, crush, degrade
(informal) put you in your place, take you down a peg

humiliating *ADJECTIVE*
*The team suffered a **humiliating** defeat.*
• embarrassing, crushing, degrading, humbling, undignified
OPPOSITE glorious

humorous *ADJECTIVE*
*My friend told me a **humorous** story.*
• amusing, funny, comic, witty, entertaining
OPPOSITE serious

humour *NOUN*
❶ *I liked the **humour** in the film.*
• comedy, wit, amusement, jokes
❷ *The ogre was in a very bad **humour**.*
• mood, temper, disposition, frame of mind, spirits

hump *NOUN*
*Camels have **humps** on their backs.*
• bump, lump, bulge, swelling

hunch *NOUN*
*The detective had a **hunch** about the murder case.*
• feeling, intuition, inkling, guess, impression, suspicion, idea

hunch *VERB*
*Will **hunched** his shoulders to keep out the cold.*
• arch, bend, curve, hump, shrug, curl up

hung *past tense see* **hang**

hunger *NOUN*
*After a week without food, the crew were faint with **hunger**.*
• lack of food, starvation, famine
Bad health caused by not having enough food is **malnutrition**.

hungry *ADJECTIVE*
*Our dog always seems to be **hungry**.*
• starving, famished, ravenous
(informal) peckish

hunt *NOUN*
*Police have begun the **hunt** for clues.*
• search, quest, chase, pursuit

a b c d e f g h i j k l m n o p q r s t u v w x y z

hunt *VERB*
❶ *Some Native Americans used to **hunt** buffalo.*
• **chase, pursue, track, trail, hound, stalk**
An animal which hunts other animals for food is a **predator.**
❷ *I **hunted** in the attic for our old photos.*
• **search, seek, look, rummage, ferret, root around**

hurdle *NOUN*
❶ *The horse jumped over the **hurdle** easily.*
• **fence, barrier, jump, barricade, obstacle**
❷ *The biggest **hurdle** facing the team is lack of experience.*
• **difficulty, problem, handicap, hindrance, snag, stumbling block**

hurl *VERB*
*I **hurled** the ball as far as I could.*
• **throw, fling, pitch, toss, cast, sling, launch** *(informal)* **chuck**

hurry *VERB*
❶ *If you want to catch the bus, you'd better **hurry**.*
• **be quick, hasten, make speed** *(informal)* **get a move on step on it**
OPPOSITE **dawdle**
❷ *Alice saw the White Rabbit **hurrying** past.*
• **rush, dash, fly, speed, hurtle, scurry**
OPPOSITES **amble, stroll**
❸ *It's no good trying to **hurry** a donkey.*
• **quicken, speed up, urge on**
OPPOSITES **slow down**

hurry *NOUN*
*In our **hurry**, we forgot the tickets.*
• **rush, haste, speed, urgency**

hurt *VERB*
❶ *Be careful not to **hurt** yourself with the scissors.*
• **harm, injure, damage, wound, maim**
To hurt someone deliberately is to **torment** or **torture** them.
❷ *My feet **hurt**.*
• **be sore, be painful, ache, throb, sting, smart**
❸ *Your letter **hurt** me deeply.*
• **upset, distress, offend, grieve**

hurtful *ADJECTIVE*
*That was a very **hurtful** remark.*
• **upsetting, unkind, cruel, mean, painful, spiteful, nasty**

hurtle *VERB*
*The train **hurtled** along at top speed.*
• **rush, speed, race, dash, fly, charge, tear, shoot, zoom**

husband *NOUN*
*Hugh is Mrs Hart's fourth **husband**.*
Another word for a person's husband or wife is **spouse.**

hush *VERB*
*The speaker tried his best to **hush** the crowd.*
• **silence, quieten, settle, still, calm**
➤ **to hush something up**
*They tried to **hush up** the scandal.*
• **cover up, hide, conceal, keep quiet, keep secret, suppress**

husky *ADJECTIVE*
*The wizard spoke in a **husky** voice.*
• **hoarse, throaty, gruff, rasping, gravelly, rough, croaky**

hut *NOUN*
*The walkers came across a **hut** in the forest.*
• **shed, shack, cabin, den, shelter, shanty, hovel**

hygienic *ADJECTIVE*
*Always use a **hygienic** surface for chopping food.*
• **sanitary, clean, disinfected, sterilised, sterile, germ-free, healthy**
OPPOSITE **unhygienic**

hysterical *ADJECTIVE*
❶ *The fans became **hysterical** when the band appeared.*
• **crazy, frenzied, mad, delirious, raving, wild, uncontrollable**
❷ *(informal) We laughed at the **hysterical** jokes in the film.*
• **hilarious, funny, amusing, comical**

Ii

ice *NOUN*

WORD WEB

VARIOUS FORMS OF ICE:

• black ice, floe, frost, glacier, iceberg, ice sheet, icicle

WAYS TO DESCRIBE ICE:

• brittle, cracked, frozen solid, glacial, glassy, gleaming, glinting, hard, packed, slippery or *(informal)* slippy, smooth, treacherous

THINGS YOU MIGHT DO ON ICE:

• glide, skate, skid, slide, slip, slither

SPORTS THAT ARE PLAYED ON ICE:

• curling, figure skating, ice skating, ice hockey, speed skating
Ice sports are played on an **ice rink**.

icy *ADJECTIVE*
❶ *You need to dress warmly in* ***icy*** *weather.*
• cold, freezing, frosty, wintry, arctic, bitter, biting
❷ ***Icy*** *roads are dangerous.*
• frozen, slippery, glacial, glassy
(informal) slippy

idea *NOUN*
❶ *I've got a great* ***idea****!*
• plan, scheme, proposal, suggestion, inspiration
❷ *She has some funny* ***ideas*** *about life.*
• belief, notion, opinion, view, theory, concept, conception, hypothesis
❸ *What's the main* ***idea*** *of this poem?*
• point, meaning, intention, thought
❹ *Give me an* ***idea*** *of what you are planning.*
• clue, hint, inkling, impression

ideal *ADJECTIVE*
It's ***ideal*** *weather for a picnic.*
• perfect, excellent, the best, faultless, suitable

identical *ADJECTIVE*
The twins were wearing ***identical*** *clothes.*
• matching, similar, alike, indistinguishable
OPPOSITE different

identify *VERB*
❶ *The police asked if I could* ***identify*** *the thief.*
• recognise, name, distinguish, pick out, single out
❷ *The doctor couldn't* ***identify*** *what was wrong.*
• diagnose, discover, spot
(informal) put a name to
➤ **to identify with**
Can you ***identify with*** *the hero of the story?*
• sympathise with, feel for, understand
(informal) put yourself in the shoes of

idiotic *ADJECTIVE*
That was an ***idiotic*** *thing to do.*
• stupid, silly, foolish, unwise, senseless, ridiculous, half-witted, unintelligent, crazy, mad, hare-brained
(informal) daft
OPPOSITE sensible

idle *ADJECTIVE*
❶ *The ogre was an* ***idle****, foul-smelling creature.*
• lazy, indolent, slothful, work-shy
OPPOSITE hard-working
❷ *The computers lay* ***idle*** *all week.*
• inactive, unused, inoperative
OPPOSITE busy, active

idol *NOUN*
❶ *The floor of the temple was littered with broken* ***idols****.*
• god, deity, image, statue
❷ *He was a pop* ***idol*** *of the fifties.*
• star, celebrity, icon, pin-up, favourite

A B C D E F G H I J K L M N O P Q R S T U V W X Y Z

idolise *VERB*
Kirsty ***idolises*** *her big brother.*
• **adore, love, worship, be devoted to, look up to**

ignite *VERB*
The matches were wet and would not ***ignite****.*
• **light, catch fire, burn, kindle, spark**

ignorant *ADJECTIVE*
Trolls are often described as ***ignorant*** *creatures.*
• **uneducated, simple, stupid**
➤ **ignorant of**
Detective Miles was ***ignorant of*** *the facts in the case.*
• **unaware of, unfamiliar with, unacquainted with, aware of**

ignore *VERB*
Ignoring *the weather, Lynn went for a walk.*
• **disregard, take no notice of, overlook, neglect, spurn, snub**
(informal) **turn a blind eye to**

ill *ADJECTIVE*
❶ *I missed school for a week when I was* ***ill****.*
• **sick, unwell, poorly, sickly, ailing, infirm, unfit, indisposed, diseased, infected, nauseous, queasy, off colour, peaky**
(informal) **under the weather**
for common illnesses see **illness**
OPPOSITES **healthy, well**
❷ *Did the plants suffer* ***ill*** *effects in the frost?*
• **bad, harmful, adverse, damaging**
OPPOSITE **good**

illegal *ADJECTIVE*
Stealing is ***illegal****.*
• **unlawful, against the law, banned, prohibited, criminal, forbidden, wrong**
OPPOSITE **legal**

illegible *ADJECTIVE*
The signature on the letter was ***illegible****.*
• **unreadable, indecipherable, unclear, indistinct**
OPPOSITES **legible, readable**

illness *NOUN*
What kind of ***illness*** *is he suffering from?*
• **abnormality, affliction, ailment, attack, complaint, condition, disability, disease, disorder, health problem, infection, infirmity, sickness**
(informal) **bug, upset**
A sudden illness is an **attack** or **fit**.
A period of illness is a **bout of illness**.
A general outbreak of illness in a particular area is an **epidemic**.

WORD WEB

SOME COMMON ILLNESSES:

• **allergy, appendicitis, asthma, bronchitis, chickenpox, chill, cold, cough, diarrhoea, eczema, fever, flu, glandular fever, hay fever, headache, indigestion, influenza, jaundice, laryngitis, measles, migraine, mumps, stomach-ache, tonsillitis, ulcer, whooping cough**
for ways to treat illness see **medicine**

illustrate *VERB*
❶ *I used some photos to* ***illustrate*** *my story.*
• **depict, picture, portray**
❷ *The accident* ***illustrates*** *the importance of road safety.*
• **show, demonstrate, make clear**

illustration *NOUN*
❶ *I like cookery books with lots of* ***illustrations****.*
• **picture, photograph, drawing, sketch, diagram**
❷ *I'll give you an* ***illustration*** *of what I mean.*
• **example, instance, demonstration, specimen**

image *NOUN*
❶ *The film contained frightening* ***images*** *of war.*
• **picture, portrayal, depiction, representation**
❷ *The temple contained* ***images*** *of the gods.*
• **figure, idol, statue, carving**
❸ *You can see your* ***image*** *in the mirror.*
• **reflection, likeness**
❹ *Alice is the* ***image*** *of her mother.*
• **double, twin**

imaginary *ADJECTIVE*
*The story takes place in an **imaginary** universe.*
• **imagined, non-existent, unreal, made-up, invented, fanciful, fictitious, fictional**
OPPOSITE **real**

imagination *NOUN*
*Use your **imagination** to draw an alien spacecraft.*
• **creativity, inventiveness, ingenuity, inspiration, originality, vision, artistry, fancy**

imaginative *ADJECTIVE*
*Roald Dahl wrote highly **imaginative** stories.*
• **creative, inventive, inspired, original, artistic, fanciful, ingenious, clever**
OPPOSITES **unimaginative, dull**

imagine *VERB*
❶ ***Imagine** what it would be like to visit Mars.*
• **picture, visualise, pretend, think up, dream up, fancy, conjure up**
❷ *I **imagine** you'd like something to eat.*
• **suppose, assume, presume, believe, guess**

imitate *VERB*
*Parrots can **imitate** the human voice.*
• **copy, reproduce, mimic, mirror, echo, simulate, impersonate, follow, match**
(informal) **send up, take off**

imitation *ADJECTIVE*
*The coat was made from **imitation** leather.*
• **artificial, synthetic, fake, sham, mock**
OPPOSITES **real, genuine**

imitation *NOUN*
*This is an **imitation** of a Viking helmet.*
• **copy, replica, reproduction, duplicate**
An imitation made to deceive someone is a **fake** or a **forgery**.

immature *ADJECTIVE*
*Tess is quite **immature** for her age.*
• **childish, babyish, infantile, juvenile**
OPPOSITE **mature**

immediate *ADJECTIVE*
❶ *Please can I have an **immediate** reply.*
• **instant, instantaneous, prompt, speedy, swift, urgent, quick, direct**
(informal) **snappy**
OPPOSITE **slow**
❷ *Are you friends with your **immediate** neighbours?*
• **closest, nearest, adjacent, next**
OPPOSITE **distant**

immediately *ADVERB*
*You must fetch a doctor **immediately**!*
• **at once, now, straight away, right away, instantly, promptly, directly**

immense *ADJECTIVE*
*The giant wiggled one of his **immense** toes.*
• **huge, great, massive, enormous, colossal, vast, giant, gigantic, mighty, mammoth, monumental**
(informal) **whopping, ginormous, humungous**
OPPOSITE **tiny**

immobile *ADJECTIVE*
*The knight stood **immobile** at the castle gate.*
• **unmoving, motionless, stationary, still**
OPPOSITE **mobile**

immoral *ADJECTIVE*
*It would be **immoral** to steal the money.*
• **wrong, wicked, bad, sinful, dishonest, corrupt**
OPPOSITES **moral, right**

immortal *ADJECTIVE*
*The ancient Greeks believed their gods were **immortal**.*
• **undying, ageless, eternal, everlasting**
OPPOSITE **mortal**

impact *NOUN*
❶ *The crater was caused by the **impact** of a meteor.*
• **crash, collision, smash, blow, bump, bang, knock, jolt**
❷ *Computers have a big **impact** on our lives.*
• **effect, influence**

A B C D E F G H I J K L M N O P Q R S T U V W X Y Z

impair *VERB*
*Very loud noise can **impair** your hearing.*
• **damage, harm, injure, weaken**

impartial *ADJECTIVE*
*Referees must be **impartial**.*
• **neutral, detached, objective, unbiased, unprejudiced, disinterested, independent, fair, fair-minded, just, even-handed, open-minded**
OPPOSITE **biased**

impatient *ADJECTIVE*
❶ *As time went on, Henry grew more and more **impatient**.*
• **restless, agitated, anxious, edgy, fidgety, irritable, snappy, testy, jumpy**
OPPOSITE **patient**
❷ *The crowd were **impatient** for the show to begin.*
• **anxious, eager, in a hurry, keen**
(informal) **itching**

imperfect *ADJECTIVE*
*The items on this shelf are **imperfect**.*
• **damaged, faulty, defective, flawed, broken, incomplete**
OPPOSITE **perfect**

impertinent *ADJECTIVE*
*The elf made some rather **impertinent** remarks.*
• **rude, cheeky, impolite, impudent, insolent, disrespectful**
OPPOSITES **respectful, polite**

implement *NOUN*
*The shed is full of garden **implements**.*
• **tool, appliance, device, utensil, gadget, instrument**
see also **tool**

implore *VERB*
*Jack **implored** the giant not to eat him.*
• **beg, entreat, plead with**

imply *VERB*
*Are you **implying** that I am a liar?*
• **suggest, hint, indicate**

WHICH WORD? Note there is a difference between **imply** and **infer**. To **infer** something is to deduce or work it out.

impolite *ADJECTIVE*
*It would be **impolite** to refuse the invitation.*
• **rude, bad-mannered, discourteous, disrespectful, insulting**
OPPOSITE **polite**

import *VERB*
*The UK **imports** tea and coffee.*
• **bring in, ship in**
OPPOSITE **export**

important *ADJECTIVE*
❶ *The World Cup is an **important** sporting event.*
• **major, significant, big, central, momentous, outstanding, historic**
❷ *I have some **important** business to attend to.*
• **serious, urgent, pressing, weighty, vital, essential, crucial**
❸ *The prime minister is an **important** person.*
• **prominent, powerful, influential, notable, eminent, distinguished**
OPPOSITES **unimportant, minor**

impose *VERB*
*The government **imposed** a tax on fuel.*
• **introduce, enforce, fix, inflict, prescribe, set**
➤ **to impose on**
*I don't want to **impose on** you.*
• **inconvenience, intrude on, take advantage of**

imposing *ADJECTIVE*
*The castle is an **imposing** building.*
• **grand, great, impressive, stately, magnificent, splendid, majestic, dignified, striking**
OPPOSITE **insignificant**

impossible *ADJECTIVE*
*We used to think that space travel was **impossible**.*
• **impractical, unthinkable, unrealistic, unachievable, unworkable, out of the question**
OPPOSITE **possible**

impress *VERB*
*Frank **impressed** the coach with his football skills.*
• make an impression on, influence, leave its mark on, stick in your mind

impression *NOUN*
❶ *I had the **impression** that something was wrong.*
• feeling, idea, sense, notion, suspicion, hunch
❷ *The film made a big **impression** on them.*
• effect, impact, influence, mark
❸ *My sister does a good **impression** of the Queen.*
• imitation, impersonation, *(informal)* send-up

impressive *ADJECTIVE*
*The film includes some **impressive** special effects.*
• striking, effective, powerful, remarkable, spectacular, exciting, inspiring
OPPOSITES unimpressive, uninspiring

imprison *VERB*
*The thief was **imprisoned** for two years.*
• send to prison, jail, lock up, incarcerate, confine, detain
(informal) put away, send down, put under lock and key
OPPOSITE liberate

improve *VERB*
❶ *Her work **improved** during the term.*
• get better, advance, progress, develop, move on
OPPOSITE deteriorate
❷ *Has he **improved** since his illness?*
• get better, recover, recuperate, pick up, rally, revive
OPPOSITE get worse
❸ *How can I **improve** this story?*
• make better, enhance, refine, amend, revise, correct, upgrade

improvement *NOUN*
❶ *Your handwriting shows signs of **improvement**.*
• getting better, advance, progress, development, recovery, upturn
❷ *The author made some **improvements** to the book.*
• amendment, correction, revision, modification, enhancement

impudent *ADJECTIVE*
*The pixie had an **impudent** grin on his face.*
• cheeky, insolent, rude, impolite, impertinent, disrespectful
OPPOSITES respectful, polite

impulse *NOUN*
*I had a sudden **impulse** to sing out loud.*
• desire, instinct, urge

impulsive *ADJECTIVE*
*She regretted her **impulsive** decision to dye her hair.*
• hasty, rash, reckless, sudden, spontaneous, thoughtless, unthinking, impetuous
OPPOSITE deliberate

inaccessible *ADJECTIVE*
*The caves were in an **inaccessible** part of the island.*
• unreachable, isolated, remote, out of the way, hard to find
OPPOSITE accessible

inaccurate *ADJECTIVE*
*That spelling of my surname is **inaccurate**.*
• wrong, incorrect, mistaken, false, inexact, untrue
OPPOSITE accurate

inadequate *ADJECTIVE*
*They had brought an **inadequate** supply of matches.*
• insufficient, not enough, limited, scarce, scanty, meagre
OPPOSITE adequate

inappropriate *ADJECTIVE*
*It's **inappropriate** to call the teacher by her first name.*
• unsuitable, improper, out of place, unfitting, unseemly
OPPOSITE appropriate

inaudible *ADJECTIVE*
see **hear**

incapable *ADJECTIVE*
➤ **incapable of**
*Miss Havers is **incapable of** making a decision.*
• unable to, incompetent at, unfit to, unsuited to, ineffective at
OPPOSITE capable of

incident *NOUN*
*There was an amusing **incident** at school this morning.*
• event, happening, occurrence, episode, affair

incidental *ADJECTIVE*
*Tell us the main story without the **incidental** details.*
• unimportant, minor, inessential, secondary, subordinate
OPPOSITE essential

incline *NOUN*
*The house was at the top of a steep **incline**.*
• hill, slope, rise, gradient

inclined *ADJECTIVE*
➤ **to be inclined to**
*Ogres are **inclined** to eat too much.*
• be disposed to, have a habit of, be liable to, tend to

include *VERB*
*Does the cost **include** postage and packing?*
• contain, incorporate, comprise, involve, take in, allow for, take into account, cover
OPPOSITE exclude

income *NOUN*
*What is your average monthly **income**?*
• pay, salary, wages, earnings
OPPOSITE expenditure

incompetent *ADJECTIVE*
*The actor was so **incompetent** that he forgot his lines.*
• unskilful, inept, ineffective, unsatisfactory, useless, hopeless
OPPOSITE competent

incomplete *ADJECTIVE*
*The new football stadium is still **incomplete**.*
• unfinished, uncompleted, not ready
OPPOSITE complete

inconsiderate *ADJECTIVE*
*It's **inconsiderate** to play the radio so loudly.*
• selfish, unthinking, thoughtless, insensitive, rude, tactless, unkind, uncaring
OPPOSITE considerate

inconsistent *ADJECTIVE*
❶ *His performance has been **inconsistent** this season.*
• changeable, unreliable, variable, unpredictable, erratic, fickle
❷ *The stories of the two witnesses are **inconsistent**.*
• contradictory, conflicting, different
OPPOSITE consistent

inconspicuous *ADJECTIVE*
*The spy wore plain clothes to be **inconspicuous**.*
• unnoticed, unobtrusive, camouflaged, out of sight
OPPOSITE conspicuous

inconvenient *ADJECTIVE*
*The guests arrived at an **inconvenient** moment.*
• awkward, difficult, unsuitable, unfortunate, untimely, inopportune
OPPOSITE convenient

incorporate *VERB*
*The show **incorporates** some well-known tunes.*
• include, contain, embrace, take in
OPPOSITE exclude

incorrect *ADJECTIVE*
*Nine out of ten of his answers were **incorrect**.*
• wrong, mistaken, inaccurate, false
OPPOSITE correct

increase *VERB*

❶ *They've **increased** the size of the tennis courts.*
• **make bigger, enlarge, expand, develop, add to, widen, broaden**
❷ *She **increased** the cooking time in the recipe.*
• **extend, lengthen, prolong**
❸ *The police **increased** their efforts to find the murderer.*
• **intensify, step up**
❹ *Will you be **increasing** the bus fares?*
• **put up, raise**
❺ *Can you **increase** the volume of the TV?*
• **turn up, amplify, boost**
❻ *The number of cars on the roads continues to **increase**.*
• **grow, mount, go up, rise, soar, build up, escalate, multiply**
for opposites see **decrease**

incredible *ADJECTIVE*

❶ *Do you expect us to believe that **incredible** story?*
• **unbelievable, unlikely, improbable, far-fetched, absurd, implausible**
OPPOSITE **credible**
❷ *The Forth Bridge is an **incredible** feat of engineering.*
• **extraordinary, amazing, astounding, magnificent, marvellous, spectacular**

independence *NOUN*

*The islanders value their **independence**.*
• **freedom, liberty, autonomy**
OPPOSITE **dependence**

independent *ADJECTIVE*

❶ *My granny is a very **independent** person.*
• **free, liberated, self-sufficient, self-reliant**
OPPOSITE **dependent**
❷ *Luxembourg is an **independent** country.*
• **autonomous, self-governing**
❸ *We need an **independent** opinion on the matter.*
• **impartial, neutral, objective, unbiased**
OPPOSITE **biased**

indicate *VERB*

❶ *The usher **indicated** where we should sit.*
• **point to or out, specify, show, reveal, make known**
❷ *A red light **indicates** danger.*
• **mean, stand for, denote, express, signal, signify, communicate, convey**

indication *NOUN*

*He gave no **indication** that he felt ill.*
• **sign, signal, hint, clue, inkling, evidence, warning, symptom, token**

indifferent *ADJECTIVE*

❶ *I felt **indifferent** as I watched the game.*
• **uninterested, detached, uncaring, unenthusiastic, unmoved, uninvolved, unconcerned**
OPPOSITE **enthusiastic**
❷ *The food in the restaurant was **indifferent**.*
• **mediocre, ordinary, unexciting, average**
OPPOSITE **excellent**

indignant *ADJECTIVE*

*The player was **indignant** when he was sent off.*
• **annoyed, angry, cross, affronted, offended, outraged, piqued**

indirect *ADJECTIVE*

*The bus took an **indirect** route into town.*
• **roundabout, winding, meandering, rambling, zigzag**
OPPOSITE **direct**

indistinct *ADJECTIVE*

❶ *The photo was rather **indistinct**.*
• **unclear, blurred, blurry, fuzzy, hazy, vague, indefinite, obscure, shadowy**
OPPOSITE **clear**
❷ *They heard **indistinct** sounds of people talking.*
• **muffled, mumbled, muted, faint, weak, inaudible, unintelligible, incoherent**
OPPOSITE **distinct**

individual *ADJECTIVE*
*Her singing has an **individual** style.*
• **characteristic, distinct, distinctive, special, unique, personal, singular**

individual *NOUN*
*Who was that odd **individual**?*
• **person, character, man, woman**

induce *VERB*
❶ *I couldn't **induce** her to come to the party.*
• **persuade, convince, prevail on, coax, tempt**
❷ *Some headaches are **induced** by stress.*
• **cause, produce, provoke, bring on, lead to, give rise to**

indulge *VERB*
*They **indulged** their children too much.*
• **spoil, pamper, mollycoddle**
➤ **to indulge in**
*I **indulged in** a nice hot bath.*
• **enjoy, revel in, wallow in**

indulgent *ADJECTIVE*
*They are very **indulgent** towards their grandchildren.*
• **tolerant, patient, permissive, lenient, easy-going, generous, liberal**
OPPOSITE **strict**

industry *NOUN*
❶ *Many people in the area work in the car **industry**.*
• **business, trade, commerce, manufacturing, production**
❷ *The elves' workshop was a hive of **industry**.*
• **hard work, effort, energy, diligence, application, busyness**
OPPOSITE **laziness**

ineffective *ADJECTIVE*
*He was an **ineffective** captain of the team.*
• **incompetent, inadequate, unsuccessful, inept** *(informal)* **useless, hopeless**
OPPOSITE **effective**

inefficient *ADJECTIVE*
❶ *Our old vacuum cleaner was very **inefficient**.*
• **ineffective, unproductive, useless, slow, sloppy**
❷ *The car is **inefficient** in its use of fuel.*
• **wasteful, uneconomical, extravagant**
OPPOSITE **efficient**

inevitable *ADJECTIVE*
*If it rains, it is **inevitable** that the pitch will get wet.*
• **certain, sure, definite, unavoidable, inescapable**

inexpensive *ADJECTIVE*
*We bought some **inexpensive** clothes in the market.*
• **cheap, low-priced, low-cost, cut-price, affordable**
OPPOSITE **expensive**

infamous *ADJECTIVE*
*Dick Turpin was an **infamous** highwayman.*
• **notorious, villainous, wicked**

infant *NOUN*
*He had blond, curly hair as an **infant**.*
• **baby, small child, tot, toddler**

infect *VERB*
*A virus may have **infected** the water supply.*
• **contaminate, pollute, poison**

infection *NOUN*
*The **infection** spread rapidly.*
• **disease, virus, contagion, contamination**

infectious *ADJECTIVE*
*Chickenpox is highly **infectious**.*
• **contagious, catching**

infer *VERB*
*What can you **infer** from the tone of her letter?*
• **conclude, deduce, gather, assume, guess, work out**
WHICH WORD? Note there is a difference between **infer** and **imply**. To **imply** something is to suggest or hint at it.

inferior *ADJECTIVE*
❶ *The clothes were of **inferior** quality.*
• **poor, bad, second-rate, mediocre, cheap, shoddy**
❷ *Officers can give orders to those of **inferior** rank.*
• **lesser, lower, junior, subordinate**

infested *ADJECTIVE*
*The attic was **infested** with mice.*
• **swarming, teeming, crawling, overrun, plagued**

infiltrate *VERB*
*Spies **infiltrated** the enemy's camp.*
• **enter secretly, penetrate**

infinite *ADJECTIVE*
*You need **infinite** patience to train a puppy.*
• **endless, limitless, unlimited, boundless, never-ending, unending, inexhaustible**
OPPOSITE **finite**

infirm *ADJECTIVE*
*Most of the patients are elderly and **infirm**.*
• **frail, weak, feeble, poorly, ill, unwell**
OPPOSITE **healthy**
People who have to stay in bed are **bedridden**.

inflammation *NOUN*
*This ointment will soothe the **inflammation**.*
• **swelling, redness, soreness, infection**

inflate *VERB*
*The tyres need to be **inflated**.*
• **blow up, pump up**
OPPOSITE **deflate**

inflict *VERB*
*I hate seeing anyone **inflict** pain on an animal.*
• **administer, deal out, apply, impose**

influence *NOUN*
*Rock music had a big **influence** on her life.*
• **effect, impact, power, dominance, guidance, authority, control**

influence *VERB*
*The money he was offered **influenced** his decision.*
• **affect, have an effect on, direct, guide, control, motivate**

influential *ADJECTIVE*
*She knows some very **influential** people.*
• **important, leading, powerful, significant**
OPPOSITE **unimportant**

inform *VERB*
*Please **inform** us if you move house.*
• **tell, let know, notify, advise**

informal *ADJECTIVE*
❶ *The party will be a very **informal** event.*
• **casual, relaxed, easy-going, friendly, homely, natural**
❷ *Emails are usually written in an **informal** style.*
• **colloquial, familiar, chatty, personal**
OPPOSITE **formal**

information *NOUN*
*There is more **information** on our website.*
• **details, particulars, facts, data, advice, guidance, knowledge**
(informal) **info**

informative *ADJECTIVE*
*That book you lent me was very **informative**.*
• **helpful, useful, instructive, illuminating, revealing**
OPPOSITE **unhelpful**

infuriate *VERB*
*He was **infuriated** by the umpire's decision.*
• **anger, enrage, incense, madden, exasperate**

ingenious *ADJECTIVE*
*It seemed like an **ingenious** plan.*
• **clever, brilliant, inspired, inventive, imaginative, original, crafty, cunning, shrewd**

inhabit *VERB*
*People **inhabited** the caves thousands of years ago.*
• **live in, occupy, dwell in, reside in, populate, settle in**

inhabitant *NOUN*
*The island has fewer than thirty **inhabitants.***
• **resident, dweller, native, occupier, occupant**
An inhabitant of a particular city or country is a **citizen.**
The inhabitants of a place are its **population.**

inhabited *ADJECTIVE*
*Is the island **inhabited?***
• **occupied, lived-in**
OPPOSITE **uninhabited**

inherit *VERB*
*She **inherited** the farm from her uncle.*
• **succeed to, be left, come into**

inherited *ADJECTIVE*
*Eye colour is an **inherited** characteristic.*
• **hereditary, passed down**

inhuman *ADJECTIVE*
*I think it's **inhuman** to hunt animals.*
• **barbaric, cruel, inhumane, merciless, heartless**
OPPOSITE **humane**

initial *ADJECTIVE*
*My **initial** reaction was to run away and hide.*
• **first, earliest, preliminary, opening, introductory**
OPPOSITES **final, eventual**

initially *ADVERB*
***Initially,** I didn't like swimming.*
• **at first, in the beginning, to begin with, to start with, at the outset**

initiative *NOUN*
*You must use your **initiative** on the treasure hunt.*
• **resourcefulness, inventiveness, originality, enterprise**

injection *NOUN*
*The nurse gave me an **injection.***
• **inoculation, vaccination**
(informal) jab

injure *VERB*
*Was anyone **injured** in the accident?*
• **hurt, harm, wound**
To injure someone causing permanent damage is to **maim** them.

injury *NOUN*
*She escaped without any serious **injury.***
• **wound, harm, hurt**

WORD WEB

SOME TYPES OF INJURY:
• **bite, bruise, burn, cut, fracture, gash, graze, scald, scratch, sprain, sting, strain**

inner *ADJECTIVE*
❶ *A passageway led to the **inner** chamber.*
• **central, inside, interior, internal, middle**
OPPOSITES **outer, exterior**
❷ *She tries to hide her **inner** feelings.*
• **innermost, inward, personal, private, intimate, secret, hidden, concealed**
OPPOSITES **outward, external**

innocent *ADJECTIVE*
❶ *The jury found the man **innocent.***
• **guiltless, blameless, free from blame**
OPPOSITE **guilty**
❷ *Baby tigers look so **innocent.***
• **angelic, harmless, faultless, virtuous, pure, simple, inexperienced, naive**
OPPOSITE **wicked**

innumerable *ADJECTIVE*
*There are **innumerable** stars in the sky.*
• **countless, numberless, uncountable, untold**

inquire *VERB*
➤ **to inquire into**
*Detectives are **inquiring into** the robbery.*
• **look into, investigate, examine, explore**

inquiry *NOUN*
*There will be an official **inquiry** into the accident.*
• **investigation, inspection, examination**

inquisitive *ADJECTIVE*
*Chimpanzees are naturally **inquisitive**.*
• curious, questioning, inquiring, probing
for uncomplimentary synonyms see **nosy**

insane *ADJECTIVE*
❶ *It was rumoured that the king had gone **insane**.*
• mentally ill, mad, crazy, deranged, demented, disturbed, unhinged
(informal) off your head, out of your mind
OPPOSITE sane
❷ *It would be **insane** to swim in the sea in January!*
• crazy, mad, daft, senseless, stupid, foolish, idiotic
OPPOSITES sensible, wise

inscription *NOUN*
*The professor read the **inscription** on the tomb.*
• engraving, carving, writing

insect *NOUN*

WORD WEB

SOME TYPES OF INSECT:

• ant, aphid, bee, beetle, bluebottle, bumblebee, butterfly, cicada, cockroach, crane fly or daddy-long-legs, cricket, dragonfly, earwig, firefly, flea, fly, glow-worm, gnat, grasshopper, greenfly, hornet, horsefly, ladybird, locust, louse, mantis, mayfly, midge, mosquito, moth, stick insect, termite, tsetse fly, wasp, weevil
see also **bee**
for groups of insects see **group**

LIFE STAGES OF SOME INSECTS:

• caterpillar, chrysalis, grub, larva, maggot, pupa

PARTS OF INSECTS' BODIES:

• abdomen, antennae, head, legs, thorax, wings

SOME CREATURES SIMILAR TO INSECTS:

• centipede, earthworm, millipede, slug, spider, woodlouse, worm

insecure *ADJECTIVE*
❶ *Be careful—that scaffolding is **insecure**.*
• unsafe, unsteady, unstable, loose, shaky, wobbly, dangerous, hazardous, precarious
❷ *Ollie felt **insecure** on his first day at school.*
• anxious, nervous, worried, apprehensive, uneasy, uncertain, unconfident
OPPOSITE secure

insensitive *ADJECTIVE*
*I'm sorry if my comments were **insensitive**.*
• thoughtless, tactless, unfeeling, uncaring, unsympathetic, callous
OPPOSITE sensitive

insert *VERB*
*Please **insert** a coin in the slot.*
• put in, place, push in, stick in, install, implant

inside *ADJECTIVE*
*The **inside** doors are all painted green.*
• indoor, inner, interior, internal
OPPOSITE outside

inside *NOUN*
*The **inside** of the nest was lined with feathers.*
• interior, inner surface, centre, core, heart, middle
OPPOSITE outside

insignificant *ADJECTIVE*
*The author made a few **insignificant** changes.*
• unimportant, minor, trivial, negligible, slight, meaningless
OPPOSITE significant

insincere *ADJECTIVE*
*The butler welcomed us with an **insincere** smile.*
• false, pretended, hypocritical, dishonest, deceitful, deceptive, lying
(informal) two-faced
OPPOSITE sincere

A B C D E F G H I J K L M N O P Q R S T U V W X Y Z

insist *VERB*
*Griselda **insisted** that she was not a witch.*
• **declare, state, assert, maintain, stress, emphasise, swear, vow, claim**
➤ **to insist on**
*The magician **insisted on** silence before he began.*
• **demand, require**

insolent *ADJECTIVE*
*The boy gave the teacher an **insolent** stare.*
• **rude, impudent, disrespectful, impolite, impertinent, arrogant, brazen**
(informal) **cheeky**
OPPOSITES **polite, respectful**

inspect *VERB*
*They **inspected** the damage done by the storm.*
• **check, examine, investigate, look over, study, survey, scrutinise**

inspection *NOUN*
*There will be a safety **inspection** this afternoon.*
• **check, check-up, examination, review, survey**

inspiration *NOUN*
❶ *What was the **inspiration** behind your story?*
• **impulse, motivation, stimulus**
❷ *The scientist had a sudden **inspiration**.*
• **idea, thought**

inspire *VERB*
*The crowd **inspired** the team to play well.*
• **motivate, prompt, stimulate, encourage, stir, arouse, spur on**

install *VERB*
*We are getting a new bathroom **installed**.*
• **put in, set up, fix, place, position, establish**
OPPOSITE **remove**

instalment *NOUN*
*I missed the first **instalment** of 'Dr Who'.*
• **episode, part**

instance *NOUN*
*Give me an **instance** of what you mean.*
• **example, illustration, case, sample**

instant *ADJECTIVE*
*Gardeners don't expect **instant** results.*
• **immediate, quick, rapid, fast, prompt, snappy, speedy, swift, direct**

instant *NOUN*
*The shooting star was gone in an **instant**.*
• **moment, second, split second, flash**
(informal) **tick, jiffy**

instinct *NOUN*
*The detective always followed his own **instincts**.*
• **impulse, inclination, intuition, hunch, feeling, urge**

instinctive *ADJECTIVE*
*Most people have an **instinctive** fear of sharks.*
• **intuitive, natural, innate, inherent, automatic, involuntary, reflex, spontaneous, impulsive, unconscious, unthinking**
OPPOSITES **deliberate, conscious**

instruct *VERB*
❶ *All the staff are **instructed** in first aid.*
• **teach, train, coach, tutor**
❷ *The police officer **instructed** the cars to wait.*
• **tell, order, direct, command**

instructions *PLURAL NOUN*
*Please follow the **instructions** carefully.*
• **directions, guidelines, orders, commands**

instructor *NOUN*
*The swimming **instructor** also teaches life-saving.*
• **teacher, trainer, coach**

instrument *NOUN*
*Dentists use special **instruments** to check your teeth.*
• **tool, implement, utensil, appliance, device, gadget, contraption**
for musical instruments see **music**

insufficient *ADJECTIVE*
*The plants died because they had **insufficient** water.*
• **inadequate, deficient, not enough, too little, scant, scanty**
OPPOSITES **enough, excessive**

insult *VERB*
*He was **insulted** not to be invited to the wedding.*
• offend, outrage, be rude to, hurt, injure, slight, snub

insult *NOUN*
*It is considered an **insult** to refuse a gift.*
• rudeness, offence, affront, slight, slur, snub

insulting *ADJECTIVE*
*She made an **insulting** comment about my clothes.*
• offensive, rude, impolite, derogatory, scornful
OPPOSITE complimentary

intact *ADJECTIVE*
*The vase has remained **intact** for centuries.*
• unbroken, whole, undamaged, unharmed, complete, perfect
(informal) in one piece

integrate *VERB*
*They decided to **integrate** the two orchestras.*
• bring together, combine, join, merge, unite, unify, amalgamate
OPPOSITE separate

integrity *NOUN*
*Do you have any reason to doubt his **integrity**?*
• honesty, honour, loyalty, trustworthiness, reliability, goodness, sincerity, virtue, fidelity
OPPOSITE dishonesty

intelligence *NOUN*
❶ *The robot shows some signs of **intelligence**.*
• cleverness, understanding, comprehension, reason, sense, wisdom, brainpower, wits
(informal) brains
❷ *The spy was sent to gather secret **intelligence**.*
• information, knowledge, data, facts, reports

intelligent *ADJECTIVE*
*The aliens from Planet Zog are highly **intelligent**.*
• clever, bright, smart, quick, sharp, perceptive, shrewd, able, brilliant, rational, thinking
(informal) brainy
OPPOSITES unintelligent, stupid

intelligible *ADJECTIVE*
*The language of the Martians was not **intelligible**.*
• understandable, comprehensible, meaningful, straightforward, unambiguous, clear, legible, plain, lucid
OPPOSITE incomprehensible

intend *VERB*
❶ *What do you **intend** to do?*
• plan, aim, mean, have in mind, plot, propose
❷ *The class is **intended** for non-swimmers.*
• design, set up, aim (at)

intense *ADJECTIVE*
❶ *I felt a sudden, **intense** pain in my chest.*
• extreme, acute, severe, sharp, great, strong, violent
OPPOSITES slight, mild
❷ *The contest aroused **intense** feelings.*
• deep, passionate, powerful, strong, profound
OPPOSITE mild

intensive *ADJECTIVE*
*Police carried out an **intensive** search of the area.*
• detailed, thorough, concentrated
OPPOSITE superficial

intent *ADJECTIVE*
*He read the letter with an **intent** look on his face.*
• concentrating, absorbed, engrossed, preoccupied, interested
➤ **intent on**
*The detective was **intent on** solving the mystery.*
• determined to, resolved to, eager to, fixed on, bent on

intention *NOUN*
*It's his **intention** to play cricket for Australia.*
• aim, objective, target, goal, ambition, plan, intent

intentional *ADJECTIVE*
*He was penalised for an **intentional** foul.*
• deliberate, conscious, calculated, planned, intended, wilful
OPPOSITE accidental

A B C D E F G H I J K L M N O P Q R S T U V W X Y Z

intercept *VERB*
The defender managed to ***intercept*** *the pass.*
• **check, stop, catch, cut off, head off, deflect**

interest *VERB*
Politics doesn't ***interest*** *me at all.*
• **appeal to, attract, capture your imagination, excite, fascinate, stimulate, absorb**
OPPOSITE **bore**

interest *NOUN*
❶ *The dog showed no* ***interest*** *in the bone.*
• **curiosity, attention, concern, involvement**
❷ *The information was of no* ***interest*** *to anyone.*
• **importance, significance, consequence, value**
❸ *My* ***interests*** *include judo and playing the trombone.*
• **hobby, pastime, pursuit, activity, diversion**

interesting *ADJECTIVE*
Everyone wanted to hear about our ***interesting*** *adventures.*
• **fascinating, absorbing, enthralling, intriguing, engrossing, stimulating, riveting, gripping, entertaining, diverting**
OPPOSITES **boring, dull**

interfere *VERB*
➤ **to interfere in**
Don't ***interfere in*** *other people's affairs.*
• **intervene in, intrude in, meddle in, pry into, encroach on, butt in on**
➤ **to interfere with**
The bad weather ***interfered with*** *our plans.*
• **hamper, hinder, get in the way of, obstruct**

interior *ADJECTIVE, NOUN*
see **inside**

intermediate *ADJECTIVE*
Should I join the ***intermediate*** *or the advanced class?*
• **middle, midway, halfway, transitional**

internal *ADJECTIVE*
Scoop out the ***internal*** *parts of the tomato.*
• **inner, inside, interior**
OPPOSITE **external**

international *ADJECTIVE*
Interpol is an ***international*** *police organisation.*
• **global, worldwide, intercontinental**

interpret *VERB*
Can you ***interpret*** *this old writing?*
• **explain, make sense of, make clear, translate, clarify, decipher, decode**

interrogate *VERB*
The police ***interrogated*** *the suspect for several hours.*
• **question, interview, examine, cross-examine**
(informal) **quiz, grill**

interrupt *VERB*
❶ *Please don't* ***interrupt*** *while I am speaking.*
• **intervene, interject, break in, butt in, cut in**
❷ *Heavy rain* ***interrupted*** *the tennis match.*
• **stop, suspend, disrupt, break off, cut short**
❸ *The new houses will* ***interrupt*** *the view.*
• **get in the way of, obstruct, spoil**

interruption *NOUN*
He wrote for an hour without any ***interruption****.*
• **break, pause, stop, gap, halt, disruption, suspension**

interval *NOUN*
❶ *There will be a short* ***interval*** *after the first act.*
• **break, pause, wait, delay, lapse, lull**
Another word for an interval in a play or film is **interlude** or **intermission**.
An interval in a meeting is a **recess**.
An interval when you take a rest is a **breather** or **breathing space**.
❷ *There were signs at regular* ***intervals*** *along the road.*
• **space, gap, distance**

intervene *VERB*
A man ***intervened*** *to stop the fight.*
• **step in, interfere, interrupt, butt in**

interview *VERB*
*He **interviewed** the author about her new book.*
• **question, talk to, interrogate, examine**

intimate *ADJECTIVE*
❶ *They have been **intimate** friends for years.*
• **close, cherished, dear, friendly, informal**
OPPOSITE **distant**
❷ *The newspaper printed **intimate** details about her life.*
• **personal, private, confidential, secret**

intimidate *VERB*
*You can't **intimidate** me into telling a lie.*
• **bully, threaten, frighten, menace, scare, terrify, terrorise, persecute**

intrepid *ADJECTIVE*
*The **intrepid** explorers finally reached the North Pole.*
• **daring, bold, fearless, courageous, brave, valiant, heroic, plucky**

intricate *ADJECTIVE*
*The clock has an **intricate** mechanism.*
• **complex, complicated, elaborate, sophisticated, involved**
OPPOSITE **simple**

intriguing *ADJECTIVE*
*The results of the experiment are **intriguing**.*
• **interesting, attractive, fascinating, captivating, beguiling**

introduce *VERB*
❶ *Let me **introduce** you to my friend.*
• **present, make known**
❷ *The director stood up to **introduce** the film.*
• **give an introduction to, announce, lead into**
❸ *They are **introducing** a new bus service next year.*
• **set up, start, begin, create, establish, initiate, bring in**

introduction *NOUN*
Something which happens as an introduction to a bigger event is a **prelude**.
An introduction to a book is a **preface**.
An introduction to a play is a **prologue**.
A piece played as an introduction to a concert or opera is an **overture**.

intrude *VERB*
➤ **to intrude on**
*I don't mean to **intrude on** your privacy.*
• **break in on, encroach on, interrupt, butt in on, interfere with, intervene in**

intruder *NOUN*
*Some **intruders** broke into the building last night.*
• **trespasser, prowler, burglar**

invade *VERB*
*The Vikings **invaded** many parts of Europe.*
• **attack, enter, occupy, overrun, march into, raid**

invalid *ADJECTIVE*
❶ *The ticket is **invalid** because it is out of date.*
• **unacceptable, unusable, worthless**
❷ *That is an **invalid** argument.*
• **false, unsound, unreasonable, illogical, irrational, unconvincing**
OPPOSITE **valid**

invaluable *ADJECTIVE*
*Steph is an **invaluable** member of the hockey team.*
• **indispensable, irreplaceable, crucial, essential, useful, valuable**
OPPOSITE **worthless**
WHICH WORD? Note that **invaluable** and **valuable** mean the same thing. They are not opposites!

invasion *NOUN*
*Fortunately, the Martian **invasion** never happened.*
• **attack, raid**

invent *VERB*
*James Dewar **invented** the Thermos flask.*
• **create, devise, think up, conceive, design, originate**

invention *NOUN*
❶ *This computer program is my own* ***invention.***
• creation, design, discovery
(informal) brainchild
❷ *Her account of what happened was pure* ***invention.***
• fantasy, fiction, lies, deceit

inventive *ADJECTIVE*
Roald Dahl's stories are full of ***inventive*** *characters.*
• creative, original, imaginative, ingenious, inspired

inventor *NOUN*
James Dewar was the ***inventor*** *of the Thermos flask.*
• creator, designer, originator, discoverer

investigate *VERB*
Police are ***investigating*** *the cause of the accident.*
• examine, explore, inquire into, look into, study, consider, follow up, probe, research, scrutinise
(informal) go into

investigation *NOUN*
An ***investigation*** *showed how the accident happened.*
• examination, inquiry, inspection, study, review, survey

invigorating *ADJECTIVE*
We went for an ***invigorating*** *walk before breakfast.*
• refreshing, stimulating, reviving, bracing, healthy
OPPOSITE tiring

invisible *ADJECTIVE*
The wizard was ***invisible*** *when he wore his magic cloak.*
• out of sight, unseen, unnoticed, hidden, concealed, covered, obscured, camouflaged, disguised, undetectable, unnoticeable, inconspicuous
OPPOSITE visible

invite *VERB*
Our neighbours ***invited*** *us round for tea.*
• ask, request your company, welcome, summon

inviting *ADJECTIVE*
An ***inviting*** *smell came from the kitchen.*
• attractive, appealing, pleasant, welcoming, agreeable, appetising, tempting
OPPOSITE repulsive

involve *VERB*
❶ *My job* ***involves*** *a lot of travel.*
• include, comprise, require, demand, necessitate, mean
❷ *Protecting the environment* ***involves*** *us all.*
• affect, concern, interest, touch

involved *ADJECTIVE*
❶ *The film has a long and* ***involved*** *plot.*
• complex, complicated, elaborate, intricate, confusing, difficult, convoluted
OPPOSITE simple
❷ *Are you* ***involved*** *in the theatre?*
• concerned, participating, engaged, caught up, mixed up

irrational *ADJECTIVE*
My aunt has an ***irrational*** *fear of hamsters.*
• unreasonable, illogical, senseless, nonsensical, absurd, crazy
OPPOSITE rational

irregular *ADJECTIVE*
❶ *The bricks were arranged in an* ***irregular*** *pattern.*
• varying, erratic, haphazard, random, unpredictable, fitful
OPPOSITE regular
❷ *It is highly* ***irregular*** *to eat pizza with a spoon!*
• abnormal, unusual, exceptional, unconventional, improper
OPPOSITE normal

irrelevant *ADJECTIVE*
Some of the information in the book is ***irrelevant.***
• inappropriate, unnecessary, inessential, pointless, unrelated, unconnected, beside the point
OPPOSITE relevant

irresistible *ADJECTIVE*
*I had an **irresistible** urge to burst out laughing.*
• **overwhelming, overpowering, uncontrollable, unavoidable, powerful, compelling**

irresponsible *ADJECTIVE*
*It's **irresponsible** to drive too fast.*
• **reckless, rash, thoughtless, inconsiderate, uncaring, unthinking, negligent**
OPPOSITE **responsible**

irritable *ADJECTIVE*
*After a bad night, he woke in an **irritable** mood.*
• **bad-tempered, grumpy, short-tempered, cross, impatient, snappy, touchy, testy, prickly, peevish**
(informal) **stroppy, shirty**
OPPOSITES **good-humoured, cheerful**

irritate *VERB*
*The noise from next door began to **irritate** me.*
• **annoy, bother, exasperate, anger, provoke, madden, vex**
(informal) **get on your nerves, bug**

island *NOUN*

WORD WEB

A small island is an **islet**.
A coral island is an **atoll**.
A group of islands is an **archipelago**.
An uninhabited island is a **desert island**.
An island which is not on a map is **uncharted**.
A person who is stranded on a desert island is a **castaway**.

ON A DESERT ISLAND YOU MIGHT BE:

• **cast adrift, beached, marooned, shipwrecked, stranded, washed ashore**

THINGS YOU MIGHT FIND OR USE ON A DESERT ISLAND:

• **beach, cave, driftwood, flotsam, footprints, lagoon, message in a bottle, palm trees, raft, shelter, tree house**

isolated *ADJECTIVE*
❶ *They sheltered in an **isolated** cave in the mountains.*
• **remote, out of the way, secluded, outlying, inaccessible, cut off, deserted**
OPPOSITE **accessible**
❷ *There have been a few **isolated** cases of cheating.*
• **single, uncommon, unusual, abnormal, exceptional, unique**
OPPOSITE **common**

issue *VERB*
❶ *They **issued** blankets to the refugees.*
• **give out, distribute, supply**
❷ *They have **issued** a new set of stamps.*
• **bring out, put out, produce, publish, release, circulate, print**
❸ *Green smoke **issued** from the dragon's nostrils.*
• **come out, emerge, appear, flow out, gush, erupt**

issue *NOUN*
❶ *The new **issue** of the magazine comes out this week.*
• **edition, number, instalment, copy**
❷ *They print stories about local **issues** in the magazine.*
• **matter, subject, topic, affair, concern, question, problem**

itch *NOUN*
❶ *I had an annoying **itch** on my foot.*
• **tickle, tingling, prickle**
❷ *Olga had a great **itch** to travel.*
• **desire, longing, urge, wish, yearning, ache, impulse**

item *NOUN*
❶ *I bought a few **items** in the jumble sale.*
• **thing, object, article**
❷ *There was an **item** about our school in the paper.*
• **article, piece, report, feature**

A B C D E F G H I J K L M N O P Q R S T U V W X Y Z

Jj

jab *VERB*
*A passer-by **jabbed** me in the ribs.*
• poke, prod, elbow, nudge, stab, thrust

jagged *ADJECTIVE*
*This dinosaur had **jagged** teeth.*
• rough, uneven, ragged, spiky, toothed, serrated
OPPOSITE smooth

jail *NOUN*
see prison

jam *NOUN*
❶ *We got stuck in a **jam** on the motorway.*
• traffic jam, hold-up, tailback, blockage
❷ *(informal) I'm in a bit of a **jam**.*
• difficulty, mess, predicament, plight
(informal) fix, tight corner

jam *VERB*
❶ *Someone had **jammed** the door open.*
• prop, wedge, stick
❷ *The roads are **jammed** at rush hour.*
• block, clog, obstruct, congest
(informal) bung up
❸ *I **jammed** my things into a backpack.*
• cram, pack, stuff, squeeze, squash, crush, ram, crowd

jangle *VERB*
*Silver bracelets **jangled** on her wrists.*
• jingle, chink, clink, tinkle

jar *NOUN*
*We collected some tadpoles in a glass **jar**.*
• pot, jug, pitcher, vase

jar *VERB*
❶ *He **jarred** his back badly when he fell.*
• jolt, jerk, shake, shock
❷ *Those paint colours **jar** with each other.*
• clash, conflict, be at odds

jaunty *ADJECTIVE*
*The seven dwarves whistled a **jaunty** tune.*
• cheerful, lively, bright, jolly, perky, breezy, sprightly
OPPOSITE gloomy

jealous *ADJECTIVE*
*Cinderella's sisters were **jealous** of her beauty.*
• envious, resentful, grudging

jeer *VERB*
*Some of the audience whistled and **jeered**.*
• boo, hiss, sneer, taunt, mock, scoff, ridicule
OPPOSITE cheer

jerk *VERB*
*The rider **jerked** on the horse's reins.*
• pull, tug, yank, pluck, wrench, tweak

jerky *ADJECTIVE*
*The stagecoach drew to a **jerky** halt.*
• jolting, jumpy, shaky, bouncy, bumpy, uneven
OPPOSITE steady

jester *NOUN*
*The king's **jester** kept the court amused.*
• fool, joker, clown

jet *NOUN*
*A **jet** of water shot high in the air.*
• spout, spurt, squirt, gush, stream, fountain

jewel and **jewellery** *NOUN*

WORD WEB

SOME ITEMS OF JEWELLERY:
• anklet, bangle, beads, body piercing, bracelet, brooch, chain, charm, choker, cufflinks, earring, engagement ring, locket, medallion, necklace, pendant, pin, ring, tiara, tiepin, wedding ring

STONES OR GEMS USED TO MAKE JEWELLERY:

• agate, amber, amethyst, aquamarine, coral, diamond, emerald, garnet, jade, jasper, jet, lapis lazuli, onyx, moonstone, opal, pearl, ruby, sapphire, topaz, turquoise

METALS USED TO MAKE JEWELLERY:

• gold, platinum, silver

jingle *VERB*
Some coins ***jingled*** *in his back pocket.*
• **jangle, chink, clink, tinkle**

job *NOUN*
❶ *My sister has a* ***job*** *as a TV reporter.*
• **post, position, profession, occupation, employment, trade, work, career**
The job you particularly want to do is your **mission** or **vocation**.
❷ *Whose* ***job*** *is it to do the washing-up?*
• **duty, task, assignment, chore, errand**

WORD WEB

SOME JOBS:

• actor, architect, artist, astronaut, author, banker, barber, blogger, bookseller, builder, bus driver, carer, chef, cleaner, coach, cook, curator, dancer, dentist, detective, doctor, editor, electrician, engineer, explorer, farmer, firefighter, fisherman, flight attendant, florist, footballer, gardener, hairdresser, imam, janitor, joiner, journalist, lawyer, lexicographer, librarian, mechanic, midwife, miner, minister, model, musician, nurse, office worker, optician, painter, paramedic, pharmacist, photographer, pilot, plumber, police officer, politician, postman, priest, printer, professor, programmer, psychiatrist, rabbi, receptionist, reporter, sailor, scientist, secretary, shepherd, shopkeeper, singer, soldier, solicitor, surgeon, tailor, teacher, train driver, translator, TV presenter, undertaker, vet, waiter or waitress, web designer, writer, zookeeper

jog *VERB*
❶ *He* ***jogs*** *round the park every morning.*
• **go jogging, run, trot**
❷ *A boy sitting next to me* ***jogged*** *my elbow.*
• **nudge, prod, jolt, knock, bump, jar, jostle**
❸ *The photograph may* ***jog*** *her memory.*
• **prompt, stir, arouse, set off, stimulate**

join *VERB*
❶ *Our families* ***joined*** *together to buy the present.*
• **combine, come together, merge, unite, amalgamate**
OPPOSITE **separate**
❷ ***Join*** *one piece of rope to the other.*
• **connect, fasten, attach, fix, link, put together, tack on**
OPPOSITE **detach**
❸ *The two roads* ***join*** *here.*
• **meet, merge, converge**
OPPOSITE **divide**
❹ *I* ***joined*** *the crowd going into the cinema.*
• **follow, go with, tag along with**
OPPOSITE **leave**
❺ *We have* ***joined*** *a local sports club.*
• **become a member of, enrol in, sign up for**
To join the army is to **enlist**.
OPPOSITES **leave, resign from**

join *NOUN*
If you look hard, you can still see the ***join****.*
• **joint, connection, link, mend, seam**

joint *ADJECTIVE*
The preparation of the meal was a ***joint*** *effort.*
• **combined, shared, common, communal, cooperative, united, collective, mutual**
OPPOSITE **individual**

joke *NOUN*
Do you know any good ***jokes****?*
• **jest, quip, crack, witticism, wisecrack** *(informal)* **gag**

joke *VERB*
Those two are always laughing and ***joking****.*
• **jest, clown, have a laugh, make jokes**

jolly *ADJECTIVE*
*We had a **jolly** time on holiday.*
• **cheerful, merry, happy, joyful, pleasant, enjoyable**
OPPOSITE **gloomy**

jolt *VERB*
*The car **jolted** over the bumps in the road.*
• **jerk, jog, bump, bounce, shake, shudder**

jostle *VERB*
*The film star was **jostled** by photographers.*
• **push, shove, hustle, press, crowd in on**

jot *VERB*
➤ **to jot down**
*I quickly **jotted down** some ideas.*
• **make a note of, write down, take down, note, scribble**

journal *NOUN*
❶ *The newsagent sells a few **journals**.*
• **magazine, newspaper, paper, periodical, publication**
❷ *The captain kept a **journal** of the voyage.*
• **diary, log, record, account, chronicle**

journalist *NOUN*
*She works as a **journalist** on the local paper.*
• **reporter, correspondent, columnist, writer**

journey *NOUN*
*On their **journey**, the astronauts will pass the Moon.*
• **voyage, trip, expedition, travels, tour, route**

jovial *ADJECTIVE*
*Our guests were in a **jovial** mood.*
• **cheerful, happy, jolly, good-humoured, merry, joyful**
OPPOSITE **sad**

joy *NOUN*
*I remember the sheer **joy** of scoring a goal!*
• **happiness, joyfulness, delight, cheerfulness, gladness, mirth, glee, jubilation, gaiety, rejoicing, bliss, ecstasy, elation**
OPPOSITE **sorrow**

joyful *ADJECTIVE*
*The wedding was a **joyful** occasion.*
• **happy, cheerful, merry, joyous, jolly, jovial, good-humoured**
OPPOSITE **sad**

judge *NOUN*
A judge in a local court is a **magistrate**.
A judge in a competition is an **adjudicator**.
A judge in a sport is a **referee** or **umpire**.

judge *VERB*
❶ *The umpire **judged** that the ball was out.*
• **rule, decide, decree, adjudicate**
❷ *Who's **judging** the flower show this year?*
• **decide on, assess, evaluate, appraise**
❸ *He **judged** the coin to be about 1000 years old.*
• **reckon, suppose, consider, gauge, guess, estimate**

judgement *NOUN*
❶ *What is the **judgement** of the court?*
• **decision, finding, ruling, verdict, decree**
❷ *His comments show a lack of **judgement**.*
• **wisdom, common sense, understanding, discrimination**
❸ *In my **judgement**, you're making a big mistake.*
• **opinion, view, belief, assessment, estimate**

juice *NOUN*
*Squeeze the **juice** from the lemons.*
• **liquid, fluid, sap**

jumble *NOUN*
*There was a **jumble** of clothes on the floor.*
• **mess, muddle, clutter, chaos, confusion, disorder**

jumble *VERB*
*Please don't **jumble** the pages.*
• **muddle, mix up, mess up, disorganise, shuffle**
OPPOSITE **arrange**

jump *VERB*
❶ *Suddenly a rabbit **jumped** in front of us.*
• **leap, spring, bound, bounce, hop**
When a cat jumps it **pounces.**
❷ *All the horses **jumped** the first hurdle.*
• **leap over, vault, clear**
❸ *The loud bang made them all **jump**.*
• **start, flinch, jolt**

jump *NOUN*
❶ *With a **jump**, the grasshopper landed on the leaf.*
• **leap, spring, bound, vault, hop**
❷ *The horse easily cleared the last **jump**.*
• **hurdle, fence, gate, barrier, obstacle**

junction *NOUN*
*There are traffic lights at the road **junction**.*
• **intersection, crossing, interchange**

jungle *NOUN*
*One of my dreams is to be a **jungle** explorer.*
• **rainforest, tropical forest**

WORD WEB

THINGS YOU MIGHT SEE IN THE JUNGLE:

• **canopy, foliage, forest floor, swamp, undergrowth**
The explorer pushed past Fred, pulling out his machete. He hacked through the foliage. 'Almost through.'—THE EXPLORER, Katherine Rundell

SOME ANIMALS WHICH LIVE IN THE JUNGLE:

• **alligator, ant, anteater, armadillo, bird of paradise, butterfly, chameleon, crocodile, gorilla, hummingbird, jaguar, leopard, macaw, monkey, mosquito, parrot, piranha, porcupine, snake, tarantula, tiger, toucan, tree frog**

SOME PLANTS WHICH ARE FOUND IN THE JUNGLE:

• **banana tree, cacao, creeper or liana, mangrove, orchid, palm tree, rubber tree**
see also **explorer**

junior *ADJECTIVE*
❶ *I'm a member of the **junior** hockey team.*
• **younger**
❷ *He's only a **junior** employee in the firm.*
• **low-ranking, minor, lesser, subordinate**
OPPOSITE **senior**

junk *NOUN*
*The garage is full of old **junk**.*
• **rubbish, clutter, garbage, jumble, trash, waste, scrap, odds and ends**

just *ADJECTIVE*
*It was a **just** punishment, considering the crime.*
• **fair, fitting, appropriate, deserved, proper, reasonable, justified**
OPPOSITES **unjust, unfair**

justice *NOUN*
❶ *The prisoners demanded to be treated with **justice**.*
• **fairness, justness, fair play, right, honesty, impartiality**
OPPOSITE **injustice**
❷ *They were tried in a court of **justice**.*
• **law**

justify *VERB*
*How can you **justify** spending so much money?*
• **defend, excuse, account for, explain**

jut *VERB*
➤ **to jut out**
*A large nail **jutted out** from the wall.*
• **stick out, project, protrude, extend, overhang**

A B C D E F G H I J K L M N O P Q R S T U V W X Y Z

juvenile *ADJECTIVE*
❶ *This part of the library is for* ***juvenile*** *fiction.*
• **children's, young people's**
OPPOSITE **adult**
❷ *His jokes are really* ***juvenile****.*
• **childish, babyish, immature**
OPPOSITE **mature**

Kk

keen *ADJECTIVE*
❶ *Rhona is a* ***keen*** *hockey player.*
• **enthusiastic, eager, fervent, avid, devoted, committed, motivated**
A common simile is **as keen as mustard.**
OPPOSITE **unenthusiastic**
❷ *A carving knife should have a* ***keen*** *edge.*
• **sharp, razor-sharp, cutting**
OPPOSITE **blunt**
❸ *Owls have* ***keen*** *eyesight.*
• **sharp, acute, piercing**
OPPOSITE **poor**
❹ *A* ***keen*** *wind was blowing from the east.*
• **bitter, cold, icy, penetrating**
OPPOSITE **mild**

keep *VERB* **keeps, keeping, kept**
❶ *Let's* ***keep*** *the rest of the cake for later.*
• **save, conserve, preserve, retain, hang on to, hold on to, guard, store**
❷ *Please* ***keep*** *still.*
• **stay, remain**
❸ *A man in the audience* ***kept*** *coughing.*
• **persist in, go on, carry on, continue**
❹ *You're late. What* ***kept*** *you?*
• **delay, detain, hold up, keep waiting**
❺ *Where do you* ***keep*** *the knives and forks?*
• **store, house, put, stow**
❻ *Will the milk* ***keep*** *until tomorrow?*
• **last, be usable, stay good**
❼ *It costs money to* ***keep*** *a pet.*
• **support, maintain, provide for, pay for**
➤ **to keep something up**
Keep ***up*** *the good work!*
• **carry on, continue, maintain**

key *NOUN*
Have you found the ***key*** *to the riddle?*
• **answer, solution, explanation, clue**

keyboard *NOUN*
for keyboard instruments see **music**

kick *NOUN*
Ben closed the gate with a ***kick****.*
• **strike, boot, hit, blow**

kick *VERB*
The goalkeeper ***kicked*** *the ball into the air.*
• **strike, boot, hit, drive, send**
for other ways to strike a ball see **ball**

kidnap *VERB*
In the story, a boy is ***kidnapped*** *by bandits.*
• **abduct, capture, seize, carry off, snatch**

kill *VERB*
Several people were ***killed*** *in the explosion.*
(informal) **bump off, do away with**
(old use) **slay**
To kill someone deliberately is to **murder** them.
To kill someone brutally is to **butcher** them.
To kill large numbers of people is to **massacre** or **slaughter** them.
To kill someone as a punishment is to **execute** them or **put them to death.**
To kill someone for political reasons is to **assassinate** them.

kind *NOUN*
*What **kind** of music do you like to play?*
• sort, type, variety, style, category, class, set

kind *ADJECTIVE*
*It was very **kind** of you to help me.*
• kind-hearted, caring, good-natured, kindly, affectionate, warm, genial, loving, sweet, gentle, lenient, amiable, friendly, generous, sympathetic, thoughtful, obliging, considerate, understanding, compassionate, unselfish, giving, gracious, merciful, benevolent, charitable, humane, neighbourly
OPPOSITE unkind

king *NOUN*
*Neptune is the mythological **King** of the Sea.*
• monarch, sovereign

kingdom *NOUN*
*King Brian the Bald ruled over a vast **kingdom**.*
• realm, monarchy

kiss *NOUN*
*The princess gave the frog a **kiss** on the cheek.*
(informal) peck

kit *NOUN*
*I've forgotten my games **kit**.*
• gear, outfit, equipment, paraphernalia, tools, tackle

kitchen *NOUN*

WORD WEB

EQUIPMENT YOU MIGHT FIND IN A KITCHEN:

• apron, blender, bread bin, cooker, crockery, cutlery, dishwasher, draining board, food processor, freezer, fridge, grill, kettle, liquidiser, microwave, mixer, oven, oven gloves, refrigerator, scales, sink, toaster
for other things used for cooking see **cook, cutlery**

kitten *NOUN*
see **cat**

knack *NOUN*
*George has a **knack** for taking photographs.*
• skill, talent, gift, flair

knead *VERB*
***Knead** the dough until it is smooth.*
• work, press, squeeze, pummel

knew *past tense see* **know**

knife *NOUN*

WORD WEB

SOME KINDS OF KNIFE:

• cleaver, dagger, dirk, machete, penknife, scalpel
for kitchen knives see **cutlery**

knight *NOUN*

WORD WEB

THINGS A MEDIEVAL KNIGHT MIGHT WEAR OR CARRY:

• armour, baldric (leather belt), chain mail, coat of arms, falcon or hawk, helmet, lance, mace (metal club), pennant, shield, surcoat, sword, tabard, tunic
for parts of a suit of armour see **armour**
He was equipped for battle, with helmet and chain mail, lance and sword. His tabard, shield, and the feathers on his helmet were as red as blood.—THE LETTER FOR THE KING, Tonke Dragt
A fight between knights on horseback was a **joust**.
A series of sporting contests between knights was a **tournament**.
A boy training to be a knight was first a **page** and then a **squire**.
An expedition made by a knight was a **quest**.

a b c d e f g h i j k l m n o p q r s t u v w x y z

A B C D E F G H I J K L M N O P Q R S T U V W X Y Z

knob *NOUN*
❶ *The **knob** had fallen off the door.*
• handle
❷ *Melt a **knob** of butter in a pan.*
• lump, piece, bit

knobbly *ADJECTIVE*
*Crocodiles have thick and **knobbly** skin.*
• lumpy, bumpy, gnarled

knock *VERB*
*I **knocked** my head as I came out of the car.*
• bump, bang, hit, strike, thump
(informal) bash

knot *VERB*
*The sailors **knotted** the two ropes together.*
• tie, bind, fasten, join, entwine, lash
OPPOSITE untie

know *VERB* **knows, knowing, knew, known**
❶ *Do you **know** how to mend a puncture?*
• understand, have knowledge of, comprehend
❷ *As soon as she saw the unicorn, she **knew** what it was.*
• recognise, realise, appreciate, be aware of
❸ *Do you **know** Oliver well?*
• be acquainted with, be familiar with, be a friend of

knowledge *NOUN*
❶ *She has a good **knowledge** of Italian.*
• understanding, grasp, command, familiarity (with)
❷ *An encyclopedia contains a lot of **knowledge**.*
• information, data, facts, learning, know-how, wisdom, scholarship

knowledgeable *ADJECTIVE*
*My dad is very **knowledgeable** about guitars.*
• familiar (with), well-informed, educated, learned
OPPOSITE ignorant

label *NOUN*
*The washing instructions are on the **label**.*
• tag, ticket, sticker

label *VERB*
*I've **labelled** all the boxes, so we'll know what's in them.*
• put a label on, tag, mark, name, identify

laborious *ADJECTIVE*
*It was a **laborious** climb to the top of the hill.*
• hard, tough, strenuous, difficult, stiff, tiring, exhausting, gruelling
OPPOSITE easy

labour *NOUN*
❶ *The workers were paid for their **labour**.*
• work, effort, industry, exertion, toil
❷ *The factory took on extra **labour**.*
• workers, employees

labour *VERB*
*They **laboured** to get the job finished on time.*
• work hard, exert yourself, toil
(informal) slave away

lack *NOUN*
*The judge dismissed the case because of a **lack** of evidence.*
• absence, shortage, scarcity, want
A general lack of food is a **famine**.
A general lack of water is a **drought**.
OPPOSITE abundance

lack *VERB*
*The game **lacked** excitement.*
• be short of, be without, want, need, require, miss

lady *NOUN*
see **woman**

lag *VERB*
*One runner was **lagging** behind the others.*
• **straggle, trail, fall behind, drop behind, dawdle, linger, loiter**

laid *past tense see* **lay**

lair *NOUN*
*The hunters tracked the animal back to its **lair**.*
• **den, refuge, shelter, hideout, hiding place**

lake *NOUN*
*We rowed across the **lake**.*
• **pond, pool,** *(Scottish)* **loch**
A saltwater lake is a **lagoon**.
A lake used to supply water is a **reservoir**.

lame *ADJECTIVE*
❶ *The **lame** horse had to be withdrawn from the race.*
• **crippled, limping**
❷ *I didn't believe her **lame** excuse.*
• **feeble, flimsy, poor, unconvincing, inadequate, weak, tame**

lamp *NOUN*
see **light**

land *NOUN*
❶ *The castle is surrounded by several acres of **land**.*
• **grounds, estate, property**
❷ *The **land** here is good for growing strawberries.*
• **ground, soil, earth**
❸ *China is a **land** with an ancient history.*
• **country, nation, state, region, territory**

land *VERB*
❶ *The plane **landed** exactly on time.*
• **touch down, arrive**
OPPOSITE **take off**
❷ *The ship will **land** at Dover.*
• **dock, berth, come ashore**
❸ *How did these papers **land** on my desk?*
• **arrive, turn up, end up, wind up, settle**

landscape *NOUN*
*We sat on the hill and admired the **landscape**.*
• **countryside, scenery, view, scene, outlook, prospect**

lane *NOUN*
see **road**

language *NOUN*
❶ *The scroll was written in an ancient **language**.*
• **tongue, speech, dialect**
❷ *The author uses very poetic **language**.*
• **wording, phrasing, vocabulary, expression, style**
The words of a language are its **vocabulary**.
see also **writing**

lap *NOUN*
❶ *My cat, Snowy, likes to sit on my **lap**.*
• **knee, knees, thighs**
❷ *The cars were on the last **lap** of the race.*
• **circuit, round, loop**

lapse *NOUN*
❶ *They made a mistake because of a **lapse** in concentration.*
• **failure, error, fault, slip, flaw, weakness, shortcoming**
❷ *I've started swimming again after a **lapse** of a year.*
• **break, gap, interval, interruption, lull, pause**

large *ADJECTIVE*
❶ *Elephants are **large** animals.*
• **big, huge, enormous, colossal, giant, gigantic, immense, great, massive, bulky, heavy, hefty, weighty, mighty, towering** *(informal)* **whopping, ginormous**
❷ *The cook gave me a **large** helping of pudding.*
• **ample, generous, plentiful, abundant, lavish**
❸ *Is this room **large** enough for dancing in?*
• **spacious, roomy, sizeable**
❹ *The gales caused damage over a **large** area.*
• **wide, broad, extensive, widespread, vast**
❺ *The meeting was attended by a **large** number of people.*
• **considerable, substantial**
OPPOSITE **small**

A B C D E F G H I J K L M N O P Q R S T U V W X Y Z

largely *ADVERB*
*The driver was **largely** to blame for the accident.*
• **mainly, chiefly, mostly, principally, to a large extent**

last *ADJECTIVE*
❶ *Z is the **last** letter of the alphabet.*
• **final, closing, concluding, terminating, ultimate**
OPPOSITE **first**
❷ *Did you see his **last** film?*
• **latest, most recent**
OPPOSITE **next**

last *NOUN*
➤ **at last**
*The holidays are here **at last**!*
• **finally, eventually, in the end**

last *VERB*
❶ *Let's hope the fine weather **lasts**.*
• **carry on, continue, keep on, stay, remain, persist, endure, hold**
❷ *The plants won't **last** long without water.*
• **hold out, keep going, live, survive**

late *ADJECTIVE*
❶ *The bus is **late**.*
• **delayed, overdue**
OPPOSITE **early, punctual, on time**
❷ *Mr Pettigrew showed us a portrait of his **late** wife.*
• **dead, deceased, departed**

lately *ADVERB*
*There has been a lot of snow **lately**.*
• **recently, latterly, of late**

later *ADJECTIVE*
*We'll study that poem in a **later** class.*
• **future, following, subsequent**

later *ADVERB*
*I'm busy now, but I'll phone you **later**.*
• **afterwards, in a while, subsequently, next**

laugh *VERB*
❶ *The children **laughed** when the clown fell over.*
• **chuckle, chortle, giggle, titter, burst out laughing, roar** or **scream with laughter, roll** or **fall about laughing, guffaw**
(informal) **have hysterics, be in stitches**
❷ *It's rude to **laugh** at his way of singing.*
• **make fun of, mock, ridicule, scoff at, tease, deride**

laughter *NOUN*
*We heard bursts of **laughter** coming from the kitchen.*
• **laughing, amusement, hilarity, mirth, merriment**

launch *VERB*
❶ *The space shuttle will be **launched** tomorrow.*
• **send off, set off, blast off, fire**
❷ *The new website was **launched** in the summer.*
• **begin, start, set up, open, establish, found, initiate**

lavatory *NOUN*
*The girls' **lavatories** are at the end of the corridor.*
• **toilet, bathroom, WC, cloakroom, washroom**
(informal) **loo**

lavish *ADJECTIVE*
*The king put on a **lavish** feast for his birthday.*
• **generous, extravagant, sumptuous, luxurious, opulent, grand, abundant, copious, plentiful, bountiful**
OPPOSITES **meagre, paltry**

law *NOUN*
A law passed by parliament is an **act**.
A proposed law to be discussed by parliament is a **bill**.
The laws of a game are **regulations** or **rules**.
A regulation which must be obeyed is a **commandment, decree, edict** or **order**.

lay *past tense see* **lie**

lay VERB **lays, laying, laid**
❶ *He **laid** the parchment carefully on his desk.*
• **put down, set down, place, position, spread, deposit, leave**
❷ *Please **lay** the table for dinner.*
• **set out, arrange**

layer NOUN
❶ *The walls needed two **layers** of paint.*
• **coat, coating, covering, thickness, film, sheet, skin**
❷ *You can see various **layers** of rock in the cliff.*
• **seam, stratum**

laze VERB
*We spent the day **lazing** in the garden.*
• **be lazy, idle, loaf, lounge, lie about, relax, loll**

lazy ADJECTIVE
*My **lazy** little brother stayed in bed all day!*
• **idle, inactive, lethargic, slack, slothful, indolent**
An informal name for a lazy person is **lazybones.**

lead VERB **leads, leading, led**
❶ *The rescuers **led** the climbers to safety.*
• **guide, conduct, escort, usher, steer, pilot, shepherd**
OPPOSITE **follow**
❷ *Dr Martez will **lead** the expedition to Peru.*
• **be in charge of, direct, command, head, manage, supervise**
❸ *The British cyclist **led** from the start of the race.*
• **be in front, be in the lead, head the field**
❹ *The animals in the zoo **lead** a peaceful life.*
• **have, pass, spend, experience**

lead NOUN
❶ *The team followed the captain's **lead**.*
• **example, guidance, leadership, direction**
❷ *The Australian swimmer is in the **lead**.*
• **first place, front position**
❸ *Charlie was given the **lead** in the play.*
• **main part, starring role, title role**
❹ *Keep the dog on a **lead**.*
• **leash, strap, chain, tether, rein**
❺ *Don't trip over the electrical **lead**.*
• **cable, flex, wire**

leader NOUN
*The **leader** of the pirates was Captain Cutlass.*
• **head, chief, commander, captain, director, principal, ruler**
(informal) **boss**
The leader of a group of wrongdoers is the **ringleader.**

leaf NOUN
❶ *Deciduous trees lose their **leaves** in autumn.*
A mass of leaves is **foliage** or **greenery.**
❷ *A single **leaf** had been torn out of the book.*
• **page, sheet**

leak NOUN
*The plumber mended a **leak** in the water tank.*
• **crack, hole, opening, drip**
A leak in a tyre is a **puncture.**

leak VERB
❶ *The juice had **leaked** all over my school bag.*
• **escape, drip, seep, ooze, trickle**
❷ *Details of a secret plan were **leaked** to the newspaper.*
• **reveal, disclose, make known, pass on, give away, let out**

lean VERB **leans, leaning, leaned** or **leant**
❶ *I **leaned** against the wall.*
• **recline, rest, prop yourself, support yourself**
❷ *The yacht **leaned** to one side in the wind.*
• **slope, tilt, tip, incline, slant, list, bank**

lean ADJECTIVE
*The athlete has a strong, **lean** figure.*
• **slim, slender, thin, wiry**
OPPOSITE **fat**

leap VERB **leaps, leaping, leapt** or **leaped**
*The dog **leaped** in the air to catch the ball.*
• **jump, spring, bound, vault**

A B C D E F G H I J K L M N O P Q R S T U V W X Y Z

learn *VERB* **learns, learning, learnt** or **learned**
❶ *We are* ***learning*** *about the Vikings this term.*
• **discover, find out, gather, grasp, pick up**
❷ *I've got to* ***learn*** *the words of this song.*
• **learn by heart, memorise, master**

learner *NOUN*
This swimming class is for ***learners*** *only.*
• **beginner, starter, novice**
Someone learning things at school or college is a **pupil** or **student**.
Someone learning a trade is an **apprentice** or **trainee**.

least *ADJECTIVE, DETERMINER*
❶ *Who got the* ***least*** *number of points?*
• **fewest, lowest**
❷ *The* ***least*** *amount of this poison is deadly.*
• **slightest, smallest, tiniest**

leave *VERB* **leaves, leaving, left**
❶ *Do you have to* ***leave*** *now?*
• **go, go away, depart, withdraw, take your leave, go out, set off, say goodbye**
(informal) **take off, disappear**
OPPOSITE **arrive**
❷ *The doctor* ***left*** *the room in a hurry.*
• **exit, go out of, depart from, quit, vacate**
OPPOSITE **enter**
❸ *Don't* ***leave*** *me here on my own!*
• **abandon, desert, forsake**
❹ *The crew* ***left*** *the sinking ship.*
• **evacuate, get out of**
❺ *My sister has* ***left*** *her job at the bank.*
• **give up, quit, resign from**
(informal) **walk out of**
❻ ***Leave*** *the milk bottles by the front door.*
• **place, position, put down, set down, deposit**
❼ *I'll just* ***leave*** *all the arrangements to you.*
• **pass on, hand over, refer, entrust**
❽ *Lady Bigwig* ***left*** *all her money to charity.*
• **bequeath, hand down, will, endow**
➤ **to leave someone** or **something out**
Eric was ***left out*** *of the basketball team.*
• **miss out, omit, exclude, reject**

leave *NOUN*
❶ *The prime minister is away on* ***leave****.*
• **holiday, vacation, time off**
❷ *Will you give me* ***leave*** *to speak?*
• **permission, freedom, liberty**

lecture *NOUN*
❶ *There is a* ***lecture*** *about dinosaurs at the museum today.*
• **talk, lesson, speech, address**
❷ *The teacher gave us a* ***lecture*** *on how to behave.*
• **reprimand, warning**
(informal) **telling-off**

led *past tense see* **lead**

ledge *NOUN*
The climbers rested on a ***ledge*** *of rock.*
• **shelf, projection**
A ledge under a window is a **windowsill**.

left *past tense see* **leave**

left *ADJECTIVE*
The left side of a ship when you face forwards is the **port** side.
see also **right**

leg *NOUN*
❶ *Boris fell and bruised his* ***leg****.*
for parts of your body see **body**
❷ *The rowers completed the first* ***leg*** *of the race.*
• **part, stage, section, phase, stretch**

legal *ADJECTIVE*
Is it ***legal*** *to park here on Sundays?*
• **lawful, legitimate, permissible, permitted, allowed**
OPPOSITE **illegal**

legend *NOUN*
I like reading ***legends*** *about ancient heroes.*
• **myth, story, folk tale, fairy tale, fable, tradition, saga**
for creatures found in myths and legends see **myth**

legendary *ADJECTIVE*
Unicorns are ***legendary*** *beasts.*
• **mythical, fabulous, fabled, fictional, fictitious, invented, made-up**
OPPOSITE **real**

legible *ADJECTIVE*
*Although the letter is old, the handwriting is **legible**.*
• **readable, clear, distinct, neat**
OPPOSITE **illegible**

legitimate *ADJECTIVE*
*Are you the **legitimate** owner of this car?*
• **legal, proper, rightful, authorised, licensed, permitted**

leisure *NOUN*
*Grandad has plenty of **leisure** since he retired.*
• **free time, spare time, relaxation, recreation, rest**

leisurely *ADJECTIVE*
*We went for a **leisurely** stroll in the park.*
• **gentle, relaxed, relaxing, unhurried, restful, slow**
OPPOSITE **fast**

lend *VERB*
*Can you **lend** me some money until the weekend?*
• **loan, advance, let you have**
OPPOSITE **borrow**

length *NOUN*
❶ *My heart sank when I saw the **length** of the queue.*
• **extent, size**
❷ *We only had to wait a short **length** of time.*
• **space, period, stretch**

lengthen *VERB*
❶ *Is it possible to **lengthen** these curtains?*
• **extend, make longer, increase, stretch**
❷ *The days **lengthen** in spring.*
• **draw out, get longer, stretch out**
OPPOSITE **shorten**

lengthy *ADJECTIVE*
*There was a **lengthy** argument over who was to blame.*
• **long, drawn-out, extended, prolonged, time-consuming**
OPPOSITE **short**

lenient *ADJECTIVE*
*The teacher was **lenient** and let us off.*
• **easy-going, soft-hearted, tolerant, forgiving, indulgent, kind, merciful**
OPPOSITE **strict**

lessen *VERB*
❶ *This medicine will **lessen** the pain.*
• **minimise, reduce, relieve**
❷ *The storm **lessened** during the night.*
• **diminish, decrease, dwindle, subside, weaken, ease off, tail off, die away** or **down**
OPPOSITE **increase**

lesson *NOUN*
*My piano **lesson** is on Friday afternoon.*
• **class, period, tutorial, instruction**

let *VERB* **lets, letting, let**
❶ *Abby's parents **let** her go to the party.*
• **allow, give permission to, permit, consent to, agree to**
OPPOSITE **forbid**
❷ *Our friends are **letting** their house for the summer.*
• **lease, rent out, hire out**

lethal *ADJECTIVE*
*This bottle contains a **lethal** potion.*
• **deadly, fatal, mortal, poisonous**

letter *NOUN*
❶ *There are twenty-six **letters** in the alphabet.*
• **character, symbol, sign, figure**
The letters a, e, i, o, u, and sometimes y, are **vowels**.
The other letters are **consonants**.
❷ *Did you remember to sign your **letter**?*
• **note, message, communication**
Letters that people send each other are **correspondence**.

level *ADJECTIVE*
❶ *You need a **level** field for playing rounders.*
• **even, flat, horizontal, smooth**
OPPOSITE **uneven**
❷ *At half-time the scores were **level**.*
• **equal, even, the same, matching**
(informal) **neck-and-neck**

A B C D E F G H I J K L M N O P Q R S T U V W X Y Z

level *VERB*
❶ *Dad **levelled** the garden to make a lawn.*
• even out, flatten, smooth
❷ *A serious earthquake **levelled** the town.*
• knock down, demolish, destroy, devastate

level *NOUN*
❶ *The water had reached a high **level**.*
• height
❷ *The lift takes you up to the sixth **level**.*
• floor, storey, tier
❸ *What **level** have you reached in judo?*
• grade, standard, stage, rank, degree

lever *VERB*
*Slowly, I **levered** open the lid of the chest.*
• prise, wrench, force

liable *ADJECTIVE*
❶ *You're **liable** to make mistakes when you're tired.*
• likely, inclined, disposed, prone, ready
OPPOSITE unlikely
❷ *If you break anything, you'll be **liable** for the cost.*
• responsible, answerable, accountable

liberal *ADJECTIVE*
❶ *We each got a **liberal** helping of ice cream.*
• generous, ample, plentiful, lavish, abundant, copious, bountiful
OPPOSITES meagre, miserly
❷ *She has a **liberal** attitude towards most things.*
• broad-minded, easy-going, lenient, tolerant, permissive
OPPOSITE strict

liberate *VERB*
*The prisoners were **liberated** at the end of the war.*
• free, release, set free, emancipate, discharge, let go, set loose
OPPOSITE imprison

liberty *NOUN*
❶ *The animals have **liberty** to wander around the park.*
• freedom, independence
❷ *The king granted the prisoners their **liberty**.*
• liberation, release, emancipation

licence *NOUN*
*He has a **licence** to practise as a doctor.*
• permit, certificate, authorisation, warrant

license *VERB*
*Are you **licensed** to drive this vehicle?*
• permit, allow, authorise, entitle

lid *NOUN*
*Can you help me get the **lid** off this jar?*
• cap, cover, covering, top

lie *VERB* **lies, lying, lay, lain**
❶ *It's twelve o'clock and he's still **lying** in bed!*
• recline, stretch out, lounge, sprawl, rest
To lie face down is to be **prone**.
To lie face upwards is to be **supine**.
❷ *The castle **lies** in a valley.*
• be sited, be situated, be located, be found

lie *VERB* **lies, lying, lied**
*I don't trust her—I think she's **lying**.*
• deceive someone, bluff
(informal) fib

lie *NOUN*
*He accused the newspaper of printing **lies**.*
• deceit, falsehood, dishonesty
(informal) fib
OPPOSITE truth

life *NOUN*
❶ *My hamster, Fluffy, leads a very easy **life**.*
• existence, being, way of life
❷ *Our **lives** depended on finding water.*
• survival
❸ *You seem to be full of **life** today!*
• energy, liveliness, vigour, vitality, spirit, sprightliness, animation
❹ *I'm reading a **life** of Elvis Presley.*
• life story, autobiography, biography

lift *VERB*
❶ *The removal men **lifted** the piano carefully.*
• pick up, raise, elevate, pull up, hoist
❷ *The plane **lifted** off the ground.*
• rise, ascend, soar

lift *NOUN*
*Take the **lift** to the top floor.*
A North American word is **elevator**.

light *NOUN*

WORD WEB

SOME KINDS OF NATURAL LIGHT:

- daylight, moonlight, starlight, sunlight, twilight

SOURCES OF ARTIFICIAL LIGHT:

- bulb, candle, chandelier, floodlight, fluorescent lamp, headlamp or headlight, lamp, lantern, laser, neon light, searchlight, spotlight, street light, torch

VARIOUS FORMS OF LIGHT:

- beam, flash, flicker, glow, halo, lustre, radiance, ray, reflection, shaft

WRITING TIPS

You can use these words to describe **light**.

TO DESCRIBE HOW LIGHT APPEARS:

- bright, brilliant, harsh, luminous, lustrous, strong; diffused, dim, muted, soft, warm

LIGHT MAY:

- beam, blaze, dazzle, flash, flicker, glare, gleam, glimmer, glint, glisten, glitter, glow, shimmer, shine, sparkle, twinkle

In the still woods, the only movements were bars of sunlight glinting like green glass through the leafy canopy.—PAX, Sara Pennypacker

light *ADJECTIVE*

❶ *The artist worked in a **light** and airy studio.*
- **bright, well-lit, illuminated**

OPPOSITES **dim, gloomy**

❷ *She was wearing **light** blue jeans.*
- **pale**

OPPOSITE **dark**

❸ *The parcel looks big, but it is quite **light**.*
- **lightweight, portable, weightless, slight**

A common simile is **as light as a feather**.

OPPOSITE **heavy**

❹ *A **light** wind rippled the surface of the water.*
- **gentle, faint, slight**

OPPOSITE **strong**

❺ *We had a **light** meal before we went out.*
- **small, modest, simple, insubstantial**

OPPOSITES **heavy, substantial**

❻ *I brought a book for some **light** reading.*
- **undemanding, entertaining, lightweight**

OPPOSITE **serious**

light *VERB* lights, lighting, lit or lighted

❶ *We **lit** the candles on my birthday cake.*
- **ignite, kindle, set alight, set fire to, switch on**

OPPOSITE **extinguish**

❷ *The fireworks **lit** the sky.*
- **light up, brighten, illuminate, shed light on, shine on**

OPPOSITE **darken**

like *VERB*

OVERUSED WORD

Try to vary the words you use for **like**. Here are some other words you could use.

TO LIKE A PERSON OR ANIMAL:

- **be fond of, be attached to, care for, love, adore, cherish, esteem, admire, hold dear** *(informal)* **have a soft spot for**

*Lauren is very **attached** to her new puppy.*

TO LIKE SOMETHING OR LIKE DOING SOMETHING:

- **be keen on, be partial to, be interested in, delight in, enjoy, appreciate, prefer, relish**

I'm not very keen on broccoli.
What sort of films do you enjoy?

OPPOSITE **dislike**

like *PREPOSITION*

*The witch's hand looked **like** a knobbly tree.*
- **similar to, the same as, resembling, identical to**

OPPOSITE **unlike**

A B C D E F G H I J K L M N O P Q R S T U V W X Y Z

likely *ADJECTIVE*
*It's **likely** that the shop will be closed tomorrow.*
• **probable, expected, anticipated, predictable, foreseeable**
OPPOSITE **unlikely**

likeness *NOUN*
❶ *There's a strong **likeness** between the two sisters.*
• **resemblance, similarity, correspondence**
OPPOSITE **difference**
❷ *This photo is a good **likeness** of my grandfather.*
• **image, representation, picture, portrait, copy**

liking *NOUN*
*Ray has a **liking** for classical music.*
• **fondness, taste, love, affection, preference**
OPPOSITE **dislike**

limb *NOUN*
Your limbs are your arms and legs.
Birds have **wings.**
Seals, whales and dolphins have **flippers.**
An octopus has **tentacles.**
The limbs of a tree are its **boughs or branches.**

limit *NOUN*
❶ *There is a **limit** of twenty pupils for this class.*
• **maximum, restriction, threshold, ceiling, cut-off point**
A limit on time is a **deadline** or **time limit.**
❷ *The fence marks the **limit** of the school grounds.*
• **border, boundary, edge, perimeter, frontier**

limit *VERB*
*I had to **limit** the invitations to my party.*
• **put a limit on, restrict, control, ration**

limited *ADJECTIVE*
❶ *The crew had a **limited** supply of water.*
• **restricted, short, inadequate, insufficient, rationed, finite, fixed**
❷ *It was hard to move about in the **limited** space.*
• **small, cramped, narrow, confined**
OPPOSITE **limitless**

limp *VERB*
*She **limped** off the pitch with an injured ankle.*
• **hobble, hop, falter, stumble**

limp *ADJECTIVE*
*The leaves on the plant are looking **limp**.*
• **drooping, floppy, sagging, wilting, soft, flabby, slack**
OPPOSITE **rigid**

line *NOUN*
❶ *I drew a pencil **line** across the page.*
• **stroke, rule, underline, stripe, streak, band, bar, dash**
A line that is cut into a surface is a **groove, score** or **scratch.**
A line on a person's skin is a **wrinkle.**
A deep groove or wrinkle is a **furrow.**
A line on fabric is a **crease.**
❷ *There was a long **line** of people waiting at the bus stop.*
• **queue, row, file, column, rank, procession, chain**
A line of police officers forming a barrier is a **cordon.**
A line of schoolchildren walking in pairs is a **crocodile.**
❸ *The clothes were drying on the washing **line**.*
• **cord, rope, string, thread, wire, cable, flex, lead**

linger *VERB*
❶ *The smell of burning wood **lingered** in the air.*
• **continue, remain, stay, last, persist**
OPPOSITE **disappear**
❷ *Don't **linger** outside in this cold weather.*
• **hang about, wait about, loiter, dawdle, dally, delay**
OPPOSITE **hurry**

link *NOUN*
*The two schools have close **links** with each other.*
• **relationship, association, connection, bond, tie**

link *VERB*
*They **linked** the trailer to the tractor.*
• **attach, connect, fasten, join, couple**
OPPOSITE **separate**

lion *NOUN*
A female lion is a **lioness**.
A young lion is a **cub**.
A group of lions is a **pride**.
The fur collar on a male lion is its **mane**.

liquid *ADJECTIVE*
*Pour the **liquid** jelly into a mould.*
• **runny, watery, wet, fluid, flowing, running, sloppy**
To make something liquid by heating it is to **melt** it.
Liquid metal or rock is **molten**.
OPPOSITE **solid**

liquid *NOUN*
*The flask contained a frothy green **liquid**.*
• **fluid, solution, juice**
The liquid inside a plant is **sap**.

list *NOUN*
A list of people's names is a **roll** or **register**.
A list of people who have tasks to do is a **rota**.
A list of books in the library or of goods for sale is a **catalogue**.
A list of topics mentioned in a book is an **index**.
A list of things to choose from is a **menu**.
A list of things to do or remember is a **checklist**.

list *VERB*
❶ *I helped to **list** the books in the library.*
• **record, write down, catalogue, index, register**
❷ *The damaged ship **listed** to one side.*
• **lean, tilt, tip, slope, incline**

listen *VERB*
➤ **to listen to something**
*The spy **listened** carefully **to** the instructions.*
• **pay attention to, take notice of, attend to, heed**
To listen secretly to a private conversation is to **eavesdrop**.

literature *NOUN*
❶ *The bookshop specialises in children's **literature**.*
• **books, writing**
for various kinds of literature see **writing**
❷ *The travel agent gave us some **literature** to read.*
• **brochures, leaflets, pamphlets, handouts**

litter *NOUN*
*The street was covered with **litter**.*
• **rubbish, waste, refuse, garbage, junk, clutter, mess, odds and ends**

litter *VERB*
*The desk was **littered** with scrunched-up paper.*
• **scatter, strew**

little *ADJECTIVE, DETERMINER*

OVERUSED WORD

Try to vary the words you use for **little**. Here are some other words you could use.

FOR SOMETHING LITTLE IN SIZE:

• **mini, miniature, minute, petite, small, tiny, compact**
(informal) **teeny, titchy**
(Scottish) **wee**
As stoves went it was a very small one, with a barred grate and a miniature oven of the kind which are built into caravans.—THE BORROWERS AFIELD, Mary Norton
OPPOSITES **big, large**
see also **small**

FOR SOMEONE LITTLE IN AGE:

• **small, young,** *(Scottish)* **wee**
*My granny lived in India when she was **young**.*
OPPOSITES **big, old**

FOR A LITTLE TIME OR A LITTLE WHILE:

• **brief, short, fleeting, passing**
*It was a **short** while before our friends arrived.*
OPPOSITES **lengthy, long**

FOR LITTLE FOOD OR LITTLE MONEY:

• **hardly any, scarcely any, insufficient, meagre, paltry**
*There was **scarcely any** food left in the house.*
OPPOSITES **ample, plenty**

a b c d e f g h i j k l m n o p q r s t u v w x y z

➤ **a little**
*Would you like **a little** milk in your tea?*
• **some, a bit of, a spot of, a touch of**
*I'm feeling **a little** tired now.*
• **a bit, slightly, rather, somewhat**

live *VERB (rhymes with* **give***)*
*Will these plants **live** through the winter?*
• **stay alive, survive, exist, flourish, last, continue, remain**
OPPOSITE die
➤ **to live in a place**
*They **live in** a basement flat.*
• **inhabit, occupy, dwell in, reside in**
➤ **to live on**
*Koalas **live on** eucalyptus leaves.*
• **eat, feed on**

live *ADJECTIVE (rhymes with* **hive***)*
*The fishermen caught a **live** octopus in their nets.*
• **alive, living, breathing**
OPPOSITE dead

lively *ADJECTIVE*
❶ *The toddlers were in a **lively** mood.*
• **active, energetic, animated, spirited, boisterous, excited, vivacious, sprightly, frisky, chirpy, perky**
OPPOSITE inactive
❷ *The city centre is always **lively** at night.*
• **busy, bustling, crowded, exciting, buzzing**
OPPOSITES quiet, dead

livid *ADJECTIVE*
*Gary was **livid** when he saw the damage to his bike.*
• **angry, furious, fuming, incensed, enraged, seething, raging**

living *ADJECTIVE*
❶ *Miss Millicent had no **living** relatives.*
• **alive**
OPPOSITE dead
❷ *There are no dinosaurs still **living**.*
• **existing, surviving**
OPPOSITE extinct

living *NOUN*
❶ *He makes a **living** from painting.*
• **income, livelihood**
❷ *What does she do for a **living**?*
• **job, occupation, profession, trade, career**

load *NOUN*
❶ *Camels can carry heavy **loads**.*
• **burden, weight**
❷ *The lorry delivered its **load** to the supermarket.*
• **cargo, consignment, goods, freight**

load *VERB*
❶ *We **loaded** the suitcases into the car.*
• **pack, pile, heap, stow**
❷ *He was **loaded** with shopping bags.*
• **weigh down, burden, saddle**

loan *NOUN*
*She needs a **loan** to pay for her holiday.*
• **advance**
A system which allows you to pay for something later is **credit**.
A loan to buy a house is a **mortgage**.

loathe *VERB*
*My brother **loathes** the colour pink.*
• **hate, detest, dislike, despise**
OPPOSITES love, adore

local *ADJECTIVE*
*Our **local** shop delivers newspapers.*
• **neighbourhood, nearby, neighbouring**

locate *VERB*
❶ *I can't **locate** the book you asked for.*
• **find, discover, track down, detect, unearth, lay your hands on**
OPPOSITE lose
❷ *The art gallery is **located** in the city centre.*
• **place, position, put, situate, set up, build, establish, station**

location *NOUN*
*The pilot made a note of his **location**.*
• **position, situation, whereabouts, place, spot**

lock *NOUN*
❶ *There was a heavy **lock** on the lid of the chest.*
• fastening, clasp, padlock, bolt, latch
❷ *The sorceress cut a **lock** from her hair.*
• tress, curl, tuft

lock *VERB*
*Make sure you **lock** the door when you go out.*
• fasten, secure, bolt, close, shut, seal

lodge *VERB*
❶ *Where are you **lodging** at present?*
• live, stay, reside, dwell
❷ *The animals are **lodged** indoors in the winter.*
• house, accommodate, board, put up
❸ *The ball was **lodged** in a tree.*
• get caught, get stuck, jam, wedge, fix, embed

log *NOUN*
❶ *They collected **logs** to burn on the fire.*
for various types of wood see **wood**
❷ *The astronauts kept a **log** of their voyage.*
• diary, journal, record, account

logical *ADJECTIVE*
*The robot always gave a **logical** answer.*
• rational, reasonable, sensible, sound, valid, intelligent, clear, lucid, methodical, systematic
OPPOSITE illogical

lone *ADJECTIVE*
*A **lone** rider galloped past.*
• single, solitary, unaccompanied, isolated

lonely *ADJECTIVE*
❶ *Cara felt **lonely** while her friends were away.*
• alone, friendless, lonesome, solitary, abandoned, neglected, forlorn, forsaken
❷ *The climbers sheltered in a **lonely** hut.*
• deserted, isolated, remote, secluded, out of the way

long *ADJECTIVE*
*It seemed a **long** time before the bus came.*
• lengthy, prolonged, extended, extensive, long-lasting
OPPOSITE short

long *VERB*
➤ **to long for something**
*I'm **longing for** a drink.*
• yearn for, crave, want, wish for, desire, fancy, hunger for, pine for, hanker after, itch for *(informal)* be dying for

look *VERB*
❶ *If you **look** carefully, you'll see an owl in the tree.*
• watch, observe, view, regard, keep your eyes open
❷ *My pet snake **looks** a bit hungry.*
• appear, seem
➤ **to look after someone** or **something**
*We **looked after** their house when they went on holiday.*
• care for, keep an eye on, mind, tend, watch, watch over, guard, protect
To look after sick people is to **nurse** them.
➤ **to look for something**
*He spent ages **looking for** his keys.*
• hunt for, search for, seek
➤ **to look out**
*If you don't **look out**, you'll get wet.*
• beware, pay attention, take care, watch out, keep an eye open

OVERUSED WORD

Try to vary the words you use for **look**. Here are some other words you could use.

TO LOOK QUICKLY:

• glance, glimpse, peek, peep
*The secret agent **glanced** at her watch.*

TO LOOK CAREFULLY OR INTENTLY:

• stare, peer, study, scrutinise, examine, inspect, take a good look at
Daniel peered out of the window, which was tinted sepia so that the outside world looked like an old photograph.—THE NOWHERE EMPORIUM, Ross MacKenzie

TO LOOK ANGRILY:

• glare, glower, frown, scowl, grimace
*The two men **glowered** at each other with menace.*

To look steadily is to **gaze**.
To look in amazement is to **gape**.
To look over a wide area is to **scan** or **survey** it.

look *NOUN*
❶ *Did you have a* ***look*** *at what she was wearing?*
• glance, glimpse, peep, sight, view
❷ *The guard had an unfriendly* ***look****.*
• appearance, bearing, manner, air, expression, face

lookout *NOUN*
Lookouts *were posted along the wall.*
• sentry, guard, sentinel, watchman

loom *VERB*
❶ *A figure* ***loomed*** *out of the mist.*
• appear, emerge, arise, take shape
❷ *The haunted mansion* ***loomed*** *above us.*
• rise, tower, stand out, hang over

loop *NOUN*
Make a ***loop*** *in the string and then tie a knot.*
• coil, hoop, circle, ring, noose, bend, curl, kink, twist

loop *VERB*
The cowboy ***looped*** *the reins round a fence post.*
• coil, wind, curl, bend, turn, twist

loose *ADJECTIVE*
❶ *Some of the cobbles on the road are* ***loose****.*
• insecure, unfixed, movable, unsteady, shaky, wobbly
OPPOSITES firm, secure
❷ *The fire was started by a* ***loose*** *wire.*
• disconnected, unattached, detached
❸ *These jeans are* ***loose*** *around the waist.*
• slack, baggy, roomy, loose-fitting
OPPOSITE tight
❹ *The chickens wander* ***loose*** *about the farm.*
• free, at large, at liberty, on the loose, unconfined, unrestricted
OPPOSITE confined

loosen *VERB*
Can you ***loosen*** *these knots?*
• undo, unfasten, untie, free, loose, slacken, release, ease
OPPOSITE tighten

loot *NOUN*
The thieves buried their ***loot*** *in a safe place.*
• haul, plunder, takings

loot *VERB*
Rioters ***looted*** *the shops.*
• raid, ransack, rob, steal from, pillage, plunder

lorry *NOUN*
for types of vehicle see **vehicle**

lose *VERB* **loses, losing, lost**
❶ *Debbie has* ***lost*** *one of her gloves.*
• be unable to find, mislay, misplace
OPPOSITE find
❷ *Unfortunately, we* ***lost*** *the game on Saturday.*
• be defeated, get beaten, suffer a defeat
OPPOSITE win

loss *NOUN*
❶ *She is suffering from* ***loss*** *of memory.*
• failure, disappearance, deprivation
❷ *The farmer was upset by the* ***loss*** *of his sheepdog.*
• death, decease, passing

lot *NOUN*
We are having another ***lot*** *of visitors this weekend.*
• group, batch, set, crowd, collection

➤ **a lot of**
My brother needs ***a lot of*** *help with his spelling.*
• a large amount of, a good or great deal of, plenty of

➤ **lots of**
There are ***lots of*** *toys to choose from in the shop.*
• a great number of, many, numerous, plenty of (*informal*) loads of, tons of, masses of, oodles of, hundreds of

loud *ADJECTIVE*
❶ *The whole house was kept awake by the* ***loud*** *music.*
• **noisy, blaring, booming, deafening, rowdy, resounding, thunderous, penetrating, piercing**
A noise which is loud enough to hear is **audible.**
OPPOSITES **quiet, soft**
❷ *The tourists wore rather* ***loud*** *shirts.*
• **bright, gaudy, garish, showy, flashy**
OPPOSITES **muted, subdued**

lounge *VERB*
They ***lounged*** *in the garden all day.*
• **relax, be lazy, idle, laze, sprawl, lie around, loll, take it easy, waste time**

lovable *ADJECTIVE*
Our friends have a ***lovable*** *new kitten.*
• **adorable, dear, sweet, charming, likeable, lovely, appealing, attractive, cuddly, enchanting, endearing**
OPPOSITE **hateful**

love *NOUN*
She often mentions her ***love*** *of the outdoors.*
• **liking, passion, fondness, affection, devotion, admiration, adoration**
(informal) **soft spot for**

love *VERB*
❶ *They* ***love*** *each other and want to get married.*
• **be in love with, care for, adore, cherish, hold dear, treasure, worship, idolise**
A relationship between two people who love each other is a **romance.**
❷ *My friend, Dot,* ***loves*** *knitting.*
• **like, have a passion for, be fond of, be partial to, enjoy**
OPPOSITE **hate**

lovely *ADJECTIVE*

OVERUSED WORD

Try to vary the words you use for **lovely.** Here are some other words you could use.

FOR A LOVELY PERSON:

• **charming, delightful, lovable, likeable, dear, sweet, enchanting, endearing**

'I told you they loved singing!' cried Mr Wonka. 'Aren't they delightful? Aren't they charming? But you mustn't believe a word they said. It's all nonsense, every bit of it!'—CHARLIE AND THE CHOCOLATE FACTORY, Roald Dahl

FOR A LOVELY DAY OR LOVELY VIEW:

• **fine, glorious**
It's a ***glorious*** *day for a bicycle trip.*

FOR A LOVELY EXPERIENCE:

• **pleasant, pleasing, enjoyable**
The girls had an ***enjoyable*** *time camping.*
OPPOSITE **nasty**

FOR SOMETHING THAT LOOKS LOVELY:

• **appealing, attractive, beautiful, pretty**
The roses look ***attractive*** *in that vase.*

loving *ADJECTIVE*
Erin gave her teddy bear a ***loving*** *hug.*
• **affectionate, kind, friendly, warm, tender, fond, devoted, passionate**
OPPOSITE **unfriendly**

low *ADJECTIVE*
❶ *The garden is surrounded by a* ***low*** *wall.*
• **short, shallow, sunken**
❷ *They were soldiers of* ***low*** *rank in the army.*
• **junior, inferior, lowly, modest, humble**
❸ *We spoke in* ***low*** *whispers.*
• **quiet, soft, muted, subdued, muffled**
❹ *The tuba plays* ***low*** *notes.*
• **bass, deep**
OPPOSITE **high**

lower *VERB*
❶ *The supermarket* ***lowered*** *its prices.*
• **reduce, cut, bring down, decrease, lessen**
(informal) **slash**
❷ *Please* ***lower*** *the volume of your radio.*
• **quieten, turn down**
❸ *At the end of the Olympic Games, they* ***lower*** *the flag.*
• **take down, let down, dip**
OPPOSITE **raise**

loyal *ADJECTIVE*
*Sir Valiant had always been a **loyal** knight.*
• **true, trusty, faithful, steadfast, reliable, dependable, devoted, constant, sincere**
OPPOSITE **disloyal**

luck *NOUN*
❶ *He found the secret entrance by **luck**.*
• **accident, chance, coincidence, fluke, fate, destiny**
❷ *She had a bit of **luck** today.*
• **good fortune, success**

lucky *ADJECTIVE*
❶ *I got the right answer by a **lucky** guess.*
• **accidental, chance, unintentional, unplanned**
❷ *Some **lucky** person won a million pounds.*
• **fortunate, favoured, successful**
OPPOSITE **unlucky**

ludicrous *ADJECTIVE*
*They laughed at such a **ludicrous** idea.*
• **ridiculous, absurd, laughable, idiotic, foolish, crazy, daft, senseless**

luggage *NOUN*
*The **luggage** can go in the boot of the car.*
• **baggage, cases, suitcases, bags**

lull *VERB*
*She **lulled** the baby by rocking it gently.*
• **calm, soothe, hush, quieten, pacify, subdue**

lull *NOUN*
*There was a brief **lull** in the conversation.*
• **pause, break, gap, interval, calm**
(informal) **let-up**

lumber *VERB*
❶ *A rhinoceros **lumbered** towards them.*
• **move clumsily, trundle, trudge, tramp, blunder, shamble**
❷ *(informal) Why am I **lumbered** with the washing up?*
• **burden**
(informal) **saddle**

lump *NOUN*
❶ *Lumps of sticky clay stuck to his boots.*
• **chunk, piece, cluster, clump, wad, mass, hunk, wedge, block**
A round lump of something is a **ball**.
A lump of gold is a **nugget**.
A lump of earth is a **clod**.
A lump of blood is a **clot**.
❷ *I could feel a **lump** where I'd bumped my head.*
• **bump, swelling, bulge, protrusion**

lump *VERB*
➤ **to lump things together**
*The books and CDs were all **lumped together**.*
• **put together, combine, merge, bunch up**

lunge *VERB*
*Robin **lunged** at the sheriff with his sword.*
• **thrust, charge, rush, dive, pounce, throw yourself**

lurch *VERB*
❶ *The bus passengers **lurched** from side to side.*
• **reel, sway, rock, stagger, stumble, totter**
❷ *The ship **lurched** as the waves pounded it.*
• **pitch, roll, heave, lean, list**

lure *VERB*
*Spiders **lure** insects into their webs.*
• **attract, entice, tempt, coax, draw, invite, persuade**
Something used to lure an animal into a trap is **bait**.

lurk *VERB*
*The jaguar **lurked** in wait for its prey.*
• **skulk, loiter, prowl, crouch, hide, lie in wait, lie low**

lush *ADJECTIVE*
*Rainforests have **lush** vegetation.*
• **rich, dense, thick, rampant, abundant**

luxurious *ADJECTIVE*
*The dress was trimmed with **luxurious** lace.*
• **grand, lavish, lush, rich, expensive, costly, de luxe, plush, magnificent, splendid, sumptuous**
OPPOSITES **simple, austere**

luxury *NOUN*
*The millionaire lived a life of **luxury**.*
• **affluence, wealth, richness, splendour, comfort, ease**
OPPOSITE **poverty**

Mm

machine *NOUN*
Do you know how this ***machine*** *works?*
• apparatus, appliance, device, engine, contraption

mad *ADJECTIVE*
1 *You must be* ***mad*** *to go out on a day like this.*
• crazy, daft, insane, senseless, stupid, foolish, idiotic
(informal) out of your mind, potty, nuts
OPPOSITE sensible, wise
2 *The emperor was* ***mad*** *with rage.*
• angry, furious, beside yourself, frenzied, hysterical
3 *(informal) Sandra is* ***mad*** *about horses.*
• enthusiastic, fanatical, passionate

made *past tense see* **make**

magazine *NOUN*
I bought a ***magazine*** *to read on the train.*
• journal, periodical, paper, comic

magic *ADJECTIVE*
1 *My uncle taught me some* ***magic*** *tricks.*
• conjuring
2 *The castle was surrounded by a* ***magic*** *spell.*
• magical, supernatural

magic *NOUN*
Do you believe in magic?
• sorcery, witchcraft, wizardry, spells, charms, enchantments

WORD WEB

PEOPLE WHO USE MAGIC:
• enchanter or enchantress, magician, sorcerer or sorceress, sorcerer's apprentice, warlock, witch, wizard
see also **fairy**

THINGS WHICH A WITCH OR WIZARD MIGHT DO:
• bewitch, enchant, cast or undo a spell, become invisible or vanish, brew a potion, put a curse on you, brandish or flick their wand

THINGS WHICH A WITCH OR WIZARD MIGHT USE:
• amulet, broomstick, cauldron, charm, curse or hex, elixir, magic potion, magic spell or incantation, spellbook, talisman, wand
Neville had somehow managed to melt Seamus's cauldron into a twisted blob and their potion was seeping across the stone floor, burning holes in people's shoes.—HARRY POTTER AND THE PHILOSOPHER'S STONE, J. K. Rowling

for magical creatures see **myth**

magical *ADJECTIVE*
see **magic**

magician *NOUN*
1 *The* ***magician*** *pulled a scarf out of his hat.*
• conjuror
2 *King Arthur was helped by the* ***magician****, Merlin.*
• sorcerer, witch, wizard

magnificent *ADJECTIVE*
1 *The mountain scenery was* ***magnificent****.*
• beautiful, glorious, splendid, spectacular, impressive, majestic
2 *The film star lived in a* ***magnificent*** *house.*
• grand, imposing, stately
(informal) posh
3 *That was a* ***magnificent*** *meal!*
• excellent, first-class, marvellous, superb
(informal) fabulous, fantastic
OPPOSITE ordinary

magnify *VERB*
Objects are ***magnified*** *through binoculars.*
• enlarge, make larger
(informal) blow up
OPPOSITES reduce, minimise

a b c d e f g h i j k l m n o p q r s t u v w x y z

mail *NOUN*
*The **mail** arrived early this morning.*
• **post, delivery, letters and parcels**

mail *VERB*
*Can you **mail** this letter for me?*
• **post, send, dispatch**

maim *VERB*
see **injure**

main *ADJECTIVE*
❶ *What was the **main** point of the story?*
• **central, chief, most important, basic, essential, fundamental, primary, predominant**
❷ *This is the **main** shopping area in the town.*
• **major, principal, biggest, foremost, largest, leading, prime**
OPPOSITES **minor, unimportant**

mainly *ADVERB*
*Chimpanzees eat **mainly** fruit and vegetables.*
• **largely, mostly, chiefly, principally, predominantly, primarily**

maintain *VERB*
❶ *The referee tried to **maintain** order.*
• **keep, preserve**
❷ *A team of gardeners **maintain** the grounds.*
• **look after, take care of, keep in order**
❸ *How much does it cost to **maintain** a family?*
• **support, keep, provide for**
❹ *He still **maintains** that he's innocent.*
• **claim, declare, assert, insist, state, contend**

majestic *ADJECTIVE*
*The town was dominated by the **majestic** castle.*
• **grand, magnificent, splendid, impressive, stately, imposing, noble**

major *ADJECTIVE*
❶ *There are delays on all the **major** roads into the city.*
• **chief, principal, primary, leading**
❷ *Writing her first novel was a **major** achievement.*
• **big, great, considerable, significant, important**
OPPOSITE **minor**

majority *NOUN*
➤ **the majority of**
*The **majority of** children walk to school.*
• **the greater number of, the bulk of, most**
OPPOSITE **minority**

make *VERB* **makes, making, made**
❶ *We **made** a shelter out of leaves and branches.*
• **build, construct, assemble, put together, produce, manufacture**
❷ *Those two are always **making** trouble.*
• **cause, bring about, give rise to, provoke**
❸ *They **made** me captain.*
• **appoint, elect, nominate**
❹ *They've **made** the attic into a games room.*
• **change, turn, convert, modify, transform, alter**
❺ *She'll **make** a good actress when she's older.*
• **become, grow into, turn into, change into**
❻ *The regulations were **made** to protect children.*
• **establish, fix, decide on, agree**
❼ *You **made** me jump!*
• **cause you to**
❽ *We can't **make** her go if she doesn't want to.*
• **force, compel, order**
❾ *He **made** a lot of money last year.*
• **gain, get, obtain, acquire, receive, earn, win**
❿ *The ship finally **made** land.*
• **reach, arrive at, get to, get as far as**
⓫ *What time do you **make** it?*
• **calculate, estimate, reckon**
⓬ *2 and 2 **make** 4.*
• **add up to, come to, total**
⓭ *I'll **make** you an offer for your old bike.*
• **propose, suggest**
⓮ *Have you **made** your bed this morning?*
• **arrange, tidy**
➤ **to make off**
*The thieves **made off** in a stolen car.*
• **leave, escape, get away, run away, disappear**
(informal) **clear off**
➤ **to make someone** or **something out**
*I can't **make out** why everything went wrong.*
• **understand, work out, comprehend, fathom, make sense of**
➤ **to make up**
*I **made up** a new flavour of ice cream.*
• **create, invent, think up, concoct**

make *NOUN*
What ***make*** *of computer do you have?*
• **brand, model, label**

male *ADJECTIVE*
for male human beings see **man**
for male animals see **animal**
OPPOSITE **female**

malicious *ADJECTIVE*
Someone had spread a ***malicious*** *rumour.*
• **malevolent, hostile, malign, spiteful, vindictive, vicious, hurtful**

mammal *NOUN*
for various kinds of animal see **animal**

man *NOUN*
A polite word for a man is **gentleman**.
Informal words are **bloke, chap, fellow** and **guy**.
A married man is a **husband**.
A man who has children is a **father**.
An unmarried man is a **bachelor**.
A man whose wife has died is a **widower**.
A man on his wedding day is a **bridegroom**.
A man who is engaged to be married is a **fiancé**.
Words for a young man are **boy, lad** and **youth**.

manage *VERB*
❶ *His eldest son* ***manages*** *the business now.*
• **be in charge of, run, direct, lead, control, govern, rule, supervise, oversee, preside over**
❷ *I can't* ***manage*** *any more work this week.*
• **cope with, deal with, take on, carry out**
❸ *We'll have to* ***manage*** *without the car.*
• **cope, make do, get along, get by**

manager *NOUN*
If you have a problem, talk to the ***manager****.*
• **chief, director, proprietor**
(informal) **boss**

mania *NOUN*
A ***mania*** *for the pop group swept the country.*
• **craze, hysteria, obsession, passion, fixation, fad**

manipulate *VERB*
❶ *He* ***manipulated*** *the dials on the robot.*
• **operate, work, handle, control**
(informal) **twiddle**
❷ *She uses her charm to* ***manipulate*** *people.*
• **take advantage of, use, exploit, impose on**

manner *NOUN*
❶ *They did the work in an efficient* ***manner****.*
• **way, style, fashion, method**
❷ *I was put off by her frosty* ***manner****.*
• **behaviour, conduct, attitude, disposition, air, look, bearing**
➤ **manners**
Trolls have no ***manners*** *at all!*
• **politeness, courtesy, graces**

manoeuvre *NOUN*
❶ *Parking a bus is a difficult* ***manoeuvre****.*
• **move, operation**
❷ *The opposing team used a clever* ***manoeuvre****.*
• **strategy, tactic, trick, dodge, plan, plot, scheme**

manoeuvre *VERB*
How do you ***manoeuvre*** *a hot-air balloon?*
• **guide, move, pilot, steer, navigate**

manufacture *VERB*
The factory ***manufactures*** *pine furniture.*
• **make, build, assemble, fabricate**

many *DETERMINER*
I've been on an aeroplane ***many*** *times.*
• **a lot of, plenty of, numerous, frequent, countless, innumerable, myriad, untold**
(informal) **umpteen, lots of**
OPPOSITE **few**

map *NOUN*
The travel agent gave us a free ***map*** *of Paris.*
• **chart, diagram, plan**
A book of maps is an **atlas**.
A person who draws maps is a **cartographer**.

mar *VERB*
The film was ***marred*** *by a terrible soundtrack.*
• **spoil, ruin, harm, impair, tarnish**

A B C D E F G H I J K L M N O P Q R S T U V W X Y Z

march *VERB*
The brass band ***marched*** *down the High Street.*
• **parade, file, troop, stride, pace**

margin *NOUN*
Don't write in the ***margin*** *of the paper.*
• **border, edge**

marginal *ADJECTIVE*
There is a ***marginal*** *difference between the two signatures.*
• **slight, small, minimal, minor, unimportant, negligible, borderline**
OPPOSITE **great**

mark *NOUN*
❶ *There were muddy paw* ***marks*** *all over the kitchen floor.*
• **spot, stain, blemish, blotch, blot, smear, smudge, streak**
A mark left by a pen or pencil is a **scribble**.
A mark left by fingers is a **fingermark**.
A mark on your skin that you are born with is a **birthmark**.
❷ *They stood in silence as a* ***mark*** *of respect.*
• **sign, token, indication, symbol, emblem**
❸ *What* ***mark*** *did you get in the spelling test?*
• **score, grade**

mark *VERB*
❶ *Please be careful not to* ***mark*** *the photographs.*
• **stain, smudge, dirty, blot**
❷ *The teacher had a pile of essays to* ***mark****.*
• **correct, grade, assess**
❸ *There will be trouble, you* ***mark*** *my words!*
• **mind, heed, attend to, listen to, note, take note of**

marked *ADJECTIVE*
There's a ***marked*** *difference in style between the paintings.*
• **noticeable, considerable, pronounced, clear, obvious, distinct, decided**
OPPOSITES **slight, minor**

market *NOUN*
see **shop**

marriage *NOUN*
❶ *My grandparents celebrated 40 years of* ***marriage****.*
• **matrimony, wedlock**
❷ *Today is the anniversary of their* ***marriage****.*
• **wedding**
see also **wedding**

marry *VERB*
In what year did your grandparents ***marry****?*
• **get married, wed**
(informal) **tie the knot, get hitched**
A couple who have promised to marry are **engaged** to each other.
A man who is engaged to be married is a **fiancé** and a woman who is engaged to be married is a **fiancée**.

marsh *NOUN*
Wading birds are found in coastal ***marshes****.*
• **swamp, bog, wetland, marshland, fen**

marvel *NOUN*
It is one of the ***marvels*** *of modern science.*
• **wonder, miracle**

marvel *VERB*
➤ **to marvel at**
The crowd ***marvelled at*** *the juggler's skill.*
• **admire, wonder at, be amazed by, be astonished by**

marvellous *ADJECTIVE*
❶ *The professor showed us his* ***marvellous*** *inventions.*
• **amazing, remarkable, extraordinary, incredible, miraculous, astonishing, phenomenal**
OPPOSITE **ordinary**
❷ *We had a* ***marvellous*** *day at the zoo.*
• **excellent, superb, tremendous, wonderful, splendid**
(informal) **brilliant, fantastic, terrific, super, smashing**
OPPOSITES **bad, awful**

masculine *ADJECTIVE*
The singer had a deep, ***masculine*** *voice.*
• **male, manly, macho, virile**
OPPOSITE **feminine**

mash *VERB*
Mash the potatoes until they're smooth.
• crush, pound, pulp, smash, squash
To make something into powder is to **grind** or **pulverise** it.

mask *VERB*
*The entrance was **masked** by an overhanging tree.*
• conceal, hide, cover, obscure, screen, veil, shroud, camouflage

mass *NOUN*
*She sifted through the **mass** of papers on her desk.*
• heap, pile, mound, stack, collection, quantity, accumulation
(informal) load

massacre *VERB*
see **kill**

massive *ADJECTIVE*
see **huge**

master *NOUN*
❶ *We played a game in which I was **master** of the castle.*
• lord, ruler, governor, chief
❷ *Sherlock Holmes was a **master** of disguises.*
• expert (at), genius, ace, wizard

master *VERB*
❶ *Have you **mastered** chess yet?*
• grasp, learn, understand
(informal) get the hang of, get to grips with
❷ *I've managed to **master** my fear of heights.*
• overcome, conquer, defeat, triumph over, get the better of, control, curb, subdue, tame

match *NOUN*
❶ *The semi-final was a really exciting **match**.*
• game, contest, competition, fixture, tournament, tie
❷ *The hat and gloves are a good **match**.*
• combination, pair

match *VERB*
*Does this tie **match** my shirt?*
• go with, suit, fit with, blend with, tone in with
OPPOSITE contrast with

matching *ADJECTIVE*
*The bed cover comes with a **matching** pillowcase.*
• coordinating, corresponding, complementary, twin
OPPOSITE contrasting

mate *NOUN (informal)*
❶ *Gary is one of my best **mates**.*
• friend
(informal) pal, chum, buddy
❷ *He's got a job as a plumber's **mate**.*
• assistant, helper, apprentice

material *NOUN*
❶ *I'm collecting **material** for the school magazine.*
• information, facts, data, ideas, notes
❷ *The cleaning **materials** are in the cupboard.*
• stuff, substances, things
❸ *The kite is made of lightweight **material**.*
• cloth, fabric
for kinds of cloth see **fabric**

mathematics *NOUN*
*This computer game makes **mathematics** fun!*
• sums
(informal) maths

WORD WEB

BRANCHES OF MATHS:
• algebra, arithmetic, geometry, statistics

THINGS YOU MIGHT DO IN MATHS:
• adding, calculating, counting, dividing, measuring, multiplying, subtracting

SOME INSTRUMENTS USED FOR MATHS:
• calculator, compasses, computer, dividers, ruler, set square
for other words used in maths see **measurement, shape**

A B C D E F G H I J K L M N O P Q R S T U V W X Y Z

matted *ADJECTIVE*
*The dog's coat was dirty and **matted**.*
• knotted, tangled, uncombed

matter *NOUN*
❶ *The manager will deal with this **matter**.*
• affair, concern, issue, business, situation, incident, subject, topic, thing
❷ *Peat consists mainly of plant **matter**.*
• material, stuff, substance
❸ *What's the **matter** with the car?*
• problem, difficulty, trouble, worry

matter *VERB*
*Will it **matter** if I'm late?*
• be important, count, make a difference

mature *ADJECTIVE*
❶ *The zoo has two **mature** gorillas.*
• adult, fully grown, well-developed
OPPOSITE young
❷ *He is very **mature** for his age.*
• grown-up, responsible, sensible
OPPOSITES immature, childish

maximum *ADJECTIVE*
*What is the **maximum** speed of the rocket?*
• greatest, top, highest, fullest, biggest, largest
OPPOSITE minimum

maximum *NOUN*
*The heat is at its **maximum** at midday.*
• highest point, peak, top, upper limit, ceiling

maybe *ADVERB*
***Maybe** you'll be picked for the football team.*
• perhaps, possibly
OPPOSITE definitely

maze *NOUN*
*We were lost in a **maze** of underground tunnels.*
• labyrinth, network, web, tangle

meadow *NOUN*
*Cows were grazing in the **meadow**.*
• field, pasture

meagre *ADJECTIVE*
*The prisoners were given **meagre** rations of food.*
• scant, sparse, poor, scanty, inadequate, insufficient, skimpy, paltry
(informal) measly, stingy
OPPOSITES generous, ample

meal *NOUN*

WORD WEB

MEALS YOU HAVE AT VARIOUS TIMES OF DAY:

• afternoon tea, breakfast, brunch, dinner, lunch, supper, tea
A big formal meal is a **banquet** or **feast**.
A quick informal meal is a **snack**.
A meal you eat out of doors is a **barbecue** or **picnic**.
A meal where you help yourself to food is a **buffet**.
A meal you buy ready cooked is a **takeaway**.

VARIOUS COURSES OF A MEAL:

• starter, main course; dessert, pudding, sweet
(informal) afters
see also **food**

mean *VERB* **means, meaning, meant**
❶ *A red traffic light **means** that cars have to stop.*
• indicate, signify, denote, express, imply, convey, communicate, stand for, symbolise
❷ *I **mean** to get better at swimming this year.*
• intend, plan, aim, propose, want

mean *ADJECTIVE*
❶ *Scrooge was too **mean** to buy any presents.*
• selfish, miserly, uncharitable
(informal) stingy, tight-fisted, penny-pinching
OPPOSITE generous
❷ *That was a **mean** trick to play.*
• unkind, unpleasant, nasty, spiteful, vicious, cruel, malicious
OPPOSITE kind

meaning *NOUN*
*What is the **meaning** of this riddle?*
• sense, significance, explanation, interpretation, definition

meaningful *ADJECTIVE*
*The two friends exchanged a **meaningful** look.*
• pointed, suggestive, significant, expressive
OPPOSITE meaningless

means *NOUN*
*Email is a popular **means** of communication.*
• method, mode, medium, channel, course, way

means *PLURAL NOUN*
*They don't have the **means** to buy a house.*
• money, resources, funds, finance, income, wherewithal

measure *VERB*
***Measure** the height of the wall.*
• calculate, gauge, assess, survey
To measure the weight of something is to **weigh** it.

measure *NOUN*
❶ *At least we now know the **measure** of the problem.*
• size, extent, magnitude
❷ *They are taking **measures** to improve the park.*
• step, action, course, procedure, means

measurement *NOUN*
*What are the **measurements** of this room?*
• dimensions, size, extent, proportions

WORD WEB

UNITS FOR MEASURING DISTANCE:
• millimetre, centimetre, metre, kilometre; inch, foot, yard, mile
The distance of an object in space is measured in **light years**.
The depth of the sea is measured in **fathoms**.

UNITS FOR MEASURING AREA:
• square centimetre or square metre, hectare; square inch or square foot, acre

UNITS FOR MEASURING VOLUME:
• millilitre, litre, kilolitre; pint, quart, gallon

UNITS FOR MEASURING WEIGHT:
• milligram, gram, kilo or kilogram, tonne, ounce, pound, stone, ton

UNITS FOR MEASURING TIME:
• second, minute, hour, day, week, month, year, decade, century

UNITS FOR MEASURING SPEED:
• kilometres per hour, miles per hour
The speed of a boat or ship is measured in **knots**.

UNITS FOR MEASURING TEMPERATURE:
• degrees Celsius, degrees centigrade, degrees Fahrenheit

OTHER MEASUREMENTS USED IN COOKING:
• cup or cupful, dessertspoon, pinch, spoonful, teaspoon, tablespoon

meat *NOUN*

WORD WEB

SOME KINDS OF MEAT:
• bacon, beef, chicken, duck, game, gammon, goose, ham, lamb, mutton, pork, turkey, veal, venison

CUTS OR JOINTS OF MEAT:
• breast, brisket, chop, cutlet, fillet, leg, loin, rib, rump, sirloin, steak

FOODS MADE FROM MEAT:
• burger, chop, corned beef, cutlet, haggis, hamburger, kebab, meatball, mince, pasty, paté, pie, sausage, sausage roll

medal *NOUN*
*Our team won a bronze **medal** in the relay race.*
• award, prize, trophy
A person who wins a medal is a **medallist**.

A B C D E F G H I J K L M N O P Q R S T U V W X Y Z

meddle *VERB*
1 *He is always **meddling** in other people's affairs.*
• **interfere, intrude, intervene, pry**
(informal) **poke your nose in**
2 *Don't **meddle** with my things.*
• **fiddle about, tinker**

medicine *NOUN*
1 *Did you take your cough **medicine**?*
• **drug, medication, treatment, remedy**
An amount of medicine taken at one time is a **dose**.
Medicine which a doctor gives you is a **prescription**.
2 *My cousin is studying herbal **medicine**.*
• **therapy, treatment, healing**

WORD WEB

SOME TYPES OF MEDICINE:

• **anaesthetic, antibiotic, antidote, antiseptic, gargle, herbs, painkiller, sedative, tincture, tonic, tranquilliser**

FORMS IN WHICH YOU TAKE MEDICINE:

• **capsule, inhaler, injection, lotion, lozenge, ointment, pill, tablet**

INSTRUMENTS AND OTHER THINGS USED IN MEDICINE:

• **bandage, dressing, forceps, gauze, lint, plaster, poultice, scalpel, sling, splint, stethoscope, syringe, thermometer, tweezers**

PLACES WHERE YOU CAN GET MEDICAL TREATMENT:

• **clinic, doctor's surgery, health centre, hospital, infirmary, nursing home, sickbay**

SOME FORMS OF ALTERNATIVE MEDICINE:

• **acupuncture, aromatherapy, herbal medicine, homeopathy, reflexology**

PEOPLE WHO PRACTISE MEDICINE:

A person trained to heal sick people is a **doctor** or **physician**.
A person trained to look after sick people is a **nurse**.
Someone who performs medical operations is a **surgeon**.
A person who puts you to sleep during operations is an **anaesthetist**.
A person who takes X-rays is a **radiographer**.
A person who tests your eyes is an **optician**.
A person who tests your hearing is an **audiologist**.
People who look after your teeth are **dentists** and **hygienists**.
A person who practises herbal medicine is a **herbalist**.
A specialist in children's health is a **paediatrician**.
A specialist in mental illnesses is a **psychiatrist**.
A person who treats you using massage and exercise is a **physiotherapist**.

mediocre *ADJECTIVE*
*I thought the film was rather **mediocre**.*
• **ordinary, average, commonplace, indifferent, second-rate, run-of-the-mill, undistinguished, uninspiring**
OPPOSITE **outstanding**

medium *ADJECTIVE*
*The man was of **medium** height.*
• **average, middle, middling, standard, moderate, normal**

medium *NOUN*
*The Internet is a great **medium** of communication.*
• **means, mode, method, way, channel**

meek *ADJECTIVE*
*Koalas look **meek**, but they have fierce claws.*
• **gentle, mild, tame, submissive, modest, docile, quiet, humble**
OPPOSITE **aggressive**

meet *VERB* **meets, meeting, met**
1 *I **met** an old friend at the party.*
• **come across, encounter, run into, see**
(informal) **bump into**

❷ *My parents **met** me at the station.*
• greet, pick up, welcome
❸ *We're **meeting** outside the cinema at eight.*
• gather, assemble, collect, muster, rally
❹ *The two roads **meet** here.*
• come together, merge, connect, join, cross, intersect
❺ *She **meets** all the requirements for the job.*
• fulfil, satisfy, match, answer, comply with

meeting *NOUN*
*The bandits held a **meeting** to discuss their plan.*
• gathering, assembly, council, forum, congress, conference
A large outdoor public meeting is a **rally**.
A formal meeting with a king or queen is an **audience**.

melancholy *ADJECTIVE*
*The princess sat alone with a **melancholy** look on her face.*
• sad, unhappy, miserable, gloomy, mournful, sorrowful, sombre, cheerless, woeful, dejected, depressed
OPPOSITE cheerful

melody *NOUN*
*The pianist played my favourite **melody**.*
• tune, air, theme

melt *VERB*
*The ice began to **melt** in the sun.*
• thaw, soften, unfreeze
To melt frozen food is to **defrost** it.
To melt ore to get metal from it is to **smelt** it.
Rock or metal that has melted because of great heat is **molten**.
OPPOSITE freeze

member *NOUN*
➤ **to be a member of something**
*Are you a **member of** the book club?*
• belong to, subscribe to

memorable *ADJECTIVE*
*The concert should be a **memorable** event.*
• unforgettable, notable, noteworthy, impressive, remarkable, outstanding
OPPOSITE ordinary

memorise *VERB*
*I have to **memorise** my words for the play.*
• learn, learn by heart, remember
OPPOSITE forget

memory *NOUN*
*She has happy **memories** of her childhood in Wales.*
• recollection, remembrance, reminiscence, reminder, impression

menace *NOUN*
❶ *Sharks can be a **menace** to divers.*
• danger, threat
❷ *That cat is an absolute **menace**!*
• nuisance, annoyance, irritation, inconvenience

mend *VERB*
*Workmen were **mending** the pavement.*
• fix, repair, put right, restore, renovate, patch

mention *VERB*
❶ *Please don't **mention** the idea to anyone.*
• refer to, speak about, touch on, hint at
❷ *You **mentioned** that you spoke Japanese.*
• say, remark, reveal, disclose
(*informal*) let out
❸ *The director **mentioned** all the cast.*
• name, acknowledge, list

mercy *NOUN*
*The evil queen showed no **mercy**.*
• compassion, humanity, sympathy, pity, leniency, kindness, charity
OPPOSITE cruelty

merge *VERB*
❶ *They plan to **merge** the two schools.*
• join together, combine, integrate, put together, unite, amalgamate
❷ *Two streams **merge** here to form a river.*
• come together, converge, join, meet
OPPOSITE separate

merit *NOUN*
*She's a writer of great **merit**.*
• excellence, quality, distinction, worth, talent, virtue, value

merit *VERB*
*The project **merits** our full attention.*
• deserve, justify, be entitled to, earn, rate, warrant

merry *ADJECTIVE*
*The postman was whistling a **merry** tune.*
• cheerful, happy, jolly, bright, joyful, light-hearted, lively, spirited
OPPOSITE gloomy

mess *NOUN*
❶ *Please clear up this **mess**.*
• muddle, untidiness, chaos, disorder, confusion, clutter, jumble, litter, dirt
(informal) shambles
❷ *Zoe made a **mess** of her audition.*
• disaster, botch
(informal) hash
❸ *They got into a **mess** over money.*
• difficulty, problem, dilemma, plight
(informal) fix, jam

mess *VERB*
➤ **to mess about**
*We spent the day **messing about** on the beach.*
• play about, fool around, lounge about
(informal) muck about
➤ **to mess things up**
*I hope you haven't **messed up** my CDs.*
• confuse, mix up, muddle, jumble, make a mess of, tangle
➤ **to mess something up**
*I think I **messed up** my interview.*
• bungle, botch
(informal) make a hash of

message *NOUN*
*Did you get my **message**?*
• note, letter, communication
for types of message see **communication**
for secret messages see **code**

messy *ADJECTIVE*
*My bedroom is really **messy**!*
• muddled, untidy, disorderly, chaotic, dirty, filthy, grubby, mucky
(informal) higgledy-piggledy
OPPOSITE neat

met *past tense see* **meet**

metal *NOUN*

WORD WEB

SOME COMMON METALS:

• aluminium, brass, bronze, copper, gold, iron, lead, magnesium, mercury, nickel, pewter, platinum, silver, steel, tin, zinc
A bar of metal is an **ingot**.
A lump of metal is a **nugget**.
Something that looks or sounds like metal is **metallic**.

method *NOUN*
*My granny has a secret **method** for making jam.*
• technique, way, procedure, process
An especially skilful method for doing something is a **knack**.

methodical *ADJECTIVE*
*Inspector Dixon is always very **methodical**.*
• organised, orderly, systematic, meticulous, careful, deliberate, efficient, businesslike, painstaking
OPPOSITE careless

middle *ADJECTIVE*
*The **middle** lane is reserved for buses.*
• central, inner, inside, midway

middle *NOUN*
*A scarecrow stood in the **middle** of the field.*
• centre, core, heart, midpoint
The middle of a wheel is the **hub**.
The middle part of an atom or cell is the **nucleus**.

might *NOUN*
*I banged at the door with all my **might**.*
• strength, power, energy, force, vigour

mighty *ADJECTIVE*
*The dragon let out a **mighty** roar.*
• powerful, forceful, vigorous, ferocious, violent, great, enormous, hefty
OPPOSITE weak

mild *ADJECTIVE*
❶ *He's a **mild** person who never complains.*
• **amiable, docile, easy-going, gentle, good-tempered, harmless, kind, lenient, merciful, placid, soft-hearted**
❷ *The weather has been **mild** for this time of year.*
• **pleasant, warm, temperate**
OPPOSITE **severe**

milk *NOUN*
Foods made from milk are **dairy products**.
see also **food**

milky *ADJECTIVE*
*The flask contained a **milky** liquid.*
• **whitish, cloudy, misty, chalky, opaque**
OPPOSITE **clear**

mimic *VERB*
*My dad is good at **mimicking** famous people.*
• **do impressions of, imitate, impersonate, pretend to be**
(informal) **take off**
If you mimic people especially to make fun of them, you **caricature** or **parody** them.

mind *NOUN*
❶ *Her **mind** was as sharp as ever.*
• **brain, intelligence, intellect, head, sense, understanding, wits, judgement, mental powers, reasoning**
❷ *Are you sure you won't change your **mind**?*
• **wishes, intention, fancy, inclination, opinion, outlook, point of view**

mind *VERB*
❶ *Will you **mind** my bag for a minute?*
• **guard, look after, watch, care for**
(informal) **keep an eye on**
❷ ***Mind** the step.*
• **look out for, watch out for, beware of, pay attention to, heed, note**
❸ *They won't **mind** if I'm late.*
• **bother, care, worry, be upset, take offence, object, disapprove**

mine *NOUN*
A coal mine is a **colliery** or **pit**.
A place where coal is removed from the surface of the ground is an **opencast mine**.
A place where stone or slate is removed is a **quarry**.

mingle *VERB*
*The secret agent **mingled** with the crowd.*
• **mix in, circulate, blend, combine, merge, fuse**

miniature *ADJECTIVE*
*A piccolo looks like a **miniature** flute.*
• **tiny, minute, diminutive, small-scale, baby, mini**
see also **small**

minimum *ADJECTIVE*
*Set the oven to the **minimum** temperature.*
• **least, smallest, littlest, lowest**
OPPOSITE **maximum**

minor *ADJECTIVE*
*I only had a **minor** part in the play.*
• **small, unimportant, insignificant, inferior, subordinate, trivial, petty**
OPPOSITE **major**

minute *ADJECTIVE*
*You can hardly see the **minute** crack.*
• **tiny, minuscule, microscopic, negligible**
OPPOSITE **large**

miraculous *ADJECTIVE*
*The patient made a **miraculous** recovery.*
• **amazing, astonishing, astounding, extraordinary, incredible, marvellous, unbelievable, wonderful, mysterious, inexplicable**

misbehave *VERB*
*My puppy has been **misbehaving** again!*
• **behave badly, be naughty, be disobedient, get up to mischief**
OPPOSITE **behave**

miscellaneous *ADJECTIVE*
*The bag contained **miscellaneous** balls of wool.*
• **assorted, various, different, mixed**

mischief *NOUN*
*The twins are always getting up to **mischief**.*
• **naughtiness, bad behaviour, disobedience, playfulness, roguishness**

miserable *ADJECTIVE*
❶ *You look **miserable**—what's the matter?*
• sad, unhappy, sorrowful, gloomy, glum, downhearted, despondent, dejected, depressed, melancholy, mournful, tearful
OPPOSITES cheerful, happy
❷ *The poor animals lived in **miserable** conditions.*
• distressing, uncomfortable, wretched, pitiful, pathetic, squalid
OPPOSITE comfortable
❸ *The weather was cold and **miserable**.*
• dismal, dreary, depressing, unpleasant
OPPOSITE pleasant

miserly *ADJECTIVE*
*He was too **miserly** to donate any money.*
• mean, selfish
(informal) grasping, stingy, tight-fisted, penny-pinching
OPPOSITE generous

misery *NOUN*
*The slaves must have led a life of **misery**.*
• sadness, sorrow, unhappiness, grief, distress, despair, anguish, wretchedness, suffering, torment, heartache, depression
OPPOSITE happiness

misfortune *NOUN*
*I heard about her family's **misfortune**.*
• bad luck, trouble, hardship, adversity, affliction, setback, mishap
OPPOSITE good luck

mishap *NOUN*
*Dad had a slight **mishap** with the car.*
• accident, problem, difficulty, setback

mislay *VERB* **mislays, mislaying, mislaid**
*I seem to have **mislaid** my purse.*
• lose
OPPOSITE find

misleading *ADJECTIVE*
*The directions he gave were quite **misleading**.*
• confusing, unreliable, deceptive, ambiguous, unclear

miss *VERB*
❶ *I **missed** the bus.*
• be too late for
❷ *The arrow **missed** the target.*
• fall short of, go wide of
❸ *If we leave now, we should **miss** the traffic.*
• avoid
❹ *I **missed** Dad when he was in hospital.*
• long for, yearn for, pine for
➤ **to miss something out**
*I **missed out** the boring bits of the story.*
• leave out, omit, ignore, overlook, skip

missile *NOUN*
see **weapon**

missing *ADJECTIVE*
*She found the **missing** keys in a drawer.*
• lost, mislaid, misplaced, absent, straying

mission *NOUN*
❶ *Her **mission** in life was to help those in need.*
• aim, purpose, objective, task, job, campaign
❷ *The astronauts are on a **mission** to Mars.*
• expedition, journey, voyage, exploration

mist *NOUN*
❶ *We drove slowly through the **mist**.*
• fog, haze, cloud, drizzle
❷ *I can't see because of the **mist** on my glasses.*
• condensation, steam

mistake *NOUN*
*This piece of writing is full of **mistakes**.*
• error, inaccuracy, blunder, slip, slip-up, lapse
A spelling mistake is a **misspelling**.
A mistake where something is left out is an **omission**.
A mistake in a printed book is a **misprint**.

mistake *VERB* **mistakes, mistaking, mistook, mistaken**
*She **mistook** my meaning entirely.*
• misunderstand, get wrong, mix up

mistrust *VERB*
*Do you have any reason to **mistrust** him?*
• distrust, have doubts about, suspect
OPPOSITE trust

misty *ADJECTIVE*
❶ *If it's **misty** outside, take a torch.*
• **foggy, hazy**
❷ *I can't see through the **misty** window.*
• **steamy, cloudy, smoky, opaque**
❸ *We saw a **misty** shape approaching.*
• **faint, fuzzy, blurred, dim, indistinct, shadowy, vague**
OPPOSITE **clear**

misunderstand *VERB* **misunderstands, misunderstanding, misunderstood**
*I think you **misunderstood** what I said.*
• **mistake, get wrong, miss the point of**
OPPOSITE **understand**

mix *VERB*
Mix the ingredients in a bowl.
• **combine, blend, mingle**
➤ **to mix something up**
*Please don't **mix up** my CDs.*
• **muddle, jumble, confuse**
To mix up playing cards is to **shuffle** them.

mixed *ADJECTIVE*
*Add a teaspoon of **mixed** herbs.*
• **assorted, various, different, miscellaneous**
OPPOSITE **separate**

mixture *NOUN*
❶ *Put the cake **mixture** in a baking tin.*
• **mix, blend, combination**
A mixture of metals is an **alloy**.
A mixture of two different species of plant or animal is a **hybrid**.
❷ *There's an odd **mixture** of things in the drawer.*
• **assortment, collection, variety, jumble, conglomeration**
A confused mixture is a **mishmash**.

moan *VERB*
❶ *The wounded warrior **moaned** in pain.*
• **cry, groan, sigh, wail, howl, whimper**
❷ *Ned's always **moaning** about the food.*
• **complain, grumble, grouse, whine**
(informal) **whinge**

mob *NOUN*
*An angry **mob** stormed the gates of the castle.*
• **crowd, horde, throng, mass, rabble, gang, pack, herd, bunch**

mob *VERB*
*Autograph hunters **mobbed** the pop star.*
• **crowd round, swarm round, surround, besiege, hem in, jostle**

mobile *ADJECTIVE*
❶ *A **mobile** library visits once a fortnight.*
• **movable, travelling**
Something that you can carry about is **portable**.
OPPOSITE **stationary**
❷ *A week after the injury, he was **mobile** again.*
• **moving about, active**
(informal) **up and about**
OPPOSITE **immobile**

mock *VERB*
*It was mean of them to **mock** his singing.*
• **jeer at, laugh at, make fun of, scoff at, sneer at, ridicule, scorn, deride**
(informal) **take the mickey out of**

model *ADJECTIVE*
❶ *We went to an exhibition of **model** railways.*
• **miniature, toy**
❷ *She's a **model** pupil.*
• **ideal, perfect**

model *NOUN*
❶ *I'm building a **model** of a space rocket.*
• **copy, replica, toy**
❷ *This is the latest **model** of skateboard.*
• **design, type, version**
❸ *She's a **model** of good behaviour.*
• **example, ideal**

model *VERB*
*The artist **models** figures in clay.*
• **make, mould, shape, construct, fashion**

moderate *ADJECTIVE*
*Her first book was a **moderate** success.*
• **average, fair, modest, medium, reasonable, passable, tolerable**
OPPOSITE **exceptional**

A B C D E F G H I J K L M N O P Q R S T U V W X Y Z

moderately *ADVERB*
*He answered the questions **moderately** well.*
• fairly, reasonably, quite, rather, somewhat
(informal) pretty

modern *ADJECTIVE*
❶ *All the equipment in their kitchen was **modern**.*
• up to date, contemporary, advanced, the latest
OPPOSITE out of date
❷ *She always dresses in **modern** clothes.*
• fashionable, stylish, modish
(informal) trendy, hip
OPPOSITE old-fashioned

modest *ADJECTIVE*
❶ *He's very **modest** about his success.*
• humble, quiet, reserved, shy, bashful, coy
OPPOSITE conceited
❷ *There has been a **modest** increase in sales.*
• moderate, reasonable, average, medium

modify *VERB*
*We've had to **modify** our travel plans.*
• adapt, alter, change, adjust, refine, revise, vary

moist *ADJECTIVE*
❶ *The walls of the dungeon were **moist**.*
• damp, wet, watery, clammy, dank
❷ *Tropical plants grow well in a **moist** atmosphere.*
• humid, muggy, steamy, rainy
OPPOSITE dry

moisture *NOUN*
*There is still a lot of **moisture** on the ground.*
• wetness, dampness, damp, dew, condensation, humidity

moment *NOUN*
❶ *I'll be ready in a **moment**.*
• minute, second, instant, flash
(informal) jiffy, tick
❷ *It was a great **moment** in the history of space travel.*
• time, occasion, period

momentary *ADJECTIVE*
*He felt a **momentary** stab of pain.*
• brief, short, fleeting, temporary
OPPOSITE permanent

monarch *NOUN*
see **ruler**

money *NOUN*
*How much **money** do you have with you?*
• cash, currency, funds, finance
(informal) dough, dosh
A large amount of money is a **fortune**, **riches** or **wealth**.

monster *NOUN*
*A sea **monster** reared its head above the waves.*
• beast, giant, ogre, brute

monstrous *ADJECTIVE*
❶ *The town was engulfed by a **monstrous** wave.*
• huge, gigantic, enormous, immense, massive, colossal, great, hulking, mighty, towering, vast
❷ *The nation was shocked by the **monstrous** crime.*
• horrifying, shocking, wicked, evil, hideous, horrible, terrible, atrocious, dreadful, gruesome, outrageous, scandalous

mood *NOUN*
*What sort of **mood** is he in today?*
• temper, humour, state of mind, disposition

moody *ADJECTIVE*
*She's been **moody** and withdrawn for weeks.*
• sulky, sullen, grumpy, bad-tempered, temperamental, touchy, miserable, gloomy, glum
OPPOSITE cheerful

moon *NOUN*

WORD WEB

FORMS IN WHICH WE SEE THE MOON:

• crescent moon, full moon, new moon; moonbeam, moonlight

THINGS YOU MIGHT FIND OR DO ON THE MOON:

• crater, moon dust, moon rock, moonscape, moonwalk

A word meaning 'to do with the moon' is **lunar**.

The time when the moon rises is **moonrise**.
The time when the moon sets is **moonset**.
see also **astronaut, space**

moor *NOUN*
The tower stood on a windswept ***moor****.*
• moorland, heath, fell

moor *VERB*
We ***moored*** *the boat in the harbour.*
• tie up, secure, fasten, anchor, berth, dock

moral *ADJECTIVE*
She tried her best to lead a ***moral*** *life.*
• good, honest, truthful, upright, decent, honourable, principled, ethical, virtuous, righteous
OPPOSITE immoral

moral *NOUN*
The ***moral*** *of this story is that crime doesn't pay.*
• lesson, message, meaning

morale *NOUN*
The new coach has improved the team's ***morale****.*
• confidence, spirit, state of mind, attitude, mood

more *DETERMINER*
The soup needs ***more*** *pepper.*
• extra, further, added, additional
OPPOSITE less

morning *NOUN*
The expedition set off in the early ***morning****.*
• daybreak, dawn, first light, sunrise
for other times of the day see **day**

morsel *NOUN*
They hadn't eaten a ***morsel*** *of food all day.*
• bite, crumb, mouthful, taste, nibble, piece, scrap, fragment

mortal *ADJECTIVE*
1 *All human beings are* ***mortal****.*
OPPOSITE immortal
2 *The knight had received a* ***mortal*** *wound.*
• deadly, fatal, lethal

mostly *ADVERB*
I spend my money ***mostly*** *on books and CDs.*
• mainly, largely, chiefly, primarily, generally, usually, normally, typically, principally, predominantly

motion *NOUN*
He summoned the waiter with a ***motion*** *of his hand.*
• gesture, movement

motivate *VERB*
What ***motivated*** *you to write a book?*
• prompt, drive, stimulate, urge, provoke, spur, influence, induce

motive *NOUN*
The police can find no ***motive*** *for the crime.*
• cause, motivation, reason, purpose, grounds

motor *NOUN*
The toy train had an electric ***motor****.*
• engine

motto *NOUN*
Her ***motto*** *has always been, 'Keep smiling'.*
• catchphrase, proverb, saying, slogan, golden rule

mould *VERB*
The sculptor ***moulded*** *the figures from clay.*
• shape, form, fashion, model, cast

mouldy *ADJECTIVE*
All I found in the fridge was some ***mouldy*** *cheese.*
• rotten, rotting, decaying, musty, damp

mound *NOUN*
❶ *Her desk was covered with **mounds** of paper.*
• **heap, pile, stack, mass**
❷ *There used to be a castle on top of that **mound**.*
• **hill, hillock, rise, hump**
An ancient mound of earth over a grave is a **barrow**.

mount *VERB*
❶ *She **mounted** the pony and rode off.*
• **get on, jump on to**
❷ *The butler slowly **mounted** the stairs.*
• **go up, climb, ascend**
❸ *The gallery is **mounting** a new exhibition.*
• **put up, set up, display**
❹ *The tension began to **mount** in the crowd.*
• **grow, increase, rise, intensify**

mountain *NOUN*

WORD WEB

The top of a mountain is the **peak** or **summit**.
A line of mountains is a **range**.
A long, narrow mountain is a **ridge**.
A mountain with a hole at the top caused by an eruption is a **volcano**.

THINGS YOU MIGHT SEE ON OR NEAR A MOUNTAIN:

• **avalanche, boulder, cave, cliff, crag, crevice, glacier, gorge, ledge, mountain pass, mountain stream, precipice, rocks, slope, valley** or *(Scottish)* **glen**

SOME WORDS TO DESCRIBE A MOUNTAIN:

• **barren, craggy, forbidding, jagged, lofty, massive, misty, rocky, rugged, snow-capped, soaring, towering, treacherous**
An area of land with many mountains is **mountainous**.

mourn *VERB*
*He was still **mourning** the loss of his friend.*
• **grieve for, lament for**

mouth *NOUN*
❶ *The crocodile slept with its **mouth** wide open.*
• **jaws**
A dog's nose and mouth is its **muzzle**.
A word meaning 'to do with your mouth' is **oral**.
❷ *They lived in a village at the **mouth** of the river.*
• **outlet**
A wide river mouth is an **estuary** or *(Scottish)* **firth**.
❸ *The **mouth** of the cave was hidden by trees.*
• **entrance, opening**

move *NOUN*
❶ *Don't make a **move**!*
• **movement**
❷ *The spy was watching their every **move**.*
• **action, step, deed, manoeuvre**
❸ *Is it my **move** next?*
• **turn, go, chance, opportunity**

move *VERB*

OVERUSED WORD

Try to vary the words you use for **move**. Here are some other words you could use.

TO MOVE FROM ONE PLACE TO ANOTHER:

• **carry, remove, transfer, transport, shift**
*They **shifted** the piano into the front room.*

TO MOVE FROM A POSITION:

• **go, leave, depart, quit, budge**
*The camel stared and refused to **budge**.*

TO MOVE RESTLESSLY:

• **toss, turn, stir, twist, shake, fidget, twitch, flap**
*Please stop **twitching** in your seat.*

TO MOVE FROM SIDE TO SIDE:

• **sway, swing, wave, wag, wiggle**
The knight ***swung*** *a sword above his helmet.*

TO MOVE ALONG:

• **travel, walk, proceed**
Few people ***travel*** *on these roads after dark.*

TO MOVE QUICKLY:

• **hurry, dash, dart, race, run, rush, hasten, hurtle, career, speed, sprint, streak, scurry, whizz, zoom**
The next stone went whizzing through a big web, snapping its cords, and taking off the spider sitting in the middle of it, whack, dead. –THE HOBBIT, J. R. R. Tolkien
see *also* **run**

TO MOVE SLOWLY:

• **amble, stroll, saunter, dawdle, slouch, crawl, drift**
Yawning and grumbling, the Weasleys slouched outside with Harry behind them.–HARRY POTTER AND THE CHAMBER OF SECRETS, J. K. Rowling

TO MOVE TOWARDS SOMETHING:

• **advance, approach, come, proceed, progress**
The lookout saw a pirate ship ***approaching.***

TO MOVE BACK OR MOVE AWAY:

• **back, retreat, reverse, withdraw**
The serpent ***retreated,*** *hissing, into its lair.*

TO MOVE DOWNWARDS:

• **drop, descend, fall, sink, swoop**
A pair of vultures ***swooped*** *down from the sky.*

TO MOVE UPWARDS:

• **rise, ascend, climb, mount, soar, arise**
A hot-air balloon ***mounted*** *into the air.*

TO MOVE GRACEFULLY:

• **flow, glide, dance**
Some swans ***glided*** *gently across the pond.*

TO MOVE CLUMSILY:

• **stumble, stagger, flounder, lurch, lumber, shuffle, totter, trundle, trip**
The ogre ***stumbled*** *up the narrow steps.*

TO MOVE STEALTHILY:

• **creep, crawl, edge, inch, slink**
The secret agent ***edged*** *carefully along the wall.*
for ways to describe how an animal or bird moves see **animal, bird**

movement *NOUN*
❶ *The robot made a sudden, jerky* ***movement.***
• **motion, move, action, gesture**
❷ *Has there been any* ***movement*** *in their attitude?*
• **progress, development, change, shift**
❸ *She was involved in the peace* ***movement.***
• **organisation, group, party, campaign**

movie *NOUN*
see **film**

moving *ADJECTIVE*
The story was so ***moving*** *that I started to cry.*
• **emotional, inspiring, stirring, touching**
(informal) **tear-jerking**

muck *NOUN*
They cleared the ***muck*** *out of the stable.*
• **dirt, filth, grime, mud, sludge, dung, manure**

mucky *ADJECTIVE*
My football boots are all ***mucky.***
• **dirty, messy, muddy, grimy, grubby, filthy, foul, soiled, squalid**
OPPOSITE **clean**

mud *NOUN*
*The tractor left a trail of **mud** on the road.*
• **dirt, muck, mire, sludge, clay, soil**

muddle *NOUN*
❶ *There was a **muddle** over the date of the party.*
• **confusion, misunderstanding**
(informal) **mix-up**
❷ *There was a **muddle** of clothes on the floor.*
• **jumble, mess, tangle**

muddle *VERB*
❶ *Who **muddled** the papers on my desk?*
• **mix up, mess up, disorder, jumble up, shuffle, tangle**
OPPOSITE **tidy**
❷ *They got **muddled** and took the wrong turning.*
• **confuse, bewilder, puzzle, perplex**

muddy *ADJECTIVE*
❶ *Take off your **muddy** shoes before you come in.*
• **dirty, messy, mucky, filthy, caked, soiled**
OPPOSITE **clean**
❷ *I got filthy walking across the **muddy** ground.*
• **boggy, marshy, waterlogged, wet, sodden**
OPPOSITE **dry, firm**

muffle *VERB*
❶ *We **muffled** ourselves up to play in the snow.*
• **wrap, cover**
❷ *She tried to **muffle** her sneeze.*
• **stifle, smother, suppress, silence, deaden, dull**

muffled *ADJECTIVE*
*They heard **muffled** voices from the next room.*
• **faint, indistinct, unclear, muted, deadened**
OPPOSITE **clear**

mug *NOUN*
see **cup**

muggy *ADJECTIVE*
*The weather is often **muggy** before a storm.*
• **humid, close, clammy, sticky, moist, damp, oppressive**
OPPOSITE **fresh**

multiply *VERB*
*Her problems seemed to be **multiplying**.*
• **increase, grow, spread, mount up**

mumble *VERB*
*We couldn't hear the actor as he was **mumbling**.*
• **mutter, talk indistinctly**

munch *VERB*
*Kim sat **munching** popcorn all through the film.*
• **chew, crunch**
for other ways to eat see **eat**

murder *VERB*
see **kill**

murky *ADJECTIVE*
*A creature loomed out of the **murky** waters of the loch.*
• **dark, clouded, cloudy, dim, dull, dingy, gloomy, grey, foggy, misty**
OPPOSITE **clear**

murmur *VERB*
*We heard voices **murmuring** in the room above.*
• **mutter, mumble, whisper**

muscular *ADJECTIVE*
*The wrestler had a **muscular** body.*
• **brawny, beefy, athletic, sinewy, strapping, strong, well-built**
OPPOSITES **puny, weak**

museum *NOUN*
*There's a new Viking exhibition at the **museum**.*
• **academy, gallery**
A person who works in a museum and looks after its collection is a **curator**.
A person who studies ancient civilisations by digging for the remains of buildings and artefacts is an **archaeologist**.

A person who studies the civilisation of ancient Egypt is an **Egyptologist**.

WORD WEB

THINGS YOU MIGHT SEE IN A MUSEUM:

- **artefact, collection, display case, exhibit**

SOME MUSEUM ARTEFACTS:

- **amphora, amulet, casket, figurine, frieze, mask, mosaic, papyrus, runes, seal, sceptre, statue, terracotta**

see also **prehistoric, pyramid**

music *NOUN*

WORD WEB

VARIOUS KINDS OF MUSIC:

- **blues, classical music, country and western, dance music, disco music, folk music, gospel, hiphop, jazz, orchestral music, pop music, punk, ragtime, rap, reggae, rock, soul, swing**

TERMS USED IN MUSIC:

- **chord, counterpoint, discord, harmony, melody, note, octave, pitch, rhythm, scale, semitone, tempo, theme, tone, tune**

NAMES OF NOTES AND SIGNS IN WRITTEN MUSIC:

- **clef, crotchet, flat, key signature, minim, natural, quaver, semibreve, semiquaver, sharp, stave, time signature**

TYPES OF MUSICAL COMPOSITION:

- **anthem, ballad, carol, concerto, folk song, fugue, hymn, lullaby, march, melody, musical, opera, operetta, sonata, song, symphony, tune**

FAMILIES OF MUSICAL INSTRUMENTS:

- **brass, keyboard, percussion, strings, woodwind**

STRINGED INSTRUMENTS THAT CAN BE PLAYED WITH A BOW:

- **cello, double bass, viola, violin** or **fiddle**

STRINGED INSTRUMENTS PLAYED BY PLUCKING OR STRUMMING:

- **banjo, cittern, guitar, harp, lute, lyre, mandolin, sitar, ukulele, zither**

BRASS INSTRUMENTS:

- **bugle, cornet, euphonium, flugelhorn, French horn, trombone, trumpet, tuba**

OTHER INSTRUMENTS PLAYED BY BLOWING:

- **bagpipes, bassoon, clarinet, cor anglais, flute, harmonica** or **mouth organ, oboe, piccolo, recorder, saxophone**

KEYBOARD INSTRUMENTS:

- **accordion, harmonium, harpsichord, keyboard, organ, piano, synthesiser**

PERCUSSION INSTRUMENTS:

- **bass drum, bongo drum, castanets, cymbals, drum, glockenspiel, gong, kettledrum, maracas, marimba, rattle, snare drum, tabor, tambour, tambourine, timpani, tom-tom, triangle, tubular bells, vibraphone, xylophone**

PEOPLE WHO PLAY VARIOUS INSTRUMENTS:

- **bugler, cellist, clarinettist, drummer, fiddler, flautist, guitarist, harpist, lutenist, oboist, organist, percussionist, pianist, piper, timpanist, trombonist, trumpeter, violinist**

SOME OTHER MUSICIANS:

- **accompanist, composer, conductor, instrumentalist, singer, vocalist**

for types of singing voice see **sing**

GROUPS OF MUSICIANS:

- **band, choir** or **chorus, duet** or **duo, ensemble, group, orchestra, quartet, quintet, trio**

A B C D E F G H I J K L M N O P Q R S T U V W X Y Z

musical *ADJECTIVE*
*Helena has a very **musical** voice.*
• tuneful, melodic, melodious, harmonious, sweet-sounding
for types of musical instrument see **music**

musty *ADJECTIVE*
*There was a **musty** smell in the cellar.*
• damp, dank, mouldy, stale, stuffy, airless
OPPOSITE fresh

mute *ADJECTIVE*
*We stared in **mute** amazement at the volcano.*
• silent, speechless, dumb, tongue-tied

mutilate *VERB*
*His right hand was **mutilated** by a firework.*
• maim, disfigure, injure, wound, mangle

mutiny *NOUN*
*The crew were plotting a **mutiny** against the captain.*
• rebellion, revolt, uprising

mutter *VERB*
*The goblin sat **muttering** to himself in the corner.*
• mumble, murmur, whisper

mutual *ADJECTIVE*
*It is in our **mutual** interest to work together.*
• joint, common, shared, reciprocal

mysterious *ADJECTIVE*
*They uncovered a **mysterious** sign on the wall.*
• strange, puzzling, baffling, mystifying, perplexing, obscure, unexplained, incomprehensible, inexplicable, curious, weird

mystery *NOUN*
*What really happened was a **mystery**.*
• puzzle, riddle, secret

mystify *VERB*
*We were **mystified** by the curious message.*
• puzzle, baffle, bewilder, perplex

myth *NOUN*

WORD WEB

CREATURES FOUND IN MYTHS AND LEGENDS

• Abominable Snowman, banshee, basilisk, brownie, chimera, centaur, Cerberus, cyclops, dragon, dwarf, elf, fairy, genie, giant, gnome, goblin, gremlin, gryphon, hippogriff, imp, kelpie, kraken, leprechaun, mermaid, merman, Minotaur, nymph, ogre, orc, Pegasus, phoenix, pixie, selkie, serpent, shapeshifter, siren, sphinx, sprite, troll, unicorn, vampire, werewolf, yeti

A native of Tibet, the yeti is believed to be related to the troll, though no one has yet got close enough to conduct the necessary tests.
—FANTASTIC BEASTS AND WHERE TO FIND THEM, J. K. Rowling

see also **dragon, fairy**

mythical *ADJECTIVE*
*The unicorn is a **mythical** beast.*
• fabulous, fanciful, imaginary, invented, fictional, legendary, mythological, non-existent, unreal
OPPOSITE real

Nn

nag *VERB*
*He was always **nagging** her to work harder.*
• **badger, pester, scold**

naive *ADJECTIVE*
*He's so **naive** that he believes her promises.*
• **innocent, inexperienced, unsophisticated, artless, gullible, simple**

naked *ADJECTIVE*
*He walked **naked** into the bathroom.*
• **bare, nude, unclothed, undressed**
OPPOSITE **clothed**

name *NOUN*
The official names you have are your **first names** or **forenames**, and **surname**.
Names a Christian is given at baptism are **Christian names**.
A false name is an **alias**.
A name people use instead of your real name is a **nickname**.
A false name an author uses is a **pen name** or **pseudonym**.
The name of a book or film is its **title**.

name *VERB*
*The zoo **named** the new lion cubs Kiara and Kovu.*
• **call**
To name someone at the ceremony of baptism is to **baptise** or **christen** them.

nap *NOUN*
*Granny always takes a **nap** on Sunday afternoons.*
• **rest, sleep, doze, lie-down, siesta**
(informal) **snooze, forty winks**

narrate *VERB*
*The famous actor **narrated** the story of his life.*
• **tell, recount, relate**

narrative *NOUN*
*The sailor wrote an exciting **narrative** of his voyage.*
• **account, history, story, tale, chronicle**
(informal) **yarn**

narrow *ADJECTIVE*
*The rabbit squeezed through a **narrow** opening in the fence.*
• **thin, slender, slim**
OPPOSITE **wide**

nasty *ADJECTIVE*
❶ *Ogres have a thoroughly **nasty** temper.*
• **unkind, unpleasant, unfriendly, disagreeable, objectionable, odious, mean, malicious, cruel, spiteful, vicious**
❷ *A **nasty** smell wafted from the laboratory.*
• **unpleasant, offensive, disgusting, repulsive, revolting, horrible, foul, rotten, sickening**
OPPOSITE **agreeable, pleasant**
❸ *The weather suddenly turned **nasty**.*
• **unpleasant, rough, stormy, squally**
for other ways to describe something you don't like see **bad**

nation *NOUN*
*People from many **nations** compete in the Olympic Games.*
• **country, state, land, race, population**

national *ADJECTIVE*
*The programme will be broadcast on **national** television.*
• **nationwide**
OPPOSITE **local**

natural *ADJECTIVE*
❶ *Karen has a **natural** gift for music.*
• **born, inborn, instinctive, intuitive, native**
❷ *It's only **natural** to be nervous before an exam.*
• **normal, common, understandable, reasonable, predictable**
OPPOSITE **unnatural**

A B C D E F G H I J K L M N O P Q R S T U V W X Y Z

nature *NOUN*
❶ *I like TV programmes about* ***nature****.*
• **natural history, wildlife**
❷ *The old sheepdog has a very kind* ***nature****.*
• **character, disposition, personality, manner**
❸ *I collect coins, medals and things of that* ***nature****.*
• **kind, sort, type, description, variety**

naughty *ADJECTIVE*
The puppies were quite ***naughty*** *when they were young.*
• **bad, badly behaved, disobedient, mischievous, uncontrollable, unmanageable, troublesome, unruly**
OPPOSITE **well-behaved**
➤ **to be naughty**
• **misbehave, behave badly, disobey**

navigate *VERB*
The captain ***navigated*** *his ship between the dangerous rocks.*
• **steer, direct, guide, manoeuvre, pilot**

navy *NOUN*
see **armed forces**

near *ADJECTIVE*
❶ *We get on well with our* ***near*** *neighbours.*
• **next-door, nearby, close, adjacent, surrounding**
❷ *My birthday is* ***near****.*
• **approaching, coming**
(informal) **round the corner**
❸ *We sent cards to all our* ***near*** *relatives.*
• **close, dear, familiar, intimate**
OPPOSITE **distant**

nearly *ADVERB*
Thank goodness, it's ***nearly*** *dinner time!*
• **almost, practically, virtually, just about, approaching**

neat *ADJECTIVE*
❶ *Please leave the room as* ***neat*** *as possible.*
• **clean, orderly, tidy, uncluttered, immaculate**
(informal) **spick and span**
❷ *Craig always looks* ***neat*** *in his school uniform.*
• **smart, elegant, spruce, trim**
❸ *Her handwriting is very* ***neat****.*
• **precise, skilful, well-formed**
OPPOSITE **untidy**

necessary *ADJECTIVE*
The recipe lists all the ***necessary*** *ingredients.*
• **essential, required, needed, needful, compulsory, obligatory, unavoidable**
OPPOSITE **unnecessary**

need *NOUN*
There's a ***need*** *for more shops in our area.*
• **call, demand, requirement**

need *VERB*
❶ *I* ***need*** *a pound coin for the locker.*
• **require, want, be short of, lack**
❷ *The charity* ***needs*** *our support.*
• **depend on, rely on**

needless *ADJECTIVE*
They went to a lot of ***needless*** *expense.*
• **unnecessary, unwanted, uncalled for, excessive, superfluous**

needlework *NOUN*
You need good eyesight for ***needlework****.*
• **sewing**

WORD WEB

SOME TYPES OF NEEDLEWORK:

• **appliqué, beadwork, cross-stitch, embroidery, patchwork, quilting, tapestry**
for other arts and crafts see **art**

needy *ADJECTIVE*
They set up a fund to help ***needy*** *children.*
• **poor, deprived, badly off, hard up**
OPPOSITE **rich**

negative *ADJECTIVE*
He has a very ***negative*** *attitude to his job.*
• **pessimistic, uncooperative, unenthusiastic, grudging, unhelpful, unwilling**
OPPOSITE **positive**

neglect *VERB*
She's been ***neglecting*** *her work.*
• **forget, ignore, overlook, abandon, disregard, pay no attention to, shirk**

negligible *ADJECTIVE*
There is a ***negligible*** *difference in price.*
• **tiny, slight, insignificant, unimportant, trivial**
OPPOSITE **considerable**

negotiate *VERB*
❶ *She* ***negotiated*** *with the car salesman.*
• **bargain, haggle, deal, confer**
❷ *The skier* ***negotiated*** *the course with ease.*
• **get past, get round, manoeuvre round**

neighbourhood *NOUN*
They live in a very nice ***neighbourhood.***
• **area, district, community, locality, vicinity**

neighbouring *ADJECTIVE*
The journey will take them to Mexico and ***neighbouring*** *countries.*
• **nearby, bordering, adjacent, adjoining, surrounding, nearest, next-door**

neighbourly *ADJECTIVE*
It was very ***neighbourly*** *of her to offer to feed the cat.*
• **friendly, helpful, kind, obliging, sociable**
OPPOSITE **unfriendly**

nerve *NOUN*
❶ *Acrobats need to have a lot of* ***nerve.***
• **bravery, courage, daring, pluck**
(informal) **bottle**
❷ *He had the* ***nerve*** *to ask for more money!*
• **cheek, impudence, rudeness, impertinence**

nervous *ADJECTIVE*
She always feels ***nervous*** *before an exam.*
• **anxious, worried, apprehensive, concerned, uneasy, fearful, edgy, fraught, tense, troubled**
(informal) **uptight, jittery**
OPPOSITE **calm**

nestle *VERB*
The cubs ***nestled*** *against their mother.*
• **cuddle, curl up, snuggle**

neutral *ADJECTIVE*
❶ *A referee has to be* ***neutral.***
• **impartial, unbiased, unprejudiced, even-handed**
OPPOSITES **biased, prejudiced**
❷ *The room was decorated in* ***neutral*** *colours.*
• **dull, drab, indefinite, colourless**
OPPOSITES **vibrant, distinctive**

new *ADJECTIVE*
❶ *Start on a* ***new*** *sheet of paper.*
• **clean, fresh, unused, brand-new**
Something new and unused is **in mint condition.**
❷ *They went to the motor show to see the* ***new*** *models.*
• **latest, current, modern, recent, up to date**
❸ *They've found a* ***new*** *bug in the computer program.*
• **additional, extra, unexpected, unfamiliar**
❹ *Haven't you got any* ***new*** *ideas?*
• **fresh, original, novel, innovative, creative, different**
OPPOSITE **old**

news *NOUN*
What's the latest ***news****?*
• **information, word, report, bulletin**
(old use) **tidings**

next *ADJECTIVE*
❶ *He lives in the house* ***next*** *to the chip shop.*
• **adjacent, closest, nearest**
OPPOSITE **distant**
❷ *If you miss this bus, you can catch the* ***next*** *one.*
• **following, subsequent**
OPPOSITE **previous**

nice *ADJECTIVE*
❶ *That's not a very* ***nice*** *thing to say!*
• **pleasant, agreeable**
OPPOSITE **nasty**
❷ *There is a* ***nice*** *distinction between borrowing and stealing.*
• **delicate, fine, precise, subtle**

OVERUSED WORD

Try to vary the words you use for **nice**. Here are some other words you could use.

FOR A NICE PERSON:

• **good, kind, friendly, helpful, generous, likeable, amiable, charming, polite, genial**
'Come with me, dear Ratty, and your amiable friend also, if he will be so very good, just as far as the stable-yard, and you shall see what you shall see!'—THE WIND IN THE WILLOWS, Kenneth Grahame

FOR A NICE EXPERIENCE:

• **delightful, enjoyable, wonderful, marvellous, splendid**
Did you have an ***enjoyable*** *time in France?*

FOR SOMETHING THAT LOOKS NICE:

• **beautiful, attractive, pleasing, lovely**
There is an ***attractive*** *view from the upstairs window.*

FOR A NICE SMELL:

• **fragrant, sweet-smelling**
The ***fragrant*** *scent of lavender filled the garden.*

FOR NICE FOOD:

• **delicious, tasty, appetising, satisfying**
They serve ***tasty*** *sandwiches in the cafe.*

FOR NICE WEATHER:

• **fine, sunny, warm**
The weather has been ***fine*** *all week.*

for other ways to describe something you like see **good**

night *NOUN*
Badgers usually come out at ***night****.*
• **night-time, dark**
Animals which are active at night are **nocturnal** animals.

nimble *ADJECTIVE*
The elves sewed the shoes with their ***nimble*** *fingers.*
• **agile, skilful, quick, deft**
OPPOSITE **clumsy**

nip *VERB*
❶ *She* ***nipped*** *her finger in the door.*
• **pinch, squeeze, clip, catch**
❷ *The dog* ***nipped*** *my leg.*
• **bite, peck, snip**
❸ *(informal) I'll just* ***nip*** *along to the post office.*
• **dash, run, rush**
(informal) **pop**

noble *ADJECTIVE*
❶ *The knight belonged to an ancient* ***noble*** *family.*
• **aristocratic, high-born, upper-class**
❷ *The rescuers were congratulated for their* ***noble*** *efforts.*
• **brave, heroic, courageous, honourable, worthy, virtuous, gallant**
OPPOSITES **cowardly, unworthy**

nod *VERB*
Simon ***nodded*** *his head in agreement.*
• **bob, bow, dip, lower**
➤ **to nod off**
He sometimes ***nods off*** *in front of the television.*
• **fall asleep, doze off, drop off, have a nap**

noise *NOUN*
Where is that dreadful ***noise*** *coming from?*
• **din, racket, row, uproar, commotion, tumult, cacophony, hullabaloo, pandemonium**

noisy *ADJECTIVE*
❶ *The people next door were playing* ***noisy*** *music.*
• **loud, blaring, booming, deafening, ear-splitting, thunderous**
❷ *The children are very* ***noisy*** *this morning.*
• **rowdy, raucous, chattering, talkative**
OPPOSITE **quiet**

nominate *VERB*
*They **nominated** her as captain.*
• appoint, elect, choose, select, name

nonsense *NOUN*
*Stop talking **nonsense**!*
• rubbish, drivel, balderdash, piffle, gibberish, claptrap, gobbledegook
(informal) rot, tripe, twaddle

non-stop *ADJECTIVE*
❶ *Their **non-stop** chattering annoyed her.*
• constant, continual, continuous, endless, ceaseless, incessant, never-ending
❷ *They took a **non-stop** train from Glasgow to Edinburgh.*
• direct, express, fast

normal *ADJECTIVE*
❶ *He had a **normal** kind of day at work.*
• average, common, customary, familiar, habitual, ordinary, predictable, regular, routine, standard, typical, unsurprising, usual
❷ *No **normal** person would sleep on a bed of nails.*
• healthy, rational, reasonable, sane
OPPOSITE abnormal

north *NOUN, ADJECTIVE, ADVERB*
The parts of a continent or country in the north are the **northern** parts.
To travel towards the north is to travel **northward** or **northwards** or **in a northerly direction**.
A wind from the north is a **northerly** wind.
A person who lives in the north of a country is a **northerner**.

nose *NOUN*
❶ *Someone punched Roger on the **nose**.*
(informal) hooter
The openings in your nose are your **nostrils**.
A word meaning 'to do with your nose' is **nasal**.
Words for an animal's nose are **muzzle** and **snout**.
❷ *I sat in the **nose** of the boat hoping to spot a dolphin.*
• front, bow, prow

WRITING TIPS

YOU CAN USE THESE WORDS TO DESCRIBE A NOSE:

• beak-like, bulbous, button, classical or Roman, crooked, pointed, snub, upturned
*The troll had bushy eyebrows and a red, **bulbous** nose.*

nosy *ADJECTIVE (informal)*
*Stop being so **nosy** and asking all these questions!*
• inquisitive, curious, prying, snooping, intrusive
An informal name for a nosy person is a **nosy parker**.

notable *ADJECTIVE*
❶ *Many **notable** artists lived and worked in Paris.*
• famous, celebrated, renowned, noted, distinguished, eminent, prominent
❷ *The fireworks concert this year was a **notable** event.*
• memorable, noteworthy, significant, major, important, remarkable
OPPOSITES insignificant, minor

notch *NOUN*
*The woodsman cut a **notch** in the tree trunk.*
• cut, nick, groove, score, incision

note *NOUN*
❶ *I sent a **note** thanking him for the present.*
• message, letter, communication
❷ *There was a **note** of anger in her voice.*
• sound, tone, feeling, quality

note *VERB*
❶ *The detective **noted** the address on a scrap of paper.*
• jot down, make a note of, write down, record, scribble
❷ *Did you **note** what she was wearing?*
• notice, see, take note of, pay attention to, heed, mark, observe

A B C D E F G H I J K L M N O P Q R S T U V W X Y Z

nothing *NOUN*
Four minus four equals ***nothing****.*
• **nought, zero**
In cricket a score of nothing is a **duck**, in tennis it is **love**, and in football it is **nil**.

notice *NOUN*
Someone put up a ***notice*** *about the meeting.*
• **sign, advertisement, placard, poster, warning**
➤ **to take notice of something**
They ***took*** *no* ***notice of*** *the warning.*
• **heed, pay attention to**

notice *VERB*
❶ *Did you* ***notice*** *what he was wearing?*
• **note, see, take note of, pay attention to, heed, mark, observe**
❷ *I* ***noticed*** *a funny smell in the room.*
• **become aware of, detect**

noticeable *ADJECTIVE*
❶ *There has been a* ***noticeable*** *improvement in the weather.*
• **definite, distinct, notable, measurable, perceptible, significant**
❷ *The tower is* ***noticeable*** *for miles around.*
• **visible, conspicuous**
❸ *He spoke with a* ***noticeable*** *foreign accent.*
• **obvious, pronounced, unmistakable, audible**
OPPOSITE **imperceptible**

notion *NOUN*
Uncle Ollie has some strange ***notions*** *about life.*
• **belief, idea, view, thought, opinion, theory, concept**

notorious *ADJECTIVE*
He is a ***notorious*** *liar as well as a thief.*
• **infamous, well-known, disgraceful, scandalous**

nought *NOUN*
see **nothing**

nourish *VERB*
Plants are ***nourished*** *by water drawn up through their roots.*
• **feed, sustain, support**

nourishing *ADJECTIVE*
The penguins live on a ***nourishing*** *diet of fish and squid.*
• **nutritious, wholesome, healthy, health-giving**

novel *ADJECTIVE*
The inventor had a ***novel*** *idea for building a robot.*
• **original, new, innovative, fresh, different, imaginative, creative, unusual, unconventional**
OPPOSITE **familiar**

novel *NOUN*
for various forms of writing see ***writing***

now *ADVERB*
❶ *My cousins are* ***now*** *living in Melbourne.*
• **at present, at the moment, currently, nowadays**
❷ *I'll give them a ring* ***now****.*
• **immediately, at once, straight away, without delay, instantly**

nude *ADJECTIVE*
The artist painted from a ***nude*** *model.*
• **naked, bare, undressed, unclothed**
OPPOSITE **clothed**

nudge *VERB*
She ***nudged*** *me with her elbow.*
• **poke, prod, shove, bump, jog, jolt**

nuisance *NOUN*
The traffic noise is a real ***nuisance****.*
• **annoyance, irritation, inconvenience, bother, menace, pest, drawback**

numb *ADJECTIVE*
My toes are ***numb*** *with cold.*
• **unfeeling, deadened, frozen, insensitive, paralysed**
OPPOSITE **sensitive**

number *NOUN*
❶ *Add the **numbers** together to get the answer.*
• **figure, numeral**
Any of the numbers from 0 to 9 is a **digit.**
A negative or positive whole number is an **integer.**
An amount used in measuring or counting is a **unit.**
❷ *A large **number** of people applied for the job.*
• **amount, quantity, collection, crowd**
❸ *I've ordered the latest **number** of the magazine.*
• **edition, issue**
❹ *The band played some well-known **numbers**.*
• **song, piece, tune**

numerous *ADJECTIVE*
*There are **numerous** spelling mistakes on this page.*
• **many, plenty of, abundant, countless, innumerable, myriad, untold**
OPPOSITE **few**

nurse *NOUN*
for people who practise medicine see **medicine**

nurse *VERB*
*The aid workers **nursed** the sick children.*
• **look after, care for, tend, treat**

nut *NOUN*

WORD WEB

SOME KINDS OF NUT:

• **acorn, almond, Brazil nut, cashew, chestnut, coconut, hazelnut, macadamia, peanut, pecan, pine nut, pistachio, walnut**

Oo

oath *NOUN*
❶ *The knights swore an **oath** of honour.*
• **pledge, promise, vow**
❷ *He let out an **oath** when he banged his head.*
• **swear word, curse, blasphemy**

obedient *ADJECTIVE*
*The dog seems very **obedient**.*
• **well-behaved, disciplined, manageable, dutiful, docile**
OPPOSITE **disobedient**

obey *VERB*
❶ *The dog **obeyed** his owner's commands.*
• **follow, carry out, execute, implement, observe, adhere to, heed**
❷ *The soldiers **obeyed** without question.*
• **do what you are told, take orders, be obedient, conform**
OPPOSITE **disobey**

object *NOUN*
❶ *We saw some strange **objects** in the museum.*
• **article, item, thing**
❷ *What is the **object** of this exercise?*
• **point, purpose, aim, goal, intention, objective**

object *VERB*
➤ **to object to something**
*Several residents have **objected to** the plan.*
• **complain about, be opposed to, disapprove of, take exception to, protest against**
OPPOSITES **accept, agree to**

objection *NOUN*
*Do you have any **objection** to my sitting here?*
• **protest, complaint, disapproval, opposition**

objectionable *ADJECTIVE*
*The drains were giving off an **objectionable** smell.*
• **unpleasant, disagreeable, disgusting, foul, offensive, repellent, revolting, obnoxious, nasty**
OPPOSITE **acceptable**

objective ADJECTIVE
*He gave an **objective** account of what happened.*
• disinterested, factual, impartial, rational, unbiased, unemotional, unprejudiced
OPPOSITE subjective

objective NOUN
*Their **objective** was to reach the top of the hill.*
• aim, goal, intention, target, ambition, object, purpose

obligatory ADJECTIVE
*The wearing of seat belts is **obligatory**.*
• compulsory, necessary, required
OPPOSITE optional

oblige VERB
*Would you **oblige** me by watering the plants?*
• help, assist, do you a favour

obliged ADJECTIVE
❶ *He felt **obliged** to help them.*
• bound, compelled, expected, required
❷ *I'm much **obliged** to you for your kindness.*
• thankful, grateful, indebted

oblong NOUN
• rectangle
for other shapes see **shape**

obscure ADJECTIVE
❶ *An **obscure** figure emerged from the mist.*
• dim, murky, shadowy, misty, blurred, unclear, vague, indistinct
OPPOSITE clear
❷ *His joke seemed rather **obscure**.*
• confusing, puzzling, incomprehensible
OPPOSITE obvious
❸ *Henry Kirke White is an **obscure** poet.*
• unknown, unheard of, unimportant, forgotten, minor
OPPOSITE famous

obscure VERB
*A tall hedge **obscured** the view.*
• block out, cover, hide, mask, screen, shroud
OPPOSITE reveal

observant ADJECTIVE
*If you're **observant**, you might see a badger tonight.*
• alert, attentive, sharp-eyed, vigilant, watchful
OPPOSITE inattentive

observation NOUN
❶ *They took him to hospital for **observation**.*
• study, watching, scrutiny
❷ *The detective made an interesting **observation**.*
• comment, remark, statement

observe VERB
❶ *Astronomers **observed** the eclipse last night.*
• watch, look at, view, study
❷ *I have **observed** a change in his behaviour.*
• notice, note, see, detect, spot, discern, perceive, witness
❸ *It's important to **observe** the rules.*
• follow, abide by, adhere to, heed, keep to, obey
❹ *My friend **observed** that I had grown taller.*
• mention, say, comment, remark, declare

obsession NOUN
*Football is Frank's **obsession**.*
• passion, fixation, addiction, mania

obsolete ADJECTIVE
*That computer software is now **obsolete**.*
• out of date, outdated, outmoded, antiquated, dated
OPPOSITE current

obstacle NOUN
❶ *They drove around the **obstacles** in the road.*
• obstruction, barrier, barricade
❷ *His age proved to be an **obstacle**.*
• problem, difficulty, hindrance, hurdle, snag, catch

obstinate ADJECTIVE
*The **obstinate** camel refused to budge.*
• stubborn, uncooperative, wilful, headstrong, pig-headed
OPPOSITE cooperative

obstruct *VERB*
*The path was **obstructed** by a fallen tree.*
• block, jam, make impassable

obstruction *NOUN*
*The fallen tree was causing an **obstruction**.*
• blockage, barrier, barricade

obtain *VERB*
*You must **obtain** a permit before you can park here.*
• get, get hold of, acquire
(informal) pick up

obvious *ADJECTIVE*
❶ *It was silly to make so many **obvious** mistakes.*
• glaring, noticeable, pronounced
❷ *The castle is an **obvious** landmark.*
• conspicuous, notable, prominent, visible
OPPOSITE inconspicuous
❸ *It was **obvious** that the woman was a spy.*
• clear, evident, apparent, plain, undeniable, unmistakable
OPPOSITE hidden

occasion *NOUN*
❶ *I've been to Italy on several **occasions**.*
• time, moment, instance, opportunity, chance
❷ *The wedding was a happy **occasion**.*
• affair, event, happening, incident, occurrence

occasional *ADJECTIVE*
*The weather forecast said there would be **occasional** showers.*
• intermittent, odd, scattered, irregular, infrequent
OPPOSITES frequent, regular

occasionally *ADVERB*
*The dragon **occasionally** lifted its head and roared.*
• sometimes, now and again, once in a while, every so often
OPPOSITES frequently, often

occupant *NOUN*
*The only **occupants** of the castle were a family of bats.*
• inhabitant, occupier, resident, tenant

occupation *NOUN*
❶ *He's not happy with his present **occupation**.*
• job, post, employment, profession, trade, work
for various occupations see **job**
❷ *Vita's favourite **occupation** is reading.*
• activity, hobby, pastime, pursuit

occupied *ADJECTIVE*
*She's very **occupied** in her work just now.*
• absorbed, involved, engrossed, busy, engaged
OPPOSITE idle

occupy *VERB*
❶ *They **occupy** the house next door.*
• live in, reside in, dwell in, inhabit
❷ *We sold the piano because it **occupied** too much space.*
• fill, take up, use up
❸ *The rebel army **occupied** the town.*
• capture, seize, take over, conquer, invade

occur *VERB*
❶ *She told us what had **occurred**.*
• happen, take place, come about, arise
❷ *The disease only **occurs** in certain plants.*
• develop, crop up, turn up

occurrence *NOUN*
*An eclipse of the sun is an unusual **occurrence**.*
• event, happening, incident, phenomenon

ocean *NOUN*

WORD WEB

THE OCEANS OF THE WORLD ARE:
• Antarctic, Arctic, Atlantic, Indian, Pacific
for creatures that live in the ocean see **sea**

odd *ADJECTIVE*
❶ *Her behaviour seemed very **odd**.*
• strange, unusual, abnormal, peculiar, curious, puzzling, queer, unconventional, eccentric, funny, weird
OPPOSITE normal
❷ *He could only find a couple of **odd** socks.*
• left over, single, spare
❸ *He does **odd** jobs to earn money.*
• occasional, casual, irregular, various

odour *NOUN*
*There's a nasty **odour** coming from the fridge.*
• smell, scent
A pleasant odour is a **fragrance** or **perfume**.
An unpleasant odour is a **reek, stench** or **stink**.
see also **smell**

offence *NOUN*
❶ *The thief was punished for his **offence**.*
• crime, wrongdoing, misdeed, fault, sin
In games, an offence is a **foul** or an **infringement**.
❷ *I didn't mean to cause any **offence**.*
• hurt, anger, annoyance, displeasure, hard feelings, disgust

offend *VERB*
❶ *I hope my letter didn't **offend** you.*
• give or cause offence to, insult, upset, hurt your feelings, anger, displease, annoy, affront, disgust, vex
❷ *You'll be punished if you **offend** again.*
• break the law, do wrong

offensive *ADJECTIVE*
❶ *The gas produces an **offensive** smell.*
• unpleasant, repellent, disgusting, revolting, nasty
OPPOSITE pleasant
❷ *He apologised for his **offensive** remarks.*
• insulting, impolite, rude, abusive

offer *VERB*
❶ *A reward was **offered** for the capture of the outlaws.*
• propose, put forward, suggest, make available
❷ *He **offered** to help with the washing-up.*
• volunteer

offer *NOUN*
*Their **offer** of help was gratefully received.*
• proposal, suggestion

office *NOUN*
❶ *The boss won't be in the **office** today.*
• workplace, bureau, department
❷ *Penny will take up the **office** of treasurer.*
• post, position, appointment, role, function

officer *NOUN*
for officers in the police force see **police officer**

official *ADJECTIVE*
*The **official** opening of the museum is next month.*
• formal, authentic, authorised, legitimate, proper, genuine, approved
OPPOSITE unofficial

official *NOUN*
*We spoke to an **official** of the organisation.*
• officer, office-holder, representative, executive

often *ADVERB*
*It **often** rains in April.*
• frequently, regularly, repeatedly, time after time, many times, again and again, constantly

oil *VERB*
*He **oiled** the hinge to stop it squeaking.*
• grease, lubricate

oily *ADJECTIVE*
*Fried food is too **oily** for me.*
• fatty, greasy

ointment *NOUN*
*The chemist gave her some **ointment** for the rash.*
• cream, lotion

old ADJECTIVE

OVERUSED WORD

Try to vary the words you use for **old**. Here are some other words you could use.

FOR AN OLD PERSON:

• **elderly, aged, senior**
Bus tickets are free for ***elderly*** *people.*
OPPOSITE **young**

FOR AN OLD BUILDING OR OLD DOCUMENT:

• **ancient, early, historical, original**
The ***ancient*** *Norman church is to be restored.*
Something that you respect because it is old is **venerable**.
OPPOSITE **new**

FOR AN OLD STYLE OR OLD TECHNOLOGY:

• **old-fashioned, out of date, antiquated, obsolete**
His clothes were curiously old-fashioned, mostly brown and black, the sort of thing people wore two or three hundred years ago.
—BILLY AND THE MINPINS, Roald Dahl
Things which are valuable because they are old are **antique** or **vintage**.
OPPOSITES **up to date, current**

FOR SOMETHING OLD AND WORN-OUT:

• **worn, scruffy, shabby, threadbare**
I put on ***scruffy*** *jeans to do some gardening.*

FOR THE OLD DAYS OR OLD TIMES:

• **past, former, earlier, previous, bygone, olden**
We did a project on how children lived in ***former*** *times.*
Times before written records were kept were **prehistoric** times.
OPPOSITE **modern**

old-fashioned ADJECTIVE

That hairstyle is quite ***old-fashioned*** *now.*
• **out of date, outdated, outmoded, antiquated**
OPPOSITES **modern, up to date**

omit VERB

❶ *His article was* ***omitted*** *from the magazine.*
• **exclude, leave out, miss out, cut, eliminate, overlook, skip**
❷ *Don't* ***omit*** *to turn off the lights.*
• **forget, fail, neglect**

one-sided ADJECTIVE

The driver gave a ***one-sided*** *account of the accident.*
• **biased, prejudiced, unbalanced, unfair**

ooze VERB

The filling started to ***ooze*** *from my sandwich.*
• **leak, seep, escape, dribble, drip**

opaque ADJECTIVE

The dirt had turned the window ***opaque****.*
• **cloudy, obscure, unclear, dull, hazy, muddy, murky**
OPPOSITE **transparent**

open ADJECTIVE

❶ *The puppy escaped through the* ***open*** *door.*
• **unlocked, unfastened, ajar, gaping**
OPPOSITE **closed**
❷ *The jam jar had been left* ***open****.*
• **uncovered, unsealed**
❸ *There is a view of* ***open*** *country from the back window.*
• **clear, unrestricted, unenclosed, extensive**
OPPOSITE **enclosed**
❹ *He was* ***open*** *about what he had done wrong.*
• **frank, honest, sincere, straightforward, candid**
OPPOSITE **deceitful**
❺ *The captain faced* ***open*** *rebellion from the crew.*
• **unconcealed, undisguised, obvious, plain**
OPPOSITE **concealed**

open VERB

❶ *Please* ***open*** *the door.*
• **unfasten, unlock, unbolt**
❷ *I can't wait to* ***open*** *my birthday presents!*
• **undo, unwrap, untie, unseal**
To open an umbrella is to **unfurl** it.
To open a wine bottle is to **uncork** it.
To open a map is to **unfold** or **unroll** it.

A B C D E F G H I J K L M N O P Q R S T U V W X Y Z

❸ *The jumble sale **opens** at 10 a.m.*
• begin, start, commence
(informal) get going
OPPOSITE close

opening *NOUN*
❶ *The sheep got out through an **opening** in the fence.*
• gap, hole, breach, break, split
❷ *The film has a very dramatic **opening**.*
• beginning, start, commencement
❸ *We are invited to the **opening** of the new sports centre.*
• launch, initiation
❹ *The job offers a good **opening** for a keen young person.*
• chance, opportunity

operate *VERB*
❶ *This watch **operates** even under water.*
• work, function, go, perform
❷ *Do you know how to **operate** this machine?*
• use, work, drive, handle, manage, deal with
❸ *The surgeon **operated** to remove her appendix.*
• carry out an operation, perform surgery

operation *NOUN*
❶ *Astronauts control the **operation** of the spacecraft.*
• performance, working, functioning
❷ *He had an **operation** to remove his appendix.*
• surgery
❸ *Trying to defuse a bomb is a dangerous **operation**.*
• task, activity, action, exercise, manoeuvre, process, procedure

opinion *NOUN*
*What was your honest **opinion** of the film?*
• view, judgement, impression, belief, attitude, point of view, thought, conclusion, assessment, notion, feeling, idea

opponent *NOUN*
*The knight fought bravely against his **opponent**.*
• enemy, foe, rival, adversary, challenger
Your opponents in a game are the **opposition**.
OPPOSITE ally

opportunity *NOUN*
❶ *There were few **opportunities** to relax.*
• chance, occasion, moment, time
❷ *The job offers a good **opportunity** for a keen young person.*
• opening
(informal) break

oppose *VERB*
*Many people **opposed** the building of the new road.*
• object to, disapprove of, be against, be hostile towards, argue against, fight against, attack, resist
OPPOSITES support, defend

opposite *ADJECTIVE*
❶ *They have **opposite** views about politics.*
• contrasting, conflicting, contradictory, opposed, opposing, different, contrary
OPPOSITE similar
❷ *My friend lives on the **opposite** side of the road.*
• facing

opposite *NOUN*
*She says one thing and does the **opposite**.*
• contrary, reverse, converse

opposition *NOUN*
❶ *There was fierce **opposition** to the new road.*
• hostility, resistance, disapproval, unfriendliness, scepticism
OPPOSITE support
❷ *The **opposition** were stronger than our team expected.*
• opponents, rivals

optical *ADJECTIVE*
for optical instruments see **glasses**

optimistic *ADJECTIVE*
*She's **optimistic** about her chances of success.*
• hopeful, positive, confident, expectant, cheerful, buoyant
OPPOSITE pessimistic

option *NOUN*
*He had the **option** of staying or leaving.*
• choice, alternative, possibility

optional *ADJECTIVE*
*The holiday includes an **optional** tour of the city.*
• voluntary, possible
OPPOSITE compulsory

oral *ADJECTIVE*
*She had to take an **oral** exam in French.*
• spoken, verbal
OPPOSITE written

orbit *VERB*
*The earth **orbits** the sun in about 365 days.*
• circle, travel round

ordeal *NOUN*
*The shipwrecked sailor told us about his **ordeal**.*
• suffering, troubles, trial, anguish, torture, nightmare

order *NOUN*
❶ *The captain gave the **order** to abandon ship.*
• command, instruction, direction
❷ *I've put in an **order** for the new book.*
• request, demand, reservation, booking
❸ *The police restored **order** after the riot.*
• peace, calm, control, quiet, harmony, law and order
❹ *The CDs are arranged in alphabetical **order**.*
• arrangement, sequence, series, succession
❺ *She keeps her bike in good **order**.*
• condition, state

order *VERB*
❶ *She **ordered** them to be quiet.*
• command, instruct, require, tell
❷ *He **ordered** the new magazine.*
• request, reserve, apply for, book

orderly *ADJECTIVE*
❶ *The library has an **orderly** system for sorting books.*
• organised, ordered, tidy, neat, systematic, methodical
OPPOSITE untidy
❷ *Please form an **orderly** queue.*
• well-behaved, controlled, disciplined
OPPOSITE disorderly

ordinary *ADJECTIVE*
❶ *It was just an **ordinary** sort of day.*
• normal, typical, usual, customary, habitual, everyday
❷ *This is more than just an **ordinary** robot.*
• standard, average, common, conventional, regular
❸ *It was a very **ordinary** game.*
• mediocre, unexceptional, run-of-the-mill, routine
OPPOSITES special, unusual

organisation *NOUN*
❶ *She works for a charitable **organisation**.*
• institution, operation, enterprise, company
(informal) outfit, set-up
❷ *Who was responsible for the **organisation** of the conference?*
• coordination, planning, arrangement, running

organise *VERB*
❶ *It took her ages to **organise** the party.*
• coordinate, plan, make arrangements for, see to, set up, run
❷ *The librarian has to **organise** the books in the library.*
• arrange, put in order, classify, sort out, tidy up

origin *NOUN*
❶ *We know very little about the **origin** of life on earth.*
• beginning, creation, start, birth, source, cause
OPPOSITE end
❷ *He became very rich, despite his humble **origins**.*
• background, ancestry, descent, family, parentage, pedigree, stock

original *ADJECTIVE*
❶ *The settlers drove out the* ***original*** *inhabitants.*
• **earliest, first, initial, native, aboriginal**
❷ *The story was very* ***original.***
• **inventive, new, novel, creative, fresh, imaginative, unusual, unconventional**
❸ *Is that an* ***original*** *work of art or a copy?*
• **genuine, real, authentic, unique**

originate *VERB*
❶ *Where did the idea* ***originate?***
• **begin, start, commence, emerge, crop up**
❷ *They* ***originated*** *a new style of dancing.*
• **invent, create, design, conceive, introduce, launch**

ornament *NOUN*
A few ***ornaments*** *will make the room more attractive.*
• **decoration, adornment, trinket, bauble**

ornamental *ADJECTIVE*
There were a few ***ornamental*** *statues in the garden.*
• **decorative, fancy, pretty, ornate**

ornate *ADJECTIVE*
The furniture in the palace was very ***ornate.***
• **elaborate, fancy, showy, ornamental, decorative**

orthodox *ADJECTIVE*
She wasn't taught to play the piano in the ***orthodox*** *way.*
• **conventional, accepted, customary, usual, standard, traditional, regular, established, approved, recognised, official**
OPPOSITE **unorthodox, unconventional**

outbreak *NOUN*
❶ *The townspeople feared an* ***outbreak*** *of violence.*
• **outburst, upsurge (in), flare-up, spate**
An outbreak of disease that spreads quickly is an **epidemic.**
❷ *The armies prepared for the* ***outbreak*** *of war.*
• **beginning, start, onset**

outburst *NOUN*
There was an ***outburst*** *of laughter from the next room.*
• **explosion, eruption, outbreak, storm**

outcome *NOUN*
What was the ***outcome*** *of the meeting?*
• **result, consequence, effect, upshot**

outcry *NOUN*
There was an ***outcry*** *over the closure of the hospital.*
• **protest, complaint, uproar, fuss, furore**

outdoor *ADJECTIVE*
The hotel had an ***outdoor*** *swimming pool.*
• **open-air, out of doors, outside**

outer *ADJECTIVE*
The fishermen wore waterproof ***outer*** *garments.*
• **external, exterior, outside**
OPPOSITE **inner**

outfit *NOUN*
❶ *Katie bought a new* ***outfit*** *for the wedding.*
• **clothes, costume, suit, ensemble**
(informal) **get-up**
❷ *The puncture repair* ***outfit*** *is in the boot.*
• **equipment, kit, gear**

outing *NOUN*
They've gone on their annual ***outing*** *to London.*
• **trip, excursion, expedition, jaunt**

outlaw *NOUN*
A band of ***outlaws*** *held up the train.*
• **bandit, brigand, robber, highwayman, criminal, fugitive**

outlet *NOUN*
❶ *The basin has an* ***outlet*** *for excess water.*
• **opening, vent, channel, way out, exit, mouth**
OPPOSITE **inlet**
❷ *The company has* ***outlets*** *throughout the UK.*
• **shop, store, market**

outline *NOUN*
❶ *We could see the **outline** of some trees in the distance.*
• profile, shape, silhouette, form, shadow
❷ *He gave us a brief **outline** of his plan.*
• summary, sketch, framework, precis, rough idea

outline *VERB*
*The detective **outlined** his plan.*
• summarise, sketch out

outlook *NOUN*
❶ *The cottage has a beautiful **outlook** over the loch.*
• view, prospect, sight, vista
❷ *He has a rather gloomy **outlook** on life.*
• point of view, view, attitude, frame of mind
❸ *The **outlook** for the weekend is bright and sunny.*
• forecast, prediction, prospect

outrage *NOUN*
❶ *There was public **outrage** at the government's decision.*
• anger, fury, disgust, indignation, horror
❷ *He said it was an **outrage** that so much money has been wasted.*
• disgrace, scandal, crime, atrocity

outrageous *ADJECTIVE*
❶ *The behaviour of the trolls was**outrageous**.*
• disgraceful, scandalous, shocking, atrocious, appalling, monstrous, shameful
❷ *They charge **outrageous** prices at that shop.*
• excessive, unreasonable
OPPOSITE acceptable, reasonable

outside *ADJECTIVE*
*Lookouts were stationed on the **outside** wall of the castle.*
• exterior, external, outer

outside *NOUN*
*Insects have their skeletons on the **outside** of their bodies.*
• exterior, shell, surface
OPPOSITE inside

outsider *NOUN*
*She's lived in the village for years, but still feels like an **outsider**.*
• newcomer, stranger, alien, foreigner, immigrant, incomer

outskirts *PLURAL NOUN*
*We live on the **outskirts** of town.*
• edge, fringe, outer areas
The outskirts of a big town are the **suburbs**.
OPPOSITE centre

outspoken *ADJECTIVE*
*She's always been **outspoken** in her views.*
• frank, honest, plain, blunt, straightforward

outstanding *ADJECTIVE*
❶ *She will be an **outstanding** tennis player in a few years.*
• excellent, exceptional, superb, extraordinary, superlative, brilliant, great, fine, distinguished, celebrated, remarkable, superior, striking, notable
OPPOSITE ordinary
❷ *There are still some **outstanding** bills to pay.*
• overdue, unpaid, owing

outward *ADJECTIVE*
*In **outward** appearance, the castle was dark and dingy.*
• outer, outside, external, exterior, visible

outwit *VERB*
*Ewan managed to **outwit** his dad at chess.*
• outsmart, get the better of, beat, defeat

oval *ADJECTIVE*
*The sandwiches were arranged on an **oval** platter.*
• egg-shaped, elliptical

oven *NOUN*
*The meat was roasting in the **oven**.*
• cooker, stove
A special oven for firing pottery is a **kiln**.

overcast *ADJECTIVE*
*The sky has been **overcast** all day.*
• cloudy, dull, grey, sunless, dark, leaden
see also **weather**

overcome *VERB* **overcomes, overcoming, overcame, overcome**
❶ *He managed to* ***overcome*** *his fear of flying.*
• conquer, defeat, master, get the better of
❷ *Some people in the building were* ***overcome*** *by fumes.*
• overpower, overwhelm

overflow *VERB*
Someone left the tap on and the bath ***overflowed.***
• spill over, run over, pour over, flood

overgrown *ADJECTIVE*
The back garden was completely ***overgrown.***
• unkempt, untidy, tangled, weedy, wild

overhaul *VERB*
The boiler was recently ***overhauled.***
• service, check over, inspect, repair, restore, refurbish

overhead *ADVERB*
A flock of geese flew ***overhead.***
• above, high up, in the sky

overlook *VERB*
❶ *He seems to have* ***overlooked*** *one important fact.*
• miss, fail to see
❷ *She's always willing to* ***overlook*** *his faults.*
• excuse, forget about, ignore, disregard, pardon, pay no attention to
(informal) turn a blind eye to
❸ *The front room of the house* ***overlooks*** *the garden.*
• have a view of, look on to, face

overpowering *ADJECTIVE*
I felt an ***overpowering*** *urge to giggle.*
• overwhelming, powerful, strong, compelling, irresistible, uncontrollable

overrun *VERB* **overruns, overrunning, overran, overrun**
The barn was ***overrun*** *with rats and mice.*
• invade, take over, spread over, swarm over

overtake *VERB* **overtakes, overtaking, overtook, overtaken**
We ***overtook*** *the car in front.*
• pass, leave behind, pull ahead of, outstrip

overthrow *VERB* **overthrows, overthrowing, overthrew, overthrown**
The rebels ***overthrew*** *the President.*
• bring down, topple, oust, defeat, drive out, depose

overturn *VERB*
❶ *The boat* ***overturned.***
• capsize, tip over, turn over, turn turtle
❷ *She leapt to her feet,* ***overturning*** *her chair.*
• knock over, tip over, topple, upset, spill

overwhelm *VERB*
❶ *The troops were* ***overwhelmed*** *by the enemy forces.*
• defeat, overcome, overpower, crush
❷ *A tidal wave* ***overwhelmed*** *the village.*
• engulf, flood, inundate, submerge, swallow up, bury

overwhelming *ADJECTIVE*
He was elected by an ***overwhelming*** *majority.*
• decisive, devastating, crushing, huge, massive, great
An overwhelming victory at an election is a **landslide.**

owe *VERB*
If you owe money to someone, you are in debt.

owing *ADJECTIVE*
➤ **owing to**
Owing to the rain, the match is cancelled.
• because of, on account of, as a result of, thanks to

own *VERB*
It was the first bike she had ***owned.***
• be the owner of, have, possess
➤ **to own up to**
No one ***owned up to*** *breaking the window.*
• confess to, admit to, tell the truth about
(informal) come clean about

Pp

pace *NOUN*
❶ *Move forward two **paces**.*
• step, stride
❷ *The front runner set a fast **pace**.*
• rate, speed
A formal word is **velocity**.

pacify *VERB*
*The zookeeper managed to **pacify** the polar bear.*
• calm, quieten, soothe, humour, appease
OPPOSITE anger, annoy

pack *NOUN*
❶ *There were four candles in each **pack**.*
• package, packet, bundle, bale
❷ *The hikers picked up their **packs** and trudged off.*
• rucksack, backpack, knapsack

pack *VERB*
❶ *She **packed** her suitcase and called a taxi.*
• fill, load up
❷ *I forgot to **pack** my hairdryer.*
• stow away, wrap up
❸ *They tried to **pack** too many passengers on to the train.*
• cram, crowd, squeeze, stuff, jam, wedge

package *NOUN*
*The postman delivered a big **package**.*
• parcel, packet, bundle

pad *NOUN*
❶ *She put a **pad** of cotton wool over the wound.*
• wad
A pad to make a chair or bed comfortable is a **cushion** or **pillow**.
❷ *There's a **pad** for messages next to the phone.*
• jotter, notebook, writing pad

pad *VERB*
*The seats are **padded** with foam rubber.*
• stuff, fill, pack
To put covers and padding on furniture is to **upholster** it.

padding *NOUN*
*The **padding** is coming out of this cushion.*
• stuffing, filling
The covers and padding on furniture are **upholstery**.

paddle *VERB*
❶ *The children **paddled** at the water's edge.*
• dabble, splash about
To walk through deep water is to **wade**.
❷ *He **paddled** his canoe along the canal.*
To move a boat along with two oars is to **row** it.

page *NOUN*
❶ *Several **pages** have been torn out of this book.*
• sheet, leaf
❷ *He wrote two **pages** of notes.*
• side

paid *past tense see* **pay**

pain *NOUN*
*Dirk felt a sudden jabbing **pain** in his foot.*
• anguish, suffering
A dull pain is an **ache** or **soreness**.
Severe pain is **agony, torment** or **torture**.
A slight pain is **discomfort**.
A slight pain which doesn't last long is a **twinge**.
A sudden pain is a **pang** or **stab**.
Pain in your head is a **headache**.
Pain in your teeth is **toothache**.

painful *ADJECTIVE*
❶ *My shoulder is still really **painful**.*
• sore, aching, tender, hurting, smarting, stinging, throbbing
OPPOSITE painless
❷ *The conversation brought back many **painful** memories.*
• unpleasant, upsetting, distressing, disagreeable, traumatic

a b c d e f g h i j k l m n o p q r s t u v w x y z

A B C D E F G H I J K L M N O P Q R S T U V W X Y Z

painless *ADJECTIVE*
❶ *The treatment is quite **painless**.*
• **comfortable, pain-free**
OPPOSITE **painful**
❷ *This is a quick and **painless** way to make a cake.*
• **easy, simple, effortless, undemanding**

paint *NOUN*

WORD WEB

KINDS OF PAINT FOR DECORATING:

• **emulsion, undercoat, whitewash**
A layer of paint is a **coat** of paint.
Paint which stays shiny when it dries is **gloss** paint.
Paint which goes dull when it dries is **matt** paint.

KINDS OF PAINT FOR ARTWORK:

• **acrylic, finger paint, oil paint, poster paint, watercolour**

paint *VERB*
❶ *The bedroom walls were **painted** green.*
• **colour, decorate**
❷ *Samantha **painted** the flowers in bright colours.*
• **depict, portray, represent**

painter *NOUN*
A person who paints houses is a **decorator**.
A person who paints pictures is an **artist**.

painting *NOUN*
A picture painted on a wall is a **fresco** or a **mural**.
A picture painted by a famous artist of the past is an **old master**.
see also **picture**

pair *NOUN*
A pair of people who go out together are a **couple**.
Two people who sing or play music together are a **duet** or a **duo**.
Two people who work together are **partners** or a **partnership**.
Two babies born together are **twins**.

palace *NOUN*
for types of building see **building**

pale *ADJECTIVE*
❶ *Are you all right? You're looking a little **pale**.*
• **white, pallid, pasty, wan, ashen, sallow, anaemic**
OPPOSITE **ruddy, flushed**
To go pale with fear is to **blanch**.
❷ *That shade of pink is too **pale**.*
• **light, pastel, faded, faint, dim, bleached, colourless**
OPPOSITE **bright**

pamper *VERB*
*The twins' grandparents liked to **pamper** them.*
• **spoil, indulge, cosset, mollycoddle, humour**

pamphlet *NOUN*
*We were given a **pamphlet** about road safety.*
• **leaflet, booklet, brochure**

pan *NOUN*
for things used for cooking see **cook**

panel *NOUN*
*A **panel** of experts judged the contest.*
• **group, team, board, committee**

panic *NOUN*
*People fled the streets in **panic**.*
• **alarm, fright, terror, frenzy, hysteria**

panic *VERB*
*If a fire starts, don't **panic**!*
• **be alarmed, take fright, become hysterical**
(informal) **lose your head, get in a flap**
To panic is also to be **panic-stricken**.

pant *VERB*
*Some of the runners were **panting** by the last lap.*
• **breathe quickly, gasp, wheeze, puff**

pants *PLURAL NOUN*
for underwear see **clothes**

paper *NOUN*
❶ *She started her diary on a fresh sheet of* ***paper****.*
A piece of paper is a **leaf** or a **sheet**.
❷ *The doctor had some important* ***papers*** *to sign.*
• **document, deed, certificate**
❸ *The story made the front page of the local* ***paper****.*
• **newspaper, journal**
(informal) **rag**

paper *NOUN*

WORD WEB

MATERIALS FOR WRITING OR DRAWING ON:

• **card, cardboard, cartridge paper, notepaper, postcard, stationery, tracing paper, writing paper**

EARLY MATERIALS FOR WRITING ON:

• **papyrus, parchment, vellum**

OTHER KINDS OF PAPER:

• **greaseproof paper, tissue paper, toilet paper, wallpaper, wrapping paper**

parade *NOUN*
A circus ***parade*** *passed along the street.*
• **procession, march, spectacle, show, display**
A parade of vehicles or of people on horseback is a **cavalcade**.
A parade of people in costume is a **pageant**.

parade *VERB*
The brass band ***paraded*** *through the town.*
• **march, troop, file past**

paralyse *VERB*
His right arm was ***paralysed*** *in the accident.*
• **disable, immobilise, cripple, deaden, numb**

parcel *NOUN*
The postman delivered a bulky ***parcel****.*
• **package, packet**

parched *ADJECTIVE*
❶ *Nothing was growing in the* ***parched*** *earth.*
• **dry, arid, baked, scorched, barren, sterile, waterless**
❷ *I need a drink of water—I'm* ***parched****!*
• **thirsty**

pardon *VERB*
The king decided to ***pardon*** *the prisoners.*
• **release, free, set free, let off, spare, excuse, forgive**
To pardon someone who is condemned to death is to **reprieve** them.

parent *NOUN*
for family relationships see **family**

park *NOUN*
At lunchtime, we went for a walk in the ***park****.*
• **public gardens, recreation ground**
A park with fields and trees around a big house is an **estate** or **parkland**.

WORD WEB

SOME KINDS OF PARK:

• **adventure park, amusement park, botanical gardens, nature reserve, play park** or **playground, safari park, skate park, theme park**

EQUIPMENT YOU MIGHT FIND IN A PLAY PARK:

• **chute** or **slide, climbing frame, flying fox, monkey bars, rope ladder, roundabout, sandpit, see-saw, swings, trampoline**

park *VERB*
The postman ***parked*** *his van around the corner.*
• **leave, position, station**

A B C D E F G H I J K L M N O P Q R S T U V W X Y Z

part *NOUN*
❶ *All the* ***parts*** *of the engine are now working properly.*
• bit, component, constituent
❷ *I only saw the first* ***part*** *of the programme.*
• section, piece, portion, element
❸ *Which* ***part*** *of the business do they own?*
• branch, department, division
❹ *Granny lives in another* ***part*** *of the town.*
• area, district, region, neighbourhood, sector
❺ *He's just right to act the* ***part*** *of Peter Pan.*
• character, role

part *VERB*
❶ *It was the first time she'd been* ***parted*** *from her parents.*
• separate, divide, remove
OPPOSITE join
❷ *They exchanged a final kiss before* ***parting****.*
• go away, leave, depart, say goodbye
OPPOSITE meet

partial *ADJECTIVE*
The play was only a ***partial*** *success.*
• limited, imperfect, incomplete
OPPOSITE complete
➤ **to be partial to**
Becky is very ***partial to*** *chocolate cake.*
• be fond of, be keen on, enjoy, like

participate *VERB*
Our school is ***participating*** *in the mini-marathon.*
• take part, join in, be involved, cooperate, help, share

particle *NOUN*
The camera lens was covered with ***particles*** *of dust.*
• speck, grain, fragment, bit, piece, scrap, shred, sliver
see also **bit**

particular *ADJECTIVE*
❶ *The tickets must be used on a* ***particular*** *day.*
• specific, certain, distinct, definite, exact
❷ *She took* ***particular*** *care not to damage the parcel.*
• special, exceptional, unusual, extreme, marked, notable
❸ *The cat's very* ***particular*** *about his food.*
• fussy, finicky, hard to please
(informal) choosy, picky

particulars *PLURAL NOUN*
The police officer took down all the ***particulars****.*
• details, facts, information, circumstances

partition *NOUN*
A ***partition*** *separates the two classrooms.*
• room divider, screen

partly *ADVERB*
It was ***partly*** *my fault that we were late.*
• in part, to some extent, up to a point
OPPOSITE entirely

partner *NOUN*
The two women have been business ***partners*** *for years.*
• colleague, associate, ally
In marriage, your partner is your **spouse**, or your **husband** or **wife**.
An animal's partner is its **mate**.

party *NOUN*
❶ *We had a class* ***party*** *at the end of term.*
• celebration, festivity, function, gathering, reception
(informal) get-together, do
❷ *A* ***party*** *of tourists was going round the museum.*
• group, band, crowd, gang
❸ *They have formed a new political* ***party****.*
• alliance, association, faction, league

party *NOUN*

WORD WEB

SOME KINDS OF PARTY:

• ball, banquet, barbecue, birthday party, ceilidh, Christmas party, cocktail party, dance, dinner party, disco, fancy dress party, garden party, Halloween party, house-warming, picnic, pot luck, reunion, sleepover, tea party, wedding

THINGS YOU MIGHT SEE AT A PARTY:

• balloons, birthday cake, birthday candles, bunting, party bags, poppers, sparklers, streamers
for party games see **game**

pass *VERB*
❶ *We watched the parade as it* ***passed****.*
• go by, move past
❷ *She tried to* ***pass*** *the car in front.*
• overtake, go ahead of
❸ *We* ***passed*** *over the bridge.*
• go, advance, proceed, progress
❹ *Could you* ***pass*** *me the sugar, please?*
• hand, give, deliver, offer, present
❺ *Do you think you will* ***pass*** *your music exam?*
• be successful in, get through, succeed in
❻ *How did you* ***pass*** *the time on holiday?*
• spend, use, occupy, fill, while away
❼ *Three years* ***passed*** *before we met again.*
• go by, elapse
❽ *The pain will soon* ***pass****.*
• go away, come to an end, disappear, fade
➤ **to pass out**
One of the runners ***passed out*** *in the heat.*
• faint, lose consciousness, black out

pass *NOUN*
❶ *We had a* ***pass*** *to get into the concert for free.*
• permit, licence, ticket
❷ *The horses filed through a* ***pass*** *between the hills.*
• gap, gorge, ravine, canyon, valley

passage *NOUN*
❶ *A secret* ***passage*** *led from the chamber to the outside.*
• passageway, corridor, tunnel
❷ *The guards forced a* ***passage*** *through the crowd.*
• path, route, way
❸ *A sea* ***passage*** *takes longer than going by air.*
• journey, voyage, crossing
❹ *Our homework is to choose a favourite* ***passage*** *from a book.*
• episode, excerpt, extract, piece, quotation, section
❺ *He hadn't changed, despite the* ***passage*** *of time.*
• passing, progress, advance

passenger *NOUN*
The bus has seats for 55 ***passengers****.*
• traveller
Passengers who travel regularly to work are **commuters**.

passion *NOUN*
❶ *'Romeo and Juliet' is a story of youthful* ***passion****.*
• love, emotion
❷ *She has a* ***passion*** *for sports.*
• enthusiasm, eagerness, appetite, desire, craving, urge, zest, thirst, mania

passionate *ADJECTIVE*
❶ *The captain gave a* ***passionate*** *speech before the battle.*
• emotional, intense, moving, heartfelt
OPPOSITE unemotional
❷ *She is a* ***passionate*** *follower of football.*
• eager, keen, avid, enthusiastic, fanatical, fervent
OPPOSITE apathetic

passive *ADJECTIVE*
Owls are normally ***passive*** *during the daytime.*
• inactive, docile
OPPOSITE active

past *NOUN*
In the ***past****, things were different.*
• past times, old days, olden days, days gone by
The study of what happened in the past is **history**.
The things and ideas that have come down to us from the past are our **heritage** or **traditions**.
OPPOSITE future

past *ADJECTIVE*
Things were very different in ***past*** *centuries.*
• earlier, former, previous, old
OPPOSITE future

pasta *NOUN*

WORD WEB

SOME TYPES OF PASTA:

• **cannelloni, lasagne, linguine, macaroni, noodles, penne, ravioli, spaghetti, tagliatelle, tortellini**

for other kinds of food see **food**

paste *NOUN*

*I used some **paste** to stick things into my scrapbook.*

• **glue, gum, adhesive**

pastime *NOUN*

*Shona's favourite **pastime** is swimming.*

• **activity, hobby, recreation, amusement, diversion, entertainment, relaxation, game, sport**

see also **game, sport**

pasture *NOUN*

*Cattle were grazing on the **pasture**.*

• **field, meadow, grassland**

pat *VERB*

*Andy **patted** the Shetland pony on the head.*

• **tap, touch, stroke, pet**

To touch something quickly and lightly is to **dab** it.

To stroke someone with an open hand is to **caress** them.

patch *VERB*

*I need some material to **patch** my jeans.*

• **mend, repair**

Another way to mend holes in clothes is to **darn** them or **stitch** them up.

patchy *ADJECTIVE*

*There will be **patchy** outbreaks of rain overnight.*

• **irregular, inconsistent, uneven, varying, unpredictable**

path *NOUN*

*Please keep to the **path** as you walk through the gardens.*

• **pathway, track, trail, footpath, walk, walkway, lane**

A path for horse-riding is a **bridleway**.

A path by the side of a road is a **pavement**.

A path above a beach is an **esplanade** or **promenade**.

A path along a canal is a **towpath**.

A path between buildings is an **alley**.

see also **road**

pathetic *ADJECTIVE*

❶ *The abandoned kittens were a **pathetic** sight.*

• **moving, touching, pitiful, distressing, heartbreaking, sad, sorry**

❷ *The goalie made a **pathetic** attempt to stop the ball.*

• **hopeless, useless, weak, feeble, inadequate, incompetent**

patience *NOUN*

*She waited with great **patience** for an hour.*

• **calmness, tolerance, self-control, endurance, restraint, perseverance, persistence, resignation**

OPPOSITE **impatience**

patient *ADJECTIVE*

❶ *The nurse was very **patient** with the children.*

• **calm, composed, even-tempered, easy-going, tolerant, lenient, mild, quiet, uncomplaining, resigned, long-suffering**

❷ *It took hours of **patient** work to restore the painting.*

• **persevering, persistent, unhurried, untiring, steady, determined**

OPPOSITE **impatient**

patrol *VERB*

*Police **patrolled** the area all night.*

• **guard, keep watch over, inspect, tour**

patter *NOUN, VERB*

for various sounds see **sound**

pattern *NOUN*
*Do you like the **pattern** on this wallpaper?*
• **design, decoration**

WORD WEB

SOME KINDS OF PATTERN:

• **checked, criss-cross, dotted** or **dotty, floral** or **flowery, geometric, gingham, paisley, polka dot, spotted** or **spotty, striped** or **stripey, tartan, wavy, zigzag**

pause *NOUN*
*There was a **pause** while the singers got their breath back.*
• **break, gap, halt, rest, lull, stop, wait, interruption, stoppage**
A pause in the middle of a performance is an **interlude** or **interval**.
A pause in the middle of a cinema film is an **intermission**.

pause *VERB*
❶ *The stranger **paused** at the door before knocking.*
• **hesitate, wait, delay, hang back**
❷ *The cyclists **paused** to let the others catch up.*
• **halt, stop, rest, take a break, break off**

paw *NOUN*
*The cat had a mouse under its **paw**.*
• **foot**
A horse's foot is a **hoof**.
A pig's feet are its **trotters**.
A bird's feet are its **claws**.

pay *VERB* pays, paying, paid
❶ *How much did you **pay** for your new bike?*
• **spend, give out, hand over**
(informal) **fork out**
❷ *Who's going to **pay** the bill?*
• **pay off, repay, settle, clear, refund**
❸ *They had to **pay** for all the damage they caused.*
• **compensate, pay back**
❹ *Do you think the new business is likely to **pay**?*
• **be profitable**
❺ *I'll make you **pay** for this!*
• **suffer**

pay *NOUN*
*We should get an increase in **pay** next year.*
• **wages, salary, income, earnings**
A payment someone gets for doing a single job is a **fee**.

payment *NOUN*
A voluntary payment to a charity is a **contribution** or **donation**.
The payment you make to travel on public transport is the **fare**.
A payment you have to make as a punishment is a **fine**.
A payment made to free a hostage or prisoner is a **ransom**.
A payment you get as a prize is a **reward**.
A payment to join a club is a **subscription**.
A voluntary payment to a waiter or waitress is a **tip**.
Payment that you receive regularly from your parents is **pocket money**.
A payment you get if you paid too much for something is a **refund**.

peace *NOUN*
❶ *After the war there was a period of **peace**.*
• **agreement, harmony, friendliness**
❷ *She enjoys the **peace** of the countryside.*
• **calmness, peacefulness, quiet, tranquillity, calm, stillness, serenity, silence**

peaceful *ADJECTIVE*
*They enjoyed a **peaceful** day fishing.*
• **calm, quiet, relaxing, tranquil, restful, serene, undisturbed, untroubled, gentle, placid, soothing, still**
OPPOSITE **noisy, troubled**

peak *NOUN*
❶ *The **peak** of the mountain was covered in snow.*
• **summit, cap, crest, crown, pinnacle, top, tip, point**
❷ *She is at the **peak** of her career as an athlete.*
• **top, height, highest point, climax**

A B C D E F G H I J K L M N O P Q R S T U V W X Y Z

peal *VERB*
for sounds made by a bell see **bell**

peculiar *ADJECTIVE*
❶ *What's that **peculiar** smell?*
• **strange, unusual, odd, curious, extraordinary, abnormal, funny, weird, bizarre**
OPPOSITE **ordinary**
❷ *He recognised her **peculiar** way of writing.*
• **characteristic, distinctive, individual, particular, personal, special, unique, identifiable**

pedigree *NOUN*
*They have a complete record of the dog's **pedigree**.*
• **ancestry, descent, family history**

peel *NOUN*
*Orange **peel** is used in marmalade.*
• **rind, skin**

peep and **peer** *VERB*
see **look**

peg *NOUN*
*Leave your coat and scarf on the **peg**.*
• **hook, knob**

pelt *VERB*
❶ *The boys **pelted** each other with snowballs.*
• **attack, bombard, shower**
see also **throw**
❷ *The rain was **pelting** down outside.*
• **pour, teem**

pen *NOUN*
❶ *My **pen** has run out of ink.*
• **ballpoint, felt-tip pen, fountain pen, gel pen**
❷ *The dog drove the sheep into the **pen**.*
• **enclosure, fold**

penalise *VERB*
*In football, you are **penalised** if you handle the ball.*
• **punish**

penalty *NOUN*
*The **penalty** for this crime is ten years in prison.*
• **punishment**
OPPOSITE **reward**

penetrate *VERB*
❶ *The bullet had **penetrated** the man's chest.*
• **make a hole in, pierce, bore through**
When something penetrates a tyre, it punctures it.
❷ *The soldiers **penetrated** the enemy's defences.*
• **get past, get through, infiltrate**

penniless *ADJECTIVE*
*The family was left **penniless** and without a home.*
• **poor, impoverished, poverty-stricken**
OPPOSITE **rich**

people *PLURAL NOUN*
❶ *How many **people** are you inviting?*
• **persons, individuals**
People as opposed to animals are **humans, human beings** or **mankind**.
❷ *The government is elected by the **people** of the country.*
• **population, citizens, the public, society, nation, race**

perceive *VERB*
❶ *They **perceived** a figure moving along the horizon.*
• **make out, notice, become aware of, catch sight of, recognise**
❷ *I began to **perceive** what she meant.*
• **realise, understand, comprehend, grasp**

perceptive *ADJECTIVE*
*It was very **perceptive** of you to spot my mistake.*
• **observant, clever, sharp, shrewd, quick, alert**
OPPOSITE **unobservant**

perch *VERB*
*A robin was **perching** on top of the postbox.*
• **sit, settle, rest, balance**

percussion *NOUN*
for percussion instruments see **music**

perfect *ADJECTIVE*
❶ *Each petal on the flower was* ***perfect****.*
• **faultless, flawless, ideal, intact, undamaged, complete, whole**
❷ *The dress is a* ***perfect*** *fit.*
• **exact, faithful, precise, accurate, correct**
OPPOSITE **imperfect**
❸ *I received a letter from a* ***perfect*** *stranger.*
• **complete, total, absolute, utter**

perfect *VERB*
Gymnasts spend years ***perfecting*** *their technique.*
• **make perfect, improve, refine, polish**

perform *VERB*
❶ *Is this your first time* ***performing*** *on stage?*
• **act, appear, play, dance, sing**
❷ *The class* ***performed*** *a play about pirates.*
• **present, stage, produce, put on**
❸ *Soldiers are expected to* ***perform*** *their duty.*
• **do, carry out, execute, fulfil**
To perform a crime is to **commit** a crime.

performance *NOUN*
❶ *Tonight's* ***performance*** *is already sold out.*
• **show, production, presentation**
❷ *He congratulated the players on their outstanding* ***performance****.*
• **effort, work, endeavour, exertion, behaviour, conduct**

performer *NOUN*
see **entertainer**

perfume *NOUN*
The ***perfume*** *of roses filled the room.*
• **smell, scent, fragrance**

perhaps *ADVERB*
Perhaps *the weather will improve soon.*
• **maybe, possibly**
OPPOSITE **definitely**

peril *NOUN*
The crew faced many ***perils*** *on their voyage.*
• **danger, hazard, risk, menace, threat**
OPPOSITE **safety**

perimeter *NOUN*
There is a fence round the ***perimeter*** *of the field.*
• **edge, border, boundary**
The distance round the edge of something is the **circumference**.

period *NOUN*
❶ *After a long* ***period*** *of hard work they had a rest.*
• **time, span, spell, stretch**
❷ *The book is about the Victorian* ***period****.*
• **age, era, epoch**

perish *VERB*
❶ *Many birds* ***perish*** *in cold weather.*
• **die, be killed, pass away**
❷ *The old tyres have started to* ***perish*** *with age.*
• **disintegrate, crumble away, rot, decay, decompose**

permanent *ADJECTIVE*
❶ *Sugar can do* ***permanent*** *damage to your teeth.*
• **lasting, long-lasting, long-term, everlasting, enduring**
❷ *Traffic noise is a* ***permanent*** *problem in the city centre.*
• **never-ending, perpetual, persistent, chronic, perennial**
❸ *She has been offered a* ***permanent*** *job in the firm.*
• **stable, steady, fixed, lifelong**
OPPOSITE **temporary**

permission *NOUN*
They had the teacher's ***permission*** *to leave.*
• **consent, agreement, approval**
(informal) **go-ahead**

a b c d e f g h i j k l m n o

p

q r s t u v w x y z

A B C D E F G H I J K L M N O P Q R S T U V W X Y Z

permit *VERB*
The council doesn't ***permit*** *fishing in the lake.*
• allow, consent to, give permission for, authorise, license, grant, tolerate, admit

permit *NOUN*
You need a ***permit*** *to fish in the river.*
• licence, pass, ticket

perpetual *ADJECTIVE*
The machine produces a ***perpetual*** *hum.*
• constant, continual, continuous, never-ending, non-stop, endless, ceaseless, incessant, persistent, unceasing, unending
OPPOSITE temporary

perplexing *ADJECTIVE*
'This is the most ***perplexing*** *case I've seen,' said the detective.*
• puzzling, confusing, bewildering, baffling, mystifying

persecute *VERB*
People were ***persecuted*** *for their religious beliefs.*
• oppress, discriminate against, harass, intimidate, bully, terrorise, torment

persevere *VERB*
The rescuers ***persevered*** *despite the bad weather.*
• continue, carry on, keep going, persist *(informal)* keep at it, stick at it
OPPOSITE give up

persist *VERB*
If your headache ***persists****, you should see a doctor.*
• continue, carry on, last, linger, remain, endure
OPPOSITE stop
➤ **to persist in**
He ***persists in*** *wearing that awful tie!*
• keep on, insist on

persistent *ADJECTIVE*
❶ *There was a* ***persistent*** *drip from the tap in the kitchen.*
• constant, continual, incessant, never-ending, steady, non-stop
❷ *That dog is very* ***persistent****—he won't go away.*
• determined, persevering, tireless, resolute, steadfast, stubborn, obstinate

person *NOUN*
Not a single ***person*** *has replied to my email.*
• individual, human being, character, soul

personal *ADJECTIVE*
❶ *The book is based on the writer's* ***personal*** *experience.*
• own, individual, particular
❷ *The contents of the letter are* ***personal****.*
• confidential, private, secret, intimate

personality *NOUN*
❶ *Like all ogres, he has an ugly* ***personality****.*
• character, nature, disposition, temperament, make-up
❷ *The show was introduced by a TV* ***personality****.*
• celebrity, star, VIP

perspire *VERB*
He ***perspires*** *a lot in hot weather.*
• sweat

persuade *VERB*
I ***persuaded*** *my friend to join the choir.*
• convince, coax, induce
To persuade someone to do something is also to **talk them into** doing it.
OPPOSITE dissuade

persuasive *ADJECTIVE*
She used some very ***persuasive*** *arguments.*
• convincing, effective, sound, strong, forceful, compelling, valid
OPPOSITE unconvincing

pessimistic *ADJECTIVE*
*The players are **pessimistic** about their chances of winning.*
• **negative, unhopeful, gloomy, despairing, resigned, cynical**
OPPOSITE **optimistic**

pest *NOUN*
❶ *I'm trying an organic method to get rid of garden **pests**.*
Pests in general are **vermin**.
An informal word for insect pests is **bugs.**
A pest which lives on or in another creature is a **parasite**.
❷ *Don't be a **pest**!*
• **nuisance, bother, annoyance**
(informal) **pain**

pester *VERB*
*Please don't **pester** me while I'm busy!*
• **annoy, bother, trouble, harass, badger, hound, nag**
(informal) **bug**

pet *NOUN*

WORD WEB
SOME ANIMALS COMMONLY KEPT AS PETS:
• **budgerigar, canary, cat, dog, ferret, fish, gerbil, goldfish, guinea pig, hamster, mouse, parrot, pigeon, rabbit, rat, tortoise**

petrified *ADJECTIVE*
*Jack stood **petrified** as the monster lumbered towards him.*
• **terrified, horrified, terror-struck, paralysed, frozen**
see also **afraid**

petty *ADJECTIVE*
*There were a lot of annoying **petty** rules.*
• **minor, trivial, unimportant, insignificant**
OPPOSITE **important**

phase *NOUN*
*Going to school is the start of a new **phase** in your life.*
• **period, time, stage, step**

phenomenal *ADJECTIVE*
*The winner of the quiz had a **phenomenal** memory.*
• **amazing, incredible, outstanding, remarkable, exceptional, extraordinary**
(informal) **fantastic**
OPPOSITE **ordinary**

phenomenon *NOUN*
❶ *Snow is a common **phenomenon** in winter.*
• **happening, occurrence, event, fact**
❷ *The six-year-old pianist was quite a **phenomenon**.*
• **wonder, curiosity, marvel**

phobia *NOUN*
see **fear**

phone *NOUN*
*Is there a **phone** in the building?*
• **telephone**
A portable phone is a **mobile phone** or **mobile**.
A phone that you use to access the Internet is a **smartphone**.
A message left on a phone is **voicemail**.

phone *VERB*
*He **phoned** to say that he'd be late.*
• **call, ring, telephone, dial**

photograph *NOUN*
*We're having our class **photograph** taken today.*
• **photo, snap** or **snapshot, shot, picture**
A photograph that you take of yourself on a phone camera is a **selfie**.
A photograph that is printed on paper is a **print**.
The art of taking photographs is **photography**.

photograph *VERB*
*Dad **photographed** some birds in the garden.*
• **take a picture of, shoot, snap**

WORD WEB

SOME OTHER TERMS USED IN PHOTOGRAPHY:

• **aperture, digital camera, flash, focus, pinhole camera, pixel, shutter, viewfinder, wide-angle lens, zoom lens**

phrase *NOUN*
*'Bon voyage' is a French **phrase** meaning 'have a good journey'.*
• **expression, saying**

phrase *VERB*
*I tried to **phrase** my letter carefully.*
• **express, put into words**

physical *ADJECTIVE*
❶ *There's a lot of **physical** contact in rugby.*
• **bodily**
Physical punishment is **corporal** punishment.
❷ *Ghosts have no **physical** presence.*
• **earthly, material, solid, substantial**

pick *VERB*
❶ *They've **picked** the players for the hockey team.*
• **choose, select, decide on, settle on, opt for, single out**
❷ *Irene **picked** some flowers from the garden.*
• **gather, collect, cut**
❸ *I **picked** an apple off the tree.*
• **pluck, pull off, take**
➤ **to pick up**
❶ *He was too weak to **pick up** the box.*
• **lift, raise, hoist**
❷ *I'll **pick up** some milk on the way home.*
• **get, collect, fetch**

picture *NOUN*
❶ *There's a **picture** of a pyramid in this book.*
• **illustration, image, print**
A picture which represents a particular person is a **portrait.**
A picture which represents the artist himself or herself is a **self-portrait.**
A picture which represents a group of objects is a **still life.**
A picture which represents a country scene is a **landscape.**
Pictures on a computer are **graphics.**
see also **painting, portrait**
❷ *Mum took some **pictures** of us building a sandcastle.*
• **photo, photograph, snapshot, snap**

picture *VERB*
❶ *The girl is **pictured** against a background of flowers.*
• **depict, illustrate, represent, show, portray**
❷ *Can you **picture** what the world will be like in 100 years?*
• **imagine, visualise**

picturesque *ADJECTIVE*
❶ *They stayed in a **picturesque** thatched cottage.*
• **attractive, pretty, charming, quaint**
OPPOSITE **ugly**
❷ *She wrote a **picturesque** account of her trip to Morocco.*
• **colourful, descriptive, imaginative, expressive, lively, poetic, vivid**

piece *NOUN*
❶ *They collected **pieces** of wood to build a raft.*
• **bar, block, length, stick, chunk, lump, hunk, bit, chip, fragment, particle, scrap, shred**
❷ *I've only got two **pieces** of chocolate left.*
• **bit, portion, part, section, segment, share, slice**
❸ *I always have a **piece** of fruit in my snack box.*
• **item**
A piece of clothing is an **article** of clothing.
❹ *I've lost one of the **pieces** of the jigsaw.*
• **part, element, unit, component, constituent**
❺ *There's a **piece** about our school in the local paper.*
• **article, item, report, feature**

pier *NOUN*
*The passengers waited at the **pier** to board the ship.*
• **quay, wharf, jetty, landing stage**

pierce *VERB*
*The arrow had **pierced** the knight's armour.*
• **enter, go through, make a hole in, penetrate, bore through**
To pierce a hole through paper is to **punch** a hole in it or **perforate** it.
To pierce a hole in a tyre is to **puncture** it.
To pierce someone with a spike is to **impale** or **spear** them.

piercing *ADJECTIVE*
*When she saw the dragon, she let out a **piercing** scream.*
• **high-pitched, shrill, penetrating, loud, shattering, deafening, ear-splitting**

pig *NOUN*
An old word for pigs is **swine**.
A wild pig is a **wild boar**.
A male pig is a **boar** or **hog**.
A female pig is a **sow**.
A young pig is a **piglet**.
A family of piglets is a **litter**.
The smallest piglet in a litter is the **runt**.

pile *NOUN*
❶ *Where did this **pile** of rubbish come from?*
• **heap, mound, mountain, stack, hoard, mass, quantity, collection, assortment**
❷ *(informal) I've still got **piles** of homework to do.*
• **plenty, a lot, a great deal**
(informal) **lots, masses**

pile *VERB*
***Pile** everything in the corner and we'll sort it out later.*
• **heap, stack, collect, gather, assemble, hoard**
➤ **to pile up**
*The bills are beginning to **pile up**.*
• **build up, mount up, accumulate**

pill *NOUN*
*Take one **pill** every four hours.*
• **tablet, capsule, pellet**

pillar *NOUN*
*The roof was supported by tall **pillars**.*
• **column, pier, post, prop, support**

pillow *NOUN*
A long kind of pillow is a **bolster**.
A kind of pillow for a chair or sofa is a **cushion**.

pilot *VERB*
*He **piloted** the hot-air balloon back to safety.*
• **fly, steer, guide, lead, navigate**

pimple *NOUN*
*The troll had a **pimple** on the end of his nose.*
• **spot, boil, swelling**

pin *NOUN*
A decorative pin to wear is a **brooch**.
A pin to fix something on a noticeboard is a **drawing pin**.
A pin to fix clothing in place is a **safety pin**.

pinch *VERB*
❶ *The baby **pinched** my arm and wouldn't let go.*
• **nip, squeeze, press, tweak, grip**
❷ *(informal) Who's **pinched** my calculator?*
• **steal, take, snatch, pilfer**
(informal) **nick, swipe, make off with**

pine *VERB*
*The dog **pined** when its master died.*
• **mope, languish, sicken, waste away**
➤ **to pine for**
*She was **pining for** her old house by the sea.*
• **long for, yearn for, miss, crave, hanker after**

pip *NOUN*
*Make sure there are no **pips** in the lemon juice.*
• **seed**

pipe *NOUN*
*The water flows away along this **pipe**.*
• **tube**
A pipe used for watering the garden is a **hose**.
A pipe in the street which supplies water for fighting fires is a **hydrant**.
A pipe which carries oil, etc., over long distances is a **pipeline**.
The system of water pipes in a house is the **plumbing**.

pipe *VERB*

❶ *Water is* ***piped*** *from the reservoir to the town.*
• **carry, convey, channel, funnel**

❷ *She began to* ***pipe*** *a tune on her recorder.*
• **play, blow, sound, whistle**

pirate *NOUN*

The ship was overrun by bloodthirsty ***pirates.***
• **buccaneer, marauder**

WORD WEB

THINGS YOU MIGHT FIND ON A PIRATE SHIP:

• **barrels, cabin, crow's nest, deck, hammock, lantern, mast, plank, pirate flag, rigging, sail, treasure chest, wheel**

A pirate flag is a **Jolly Roger** or **skull-and-crossbones.**

A pirate ship might sail on the **high seas** or the **Spanish Main.**

see also **boat**

PEOPLE YOU MIGHT FIND ON A PIRATE SHIP:

• **cabin boy** or **girl, captain, captives, cook, crew, first mate, lookout, stowaway**

PIRATE TREASURE MIGHT CONTAIN:

• **doubloons** or **ducats, gold bullion, pieces of eight**

Goods or treasure seized by pirates is **booty.**

see also **treasure**

WEAPONS A PIRATE MIGHT USE:

• **cannon, cutlass, dagger, gunpowder, musket, pistol**

Silver had two guns slung about him—one before and one behind—besides the great cutlass at his waist, and a pistol in each pocket of his square-tailed coat.—TREASURE ISLAND, Robert Louis Stevenson

OTHER THINGS A PIRATE MIGHT WEAR OR CARRY:

• **bandanna** or **kerchief, bottle of rum, breeches, cocked hat, earrings, eye patch, hook, parrot** or **cockatoo, pigtail, sea chart, spyglass** or **telescope, treasure map, wooden leg** or **peg leg**

SOME WORDS TO DESCRIBE A PIRATE:

• **barbaric, black-hearted, bloodthirsty, cut-throat, daring, dastardly, fearless, heartless, lawless, merciless, murderous, pitiless, ruthless, savage, swashbuckling, vengeful, vicious, villainous**

pit *NOUN*

❶ *They dug a deep* ***pit*** *to bury the treasure.*
• **hole, crater, cavity, hollow, depression, pothole, chasm, abyss**

❷ *Coal used to be mined from the* ***pits*** *in this area.*
• **mine, coal mine, colliery, quarry**

pitch *NOUN*

❶ *The* ***pitch*** *was waterlogged, so the match was called off.*
• **ground, field, playing field**

❷ *She can sing at a very high* ***pitch.***
• **tone, frequency**

pitch *VERB*

❶ *Scott* ***pitched*** *the ball back over the fence.*
• **throw, toss, fling, hurl, sling, cast, lob** *(informal)* **chuck**

❷ *It was hard trying to* ***pitch*** *the tent in the rain!*
• **erect, put up, set up**

❸ *He lost his balance and* ***pitched*** *headlong into the water.*
• **plunge, dive, drop, topple, plummet**

❹ *The rowing boat* ***pitched*** *about in the storm.*
• **lurch, rock, roll, toss**

pitfall *NOUN*

The author described some of the ***pitfalls*** *of being famous.*
• **difficulty, problem, hazard, danger, snag, catch, trap**

pitiful *ADJECTIVE*

❶ *We could hear* ***pitiful*** *cries for help.*
• **sad, sorrowful, mournful, pathetic, plaintive, heart-rending, moving, touching**

A B C D E F G H I J K L M N O P Q R S T U V W X Y Z

❷ *The goalie made a **pitiful** attempt to stop the ball.*
• **hopeless, useless, feeble, inadequate, incompetent, pathetic**

pity *NOUN*
*The pirates showed no **pity** towards the captives.*
• **mercy, compassion, sympathy, humanity, kindness, concern, feeling**
OPPOSITE **cruelty**
➤ **a pity**
*It's **a pity** that you have to leave so early.*
• **a shame, unfortunate, bad luck**

pity *VERB*
*We **pitied** anyone who was caught up in the storm.*
• **feel sorry for, feel for, sympathise with, take pity on**

pivot *NOUN*
The point on which a lever turns is the **fulcrum**.
The point on which a spinning object turns is its **axis**.
The point on which a wheel turns is the axle or **hub**.

place *NOUN*
❶ *This is a good **place** to park.*
• **site, venue, spot, location, position, situation**
❷ *They are looking for a quiet **place** to live.*
• **area, district, locality, neighbourhood, region, vicinity**
❸ *Save me a **place** on the bus.*
• **seat, space**

place *VERB*
❶ *The hotel is **placed** next to the beach.*
• **locate, situate, position, station**
❷ *You can **place** your coats on the bed.*
• **put down, set down, leave, deposit, lay**
(informal) **dump, plonk**

placid *ADJECTIVE*
❶ *The dog has a **placid** nature and would make an ideal pet.*
• **calm, composed, unexcitable, even-tempered**
OPPOSITE **excitable**
❷ *The sea was **placid** at that time of the day.*
• **calm, quiet, tranquil, peaceful, undisturbed, unruffled**
OPPOSITE **stormy**

plague *NOUN*
❶ *Doctors worked hard to prevent the **plague** from spreading.*
• **pestilence, epidemic, contagion, outbreak**
❷ *There was a **plague** of wasps this summer.*
• **invasion, infestation, swarm**

plague *VERB*
❶ *Stop **plaguing** me with questions!*
• **bother, pester, trouble, annoy, badger, harass**
(informal) **nag, bug**
❷ *Celia has been **plagued** by bad luck recently.*
• **afflict, beset, torment, hound**

plain *ADJECTIVE*
❶ *The furniture in the room was very **plain**.*
• **simple, modest, basic**
OPPOSITE **elaborate**
❷ *Some people say she looks **plain** compared with her sister.*
• **unattractive, ordinary**
OPPOSITE **attractive**
❸ *It is **plain** to me that you are not interested.*
• **clear, evident, obvious, apparent, unmistakable**
OPPOSITE **unclear**
❹ *She told us what she thought in very **plain** terms.*
• **direct, frank, blunt, outspoken, honest, sincere, straightforward**
❺ *We need to wear a **plain** T-shirt for sports.*
• **self-coloured**

plain *NOUN*
A grassy plain in a hot country is called **savannah**.
The large plains of North America are the **prairies**.
The large plains of Russia are the **steppes**.

A B C D E F G H I J K L M N O P Q R S T U V W X Y Z

plan *NOUN*

❶ *The captain explained her **plan** to the rest of the team.*
• **idea, proposal, scheme, strategy, project, suggestion, proposition**
A plan to do something bad is a **plot.**
❷ *They looked at the **plans** for the new sports centre.*
• **design, diagram, chart, map, drawing, blueprint**

plan *VERB*

❶ *The outlaws **planned** an attack upon the sheriff.*
• **scheme, design, devise, work out, formulate, prepare, organise**
To plan to do something bad is to **plot.**
❷ *What do you **plan** to do next?*
• **aim, intend, propose, mean**

plane *NOUN*

see **aircraft**

planet *NOUN*

*The new space probe will travel to distant **planets.***
• **world**

WORD WEB

THE PLANETS OF THE SOLAR SYSTEM (IN ORDER FROM THE SUN) ARE:

• **Mercury, Venus, Earth, Mars, Jupiter, Saturn, Uranus, Neptune**
The path followed by a planet is its **orbit.**
Minor planets orbiting the sun are **asteroids.**
Pluto is classified as a **dwarf planet.**
A planet, such as Jupiter or Saturn, that is made up of gases is a **gas giant.**
Something which orbits a planet is a **satellite.**
The earth's large satellite is the **Moon.**
see also **space**

WRITING TIPS

You can use these words to describe an alien planet:
• **Earth-like, gaseous, inhospitable, uninhabitable, uninhabited**

TO DESCRIBE ITS SURFACE:

• **barren, desolate, dusty, frozen, icy, molten, rocky, volcanic**

TO DESCRIBE ITS ATMOSPHERE OR AIR:

• **airless, noxious, poisonous, thin, toxic, unbreathable**

TO DESCRIBE ITS LIFE:

• **beings, extraterrestrials, inhabitants, life forms**
see also **alien**
On Uriel there had been the magnificent creatures. On Camazotz the inhabitants had at least resembled people. But what were these three strange things approaching?—A WRINKLE IN TIME, Madeleine L'Engle

plant *NOUN*

WORD WEB

SOME TYPES OF PLANT:

• **algae, bush, cactus, cereal, evergreen, fern, flower, fungus, grass, herb, house plant, ivy, lichen, moss, pot plant, shrub, tree, vegetable, vine, weed, wildflower**
see also **flower, fruit, herb, tree, vegetable**

PARTS OF VARIOUS PLANTS:

• **bloom, blossom, branch, bud, flower, fruit, leaf, petal, pod, root, shoot, stalk, stem, trunk, twig**
A young plant is a **seedling.**
A piece cut off a plant to form a new plant is a **cutting.**
A word for plants in general is **vegetation.**
A person who studies plants is a **botanist.**
A word meaning 'to do with plants' is **botanical.**

plant *VERB*

*These seeds should be **planted** in the spring.*
• **sow, put in the ground**
To move a plant from where it was growing and plant it somewhere else is to **transplant** it.

plaster *NOUN*
*The nurse put a **plaster** on the cut.*
• dressing, sticking plaster, bandage

plate *NOUN*
❶ *She piled their **plates** with food.*
for items of crockery see **crockery**
❷ *The robot's body was formed of metal **plates**.*
• panel, sheet
❸ *The book includes colour **plates** of various flowers.*
• illustration, photo, picture

platform *NOUN*
*The conductor stood on a **platform** to address the audience.*
• dais, podium, stage, stand

play *NOUN*
❶ *The school **play** this year is 'Peter Pan'.*
• drama, performance, production
❷ *It is important to balance work and **play**.*
• playing, recreation, amusement, fun, games, sport
for various games and sports see **game, sport**

play *VERB*
❶ *We went out to **play** after lunch.*
• amuse yourself, have fun, romp about
❷ *My sister loves **playing** football.*
• take part in, participate in, compete in
❸ *We're **playing** the home team next week.*
• compete against, oppose, challenge, take on
❹ *I'm learning to **play** the guitar.*
• perform on
❺ *Who will be **playing** Peter Pan?*
• act, take the part of, portray, represent

player *NOUN*
❶ *You need four **players** for this game.*
• contestant, participant, competitor
❷ *How many **players** are in the orchestra?*
• performer, instrumentalist, musician
Someone who plays music on their own is a **soloist**.
for various performers see **entertainer, music**

playful *ADJECTIVE*
*The kittens were in a **playful** mood.*
• lively, spirited, frisky, mischievous, roguish, impish, joking, teasing
OPPOSITE serious

playground *NOUN*
for playground games see **game**

playing field *NOUN*
*There is a training session on the **playing field** tomorrow.*
• ground, pitch, sports ground

play park *NOUN*
see **park**

plea *NOUN*
*The king ignored the captives' **plea** for mercy.*
• appeal, request, entreaty, petition

plead *VERB*
➤ **to plead with**
*The children **pleaded with** the witch to let them go.*
• beg, entreat, implore, appeal to, ask, request, petition

pleasant *ADJECTIVE*
❶ *The owner of the shop is always **pleasant** to us.*
• kind, friendly, likeable, charming, amiable, amicable, cheerful, genial, good-natured, good-humoured, approachable, hospitable, welcoming
❷ *We spent a very **pleasant** evening playing cards.*
• pleasing, enjoyable, agreeable, delightful, lovely, entertaining
❸ *The weather is quite **pleasant** today.*
• fine, mild, sunny, warm
OPPOSITE unpleasant

please *VERB*
❶ *I hope my present will **please** you.*
• give pleasure to, make happy, satisfy, delight, amuse, entertain
❷ *Do as you **please**.*
• want, wish

pleased *ADJECTIVE*
*Why do you look so **pleased** today?*
• **contented, delighted, elated, glad, grateful, happy, satisfied, thankful, thrilled**
OPPOSITE **annoyed**

pleasure *NOUN*
❶ *Mrs Ramsay gets a lot of **pleasure** from her garden.*
• **delight, enjoyment, happiness, joy, satisfaction, comfort, contentment, gladness**
Very great pleasure is **bliss** or **ecstasy**.
❷ *He talked about the **pleasures** of living in the country.*
• **joy, comfort, delight**

pleat *NOUN*
*It takes ages to iron the **pleats** in the skirt.*
• **crease, fold, tuck**

pledge *NOUN*
*The knights swore a **pledge** of loyalty to the king.*
• **oath, vow, promise, word**

plentiful *ADJECTIVE*
*There is a **plentiful** supply of berries in the forest.*
• **abundant, ample, generous, inexhaustible, lavish, liberal, profuse**
OPPOSITE **scarce**

plenty *NOUN*
*Don't buy any milk—there's **plenty** in the fridge.*
• **a lot, a large amount, an abundance, a profusion**
A lot more than you need is a **glut** or **surplus**.
OPPOSITE **scarcity**
➤ **plenty of**
*We've still got **plenty of** time.*
• **a lot of, lots of, ample, abundant**
(informal) **loads of, masses of, tons of**

plight *NOUN*
*He was concerned about the **plight** of the homeless.*
• **predicament, trouble, difficulty, problem, dilemma**

plod *VERB*
❶ *The hikers **plodded** on through the mud.*
• **tramp, trudge, lumber**
❷ *She's still **plodding** away at her violin lessons.*
• **slog, labour, persevere**

plot *NOUN*
❶ *Guy Fawkes was part of a **plot** against the government.*
• **conspiracy, scheme, secret plan**
❷ *It was hard to follow the **plot** of the film.*
• **story, storyline, narrative, thread**
for ways to describe a plot or storyline
see **writing**
❸ *They bought a **plot** of ground to build a new house.*
• **area, piece, lot, patch**
A plot of ground for growing flowers or vegetables is an **allotment**.
A large plot of land is a **tract** of land.

plot *VERB*
❶ *The gang were **plotting** a daring bank raid.*
• **plan, devise, concoct, hatch**
(informal) **cook up**
❷ *They were accused of **plotting** against the queen.*
• **conspire, intrigue, scheme**
❸ *The captain **plotted** the course of the ship.*
• **chart, map, mark**

plough *VERB*
❶ *Tractors are used to **plough** the fields.*
• **cultivate, till, turn over**
❷ *Are you still **ploughing** through that book?*
• **wade, labour, toil**

pluck *VERB*
❶ *They **plucked** the apples off the tree.*
• **pick, pull off, gather, collect, harvest**
❷ *A seagull **plucked** the sandwich out of her hand.*
• **grab, seize, snatch, jerk, pull, tug, yank**
❸ *The guitarist **plucked** the strings very gently.*
To run your finger or plectrum across the strings of a guitar is to **strum**.
To pluck the strings of a violin or cello is to play **pizzicato**.

plug *NOUN*
*They removed the **plug** in the side of the barrel.*
• stopper, cork, bung

plug *VERB*
❶ *Dad managed to **plug** the leak in the pipe.*
• stop up, block, close, fill, seal, bung up
❷ *(informal) We asked the local radio station to **plug** our concert.*
• advertise, publicise, promote, push

plump *ADJECTIVE*
*The goblin was short and **plump**, with pointy ears.*
• chubby, dumpy, fat, tubby, podgy, round, stout, portly
OPPOSITE skinny

plunder *VERB*
*Viking raiders **plundered** the village.*
• loot, pillage, raid, ransack, rob, steal from

plunge *VERB*
❶ *One by one, the girls **plunged** into the pool.*
• dive, jump, leap, throw yourself
❷ *As the wind died down, the kite **plunged** to the ground.*
• drop, fall, pitch, tumble, plummet, swoop
❸ *I **plunged** my hand in the cold water.*
• dip, lower, sink, immerse, submerge
❹ *Finn **plunged** his spear into the dragon's throat.*
• thrust, stab, push, stick, shove, force

plural *ADJECTIVE*
OPPOSITE singular

poem *NOUN*
*We each wrote a **poem** about the seaside.*
• rhyme
Poems are **poetry** or **verse**.
A group of lines forming a section of a poem is a **stanza**.
A pair of rhyming lines within a poem is a **couplet**.
The rhythm of a poem is its **metre**.

WORD WEB

SOME KINDS OF POEM:

• ballad, concrete poem, elegy, epic, free verse, haiku, limerick, lyric, narrative poem, nonsense verse, nursery rhyme, ode, sonnet

poetic *ADJECTIVE*
*The opening chapter is written in a **poetic** style.*
• expressive, imaginative, lyrical, poetical
An uncomplimentary synonym is **flowery**.

point *NOUN*
❶ *Be careful—that knife has a very sharp **point**.*
• tip, end, spike, prong
❷ *The stars looked like **points** of light in the sky.*
• dot, spot, speck, fleck
❸ *He marked on the map the exact **point** where the treasure lay.*
• location, place, position, site
❹ *At that **point** the rain started to come down.*
• moment, instant, time
❺ *I agree with your last **point**.*
• idea, argument, thought
❻ *His sense of humour is one of his good **points**.*
• characteristic, feature, attribute
❼ *There is no **point** in phoning at this hour.*
• purpose, reason, aim, object, use, usefulness
❽ *I think I missed the **point** of that film.*
• meaning, essence, core, gist

point *VERB*
❶ *She **pointed** the way.*
• draw attention to, indicate, point out, show, signal
❷ *Can you **point** me in the right direction for the station?*
• aim, direct, guide, lead, steer

A B C D E F G H I J K L M N O P Q R S T U V W X Y Z

pointless *ADJECTIVE*
It's ***pointless*** *to argue with him—he's so stubborn.*
• **useless, futile, vain**
OPPOSITE **worthwhile**

poise *NOUN*
The young actress showed great ***poise*** *for her age.*
• **calmness, composure, assurance, self-confidence**

poised *ADJECTIVE*
The jaguar was ***poised*** *to pounce on its prey.*
• **ready, waiting, prepared, set**

poison *NOUN*
A poison to kill plants is **herbicide** or **weedkiller.**
A poison to kill insects is **insecticide** or **pesticide.**
The poison in a snake bite is **venom.**
A substance which can save you from the effects of a poison is an **antidote.**

poisonous *ADJECTIVE*
Some of those mushrooms may be ***poisonous.***
• **toxic, venomous, deadly, lethal**

poke *VERB*
Someone ***poked*** *me in the back with an umbrella.*
• **prod, dig, jab, stab, thrust**
➤ **to poke out**
The kitten's head was ***poking out*** *of the basket.*
• **stick out, project, protrude**

polar *ADJECTIVE*
The ***polar*** *expedition will study birds and sea life.*
• **Antarctic** or **Arctic**

WORD WEB

THINGS YOU MIGHT SEE IN POLAR REGIONS:
• **glacier, iceberg, ice field or ice cap, moss, permafrost, pack ice, sheet ice, tundra**
see also **ice**

SOME ANIMALS WHICH LIVE IN POLAR REGIONS:
• **albatross, arctic fox, arctic tern, narwhal, penguin, polar bear, reindeer, seal, walrus, whale, wolf**

THINGS A POLAR EXPLORER MIGHT USE:
• **goggles, huskies, ice pick, kayak, mittens, parka, skis, ski pole, sledge, snowmobile, snowshoes**

pole *NOUN*
Four ***poles*** *marked the corners of the field.*
• **post, bar, rod, stick, shaft**
A pole that you use when walking or as a weapon is a **staff.**
A pole for a flag to fly from is a **flagpole.**
A pole to support sails on a boat or ship is a **mast** or **spar.**
A pole with a pointed end to stick in the ground is a **stake.**
Poles which a circus entertainer walks on are **stilts.**

police officer *NOUN*
Several ***police officers*** *were patrolling the football ground.*
• **policeman** or **policewoman, officer, constable**
(informal) **cop, copper**
Police officers of higher rank are **sergeant, inspector** and **superintendent.**
The head of a police force is the **chief constable.**
Someone training for the police force is a **cadet.**
Someone who investigates crimes is a **detective.**
see also **detective**

policy *NOUN*
The leaflet explains the school's ***policy*** *on bullying.*
• **approach, strategy, stance, plan of action**

polish *VERB*
Beeswax is used to ***polish*** *furniture.*
• **rub down, shine, buff, burnish, wax**

➤ to polish something off
*The girls **polished off** a whole plate of sandwiches.*
• **finish, get through, eat up**

polish *NOUN*
*The silverware had been cleaned to give it a good **polish**.*
• **shine, sheen, gloss, lustre, sparkle, brightness, glaze, finish**

polished *ADJECTIVE*
❶ *She could see her face in the **polished** surface.*
• **shining, shiny, bright, glassy, gleaming, glossy, lustrous**
OPPOSITE **dull, tarnished**
❷ *The orchestra gave a **polished** performance.*
• **accomplished, skilful, faultless, perfect, well-prepared**

polite *ADJECTIVE*
*My aunt is always **polite** to visitors.*
• **courteous, well-mannered, respectful, civil, well-behaved, gracious, gentlemanly** or **ladylike, chivalrous, gallant**
OPPOSITE **rude, impolite**

politics *NOUN*

WORD WEB

SOME WORDS USED IN POLITICS:

• **alliance, assembly, ballot, by-election, cabinet, campaign, council, election, first minister, government, left-wing, lobby, majority, manifesto, minister, MP, MSP, parliament, party, poll, president, prime minister, referendum, right-wing, vote**

poll *NOUN*
*The result of the **poll** has been declared.*
• **election, vote, ballot**
A vote on a particular question by all the people in a country is a **referendum**.
An official survey to find out about the population is a **census**.

pollute *VERB*
*The river has been **polluted** by chemicals.*
• **contaminate, infect, poison**

pompous *ADJECTIVE*
*The giant spoke in a rather **pompous** manner.*
• **arrogant, self-important, haughty, snobbish**
(informal) **stuck-up**
OPPOSITE **modest**

pond *NOUN*
see **pool**

pool *NOUN*
❶ *The surface of the **pool** was covered with frogspawn.*
• **pond**
A larger area of water is a **lake** or (in Scotland) a **loch**.
A small shallow area of water is a **puddle**.
A pool of water in the desert is an **oasis**.
A pool among rocks on a seashore is a **rock pool**.
❷ *The sports centre has an indoor and an outdoor **pool**.*
• **swimming pool, swimming baths**
A public open-air swimming pool is a **lido**.

poor *ADJECTIVE*
❶ *You can't afford luxuries if you're **poor**.*
• **impoverished, poverty-stricken, penniless, needy, badly off, hard up**
OPPOSITE **rich**
❷ *His handwriting is very **poor**.*
• **bad, inferior, inadequate, incompetent, unsatisfactory, shoddy, weak, worthless**
OPPOSITE **good, superior**
❸ *They pitied the **poor** animals standing in the rain.*
• **unlucky, unfortunate, pitiful, wretched**
OPPOSITE **lucky**

poorly *ADJECTIVE*
*He stayed at home because he felt **poorly**.*
• **ill, sick, unwell, unfit**
OPPOSITE **well**

pop *NOUN, VERB*
for various sounds see **sound**

popular *ADJECTIVE*
❶ *Disney has made a lot of* ***popular*** *children's films.*
• **well-liked, well-loved, celebrated, favourite**
OPPOSITE **unpopular**
❷ *Rollerblades are very* ***popular*** *just now.*
• **fashionable, widespread, current, in demand**
(informal) **trendy**
OPPOSITE **unpopular**

population *NOUN*
About ten per cent of the world's ***population*** *is left-handed.*
• **inhabitants, residents, occupants, citizens, people, community**

pore *VERB*
➤ **to pore over**
The detective ***pored over*** *the evidence on his desk.*
• **examine, study, inspect, look closely at, scrutinise**

port *NOUN*
A large cruise ship sailed into the ***port****.*
• **harbour, dock, anchorage**
A harbour for yachts and pleasure boats is a **marina**.

portable *ADJECTIVE*
We brought a ***portable*** *DVD player.*
• **transportable, mobile, compact, lightweight**
A portable phone is a **mobile phone** or **mobile**
A portable computer is a **laptop** or **notebook**.

portion *NOUN*
Violet asked for a large ***portion*** *of trifle.*
• **helping, serving, ration, share, quantity, piece, part, bit, slice**

portrait *NOUN*
There's a ***portrait*** *of the Queen on every stamp.*
• **picture, image, likeness, representation**
A portrait which shows a side view of someone is a **profile**.
A portrait which shows just the outline of someone is a **silhouette**.
A portrait which exaggerates some aspect of a person is a **caricature**.

portray *VERB*
The film ***portrays*** *life in Victorian England.*
• **depict, represent, show, describe, illustrate**

pose *VERB*
The film star ***posed*** *in front of the camera.*
• **model, sit**
➤ **to pose as someone**
The spy ***posed as*** *a newspaper reporter.*
• **impersonate, pretend to be, pass yourself off as**

posh *ADJECTIVE*
We went to a ***posh*** *restaurant for a treat.*
• **smart, stylish, high-class, elegant, fashionable, up-market, luxurious, luxury, de luxe, plush**
(informal) **classy, swanky, swish, snazzy**

position *NOUN*
❶ *Mark the* ***position*** *on the map.*
• **location, place, point, spot, site, whereabouts**
❷ *He shifted his* ***position*** *to avoid getting cramp.*
• **pose, posture, stance**
❸ *Losing all her money put her in a difficult* ***position****.*
• **situation, state, condition, circumstances**
❹ *A referee should adopt a neutral* ***position****.*
• **opinion, attitude, outlook, view**
❺ *Being a head teacher is an important* ***position****.*
• **job, post, appointment, function**

positive *ADJECTIVE*
❶ *The detective was **positive** that the cook was lying.*
• **certain, sure, convinced, assured, confident**
OPPOSITE **uncertain**
❷ *Miss Andrews made some **positive** comments on my singing.*
• **helpful, useful, worthwhile, beneficial, constructive**
OPPOSITE **negative**

possess *VERB*
❶ *They don't **possess** a computer.*
• **have, own**
❷ *What **possessed** you to take up diving?*
• **make you think of, come over you**

possessions *PLURAL NOUN*
*The refugees had lost all of their **possessions**.*
• **belongings, goods, property**

possibility *NOUN*
*There's a **possibility** that it may rain later.*
• **chance, likelihood, danger, risk**

possible *ADJECTIVE*
❶ *Is it **possible** that life exists on other planets?*
• **likely, probable, conceivable, credible**
❷ *It wasn't **possible** to shift the piano.*
• **feasible, practicable, practical**
OPPOSITE **impossible**

possibly *ADVERB*
*'Will you finish your homework today?' '**Possibly**.'*
• **maybe, perhaps**

post *NOUN*
❶ *The farmer put up some **posts** for a new fence.*
• **pole, pillar, shaft, stake, support, prop**
❷ *The **post** was delivered late.*
• **mail, letters, delivery**
❸ *Are you thinking of applying for the **post**?*
• **job, position, situation, appointment, vacancy**

post *VERB*
❶ *Did you **post** those letters?*
• **mail, send, dispatch**
❷ *The names of the winners will be **posted** on the noticeboard.*
• **display, put up, announce, advertise**

poster *NOUN*
*We saw a **poster** about a missing cat.*
• **advertisement, announcement, bill, notice, sign, placard**

postpone *VERB*
*They **postponed** the match because of bad weather.*
• **put off, defer, delay**
To stop a meeting or game that you intend to start again later is to **adjourn** or **suspend** it.

pot *NOUN*
*On the table were little **pots** of jam and honey.*
• **jar, dish, bowl, pan**

potent *ADJECTIVE*
❶ *The magic potion is very **potent**, so you only need a single drop.*
• **strong, powerful, intoxicating, pungent, heady**
❷ *She persuaded us with her **potent** arguments.*
• **effective, forceful, strong, compelling**
OPPOSITE **weak**

potential *ADJECTIVE*
❶ *He's a **potential** champion.*
• **budding, future, likely, possible, probable, promising**
❷ *These floods are a **potential** disaster for the farmers.*
• **looming, threatening**

potion *NOUN*
*A magic **potion** was brewing in the wizard's cauldron.*
• **drug, medicine, mixture**

pottery *NOUN*

WORD WEB

Someone who creates pottery is a **potter**.
A formal word for pottery is **ceramics**.

TYPES OF POTTERY:

• **bone china, china, earthenware, porcelain, stoneware, terracotta**
The kind of pottery we eat and drink from is **crockery**.

pouch *NOUN*
The pirate kept his gunpowder in a leather ***pouch****.*
• **bag, purse, sack**

poultry *NOUN*

WORD WEB

KINDS OF POULTRY:

• **bantam, chicken, duck, fowl, goose, guinea fowl, hen, pullet, turkey**
A male chicken specially fattened for eating is a **capon**.

pounce *VERB*
➤ **to pounce on**
The cat ***pounced on*** *the mouse.*
• **jump on, leap on, spring on, swoop down on, lunge at, ambush, attack**

pound *VERB*
Huge waves ***pounded*** *the stranded ship.*
• **beat, hit, batter, smash**
To pound something hard until it is powder is to **crush, grind** or **pulverise** it.
To pound something soft is to **knead, mash** or **pulp** it.

pour *VERB*
❶ *Water* ***poured*** *through the hole.*
• **flow, run, gush, stream, spill, spout**
❷ *I* ***poured*** *some milk into my cup.*
• **tip, serve**

poverty *NOUN*
Many of the townspeople were living in ***poverty****.*
• **pennilessness, hardship, need, want**
Extreme poverty is **abject poverty**.
OPPOSITE **wealth**

powder *NOUN*
The fairy sprinkled some magic ***powder*** *in the air.*
• **dust, particles**

powdery *ADJECTIVE*
The wind blew the ***powdery*** *soil away.*
• **dusty, fine, loose, grainy, sandy**

power *NOUN*
❶ *They were amazed by the* ***power*** *of the robot.*
• **strength, force, might, energy**
❷ *The storyteller has the* ***power*** *to enthrall an audience.*
• **skill, talent, ability, competence**
❸ *A policeman has the* ***power*** *to arrest someone.*
• **authority, right**
❹ *The empress had* ***power*** *over all the people.*
• **authority, command, control, dominance, domination**

powerful *ADJECTIVE*
❶ *Sir Joustalot was the most* ***powerful*** *knight in the kingdom.*
• **influential, leading, commanding, dominant, high-powered**
❷ *The wrestler had a* ***powerful*** *punch.*
• **strong, forceful, hard, mighty, vigorous, formidable, potent**
❸ *He used some* ***powerful*** *arguments.*
• **strong, convincing, effective, persuasive, impressive**
OPPOSITE **weak**

powerless *ADJECTIVE*
The good witch was ***powerless*** *to undo the spell.*
• **helpless, ineffective, weak, feeble, defenceless**

practical *ADJECTIVE*
❶ *I'll ask Katie what to do—she is always very* ***practical****.*
• **down-to-earth, matter-of-fact, sensible, level-headed**
OPPOSITE **impractical**
❷ *The robbers' plan was not very* ***practical****.*
• **workable, realistic, sensible, feasible, viable, achievable**
OPPOSITE **impractical**
❸ *Do you have any* ***practical*** *experience of child-minding?*
• **real, actual, hands-on**
OPPOSITE **theoretical**

practically *ADVERB*
Keep going—we're ***practically*** *there!*
• **almost, just about, nearly, virtually**

practice *NOUN*
❶ *We have extra football* ***practice*** *this week.*
• **training, exercises, preparation, rehearsal, drill**
❷ *Is it the* ***practice*** *amongst ogres to eat grubs for breakfast?*
• **custom, habit, convention, routine**
➤ **in practice**
What will the plan involve ***in practice****?*
• **in effect, in reality, actually, really**

practise *VERB*
❶ *My piano teacher asked me to* ***practise*** *for longer.*
• **do exercises, rehearse, train, drill**
To practise just before the start of a performance is to **warm up**.
❷ *My sister wants to* ***practise*** *veterinary medicine.*
• **do, perform, carry out, put into practice, follow, pursue, work in**

praise *VERB*
The critics ***praised*** *the actress for her outstanding performance.*
• **commend, applaud, admire, compliment, congratulate, pay tribute to**
(informal) **rave about**
OPPOSITE **criticise**

praise *NOUN*
She received a lot of ***praise*** *for her painting.*
• **approval, admiration, compliments, congratulations, applause**

prance *VERB*
Milly started ***prancing*** *about in a silly way.*
• **dance, skip, hop, leap, romp, cavort, caper, frolic, gambol**

precarious *ADJECTIVE*
❶ *The diver was in a* ***precarious*** *situation, surrounded by sharks.*
• **dangerous, perilous, risky**
OPPOSITE **safe**
❷ *Take care—that ladder looks* ***precarious****!*
• **unsafe, unstable, unsteady, insecure, shaky, wobbly, rickety**
OPPOSITE **secure**

precede *VERB*
A fireworks display ***preceded*** *the concert.*
• **come before, go before, lead**
OPPOSITE **follow, succeed**

precious *ADJECTIVE*
❶ *Her most* ***precious*** *possession was an old photograph.*
• **treasured, cherished, valued, prized, dearest, beloved**
❷ *The throne glittered with* ***precious*** *gems and gold.*
• **valuable, costly, expensive, priceless**
for precious stones see **jewel**
OPPOSITE **worthless**

precise *ADJECTIVE*
❶ *Can you tell me the* ***precise*** *time, please?*
• **exact, accurate, correct, true, right**
OPPOSITE **rough**
❷ *The map gave* ***precise*** *directions for finding the treasure.*
• **careful, detailed, specific, particular, definite**
OPPOSITE **vague**

predict *VERB*
*You can't **predict** what may happen in the future.*
• **forecast, foresee, foretell, prophesy**

predictable *ADJECTIVE*
*It was **predictable** that it would rain.*
• **expected, foreseeable, likely, probable**
OPPOSITE **unpredictable**

preface *NOUN*
*The story behind the book is explained in the **preface**.*
• **introduction, prologue**

prefer *VERB*
*Would you **prefer** juice or lemonade?*
• **rather have, go for, opt for, plump for, choose, fancy**

preferable *ADJECTIVE*
➤ **preferable to**
*She finds country life **preferable to** living in the city.*
• **better than, superior to, more attractive than, more suitable than**

preference *NOUN*
❶ *Sandy has a **preference** for sweet things.*
• **liking, fancy, inclination**
❷ *My **preference** is to walk rather than take the bus.*
• **choice, option, selection, pick, wish**

prefix *NOUN*
OPPOSITE **suffix**

pregnant *ADJECTIVE*
*One of the giraffes in the zoo is **pregnant**.*
• **expecting a baby, carrying a baby** *(informal)* **expecting**
A pregnant woman is an **expectant mother.**

prehistoric *ADJECTIVE*

WORD WEB

PREHISTORIC REMAINS YOU MIGHT VISIT:

• **barrow** or **tumulus, cromlech** or **stone circle, dolmen, hill fort, menhir** or **standing stone**
A person who studies prehistory by excavating and analysing remains is an **archaeologist.**

NAMES OF PREHISTORIC PERIODS:

The best tools and weapons were made of stone in the **Stone Age**, of bronze in the **Bronze Age**, and of iron in the **Iron Age.**
Formal names for the Old, Middle and New Stone Ages are **Palaeolithic**, **Mesolithic** and **Neolithic** periods.
Prehistoric people who lived during the Stone Age were **Neanderthals.**
Most of the earth's surface was covered with ice in the **Ice Age.**
see also **cave**

SOME PREHISTORIC ANIMALS:

• **cave bear, dinosaur, glyptodont, ground sloth, sabre-toothed cat** or **smilodon, sabre-toothed squirrel, woolly mammoth, woolly rhinoceros**
A person who studies fossils of prehistoric life is a **palaeontologist.**
see also **dinosaur**

prejudice *NOUN*
*The school has a policy against racial **prejudice**.*
• **bias, discrimination, intolerance, narrow-mindedness, bigotry**
Prejudice against other races is **racism.**
Prejudice against other nations is **xenophobia.**
Prejudice against the other sex is **sexism.**
OPPOSITE **fairness, tolerance**

preliminary *ADJECTIVE*
They were knocked out in the ***preliminary*** *round of the competition.*
• **first, initial, introductory, early, opening, preparatory**

prelude *NOUN*
see **introduction**

premises *PLURAL NOUN*
Keep out—these are private ***premises.***
• **buildings, property, grounds**

preoccupied *ADJECTIVE*
➤ **preoccupied with something**
She was so ***preoccupied with*** *her work that she forgot the time.*
• **absorbed in, engrossed in, wrapped up in, intent on, obsessed with**

prepare *VERB*
The museum staff are ***preparing*** *for the new exhibition.*
• **get ready, make arrangements for, organise, plan, set up**
To prepare for a play is to **rehearse.**
To prepare to take part in a sport is to **train.**

prepared *ADJECTIVE*
The knights were ***prepared*** *to fight for the Queen.*
• **be able, be ready, be willing**

presence *NOUN*
Your ***presence*** *is required upstairs.*
• **attendance**

present *ADJECTIVE (say* **prez-ent***)*
❶ *Is everyone* ***present?***
• **here, in attendance, at hand**
❷ *Who is the* ***present*** *world chess champion?*
• **current, existing**

present *NOUN (say* **prez-ent***)*
What would you like for your birthday ***present?***
• **gift**
(informal) **prezzie**

present *VERB (say* **pri-zent***)*
❶ *The head* ***presents*** *the prizes on sports day.*
• **award, hand over**
❷ *Our class is* ***presenting*** *a play about the Vikings.*
• **put on, perform, stage, mount**
❸ *Dr Smart* ***presented*** *her amazing invention to the world.*
• **put forward, show, display, exhibit, make known**

preserve *VERB*
❶ *It's more difficult to* ***preserve*** *food in hot weather.*
• **keep, save, store**
❷ *It's important to* ***preserve*** *wildlife.*
• **look after, protect, conserve, defend, safeguard, maintain**

press *VERB*
❶ ***Press*** *the fruit through a sieve to get rid of the seeds.*
• **push, force, squeeze, squash, crush, shove, cram, compress**
❷ *She* ***pressed*** *her blouse for the party.*
• **iron, flatten, smooth**
❸ *Our friends* ***pressed*** *us to stay a bit longer.*
• **beg, urge, entreat, implore**

press *NOUN*
❶ *We read about the competition in the* ***press.***
• **newspapers, magazines**
❷ *The* ***press*** *came to the opening of the new arts centre.*
• **journalists, reporters, the media**

pressure *NOUN*
❶ *The nurse applied* ***pressure*** *to the wound.*
• **force, compression, squeezing, weight, load**
❷ *In the final, the home team were under a lot of* ***pressure.***
• **stress, strain, tension**

prestige *NOUN*
There's a lot of ***prestige*** *in winning an Olympic medal.*
• **credit, glory, fame, honour, renown, distinction, status, kudos**

a b c d e f g h i j k l m n o p q r s t u v w x y z

A B C D E F G H I J K L M N O P Q R S T U V W X Y Z

presume *VERB*
❶ *I* ***presume*** *you'd like something to eat.*
• **assume, take it, imagine, suppose, think, believe, guess**
❷ *He wouldn't* ***presume*** *to tell her what to do!*
• **be bold enough, dare, venture**

pretend *VERB*
She's not really crying—she's only ***pretending.***
• **put on an act, bluff, fake, sham, pose**
(informal) **kid, put it on**

pretend *ADJECTIVE*
That's not a real spider—it's just a ***pretend*** *one!*
• **fake, false, artificial, made-up**
OPPOSITE **real**

pretty *ADJECTIVE*
The doll was dressed in a ***pretty*** *blue outfit.*
• **attractive, beautiful, lovely, nice, pleasing, charming, dainty, picturesque, quaint**
(informal) **cute**
A common simile is **as pretty as a picture.**
OPPOSITE **ugly**

prevent *VERB*
❶ *The driver could do nothing to* ***prevent*** *the accident.*
• **stop, avert, avoid, head off**
❷ *The police* ***prevented*** *an attempted bank raid.*
• **block, foil, frustrate, thwart**
❸ *There's not much you can do to* ***prevent*** *colds.*
• **stave off, ward off**

previous *ADJECTIVE*
❶ *The couple had met on a* ***previous*** *occasion.*
• **earlier, former, preceding**
❷ *The* ***previous*** *owners of the house have gone abroad.*
• **former**
OPPOSITE **subsequent**

prey *NOUN*
The lion killed its ***prey.***
• **quarry, victim**

prey *VERB*
➤ **to prey on**
Owls ***prey on*** *small animals.*
• **hunt, kill, feed on**

price *NOUN*
What is the ***price*** *of a return ticket to Sydney?*
• **cost, amount, figure, expense, payment, sum, charge, rate**
The price you pay for a journey on public transport is the **fare.**
The price you pay to send a letter is the **postage.**
The price you pay to use a private road, bridge or tunnel is a **toll.**

priceless *ADJECTIVE*
❶ *The museum contained many* ***priceless*** *antiques.*
• **precious, rare, valuable, costly, expensive, dear**
❷ *(informal) The joke she told was* ***priceless.***
• **funny, amusing, comic, hilarious, witty**

prick *VERB*
Jamie burst the balloon by ***pricking*** *it with a pin.*
• **pierce, puncture, stab, jab, perforate**

prickle *NOUN*
A hedgehog uses its ***prickles*** *for defence.*
• **spike, spine, needle, barb, thorn**
The prickles on a hedgehog or porcupine are also called **quills.**

prickly *ADJECTIVE*
Holly leaves are very ***prickly.***
• **spiky, spiny, thorny, bristly, sharp, scratchy**

pride *NOUN*
❶ *Mr Dodds takes great* ***pride*** *in his garden.*
• **satisfaction, pleasure, delight**
❷ *The medal winner was a source of great* ***pride*** *to his family.*
• **self-esteem, self-respect, dignity, honour**
❸ ***Pride*** *comes before a fall.*
• **arrogance, conceit, big-headedness, vanity, snobbery**
OPPOSITE **humility**

priest *NOUN*
*The **priest** conducted the wedding ceremony.*
• **minister, vicar, pastor, padre**
A Buddhist religious leader is a **lama.**
A Hindu or Sikh religious leader is a **guru.**
A Jewish religious leader is a **rabbi.**
A Muslim religious leader is an **imam.**
An ancient Celtic priest was a **Druid.**

prim *ADJECTIVE*
*Aunt Jemima is always very **prim** and proper.*
• **prudish, strait-laced, formal, demure**

primarily *ADVERB*
*The website is aimed **primarily** at teenagers.*
• **chiefly, especially, mainly, mostly, predominantly, principally, above all**

primary *ADJECTIVE*
*Their **primary** aim was to win the match.*
• **main, chief, principal, foremost, major, most important, top, prime**
for primary colours see **colour**

prime *ADJECTIVE*
❶ *The penguins' **prime** concern is to protect their chicks.*
see also **primary**
❷ *The dish is made with **prime** cuts of meat.*
• **best, superior, first-class, choice, select, top**

primitive *ADJECTIVE*
❶ ***Primitive** humans were hunters rather than farmers.*
• **ancient, early, prehistoric, primeval**
OPPOSITE **civilised**
❷ *These days steam engines seem very **primitive**.*
• **crude, basic, simple, rudimentary, undeveloped**
OPPOSITE **advanced**

prince and **princess** *NOUN*
see **royalty**

principal *ADJECTIVE*
*The **principal** aim of the race is to raise money for charity.*
• **main, chief, primary, foremost, most important, leading, major, dominant, fundamental, supreme, top**

principle *NOUN*
*Both teams agreed to follow the **principles** of fair play.*
• **rule, standard, code, ethic**

print *NOUN*
❶ *She found the tiny **print** difficult to read.*
• **lettering, letters, printing, type, characters**
❷ *The detective searched the building for **prints**.*
• **mark, impression, footprint, fingerprint**
❸ *Is that a **print** or an original painting?*
• **copy, reproduction, duplicate**

priority *NOUN*
*Traffic on the main road has **priority**.*
• **precedence, right of way**

prise *VERB*
*He tried to **prise** the lid off the treasure chest.*
• **lever, force, wrench**

prison *NOUN*
*He was sentenced to six months in **prison**.*
• **jail, imprisonment, confinement**

prisoner *NOUN*
*The **prisoner** tried to escape from jail.*
• **convict, captive, inmate**
A person who is held prisoner until a demand is met is a **hostage.**

private *ADJECTIVE*
❶ *Everything I write in my diary is **private**.*
• **secret, confidential, personal, intimate**
Secret official documents are **classified** documents.
❷ *Can we go somewhere a little more **private**?*
• **quiet, secluded, hidden, concealed**
OPPOSITE **public**

privilege *NOUN*
Club members enjoy special ***privileges.***
• **advantage, benefit, concession, right**

privileged *ADJECTIVE*
She comes from a ***privileged*** *family background.*
• **advantaged, wealthy, fortunate, affluent, prosperous**

prize *NOUN*
Our team won first ***prize*** *in the relay race.*
• **award, reward, trophy**
Money that you win as a prize is your **winnings.**
Prize money that keeps increasing until someone wins it is a **jackpot.**

prize *VERB*
Chrissie ***prized*** *her grandmother's ring above all else.*
• **treasure, value, cherish, hold dear, esteem, revere**
OPPOSITE **dislike**

probable *ADJECTIVE*
A burst pipe was the most ***probable*** *cause of the flood.*
• **likely, feasible, possible, predictable, expected**
OPPOSITE **improbable**

probe *VERB*
❶ *The submarine can* ***probe*** *the depths of the ocean.*
• **explore, penetrate, see into, plumb**
❷ *Detectives* ***probed*** *the circumstances surrounding the crime.*
• **investigate, inquire into, look into, examine, study**

problem *NOUN*
❶ *Our maths teacher set us a difficult* ***problem.***
• **puzzle, question**
(informal) **brain-teaser, poser**
❷ *I'm having a* ***problem*** *with my computer.*
• **difficulty, trouble, snag, worry**
(informal) **headache**

procedure *NOUN*
The recipe explains the ***procedure*** *for making bread.*
• **method, process, system, technique, way**
A procedure which you follow regularly is a **routine.**

proceed *VERB*
❶ *The sheep* ***proceeded*** *slowly along the path.*
• **go on, advance, move forward, progress**
❷ *We advised them not to* ***proceed*** *with their plan.*
• **go ahead, carry on**

proceedings *PLURAL NOUN*
A thunderstorm interrupted the day's ***proceedings.***
• **events, happenings, activities, affairs**
(informal) **goings-on**

proceeds *PLURAL NOUN*
They added up the ***proceeds*** *from the jumble sale.*
• **income, takings, money, earnings, profit**

process *NOUN*
The inventor showed us a new ***process*** *for creating electricity.*
• **method, procedure, operation, system, technique**

process *VERB*
The dairy ***processes*** *milk to make butter and cheese.*
• **deal with, prepare, treat, refine, transform**

procession *NOUN*
The ***procession*** *made its way slowly down the hill.*
• **parade, march, column, line**

proclaim *VERB*
The judges ***proclaimed*** *that the winner was disqualified.*
• **declare, announce, pronounce**

prod *VERB*
Someone ***prodded*** *me in the back with an umbrella.*
• **poke, dig, jab, nudge, push**

produce *VERB*
❶ *Some lorries **produce** a lot of fumes.*
• create, generate, cause, give rise to
❷ *The tree **produced** a good crop of apples this year.*
• yield, grow
❸ *The factory **produces** cars and vans.*
• make, manufacture, construct
❹ *The referee's decision **produced** whistles from the crowd.*
• provoke, result in, arouse, stimulate
❺ *The writers have **produced** an award-winning comedy.*
• compose, invent, think up
❻ *The magician **produced** a rabbit from his hat.*
• bring out, present, reveal

produce *NOUN*
*The shop sells organic **produce**.*
• food, crops, fruit and vegetables

product *NOUN*
❶ *The company launched a new range of beauty **products**.*
• item, article, substance
❷ *The famine is the **product** of years of drought.*
• result, consequence, outcome, upshot

production *NOUN*
❶ ***Production** at the factory has increased this year.*
• output
❷ *We went to see a **production** of 'The Sound of Music.'*
• performance, show

productive *ADJECTIVE*
❶ *The soil here is rich and **productive**.*
• fertile, fruitful
❷ *It wasn't a very **productive** meeting.*
• useful, valuable, worthwhile, constructive, profitable, fruitful
OPPOSITE unproductive

profession *NOUN*
*Nursing is a worthwhile **profession**.*
• career, job, occupation, work, employment, business

professional *ADJECTIVE*
❶ *The plans were drawn by a **professional** architect.*
• qualified, skilled, trained, experienced
❷ *This is a very **professional** piece of work.*
• skilled, expert, proficient, competent, efficient
OPPOSITE incompetent
❸ *His ambition is to be a **professional** footballer.*
• paid, full-time
OPPOSITE amateur

proficient *ADJECTIVE*
*Olga is a **proficient** tap dancer.*
• skilful, skilled, accomplished, capable, expert, able
OPPOSITE incompetent

profile *NOUN*
see portrait

profit *NOUN*
*They sold the business and bought a yacht with the **profit**.*
• gain, surplus, excess
The extra money you get on your savings is **interest**.
OPPOSITE loss

programme *NOUN*
❶ *We worked out a **programme** for sports day.*
• plan, schedule, timetable
A list of things to be done at a meeting is an **agenda**.
❷ *There was a really good **programme** on TV last night.*
• broadcast, show, production, transmission

progress *NOUN*
❶ *I traced their **progress** on the map.*
• journey, route, movement, travels
❷ *I'm not making much **progress** learning Dutch.*
• advance, development, growth, improvement, headway
An important piece of progress is a **breakthrough**.

progress *VERB*
*Work on the new building is **progressing** well.*
• proceed, advance, move forward, make progress, make headway, continue, develop, improve
(informal) come along

prohibit *VERB*
*Skateboarding is **prohibited** in the school grounds.*
• ban, forbid, outlaw, rule out, veto
OPPOSITE permit, allow

project *NOUN*
❶ *We did a history **project** on the Victorians.*
• activity, task, assignment, piece of research
❷ *There is a **project** to create a bird sanctuary in the area.*
• plan, proposal, scheme

project *VERB*
❶ *A narrow ledge **projects** from the cliff.*
• extend, protrude, stick out, jut out, overhang
❷ *The lighthouse **projects** a beam of light.*
• cast, shine, throw out

prolong *VERB*
*Our guests **prolonged** their visit by a few days.*
• extend, lengthen, make longer, stretch out, draw out
OPPOSITE shorten

prominent *ADJECTIVE*
❶ *The clown had a very **prominent** nose.*
• noticeable, conspicuous, obvious, striking, eye-catching
OPPOSITE inconspicuous
❷ *He is a **prominent** Hollywood actor.*
• well-known, famous, celebrated, major, leading, notable, distinguished, eminent
OPPOSITE unknown

promise *NOUN*
❶ *We had **promises** of help from many people.*
• assurance, pledge, guarantee, commitment, vow, oath, word of honour
❷ *That young pianist shows **promise**.*
• potential, talent

promise *VERB*
*Dad **promised** that we'd go camping this summer.*
• assure someone, give your word, guarantee, swear, take an oath, vow

promising *ADJECTIVE*
❶ *The weather looks **promising** for tomorrow.*
• encouraging, hopeful
❷ *Sheena is a **promising** young singer.*
• bright, talented, gifted, budding
(informal) up-and-coming

promote *VERB*
❶ *Gareth has been **promoted** to captain.*
• move up, advance, upgrade, elevate
❷ *The singer is here to **promote** her new album.*
• advertise, publicise, market, push, sell
(informal) plug
❸ *The school is trying to **promote** healthy eating.*
• encourage, foster, advocate, back, support

prompt *ADJECTIVE*
*I received a **prompt** reply to my email.*
• punctual, quick, rapid, swift, immediate, instant
OPPOSITE delayed

prompt *VERB*
*Having a dog **prompted** her to take more exercise.*
• cause, lead, induce, motivate, stimulate, encourage, provoke

prone *ADJECTIVE*
❶ *The victim was lying **prone** on the floor.*
• face down, on the front
To lie face upwards is to be **supine**.
❷ *He is **prone** to exaggerate his health problems.*
• inclined, apt, liable, likely

pronounce *VERB*
❶ *Try to **pronounce** the words clearly.*
• say, speak, utter, articulate, sound
❷ *The doctor **pronounced** her fully recovered.*
• declare, announce, proclaim, judge

pronounced *ADJECTIVE*
*She spoke with a **pronounced** Australian accent.*
• clear, marked, distinct, definite, noticeable, obvious, striking, unmistakable, prominent
OPPOSITE imperceptible

proof *NOUN*
*There is no **proof** that he is a secret agent.*
• evidence, confirmation

prop *NOUN*
*The bridge is supported by steel **props**.*
• support, strut
A stick to prop yourself on when you hurt a leg is a **crutch**.
Part of a building which props up a wall is a **buttress**.

prop *VERB*
*Kenny **propped** his bike against the kerb.*
• lean, rest, stand
➤ **to prop something up**
*The shelf was **propped up** with sticks of wood.*
• support, hold up, reinforce

propel *VERB*
*The steamboat was **propelled** by a huge paddle wheel.*
• drive forward, push forward, power, impel

proper *ADJECTIVE*
❶ *The nurse showed them the **proper** way to tie a bandage.*
• correct, right, accurate, precise, true, genuine
OPPOSITE wrong, incorrect
❷ *It's only **proper** that he should pay for the broken window.*
• fair, just, fitting, appropriate, deserved, suitable
OPPOSITE inappropriate
❸ *It's not **proper** to speak with your mouth full.*
• decent, respectable, tasteful
OPPOSITE rude
❹ *(informal) I looked a **proper** idiot wearing two different socks!*
• complete, total, utter, absolute, thorough

property *NOUN*
❶ *This office deals with lost **property**.*
• belongings, possessions, goods
❷ *The website lists **property** that is for sale in the city.*
• buildings, houses, land, premises
❸ *Many herbs have healing **properties**.*
• quality, characteristic, feature, attribute, trait

prophecy *NOUN*
*The witch's **prophecy** came true.*
• prediction, forecast

prophesy *VERB*
*The witch **prophesied** that there would be a great battle.*
• predict, forecast, foresee, foretell

proportion *NOUN*
❶ *A large **proportion** of wild elephants live on nature reserves.*
• part, section, share, fraction
❷ *What is the **proportion** of girls to boys in your class?*
• balance, ratio
➤ **proportions**
*The dining hall was a room of large **proportions**.*
• measurements, size, dimensions

proposal *NOUN*
*What do you think of the **proposal** to build a skate park?*
• plan, project, scheme, suggestion, recommendation

propose *VERB*
❶ *He **proposed** a change in the rules.*
• suggest, ask for, recommend
❷ *How do you **propose** to pay for the holiday?*
• intend, mean, plan, aim
❸ *The class **proposed** two pupils to represent them on the school council.*
• nominate, put forward

proprietor *NOUN*
*Who is the **proprietor** of the bicycle shop?*
• **manager, owner**
(informal) **boss**

prosecute *VERB*
*Anyone caught shoplifting will be **prosecuted**.*
• **bring to trial, charge, take to court**
To take someone to court to try to get money from them is to **sue** them.

prospect *NOUN*
❶ *What are their **prospects** of winning the tournament?*
• **chance, hope, expectation, likelihood, possibility, probability**
❷ *The hotel has a lovely **prospect** across the valley.*
• **outlook, view, vista**

prosper *VERB*
*We expect our business to **prosper** this year.*
• **do well, be successful, flourish, succeed, thrive, grow, boom**
OPPOSITE **fail**

prosperity *NOUN*
*Tourism has brought **prosperity** to the region.*
• **wealth, affluence, growth, success**
(informal) **boom**

prosperous *ADJECTIVE*
*She used to be married to a **prosperous** businessman.*
• **wealthy, rich, well-off, well-to-do, affluent, successful, thriving**
OPPOSITE **poor**

protect *VERB*
❶ *A sentry was posted outside to **protect** the palace.*
• **defend, guard, safeguard, keep safe, secure**
❷ *I wore a hat to **protect** myself from the sun.*
• **shield, shade, screen, insulate**

protection *NOUN*
*The waterproof hood gives **protection** from the rain.*
• **shelter, cover, defence, insulation**

protest *NOUN*
❶ *There were **protests** at the plan to close the cinema.*
• **complaint, objection**
A general protest is an **outcry**.
❷ *Some streets will be closed for a **protest** in the city centre.*
• **demonstration, march, rally**
(informal) **demo**

protest *VERB*
*We wrote a letter **protesting** about the closure of the cinema.*
• **complain, make a protest, object (to), take exception (to), express disapproval (of)**

protrude *VERB*
*His stomach **protrudes** above his waistband.*
• **stick out, poke out, bulge, swell, project, stand out, jut out**

proud *ADJECTIVE*
❶ *Jennie's father was very **proud** when she passed her music exam.*
• **delighted (with), pleased (with)**
A common simile is **as proud as a peacock**.
❷ *He's too **proud** to mix with the likes of us!*
• **conceited, big-headed, arrogant, vain, haughty, self-important, snobbish, superior**
(informal) **stuck-up**
OPPOSITE **humble**

prove *VERB*
*The evidence will **prove** that he is innocent.*
• **confirm, demonstrate, establish, verify**
OPPOSITE **disprove**

proverb *NOUN*
see **saying**

provide *VERB*
❶ *We'll **provide** the juice if you bring the sandwiches.*
• bring, contribute, arrange for, lay on
To provide food and drink for people is to **cater** for them.
❷ *The ski centre can **provide** you with boots and skis.*
• supply, equip, furnish

provisions *PLURAL NOUN*
*We had enough **provisions** for two weeks.*
• food, rations, stores, supplies

provoke *VERB*
❶ *Don't do anything to **provoke** the lions!*
• annoy, irritate, anger, incense, infuriate, exasperate, tease, taunt, goad
(informal) wind up
OPPOSITE pacify
❷ *The referee's decision **provoked** anger from the crowd.*
• arouse, produce, prompt, cause, generate, induce, stimulate, spark off, stir up, whip up

prowl *VERB*
*Guard dogs **prowled** about the grounds of the palace.*
• roam, slink, sneak, creep, steal

prudent *ADJECTIVE*
*It would be **prudent** to start saving some money.*
• wise, sensible, shrewd, thoughtful, careful, cautious
OPPOSITE reckless, unwise

prune *VERB*
*Mum **prunes** her roses every spring.*
• cut back, trim

pry *VERB*
*I didn't mean to **pry**, but I overheard your conversation.*
• be curious, be inquisitive, interfere
(informal) be nosy, nose about or around, snoop
➤ **to pry into something**
*Mrs Snout was always **prying into** other people's business.*
• interfere in, meddle in, spy on
(informal) poke your nose into

psychological *ADJECTIVE*
*The doctor thinks her illness is **psychological**.*
• mental, emotional
OPPOSITE physical

public *ADJECTIVE*
❶ *The **public** entrance is at the front of the gallery.*
• common, communal, general, open, shared
OPPOSITE private
❷ *The name of the author is now **public** knowledge.*
• well-known, acknowledged, published, open, general, universal
OPPOSITE secret

public *NOUN*
➤ **the public**
*This part of the castle is not open to **the public**.*
• people in general, everyone, the community, society, the nation

publication *NOUN*
*She's celebrating the **publication** of her first novel.*
• issuing, printing, production
Various publications are **books** and **magazines**.

publicity *NOUN*
❶ *Did you see the **publicity** for the book fair?*
• advertising, advertisements, promotion
❷ *Famous people don't always enjoy **publicity**.*
• fame, exposure, limelight

publish *VERB*
❶ *The magazine is **published** every week.*
• **issue, print, produce, bring out, release, circulate**
❷ *When will they **publish** the results?*
• **announce, declare, disclose, make known, make public, report, reveal**
To publish information on radio or TV is to **broadcast** it.

pudding *NOUN*
*Do you want any **pudding**?*
• **dessert, sweet**
(informal) **afters**
for types of pudding see **food**

puff *NOUN*
❶ *A **puff** of wind caught his hat.*
• **gust, breath, flurry**
❷ *A **puff** of smoke rose from the chimney.*
• **cloud, whiff**

puff *VERB*
❶ *The dragon **puffed** green smoke from its nostrils.*
• **blow out, send out, emit, belch**
❷ *By the end of the race I was **puffing**.*
• **breathe heavily, pant, gasp, wheeze**
❸ *The sails **puffed** out as the wind rose.*
• **become inflated, billow, swell**

pull *VERB*
❶ *She **pulled** her chair nearer to the desk.*
• **drag, draw, haul, lug, trail, tow**
OPPOSITE **push**
❷ *Be careful—you nearly **pulled** my arm off!*
• **tug, rip, wrench, jerk, pluck**
➤ **to pull out**
❶ *The dentist **pulled out** one of my teeth.*
• **extract, take out, remove**
❷ *He had to **pull out** of the race.*
• **back out, withdraw, retire**
➤ **to pull someone's leg**
*I hope you aren't **pulling my leg**!*
• **make fun of, play a trick, tease**
➤ **to pull through**
*It was a bad accident, but the doctors expect him to **pull through**.*
• **get better, recover, revive, survive**
➤ **to pull up**
*The bus **pulled up** at the traffic lights.*
• **draw up, stop, halt**

pulse *NOUN*
*You can feel the **pulse** of blood in your veins.*
• **beat, throb, drumming**

pump *VERB*
*The fire brigade **pumped** water out of the cellar.*
• **drain, draw off, empty**
To move liquid from a higher container to a lower one through a tube is to **siphon** it.

punch *VERB*
❶ *Mrs Rafferty **punched** the robber on the nose.*
• **jab, poke, prod, thump**
for other ways of hitting see **hit**
❷ *I need to **punch** a hole through the card.*
• **bore, pierce**

punctual *ADJECTIVE*
*The bus was **punctual** today.*
• **in good time, on time, prompt**
OPPOSITE **late**

punctuation *NOUN*

WORD WEB

PUNCTUATION MARKS:
• **apostrophe, brackets, colon, comma, dash, exclamation mark, full stop, hyphen, question mark, quotation marks or speech marks, semicolon, square brackets**

OTHER SYMBOLS USED IN WRITING:
• **accent, asterisk, bullet point, emoji, hashtag, slash**

puncture *NOUN*
❶ *I had a **puncture** on the way home.*
• **burst tyre, flat tyre**
❷ *I found the **puncture** in my tyre.*
• **hole, leak**

puncture *VERB*
*A nail **punctured** my tyre.*
• **perforate, pierce, deflate, let down**

punish *VERB*
*Those responsible for the crime will be **punished**.*
• **penalise, discipline, chastise**

punishment *NOUN*
*The **punishment** for dropping litter is a hefty fine.*
• **penalty**
Punishing someone by taking their life is **capital punishment** or **execution**.

puny *ADJECTIVE*
*Miles was rather a **puny** child.*
• **delicate, weak, feeble, frail, weedy**
OPPOSITE **strong, sturdy**

pupil *NOUN*
*There are 33 **pupils** in our class.*
• **schoolchild, student, learner, scholar**
Someone who follows a great teacher is a **disciple**.

purchase *VERB*
*I'm saving my pocket money to **purchase** a bike.*
• **buy, pay for, get, obtain, acquire**

purchase *NOUN*
❶ *She opened her bag and examined her **purchases**.*
• **acquisition**
❷ *The climbers had difficulty getting any **purchase** on the ice.*
• **grasp, hold, leverage**

pure *ADJECTIVE*
❶ *The bracelet is made of **pure** gold.*
• **authentic, genuine, real**
❷ *He was talking **pure** nonsense.*
• **complete, absolute, utter, sheer, total**
❸ *All our dishes are made from **pure** ingredients.*
• **natural, wholesome**
❹ *They swam in the **pure**, clear water of the lake.*
• **clean, fresh, unpolluted**
OPPOSITE **impure**

purify *VERB*
*You can't drink this water unless you **purify** it.*
• **clean, make pure**
You destroy germs by **disinfecting** or **sterilising** things.
You take solid particles out of a liquid by **filtering** it.
To purify water by boiling it and condensing the vapour is to **distil** it.
To purify crude oil is to **refine** it.

purpose *NOUN*
❶ *Have you got a particular **purpose** in mind?*
• **intention, aim, end, goal, target, objective, outcome, result**
❷ *What's the **purpose** of your invention?*
• **point, use, usefulness, value**

purposeful *ADJECTIVE*
*Sam barged into the room with a **purposeful** look on her face.*
• **determined, decisive, positive**
OPPOSITE **aimless**

purse *NOUN*
*I always keep some loose change in my **purse**.*
• **money bag, pouch**
A purse which holds paper money and credit cards is a **wallet**.

pursue *VERB*
❶ *The thief ran off, **pursued** by two police officers.*
• **chase, follow, run after, tail, track, hunt, trail, shadow**
❷ *She wants to **pursue** a career as a dancer.*
• **follow, undertake, practise, conduct, carry on, continue, maintain, proceed with**

pursuit *NOUN*
❶ *The **pursuit** of the criminals lasted for months.*
• **hunt (for), search (for), tracking, chase, trail**
❷ *The family enjoy many outdoor **pursuits**.*
• **activity, pastime, hobby, interest**

a b c d e f g h i j k l m n o p q r s t u v w x y z

A B C D E F G H I J K L M N O P Q R S T U V W X Y Z

push *VERB*
❶ *We **pushed** our way through the crowd.*
• shove, thrust, force, propel, barge, elbow, jostle
OPPOSITE pull
❷ *Pete **pushed** his things into a bag.*
• pack, press, cram, crush, compress, ram, squash, squeeze
❸ *They **pushed** him to work even harder.*
• pressurise, press, drive, urge, compel, bully
(informal) lean on
❹ *The actress is **pushing** her latest film.*
• promote, publicise, advertise
(informal) plug

put *VERB* **puts, putting, put**
❶ *You can **put** your school bags in the corner.*
• place, set down, leave, deposit, dump, stand
❷ *The dog **put** its head on my lap.*
• lay, lean, rest
❸ *I'll **put** some pictures on the wall.*
• attach, fasten, fix, hang
❹ *Where are they planning to **put** the car park?*
• locate, situate
❺ *They **put** guards outside the bank.*
• position, post, station
❻ *I'm not sure of the best way to **put** this.*
• express, word, phrase, say, state
➤ **to put someone off**
*The colour of the food **put** me **off** eating.*
• deter, discourage, distract
➤ **to put something off**
*They **put off** their journey because of the fog.*
• delay, postpone, defer
➤ **to put something out**
*The firefighters quickly **put out** the blaze.*
• extinguish, quench, smother
➤ **to put something up**
*It doesn't take long to **put up** the tent.*
• set up, construct, erect
*I'm going to buy a new bike before they **put up** the price.*
• increase, raise
➤ **to put up with something**
*I don't know how you **put up with** that noise.*
• bear, stand, tolerate, endure

puzzle *NOUN*
*Has anyone managed to solve the **puzzle**?*
• question, mystery, riddle, conundrum, problem
(informal) brain-teaser, poser

puzzle *VERB*
❶ *Phil was **puzzled** by the mysterious message.*
• confuse, baffle, bewilder, bemuse, mystify, perplex, fox
❷ *We **puzzled** over the problem for hours.*
• ponder, think, meditate, worry, brood

puzzled *ADJECTIVE*
*Why are you looking so **puzzled**?*
• confused, baffled, bewildered, mystified, perplexed

puzzling *ADJECTIVE*
*There was something **puzzling** about the signature on the letter.*
• confusing, baffling, bewildering, mystifying, perplexing, mysterious, inexplicable
OPPOSITE straightforward

pyramid *NOUN*

WORD WEB

THINGS FOUND INSIDE OR NEAR ANCIENT EGYPTIAN PYRAMIDS:

• burial chamber, Canopic jar, frieze, hieroglyphics, mummy (of a pharaoh), papyrus, sarcophagus, sphinx, tomb
A pyramid which does not have smooth sides is a **stepped pyramid**.

Qq

quaint *ADJECTIVE*
*They stayed in a **quaint** thatched cottage.*
• charming, picturesque, sweet, old-fashioned, old-world

quake *VERB*
*The ground **quaked** with the thud of the giant's footsteps.*
• shake, shudder, tremble, quiver, shiver, vibrate, rock, sway, wobble

qualification *NOUN*
❶ *What kind of **qualification** do you need to be a vet?*
• diploma, certificate, degree, knowledge, training, skill
❷ *The committee approved the plan, but with some **qualifications**.*
• condition, reservation

qualified *ADJECTIVE*
❶ *This job needs a **qualified** electrician.*
• experienced, skilled, trained, professional
OPPOSITE amateur
❷ *He received **qualified** praise for his efforts.*
• limited, cautious, half-hearted

qualify *VERB*
❶ *The licence **qualifies** him to work as a private detective.*
• authorise, permit, allow, entitle
❷ *The first three runners will **qualify** to take part in the final.*
• get through, pass, be eligible
❸ *She felt the need to **qualify** her remarks.*
• limit, modify, restrict, soften, weaken

quality *NOUN*
❶ *We only use ingredients of the highest **quality**.*
• grade, class, standard
❷ *The most obvious **quality** of rubber is that it stretches.*
• characteristic, feature, property, attribute, trait

quantity *NOUN*
❶ *She receives a huge **quantity** of fan mail every week.*
• amount, mass, volume, bulk, weight
(informal) load
❷ *We recycled a large **quantity** of empty bottles.*
• number
When you add up numbers, you get a **sum** or **total**.

quarrel *NOUN*
*We have **quarrels**, but really we are good friends.*
• argument, disagreement, dispute, difference of opinion, row, squabble, clash, tiff
Continuous quarrelling is **strife**.
A long-lasting quarrel is a **feud** or **vendetta**.
A quarrel in which people become violent is a **brawl** or **fight**.

quarrel *VERB*
*The twins **quarrelled** over who should sit in the front.*
• disagree, argue, row, squabble, bicker, clash, fight, fall out
➤ **to quarrel with something**
*I can't **quarrel with** your decision.*
• disagree with, object to, take exception to, oppose

quarrelsome *ADJECTIVE*
*Goblins can be very **quarrelsome** creatures.*
• bad-tempered, irritable, aggressive, argumentative
OPPOSITE placid

quaver *VERB*
*The boy's voice **quavered** with fear.*
• shake, tremble, waver, quake, quiver, falter

quay *NOUN*
*The ship unloaded its cargo on to the **quay**.*
• dock, harbour, pier, wharf, jetty, landing stage

a b c d e f g h i j k l m n o p q r s t u v w x y z

queer *ADJECTIVE*
❶ *The engine made a **queer** rattling noise.*
• **curious, strange, unusual, weird, funny, mysterious, puzzling**
❷ *There's something **queer** going on.*
• **odd, peculiar, abnormal, suspicious, shady** *(informal)* **fishy**
OPPOSITES **normal, ordinary**

quench *VERB*
❶ *The iced lemonade soon **quenched** her thirst.*
• **cool, satisfy**
❷ *They dumped sand on the embers to **quench** the fire.*
• **extinguish, put out, smother**

query *NOUN*
*If you have any **queries**, please phone this number.*
• **question, enquiry, problem**

query *VERB*
*The manager **queried** the referee's decision.*
• **question, challenge, dispute, argue over, quarrel with, object to**

quest *NOUN*
*The knights set out on a **quest** to find the enchanted tower.*
• **search, hunt, expedition, mission**

question *NOUN*
❶ *Does anyone have any **questions**?*
• **enquiry, query, problem**
A question which someone sets as a puzzle is a **brain-teaser, conundrum** or **riddle**.
A series of questions asked as a game is a **quiz**.
A set of questions which someone asks to get information is a **questionnaire** or **survey**.
❷ *There's some **question** over the player's fitness.*
• **uncertainty, doubt, argument, debate, dispute**

question *VERB*
❶ *The detective decided to **question** the suspect.*
• **ask, examine, interview, quiz, interrogate**
To question someone intensively is to **grill** them.
❷ *He **questioned** the referee's decision.*
• **challenge, dispute, argue over, quarrel with, object to, query**

queue *NOUN*
*There was a **queue** of people outside the cinema.*
• **line, file, column, string**
A long queue of traffic on a road is a **tailback**.

queue *VERB*
*Please **queue** at the door.*
• **line up, form a queue**

quick *ADJECTIVE*
❶ *You'd better be **quick**—the bus leaves in 10 minutes.*
• **fast, swift, rapid, speedy, hasty** *(informal)* **nippy**
A common simile is **as quick as a flash**.
OPPOSITE **slow**
❷ *Do you mind if I make a **quick** phone call?*
• **short, brief, momentary, immediate, instant, prompt, snappy**
OPPOSITES **long, lengthy**
❸ *She's very **quick** at mental arithmetic.*
• **bright, clever, sharp, acute, alert** *(informal)* **on the ball**
OPPOSITE **slow**

quicken *VERB*
*The front runners **quickened** their pace.*
• **accelerate, speed up, hurry up, hasten**

quiet *ADJECTIVE*
❶ *The deserted house was still and **quiet**.*
• **silent, noiseless, soundless**
A common simile is **as quiet as a mouse**.
OPPOSITE **noisy**
❷ *The children spoke in **quiet** whispers.*
• **hushed, low, soft**
Something that is so quiet that you can't hear it is **inaudible**.
OPPOSITE **loud**
❸ *Amy has always been a **quiet** child.*
• **shy, reserved, subdued, placid, uncommunicative, retiring, withdrawn,**
OPPOSITE **talkative**

❹ *We found a **quiet** place for a picnic.*
• **peaceful, secluded, isolated, restful, tranquil, calm, serene**
OPPOSITE **busy**

quieten *VERB*
❶ *The mother tried to **quieten** her baby.*
• **calm, soothe, hush, pacify**
❷ *Turn this dial to **quieten** the volume.*
• **deaden, muffle, mute, soften, suppress**

quit *VERB* **quits, quitting, quitted** or **quit**
❶ *She **quit** her teaching job to travel round the world.*
• **leave, give up, resign from**
(informal) **pack in**
❷ *(informal) **Quit** pushing me!*
• **stop, cease, leave off**

quite *ADVERB*
❶ *The two puppies have **quite** different personalities.*
• **completely, totally, utterly, entirely, absolutely, very, wholly**
❷ *They played **quite** well, but far from their best.*
• **fairly, reasonably, moderately, rather**
WHICH WORD? Note that **quite** has two different meanings, which are almost opposites, so be sure to choose the correct synonyms!

quiver *VERB*
*The jelly **quivered** when the table was banged.*
• **shake, wobble, quake, shiver, quaver, tremble, shudder, vibrate**

quiz *NOUN*
*Our class took part in a general knowledge **quiz**.*
• **test, competition, questionnaire, exam, examination**

quiz *VERB*
*The teacher **quizzed** us on our times tables.*
• **question, ask, examine, interrogate**

quota *NOUN*
*I've had my **quota** of chocolate for this week.*
• **ration, share, portion, allowance, helping**

quotation *NOUN*
*I copied a short **quotation** from the book.*
• **extract, excerpt, passage, piece**
A piece taken from a newspaper is a **cutting**.
A piece taken from a film or TV programme is a **clip**.

quote *VERB*
*He **quoted** some lines from a poem.*
• **recite, repeat**

Rr

race *NOUN*
❶ *We had a **race** to see who was the fastest runner.*
• **competition, contest, chase**
A race to decide who will take part in the final is a **heat**.
❷ *We belong to different **races** but we're all humans.*
• **nation, people, ethnic group**

race *VERB*
❶ *We **raced** each other to the end of the road.*
• **have a race with, run against, compete with**
❷ *She had to **race** home because she was late.*
• **run, rush, dash, hurry, sprint, fly, tear, whizz, zoom**

rack *NOUN*
*Cooking pots hung from a **rack** on the wall.*
• **frame, framework, shelf, support**

racket *NOUN*
❶ *A **racket** is used to hit the ball in tennis.*
In cricket and some other games you hit the ball with a **bat**.
In golf you hit the ball with a **club**.
❷ *Please stop making that awful **racket**!*
• **noise, row, din, commotion, disturbance, uproar, rumpus**

radiate *VERB*
❶ *This fire* ***radiates*** *a lot of heat.*
• give off, send out, emit
❷ *The bus routes* ***radiate*** *from the centre of town.*
• spread out

radical *ADJECTIVE*
❶ *They have made* ***radical*** *changes to school meals.*
• fundamental, drastic, thorough, sweeping
OPPOSITE superficial
❷ *The politician was known for her* ***radical*** *views.*
• extreme, revolutionary
OPPOSITE moderate

rage *NOUN*
Derek slammed the door in a show of ***rage****.*
• anger, fury, indignation, ire
(old use) wrath
A child's rage is a **tantrum** or fit of **temper**.

rage *VERB*
❶ *He was still* ***raging*** *about the cost of the meal.*
• be angry, be fuming, seethe, rant
❷ *The hurricane* ***raged*** *for three days.*
• blow, storm, rampage

ragged *ADJECTIVE*
❶ *They met a traveller wearing* ***ragged*** *clothes.*
• tattered, tatty, threadbare, torn, frayed, patched, ripped, shabby, worn-out
❷ *A* ***ragged*** *line of people waited in the rain.*
• irregular, uneven

raid *NOUN*
The enemy ***raid*** *caught them by surprise.*
• attack, assault, strike, onslaught, invasion, blitz

raid *VERB*
❶ *Long ago, Vikings* ***raided*** *the towns on the coast.*
• attack, invade, ransack, plunder, loot, pillage
Someone who raids ships at sea is a **pirate**.
Someone who raids and steals cattle is a **rustler**.
❷ *Police* ***raided*** *the house at dawn.*
• descend on, rush, storm, swoop on

rail *NOUN*
The fence was made of iron ***rails****.*
• bar, rod, spar
A fence made of rails is also called **railings**.

railway *NOUN*

WORD WEB

VARIOUS TYPES OF RAILWAY:

• branch line, cable railway, funicular, main line, metro, monorail, mountain railway, tramway, underground railway

TYPES OF RAILWAY TRAIN:

• diesel, electric train, express, freight train or goods train, intercity, sleeper, steam train, tram, underground train
Vehicles which run on the railway are **locomotives and rolling stock**.

PARTS OF A RAILWAY TRAIN:

• buffet car, carriage or coach, dining car, engine, goods van, guard's van, locomotive, sleeping car

THINGS YOU MIGHT SEE ON OR NEAR A RAILWAY:

• buffers, cutting, level crossing, platform, points, signals, signal box, sleepers, station, track, trolley, tunnel, viaduct
The rails which trains run on are the **line** or **track**.
The end of the line is the **terminus**.

PEOPLE WHO WORK ON A TRAIN OR RAILWAY:

• conductor, driver, engineer, guard, porter, signalman, station manager, stationmaster, steward

rain *NOUN*
A formal word for rain is **precipitation**.
The rainy season in south and south-east Asia is the **monsoon**.

When there is no rain for a long time there is a **drought**.
for ways to describe rain see **weather**

raise *VERB*
❶ ***Raise** your hand if you need help.*
• **hold up, put up, lift**
❷ *The box was too heavy for him to **raise**.*
• **lift, pick up, elevate, hoist, jack up**
❸ *The Post Office is **raising** the price of stamps.*
• **increase, put up**
❹ *The runners hope to **raise** £1000 for charity.*
• **collect, gather, take in, make**
❺ *He **raised** some objections to the plan.*
• **bring up, mention, put forward, present, introduce**
❻ *The doctor didn't want to **raise** their hopes.*
• **encourage, build up, arouse**
❼ *It's hard work trying to **raise** a family.*
• **bring up, care for, look after, nurture, rear**

rally *NOUN*
*Some demonstrators held a **rally** in the town square.*
• **demonstration, meeting, march, protest**
(informal) **demo**

ram *VERB*
*The car skidded and **rammed** into a lamp post.*
• **bump, hit, strike, crash into, collide with, smash into**

ramble *VERB*
❶ *They **rambled** round the country park.*
• **walk, stroll, wander, roam, rove, range, hike, trek**
❷ *The speaker **rambled** on for hours.*
• **chatter, babble, drift**
(informal) **rabbit, witter**

rampage *VERB*
*An angry mob **rampaged** through the streets.*
• **run riot, run amok, go berserk, go wild, race about, rush about**

ran *past tense see* **run**

random *ADJECTIVE*
*They picked a **random** selection of pupils.*
• **arbitrary, chance, haphazard, casual, unplanned**
OPPOSITE **deliberate**

rang *past tense see* **ring**

range *NOUN*
❶ *There is a **range** of mountains to the south.*
• **chain, line, row, series, string**
❷ *Supermarkets sell a wide **range** of goods.*
• **variety, assortment, selection, choice, spectrum**
❸ *The shop caters for all age **ranges** from toddlers to teenagers.*
• **span, scope**

range *VERB*
❶ *Prices **range** from five to twenty euros.*
• **vary, differ, extend, fluctuate**
❷ *Rows of jam jars were **ranged** on the shelf.*
• **arrange, order, lay out, set out, line up**
❸ *Wild deer **range** over the hills.*
• **wander, ramble, roam, rove, stray**

rank *NOUN*
❶ *The soldiers formed themselves into **ranks**.*
• **column, line, file, row**
❷ *A black belt is the highest **rank** in judo.*
• **grade, level, position, status**
To raise someone to a higher rank is to **promote** them.
To reduce someone to a lower rank is to **demote** them.

ransack *VERB*
❶ *Mrs Hogg **ransacked** the house looking for her keys.*
• **search, scour, rummage through, comb**
(informal) **turn upside down**
❷ *Thieves had **ransacked** the building.*
• **loot, pillage, plunder, wreck**

rap *VERB*
*Someone **rapped** urgently on the door.*
• **knock, tap**

rapid *ADJECTIVE*
*The cyclists set off at a **rapid** pace.*
• **fast, quick, speedy, swift, brisk**
OPPOSITE **slow**

rare *ADJECTIVE*
❶ *These flowers are now very **rare** in the wild.*
• **uncommon, unusual, infrequent, scarce, sparse**
OPPOSITE **common**
❷ *He has a **rare** ability to make people laugh.*
• **exceptional, remarkable, special**

rarely *ADVERB*
*Our next-door neighbour **rarely** goes out.*
• **seldom, infrequently, hardly ever**
OPPOSITE **often**

rash *ADJECTIVE*
*Don't make any **rash** promises.*
• **reckless, foolhardy, hasty, hurried, impulsive, unthinking**
OPPOSITE **careful**

rash *NOUN*
❶ *Rory had an itchy red **rash** on his leg.*
• **spots**
❷ *There has been a **rash** of break-ins lately.*
• **outbreak, series, succession, spate**

rate *NOUN*
❶ *The cyclists were pedalling at a furious **rate**.*
• **pace, speed**
❷ *What's the usual **rate** for washing a car?*
• **charge, cost, fee, payment, price, figure, amount**

rate *VERB*
*How do you **rate** their chance of winning?*
• **judge, regard, consider, estimate, evaluate**

rather *ADVERB*
❶ *It's **rather** chilly today.*
• **quite, fairly, moderately, slightly, somewhat, a bit, a little**
❷ *I'd **rather** not go out tonight.*
• **preferably, sooner**

ratio *NOUN*
*The **ratio** of boys to girls is about 50-50.*
• **proportion, balance**
You can express a ratio as a **percentage**.

ration *NOUN*
*The pirates each had a daily **ration** of rum.*
• **portion, quota, share, allowance, helping, measure**
➤ **rations**
*The astronauts took enough **rations** to last a month.*
• **food, provisions, stores, supplies**

ration *VERB*
*During the war, the government had to **ration** food.*
• **limit, restrict, share out, allot**

rattle *NOUN, VERB*
*for various sounds see **sound***

rave *VERB*
❶ *Connie **raved** about the film she saw last week.*
• **be enthusiastic, talk wildly**
❷ *The head **raved** on about their bad behaviour.*
• **shout, rage, storm, yell, roar**

ravenous *ADJECTIVE*
*The children were **ravenous** after their walk.*
• **hungry, starved, starving, famished**

raw *ADJECTIVE*
❶ ***Raw** vegetables are supposed to be good for you.*
• **uncooked**
OPPOSITE **cooked**
❷ *The factory imports a lot of **raw** materials from abroad.*
• **crude, natural, unprocessed, untreated**
OPPOSITES **manufactured, processed**
❸ *Her knee felt **raw** after she fell off her bike.*
• **red, rough, sore, tender, inflamed**
❹ *There was a **raw** wind blowing from the east.*
• **bitter, cold, chilly, biting, freezing, piercing**

ray *NOUN*
A ray of light shone into the dark cave.
• beam, shaft, stream

reach *VERB*
❶ *They hoped to* ***reach*** *Oxford by lunchtime.*
• arrive at, go as far as, get to, make
❷ *The appeal fund has* ***reached*** *its target.*
• achieve, attain
❸ *I'm not tall enough to* ***reach*** *the top shelf.*
• get hold of, grasp, touch
➤ **to reach out**
Reach out your hands.
• extend, hold out, put out, stick out, stretch out

reach *NOUN*
❶ *The shelf was just within his* ***reach****.*
• grasp
❷ *The shops are within easy* ***reach****.*
• distance, range

react *VERB*
How did he ***react*** *when he read the letter?*
• respond, behave, answer, reply

reaction *NOUN*
What was her ***reaction*** *when you said you were sorry?*
• response, answer, reply

read *VERB* **reads, reading, read**
They couldn't ***read*** *the doctor's handwriting.*
• make out, understand, decipher
To read through something very quickly is to **skim through** it.
To read here and there in a book is to **dip into** it.
To read something intently is to **pore over** it.

readily *ADVERB*
❶ *My friends* ***readily*** *agreed to help.*
• willingly, gladly, happily, eagerly
❷ *The recipe uses ingredients which are* ***readily*** *available.*
• easily, conveniently, quickly

ready *ADJECTIVE*
❶ *When will tea be* ***ready****?*
• prepared, set, done, available, in place
OPPOSITE not ready
❷ *He's always* ***ready*** *to help.*
• willing, glad, pleased, happy, keen, eager
OPPOSITE reluctant
❸ *She's always got a* ***ready*** *reply.*
• quick, prompt, immediate
OPPOSITE slow

real *ADJECTIVE*
❶ *History is about* ***real*** *events.*
• actual, true, factual, verifiable
OPPOSITES fictitious, imaginary
❷ *The necklace was made from* ***real*** *rubies.*
• authentic, genuine, bona fide, natural
OPPOSITES artificial, fake
❸ *She doesn't often show her* ***real*** *feelings.*
• true, honest, sincere, genuine, heartfelt
OPPOSITE insincere

realise *VERB*
It took him a long time to ***realise*** *what she meant.*
• understand, appreciate, grasp, comprehend, recognise, see
(informal) catch on to, tumble to, twig

realistic *ADJECTIVE*
❶ *The portrait of the artist is very* ***realistic****.*
• lifelike, true to life, faithful, convincing, recognisable
❷ *It's not* ***realistic*** *to expect a puppy to be quiet.*
• feasible, practical, sensible, possible, workable
OPPOSITE unrealistic

reality *NOUN*
Stop daydreaming and face ***reality****.*
• the facts, the real world, the truth

really *ADVERB*
❶ *Are you* ***really*** *going to Peru?*
• actually, definitely, truly, in fact, certainly, genuinely, honestly
❷ *I saw a* ***really*** *good film last night.*
• very, extremely, exceptionally

A B C D E F G H I J K L M N O P Q R S T U V W X Y Z

realm *NOUN*
*The king ruled the **realm** for fifty years.*
• **country, kingdom, domain, empire**

rear *ADJECTIVE*
*They found seats in the **rear** coach of the train.*
• **back, end, last**
The rear legs of an animal are its **hind** legs.
OPPOSITE **front**

rear *NOUN*
*The buffet car is at the **rear** of the train.*
• **back, end, tail end**
The rear of a ship is the **stern**.

rear *VERB*
❶ *The couple have **reared** three children.*
• **bring up, raise, nurture**
❷ *The deer **reared** their heads when they caught his scent.*
• **hold up, lift, raise**

reason *NOUN*
❶ *What was the **reason** for the delay?*
• **cause, grounds, explanation, motive, justification, excuse**
❷ *It was clear that the poor woman had lost her **reason**.*
• **mind, sanity, senses, wits**
❸ *They tried to make him see **reason**.*
• **sense, common sense, logic**

reason *VERB*
➤ **to reason with someone**
*We tried to **reason with** him, but he wouldn't change his mind.*
• **argue with, persuade, talk round**

reasonable *ADJECTIVE*
❶ *That seems like a **reasonable** plan.*
• **sensible, intelligent, rational, logical, sane, sound**
OPPOSITE **irrational**
❷ *They bought the house for a **reasonable** price.*
• **fair, acceptable, average, moderate, respectable, normal, proper**
OPPOSITE **excessive**

reassure *VERB*
*The doctor **reassured** her that the wound was not serious.*
• **calm, comfort, encourage, hearten, give confidence to**
OPPOSITE **threaten**

rebel *VERB*
*The king feared that the people would **rebel**.*
• **revolt, rise up**
To rebel against the captain of a ship is to **mutiny** and someone who does this is a **mutineer**.
OPPOSITE **obey**

rebellion *NOUN*
*The protest soon became a widespread **rebellion**.*
• **revolt, revolution, uprising, resistance**
A rebellion on a ship is a **mutiny**.

rebound *VERB*
*The ball **rebounded** off the wall.*
• **bounce back, spring back**
If a bullet rebounds off a surface, it **ricochets**.

recall *VERB*
*Try to **recall** what happened.*
• **remember, recollect, think back to**

recede *VERB*
*When the rain stopped, the flood **receded**.*
• **go back, retreat, decline, subside, ebb**

receive *VERB*
❶ *The captain went up to **receive** the winners' cup.*
• **collect, take, accept, be given**
OPPOSITES **give, present**
❷ *Some passengers **received** minor injuries.*
• **experience, suffer, undergo, sustain**
OPPOSITE **inflict**
❸ *We went to the front door to **receive** our visitors.*
• **greet, meet, welcome**

recent *ADJECTIVE*
*We watch the news to keep up with **recent** events.*
• current, up-to-date, contemporary, new, the latest, fresh

reception *NOUN*
❶ *The home crowd gave the team a friendly **reception**.*
• greeting, welcome
❷ *Who are they inviting to the wedding **reception**?*
• party, gathering, celebration, function *(informal)* do

recipe *NOUN*
*I followed my granny's **recipe** for making apple pie.*
• directions, instructions
The items you use for a recipe are the **ingredients**.

recital *NOUN*
*There will be a short **recital** of piano music at noon.*
• concert, performance

recite *VERB*
*Zoe **recited** a poem she had written.*
• say aloud, read out, narrate

reckless *ADJECTIVE*
*A man has been charged with **reckless** driving.*
• careless, irresponsible, mindless, thoughtless, negligent, foolhardy, rash, wild
OPPOSITE careful

reckon *VERB*
❶ *I tried to **reckon** how much she owed me.*
• calculate, work out, add up, figure out, assess, estimate
❷ *Do you **reckon** it's going to rain?*
• think, believe, guess, imagine, feel

recline *VERB*
*Paula **reclined** lazily on the sofa.*
• lean back, lie, lounge, rest, stretch out, sprawl, loll

recognise *VERB*
❶ *I didn't **recognise** her with her new haircut.*
• identify, know, distinguish, make out, recall, recollect, remember
❷ *He refused to **recognise** that he was to blame.*
• acknowledge, admit, accept, grant, concede, confess, realise

recoil *VERB*
*Chloe **recoiled** as a spider scuttled towards her.*
• draw back, flinch, quail, wince, shrink back

recollect *VERB*
❶ *Do you **recollect** what happened?*
• remember, recall, have a memory of
❷ *The two friends sat for hours **recollecting** the past.*
• reminisce about, think back to, cast your mind back to
OPPOSITE forget

recommend *VERB*
❶ *The doctor **recommended** complete rest.*
• advise, counsel, propose, suggest, advocate, prescribe, urge
❷ *The restaurant was **recommended** by a friend of mine.*
• approve of, endorse, praise, commend

record *NOUN*
*The zookeepers keep a **record** of the animals' diet.*
• account, report
A record of daily events is a **diary** or **journal**.
The record of a voyage at sea or in space is the **log**.
The record of what happened at a meeting is the **minutes**.
A record of people's names is a **register**.
Records consisting of historical documents are **archives**.

record *VERB*
❶ *The concert is being **recorded** by the BBC.*
• tape, video, film
❷ *She **recorded** our interview in a notebook.*
• write down, note, set down, put down, enter

A B C D E F G H I J K L M N O P Q R S T U V W X Y Z

recover *VERB*
❶ *It took a long time to **recover** after my illness.*
• get better, heal, improve, recuperate, pick up, mend, come round, pull through, revive, rally
❷ *The police have **recovered** the stolen vehicles.*
• get back, retrieve, reclaim, repossess, find, trace

recovery *NOUN*
*The doctors were surprised at her speedy **recovery**.*
• healing, cure, revival, recuperation, convalescence

recreation *NOUN*
*What do you do for **recreation** around here?*
• fun, enjoyment, pleasure, relaxation, leisure, amusement, diversion, entertainment, play
A particular activity you do as recreation is a **hobby** or **pastime**.

recruit *NOUN*
*The police **recruits** were very inexperienced.*
• beginner, learner, novice
A recruit learning a trade is an **apprentice** or **trainee**.
A recruit training to be in the armed services is a **cadet**.

recruit *VERB*
*The book club has **recruited** two new members.*
• bring in, take on, attract, enrol
To be recruited into the armed services is to **enlist** or **sign up**.

rectangle *NOUN*
• oblong

recur *VERB*
*Go to the doctor if the symptoms **recur**.*
• happen again, come again, reappear, return

recycle *VERB*
*You can **recycle** glass by putting it in the bottle bank.*
• reuse, reprocess, salvage, use again

red *ADJECTIVE, NOUN*
❶ *I chose a **red** ribbon for my doll.*
Something which is rather red is **reddish**.
A common simile is **as red as a beetroot**.
❷ *My nose and cheeks were **red** with cold.*
• flushed, glowing, rosy, ruddy, blushing
❸ *Her eyes were **red** from lack of sleep.*
• bloodshot, inflamed, red-rimmed
❹ *The fairy queen had flaming **red** hair.*
• ginger, auburn, coppery
(informal) carroty

WORD WEB

SOME SHADES OF RED:

• brick red, cherry, crimson, maroon, pillar-box red, pink, rose, ruby, scarlet, vermilion

reduce *VERB*
*She's **reduced** the amount of sugar in her diet.*
• decrease, lessen, lower, cut, cut back, slash
To reduce something by half is to **halve** it.
To reduce the width of something is to **narrow** it.
To reduce the length of something is to **shorten** or **trim** it.
To reduce speed is to **decelerate**.
To reduce the strength of a liquid is to **dilute** it.
OPPOSITE increase

reel *NOUN*
*I bought a **reel** of white cotton thread.*
• spool

reel *VERB*
❶ *The blow made his head **reel**.*
• spin, whirl
❷ *The injured man **reeled** as if he was drunk.*
• stagger, stumble, sway, rock, totter, lurch, roll
➤ **to reel off**
*The chef **reeled off** a long list of ingredients.*
• recite, rattle off, fire off

refer *VERB*
*The shop assistant **referred** me to another department.*
• hand over, pass on, direct, send

➤ **to refer to**
❶ *Please don't **refer to** this matter again.*
• **mention, speak of, make reference to, allude to, bring up**
❷ *If you can't spell a word, **refer to** a dictionary.*
• **look up, consult, go to, turn to**

referee *NOUN*
*The **referee** blew his whistle.*
• **umpire, adjudicator**
(informal) **ref**
A person who helps the referee in football is a **linesman** or **touch judge**.

refill *VERB*
*The waiter **refilled** our glasses of water.*
• **top up**
To refill a fuel tank is to **refuel**.

reflect *VERB*
❶ *Catseyes™ **reflect** the light from car headlights.*
• **send back, throw back, shine back**
❷ *Their success **reflects** their hard work.*
• **show, indicate, demonstrate, exhibit, reveal**
➤ **to reflect on**
*We need time to **reflect on** what to do next.*
• **think about, contemplate, consider, ponder, mull over**

reflection *NOUN*
❶ *Gus could see his **reflection** in the pond.*
• **image, likeness**
❷ *Their success is a **reflection** of their hard work.*
• **indication, demonstration, evidence, result**
❸ *We need more time for **reflection**.*
• **thinking, contemplation, meditation**

reform *NOUN*
*They're making **reforms** to the school curriculum.*
• **change, improvement, modification, amendment**

refrain *VERB*
➤ **to refrain from**
*Please **refrain from** talking in the library.*
• **avoid, abstain from, stop**
(informal) **leave off, quit**

refresh *VERB*
❶ *They **refreshed** themselves with a glass of lemonade.*
• **cool, freshen, revive, restore, invigorate, stimulate**
❷ *Let me **refresh** your memory.*
• **jog, prompt, prod**

refreshing *ADJECTIVE*
*We went for a **refreshing** dip in the pool.*
• **reviving, invigorating, restorative, bracing, stimulating**

refuge *NOUN*
❶ *The climbers looked for **refuge** from the blizzard.*
• **shelter, cover, protection, safety**
❷ *The outlaws stayed hidden in their mountain **refuge**.*
• **hideaway, hideout, retreat, haven, sanctuary**

refund *VERB*
*She asked them to **refund** her money.*
• **give back, pay back, repay, return**

refuse *VERB*
❶ *Why did you **refuse** my offer of help?*
• **decline, reject, turn down, say no to**
OPPOSITE **accept**
❷ *They were **refused** permission to enter the building.*
• **deny, deprive of**
OPPOSITES **give, allow**

refuse *NOUN*
*The **refuse** was taken to the local tip.*
• **rubbish, garbage, trash, waste, litter, junk**

regain *VERB*
*The patient began to **regain** consciousness.*
• **get back, get back to, return to**

regard *VERB*
❶ *Do you still **regard** him as your friend?*
• **think of, consider, judge, value**
❷ *The cat **regarded** us curiously.*
• **look at, gaze at, stare at, eye, view, scrutinise, watch**

regarding *PREPOSITION*
I must speak with you ***regarding*** *a private matter.*
• **about, concerning, on the subject of, with reference to, with regard to**

region *NOUN*
❶ *The Arctic and Antarctic are polar* ***regions****.*
• **area, place, land, territory, part of the world**
❷ *There are two local radio stations serving this* ***region****.*
• **area, district, neighbourhood, locality, vicinity, zone**

register *VERB*
❶ *The parents* ***registered*** *the birth of their child.*
• **record, set down, write down**
❷ *The thermometer* ***registered*** *a very high temperature.*
• **show, indicate, display, read**

regret *VERB*
She ***regretted*** *her decision to leave Ireland.*
• **be sorry for, repent, feel sad about**

regular *ADJECTIVE*
❶ *Signs are placed at* ***regular*** *intervals along the cycle path.*
• **evenly spaced, fixed**
OPPOSITES **irregular, uneven**
❷ *The drummer kept up a* ***regular*** *rhythm.*
• **constant, consistent, steady, uniform, unvarying**
A common simile is **as regular as clockwork.**
OPPOSITE **erratic**
❸ *Is this your* ***regular*** *route to school?*
• **normal, usual, customary, habitual, ordinary, routine**
OPPOSITE **unusual**
❹ *Craig is a* ***regular*** *customer at the sweet shop.*
• **frequent, familiar, persistent**
OPPOSITES **rare, unusual**

regulate *VERB*
❶ *Just turn the knob to* ***regulate*** *the volume.*
• **control, set, adjust, alter, change, moderate**
❷ *The new roundabout is meant to* ***regulate*** *the traffic.*
• **control, manage, direct, govern, monitor**

regulation *NOUN*
There are new ***regulations*** *on school uniform.*
• **rule, law, order, decree, requirement**

rehearsal *NOUN*
The actors had to learn their words before the ***rehearsal****.*
• **practice, preparation**
(informal) **try-out**
A final rehearsal in which actors wear their costumes is a **dress rehearsal.**

rehearse *VERB*
We had to ***rehearse*** *the scene all over again.*
• **go over, practise, try out**

reign *VERB*
Which British monarch ***reigned*** *the longest?*
• **be king** or **queen, be on the throne, govern, rule**

reject *VERB*
❶ *At first, she* ***rejected*** *their offer of help.*
• **decline, refuse, turn down, say no to**
OPPOSITE **accept**
❷ *As we picked the berries, we* ***rejected*** *any bad ones.*
• **discard, get rid of, throw out, scrap**

rejoice *VERB*
The people ***rejoiced*** *when the wicked queen died.*
• **celebrate, delight, be happy, exult**
OPPOSITE **grieve**

relate *VERB*
❶ *Do you think the two crimes are* ***related****?*
• **connect, link, associate**
❷ *The travellers* ***related*** *the story of their adventures.*
• **tell, narrate, report, describe**

➤ **relate to**
The letter ***relates to*** *your great-grandfather.*
• be about, refer to, have to do with, concern

relation *NOUN*
❶ *The stolen car has no* ***relation*** *to the robbery.*
• connection, link, association, bond
❷ *Are you a* ***relation*** *of hers?*
• relative, member of the family, kinsman or kinswoman
for members of a family see **family**

relationship *NOUN*
❶ *There is a* ***relationship*** *between your diet and health.*
• connection, link, association, bond
The relationship between two numbers is a **ratio**.
❷ *The twins have a close* ***relationship.***
• friendship, attachment, understanding

relative *NOUN*
see **relation**

relax *VERB*
❶ *I like to* ***relax*** *by listening to music.*
• unwind, rest, take it easy
❷ *This exercise will* ***relax*** *your shoulder muscles.*
• loosen, ease
OPPOSITE tighten
❸ *He* ***relaxed*** *his hold on the dog's leash.*
• slacken, loosen, ease, lessen, reduce
OPPOSITE tighten

relaxed *ADJECTIVE*
They liked the ***relaxed*** *atmosphere of village life.*
• informal, casual, carefree, leisurely, easy-going, peaceful, restful, unhurried, calm
(informal) laid-back
OPPOSITES tense, stressful

release *VERB*
❶ *The prisoners were* ***released*** *early.*
• free, let go, discharge, liberate, set free
To release slaves is to **emancipate** them.
OPPOSITE imprison
❷ *The dog was tied up—who* ***released*** *him?*
• let loose, set loose, unfasten, unleash, untie
❸ *The band will* ***release*** *their new album in April.*
• issue, publish, put out

relent *VERB*
Her parents ***relented*** *and let her stay up late.*
• give in, give way, yield, soften, weaken

relentless *ADJECTIVE*
The footballer faced ***relentless*** *questions from the press.*
• constant, continuous, incessant, perpetual, persistent, never-ending, unrelenting, remorseless, ruthless

relevant *ADJECTIVE*
❶ *The detective noted everything that was* ***relevant*** *to the case.*
• applicable, pertinent, appropriate, suitable, significant, related, connected
❷ *Don't interrupt unless your comments are* ***relevant.***
• to the point, pertinent
OPPOSITE irrelevant

reliable *ADJECTIVE*
❶ *The king summoned his most* ***reliable*** *knights.*
• faithful, dependable, trustworthy, loyal, constant, devoted, staunch, true
❷ *The secret agent always sent* ***reliable*** *information.*
• dependable, valid, trustworthy, safe, sound, steady, sure
OPPOSITE unreliable

relief *NOUN*
❶ *The pills gave some* ***relief*** *from the pain.*
• comfort, ease, help, release
❷ *I watched a film for some light* ***relief*** *after work.*
• relaxation, rest

A B C D E F G H I J K L M N O P Q R S T U V W X Y Z

relieve *VERB*

❶ *The doctor said the pills would **relieve** the pain.*
• ease, help, lessen, diminish, relax, soothe, comfort
❷ *We played cards to **relieve** the boredom of waiting.*
• reduce, lighten, dispel, counteract
OPPOSITE intensify

religion *NOUN*

*People from all **religions** went to the service.*
• faith, belief, creed, denomination, sect

WORD WEB

MAJOR WORLD RELIGIONS:

• Buddhism, Christianity, Hinduism, Islam, Judaism, Shintoism, Sikhism, Taoism, Zen

MAJOR RELIGIOUS FESTIVALS:

• Buddhist: Buddha Day, Nirvana Day
• Christian: Lent, Easter, Christmas Day
• Hindu: Holi, Diwali
• Muslim: Ramadan, Eid
• Jewish: Passover, Rosh Hashanah, Yom Kippur, Hanukkah
• Sikh: Baisakhi, Birth of Guru Nanak

The study of religion is **divinity** or **theology**.
for religious leaders see **priest**

religious *ADJECTIVE*

❶ *The choir sang a selection of **religious** music.*
• sacred, holy, divine
OPPOSITE secular
❷ *My grandparents were very **religious**.*
• devout, pious, reverent, spiritual, godly
OPPOSITE ungodly

relish *VERB*

*He would **relish** the chance to appear on television.*
• enjoy, delight in, appreciate

reluctant *ADJECTIVE*

*The old woman was **reluctant** to open the door.*
• unwilling, hesitant, slow, grudging, loth, half-hearted, resistant
OPPOSITE eager

rely *VERB*

*Are you sure that we can **rely** on their help?*
• depend on, count on, have confidence in, trust
(informal) bank on

remain *VERB*

❶ *The boys were told to **remain** behind after school.*
• stay, wait, linger
(informal) hang about
❷ *It will **remain** warm and sunny all weekend.*
• continue, persist, keep on, carry on
❸ *Little **remained** of the house after the fire.*
• be left, survive

remainder *NOUN*

*We played games for the **remainder** of the afternoon.*
• rest, what is left, surplus, remains

remains *PLURAL NOUN*

*They cleared away the **remains** of the picnic.*
• remnants, leftovers, fragments, traces, scraps, debris

The remains at the bottom of a cup are the **dregs**.
Remains still standing after a building has collapsed are **ruins**.
Historic remains are **relics**.

remark *VERB*

*He **remarked** that it was a nice day.*
• say, state, comment, note, declare, mention, observe
see also **say**

remark *NOUN*

*They exchanged a few **remarks** about the weather.*
• comment, observation, word, statement, thought, mention

remarkable *ADJECTIVE*
❶ *He described his **remarkable** escape from the island.*
• **amazing, extraordinary, astonishing, memorable, wonderful, incredible, unforgettable, breathtaking**
❷ *The young violinist shows **remarkable** skill for her age.*
• **exceptional, notable, noteworthy, striking, outstanding, impressive, phenomenal**
OPPOSITE **ordinary**

remedy *NOUN*
❶ *There is no known **remedy** for his illness.*
• **cure, treatment, medicine, therapy, relief**
A remedy to act against a poison is an **antidote**.
❷ *We may have found a **remedy** for the problem.*
• **solution, answer**

remember *VERB*
❶ *Can you **remember** what she looked like?*
• **recall, recollect, recognise, place**
❷ *He was trying to **remember** his lines for the play.*
• **learn, memorise, keep in mind**
OPPOSITE **forget**
❸ *My granny likes to **remember** the old days.*
• **reminisce about, think back to**

remind *VERB*
***Remind** me to buy a newspaper.*
• **prompt, jog your memory**
➤ **to remind you of something**
*What does this tune **remind** you **of**?*
• **make you think of, take you back to**

reminder *NOUN*
❶ *They sent him a **reminder** to pay the bill.*
• **prompt, cue, hint, nudge**
❷ *The photographs are a **reminder** of our holiday.*
• **souvenir, memento**

reminiscent *ADJECTIVE*
➤ **be reminiscent of something**
*The tune is **reminiscent of** an old folk song.*
• **remind you of, make you think of, call to mind**

remnants *PLURAL NOUN*
*They had to clear up the **remnants** of the party.*
• **remains, scraps, traces, fragments, debris, leftovers**

remorse *NOUN*
*He showed no **remorse** for stealing the money.*
• **regret, repentance, guilt, guilty conscience, sorrow, shame**

remote *ADJECTIVE*
❶ *The tour will explore a **remote** part of Brazil.*
• **distant, faraway, isolated, cut-off, inaccessible, out of the way, unfrequented**
OPPOSITE **accessible**
❷ *The chances of us winning are **remote**.*
• **poor, slender, slight, small, faint, doubtful**
OPPOSITE **likely**

remove *VERB*
❶ *Please **remove** your rubbish.*
• **clear away, take away**
❷ *The rowdy passengers were **removed** from the bus.*
• **throw out, turn out, eject, expel** *(informal)* **kick out**
To remove people from a house where they are living is to **evict** them.
To remove a monarch from the throne is to **depose** him or her.
❸ *The author decided to **remove** the last paragraph.*
• **cut out, delete, erase, get rid of, do away with, eliminate**
❹ *The dentist **removed** my bad tooth.*
• **extract, pull out, take out, withdraw**
❺ *The divers slowly **removed** their wetsuits.*
• **take off, peel off, strip off, shed, cast off**

a b c d e f g h i j k l m n o p q r s t u v w x y z

A B C D E F G H I J K L M N O P Q R S T U V W X Y Z

render *VERB*
❶ *The shock **rendered** her speechless.*
• make, leave, cause to be
❷ *Many volunteers **rendered** their assistance.*
• give, provide, offer, furnish, supply

renew *VERB*
❶ *The church roof has been completely **renewed**.*
• repair, renovate, restore, replace, rebuild, reconstruct, revamp, refurbish, overhaul (*informal*) do up
❷ *We stopped for a cup of tea to **renew** our energy.*
• refresh, revive, restore, replenish, revitalise
❸ *You must **renew** your passport before you go abroad.*
• bring up to date, update

rent *VERB*
*We **rented** a couple of bikes to tour the Lake District.*
• hire, charter, lease

repair *VERB*
*It took them a week to **repair** the damaged car.*
• mend, fix, put right, patch up

repay *VERB* **repays, repaying, repaid**
❶ *I can **repay** you the money next week.*
• pay back, refund
❷ *How can we ever **repay** your kindness?*
• return, reciprocate

repeat *VERB*
❶ *The parrot **repeated** everything he said.*
• say again, copy, duplicate, reproduce, echo
❷ *The actors had to **repeat** the opening scene.*
• do again, redo

repeatedly *ADVERB*
*We warned them **repeatedly** about the danger.*
• again and again, over and over, regularly, time after time, frequently, often

repel *VERB*
❶ *The humans managed to **repel** the Martian invasion.*
• drive back, beat back, push back, fend off, resist
❷ *This spray will **repel** wasps and other insects.*
• keep away, scare off, deter, ward off
❸ *They were **repelled** by the smell of the dragon's lair.*
• disgust, revolt, sicken, offend (*informal*) turn you off

repellent *ADJECTIVE*
*The princess found the ogre quite **repellent**.*
• disgusting, repulsive, revolting, hideous, horrible, loathsome, objectionable, foul, offensive, vile
OPPOSITE attractive

replace *VERB*
❶ *The spy carefully **replaced** the missing document.*
• put back, return, restore, reinstate
❷ *Who will **replace** the head teacher when she retires?*
• follow, succeed, take over from, take the place of
❸ *I need to **replace** one of the tyres on my bike.*
• change, renew

replacement *NOUN*
*They found a **replacement** for the injured player.*
• substitute, standby, stand-in, reserve
Someone who can take the place of an actor is an **understudy**.

replica *NOUN*
*In the garden, there's a **replica** of a Roman statue.*
• copy, reproduction, duplicate, model, imitation, likeness
An exact copy of a document is a **facsimile**.

reply *NOUN*
*He has received no **replies** to his email.*
• response, answer, reaction, acknowledgement
An angry reply is a **retort**.

reply *VERB*
➤ **to reply to**
*She took a long time to **reply to** my letter.*
• **answer, respond to, give a reply to, react to, acknowledge**

report *VERB*
❶ *The newspapers **reported** what happened.*
• **give an account of, record, state, describe, announce, publish**
❷ *We were told to **report** to reception when we arrived.*
• **present yourself, make yourself known, check in**
❸ *If you cause any damage, I'll **report** you to the police.*
• **complain about, inform on, denounce**

report *NOUN*
❶ *There was a **report** in the paper about the crash.*
• **account, record, story, article, description**
❷ *The deer were startled by the **report** of the gun.*
• **bang, blast, crack, noise**

reporter *NOUN*
*The film star was being interviewed by a TV **reporter**.*
• **journalist, correspondent**

represent *VERB*
❶ *The picture **represents** an ancient legend.*
• **depict, illustrate, portray, picture, show, describe**
❷ *A dove is often said to **represent** peace.*
• **stand for, symbolise**
❸ *He appointed a lawyer to **represent** him.*
• **speak for**

reprimand *VERB*
*He **reprimanded** them for their bad behaviour.*
• **reproach, scold, criticise**
(informal) **tell off, tick off**
OPPOSITE **praise**

reproduce *VERB*
❶ *The robot can **reproduce** a human voice.*
• **copy, duplicate, imitate, simulate, mimic**
❷ *Mice **reproduce** very quickly.*
• **breed, produce offspring, multiply, procreate**
Fish reproduce by **spawning.**
To reproduce plants is to **propagate** them.

reproduction *NOUN*
❶ *Vets have to know about animal **reproduction**.*
• **breeding, procreation**
❷ *Is that an original painting or a **reproduction**?*
• **copy, replica, imitation, likeness, duplicate, print**
A reproduction of something which is intended to deceive people is a **fake** or **forgery.**
An exact reproduction of a document is a **facsimile.**

reptile *NOUN*

WORD WEB

SOME ANIMALS WHICH ARE REPTILES:

• **alligator, chameleon, crocodile, gecko, iguana, lizard, salamander, slow-worm, snake, terrapin, tortoise, turtle**
see also **snake**
A reptile found in myths and legends is a **basilisk.**
for other animals see **animal**

repulsive *ADJECTIVE*
*We were put off eating by the **repulsive** smell.*
• **disgusting, revolting, offensive, repellent, disagreeable, foul, repugnant, obnoxious, sickening, hateful, hideous, horrible, loathsome, objectionable, vile**
OPPOSITE **attractive**

reputation *NOUN*
*The singer's **reputation** spread throughout the world.*
• **fame, celebrity, name, renown, eminence, standing, stature**

a b c d e f g h i j k l m n o p q r s t u v w x y z

request *VERB*
*She has **requested** a transfer to a different job.*
• **ask for, appeal for, apply for, beg for, call for, entreat, implore, invite, pray for, seek**

request *NOUN*
*They have ignored our **request** for help.*
• **appeal, plea, entreaty, call, cry**
A request for a job or membership is an **application.**
A request signed by a lot of people is a **petition.**

require *VERB*
❶ *They **require** a draw to win the championship.*
• **need, must have**
❷ *Visitors are **required** to sign the register.*
• **instruct, oblige, request, direct, order, command**

rescue *VERB*
❶ *A helicopter was sent to **rescue** the trapped climbers.*
• **free, liberate, release, save, set free**
To rescue someone by paying money is to **ransom** them.
❷ *The divers **rescued** some items from the sunken ship.*
• **retrieve, recover, salvage**

resemblance *NOUN*
*It's easy to see the **resemblance** between the two sisters.*
• **likeness, similarity, closeness**
OPPOSITE **difference**

resemble *VERB*
*The twins closely **resemble** their mother.*
• **look like, be similar to**
(informal) **take after**

resent *VERB*
*She **resents** having to work such long hours.*
• **be annoyed about, take exception to, be resentful about, begrudge, grudge**

reservation *NOUN*
❶ *We have a **reservation** for two nights in the hotel.*
• **booking**
❷ *They saw giraffes on the wildlife **reservation.***
• **reserve, park, preserve, sanctuary**
❸ *She had **reservations** about whether the plan would work.*
• **doubt, misgiving, hesitation, qualm**
If you have reservations about something, you are **sceptical** about it.

reserve *VERB*
❶ *The astronauts had to **reserve** fuel for the return voyage.*
• **keep, put aside, set aside, save, preserve, retain, hold back**
❷ *Have you **reserved** your seats on the train?*
• **book, order, secure**

reserve *NOUN*
❶ *The climbers kept a **reserve** of food in their base camp.*
• **stock, store, supply, hoard, stockpile**
A reserve of money is a **fund** or **savings.**
❷ *They put him down as a **reserve** for Saturday's game.*
• **substitute, standby, stand-in, replacement**
Someone who can take the place of an actor is an **understudy.**
❸ *The wildlife **reserve** has a new baby rhino.*
• **reservation, park, preserve, sanctuary**

reserved *ADJECTIVE*
❶ *These seats are **reserved.***
• **booked, set aside, ordered**
❷ *She is too **reserved** to speak up for herself.*
• **shy, timid, quiet, bashful, modest, retiring, reticent**
OPPOSITE **outgoing**

residence *NOUN*
*The palace is the official **residence** of the queen.*
• **dwelling, home, house**
(formal) **abode**

resident *NOUN*
*The **residents** of New York are proud of their city.*
• **citizen, inhabitant, occupant**
A temporary resident in a hotel is a **guest.**
A resident in rented accommodation is a **boarder, lodger** or **tenant.**

resign *VERB*
*The manager of the football team was forced to **resign**.*
• leave, quit, stand down, step down, give in your notice
When a monarch resigns from the throne, he or she **abdicates**.

resist *VERB*
❶ *They were too weak to **resist** the sorcerer's magic.*
• stand up to, defend yourself against, withstand, defy, oppose, fend off
OPPOSITES yield to, surrender to
❷ *I couldn't **resist** having another piece of chocolate.*
• avoid, hold back from, refuse
OPPOSITES give in, accept

resolve *VERB*
❶ *I **resolved** to try harder next time.*
• decide, determine, make up your mind
❷ *They held a meeting to try to **resolve** the dispute.*
• settle, sort out, straighten out, end, overcome

resort *NOUN*
*As a last **resort**, we could always walk.*
• option, choice, course of action

resort *VERB*
*He didn't want to **resort** to violence.*
• start using, turn to, fall back on, rely on, stoop to

resound *VERB*
*The howling of the wolves **resounded** through the forest.*
• echo, boom

resources *PLURAL NOUN*
❶ *The country is rich in natural **resources**.*
• materials, raw materials, reserves
❷ *The library has limited **resources** for buying CDs.*
• funds, money, capital, assets, means, wealth

respect *NOUN*
❶ *Her colleagues have the deepest **respect** for her.*
• admiration, esteem, regard, reverence, honour
❷ *Have some **respect** for other people's feelings.*
• consideration, sympathy, thought, concern
❸ *In some **respects**, he's a better player than I am.*
• way, point, aspect, feature, characteristic, detail, particular

respect *VERB*
❶ *Everyone **respects** her for her courage.*
• admire, esteem, revere, honour, look up to, value
OPPOSITES scorn, despise
❷ *She tried to **respect** the wishes of her dead husband.*
• obey, follow, observe, adhere to, comply with
OPPOSITE ignore

respectable *ADJECTIVE*
❶ *He came from a very **respectable** family.*
• decent, honest, upright, honourable, worthy
❷ *I finished the race in a **respectable** time.*
• reasonable, satisfactory, acceptable, passable, adequate, fair, tolerable

respective *ADJECTIVE*
*We all returned to our **respective** homes.*
• separate, individual, own, particular, personal, specific

respond *VERB*
➤ **to respond to**
*He didn't **respond to** my question.*
• reply to, answer, react to, acknowledge

response *NOUN*
*Did you get a **response** to your letter?*
• reply, answer, reaction, acknowledgement
An angry response is a retort.

responsible *ADJECTIVE*
❶ *Parents are legally **responsible** for their children.*
• in charge
OPPOSITE not responsible
❷ *He's a very **responsible** sort of person.*
• reliable, sensible, trustworthy, dependable, conscientious, dutiful, honest
OPPOSITE irresponsible
❸ *Looking after people's money is a **responsible** job.*
• important, serious
❹ *Who is **responsible** for all this mess?*
• to blame, guilty (of), at fault

rest *NOUN*
❶ *The actors had a short **rest** in the middle of the rehearsal.*
• break, breather, breathing space, pause, respite, lie-down, nap
❷ *The doctor said the patient needed complete **rest**.*
• relaxation, leisure, inactivity, ease, quiet, time off

rest *VERB*
❶ *I think we should stop and **rest** for a while.*
• have a rest, lie down, relax, lounge, have a nap
❷ ***Rest** the ladder against the wall.*
• lean, prop, stand, place, support

rest *NOUN*
➤ **the rest**
*Take a few sweets now, but leave **the rest** for later.*
• the remainder, the surplus, the others, the remains

restaurant *NOUN*

WORD WEB

SOME TYPES OF RESTAURANT:

• buffet, cafe, cafeteria, canteen, chip shop, coffee shop, diner, grill, snack bar, steakhouse, takeaway, tea room
A French-style restaurant is a **bistro**.
A restaurant which serves pizza is a **pizzeria**.

restful *ADJECTIVE*
*We spent a **restful** Sunday morning reading magazines.*
• peaceful, quiet, relaxing, leisurely, calm, tranquil, undisturbed
OPPOSITE stressful

restless *ADJECTIVE*
❶ *The animals became **restless** during the storm.*
• agitated, nervous, anxious, edgy, fidgety, excitable, jumpy
(informal) jittery
OPPOSITE relaxed
❷ *I'm tired—I had a **restless** night.*
• sleepless, troubled, disturbed, unsettled, interrupted
OPPOSITE restful

restore *VERB*
❶ *Please **restore** the book to its proper place on the shelf.*
• put back, replace, return
❷ *They are going to **restore** the Sunday bus service.*
• bring back, reinstate
To restore someone to health is to cure them.
❸ *My uncle loves to **restore** old cars.*
• renew, repair, renovate, fix, mend, rebuild

restrain *VERB*
❶ *Dogs must be **restrained** on a lead in the park.*
• hold back, keep back, keep under control, subdue, repress, restrict
❷ *She tried to **restrain** her anger.*
• control, curb, suppress, stifle

restrict *VERB*
*The new law **restricts** the sale of fireworks.*
• control, limit, regulate
➤ **to restrict to**
*In a safari park, animals are not **restricted to** enclosures.*
• confine to, enclose in, keep in, shut in, imprison in

result *NOUN*

❶ *The water shortage is a **result** of a long drought.*

• **consequence, effect, outcome, sequel, upshot**

The result of a game is the **score**.

The result of a trial is the **verdict**.

❷ *If you multiply 9 by 12, what is the **result**?*

• **answer, product**

result *VERB*

*The bruising on his leg **resulted** from a bad fall.*

• **come about, develop, emerge, happen, occur, follow, ensue, take place, turn out**

➤ **to result in**

*Severe flooding **resulted in** chaos on the roads.*

• **cause, bring about, give rise to, lead to, develop into**

resume *VERB*

*We'll **resume** work after lunch.*

• **restart, start again, recommence, proceed with, continue, carry on**

retain *VERB*

❶ *Please **retain** your ticket.*

• **hold on to, keep, preserve, reserve, save** *(informal)* **hang on to**

OPPOSITE **surrender**

❷ *This type of soil is good at **retaining** water.*

• **hold in, keep in, hold back**

OPPOSITE **release**

retire *VERB*

❶ *The manager plans to **retire** at the end of the season.*

• **give up work, stop working**

To leave your job voluntarily is to **resign**.

❷ *Mrs Doyle **retired** to her room with a headache.*

• **withdraw, adjourn**

retort *VERB*

*'There's no need to be rude!' **retorted** Hannah.*

• **reply, answer, respond, react**

for other ways to say something see **say**

retreat *VERB*

❶ *The army **retreated** to a safe position.*

• **move back, draw back, fall back, withdraw, retire**

To retreat in a shameful way is to **run away** or *(informal)* **turn tail**.

❷ *The snail **retreated** into its shell.*

• **shrink back, recoil**

retrieve *VERB*

*I had to climb the fence to **retrieve** our ball.*

• **get back, bring back, fetch, recover, rescue, salvage**

return *VERB*

❶ *We hope to **return** to Paris next summer.*

• **go back, revisit**

❷ *My husband **returns** on Friday.*

• **get back, come back, come home**

❸ *I **returned** the book to its rightful owner.*

• **give back, restore**

❹ *Faulty goods may be **returned** to the shop.*

• **send back, take back**

❺ *Please **return** the money I lent you.*

• **give back, repay, refund**

❻ *We hoped that the fever would not **return**.*

• **happen again, recur**

return *NOUN*

❶ *She looked forward to her friends' **return**.*

• **reappearance, homecoming**

❷ *Did you get a good **return** from your investment?*

• **profit, interest, gain**

reveal *VERB*

❶ *The spy refused to **reveal** his real identity.*

• **declare, disclose, make known, confess, admit, announce, proclaim, publish, tell**

❷ *She swept aside the curtain to **reveal** a secret door.*

• **uncover, unveil, expose**

OPPOSITE **hide**

revenge *NOUN*
*He sought **revenge** for the killing of his brother.*
• **reprisal, vengeance**
➤ **to take revenge on someone**
*He declared that he would **take revenge on** them all.*
• **get even with, repay**
(informal) **get your own back on**

revere *VERB*
*The painter was greatly **revered** by his fellow artists.*
• **admire, respect, honour, esteem, worship, adore**
OPPOSITE **despise**

reverse *NOUN*
*The letter had a handwritten note on the **reverse**.*
• **other side, back**

reverse *VERB*
❶ *You can use tracing paper to **reverse** a drawing.*
• **turn round, swap round, transpose, invert**
❷ *The driver tried to **reverse** into the parking space.*
• **back, drive backwards, go backwards**

review *NOUN*
❶ *They are carrying out a **review** of after-school clubs.*
• **study, survey, examination, inspection**
❷ *We had to write **reviews** of our favourite books.*
• **report, criticism, appraisal, critique**

review *VERB*
❶ *The judge began to **review** the evidence.*
• **examine, go over, study, survey, consider, assess, appraise, evaluate, weigh up**
❷ *He **reviews** the latest films for the Sunday paper.*
• **criticise, write a review of**

revise *VERB*
❶ *We **revised** the work we did last term.*
• **go over, review, study**
❷ *The new evidence forced me to **revise** my opinion.*
• **change, modify, alter, reconsider, re-examine**
❸ *The last chapter has been **revised** by the author.*
• **correct, amend, edit, rewrite, update**

revive *VERB*
❶ *The patient **revived** slowly after the operation.*
• **come round, come to, recover, rally, wake up**
❷ *A cold drink will **revive** you.*
• **refresh, restore, invigorate, bring back to life, revitalise**

revolt *VERB*
❶ *The people **revolted** against the cruel king.*
• **rebel, riot, rise up**
To revolt on a ship is to **mutiny**.
❷ *They were **revolted** by the stench in the dungeon.*
• **disgust, repel, sicken, nauseate, offend, appal**

revolting *ADJECTIVE*
*What is that **revolting** smell?*
• **disgusting, foul, horrible, nasty, loathsome, offensive, obnoxious, repulsive, repugnant, sickening, nauseating, vile, unpleasant**
OPPOSITES **pleasant, attractive**

revolution *NOUN*
❶ *The **revolution** brought in a new government.*
• **rebellion, revolt, uprising**
❷ *Computers brought about a **revolution** in the way people work.*
• **change, transformation, shift**
❸ *One **revolution** of the earth takes 24 hours.*
• **rotation, turn, circuit, cycle**

revolutionary *ADJECTIVE*
*The inventor had come up with a **revolutionary** design.*
• **new, novel, innovative, radical**

revolve *VERB*
*The earth **revolves** once every 24 hours.*
• **rotate, turn**
To revolve quickly is to **spin** or **whirl**.
To move round something is to **circle** or **orbit** it.

reward *NOUN*
*There is a **reward** for finding the missing cat.*
• **prize, bonus, payment, award, decoration**
OPPOSITE **punishment**

reward *VERB*
❶ *The firefighters were **rewarded** for their bravery.*
• **honour, decorate**
❷ *She was generously **rewarded** for her work.*
• **compensate, pay**

rewarding *ADJECTIVE*
*Being a vet must be a **rewarding** job.*
• **satisfying, pleasing, gratifying, worthwhile**
OPPOSITE **thankless**

rhyme *NOUN*
*The children like listening to nursery **rhymes**.*
• **poem, verse**

rhythm *NOUN*
*We tapped our feet to the **rhythm** of the music.*
• **beat, pulse**
The speed or type of rhythm of a piece of music is the **tempo**.
The type of rhythm of a piece of poetry is its **metre**.

rich *ADJECTIVE*
❶ *They must be **rich** to live in a castle.*
• **wealthy, affluent, prosperous, well-off, well-to-do**
OPPOSITE **poor**
❷ *The palace was full of **rich** furnishings.*
• **expensive, costly, luxurious, sumptuous, opulent, lavish, splendid, ornate**
❸ *The dancer wore a dress of a **rich** red colour.*
• **deep, strong, vivid, intense**
❹ *The soil in this area is very **rich**.*
• **fertile, productive**

riches *PLURAL NOUN*
*They acquired **riches** beyond their wildest dreams.*
• **wealth, money, affluence, prosperity, fortune, treasure**

rickety *ADJECTIVE*
*Take care—that ladder looks **rickety**.*
• **shaky, unsteady, unstable, wobbly, flimsy**
OPPOSITE **solid**

rid *VERB* **rids, ridding, rid**
*The new vaccine may **rid** the world of the disease.*
• **clear, free, empty, strip, purge**
➤ **to get rid of**
*He decided to **get rid of** his old guitar.*
• **dispose of, throw away** or **out, scrap**
(informal) **dump**

riddle *NOUN*
*They had to solve the **riddle** to find the treasure.*
• **puzzle, mystery, question, conundrum, problem**

ride *VERB* **rides, riding, rode, ridden**
*My little brother is learning to **ride** a bike.*
• **control, handle, manage, steer**

ride *NOUN*
*They took us for a **ride** in their new car.*
• **drive, run, journey, trip**
(informal) **spin**

ridicule *VERB*
*The inventor was **ridiculed** for his wacky ideas.*
• **laugh at, make fun of, mock, scoff at, jeer at, sneer at, taunt, tease, deride**

ridiculous *ADJECTIVE*
❶ *My little sister looked **ridiculous** in high-heeled shoes.*
• **silly, stupid, foolish, daft, absurd, funny, laughable**
❷ *That is a **ridiculous** price for a pair of trainers!*
• **ludicrous, senseless, nonsensical, preposterous, outrageous, absurd, unreasonable, crazy**
OPPOSITE **sensible**

A B C D E F G H I J K L M N O P Q R S T U V W X Y Z

right *ADJECTIVE*
❶ *The entrance is on the the **right** side of the building.*
The right side of a ship when you face forwards is the **starboard** side.
OPPOSITE left
❷ *Put up your hand if you got the **right** answer.*
• **correct, accurate, true, exact**
OPPOSITE wrong
❸ *She was waiting for the **right** moment to tell him.*
• **proper, appropriate, fitting, suitable, ideal**
OPPOSITE wrong
❹ *It's not **right** to steal.*
• **fair, honest, decent, just, honourable, lawful, moral, upright, virtuous, ethical**
OPPOSITE wrong

right *ADVERB*
❶ *Turn **right** at the corner.*
OPPOSITE left
❷ *Turn **right** round.*
• **all the way, completely**
❸ *She stood **right** in the middle.*
• **exactly, precisely**
❹ *Go **right** ahead.*
• **directly, straight**

right *NOUN*
❶ *The post office is on the **right** along the High Street.*
OPPOSITE left
❷ *People have the **right** to walk across the common.*
• **freedom, liberty**
❸ *You don't have the **right** to tell me what to do.*
• **authority, power**

rigid *ADJECTIVE*
❶ *The tent was supported by a **rigid** framework.*
• **solid, stiff, firm, hard**
❷ *The referee was **rigid** in applying the rules.*
• **strict, inflexible, harsh, stern, uncompromising**
OPPOSITE flexible

rigorous *ADJECTIVE*
*The detective carried out a **rigorous** investigation.*
• **thorough, careful, meticulous, painstaking**

rim *NOUN*
*Mrs Sharpe peered at us over the **rim** of her glasses.*
• **brim, edge, lip, brink**

ring *NOUN*
❶ *The dancers linked arms in a **ring**.*
• **circle, round, loop, circuit**
❷ *The wooden barrel had metal **rings** round it.*
• **band, hoop**

ring *VERB* **rings, ringing, ringed**
*The ancient city is **ringed** by mountains.*
• **surround, encircle, enclose, circle**

ring *VERB* **rings, ringing, rang, rung**
❶ *The doorbell **rang**.*
• **chime, peal, toll, jangle, tinkle, sound, buzz**
see also **bell**
❷ ***Ring** me tomorrow evening.*
• **phone, call, telephone, ring up**
(informal) **give a buzz**

rinse *VERB*
*After shampooing your hair, **rinse** it in clean water.*
• **wash, clean, bathe, swill**
To rinse out a toilet is to **flush** it.

riot *NOUN*
*The police moved in to stop the **riot**.*
• **commotion, disorder, disturbance, turmoil, uproar, uprising**

riot *VERB*
*The crowds were **rioting** in the streets.*
• **run riot, run wild, run amok, rampage, revolt, rise up, rebel**

rip *VERB*
*She snatched the letter and **ripped** it to pieces.*
• **tear**

ripe *ADJECTIVE*
*Some of the plums on the tree are **ripe** now.*
• **mature, ready to eat**
To become ripe is to **ripen**.

ripple *VERB*
*The wind **rippled** the surface of the pond.*
• **ruffle, stir, disturb, make waves on**

rise *VERB* **rises, rising, rose, risen**
❶ *The kite **rose** high into the air.*
• **climb, mount, fly up, ascend, soar**
When a plane rises into the air, it **takes off**.
When a rocket rises into the air, it **lifts off**.
OPPOSITE **descend**
❷ *The outer wall of the castle **rose** before us.*
• **tower, loom, reach up, stick up**
❸ *House prices **rose** again last year.*
• **go up, increase**
OPPOSITE **fall**
❹ *The audience **rose** and applauded wildly.*
• **stand up, get up**
OPPOSITE **sit**

rise *NOUN*
❶ *There will be a **rise** in temperature over the next few days.*
• **increase, jump**
OPPOSITE **fall**
❷ *At the top of the **rise** they paused for a break.*
• **hill, slope, ascent, incline, bank, ramp**
(Scottish) **brae**

risk *VERB*
❶ *If you place a bet, you **risk** losing the money.*
• **chance, dare, gamble, venture**
❷ *The firefighter **risked** his life to save them.*
• **endanger, put at risk, jeopardise, hazard**

risk *NOUN*
❶ *All outdoor activities carry an element of **risk**.*
• **danger, hazard, peril**
❷ *Starting a business involves **risk**.*
• **a gamble, uncertainty**
❸ *The forecast says there's a **risk** of snow.*
• **chance, likelihood, possibility**

risky *ADJECTIVE*
*Cycling on icy roads is **risky**.*
• **dangerous, hazardous, perilous, unsafe**
OPPOSITE **safe**

ritual *NOUN*
*The temple was used for ancient religious **rituals**.*
• **ceremony, rite, service**

rival *NOUN*
*He has no serious **rival** for the championship.*
• **competitor, adversary, challenger, opponent, contender, contestant**

rival *VERB*
*Few countries can **rival** Scotland for mountainous scenery.*
• **compete with, contend with**

rivalry *NOUN*
*There was fierce **rivalry** between the two local teams.*
• **competition, competitiveness, opposition**
OPPOSITE **cooperation**

river *NOUN*
A small river is a **stream** or **rivulet** or *(Scottish)* **burn**.
A small river which flows into a larger river is a **tributary**.
The place where a river begins is its **source**.
The place where a river goes into the sea is its **mouth**.
A wide river mouth is an **estuary** or *(Scottish)* **firth**.
The place where the mouth of a river splits before going into the sea is a **delta**.
A river of ice is a **glacier**.
This rivulet ... broadens out into salt marshes below the village, and loses itself at last in a lake of brackish water.—MOONFLEET, J. Meade Faulkner

WRITING TIPS

You can use these words to describe a river.

TO DESCRIBE HOW A RIVER FLOWS:

• **cascade, eddy, flood, glide, gush, meander, plunge, run, rush, snake, sweep, swirl, twist, wind**

TO DESCRIBE HOW A RIVER SOUNDS:

• **babble, burble, gurgle, murmur, ripple, roar, splash, thunder**

A B C D E F G H I J K L M N O P Q R S T U V W X Y Z

road *NOUN*

WORD WEB

KINDS OF ROAD:

• **bypass, dual carriageway, highway, main road, motorway, one-way street, ring road, trunk road**
A road which is closed at one end is a **dead end**.
A private road up to a house is a **drive**.

KINDS OF ROAD IN A TOWN:

• **alley, avenue, boulevard, crescent, cul-de-sac, lane, street, terrace**
see also **path**

roam *VERB*
❶ *We **roamed** about town aimlessly.*
• **wander, ramble, drift, stroll, amble, meander**
❷ *Herds of wild deer **roamed** over the hills.*
• **range, rove, prowl**

roar *NOUN, VERB*
*The dragon lifted its mighty head and **roared**.*
• **bellow, cry, yell, bawl, howl, thunder**

rob *VERB*
*The thieves planned to **rob** several banks in the city.*
• **steal from, break into, burgle, hold up, raid, loot, ransack, rifle**

robber *NOUN*
see **thief**

robbery *NOUN*
see **stealing**

robe *NOUN*
A kind of robe you might wear in your bedroom is a **dressing gown** or **bathrobe**.
Robes worn by a priest are **vestments**.
The robe worn by a monk or nun is a **habit**.
A robe an official might wear at a ceremony is a **gown**.
Robe is also a formal word for a woman's **dress**.

robot *NOUN*
*The **robot** spoke in a flat, metallic voice.*
• **automaton, android**
A robot which is part-human is a **cyborg**.
A word meaning 'to do with robots' is **robotic**.
The study and design of robots is **robotics**.

WORD WEB

PARTS A ROBOT MIGHT HAVE:

• **antenna, buttons, computer brain** or **chip, control panel, flashing lights, arm** or **limb, gripper, laser, motor, sensor, wheels**

SOME WAYS TO DESCRIBE A ROBOT:

• **bionic, intelligent, machine-like, mechanical, metallic, superhuman**

robust *ADJECTIVE*
❶ *To be an explorer, you must be **robust**.*
• **strong, vigorous, fit, hardy, healthy, rugged**
OPPOSITE **weak**
❷ *I bought a **robust** pair of boots for hiking.*
• **sturdy, tough, durable, hard-wearing**
OPPOSITE **flimsy**

rock *NOUN*
*We clambered over the **rocks** on the seashore.*
• **boulder, stone**

WORD WEB

A small rock is a **pebble**.
A steep face of rock is a **cliff** or **crag**.

SOME KINDS OF ROCK:

• **basalt, chalk, flint, granite, gypsum, lava, limestone, marble, quartz, sandstone, shale, slate**
Rock from which metal or valuable minerals can be extracted is **ore**.
A layer of rock is a **stratum**.
A person who studies rocks is a **geologist**.

rock *VERB*
❶ *I **rocked** the baby's cradle to and fro.*
• **sway, swing**
❷ *The ship **rocked** in the storm.*
• **roll, toss, lurch, pitch, tilt, reel**

rocky *ADJECTIVE*
❶ *Nothing was growing in the **rocky** ground.*
• **barren, stony, pebbly**
❷ *Take care—that chair's a bit **rocky**.*
• **rickety, shaky, unsteady, unstable, wobbly**

rod *NOUN*
*The framework is held together by steel **rods**.*
• **bar, rail, pole, strut, shaft, stick, spoke, staff**

rode *past tense see* **ride**

rodent *NOUN*
for various kinds of animal see **animal**

rogue *NOUN*
*Don't trust him—he's a **rogue**.*
• **rascal, scoundrel, villain, cheat, fraud, swindler, charlatan**

role *NOUN*
❶ *Who is playing the lead **role** in the play?*
• **character, part**
❷ *Each player has an important **role** in the team.*
• **job, task, function, position**

roll *VERB*
❶ *The wheels of the carriage began to **roll**.*
• **move round, turn, revolve, rotate, spin, twirl, whirl**
❷ ***Roll** the paper around your finger.*
• **curl, wind, wrap, twist, coil**
To roll up a sail on a yacht is to **furl** it.
❸ ***Roll** the pastry into a large circle.*
• **flatten, level out, smooth**
❹ *The ship **rolled** about in the storm.*
• **pitch, rock, sway, toss, wallow, lurch**

romantic *ADJECTIVE*
❶ *The film had a very **romantic** ending.*
• **sentimental, emotional, tender**
(informal) **soppy, mushy**
❷ *The life of an explorer sounds very **romantic**.*
• **exotic, glamorous, exciting**

romp *VERB*
*The children **romped** around the playground.*
• **leap about, run about, skip about, caper, frisk, frolic**

roof *NOUN*
The sloping beams in the framework of a roof are **rafters**.
The overhanging edge of a roof is the **eaves**.
A building without a roof is an **open-air building**.
A vehicle without a roof is an **open-top vehicle**.

room *NOUN*
❶ *How many **rooms** are there in your house?*
An old word for room is **chamber**.
❷ *Is there **room** in the car for another suitcase?*
• **space, capacity**

WORD WEB

ROOMS YOU MIGHT FIND IN A HOUSE OR FLAT:

• **bathroom, bedroom, box room, conservatory, dining room, drawing room, hall, kitchen** or **kitchenette, living room, lounge, nursery, pantry, parlour, sitting room, spare room** or **guest room, study, toilet** or **lavatory** or *(informal)* **loo, utility room**

ROOMS YOU MIGHT FIND IN A SCHOOL:

• **assembly hall, classroom, cloakroom, corridor, drama room, laboratory, library, music room, office, sickroom, staffroom, storeroom, toilets** or **lavatories** or *(informal)* **loos**
A small room in a monastery or prison is a **cell**.
An underground room is a **basement** or **cellar**. In a church it is a **vault**.

The space in the roof of a house is the **attic** or **loft**.
A room where an artist works is a **studio**.
A room where you wait to see a doctor or dentist is a **waiting room**.
A room in a boarding school where pupils sleep is a **dormitory**.
A room in a hospital for patients is a **ward**.

roomy *ADJECTIVE*
*The flat is surprisingly **roomy** inside.*
• **big, large, spacious, sizeable**

root *NOUN*
*We need to get to the **root** of the problem.*
• **origin, source, cause, basis, starting point**

rope *NOUN*
*The sailors threw a **rope** to the men in the water.*
• **cable, cord, line**
The ropes that support a ship's mast and sails are the **rigging**.
A rope with a loop at one end used for catching cattle is a **lasso**.

rose *past tense see* **rise**

rot *VERB*
*The wooden fence had begun to **rot**.*
• **decay, decompose, become rotten, crumble, disintegrate**
If metal rots it is said to **corrode**.
If rubber rots it is said to **perish**.
If food rots it is said to **go bad** or **putrefy**.

rotate *VERB*
*The globe **rotates** on its axis.*
• **revolve, turn, spin, pivot, wheel, swivel, twirl, twist, whirl**

rotten *ADJECTIVE*
❶ *The window frame is **rotten**.*
• **decayed, decaying, decomposed, crumbling, disintegrating**
Rotten metal is **corroded** or **rusty** metal.
OPPOSITE **sound**
❷ *The fridge smelled of **rotten** eggs.*
• **bad, mouldy, mouldering, foul, putrid, smelly**
OPPOSITE **fresh**
❸ *(informal) The weather has been **rotten** all week.*
• **bad, unpleasant, disagreeable, awful, abysmal, dreadful, nasty**
(informal) **lousy**
OPPOSITE **good**

rough *ADJECTIVE*
❶ *A **rough** track led to the farm.*
• **bumpy, uneven, irregular, rocky, stony, rugged, craggy, jagged**
OPPOSITES **even, smooth**
❷ *The sea was **rough** and the boat lurched from side to side.*
• **stormy, turbulent, heaving**
If the sea is rough with small waves it is said to be **choppy**.
OPPOSITE **calm**
❸ *The woman wore a **rough** woollen cloak.*
• **coarse, harsh, scratchy, bristly**
OPPOSITE **soft**
❹ *The prisoners had suffered **rough** treatment.*
• **harsh, severe, cruel, hard, tough, violent**
OPPOSITES **gentle, mild**
❺ *I had only a **rough** idea of where we were.*
• **approximate, vague, inexact, imprecise, hazy**
OPPOSITE **exact**
❻ *Our guide made a **rough** sketch of the route.*
• **quick, hasty, crude, basic**
OPPOSITES **detailed, careful**

roughly *ADVERB*
*The cinema can seat **roughly** a hundred people.*
• **approximately, about, around, close to, nearly**

round *ADJECTIVE*
*Holly bushes have small **round** berries.*
• **rounded, spherical**
A flat round shape is **circular**.

round *NOUN*
*Our team got through to the second **round** of the competition.*
• **stage, heat, bout, contest, game**

round *VERB*
*The motorbike **rounded** the corner at top speed.*
• go round, travel round, turn
➤ **to round something off**
*They **rounded** the evening **off** with some songs.*
• bring to an end, conclude, end, finish, complete
➤ **to round up people** or **things**
*The captain **rounded up** his players.*
• assemble, gather, bring together, collect, muster, rally

roundabout *ADJECTIVE*
*We went by a **roundabout** route to avoid the traffic.*
• indirect, circuitous, long, winding, twisting
OPPOSITE direct

rouse *VERB*
❶ *We were **roused** by the sound of birds singing.*
• arouse, awaken, call, wake up
❷ *He was a quiet man, not easily **roused** to anger.*
• provoke, agitate, excite, stimulate, stir up

route *NOUN*
*We drove home by the quickest **route**.*
• path, road, way, course, direction, journey

routine *NOUN*
❶ *Brushing my teeth is part of my morning **routine**.*
• pattern, procedure, way, custom, habit, practice, order
❷ *The ice-skaters practised their new **routine**.*
• act, programme, performance, number

row *NOUN (rhymes with* **go***)*
*The gardener planted the vegetables in **rows**.*
• column, line, string, series, sequence
A row of people waiting for something is a **queue**.
A row of people walking behind each other is a **file**.
A row of soldiers standing side by side on parade is a **rank**.

row *NOUN (rhymes with* **cow***)*
❶ *The class next door was making a terrible **row**.*
• noise, racket, din, commotion, disturbance, uproar, rumpus
❷ *One of the pirates had a **row** with the captain.*
• argument, fight, quarrel, squabble, disagreement, dispute

rowdy *ADJECTIVE*
*Later in the evening, the party became **rowdy**.*
• noisy, unruly, wild, disorderly, boisterous, riotous
OPPOSITE quiet

royalty *NOUN*

WORD WEB

SOME MEMBERS OF A ROYAL FAMILY:

• king, monarch, prince, princess, queen, sovereign
The husband or wife of a royal person is a **consort**.
The way to address a king or queen is **Your Majesty**.
The way to address a prince or princess is **Your Highness**.
see also **ruler**

rub *VERB*
❶ *Kathy **rubbed** her sore elbow.*
• stroke, knead, massage
❷ *I **rubbed** some suncream on my arms.*
• spread, smooth, smear, apply (to)
❸ *These boots are **rubbing** against my ankles.*
• graze, scrape, chafe
❹ *She **rubbed** the mirror until it gleamed.*
• polish, wipe, shine, buff
➤ **to rub something out**
*Can you **rub out** those pencil marks?*
• erase, wipe out, delete, remove

A B C D E F G H I J K L M N O P Q R S T U V W X Y Z

rubbish *NOUN*
❶ *Mike took the **rubbish** out to the bin.*
• refuse, waste, trash, garbage, junk, litter, scrap
❷ *Don't talk **rubbish**!*
• nonsense, drivel, balderdash, piffle, gibberish, claptrap, gobbledegook
(informal) rot, tripe, twaddle

rude *ADJECTIVE*
❶ *It's very **rude** to talk with your mouth full.*
• impolite, discourteous, disrespectful, impertinent, impudent, insolent, offensive, insulting, bad-mannered, ill-bred
To be rude to someone is to **insult** or **snub** them.
To be rude about sacred things is to be **blasphemous** or **irreverent**.
OPPOSITE polite
❷ *Some of the jokes in the film are rather **rude**.*
• indecent, improper, offensive, coarse, crude
OPPOSITES decent, clean

ruffle *VERB*
*The peacock shook and **ruffled** its tail feathers.*
• stir, ripple, rumple, tousle

ruin *VERB*
*The storm had **ruined** the farmer's crops.*
• damage, destroy, spoil, wreck, devastate, demolish, lay waste, shatter

ruin *NOUN*
*When they lost the match, it was the **ruin** of their dream.*
• collapse, failure, breakdown
Financial ruin is **bankruptcy**.
➤ **ruins**
*Archaeologists have discovered the **ruins** of a Roman fort.*
• remains, remnants, fragments

ruined *ADJECTIVE*
*Bats flew in and out of the **ruined** abbey.*
• wrecked, crumbling, derelict, dilapidated, tumbledown, ramshackle

rule *NOUN*
❶ *Players must stick to the **rules** of the game.*
• law, regulation, principle
A set of rules is a **code**.
❷ *The country was formerly under French **rule**.*
• control, authority, command, power, government, reign

rule *VERB*
❶ *The Romans **ruled** a vast empire.*
• command, govern, control, direct, lead, manage, run, administer
❷ *Queen Victoria continued to **rule** for many years.*
• reign, be ruler
❸ *The umpire **ruled** that the batsman was out.*
• judge, decree, pronounce, decide, determine, find

ruler *NOUN*

WORD WEB

SOME KINDS OF RULER:

• emir, emperor, empress, governor, head of state, king, lord, monarch, president, prince, princess, queen, sovereign
A person who rules while a monarch is too young or too ill to rule is a **regent**.

SOME RULERS IN PAST TIMES:

• Caesar, pharaoh, raja or rani, sultan or sultana, tsar or tsarina

rummage *VERB*
*I **rummaged** through my bag looking for my purse.*
• search, hunt, ransack, scour

rumour *NOUN*
*There was a **rumour** that the queen was a witch in disguise.*
• gossip, hearsay, talk
(informal) tittle-tattle

run *VERB* **runs, running, ran, run**

❶ *We* ***ran*** *as fast as our legs could carry us.*

• **race, sprint, dash, tear, bolt, career, speed, hurry, rush, streak, fly, whizz, zoom, scurry, scamper, scoot**

To run at a gentle pace is to **jog**.

When a horse runs, it **gallops, canters** or **trots**.

❷ *Tears* ***ran*** *down the mermaid's cheeks.*

• **stream, flow, pour, gush, flood, cascade, spill, trickle, dribble, leak**

❸ *That old sewing machine still* ***runs*** *well.*

• **function, operate, work, go, perform**

❹ *My uncle* ***runs*** *a restaurant in Leeds.*

• **manage, be in charge of, direct, control, supervise, govern, rule**

❺ *The High Street* ***runs*** *through the city centre.*

• **pass, go, extend, stretch, reach**

➤ **to run away** or **off**

The thieves ***ran off*** *when they heard footsteps.*

• **bolt, fly, flee, escape, take off, hurry off** *(informal)* **make off, clear off, scarper**

➤ **to run into**

Guess who I ***ran into*** *the other day?*

• **meet, come across, encounter** *(informal)* **bump into**

A cyclist skidded and ***ran into*** *a tree.*

• **hit, collide with**

run *NOUN*

❶ *She goes for a* ***run*** *in the park every morning.*

A fast run is a **dash, gallop, race** or **sprint**.

A gentle run is a **jog**.

❷ *We went for a* ***run*** *in the car.*

• **drive, journey, ride**

❸ *They've had a* ***run*** *of good luck recently.*

• **sequence, stretch, series**

❹ *The farmer built a new chicken* ***run****.*

• **enclosure, pen, coop**

runaway *NOUN*

A person who has run away from the army is a **deserter**.

A person who is running away from the law is a **fugitive** or **outlaw**.

runner *NOUN*

The ***runners*** *were ready to start the race.*

• **athlete, competitor**

Someone who runs fast over short distances is a **sprinter**.

Someone who runs to keep fit is a **jogger**.

runny *ADJECTIVE*

This custard is too ***runny****.*

• **watery, thin, liquid, fluid**

OPPOSITE **thick**

rural *ADJECTIVE*

They live in a peaceful ***rural*** *area.*

• **country, rustic, agricultural, pastoral**

OPPOSITE **urban**

rush *VERB*

I ***rushed*** *home with the good news.*

• **hurry, hasten, race, run, dash, fly, bolt, charge, shoot, speed, sprint, tear, zoom**

When cattle or other animals rush along together they **stampede**.

rush *NOUN*

❶ *We've got plenty of time, so what's the* ***rush****?*

• **hurry, haste, urgency**

❷ *There was a sudden* ***rush*** *of water.*

• **flood, gush, spurt, stream, spate**

rustic *ADJECTIVE*

The village had a ***rustic*** *charm.*

• **country, rural, pastoral, countrified**

rut *NOUN*

The tractor left ***ruts*** *along the track.*

• **furrow, groove, channel, trough**

ruthless *ADJECTIVE*

The pirates launched a ***ruthless*** *attack.*

• **cruel, brutal, bloodthirsty, barbaric, heartless, pitiless, merciless, callous, ferocious, fierce, savage, vicious, violent**

OPPOSITE **merciful**

A B C D E F G H I J K L M N O P Q R S T U V W X Y Z

Ss

sack *NOUN*
The farmer delivered a large ***sack*** *of potatoes.*
• bag, pack

sack *VERB*
The manager threatened to ***sack*** *the whole team.*
• dismiss, discharge
(informal) fire, give you the sack

sacred *ADJECTIVE*
The Koran is a ***sacred*** *book.*
• holy, religious, divine, heavenly

sacrifice *VERB*
❶ *I* ***sacrificed*** *my lunch break to practise guitar.*
• give up, surrender, go without
❷ *The ancient Greeks* ***sacrificed*** *animals to please the gods.*
• offer up, kill, slaughter

sad *ADJECTIVE*

OVERUSED WORD

Try to vary the words you use for **sad**. Here are some other words you could use.

FOR A SAD MOOD OR SAD PERSON:

• unhappy, sorrowful, miserable, depressed, downcast, downhearted, despondent, crestfallen, dismal, gloomy, glum, blue, low, dejected, forlorn, desolate, doleful, wretched, woebegone, tearful, heartbroken, broken-hearted
The Big Friendly Giant looked suddenly so forlorn that Sophie got quite upset. 'I'm sorry,' she said. 'I didn't mean to be rude.'—THE BFG, Roald Dahl
If you are sad because you are away from home, you are **homesick**.
OPPOSITE happy

FOR A SAD STORY OR SAD TUNE:

• depressing, melancholy, mournful, moving, touching, plaintive, wistful, sorrowful, woeful
The pirate related the ***mournful*** *tale of Billy Bones.*
OPPOSITE cheering

FOR A SAD SITUATION OR SAD NEWS:

• unfortunate, unpleasant, painful, regrettable, lamentable, grim, serious, grave, tragic, grievous
The letter contained some ***painful*** *news.*
OPPOSITES cheerful, pleasant

FOR SOMETHING THAT MAKES YOU FEEL SAD:

• upsetting, distressing, heartbreaking, heart-rending, pitiful, pathetic
It was ***heartbreaking*** *to watch the injured bird.*

sadden *VERB*
The news of her friend's illness ***saddened*** *her.*
• distress, upset, depress, grieve, disappoint
(informal) break your heart
OPPOSITE cheer up

sadness *NOUN*
see **sorrow**

safe *ADJECTIVE*
❶ *The kitten was found* ***safe*** *and well in a neighbour's garden.*
• unharmed, unhurt, uninjured, undamaged, sound, intact
(informal) in one piece
OPPOSITES hurt, damaged
❷ *They felt* ***safe*** *indoors as the storm raged outside.*
• protected, guarded, defended, secure
OPPOSITE vulnerable

❸ *The secret code is in **safe** hands.*
• **reliable, trustworthy, dependable**
❹ *Is the tap water **safe** to drink?*
• **harmless, uncontaminated, innocuous**
OPPOSITE **dangerous**

safety *NOUN*
*You must wear a seat belt for your own **safety**.*
• **protection, security, well-being**
OPPOSITE **danger**

sag *VERB*
*The settee was old and stained and **sagged** in the middle.*
• **sink, dip, droop, flop, slump**

said *past tense see* **say**

sail *VERB*
❶ *We **sailed** to Norway rather than going by air.*
• **travel by ship**
To have a holiday sailing on a ship is to **cruise** or **go on a cruise**.
To begin a sea voyage is to **put to sea** or **set sail**.
❷ *None of the survivors knew how to **sail** the ship.*
• **pilot, steer, navigate**

sailor *NOUN*
*The crew comprised three **sailors** and a cook.*
• **seaman, seafarer, mariner, boatman**
A person who sails a yacht is a **yachtsman** or **yachtswoman**.

sake *NOUN*
➤ **for the sake of**
*He put some money aside **for the sake of** his children.*
• **for the good of, on behalf of, in the interests of, to help**

salary *NOUN*
*The job has an annual **salary** of £30,000.*
• **income, pay, earnings**
If your pay is paid week by week, it is called **wages**.

sale *NOUN*
*They made a lot of money from the **sale** of their house.*
• **selling, marketing, vending**
OPPOSITE **purchase**

salvage *VERB*
*The crew tried to **salvage** some supplies from the wreck.*
• **rescue, save, recover, retrieve, reclaim**

same *ADJECTIVE*
➤ **the same**
❶ *Each pirate was given **the same** ration of rum.*
• **equal, identical, equivalent**
❷ *Everyone in the choir wore **the same** outfit.*
• **matching, similar, alike, uniform**
❸ *Her feelings have remained **the same**.*
• **unaltered, unchanged, constant**
Words which mean the same are **synonymous** with each other.
OPPOSITE **different**

sample *NOUN*
*The detective asked for a **sample** of her handwriting.*
• **specimen, example, instance, illustration, selection**

sample *VERB*
*Would you like to **sample** some home-made jam?*
• **taste, test, try**

sand *NOUN*
*We built a huge castle out of **sand** and seashells.*
Hills of sand along the coast are **dunes**.
➤ **sands**

*They played on the **sands** until the tide came in.*
• beach, shore

sane *ADJECTIVE*
*No **sane** person would stand out in the pouring rain!*
• sensible, rational, reasonable
OPPOSITE insane

sang *past tense see* **sing**

sank *past tense see* **sink**

sarcastic *ADJECTIVE*
*He made a **sarcastic** remark about my hat.*
• mocking, satirical, ironical, sneering, taunting

sat *past tense see* **sit**

satisfaction *NOUN*
*He gets a lot of **satisfaction** from growing vegetables.*
• happiness, pleasure, enjoyment, contentment, fulfilment, sense of achievement, pride
OPPOSITE dissatisfaction

satisfactory *ADJECTIVE*
*I'm afraid this work is not **satisfactory**.*
• acceptable, adequate, passable, good enough, tolerable, competent
(informal) all right, up to scratch
OPPOSITE unsatisfactory

satisfy *VERB*
*Nothing **satisfies** him—he's always complaining.*
• please, content, make happy
OPPOSITE dissatisfy
To satisfy your thirst is to **quench** or slake it.

savage *ADJECTIVE*
❶ *The invaders launched a **savage** attack on the town.*
• vicious, cruel, barbaric, brutal, bloodthirsty, pitiless, ruthless, merciless, inhuman
OPPOSITE humane
❷ *A **savage** beast is said to live in the cave.*
• untamed, wild, ferocious, fierce
OPPOSITE domesticated

save *VERB*
❶ *They managed to **save** most of the books from the fire.*
• rescue, recover, retrieve, salvage
❷ *The knight pledged to **save** the princess from the witch's curse.*
• protect, defend, guard, shield, preserve
❸ *She **saved** him from making a fool of himself.*
• stop, prevent, deter
❹ *I **saved** you a piece of my birthday cake.*
• keep, reserve, set aside, hold on to
❺ *If you share a car, then you can **save** petrol.*
• be sparing with, conserve, use wisely

savings *PLURAL NOUN*
*They used all their **savings** to go on a cruise.*
• reserves, funds, resources, investments

saw *past tense see* **see**

saw *NOUN*
for various tools see **tool**

say *VERB* **says, saying, said**
❶ *He found it hard to **say** what he meant.*
• express, communicate, put into words, convey
❷ *I would like to **say** a few words before we start.*
• utter, speak, recite, read

OVERUSED WORD

Try to vary the words you use for **say**, especially with direct speech.
Here are some other words you could use.

TO SAY LOUDLY:

• **call, cry, exclaim, bellow, bawl, shout, yell, roar**
*'Land ahoy!' **bellowed** the cabin boy.*

TO SAY QUIETLY:

• **whisper, mumble, mutter**
*'That woman,' I **whispered**, 'is a secret agent.'*

TO SAY STRONGLY:

• **state, announce, assert, declare, pronounce, insist, maintain, profess**
'You may leave us,' Miss Minchin announced to the servants with a wave of her hand.–A LITTLE PRINCESS, Frances Hodgson Burnett

TO SAY CASUALLY:

• **remark, comment, observe, note, mention**
*'It's very warm for this time of year,' Mr Lewis **remarked**.*

TO SAY ANGRILY:

• **snap, snarl, growl, thunder, bark, rasp, rant, rave**
*'Give me that piece of paper!' **snapped** Miss Crabbit.*

TO SAY SUDDENLY:

• **blurt out**
*'That's just a pretend dinosaur!' Ben **blurted out**.*

TO SAY UNCLEARLY:

• **babble, burble, gabble, stammer, stutter**
*The stranger kept **babbling** about hidden treasure.*

TO SAY IN SURPRISE OR ALARM:

• **gasp, cry, squeal**
*'The tunnel is sealed! There's no way out!' **gasped** Alex.*

TO SAY SOMETHING FUNNY:

• **joke, quip, tease**
*'Were you singing? I thought it was a cat,' **teased** my big sister.*

TO GIVE AN ORDER:

• **command, demand, order**
*A voice outside **demanded**, 'Open the door at once!'*

TO ASK A QUESTION:

• **enquire, demand, query**
*'How do you spell your name?' the judge **enquired**.*

TO GIVE A REPLY:

• **answer, reply, respond, retort**
*'Certainly not!' **retorted** Lady Dimsley.*

TO MAKE A REQUEST OR AN EXCUSE:

• **beg, entreat, implore, plead, urge**
'I didn't mean it!' pleaded poor Alice. 'But you're so easily offended, you know!'–ALICE'S ADVENTURES IN WONDERLAND, Lewis Carroll

TO MAKE A SUGGESTION:

• **suggest, propose**
*'Let's make them walk the plank,' **suggested** Captain Hook.*

TO SAY AGAIN:

• **repeat, reiterate, echo**
*The Martians **repeated**, 'Take us to your leader!'*

saying *NOUN*
*'Many hands make light work' is a common **saying**.*
• **expression, phrase, motto, proverb, catchphrase**
An overused saying is a **cliché**.

scamper *VERB*
The rabbits ***scampered*** *away to safety.*
• **hurry, dash, run, rush, hasten, scuttle**

scan *VERB*
❶ *The lookout* ***scanned*** *the horizon, hoping to see land.*
• **search, study, survey, examine, scrutinise, stare at, eye**
❷ *I* ***scanned*** *through some magazines in the waiting room.*
• **skim, glance at, flick through**

scandal *NOUN*
❶ *The waste of food after the party was a* ***scandal.***
• **disgrace, embarrassment, shame, outrage**
❷ *Some newspapers like to publish the latest* ***scandal.***
• **gossip, rumours, dirt**

scar *NOUN*
The warrior had a ***scar*** *across his forehead.*
• **mark, blemish, wound**

scar *VERB*
The injuries he received ***scarred*** *him for life.*
• **mark, disfigure, deface**

scarce *ADJECTIVE*
Water is very ***scarce*** *in the desert.*
• **hard to find, in short supply, lacking, sparse, scanty, rare, uncommon**
(informal) **thin on the ground**
OPPOSITE **plentiful**

scarcely *ADVERB*
She was so tired that she could ***scarcely*** *walk.*
• **barely, hardly, only just**

scare *NOUN*
The explosion gave them a nasty ***scare.***
• **fright, shock, alarm**

scare *VERB*
My brother tried to ***scare*** *us by making ghost noises.*
• **frighten, terrify, petrify, alarm, startle, panic**
OPPOSITE **reassure**

scared *ADJECTIVE*
When she heard the footsteps, Lily was too ***scared*** *to move.*
• **frightened, terrified, petrified, horrified, alarmed, fearful, panicky**
see also **afraid**

scary *ADJECTIVE (informal)*
I had to close my eyes at the ***scary*** *bits in the film.*
• **frightening, terrifying, horrifying, alarming, nightmarish, fearsome, chilling, spine-chilling, hair-raising, blood-curdling, chilling, eerie, sinister**

scatter *VERB*
❶ *She* ***scattered*** *the seeds on the ground.*
• **spread, sprinkle, sow, strew, throw about, shower**
OPPOSITE **collect**
❷ *The animals* ***scattered*** *when the children ran towards them.*
• **break up, separate, disperse, disband**
OPPOSITE **gather**

scene *NOUN*
❶ *The police arrived quickly at the* ***scene*** *of the crime.*
• **location, position, site, place, situation, spot**
❷ *They were rehearsing a* ***scene*** *from the play.*
• **episode, part, section, act**

❸ *I gazed out of the window at the moonlit scene.*
• **landscape, scenery, view, sight, outlook, prospect, spectacle, setting, backdrop**
❹ *He didn't want to create a **scene** in the restaurant.*
• **fuss, commotion, disturbance, quarrel, row**

scenery NOUN
*We admired the **scenery** from the top of the hill.*
• **landscape, outlook, prospect, scene, view, panorama**

scent NOUN
*Rowena loves the **scent** of roses.*
• **smell, fragrance, perfume, aroma**
see also **smell**

sceptical ADJECTIVE
*At first, I was **sceptical** about the legend of the ghost.*
• **disbelieving, doubtful, doubting, unconvinced, dubious, incredulous, suspicious, uncertain, unsure**
OPPOSITE **trustful**

schedule NOUN
*The athletes had a rigorous training **schedule**.*
• **programme, timetable, plan, calendar, diary**
A schedule of topics to be discussed at a meeting is an **agenda.**
A schedule of places to be visited on a journey is an **itinerary.**

scheme NOUN
*They worked out a **scheme** to raise some money.*
• **plan, proposal, project, procedure, method, system**

scheme VERB
*The smugglers were **scheming** against each other.*
• **plot, conspire, intrigue**

school NOUN

WORD WEB

VARIOUS KINDS OF SCHOOL:

• **academy, boarding school, comprehensive school, faith school, grammar school, high school, independent school, infant school, junior school, kindergarten, nursery school, preparatory or prep school, primary school, private school, public school, secondary school**
for rooms in a school see **room**

science NOUN

WORD WEB

SOME BRANCHES OF SCIENCE:

• **aeronautics, anatomy, astronomy, biology, botany, chemistry, computer science, earth sciences, electronics, engineering, genetics, geology, information technology, mechanics, medicine, meteorology, physics, psychology, veterinary science, zoology**

scoff VERB
➤ **to scoff at**
*Everyone **scoffed at** her ideas.*
• **mock, ridicule, sneer at, jeer at, deride, make fun of, poke fun at**

scold VERB
*He **scolded** the paperboy for being late.*
• **reprimand, reproach, tell off**
(informal) **tick off**

scoop VERB
*We **scooped** out a moat for our sandcastle.*
• **dig, gouge, scrape, excavate, hollow**

A B C D E F G H I J K L M N O P Q R S T U V W X Y Z

scope *NOUN*
❶ *The park offers plenty of* ***scope*** *for children to play.*
• **opportunity, room, space, freedom, liberty**
❷ *These things are outside the* ***scope*** *of the project.*
• **range, extent, limit, reach, span**

scorch *VERB*
The dragon's breath ***scorched*** *the wizard's beard.*
• **burn, singe, sear, blacken, char**

score *NOUN*
We added up each other's ***scores****.*
• **marks, points, total**
The final score is the **result**.

score *VERB*
❶ *How many goals did you* ***score****?*
• **win, get, make, gain, earn**
❷ *Some lines were* ***scored*** *into the bark of the tree.*
• **cut, gouge, mark, scrape, scratch**

scorn *NOUN*
She dismissed my suggestion with ***scorn****.*
• **contempt, derision, disrespect, mockery, ridicule**
OPPOSITE **admiration**

scour *VERB*
❶ *He* ***scoured*** *the pan until it shone.*
• **scrape, scrub, rub, clean, polish**
❷ *Edith* ***scoured*** *the room looking for her glasses.*
• **search, hunt through, ransack, comb**

scowl *VERB*
The witch ***scowled*** *under her floppy black hat.*
• **frown, glower**
for other facial expressions see **expression**

scramble *VERB*
❶ *The smugglers escaped by* ***scrambling*** *over the rocks.*
• **clamber, climb, crawl, scrabble**
❷ *The children* ***scrambled*** *to get the best seats.*
• **push, jostle, struggle, fight, scuffle**

scrap *NOUN*
❶ *They fed the* ***scraps*** *of food to the birds.*
• **bit, piece, fragment, morsel, crumb, speck, particle**
❷ *He took a pile of* ***scrap*** *to the tip.*
• **rubbish, waste, junk, refuse, litter**
Scraps of cloth are **rags** or **shreds**.
❸ *(informal) There was a* ***scrap*** *between the two gangs.*
• **fight, brawl, scuffle, tussle, squabble**

scrap *VERB*
❶ *The author* ***scrapped*** *the last paragraph.*
• **discard, throw away, abandon, cancel, drop, give up**
(informal) **dump**
❷ *(informal) The cubs enjoy* ***scrapping*** *with each other.*
• **fight, brawl, tussle, scuffle**

scrape *VERB*
❶ *She* ***scraped*** *her knee when she fell over.*
• **graze, scratch, scuff**
❷ *I tried to* ***scrape*** *the mud off my trainers.*
• **rub, scour, scrub, clean**

scrape *NOUN*
My little brother is always getting into ***scrapes****.*
• **trouble, mischief**
(informal) **jam, pickle**

scratch *VERB*
❶ *Someone* ***scratched*** *the side of the car.*
• **mark, score, scrape, gouge, graze**
❷ *The cat tried to* ***scratch*** *me.*
• **claw**

scratch *NOUN*
*Who made this **scratch** on the side of the car?*
• gash, groove, line, mark, scrape

scrawl *VERB*
*She **scrawled** his phone number on a scrap of paper.*
• jot down, scribble, write

scream *NOUN, VERB*
*We heard a woman's **scream** in the distance.*
*A woman ran out of the house **screaming**.*
• shriek, screech, shout, yell, cry, bawl, howl, wail, squeal, yelp

screen *NOUN*
*The room was divided into two by a **screen**.*
• curtain, partition, divider

screen *VERB*
❶ *Miss Bennett used a parasol to **screen** her face from the sun.*
• shield, protect, shelter, shade, cover, hide, mask, veil
❷ *All employees are **screened** before being appointed.*
• examine, investigate, test, check

scribble *VERB*
*He **scribbled** his phone number on a scrap of paper.*
• scrawl, jot down, dash off, write
To scribble a rough drawing, especially when you are bored, is to **doodle**.

script *NOUN*
The script for a film is a **screenplay**.
A handwritten or typed script is a **manuscript**.

scrub *VERB*
*She **scrubbed** the floor clean.*
• rub, brush, clean, wash, scour

scruffy *ADJECTIVE*
*Magnus wore an old jumper and **scruffy** jeans.*
• untidy, messy, ragged, tatty, tattered, worn-out, shabby
OPPOSITE smart

scrutinise *VERB*
*She **scrutinised** the handwriting on the letter.*
• examine, inspect, look at, study, investigate, explore

sculpture *NOUN*
*The temple was full of marble **sculptures**.*
• carving, figure, statue

sea *NOUN*

WORD WEB

The very large seas of the world are called **oceans**.
An area of sea partly enclosed by land is a **bay** or **gulf**.
A wide inlet of the sea is a **sound**.
A wide inlet where a river joins the sea is an **estuary**, or *(in Scotland)* a **firth**.
A long narrow sea inlet between cliffs is a **fjord**.
A narrow stretch of water linking two seas is a **strait**.
The bottom of the sea is the **seabed**.
The land near the sea is the **coast** or the **seashore**.
Creatures that live in the sea are **marine** creatures.

THINGS YOU MIGHT SEE ON THE SEA:
• breaker, iceberg, sea spray, surf, swell, waves
• boat, cruise ship, ocean liner, yacht

SOME CREATURES THAT LIVE IN THE SEA:
• cuttlefish, dolphin, eel, fish, jellyfish, killer whale, octopus, porpoise, seahorse, seal, sea lion, shark, squid, stingray, turtle, whale

see also **seashore**

WRITING TIPS

You can use these words to describe the sea.

TO DESCRIBE A CALM SEA:

- **calm, crystal clear, glassy, sparkling, tranquil, unruffled**

TO DESCRIBE A ROUGH SEA:

- **choppy, raging, rough, stormy, tempestuous, turbulent, wild**

The Tankadere started to move fast over the raging sea whose waves were now colliding with those previously produced by the wind.
—AROUND THE WORLD IN EIGHTY DAYS, Jules Verne

WAVES ON THE SEA MIGHT:

- **billow, break, crash, heave, pound, roll, surge, swell, tumble, wash**

seal *VERB*

The entrance to the burial chamber had been sealed.
- **close, fasten, shut, lock, secure**

To seal a leak is to **plug** it or **stop** it.

seam *NOUN*

❶ *The **seam** on his trousers split.*
- **join, stitching**

❷ *Geologists discovered a **seam** of coal.*
- **layer, stratum**

search *VERB*

❶ *He was **searching** for the book he had lost.*
- **hunt, look, seek**

To search for gold or some other mineral is to **prospect**.

❷ *The police **searched** the house but didn't find anything.*
- **explore, scour, ransack, rummage through, comb**

❸ *Security staff **searched** all the passengers.*
- **check, inspect, examine, scrutinise** *(informal)* **frisk**

search *NOUN*

*After a long **search**, she found her keys.*
- **hunt, look, check**

A long journey in search of something is a **quest**.

seashore *NOUN*

*We explored the **seashore**, looking for shells and fossils.*
- **seaside, beach, shore, coast**

WORD WEB

THINGS YOU MIGHT SEE ON THE SEASHORE:

- **cave, cliff, coral reef, driftwood, dunes, lighthouse, mudflats, pebbles, rock pool, rocks, sand, seashell, seaweed, shingle**

see also **seaside**

CREATURES THAT LIVE ON THE SEASHORE:

- **barnacle, clam, cockle, coral, crab, limpet, mussel, oyster, prawn, razor shell, sea anemone, seabird, seagull, sea urchin, shrimp, sponge, starfish, whelk**

for names of seabirds see **bird**
for other sea creatures see **sea**

seaside *NOUN*

*If it's sunny tomorrow, we might go to the **seaside**.*
- **beach, sands, seashore**

WORD WEB

THINGS YOU MIGHT SEE AT THE SEASIDE:

- **beach huts, funfair, harbour, ice cream van, jetty, lifeguard, pier, promenade**

A town where you go to have fun by the sea is a **seaside resort**.

THINGS YOU MIGHT TAKE TO THE SEASIDE:

- **beach ball, bucket and spade, deckchair, fishing net, snorkel, sunglasses, sunhat, sunshade, suncream, surfboard, wetsuit, swimming costume, towel, windbreak**

THINGS YOU MIGHT DO AT THE SEASIDE:

• ball games, beachcombing, building sandcastles, collecting shells, fishing, paddling, scuba diving, snorkelling, sunbathing, surfing, swimming, waterskiing, windsurfing

season *NOUN*
The hotels are full during the holiday season.
• period, time

seat *NOUN*
*We found two empty **seats** at the back of the cinema.*
• chair, place
A long seat for more than one person is a **bench**.
A long wooden seat in a church is a **pew**.
A seat on a bicycle or horse is a **saddle**.
A special seat for a king or queen is a **throne**.

seat *VERB*
❶ *The guests **seated** themselves around the table.*
• place, position, sit down, settle
❷ *The theatre can **seat** two hundred people.*
• have seats for, accommodate, hold, take

second *ADJECTIVE*
*Would anyone like a **second** helping of pudding?*
• another, additional, extra, further

second *NOUN*
❶ *The magic potion only takes a **second** to work.*
• instant, moment, flash
(informal) jiffy, tick
❷ *Inga was **second** in the cross-country race.*
• runner-up

second *VERB*
*We need someone to **second** the proposal.*
• back, support

secondary *ADJECTIVE*
*She loves to run and winning is of **secondary** importance to her.*
• lesser, lower, minor, inferior, subordinate

second-hand *ADJECTIVE*
*The shop sells **second-hand** computers.*
• used, pre-owned
OPPOSITE new

secret *ADJECTIVE*
❶ *The spy managed to get hold of a **secret** document.*
• confidential, classified, restricted
(informal) hush-hush
❷ *The detectives are part of a **secret** operation.*
• undercover, covert
❸ *The things I write in my diary are **secret**.*
• private, confidential, personal, intimate
❹ *The cook showed us a **secret** passageway into the castle.*
• hidden, concealed, disguised
for secret agents see **spy**

secretive *ADJECTIVE*
*Why is she being so **secretive** about her past?*
• uncommunicative, tight-lipped, reticent, reserved, mysterious, quiet
(informal) cagey
OPPOSITES communicative, open

section *NOUN*
*The website has a special **section** aimed at children.*
• part, division, sector, portion, segment, bit, fragment
A section of a book is a **chapter**.
A section from a piece of classical music is a **movement**.
A section taken from a book or long piece of music is a **passage**.
A section of a journey is a **stage**.

secure *ADJECTIVE*
❶ *The ladder was not very* ***secure****.*
• steady, firm, solid, fixed, fast, immovable
OPPOSITES insecure, unsafe
❷ *She is still trying to find a* ***secure*** *job.*
• permanent, regular, steady
❸ *They bolted the doors to make the castle* ***secure****.*
• safe, guarded, protected, defended

secure *VERB*
❶ *The door wasn't properly* ***secured****.*
• fasten, lock, seal, bolt
❷ *He managed to* ***secure*** *two tickets for the match.*
• get hold of, acquire, obtain

security *NOUN*
You must wear a seat belt for your own ***security****.*
• protection, safety

see *VERB* **sees, seeing, saw, seen**
❶ *If you look closely, you might* ***see*** *a dragonfly.*
• catch sight of, spot, notice, observe, make out, distinguish, note, perceive, recognise, sight, spy
(old use) behold
To see something briefly is to **glimpse** it.
To see an accident or an unusual event is to **witness** it.
❷ *Did you* ***see*** *the news yesterday?*
• watch, look at, view
❸ ***See*** *me in my office after school.*
• go to, report to
❹ *I didn't expect to* ***see*** *you here!*
• meet, run into, encounter
(informal) bump into
❺ *Will we have time to* ***see*** *them on the way home?*
• visit, call on, drop in on
❻ *I* ***see*** *what you mean.*
• understand, appreciate, comprehend, follow, grasp, realise, take in
❼ *I find it hard to* ***see*** *him in the role of Peter Pan.*
• imagine, picture, visualise
❽ *Please* ***see*** *that the windows are shut.*
• make sure, make certain, ensure
❾ *I'll* ***see*** *what I can do.*
• think about, consider, ponder, reflect on, weigh up
❿ *I'll* ***see*** *you to the door.*
• conduct, escort, accompany, guide, lead, take
➤ **to see to something**
Who's going to ***see to*** *the refreshments?*
• deal with, attend to, take care of, sort out

seed *NOUN*
The seeds in an orange, lemon, etc., are the **pips**.
The seed in a date, plum, etc., is the **stone**.

seek *VERB* **seeks, seeking, sought**
❶ *For many years he* ***sought*** *his long-lost brother.*
• search for, hunt for, look for
❷ *The king* ***sought*** *only to make his daughter happy.*
• try, attempt, strive, want, wish, desire

seem *VERB*
Everything ***seems*** *to be all right.*
She is far more friendly than she ***seems****.*
• appear, look, give the impression of being

seep *VERB*
Oil began to ***seep*** *through the crack.*
• leak, ooze, escape, flow, dribble, trickle, soak

seethe *VERB*
The mixture in the cauldron began to ***seethe****.*
• boil, bubble, foam, froth up
➤ **to be seething**
Greg ***was seething*** *when I crashed his bike.*
• be angry, be furious, rage, storm

segment *NOUN*
*Divide the orange into **segments**.*
• **section, portion, piece, part, bit, wedge, slice**

seize *VERB*
❶ *The climber stretched out to **seize** the rope.*
• **grab, catch, snatch, take hold of, grasp, grip, clutch**
❷ *The police **seized** the robbers as they left the bank.*
• **arrest, capture**
(informal) **collar, nab**
To seize someone's property as a punishment is to **confiscate** it.
To seize someone's power or position is to **usurp** it.
To seize an aircraft or vehicle during a journey is to **hijack** it.

seldom *ADVERB*
*It **seldom** rains in the desert.*
• **rarely, infrequently**
OPPOSITE **often**

select *VERB*
*They had to **select** a new captain.*
• **choose, pick, decide on, opt for, settle on, appoint, elect**

select *ADJECTIVE*
*Only a **select** few were invited to the party.*
• **privileged, chosen, special, hand-picked**

selection *NOUN*
*The shop has a wide **selection** of roller skates.*
• **choice, range, variety, assortment**

selfish *ADJECTIVE*
*He's so **selfish** that he kept all the chocolate to himself.*
• **greedy, mean, miserly, grasping, self-centred, thoughtless**
OPPOSITES **unselfish, generous**

sell *VERB* **sells, selling, sold**
*The corner shop **sells** newspapers and sweets.*
• **deal in, trade in, stock, retail**
Uncomplimentary synonyms are **peddle** and **hawk**.
for people who sell things see **shop**
OPPOSITE **buy**

send *VERB* **sends, sending, sent**
❶ *I **sent** each of my friends a postcard.*
• **post, mail, dispatch**
❷ *They plan to **send** a rocket to Mars.*
• **launch, propel, direct, fire, shoot**
➤ **to send for someone**
*I think we should **send for** a doctor.*
• **call, summon, fetch**
➤ **to send something out**
*The device was **sending out** weird noises.*
• **emit, issue, give off, discharge**

senior *ADJECTIVE*
❶ *She's one of the **senior** players in the squad.*
• **older, long-standing, principal**
❷ *He is a **senior** officer in the navy.*
• **high-ranking, superior**
OPPOSITE **junior**

sensation *NOUN*
❶ *She had a tingling **sensation** in her fingers.*
• **feeling, sense**
❷ *The unexpected news caused a **sensation**.*
• **excitement, thrill**
A sensation caused by something bad is an **outrage** or a **scandal**.

sensational *ADJECTIVE*
❶ *The newspaper printed a **sensational** account of the murder.*
• **shocking, horrifying, startling, lurid**
❷ *(informal) Did you hear the **sensational** result of yesterday's match?*
• **amazing, extraordinary, remarkable, fantastic, spectacular, stupendous**

sense *NOUN*

❶ *A baby learns about the world through its senses.*

Your five senses are **hearing**, **sight**, **smell**, **taste** and **touch**.

❷ *A drummer needs to have a good* ***sense*** *of rhythm.*

• **awareness, consciousness, perception, feeling (for)**

❸ *If you had any* ***sense*** *you'd stay at home.*

• **common sense, intelligence, wisdom, wit, brains**

❹ *The* ***sense*** *of the word is not clear.*

• **meaning, significance, import**

➤ **to make sense of something**

They couldn't ***make sense of*** *the garbled message.*

• **understand, make out, interpret, follow**

sense *VERB*

❶ *He* ***sensed*** *that she didn't like him.*

• **be aware, realise, perceive, feel, guess, notice, suspect**

❷ *The device* ***senses*** *any change of temperature.*

• **detect, respond to**

senseless *ADJECTIVE*

❶ *Smashing the window was a* ***senseless*** *act.*

• **foolish, stupid, crazy, daft, irrational, mad, illogical, pointless, futile**

OPPOSITE **sensible**

❷ *The blow on the head left the ogre* ***senseless****.*

• **unconscious, knocked out**

OPPOSITE **conscious**

sensible *ADJECTIVE*

❶ *It would be* ***sensible*** *to wait until the weather improves.*

• **wise, intelligent, shrewd, rational, reasonable, careful, prudent, logical, sane, sound**

OPPOSITE **stupid**

❷ *You will need* ***sensible*** *shoes for the hiking trip.*

• **comfortable, practical**

OPPOSITE **impractical**

sensitive *ADJECTIVE*

❶ *She has* ***sensitive*** *skin which gets sunburnt.*

• **delicate, tender, fine, soft**

❷ *Take care what you say—he's very* ***sensitive****.*

• **easily offended, easily upset, touchy**

❸ *She's very* ***sensitive*** *towards other people.*

• **tactful, considerate, thoughtful, sympathetic, understanding**

OPPOSITE **insensitive**

sentence *VERB*

The judge ***sentenced*** *him to five years in prison.*

• **pass judgement on, pronounce sentence on, condemn**

sentimental *ADJECTIVE*

❶ *He gets* ***sentimental*** *looking at old photographs.*

• **emotional, nostalgic, tearful**

❷ *I hate* ***sentimental*** *messages on birthday cards.*

• **romantic, tender**

(informal) **soppy, mushy**

sentry *NOUN*

A ***sentry*** *was on duty at the gate.*

• **guard, lookout, sentinel, watchman**

separate *ADJECTIVE*

❶ *The zoo kept the male lions* ***separate*** *from the cubs.*

• **apart, separated, distinct, independent**

OPPOSITE **together**

❷ *They slept in* ***separate*** *rooms.*

• **different, detached, unattached**

OPPOSITES **attached, joined**

separate *VERB*

❶ *The sheepdog* ***separated*** *the sheep from the lambs.*

• **cut off, divide, fence off, isolate, keep apart, remove, segregate, set apart, take away**

OPPOSITES **combine, mix**

To separate something which is connected to something else is to **detach** or **disconnect** it.
To separate things which are tangled together is to **disentangle** them.
❷ *They walked along together until their paths* ***separated.***
• **split, branch, fork**
OPPOSITE **merge**
❸ *Her friend's parents have* ***separated.***
• **split up, break up, part company**
To end a marriage legally is to **divorce.**

sequence *NOUN*
The detective tried to piece together the ***sequence*** *of events.*
• **order, progression, series, succession, string, chain, train**

serene *ADJECTIVE*
The woman in the painting had a ***serene*** *smile on her face.*
• **calm, contented, untroubled, peaceful, quiet, placid, tranquil**
OPPOSITE **agitated**

series *NOUN*
❶ *We had to answer a* ***series*** *of questions in our exam.*
• **succession, sequence, string, set, chain, train**
❷ *Are you watching the new* ***series*** *on TV?*
• **serial**

serious *ADJECTIVE*
❶ *His* ***serious*** *expression told them something was wrong.*
• **solemn, sombre, unsmiling, grave, grim**
OPPOSITE **cheerful**
❷ *She is writing a* ***serious*** *book about global warming.*
• **learned, intellectual, scholarly**
(informal) **heavy**
OPPOSITE **light**
❸ *Are you* ***serious*** *about wanting to learn to ski?*
• **sincere, genuine, in earnest**
❹ *This hospital ward is for people with* ***serious*** *injuries.*
• **severe, acute, critical, bad, terrible, appalling, dreadful, major, grave**
OPPOSITES **minor, trivial**

servant *NOUN*
This part of the house was where the ***servants*** *lived.*
• **attendant, retainer, helper, domestic, manservant, maid**
The chief manservant in a private house is a **butler.**
The servant of a medieval knight was a **page** or **squire.**

serve *VERB*
❶ *The shopkeeper was busy* ***serving*** *customers.*
• **help, assist, aid**
❷ *When everyone had sat down they* ***served*** *the first course.*
• **give out, dish up, pass round, distribute**
❸ *This room will* ***serve*** *as a study.*
• **be suitable, be useful, function**

service *NOUN*
❶ *The genie bowed and said he was glad to be of* ***service.***
• **help, assistance, aid, use, usefulness, benefit**
❷ *Their marriage* ***service*** *was held in the local church.*
• **ceremony, ritual, rite**
A service in church is a meeting for **worship.**
❸ *Mum says her car needs a* ***service.***
• **check-over, maintenance, servicing**

service *VERB*
The garage ***serviced*** *her car.*
• **maintain, check, repair, mend, overhaul**

session *NOUN*
❶ *We have a training* ***session*** *on Saturday mornings.*
• **period, time**

❷ *The Queen will open the next* ***session*** *of Parliament.*
• **meeting, sitting**

set *VERB* sets, setting, set

❶ *The removal men* ***set*** *the piano on the floor.*
• **place, put, stand, position**
❷ *I helped Dad to* ***set*** *the table.*
• **arrange, lay, set out**
❸ *Have they* ***set*** *a date for the wedding yet?*
• **appoint, specify, name, decide, determine, choose, fix, establish, settle**
❹ *The jelly will* ***set*** *quicker in the fridge.*
• **become firm, solidify, harden, stiffen**
❺ *The sun was just beginning to* ***set****.*
• **do down, sink**

➤ to set about something

We ***set about*** *clearing the table immediately.*
• **begin, start, commence**

➤ to set off

❶ *The knights* ***set off*** *on their quest.*
• **depart, get going, leave, set out, start out**
❷ *The burnt toast* ***set off*** *the smoke alarm.*
• **activate, start, trigger**

➤ to set something out

The information is clearly ***set out*** *on the page.*
• **lay out, arrange, display, present**

➤ to set something up

They're trying to ***set up*** *an after-school club.*
• **establish, create, start, begin, introduce, organise**

set *NOUN*

❶ *There is a* ***set*** *of measuring spoons in the drawer.*
• **collection, batch, kit**
❷ *Is there something wrong with the TV* ***set****?*
• **apparatus, receiver**
❸ *Our class painted the* ***set*** *for the play.*
• **scenery, setting**

setting *NOUN*

The house stood in a rural ***setting****.*
• **surroundings, location, place, position, site, background**
for ways to describe the setting of a story see **writing**

settle *VERB*

❶ *The brothers tried to* ***settle*** *their differences.*
• **resolve, sort out, deal with, end**
❷ *The cat had just* ***settled*** *on the sofa.*
• **sit down, relax, rest**
❸ *A robin* ***settled*** *on a nearby branch.*
• **land, alight**
❹ *The family is planning to* ***settle*** *in Canada.*
• **emigrate (to), move (to), set up home**
❺ *You can see lots of fish when the mud* ***settles****.*
• **sink to the bottom, clear, subside**
❻ *We'll* ***settle*** *the hotel bill in the morning.*
• **pay, clear, square**

➤ to settle on

Have you ***settled on*** *a date for the wedding?*
• **agree on, decide on, choose, name, fix**

settlement *NOUN*

There was once a Viking ***settlement*** *in this area.*
• **community, colony, encampment, village**

sever *VERB*

The couple decided to ***sever*** *their relationship.*
• **break off, end, terminate**
To sever a branch of a tree is to **cut it off** or **remove it**.
To sever a limb is to **amputate** it.

several *DETERMINER*

The spy was able to adopt ***several*** *disguises.*
• **a number of, some, a few, various**

severe *ADJECTIVE*

❶ *The jailer was very* ***severe*** *with the prisoners.*
• **harsh, strict, hard, stern**
OPPOSITE **lenient**

❷ *The traffic warden gave him a **severe** look.*
• **unkind, unsympathetic, disapproving, grim**
OPPOSITE **kind**
❸ *Ruby has a **severe** case of chickenpox.*
• **bad, serious, acute, grave**
OPPOSITE **mild**
❹ *The Arctic has a **severe** climate.*
• **extreme, tough, harsh, hostile**
A severe frost is a **sharp** frost.
Severe cold is **intense** cold.
A severe storm is a **violent** storm.

sew *VERB* **sews, sewing, sewed, sewn** or **sewed**
*Mum **sewed** a name tag on to my coat.*
• **stitch, tack**
To sew a picture or design is to **embroider** it.
see also **needlework**

sex *NOUN*
*What **sex** is the hamster?*
• **gender**

shabby *ADJECTIVE*
❶ *The witch disguised herself in a **shabby** cloak.*
• **ragged, scruffy, tattered, worn, worn-out, threadbare, frayed, tatty, seedy, dingy**
OPPOSITE **smart**
❷ *That was a **shabby** trick!*
• **mean, nasty, unfair, unkind, dishonest, shameful, low, cheap**

shade *NOUN*
❶ *They sat in the **shade** of a chestnut tree.*
• **shadow**
❷ *The porch had a **shade** to keep out the sun.*
• **screen, blind, canopy**
A type of umbrella used as a sunshade is a **parasol**.
❸ *The bathroom walls are a pale **shade** of blue.*
• **hue, tinge, tint, tone, colour**

shade *VERB*
❶ *Wearing a cap will **shade** your eyes from the sun.*
• **shield, screen, protect, hide, mask**
❷ *He **shaded** the background of the picture with a pencil.*
• **fill in, make darker, darken**

shadow *NOUN*
*Her face was deep in **shadow**.*
• **shade, darkness, gloom**

shadow *VERB*
*The detective was **shadowing** the suspect.*
• **follow, pursue, tail, stalk, track, trail**

shady *ADJECTIVE*
❶ *They found a **shady** spot under a tree.*
• **shaded, shadowy, sheltered, dark, sunless**
OPPOSITE **sunny**
❷ *He took part in some **shady** business deals.*
• **dishonest, disreputable, suspicious, dubious, suspect, untrustworthy**
(informal) **fishy, dodgy**
OPPOSITE **honest**

shaft *NOUN*
❶ *Modern arrow **shafts** are made of wood.*
• **spine, stick, pole, rod, staff**
❷ *He nearly fell into an old mine **shaft**.*
• **pit, tunnel, hole**
❸ *A **shaft** of moonlight shone through the window.*
• **beam, ray**

shaggy *ADJECTIVE*
*Llamas have long **shaggy** coats.*
• **bushy, woolly, fleecy, hairy, thick**

shake *VERB* **shakes, shaking, shook, shaken**
❶ *The hurricane made the whole house **shake**.*
• **quake, shudder, shiver, rock, sway, totter, wobble, quiver, vibrate, rattle**
❷ *He was so upset that his voice was **shaking**.*
• **tremble, quaver**

❸ *The giant **shook** his fist and growled angrily.*
• **wave, brandish, flourish, wag, waggle, joggle**
❹ *They were **shaken** by the terrible news.*
• **shock, startle, distress, upset, disturb, alarm, frighten**

shaky *ADJECTIVE*
❶ *Be careful—the table is rather **shaky**.*
• **unsteady, wobbly, insecure, rickety, flimsy, weak**
❷ *He was so nervous that his hands were **shaky**.*
• **shaking, trembling, quivering**
❸ *He spoke in a **shaky** voice.*
• **quavering, faltering, nervous, tremulous**
OPPOSITE **steady**

shallow *ADJECTIVE*
*The children paddled about in the **shallow** water.*
OPPOSITE **deep**

sham *NOUN*
*The story he told about his family was all a **sham**.*
• **pretence, deception, lie**

shame *NOUN*
*The guilty man hung his head in **shame**.*
• **disgrace, dishonour, humiliation, embarrassment, guilt**
➤ **a shame**
*It's a **shame** that you can't stay for longer.*
• **a pity, unfortunate**

shameful *ADJECTIVE*
*The player was sent off for his **shameful** conduct on the pitch.*
• **disgraceful, outrageous, scandalous, contemptible, despicable, wicked**
OPPOSITE **honourable**

shape *NOUN*
*The Halloween cake was in the **shape** of a bat.*
• **form, figure**

A line showing the shape of a thing is the **outline**.
A dark outline seen against a light background is a **silhouette**.
A container for making things in a special shape is a **mould**.

WORD WEB

FLAT SHAPES:
• **circle, diamond, ellipse, heptagon, hexagon, oblong, octagon, oval, parallelogram, pentagon, polygon, quadrilateral, rectangle, rhombus, ring, semicircle, square, trapezium, triangle**

THREE-DIMENSIONAL SHAPES:
• **cone, cube, cylinder, hemisphere, polyhedron, prism, pyramid, sphere**

shape *VERB*
*The potter **shaped** the clay into a tall vase.*
• **form, mould, fashion**
To shape something in a mould is to **cast** it.

share *NOUN*
*Each of the pirates got a **share** of rum.*
• **ration, allowance, portion, quota, helping, division, part**
(informal) **cut**

share *VERB*
*The robbers **shared** the loot between them.*
• **divide, split, distribute, allot, allocate, deal out, ration out**

sharp *ADJECTIVE*
❶ *Use a pair of **sharp** scissors.*
• **keen, sharpened, razor-sharp**
OPPOSITE **blunt**
❷ *Barbed wire has **sharp** points all along it.*
• **pointed, spiky, jagged**
OPPOSITE **smooth**
❸ *He felt a **sharp** pain in his side.*
• **acute, piercing, stabbing**
OPPOSITE **dull**

❹ *Eagles have **sharp** eyes to see far in the distance.*
• **keen, keen-sighted, observant, perceptive**
OPPOSITE **unobservant**
❺ *You need to focus the camera to get a **sharp** picture.*
• **clear, distinct, well defined, crisp**
OPPOSITE **blurred**
❻ *Sherlock Holmes had a very **sharp** intelligence.*
• **clever, quick, shrewd, perceptive**
OPPOSITES **dull, slow**
❼ *The bus slowed down before a **sharp** bend in the road.*
• **abrupt, sudden, steep**
A bend that doubles back on itself is a **hairpin** bend.
OPPOSITE **gradual**
❽ *The **sharp** frost killed our geraniums.*
• **severe, extreme, intense, serious**
OPPOSITES **slight, mild**
❾ *This salad dressing is a bit **sharp**.*
• **sour, tart, bitter**
OPPOSITES **mild, sweet**

sharpen *VERB*
*I need to **sharpen** these crayons.*
• **make sharp, grind, whet, hone**

shatter *VERB*
❶ *The ball **shattered** a window.*
• **break, smash, destroy, wreck**
❷ *The windscreen **shattered** when a stone hit it.*
• **break, splinter, disintegrate**

sheaf *NOUN*
*She had a **sheaf** of papers in her hand.*
• **bunch, bundle**

sheath *NOUN*
*The knight put his sword back in its **sheath**.*
• **casing, covering, sleeve**
A sheath for a sword or dagger is a **scabbard**.

shed *NOUN*
*They kept their lawnmower in the garden **shed**.*
• **hut, shack, outhouse**

shed *VERB* **sheds, shedding, shed**
*A lorry **shed** its load on the motorway.*
• **drop, let fall, spill, scatter**

sheen *NOUN*
*He waxed the table to give it a nice **sheen**.*
• **shine, polish, gloss, gleam, lustre**

sheep *NOUN*
A male sheep is a **ram**.
A female sheep is a **ewe**.
A young sheep is a **lamb**.
Meat from sheep is **mutton** or **lamb**.
The woolly coat of a sheep is its **fleece**.

sheer *ADJECTIVE*
❶ *The story he told was **sheer** nonsense.*
• **complete, total, utter, absolute, pure**
❷ *Don't try to climb that **sheer** cliff.*
• **vertical, perpendicular**
❸ *The ballgown was made of **sheer** silk.*
• **fine, thin, transparent, see-through**

sheet *NOUN*
❶ *She started her diary on a fresh **sheet** of paper.*
• **page, leaf, piece**
❷ *The pond was covered with a thin **sheet** of ice.*
• **layer, film, covering, surface**
❸ *The glazier came to fit a new **sheet** of glass.*
• **panel, pane, plate**

shelf *NOUN*
*She put the books back on the **shelf**.*
• **ledge, rack**
A shelf above a fireplace is a **mantelpiece**.

shell *NOUN*
*Tortoises have hard **shells**.*
• **covering, case, casing, outside, exterior**

A B C D E F G H I J K L M N O P Q R S T U V W X Y Z

shellfish *NOUN*

WORD WEB

SOME TYPES OF SHELLFISH:

• **barnacle, clam, cockle, conch, crab, crayfish, cuttlefish, limpet, lobster, mussel, oyster, prawn, razor shell, scallop, shrimp, whelk, winkle**

Shellfish with legs, such as crabs, lobsters and shrimps are **crustaceans**.

shelter *NOUN*

They reached ***shelter*** *just before the storm broke.*

• **cover, protection, safety, refuge, sanctuary**

shelter *VERB*

❶ *The hedge* ***shelters*** *the garden from the wind.*

• **protect, screen, shield, guard, defend, safeguard**

❷ *We* ***sheltered*** *from the rain under the trees.*

• **hide, take refuge**

shelve *VERB*

They had to ***shelve*** *their plans for a summer holiday.*

• **postpone, put off, defer, suspend**
(informal) **put on ice**

shield *NOUN*

The trees act as an effective wind ***shield.***

• **screen, barrier, defence, guard, protection**

The part of a helmet that shields your face is the **visor**.

shield *VERB*

The mother bear ***shielded*** *her cubs from danger.*

• **protect, defend, guard, safeguard, keep safe, shelter**

shift *VERB*

❶ *I need some help to* ***shift*** *the furniture.*

• **move, rearrange, reposition**

❷ *It was hard work* ***shifting*** *the mud off the tyres.*

• **remove, dislodge, budge**

shine *VERB* **shines, shining, shone** or (in sense 2) **shined**

❶ *A light* ***shone*** *from an upstairs window.*

• **beam, glow, blaze, glare, gleam**

for other ways to describe light see **light**

❷ *He* ***shines*** *his shoes every morning.*

• **polish, rub, brush**

❸ *She's good at all sports, but she* ***shines*** *at tennis.*

• **be outstanding, excel, stand out**

shiny *ADJECTIVE*

She polished the mirror until it was ***shiny.***

• **shining, bright, gleaming, glistening, glossy, polished, burnished, lustrous**

OPPOSITE **dull**

ship *NOUN*

Ships that travel long distances at sea are **ocean-going** or **seagoing** ships.

People who work on ships at sea are **nautical** or **seafaring** people.

for types of boat or ship see **boat**

ship *VERB*

The firm ***ships*** *goods all over the world.*

• **transport, send, post, mail**

shirk *VERB*

He always ***shirks*** *the unpleasant tasks.*

• **avoid, evade, get out of, dodge, duck**

shiver *VERB*

Ali waited outside, ***shivering*** *with cold.*

• **tremble, quiver, shake, shudder, quake**

shock *NOUN*

❶ *The news of his death came as a great* ***shock.***

• **blow, surprise, fright, upset**

❷ *People felt the* ***shock*** *of the explosion miles away.*

• **bang, impact, jolt**

❸ *The driver involved in the accident was in a state of* ***shock.***

• **distress, trauma**

shock *VERB*
*The whole town was **shocked** by the news.*
• horrify, appal, startle, alarm, stun, stagger, shake, astonish, astound, surprise, dismay, upset
A formal synonym is **traumatise**.

shoe *NOUN*

WORD WEB

SOME TYPES OF SHOE OR BOOT:

• ankle boot, ballet shoe, baseball boot, boot, brogue, clog, court shoe, espadrille, flat shoe, flip-flop, football boot, gym shoe, high-heel shoe, moccasin, mule, plimsoll, pump, sandal, slipper, sneaker, stiletto, tap shoe, tennis shoe, trainer, wedge, wellington or *(informal)* wellie

shone *past tense see* **shine**

shook *past tense see* **shake**

shoot *VERB* **shoots, shooting, shot**
❶ *Robin Hood **shot** an arrow into the air.*
• fire, discharge, launch, aim
❷ *It is now illegal to hunt and **shoot** tigers.*
• fire at, hit, open fire on, gun down
❸ *They watched the racing cars **shoot** past.*
• race, speed, dash, rush, streak, hurtle, fly, whizz, zoom
❹ *Part of the film was **shot** in Canada.*
• film, photograph

shoot *NOUN*
*Young **shoots** grow in the spring.*
• bud, sprout

shop *NOUN*

WORD WEB

VARIOUS TYPES OF SHOP:

• boutique, corner shop, department store, market, online store, shopping centre, supermarket

SPECIALIST SHOPS:

• antique shop, baker, bookshop, butcher, charity shop, cheesemonger, chemist, clothes shop, delicatessen, DIY or do-it-yourself store, fishmonger, florist, garden centre, gift shop, greengrocer, grocer, health-food shop, ironmonger, jeweller, music shop, newsagent, pharmacy, post office, shoe shop, sweet shop, toy shop

PEOPLE WHO WORK IN SHOPS:

• cashier, sales assistant, shopkeeper or storekeeper

shopping *NOUN*
*Just put the **shopping** in the boot of the car.*
• goods, purchases

shore *NOUN*
see **seashore**

short *ADJECTIVE*
❶ *They live a **short** distance from the shops.*
• little, small
OPPOSITE long
❷ *It was a very **short** visit.*
• brief, quick, fleeting, hasty, temporary
OPPOSITE long
❸ *The troll was very **short** and fat.*
• small, tiny, little, squat, dumpy, diminutive, petite
OPPOSITE tall
❹ *The supply of water was getting **short**.*
• low, meagre, scant, limited, inadequate, insufficient
OPPOSITE plentiful
❺ *There is no need to be **short** with me!*
• abrupt, rude, sharp, curt, impolite, snappy
OPPOSITES patient, polite

shortage *NOUN*
*The **shortage** of water is worrying.*
• scarcity, deficiency, lack, want, dearth
A shortage of water is a **drought**.
A shortage of food is a **famine**.

A B C D E F G H I J K L M N O P Q R S T U V W X Y Z

shortcoming *NOUN*
*As an actor, he has some **shortcomings**.*
• defect, failing, fault, weakness, limitation, drawback

shorten *VERB*
*She had to **shorten** the essay because it was too long.*
• cut down, reduce, cut, trim, abbreviate, abridge, condense, compress, curtail
OPPOSITE lengthen

shortly *ADVERB*
*The post should arrive **shortly**.*
• soon, before long, presently

shot *past tense see* **shoot**

shot *NOUN*
❶ *I heard a noise like the **shot** of a pistol.*
• bang, blast, crack
❷ *The archer was an excellent **shot**.*
A person who is good at shooting with a gun is a **marksman**.
❸ *The striker had an easy **shot** at the goal.*
• hit, strike, kick
❹ *The photographer took some unusual **shots**.*
• photograph, picture, snap, snapshot
❺ *(informal) We each had a **shot** at solving the riddle.*
• try, go, attempt
(informal) bash

shout *VERB*
*The ogre was **shouting** and stamping with rage.*
• call, cry out, bawl, yell, bellow, roar, howl, yelp, scream, screech, shriek
OPPOSITE whisper

shout *NOUN*
*We heard a **shout** from far away.*
• call, cry, yell, yelp, bellow, roar, howl

shove *VERB*
*A man ran past and **shoved** me to the side.*
• push, thrust, force, barge, elbow, jostle, shoulder

shovel *VERB*
*We **shovelled** the snow into a huge heap.*
• dig, scoop, shift, clear, move

show *VERB* **shows, showing, showed, shown**
❶ *My uncle **showed** us his coin collection.*
• present, reveal, display, exhibit
❷ *The photo **shows** my grandparents on holiday.*
• portray, picture, depict, illustrate, represent
❸ *The dance tutor **showed** them what to do.*
• explain to, make clear to, instruct, teach, tell
❹ *The evidence **shows** that he was right.*
• prove, demonstrate
❺ *A nurse **showed** them into the waiting room.*
• direct, guide, conduct, escort, usher
❻ *The signpost **shows** the way.*
• indicate, point out
❼ *His vest **showed** through his shirt.*
• be seen, be visible, appear

➤ **to show off**
*Walter is always **showing off**.*
• boast, brag, crow, gloat, swagger
(informal) blow your own trumpet
A person who shows off is a **show-off**.

show *NOUN*
❶ *There is a **show** of artwork at the end of term.*
• display, exhibition, presentation
❷ *There's a good **show** on at the theatre.*
• performance, production, entertainment

shower *NOUN*
for various types of rain see **weather**

shower *VERB*
*A passing bus **showered** mud over them.*
• spray, splash, spatter, sprinkle

showy *ADJECTIVE*
*She was wearing very **showy** earrings.*
• gaudy, flashy, bright, loud, garish, conspicuous
OPPOSITE plain

shred *NOUN*
*The police couldn't find a **shred** of evidence.*
• **bit, piece, scrap, trace**
➤ **shreds**
*The gale ripped the tent to **shreds**.*
• **tatters, ribbons, rags, strips**

shrewd *ADJECTIVE*
*The spy was too **shrewd** to be caught.*
• **clever, quick-witted, intelligent, sharp, cunning, crafty, artful, ingenious, wily, canny**
OPPOSITE **stupid**

shriek *NOUN, VERB*
*'Quick!' **shrieked** Alice. 'Open the door!'*
• **cry, scream, screech, shout, howl, bawl, squeal, wail, yell**

shrill *ADJECTIVE*
*They heard the **shrill** sound of a whistle.*
• **high, high-pitched, piercing, sharp, screechy**
OPPOSITES **low, soft**

shrink *VERB*
*My jeans have **shrunk** in the wash.*
• **become smaller, contract**
OPPOSITE **expand**

shrivel *VERB*
*The plants **shrivelled** in the heat.*
• **wilt, wither, droop, dry up, wrinkle, shrink**

shroud *VERB*
*The mountain was **shrouded** in mist.*
• **cover, envelop, wrap, blanket, hide, conceal, mask, screen, veil**

shrub *NOUN*
*She bought some **shrubs** at the garden centre.*
• **bush**

shudder *VERB*
*They **shuddered** with fear when they heard the creature roar.*
• **tremble, quake, quiver, shake, shiver**

shuffle *VERB*
❶ *She **shuffled** along the corridor in her slippers.*
• **shamble, scuffle, hobble, scrape**
❷ *Did you remember to **shuffle** the cards?*
• **mix, mix up, jumble**

shut *VERB* **shuts, shutting, shut**
*Please **shut** the door behind you.*
• **close, fasten, seal, secure, lock, bolt, latch**
To shut a door with a bang is to **slam** it.
➤ **to shut down**
*The restaurant may have to **shut down**.*
• **close down**
➤ **to shut someone up**
*He had been **shut up** in a dungeon for five years.*
• **imprison, confine, detain**
➤ **to shut up** *(informal)*
*I wish those people behind us would **shut up**!*
• **be quiet, be silent, stop talking, hold your tongue**

shy *ADJECTIVE*
*The little girl was too **shy** to say anything.*
• **bashful, timid, coy, reserved, hesitant, self-conscious, inhibited, modest**
OPPOSITE **bold**

sick *ADJECTIVE*
❶ *Katie is off school because she's **sick**.*
• **ill, unwell, poorly, sickly, ailing, indisposed, off colour, peaky**
OPPOSITE **healthy**
❷ *The sea was rough and the cabin boy felt **sick**.*
• **nauseous, queasy**
➤ **to be sick of**
*I'm **sick of** this miserable weather!*
• **be fed up with, be tired of, have had enough of**

sicken *VERB*
*They were **sickened** by the smell in the dungeon.*
• **disgust, revolt, repel, offend**
(informal) **turn your stomach**

sickly *ADJECTIVE*
*He has always been a **sickly** child.*
• **unhealthy, weak, delicate, frail**
OPPOSITES **healthy, strong**

sickness *NOUN*
see **illness**

side *NOUN*
❶ *A cube has six **sides**.*
• **face, surface**
❷ *The path runs along the **side** of the field.*
• **edge, border, boundary, fringe, perimeter**
The side of a page is the **margin**.
The side of a road is the **verge**.
❸ *I could see both **sides** of the argument.*
• **point of view, view, angle, aspect**
❹ *The football club has a strong **side** this year.*
• **team**

side *VERB*
➤ **to side with someone**
*Some of the townspeople **sided with** the enemy.*
• **support, favour, take the side of, agree with, back**

siege *NOUN*
*The town held out against the **siege** for months.*
• **blockade**

sift *VERB*
***Sift** the flour to get rid of any lumps.*
• **sieve, strain, filter**
➤ **to sift through something**
*The detective began to **sift through** the evidence.*
• **examine, inspect, sort out, analyse, scrutinise, review**

sigh *NOUN, VERB*
*'I'll never be good at tennis,' **sighed** Libby.*
• **moan, lament, grumble, complain**

sight *NOUN*
❶ *Weasels have sharp **sight** and excellent hearing.*
• **eyesight, vision**
❷ *The woods in autumn are a lovely **sight**.*
• **spectacle, display, show, scene**
❸ *By the third day, the ship was in **sight** of land.*
• **view, range**
❹ *We went to London to see the **sights**.*
• **attraction, landmark**

sight *VERB*
*The lookout **sighted** a ship on the horizon.*
• **see, spot, spy, make out, observe, notice, distinguish, recognise, glimpse**

sign *NOUN*
❶ *A **sign** pointed to the exit.*
• **notice, placard, poster, signpost**
The sign belonging to a particular business or organisation is its **logo**.
The sign on a particular brand of goods is a **trademark**.
❷ *The witch gave no **sign** that she was angry.*
• **indication, clue, hint, warning, signal, portent**
❸ *The guard gave us a **sign** to pass through the gates.*
• **signal, gesture, cue, reminder**

sign *VERB*
❶ *Please **sign** your name on the form.*
• **write, inscribe**
❷ *The club **signed** a new player last week.*
• **take on, engage, recruit, enrol**

signal *NOUN*
*The spy waited for the **signal** that all was clear.*
• **sign, indication, prompt, cue**
A signal that tells you not to do something is a **warning**.

signal *VERB*
*The pilot **signalled** that he was going to descend.*
• **give a sign or signal, gesture, indicate, motion**

significance *NOUN*
*What's the **significance** of that symbol?*
• **importance, meaning, message, point, relevance**

significant *ADJECTIVE*
❶ *The book describes the **significant** events of last century.*
• **important, major, noteworthy, influential**
❷ *Global warming is having a **significant** effect on wildlife.*
• **noticeable, considerable, perceptible, striking**
OPPOSITE **insignificant**

signify *VERB*
❶ *A red light **signifies** danger.*
• **represent, stand for, symbolise, indicate, denote, mean**
❷ *The crew **signified** their agreement by raising their hands.*
• **show, express, communicate, convey**

silence *NOUN*
*There was **silence** while we sat the exam.*
• **quiet, quietness, hush, stillness, calm, peace**
OPPOSITE **noise**

silence *VERB*
*He **silenced** the audience by ringing a gong.*
• **deaden, muffle, quieten, suppress**
To silence someone by putting something over their mouth is to **gag** them.

silent *ADJECTIVE*
❶ *At night, the desert was cold and **silent**.*
• **quiet, noiseless, soundless, still, hushed**
Something you can't hear is **inaudible**.
A common simile is **as silent as the grave**.
OPPOSITE **noisy**
❷ *Morris kept **silent** throughout the meeting.*
• **quiet, speechless, mute**
(informal) **mum**
To be too shy to speak is to be **tongue-tied**.
OPPOSITE **talkative**

silky *ADJECTIVE*
*Some types of rabbit have long, **silky** fur.*
• **smooth, soft, fine, sleek, velvety**

silly *ADJECTIVE*
*It was **silly** of me to lock myself out of the house.*
• **foolish, stupid, idiotic, senseless, thoughtless, brainless, unwise, unintelligent, half-witted, hare-brained, scatterbrained**
(informal) **daft**
OPPOSITE **sensible**

similar *ADJECTIVE*
*The puppies are **similar** in appearance.*
• **alike, identical, indistinguishable, matching, the same**
OPPOSITES **dissimilar, different**
➤ **similar to**
*The new book is **similar to** the previous one.*
• **like, close to, comparable tounlike, different from**

similarity *NOUN*
*It's easy to see the **similarity** between the twins.*
• **likeness, resemblance**
OPPOSITE **difference**

simple *ADJECTIVE*
❶ *Can you answer this **simple** question?*
• **easy, elementary, straightforward**
OPPOSITE **difficult**
❷ *The help file is written in **simple** language.*
• **clear, plain, uncomplicated, understandable, intelligible**
OPPOSITE **complicated**
❸ *The girl wore a **simple** cotton dress.*
• **plain, undecorated**
OPPOSITE **elaborate**
❹ *He enjoys **simple** pleasures like walking and gardening.*
• **ordinary, unsophisticated, humble, modest, homely**
OPPOSITE **sophisticated**

simply *ADVERB*
❶ *I found his story **simply** unbelievable.*
• **absolutely, wholly, completely, totally, utterly**
❷ *He won't eat peas **simply** because they're green!*
• **just, merely, purely, only, solely**

sin *NOUN*
Some people believe that lying is a ***sin****.*
• **wrong, evil, wickedness, wrongdoing**

sincere *ADJECTIVE*
Please accept my ***sincere*** *apologies.*
• **genuine, honest, true, truthful, real, earnest, wholehearted, frank**
OPPOSITE **insincere**

sing *VERB* **sings, singing, sang, sung**

WORD WEB

SOME WAYS TO SING:
• **chant, chirp, croon, hum, trill, warble, yodel**

TYPES OF SINGING VOICE:
• **alto, baritone, bass, contralto, soprano, tenor, treble**
for kinds of music for singing see **song**

singe *VERB*
The iron was too hot and ***singed*** *my T-shirt.*
• **burn, scorch, sear, blacken, char**

singer *NOUN*
The band comprises two guitarists and a ***singer****.*
• **vocalist**
A group of singers is a **choir** or **chorus**.
A member of a choir is a **chorister**.

single *ADJECTIVE*
❶ *We saw a* ***single*** *house high on the moors.*
• **solitary, isolated**
When only a single example of something exists, it is **unique**.
❷ *Miss Dempster was quite content to stay* ***single****.*
• **unmarried**
An unmarried man is a **bachelor**.
An unmarried woman is a **spinster**.

single *VERB*
➤ **to single someone out**
They ***singled her out*** *as the best player in the team.*
• **pick out, select, choose, identify**

sinister *ADJECTIVE*
He looked up with a ***sinister*** *smile on his face.*
• **menacing, threatening, malevolent, evil, disturbing, unsettling, eerie**
(informal) **creepy**

sink *VERB* **sinks, sinking, sank, sunk**
❶ *The ship hit the rocks and* ***sank****.*
• **go down, become submerged, founder, capsize**
To let water into a ship to sink it deliberately is to **scuttle** it.
❷ *The sun began to* ***sink*** *below the horizon.*
• **drop, fall, descend, subside, dip**
When the sun sinks to the horizon it **sets**.

sit *VERB* **sits, sitting, sat**
❶ *Rachel* ***sat*** *on the sofa reading a magazine.*
• **have a seat, settle down, rest, perch**
To sit on your heels is to **squat**.
To sit to have your portrait painted is to **pose**.
❷ *My brother is* ***sitting*** *his driving test next week.*
• **take**
(informal) **go in for**

site *NOUN*
This is the ***site*** *of an ancient burial ground.*
• **location, place, position, situation, setting, plot**

site *VERB*
The new cinema will be ***sited*** *in the middle of the town.*
• **locate, place, position, situate**

situation *NOUN*
❶ *The house is in a pleasant* ***situation****.*
• **location, locality, place, position, setting, site, spot**
❷ *I found myself in an awkward* ***situation****.*
• **position, circumstances, condition, state of affairs**

A bad situation is a **plight** or **predicament**.
❸ *She applied for a **situation** in the bank.*
• **job, post, position, appointment**

size NOUN

❶ *What **size** is the garden?*
• **dimensions, proportions, area, extent**
❷ *They were amazed by the sheer **size** of the pyramids.*
• **scale, magnitude, immensity**

skeleton NOUN

❶ *Inside the crypt, they found several human **skeletons**.*
• **bones**
❷ *So far they've only put up the **skeleton** of the building.*
• **frame, framework, shell**

sketch NOUN

❶ *She drew a quick **sketch** of her cat.*
• **drawing, picture, outline**
A sketch you do while you think of other things is a **doodle**.
❷ *The actors performed a comic **sketch**.*
• **scene, turn, routine**

sketch VERB

*He **sketched** a rough design for the poster.*
• **draw, draft, outline, rough out**

skid VERB

*The postman **skidded** on the icy pavement.*
• **slide, slip**

skilful ADJECTIVE

*Dickens was a **skilful** writer.*
• **expert, skilled, accomplished, able, capable, talented, brilliant, clever, masterly, deft**
If you are skilful at a lot of things, you are **versatile**.
OPPOSITE **incompetent**

skill NOUN

*It takes a lot of **skill** to build a boat.*
• **expertise, ability, aptitude, capability, competence, accomplishment, talent, proficiency, deftness**

skim VERB

*The stone **skimmed** across the surface of the pond.*
• **glide, slide, skid, slip**
➤ **to skim through**
*Luke **skimmed through** the newspaper.*
• **scan, look through, skip through, flick through**

skin NOUN

*The cave people were dressed in animal **skins**.*
• **coat, fur, hide, pelt**
The type of skin you have on your face is your **complexion**.
Skin on fruit or vegetables is **peel** or **rind**.
Skin that might form on top of a liquid is a **coating**, **film** or **membrane**.

skinny ADJECTIVE

*A **skinny** girl in bare feet answered the door.*
• **thin, lean, bony, gaunt, lanky, scrawny, scraggy**
OPPOSITE **plump**

skip VERB

❶ *The children **skipped** along the pavement.*
• **hop, jump, leap, bound, caper, dance, prance**
❷ *I **skipped** the boring bits in the book.*
• **pass over, miss out, ignore, omit, leave out**

skirt VERB

*The path **skirts** the playing field.*
• **circle, go round, pass round**

sky NOUN

*Clouds drifted slowly across the **sky**.*
• **air, heavens**

WRITING TIPS

You can use these words to describe the sky.

TO DESCRIBE THE SKY BY DAY:

• **blue, clear, cloudless, cloudy, grey, overcast, stormy, sunless, sunny, thundery**
see also **weather**
The sky was overcast and still. Thin wisps of mist clung to the tops of the pine trees, and the oak and wild cherry were bare-leaved, waiting for spring.—SKY HAWK, Gill Lewis

TO DESCRIBE THE SKY AT NIGHT:

• **moonless, moonlit, pitch-black, starless, starlit, starry, star-studded**

slab *NOUN*
The words were engraved on a ***slab*** *of marble.*
• **block, piece, tablet, slice, chunk, hunk, lump**

slack *ADJECTIVE*
❶ *One of the ropes on the tent was* ***slack****.*
• **loose, limp**
OPPOSITE **tight**
❷ *The team looked very* ***slack*** *in defence.*
• **lazy, lax, negligent, casual, relaxed, easy-going**
OPPOSITE **alert**

slacken *VERB*
❶ *The climber* ***slackened*** *the rope around his waist.*
• **loosen, relax, release, ease off**
OPPOSITE **tighten**
❷ *The pace of the game* ***slackened*** *after half-time.*
• **lessen, reduce, decrease, slow down**
OPPOSITE **increase**

slam *VERB*
Don't ***slam*** *the door!*
• **bang, shut loudly**

slant *VERB*
❶ *Her handwriting* ***slants*** *backwards.*
• **lean, slope, tilt, incline, be at an angle**
❷ *He* ***slanted*** *his story to make it more dramatic.*
• **distort, twist, warp**

slant *NOUN*
❶ *The floor of the caravan was at a* ***slant****.*
• **slope, angle, tilt, incline, gradient**
A slant on a damaged ship is a **list**.
A slanting line joining opposite corners of a square, etc., is a **diagonal**.
A surface slanting up to a higher level is a **ramp**.
❷ *The film brings a new* ***slant*** *to an old story.*
• **point of view, angle, emphasis, bias**

slap *VERB*
He ***slapped*** *his hand against his thigh and laughed.*
• **smack, strike, spank, hit, clout**
(informal) **whack**

slash *VERB*
for various ways to cut things see **cut**

slaughter *VERB*
They had to ***slaughter*** *the diseased cattle.*
• **kill, butcher, massacre**

slaughter *NOUN*
The battle ended in terrible ***slaughter****.*
• **bloodshed, killing, massacre, butchery**

slave *VERB*
They ***slaved*** *all day to get the job done.*
• **work hard, labour, toil, grind, sweat**

slavery *NOUN*
The prisoners were sold into ***slavery****.*
• **captivity, bondage**
OPPOSITE **freedom**

sledge *NOUN*
We dragged our ***sledges*** *up the snowy slope.*
• **toboggan**
(North American) **sled**
A large sledge pulled by horses is a **sleigh**.
A sledge used in winter sports is a **bobsleigh**.

sleek *ADJECTIVE*
Otters have ***sleek*** *coats.*
• **smooth, glossy, shiny, silky, soft, velvety**
OPPOSITE **coarse**

sleep *VERB* **sleeps, sleeping, slept**
The baby is ***sleeping*** *in the next room.*
• **be asleep, take a nap, doze**
(informal) **snooze**
To go to sleep is to **drop off** or **nod off**.

sleep *NOUN*
*Mr Khan had a short **sleep** after lunch.*
• **nap, rest, doze, catnap**
(informal) **snooze, forty winks, shut-eye**
An afternoon sleep is a **siesta**.
The long sleep some animals have through the winter is **hibernation**.

sleepless *ADJECTIVE*
*The wanderers spent a **sleepless** night.*
• **restless, wide awake**
The formal name for sleeplessness is **insomnia**.

sleepy *ADJECTIVE*
*The giant was usually **sleepy** after dinner.*
• **drowsy, tired, weary, heavy-eyed, lethargic, ready to sleep**
(informal) **dopey**
OPPOSITE **wide awake**

slender *ADJECTIVE*
❶ *The ballerina had a **slender** figure.*
• **slim, lean, slight, graceful, trim, svelte**
OPPOSITE **fat**
❷ *The spider dangled on a **slender** thread.*
• **thin, fine, fragile, delicate**
OPPOSITE **thick**
❸ *They only had a **slender** chance of winning.*
• **poor, slight, slim, faint, negligible, remote**
OPPOSITE **good**
❹ *The team won by a **slender** margin.*
• **narrow, small, slim**
OPPOSITE **wide**

slice *VERB*
To slice meat is to **carve** it.
see also **cut**

slick *ADJECTIVE*
*He was very **slick** at shuffling cards.*
• **skilful, artful, clever, cunning, deft, quick**
OPPOSITE **clumsy**

slide *VERB*
*I like **sliding** down the chute in the playground.*
• **glide, skid, slip, slither**

slight *ADJECTIVE*
❶ *There's a **slight** problem with the computer.*
• **minor, unimportant, insignificant, negligible, superficial, trifling, trivial**
OPPOSITE **important**
❷ *A **slight** elderly lady met us at the door.*
• **delicate, fragile, frail, slender, slim, small, spare, thin, tiny**
OPPOSITES **stout, tall**

slightly *ADVERB*
*She was **slightly** hurt in the accident.*
• **a little, a bit, somewhat, rather**
OPPOSITES **very, seriously**

slim *ADJECTIVE*
❶ *A tall, **slim** figure appeared out of the fog.*
• **graceful, lean, slender, spare, thin, trim**
OPPOSITE **fat**
❷ *Their chances of winning are **slim**.*
• **faint, poor, slight, slender, negligible, remote**
OPPOSITE **good**
❸ *They won by a **slim** margin.*
• **narrow, small, slender**
OPPOSITE **wide**

slimy *ADJECTIVE*
*The floor of the tunnel was covered with **slimy** mud.*
• **slippery, slithery, sticky, oozy**
(informal) **gooey, icky**

sling *VERB* **slings, slinging, slung**
*Robin Hood **slung** his quiver over his shoulder.*
• **throw, cast, fling, hurl, pitch, heave, toss, lob**
(informal) **chuck**

slink *VERB* **slinks, slinking, slunk**
*The spy **slunk** away without being seen.*
• **slip, sneak, steal, creep, edge, sidle**

A B C D E F G H I J K L M N O P Q R S T U V W X Y Z

slip *VERB*
❶ *The paperboy **slipped** on the ice.*
• **skid, slither, skate**
❷ *The lifeboat **slipped** into the water.*
• **glide, slide**
❸ *Marion **slipped** out while everyone was talking.*
• **sneak, steal, slink, tiptoe, creep, edge, sidle**

slip *NOUN*
❶ *She wrote her phone number on a **slip** of paper.*
• **piece, scrap**
❷ *The pianist made a tiny **slip** at the start of the concert.*
• **mistake, error, fault, blunder, gaffe, lapse**
➤ **to give someone the slip**
*The robber **gave them all the slip**.*
• **escape, get away, run away**

slippery *ADJECTIVE*
*Take care—the floor is **slippery**.*
• **slithery, slippy, smooth, glassy**
A surface slippery with frost is **icy**.
A surface slippery with grease is **greasy** or **oily**.
A common simile is **as slippery as an eel**.

slit *NOUN*
*The archers shot arrows through the **slits** in the castle wall.*
• **opening, chink, gap, slot, split, tear, cut**

slit *VERB*
for various ways to cut things see **cut**

slither *VERB*
*The rattlesnake **slithered** through the long grass.*
• **slide, slip, glide, slink, snake**

slope *VERB*
*The beach **slopes** gently down to the sea.*
• **fall or rise, incline, bank, shelve**

slope *NOUN*
❶ *It was hard work pushing my bike up the **slope**.*
• **hill, rise, bank, ramp**
An upward slope is an **ascent**.
A downward slope is a **descent**.
❷ *Rain runs down the roof because of the **slope**.*
• **incline, slant, tilt, gradient**

sloppy *ADJECTIVE*
❶ *For breakfast, there was a bowl of steaming, **sloppy** porridge.*
• **runny, slushy, watery, liquid, wet**
(*informal*) **gloopy**
❷ *His handwriting is very **sloppy**.*
• **untidy, messy, careless, slovenly, slapdash, slipshod**

slot *NOUN*
❶ *To use the locker, put a pound coin into the **slot**.*
• **slit, chink, hole, opening**
❷ *The programme has been moved from its usual **slot**.*
• **time, spot, space, place**

slouch *VERB*
*Sue sat at her desk, **slouched** over the computer.*
• **hunch, stoop, slump, droop, flop**

slow *ADJECTIVE*
❶ *Tortoises move at a **slow** but steady pace.*
• **unhurried, leisurely, gradual, plodding, dawdling, sluggish**
❷ *They took the train to London, followed by a **slow** bus journey.*
• **lengthy, prolonged, drawn-out, tedious**
❸ *The prisoner was **slow** to answer.*
• **hesitant, reluctant, tardy**
OPPOSITE **quick**

slow *VERB*
➤ **to slow down**
***Slow down**—you're driving too fast!*
• **go slower, brake, reduce speed, decelerate**
OPPOSITE **accelerate**

sludge *NOUN*
*They cleared a lot of **sludge** out of the pond.*
• **muck, mud, ooze, slime**
(*informal*) **gunk**

slump *VERB*
❶ *Sales of music CDs have* ***slumped*** *recently.*
• **decline, fall, drop, plummet, plunge, crash, collapse**
❷ *The professor* ***slumped*** *into an armchair.*
• **flop, collapse, sink, sag, slouch**

slump *NOUN*
There was a ***slump*** *in trade after Christmas.*
• **collapse, drop, fall, decline**
A general slump in trade is a **depression** or **recession.**
OPPOSITE **boom**

sly *ADJECTIVE*
The chess player knew several ***sly*** *moves.*
• **crafty, cunning, artful, clever, wily, tricky, sneaky, devious, furtive, secretive, stealthy, underhand**
A common simile is **as sly as a fox.**
OPPOSITE **straightforward**

smack *VERB*
He ***smacked*** *the other player on the head by accident.*
• **slap, strike, hit, cuff**
(informal) **whack**
for other ways of hitting see **hit**

small *ADJECTIVE*

OVERUSED WORD

Try to vary the words you use for **small**. Here are some other words you could use.

FOR A SMALL OBJECT:

• **little, tiny, minute, compact, miniature, microscopic, minuscule, mini, baby**
(informal) **teeny, titchy**
(Scottish) **wee**
OPPOSITES **big, large**
'Put vun drop, just vun titchy droplet, of this liqvid into a chocolate or a sveet, and at nine o'clock the next morning the child who ate it vill turn into a mouse in tventy-six seconds!' —THE WITCHES, Roald Dahl

FOR A SMALL PERSON OR CREATURE:

• **little, short, petite, slight, dainty, diminutive, undersized**
(informal) **pint-sized**
Although ***slight*** *in stature, Ellie was remarkably strong.*
OPPOSITES **big, tall, large**

FOR A SMALL HELPING OR PORTION:

• **meagre, inadequate, insufficient, paltry, scanty, stingy, skimpy**
(informal) **measly**
OPPOSITES **large, generous, ample**
Interesting smells rose from the camp-kitchens, and Snibril thought sadly of the meagre rations he carried in his pack.—DRAGONS AT CRUMBLING CASTLE, Terry Pratchett

FOR A SMALL PROBLEM OR CHANGE:

• **minor, slight, unimportant, insignificant, trivial, trifling, negligible**
OPPOSITES **major, substantial**
Don't worry about the ***trivial*** *details.*

smart *ADJECTIVE*
❶ *Everyone looked* ***smart*** *at the wedding.*
• **elegant, well-dressed, well-groomed, stylish, spruce, fashionable, chic, neat, trim**
To make yourself smart is to **smarten up.**
OPPOSITE **scruffy**
❷ *They booked a table in a very* ***smart*** *restaurant.*
• **fashionable, high-class, exclusive, fancy**
(informal) **posh**
❸ *The detective made a very* ***smart*** *move.*
• **clever, ingenious, intelligent, shrewd, crafty**
OPPOSITE **stupid**
❹ *The cyclists set off at a* ***smart*** *pace.*
• **fast, quick, rapid, speedy, swift, brisk**
OPPOSITE **slow**

smart *VERB*
The smoke from the barbecue made our eyes ***smart.***
• **hurt, sting, prick, prickle, tingle**

smash *VERB*
*The vase rolled off the table and **smashed** to pieces on the floor.*
• **break, crush, shatter, crack**
When wood smashes it **splinters.**
To smash something completely is to **demolish, destroy** or **wreck** it.
➤ **to smash into**
*A lorry had **smashed into** the side of a bus.*
• **crash into, collide with, bang into, bump into**

smear *VERB*
*First **smear** the dish with butter.*
• **spread, wipe, plaster, rub, dab, smudge, daub**

smear *NOUN*
*There were **smears** of paint all over the carpet.*
• **streak, smudge, blotch, splodge, splotch, daub, mark**

smell *VERB* **smells, smelling, smelt** or **smelled**
❶ *I could **smell** something baking in the oven.*
• **scent, sniff**
(informal) **get a whiff of**
❷ *After walking all day, my feet were beginning to **smell**.*
• **stink, reek**
(informal) **pong**

smell *NOUN*
❶ *The air was filled with the **smell** of roses.*
• **scent, aroma, perfume, fragrance**
❷ *The **smell** of mouldy cheese was unbearable.*
• **odour, stench, stink, reek, whiff**
(informal) **pong, niff**

WRITING TIPS

You can use these words to describe a **smell**.

TO DESCRIBE A GOOD SMELL:

• **aromatic, fragrant, perfumed, scented, sweet, sweet-smelling**
In the garden below were lilac-trees purple with flowers, and their dizzily sweet fragrance drifted up to the window on the morning wind.–ANNE OF GREEN GABLES, L. M. Montgomery

TO DESCRIBE A BAD SMELL:

• **evil-smelling, fetid, foul, musty, odorous, rancid, reeking, rotten, smelly, stinking**
(informal) **stinky, pongy, whiffy**
There was the same musty smell about the place that I had noticed in the Ballroom. It was the stench of witches.–THE WITCHES, Roald Dahl

TO DESCRIBE A STRONG SMELL:

• **heady, overpowering, pungent**
*The **heady** scent of spices hung in the air.*

smile *VERB, NOUN*
*The stranger **smiled** and introduced himself.*
• **grin, beam**
To smile in a silly way is to **simper.**
To smile in a self-satisfied way is to **smirk.**
To smile in an insulting way is to **sneer.**

smoke *NOUN*
*Puffs of green **smoke** came from the dragon's nostrils.*
• **fumes, gas, steam, vapour**
The smoke given out by a car is **exhaust.**
A mixture of smoke and fog is **smog.**

smoke *VERB*
❶ *The bonfire was still **smoking** next morning.*
• **smoulder**
❷ *A man stood silently **smoking** a cigar.*
• **puff at**

smooth *ADJECTIVE*
❶ *This part of the road is **smooth** and good for cycling.*
• **flat, even, level**
OPPOSITE **uneven**
❷ *In the early morning, the lake was perfectly **smooth**.*
• **calm, still, unruffled, undisturbed, glassy**
OPPOSITE **rough**
❸ *Otters have **smooth** and shiny coats.*
• **silky, sleek, velvety**
OPPOSITE **coarse**

❹ *The journey by train is very quick and smooth.*
- comfortable, steady

OPPOSITE bumpy

❺ *Stir the cake mixture until it is smooth.*
- creamy, flowing, runny

OPPOSITE lumpy

smooth *VERB*

*Mia stood up and **smoothed** her dress.*
- flatten, level, even out

To smooth cloth you can **iron** or **press** it.
To smooth wood you can **plane** or **sand** it.

smother *VERB*

❶ *Pythons **smother** their prey to death.*
- suffocate, choke, stifle

❷ *The pudding was **smothered** with cream.*
- cover, coat

smoulder *VERB*

see **burn**

smudge *NOUN*

*There were **smudges** of ink all over the page.*
- smear, blot, streak, stain, mark

smudge *VERB*

*Don't **smudge** the icing on the cake!*
- smear, blur, streak

snack *NOUN*

*I usually bring an apple or banana for a **snack**.*
- bite, refreshments

(informal) nibble

snag *NOUN*

*We've hit a **snag** with our holiday plans.*
- problem, difficulty, obstacle, hitch, complication, setback

snake *NOUN*

*The **snake** coiled itself around a branch.*
- serpent

WORD WEB

SOME KINDS OF SNAKE:
- adder, asp, anaconda, boa constrictor, cobra, coral snake, grass snake, mamba, puff adder, python, rattlesnake, sand snake, sea snake, sidewinder, tree snake, viper

PARTS OF A SNAKE:
- fangs, hood, scales, skin, venom

A snake **sheds** or **sloughs off** its old skin.
Snakes are **oviparous**, meaning that they lay eggs.
A route or river that twists like a snake is **serpentine**.

snap *VERB*

❶ *A twig **snapped** under one of my boots.*
- break, crack

❷ *The dog **snapped** at the postman's ankles.*
- bite, nip

❸ *Mr Doyle was in a bad mood and **snapped** at everyone.*
- snarl, bark

snare *NOUN*

*A bird had got caught in the **snare**.*
- trap

snarl *VERB*

❶ *The guard dog **snarled** as we approached.*
- growl, bare its teeth

❷ *'Go away!' **snarled** a voice inside the cave.*
- snap, growl, thunder, bark

snatch *VERB*

*The thief **snatched** the jewels and ran off.*
- grab, seize, grasp, pluck, wrench away, wrest away

a b c d e f g h i j k l m n o p q r s t u v w x y z

sneak *VERB* **sneaks, sneaking, sneaked** or *(North American)* **snuck**
*I managed to **sneak** in without anyone seeing.*
• slip, steal, creep, slink, tiptoe, sidle, skulk

sneaky *ADJECTIVE*
*That was a really **sneaky** trick.*
• sly, underhand, cunning, crafty, devious, furtive, untrustworthy
OPPOSITE honest

sneer *VERB*
➤ **to sneer at**
*He **sneered at** my attempt to write a poem.*
• make fun of, mock, ridicule, scoff at, jeer at, deride

sniff *NOUN, VERB*
for various sounds see **sound**

snigger *VERB*
*Please stop **sniggering** at the back of the room.*
• laugh, giggle, titter, chuckle

snip *VERB*
*Remember to **snip** off any loose threads.*
• cut, chop, clip, trim

snippet *NOUN*
*We could hear **snippets** of their conversation.*
• piece, fragment, bit, scrap, morsel, snatch

snivel *VERB*
*For goodness' sake, stop **snivelling**!*
• cry, sob, weep, sniff, whimper, whine

snobbish *ADJECTIVE*
*She's too **snobbish** to mix with us.*
• arrogant, pompous, superior, haughty
(informal) stuck-up, snooty, toffee-nosed
OPPOSITE humble

snoop *VERB*
*They caught a man **snooping** round the building.*
• sneak, pry, poke, rummage, spy

snort *NOUN, VERB*
for various sounds see **sound**

snout *NOUN*
*Aardvarks have long, narrow **snouts**.*
• muzzle, nose

snub *VERB*
*She **snubbed** the neighbours by not inviting them to the party.*
• insult, offend, be rude to, brush off
(informal) put down

snuck *(North American)*
past tense see **sneak**

snug *ADJECTIVE*
*The girls were tucked up **snug** in bed.*
• cosy, comfortable, warm, relaxed
(informal) comfy
A common simile is **as snug as a bug in a rug**.
OPPOSITE uncomfortable

soak *VERB*
❶ *Days of rain had **soaked** the cricket pitch.*
• wet thoroughly, drench, saturate
❷ *Leave the beans to **soak** in water overnight.*
• steep, immerse, submerge

soaking *ADJECTIVE*
*My socks are absolutely **soaking**!*
• wet through, drenched, dripping, wringing, saturated, sodden, sopping, soggy
Ground that has been soaked by rain is **waterlogged**.

soar *VERB*
❶ *The seagull spread its wings and **soared** upwards.*
• climb, rise, ascend, fly, wing
❷ *Prices have continued to **soar**.*
• go up, rise, increase, shoot up

sob *VERB*
*Tina threw herself on the bed, **sobbing** loudly.*
• cry, weep, bawl, blubber, shed tears, snivel

sober *ADJECTIVE*
❶ *He drank a little wine, but he stayed **sober**.*
• **clear-headed**
OPPOSITE **drunk**
❷ *The funeral was a **sober** occasion.*
• **serious, solemn, sombre, grave, dignified, sedate**
OPPOSITES **light-hearted, frivolous**

sociable *ADJECTIVE*
*Our new neighbours are very **sociable**.*
• **friendly, outgoing, amiable, hospitable, neighbourly**
OPPOSITE **unfriendly**

social *ADJECTIVE*
❶ *Elephants are **social** animals.*
People and creatures that like to be in groups or communities are **gregarious**.
OPPOSITE **solitary**
❷ *The club organised several **social** activities.*
• **communal, community, public, group**

society *NOUN*
❶ *Ancient Egypt was a **society** ruled by pharaohs.*
• **community, civilisation**
❷ *Mrs Byrd is head of the local music **society**.*
• **association, group, organisation, club**
❸ *She enjoys the **society** of her friends.*
• **companionship, company, fellowship, friendship**

soft *ADJECTIVE*
❶ *The kittens can only eat **soft** food.*
• **pulpy, spongy, squashy**
(informal) **squidgy**
OPPOSITES **hard, dry**
❷ *My head sank into the **soft** pillow.*
• **supple, pliable, springy, yielding, flexible**
OPPOSITES **firm, rigid**
❸ *The rabbit's fur felt very **soft**.*
• **smooth, silky, sleek, velvety, downy, feathery**
OPPOSITE **coarse**
❹ *A **soft** breeze stirred the leaves.*
• **gentle, light, mild, delicate**
OPPOSITES **rough, strong**
❺ *The smugglers spoke in **soft** whispers.*
• **quiet, low, faint**
OPPOSITE **loud**
❻ *It was hard to see clearly in the **soft** light.*
• **subdued, muted, pale, dim, low**
OPPOSITES **bright, dazzling**
❼ *You are being too **soft** with that puppy.*
• **lenient, easy-going, tolerant, indulgent**
OPPOSITES **strict, tough**

soggy *ADJECTIVE*
❶ *The pitch was **soggy** after all the rain.*
• **wet, drenched, soaked, saturated, sodden, waterlogged**
❷ *The bread had started to go **soggy**.*
• **moist, soft, mushy, pulpy, squelchy**
(informal) **squidgy**
OPPOSITE **dry**

soil *NOUN*
*The plants grow best in well-drained **soil**.*
• **earth, ground, land**
Good fertile soil is **loam**.
The fertile top layer of soil is **topsoil**.
Rich soil made by decaying leaves and plants is **humus**.

soil *VERB*
*My trainers were **soiled** with mud and grass.*
• **dirty, make dirty, stain, muddy, tarnish**

sold *past tense see* **sell**

soldier *NOUN*
*Three **soldiers** stood guard outside the building.*
• **serviceman** or **servicewoman**
A soldier paid to fight for a foreign country is a **mercenary**.
An old word for a soldier is **warrior**.
Soldiers who use heavy guns are the **artillery**.
Soldiers who fight on horseback are the **cavalry**.
Soldiers who fight on foot are the **infantry**.
see also **armed forces**

sole *ADJECTIVE*
*The castaway was the **sole** inhabitant of the island.*
• only, single, one, solitary, lone, unique

solemn *ADJECTIVE*
❶ *Inspector Fry always wore a **solemn** expression.*
• serious, grave, sober, sombre, unsmiling, glum
OPPOSITE cheerful
❷ *The funeral was a **solemn** occasion.*
• formal, dignified, grand, stately, majestic, pompous
OPPOSITE frivolous

solid *ADJECTIVE*
❶ *A cricket ball is **solid**.*
OPPOSITE hollow
❷ *The water turned into **solid** ice.*
• hard, firm, dense, compact, rigid, unyielding
A common simile is **as solid as a rock**.
OPPOSITE soft
❸ *The bars of the climbing frame are quite **solid**.*
• firm, robust, sound, strong, stable, sturdy
OPPOSITES weak, unstable
❹ *The crown was made of **solid** gold.*
• pure, genuine
❺ *He got **solid** support from his teammates.*
• firm, reliable, dependable, united, unanimous
OPPOSITES weak, divided

solidify *VERB*
*The lava **solidifies** as it cools.*
• harden, become solid, set, stiffen
OPPOSITES soften, liquify

solitary *ADJECTIVE*
❶ *He was a **solitary** man and rarely spoke to others.*
• isolated, secluded, lonely, unsociable
To be solitary is to be alone.
OPPOSITE sociable.
❷ *There was a **solitary** tree in the middle of the field.*
• single, sole, one, only

solitude *NOUN*
*On the island, there was total peace and **solitude**.*
• privacy, seclusion, isolation, loneliness

solve *VERB*
*No one has been able to **solve** this ancient riddle.*
• interpret, explain, answer, work out, find the solution to, unravel, decipher

sombre *ADJECTIVE*
❶ *The hall was decorated in **sombre** hues.*
• dark, dull, dim, dismal, dingy, drab, cheerless
OPPOSITE bright
❷ *A messenger arrived with a **sombre** look on his face.*
• gloomy, serious, grave, sober, sad, melancholy, mournful
OPPOSITE cheerful

song *NOUN*

WORD WEB

SOME KINDS OF SONG:

• anthem, aria, ballad, calypso, carol, chant, ditty, folk song, hymn, jingle, lament, lay, love song, lullaby, madrigal, nursery rhyme, pop song, psalm, rap, round, shanty, spiritual
A play or film that includes many songs is a **musical**.
A song from a musical is a **number**.
The words for a song are the **lyrics**.
for other musical terms see **music**

soon *ADVERB*
*Dinner will be ready **soon**.*
• before long, in a minute, shortly, presently, quickly

soothe *VERB*
❶ *The quiet music **soothed** her nerves.*
• calm, comfort, relax, pacify
❷ *This cream will **soothe** the pain.*
• ease, lessen, relieve

soothing *ADJECTIVE*
*They played **soothing** music.*
• calming, relaxing, restful, peaceful, gentle, pleasant

sophisticated *ADJECTIVE*
❶ *Frida looked very **sophisticated** with her hair up.*
• grown-up, mature, cultivated, cultured, refined
OPPOSITE naive
❷ *This is our most **sophisticated** camera.*
• advanced, complex, complicated, intricate, elaborate
OPPOSITES primitive, simple

sorcerer and **sorceress** *NOUN*
see **magic**

sore *ADJECTIVE*
*My feet are still **sore** from the walk.*
• painful, aching, hurting, smarting, tender, sensitive, inflamed, raw, red

sore *NOUN*
*A nurse put a dressing on the **sore**.*
• wound, inflammation, swelling

sorrow *NOUN*
❶ *Those were years of **sorrow** for the family.*
• sadness, unhappiness, misery, woe, grief, anguish, despair, distress, heartache, heartbreak, melancholy, gloom, depression, desolation, wretchedness
Sorrow because of someone's death is **mourning.**
Sorrow at being away from home is **homesickness.**
OPPOSITE happiness
❷ *Jo felt no **sorrow** for what she had done.*
• regret, remorse, repentance, apologies

sorry *ADJECTIVE*
❶ *I am so **sorry** I forgot your birthday!*
• apologetic, regretful, remorseful, ashamed (of), repentant
OPPOSITE unapologetic
❷ *Everyone felt **sorry** for the losers.*
• sympathetic, pitying, understanding, compassionate
OPPOSITE unsympathetic

sort *NOUN*
*What **sort** of music do you like?*
• kind, type, variety, form, nature, style, genre, category, order, class
A sort of animal is a **breed** or **species.**

sort *VERB*
*The books are **sorted** according to size.*
• arrange, organise, class, group, categorise, classify, divide
OPPOSITE mix
➤ **to sort something out**
*Did you manage to **sort out** the problem?*
• settle, resolve, clear up, cope with, deal with

sought *past tense see* **seek**

sound *NOUN*
*We heard the **sound** of footsteps approaching.*
• noise, tone
A loud, harsh sound is a **din** or **racket.**
A harsh mixture of sounds is a **cacophony.**

WORD WEB

SOUNDS MADE BY PEOPLE:

• achoo, bawl, bellow, boo, boom, cackle, chortle, clap, croak, cry, gasp, groan, gurgle, hiccup, hiss, howl, hum, moan, murmur, puff, scream, shout, shriek, sigh, sing, sniff, snore, snort, sob, splutter, stammer, stutter, wail, wheeze, whimper, whine, whisper, whistle, whoop, yell, yodel
see also **say**
for sounds made by animals and birds see **animal, bird**

SOUNDS MADE BY THINGS:

• bang, blare, beep, bleep, boing, bong, boom, burble, buzz, chime, chink, chug, clang, clank, clash, clatter, click, clink, clunk, crack, crackle, crash, creak, crunch, ding, drone, drum, fizz, grate, gurgle, hum, jangle, jingle, kaboom, patter, peal, ping, plink, plop, pop, purr, putter, rattle, ring, rumble, rustle, scrunch, sizzle, slam, snap, splash, squeak, squelch, swish, throb, thud, thunder, tick, ting, tinkle, twang, wham, whirr, whoosh, whistle, whizz, zap, zoom

Great whooshes of sound filled the air as the beam engine started to move, then generators started to hum, and power surged through the sizing machine.—HERE BE MONSTERS!, Alan Snow

WRITING TIPS

You can use these words to describe a sound.

TO DESCRIBE A PLEASANT SOUND:

- **sweet, harmonious, melodious, mellifluous, dulcet**

*It sounded like the **sweet** singing of a mermaid.*

TO DESCRIBE AN UNPLEASANT SOUND:

- **grating, harsh, jarring, piercing, rasping, raucous, shrill, thin, tinny**

A startled raven burst upward uttering its harsh, grating alarm cry, and flew off northward with slow, indignant wing-beats, caaking as it went.—THE EAGLE OF THE NINTH, Rosemary Sutcliff

TO DESCRIBE A LOUD SOUND:

- **blaring, deafening, noisy, thunderous**

TO DESCRIBE A QUIET SOUND:

- **low, muffled, muted, soft**

In the distance they could hear the muted sound of traffic going round Hyde Park Corner.—THE BFG, Roald Dahl

sound *VERB*
*A trumpet **sounded** in the distance.*
- **make a noise, resound, be heard**

sound *ADJECTIVE*
❶ *The walls of the fortress seemed **sound**.*
- **firm, solid, stable, safe, secure, intact, undamaged**

OPPOSITES **unsound, unstable**

❷ *She gave us some **sound** advice.*
- **good, sensible, wise, reasonable, trustworthy**

OPPOSITE **unwise**

❸ *The travellers returned safe and **sound**.*
- **strong, well, fit, healthy**

OPPOSITES **weak, unfit**

sour *ADJECTIVE*
❶ *These apples are a bit **sour**.*
- **tart, bitter, sharp, acid**

OPPOSITE **sweet**

❷ *The guard opened the door with a **sour** look on his face.*
- **cross, bad-tempered, grumpy, disagreeable, peevish**

source *NOUN*
*The vet has found the **source** of the infection.*
- **origin, start, starting point, head, root, cause**

The source of a river or stream is usually a **spring**.

south *NOUN, ADJECTIVE, ADVERB*
The parts of a continent or country in the south are the **southern** parts.
To travel towards the south is to travel **southward** or **southwards** or **in a southerly direction**.
A wind from the south is a **southerly** wind.
A person who lives in the south of a country is a **southerner**.

sow *VERB* **sows, sowing, sowed, sown** or **sowed**
To sow seeds in the ground is to **plant** them.
To sow an area of ground with seeds is to **seed** it.

space *NOUN*
❶ *There wasn't much **space** to move about.*
- **room, freedom, scope**

❷ *He peered through the tiny **space** in the curtains.*
- **gap, hole, opening, break**

A space without any air in it is a **vacuum**.
A space of time is an **interval** or **period**.
❸ *The astronauts will spend ten days in **space**.*
• outer space

WORD WEB

Everything that exists in space is the **universe** or **cosmos**.
Distances in space stretch to **infinity**.
Travel to other planets is **interplanetary** travel.
Travel to other stars is **interstellar** travel.
Travel to other galaxies is **intergalactic** travel.
A traveller in space is an **astronaut**.
A Russian astronaut is a **cosmonaut**.
In stories, beings from other planets are **aliens** or **extraterrestrials**.
see also **alien, astronaut**

NATURAL OBJECTS FOUND IN SPACE:

• **asteroid, black hole, comet, constellation, galaxy, meteor, meteorite, Milky Way, moon, nebula, nova, planet, red dwarf, red giant, shooting star, solar system, star, sun, supernova**
see also **moon, planet**

WORDS TO DO WITH TRAVEL IN SPACE:

• **blast-off, countdown, launch, mission, orbit, re-entry, rocket, satellite, spacecraft, spaceship, space station, spacesuit, spacewalk**
A robot spacecraft is a **probe**.
A vehicle which can travel on the surface of a planet is a **buggy** or **rover**.

THINGS YOU MIGHT FIND ON A SPACECRAFT:

• **airlock, booster rocket, bridge, cargo bay, capsule, computer, docking bay, fuel tank, heat shield, instrument panel, life support system, module, pod, solar panel, thruster**

THINGS A SPACECRAFT MIGHT DO:

• **blast off, burn up, drift off-course, jettison parts, land, lift off, malfunction, orbit, re-enter the earth's atmosphere, splash down, touch down**

spacious *ADJECTIVE*
*The living room is **spacious** and bright.*
• **big, large, roomy, sizeable**
OPPOSITES **small, cramped**

span *NOUN*
*The bridge has a **span** of 200 metres.*
• **breadth, extent, length, width, distance, reach**
A span of time is a **period** or **stretch**.

span *VERB*
*A rickety footbridge **spanned** the river.*
• **cross, stretch over, extend across, straddle, bridge, traverse**

spare *VERB*
❶ *Can you **spare** any money for a good cause?*
• **afford, part with, give, provide, do without**
❷ *Gretel begged the witch to **spare** her brother.*
• **show mercy to, pardon, reprieve, let off, release, free**

spare *ADJECTIVE*
❶ *The **spare** tyre is in the boot.*
• **additional, extra, reserve, standby**
❷ *Have you any **spare** change?*
• **leftover, surplus, odd, remaining, unused, unwanted**
❸ *The ghostly figure was tall and **spare**.*
• **lean, thin, slender, slim, trim**

spark *NOUN*
*There was a **spark** of light as he struck the match.*
• **flash, gleam, glint, flicker, sparkle**

sparkle *VERB*
*The diamond ring **sparkled** in the sunlight.*
• **glitter, glisten, glint, twinkle**

sparse *ADJECTIVE*
*In the desert, vegetation is very **sparse**.*

a b c d e f g h i j k l m n o p q r s t u v w x y z

A B C D E F G H I J K L M N O P Q R S T U V W X Y Z

• scarce, scanty, scattered, inadequate, infrequent
OPPOSITE plentiful

spatter *VERB*
*The bus **spattered** mud all over us.*
• splash, spray, sprinkle, scatter, shower

speak *VERB* **speaks, speaking, spoke, spoken**
*The robot opened its mouth and began to **speak**.*
• communicate, express yourself, say something, talk, utter

speaker *NOUN*
A person who gives a talk is a **lecturer**.
A person who makes formal speeches is an **orator**.
A person who speaks on behalf of an organisation is a **spokesperson**.

spear *NOUN*
A spear used in whaling is a **harpoon**.
A spear thrown as a sport is a **javelin**.
A spear carried by a medieval knight on horseback was a **lance**.

special *ADJECTIVE*
❶ *Are you keeping the champagne for a **special** occasion?*
• important, significant, memorable, noteworthy, momentous, exceptional, extraordinary, out of the ordinary
OPPOSITE ordinary
❷ *My granny has her own **special** way of making porridge.*
• unique, individual, characteristic, distinctive, different, peculiar
❸ *You need a **special** camera to film underwater.*
• particular, specific, proper, specialised

speciality *NOUN*
*The chef's **speciality** is sticky toffee pudding.*
• strength, strong point, expertise, forte

specific *ADJECTIVE*
*The treasure map gave **specific** directions.*
• detailed, precise, exact, definite, particular, clear-cut
OPPOSITES general, vague

specify *VERB*
*Please **specify** your shoe size.*
• be specific about, identify, name, define

specimen *NOUN*
*The police asked for a **specimen** of his handwriting.*
• sample, example, illustration, instance

speck *NOUN*
*She brushed a **speck** of dust from her shoes.*
• bit, dot, spot, fleck, grain, particle, trace, mark
see also **bit**

speckled *ADJECTIVE*
*A brown, **speckled** egg lay on the nest.*
• flecked, spotted, spotty, mottled
If you have a lot of brown spots on your skin you are **freckled**.
Something with patches of colour is **dappled** or **patchy**.

spectacle *NOUN*
*The fireworks for Diwali will be a great **spectacle**.*
• display, show, performance, exhibition, extravaganza

spectacles *PLURAL NOUN*
see **glasses**

spectacular *ADJECTIVE*
❶ *The acrobats gave a **spectacular** performance.*
• dramatic, exciting, impressive, thrilling, magnificent, sensational
❷ *The tulips are **spectacular** at this time of year.*
• eye-catching, showy, splendid, breathtaking, colourful

spectator *NOUN*
The spectators at a show are the **audience**.
The spectators at a football match are the **crowd**.
A person watching TV is a **viewer**.
If you see an accident or a crime you are an **eyewitness** or **witness**.
If you just happen to see something going on you are a **bystander** or **onlooker**.

speech *NOUN*
❶ *His **speech** was slurred and he looked tired.*
• **speaking, talking, articulation, pronunciation**
❷ *She was invited to give an after-dinner **speech**.*
• **talk, address, lecture, oration**
A talk in church is a **sermon**.
Speech between actors in a play is **dialogue**.
A speech delivered by a single actor is a **monologue**.

speechless *ADJECTIVE*
*She was **speechless** with surprise.*
• **dumbstruck, dumbfounded, tongue-tied**

speed *NOUN*
❶ *Could a spacecraft travel faster than the **speed** of light?*
• **pace, rate**
A formal synonym is **velocity**.
The speed of a piece of music is its **tempo**.
To increase speed is to **accelerate**.
To reduce speed is to **decelerate**.
❷ *They finished clearing up with amazing **speed**.*
• **quickness, rapidity, swiftness**
OPPOSITE **slowness**

speed *VERB* **speeds, speeding, sped**
*The skiers **sped** down the mountain.*
• **race, rush, dash, dart, hurry, hurtle, career, fly, streak, tear, shoot, zoom, zip**

speedy *ADJECTIVE*
*They sent their best wishes for a **speedy** recovery.*
• **fast, quick, swift, rapid, prompt, brisk**
OPPOSITE **slow**

spell *NOUN*
❶ *We're hoping for a **spell** of dry weather.*
• **period, interval, time, stretch, run**
❷ *A magic **spell** had turned the knight into a toad.*
• **charm, incantation**
Making magic spells is **sorcery, witchcraft** or **wizardry**.
for other words to do with magic see **magic**

spend *VERB* **spends, spending, spent**
❶ *Have you **spent** all your pocket money already?*
• **pay out, use up, get through, exhaust** *(informal)* **fork out, shell out**
To spend money unwisely is to **fritter** or **squander** it.
❷ *She **spends** a lot of time working in the garden.*
• **pass, occupy, fill**
To spend time doing something useless is to **waste** it.

sphere *NOUN*
❶ *The earth has the shape of a **sphere**.*
• **ball, globe, orb**
❷ *He's an expert in the **sphere** of photography.*
• **subject, area, field**

spherical *ADJECTIVE*
*The earth is **spherical**.*
• **round, ball-shaped**

spice *NOUN*

WORD WEB

SOME SPICES USED IN COOKING:

• **allspice, aniseed, bay leaf, capsicum, cardamom, cayenne, chilli, cinnamon, cloves, coriander, cumin, curry powder, ginger, juniper, mace, nutmeg, paprika, pepper, pimento, saffron, sesame, turmeric**

spicy *ADJECTIVE*
*The meat was cooked in a **spicy** chilli sauce.*
• **hot, peppery, fiery**

spike *NOUN*
His shirt got caught on a metal ***spike****.*
• point, prong, spear, stake, barb

spill *VERB*
❶ *Katie* ***spilled*** *her juice all over the table.*
• overturn, upset, tip over
❷ *Milk* ***spilled*** *on to the floor.*
• overflow, pour, slop, slosh, splash
❸ *The treasure chest fell open,* ***spilling*** *gold coins everywhere.*
• shed, tip, scatter, drop

spin *VERB* **spins, spinning, spun**
The rear wheels of the jeep ***spun*** *round.*
• turn, rotate, revolve, whirl, twirl

spine *NOUN*
❶ *Your* ***spine*** *runs down the middle of your back.*
• backbone, spinal column
The bones in your spine are your **vertebrae**.
❷ *A porcupine has sharp* ***spines****.*
• needle, quill, point, spike, bristle

spiral *NOUN*
The staircase wound upwards in a long ***spiral****.*
• coil, twist, corkscrew, whorl
A tight spiral of swirling air or water is a **vortex**.

spirit *NOUN*
❶ *He carried a charm to keep evil* ***spirits*** *away.*
• ghost, ghoul, phantom, spectre, demon
see also **ghost**
❷ *The orchestra played the piece with great* ***spirit****.*
• energy, liveliness, enthusiasm, vigour, zest, zeal, fire
❸ *There is a real* ***spirit*** *of cooperation in the team.*
• feeling, mood, atmosphere

spiritual *ADJECTIVE*
The Dalai Lama is the ***spiritual*** *leader of Tibet.*
• religious, holy, sacred
OPPOSITE **worldly**

spite *NOUN*
I believe that she ripped my book out of ***spite****.*
• malice, spitefulness, ill will, ill feeling, hostility, bitterness, resentment, venom

spiteful *ADJECTIVE*
He made some really ***spiteful*** *comments.*
• malicious, malevolent, ill-natured, hostile, venomous, vicious, nasty, unkind
OPPOSITE **kind**

splash *VERB*
❶ *The bus* ***splashed*** *water over us.*
• shower, spray, spatter, sprinkle, squirt, slop, slosh, spill, splatter
(informal) splosh
❷ *The children* ***splashed*** *about in the playing pool.*
• paddle, wade, dabble, bathe

splendid *ADJECTIVE*
❶ *There was a* ***splendid*** *banquet on the eve of the wedding.*
• magnificent, lavish, luxurious, impressive, imposing, grand, great, dazzling, glorious, gorgeous, elegant, rich, stately, majestic
❷ *That's a* ***splendid*** *idea!*
• excellent, first-class, admirable, superb, wonderful, marvellous

splendour *NOUN*
They admired the ***splendour*** *of the cathedral.*
• magnificence, glory, grandeur, majesty, richness, brilliance, spectacle

splinter *NOUN*
There were ***splinters*** *of glass all over the floor.*
• fragment, sliver, chip, flake

splinter *VERB*
The glass ***splintered*** *into pieces.*
• shatter, smash, fracture, chip, crack, split

split *VERB*
❶ *He* ***split*** *the log in two.*
• chop, cut up, crack open, splinter
❷ *He* ***split*** *his trousers climbing over the fence.*
• rip open, tear

❸ *The pirates **split** the gold between them.*
• distribute, share out
❹ *The path **splits** here.*
• branch, fork, separate

➤ **to split up**
*The search party decided to **split up**.*
• break up, part, separate, divide
If a married couple splits up, they may divorce.

split *NOUN*
*He had a **split** in the seat of his trousers.*
• rip, tear, slash, slit

spoil *VERB*
❶ *Bad weather **spoiled** the holiday.*
• ruin, wreck, upset, mess up, mar, scupper
❷ *The graffiti **spoils** the look of the new building.*
• damage, harm, hurt, disfigure, deface
❸ *His parents have **spoiled** him since he was a baby.*
• indulge, pamper, make a fuss of

spoke *past tense see* **speak**

spoken *ADJECTIVE*
*Her **spoken** French is excellent.*
• oral, spoken
OPPOSITE written

spongy *ADJECTIVE*
*The mossy ground felt **spongy** to walk on.*
• soft, springy, squashy, absorbent, porous

spoon *NOUN*
see **cutlery**

sport *NOUN*
*I enjoy playing **sport** at the weekend.*
• exercise, games

WORD WEB

TEAM SPORTS INCLUDE:

• American football, baseball, basketball, bowls, cricket, football or soccer, hockey, lacrosse, netball, polo, rounders, rugby, volleyball, water polo

INDIVIDUAL SPORTS INCLUDE:

• angling, archery, athletics, badminton, billiards, boxing, bowling, canoeing, climbing, croquet, cross-country running, cycling, darts, diving, fencing, golf, gymnastics, horse racing, jogging, judo, karate, motor racing, mountaineering, orienteering, pool, rowing, sailing, showjumping, snooker, squash, surfing, swimming, table tennis, taekwondo, tennis, waterskiing, weightlifting, windsurfing, wrestling
for individual athletic events see **athletics**

WINTER SPORTS INCLUDE:

• bobsleigh, cross-country skiing, curling, downhill skiing, ice hockey, ice skating, luge, skeleton, ski jumping, slalom, snowboarding, speed skating, tobogganing

PEOPLE WHO TAKE PART IN SPORT:

• athlete, coach, competitor, Olympian, Paralympian, player, sportsman or sportswoman

PLACES WHERE SPORT TAKES PLACE:

• arena, field, ground, park, pitch, pool, ring, rink, run, slope, stadium, track

sporting *ADJECTIVE*
*It was **sporting** of him to admit the ball was out.*
• sportsmanlike, fair, generous, honourable
OPPOSITE unsporting

spot *NOUN*
❶ *There were several **spots** of paint on the carpet.*
• mark, stain, blot, blotch, smudge, dot, fleck, speck
Small brown spots on your skin are freckles.

A small dark spot on your skin is a **mole**.
A mark you have had on your skin since you were born is a **birthmark**.
A small round swelling on your skin is a **pimple**.
A lot of spots is a **rash**.
❷ *We felt a few* ***spots*** *of rain.*
• **drop, blob, bead**
❸ *Here's a nice* ***spot*** *for a picnic.*
• **place, position, location, site, situation, locality**

spot *VERB*
❶ *Nina* ***spotted*** *her friend in the crowd.*
• **see, sight, spy, catch sight of, notice, observe, make out, recognise, detect**
❷ *The tyres were* ***spotted*** *with mud.*
• **mark, stain, blot, spatter, fleck, speckle, mottle**

spotless *ADJECTIVE*
Mr Travis washed his car until it was ***spotless****.*
• **clean, unmarked, immaculate, gleaming**
OPPOSITE **dirty**

spout *VERB*
Molten lava and ash ***spouted*** *from the volcano.*
• **gush, spew, pour, stream, spurt, squirt, jet**

sprawl *VERB*
❶ *We* ***sprawled*** *on the lawn.*
• **flop, lean back, lie, loll, lounge, recline, relax, slouch, slump, spread out, stretch out**
❷ *New houses have started to* ***sprawl*** *across the countryside.*
• **spread, stretch**

spray *VERB*
A passing bus ***sprayed*** *mud over us.*
• **shower, spatter, splash, sprinkle, scatter**

spray *NOUN*
❶ *We gave the plants a* ***spray*** *of water with the hose.*
• **shower, sprinkling, fountain, mist**
❷ *She picked a* ***spray*** *of snowdrops from the garden.*
• **bunch, posy**

spread *VERB*
❶ *I* ***spread*** *the map on the table.*
• **lay out, open out, fan out, unfold, unfurl, unroll**
❷ *The milk spilled and* ***spread*** *all over the floor.*
• **expand, extend, stretch, broaden, enlarge, swell**
❸ *The school website is a good way of* ***spreading*** *news.*
• **communicate, circulate, distribute, transmit, make known, pass on, pass round**
❹ *She* ***spread*** *jam on a piece of toast.*
• **smear**
❺ *He* ***spread*** *the seeds evenly over the ground.*
• **scatter, strew**

sprightly *ADJECTIVE*
My granny is quite ***sprightly*** *for her age.*
• **lively, energetic, active, agile, nimble, frisky, spry**
OPPOSITE **inactive**

spring *VERB* **springs, springing, sprang, sprung**
Suddenly a rabbit ***sprang*** *over the fence.*
• **jump, leap, bound, hop, vault**
When a cat springs at a mouse, it **pounces**.
➤ **to spring up**
Weeds ***spring up*** *quickly in damp weather.*
• **appear, develop, emerge, shoot up, sprout**

springy *ADJECTIVE*
The bed felt soft and ***springy****.*
• **bouncy, elastic, stretchy, flexible, pliable**
OPPOSITE **rigid**

sprinkle *VERB*
She ***sprinkled*** *flakes of chocolate over the cake.*
• **scatter, shower, spray, dust, powder**

sprout *VERB*
The seeds will ***sprout*** *if they are warm and damp.*
• **grow, germinate, shoot up, spring up, develop, emerge**

spruce *ADJECTIVE*
*He looked very **spruce** in a clean white shirt.*
• smart, well-dressed, well-groomed, elegant, neat, trim
OPPOSITE scruffy

spun *past tense see* **spin**

spur *VERB*
➤ **to spur someone on**
*The cheers of the crowd **spurred on** the athletes.*
• egg on, encourage, inspire, prompt, stimulate, urge

spurt *VERB*
*Water **spurted** from the hole in the pipe.*
• gush, spout, shoot out, stream, squirt, jet

spy *NOUN*
*The **spy** was on a top secret mission.*
• agent, secret agent
The work of a spy is **spying** or **espionage**.
A spy who works for two rival countries or organizations is a **double agent**.
An informal name for a spy who works undercover is a **mole**.

WORD WEB

THINGS A SPY MIGHT DO:

• adopt a disguise or cover, assume a secret identity, carry out a secret mission, crack or decipher a code, gather intelligence, keep someone under surveillance, report to headquarters, uncover an enemy agent, work undercover
see also **code**

THINGS A SPY MIGHT USE OR CARRY:

• coded message, false passport, hidden camera or microphone, listening device, motion detector, night-vision goggles, password, torch, walkie-talkie

A SPY'S MISSION MIGHT BE:

• clandestine, covert, secret, stealthy, surreptitious, top secret, undercover, *(informal)* cloak-and-dagger, hush-hush

spy *VERB*
*The lookout **spied** a ship on the horizon.*
• see, sight, spot, catch sight of, notice, observe, make out, detect

squabble *VERB*
*The twins are always **squabbling** in the car.*
• argue, fight, quarrel, bicker, wrangle

squalid *ADJECTIVE*
*The prisoners were kept in a **squalid** underground cell.*
• degrading, dingy, dirty, filthy, foul, mucky, nasty, unpleasant
OPPOSITE clean

squander *VERB*
*He **squandered** his money on an expensive watch.*
• waste, fritter away, misuse
(informal) blow
OPPOSITE save

square *ADJECTIVE*
*All the tiles have **square** corners.*
• right-angled
A pattern of squares is a **chequered** pattern.

squarely *ADVERB*
*The ball hit him **squarely** in the face.*
• directly, straight, head-on
OPPOSITE obliquely

squash *VERB*
❶ *My sandwich got **squashed** at the bottom of my school bag.*
• crush, flatten, press, compress, mangle
To squash food deliberately is to **mash** or **pulp** or **purée** it.
❷ *We **squashed** our sleeping bags into our rucksacks.*
• squeeze, stuff, force, cram, pack, ram

squat *VERB*
*We **squatted** on the ground to watch the puppet show.*
• crouch, sit

squat *ADJECTIVE*
*The alien had a **squat** little body on three short legs.*
• **dumpy, stocky, plump, podgy, portly**

squeak and **squeal** *NOUN, VERB*
for various sounds see **sound**

squeeze *VERB*
❶ *She **squeezed** the water out of the sponge.*
• **press, wring, compress, crush**
❷ *Five of us **squeezed** into the back of the car.*
• **squash, cram, crowd, stuff, push, ram, shove, wedge**
❸ *Holly **squeezed** her sister affectionately.*
• **clasp, hug, embrace, cuddle**
To squeeze something between your thumb and finger is to **pinch** it.

squirm *VERB*
*The guinea pig **squirmed** out of the vet's grasp.*
• **wriggle, writhe, twist**

squirt *VERB*
*My little brother made the tap water **squirt** all over me.*
• **spurt, spray, gush, spout, shoot, jet**

stab *VERB*
❶ *He **stabbed** the sausage with his fork.*
• **spear, jab, pierce, impale**
❷ *She **stabbed** a finger at him.*
• **stick, thrust, push, jab**

stab *NOUN*
*Jake felt a sudden **stab** of pain in his chest.*
• **pang, prick, sting**

stable *ADJECTIVE*
❶ *The ladder doesn't look very **stable**.*
• **steady, secure, firm, fixed, solid, balanced**
OPPOSITES **wobbly, shaky**
❷ *He's been in a **stable** relationship for years.*
• **steady, established, lasting, durable, strong**
OPPOSITE **temporary**

stack *NOUN*
*There were **stacks** of books all over the floor.*
• **pile, heap, mound, tower**
Another word for a stack of hay is a **rick** or **hayrick**.

stack *VERB*
Stack the papers on the desk.
• **gather, assemble, collect, heap up, pile up**

staff *NOUN*
*There was a party at the hospital for all the **staff**.*
• **workers, employees, personnel, workforce, team**
The staff on a ship or aircraft are the **crew**.

stage *NOUN*
❶ *They went up on the **stage** to collect their prizes.*
• **platform**
❷ *The final **stage** of the journey was made by coach.*
• **leg, step, phase, portion, stretch**
❸ *At this **stage** in her life, she wants to try something new.*
• **period, point, time, juncture**

stagger *VERB*
❶ *The wounded knight **staggered** and fell.*
• **reel, stumble, lurch, totter, sway, falter, waver, wobble**
❷ *We were **staggered** at the size of the pyramid.*
• **amaze, astonish, astound, surprise, flabbergast, stupefy, startle, stun**

stagnant *ADJECTIVE*
*Mosquitoes swarmed around the pool of **stagnant** water.*
• **still, motionless, static**
OPPOSITES **flowing, fresh**

stain *NOUN*
*There were several coffee **stains** on the tablecloth.*
• **mark, spot, blot, blotch, blemish, smear, smudge**

stain *VERB*
❶ *Her trainers were **stained** with mud.*
• **discolour, mark, soil, dirty, blacken, tarnish**
❷ *The wood can be **stained** a darker shade.*
• **dye, colour, paint, tint, tinge**

stairs *PLURAL NOUN*
*The **stairs** up to the front door were worn with age.*
• **steps**
A set of stairs taking you from one floor to another is a **flight** of stairs, or a **staircase** or **stairway**.
A moving staircase is an **escalator**.
A handrail at the side of a staircase is a **banister**.

stake *NOUN*
*The fence was made from sharp wooden **stakes**.*
• **pole, post, stick, spike, stave, pile**

stale *ADJECTIVE*
*The bread had gone **stale**.*
• **dry, hard, old, mouldy, musty**
OPPOSITE **fresh**

stalk *NOUN*
*The recipe requires half a **stalk** of celery.*
• **stem, shoot, twig**

stalk *VERB*
❶ *The cheetah **stalked** its prey.*
• **hunt, pursue, track, trail, follow, shadow, tail**
❷ *Miss Foster turned and **stalked** out of the room.*
• **stride, strut**
for other ways to walk see **walk**

stall *VERB*
*The man was **stalling** to give his friends time to escape.*
• **play for time, delay, hesitate, hedge**

stammer *VERB*
*Angela went red and started **stammering**.*
• **stutter, falter, stumble, splutter**

stamp *VERB*
❶ *He **stamped** on the flower by mistake.*
• **step, tread, trample**
❷ *The librarian **stamped** my library book.*
• **mark, print**
To stamp a postmark on a letter is to **frank** it.
To stamp a mark on cattle with a hot iron is to **brand** them.

stamp *NOUN*
*I put a first-class **stamp** on the letter.*
A person who studies or collects stamps is a **philatelist**.

stand *VERB* **stands, standing, stood**
❶ *The newborn pup was too weak to **stand**.*
• **get to your feet, get up, rise**
❷ *They **stood** the ladder against the wall.*
• **put, place, set, position, station, erect**
❸ *The offer still **stands**.*
• **remain valid, be unchanged, continue**
❹ *I can't **stand** the smell any longer.*
• **bear, abide, endure, put up with, tolerate, suffer**
➤ **to stand for something**
*She won't **stand for** any nonsense.*
• **put up with, tolerate, accept, allow, permit**
*What do these initials **stand for**?*
• **mean, indicate, signify, represent**
➤ **to stand out**
*Among all the photographs, this one really **stood out**.*
• **catch your eye, stick out, be prominent**
➤ **to stand up for someone**
*He always **stands up for** his friends.*
• **support, defend, side with, speak up for** *(informal)* **stick up for**

stand *NOUN*
A three-legged stand for a camera or telescope is a **tripod**.
A stand for a Bible or other large book is a **lectern**.
A stand to put a statue on is a **pedestal** or **plinth**.

standard *NOUN*
❶ *Their writing is of a very high **standard**.*
• **grade, level, quality**
❷ *He considered the book good by any **standard**.*
• **guidelines, ideal, measurement, model**

a b c d e f g h i j k l m n o p q r s t u v w x y z

❸ *The soldiers carried their **standard** proudly.*
• **colours, flag, banner**

standard *ADJECTIVE*
*The teacher showed us the **standard** way to write a letter.*
• **normal, usual, common, conventional, typical, customary, accepted, approved, established, orthodox, regular, traditional**
OPPOSITE **abnormal**

standby *NOUN*
*We need a **standby** in case someone drops out.*
• **reserve, substitute, replacement**

standstill *NOUN*
➤ **to come to a standstill**
*The traffic had **come to a standstill**.*
• **stop moving, draw up, halt, stop**

staple *ADJECTIVE*
*Rice is the **staple** food in many countries.*
• **chief, main, principal, standard, basic**

star *NOUN*
❶ *Astronomers study the **stars**.*
for objects found in space see **space**
for signs of the zodiac see **zodiac**
Words meaning 'to do with stars' are **astral** and **stellar**.
A night sky in which you can see stars is **starry** or **star-studded**.
A mark in the shape of a star in a piece of writing is an **asterisk**.
❷ *Several Hollywood **stars** attended the premiere of the film.*
• **celebrity, idol, superstar**

stare *VERB*
*The guard **stared** straight ahead, not blinking.*
• **gaze, gape, peer, look**
➤ **to stare at someone**
*The wolf was **staring** hungrily **at** us.*
• **gaze at, gawp at, goggle at, eye, ogle, scrutinise, watch**
To stare angrily at someone is to **glare** at them.

start *VERB*
❶ *The new course will **start** in the autumn.*
• **begin, commence**
(informal) **get going, get cracking, kick off**
OPPOSITES **finish, end**
❷ *We are planning to **start** a book club.*
• **create, set up, establish, found, institute, originate, introduce, initiate, open, launch**
OPPOSITE **close**
❸ *The horses **started** when the gun went off.*
• **jump, flinch, jerk, twitch, recoil, wince**

start *NOUN*
❶ *Try not to miss the **start** of the film.*
• **beginning, opening, introduction, commencement**
OPPOSITES **end, close, finish**
❷ *She has been with the theatre company right from the **start**.*
• **beginning, outset, creation, inception, birth, dawn, launch**
❸ *The explosion gave us all a nasty **start**.*
• **jump, jolt, shock, surprise**

startle *VERB*
*The sudden noise **startled** the deer.*
• **alarm, panic, frighten, scare, make you start, make you jump, surprise, take you by surprise**

starve *VERB*
*Many animals will **starve** if the drought continues.*
• **die of starvation, go hungry**
To choose to go without food is to **fast**.

starving *ADJECTIVE (informal)*
*What's for dinner? I'm **starving**!*
• **hungry, famished, ravenous**
To be slightly hungry is to be **peckish**.

state *NOUN*
❶ *The roof of the cottage is in a bad **state**.*
• **condition, shape**

The state of a person or animal is their **fitness** or **health.**
❷ *He gets into a terrible* ***state*** *before an exam.*
• **panic, fluster**
(informal) **flap**
❸ *The Queen is the head of* ***state.***
• **country, nation**

state *VERB*
Her passport ***states*** *that she is an Australian citizen.*
• **declare, announce, report, say, proclaim, pronounce, communicate**

stately *ADJECTIVE*
The royal banquet will be a ***stately*** *occasion.*
• **grand, dignified, formal, imposing, majestic, noble, splendid**

statement *NOUN*
The prime minister made a ***statement*** *to the press.*
• **announcement, declaration, communication, report, testimony**

station *NOUN*
❶ *Does the train stop at the next* ***station?***
The station at the end of a line is the **terminus.**
for other words to do with trains see **railway.**
❷ *He was taken to the police* ***station*** *for questioning.*
• **depot, headquarters**
❸ *There are two local radio* ***stations.***
• **channel**

station *VERB*
A lookout was ***stationed*** *on the roof of the building.*
• **place, position, put, stand, situate, locate**

stationary *ADJECTIVE*
The bus was stuck behind a ***stationary*** *vehicle.*
• **still, static, unmoving, immobile, motionless, standing, at rest**
OPPOSITE **moving**

statue *NOUN*
There is a ***statue*** *of Millicent Fawcett in Parliament Square.*
• **figure, sculpture, carving**
A small statue is a **statuette.**

status *NOUN*
Slaves had a very low ***status*** *in Ancient Rome.*
• **rank, level, position, grade, importance, prestige**

staunch *ADJECTIVE*
The Black Knight was a ***staunch*** *ally of the prince.*
• **firm, strong, faithful, loyal, true, reliable, dependable, steadfast, trusty**
OPPOSITE **unreliable**

stay *VERB*
❶ *Can you* ***stay*** *there while I park the car?*
• **wait, hang about, remain**
OPPOSITES **leave, depart**
❷ *We tried to* ***stay*** *warm by stamping our feet.*
• **keep, carry on being, continue**
❸ *Do you plan to* ***stay*** *in Scotland for long?*
• **live, reside, dwell, lodge, settle, stop**

stay *NOUN*
Our friends came for a short ***stay.***
• **visit, stopover, holiday, break**

steady *ADJECTIVE*
❶ *You need a* ***steady*** *hand to be a surgeon.*
• **stable, balanced, settled, secure, fixed, firm, fast, solid**
A common simile is **as steady as a rock.**
OPPOSITES **unsteady, shaky**
❷ *The plants need a* ***steady*** *supply of water.*
• **continuous, uninterrupted, non-stop, consistent**
OPPOSITE **intermittent**
❸ *The runners kept up a* ***steady*** *pace.*
• **regular, constant, even, smooth, rhythmic, unvarying**
OPPOSITE **irregular**

steady *VERB*
The crew managed to ***steady*** *the yacht.*
• **balance, stabilise**

steal *VERB* **steals, stealing, stole, stolen**

❶ *The thieves **stole** several valuable paintings.*
• **rob, thieve, take, lift, make off with** *(informal)* **pinch, nick, swipe, snaffle**

❷ *The children **stole** quietly upstairs.*
• **creep, sneak, tiptoe, slip, slink**

stealing *NOUN*

*The police have accused him of **stealing**.*
• **robbery, theft**

Stealing from someone's home is **burglary** or **housebreaking.**
Stealing from a shop is **shoplifting.**
Stealing small things is **pilfering.**

stealthy *ADJECTIVE*

*We heard **stealthy** footsteps going upstairs.*
• **furtive, secretive, surreptitious, sly, sneaky, underhand**

OPPOSITES **conspicuous, open**

steam *NOUN*

*Clouds of **steam** were coming from the cauldron.*
• **vapour, mist, haze**

Steam on a cold window is **condensation.**

steamy *ADJECTIVE*

❶ *The climate in a jungle is hot and **steamy**.*
• **humid, muggy, close, damp, moist**

❷ *She wiped the **steamy** mirror.*
• **misty, hazy, cloudy**

steep *ADJECTIVE*

*The bus inched its way slowly up the **steep** slope.*
• **abrupt, sudden, sharp**

A cliff or drop which is straight up and down is **sheer** or **vertical.**

OPPOSITES **gradual, gentle**

steer *VERB*

*She **steered** the car into the parking space.*
• **direct, guide**

To steer a vehicle is to **drive** it.
To steer a boat is to **navigate** or **pilot** it.

stem *NOUN*

*The gardener pulled out the dead **stems**.*
• **stalk, shoot, twig, branch**

The main stem of a tree is its **trunk.**

stem *VERB*

*Chloe blinked, trying to **stem** the flow of her tears.*
• **stop, check, hold back, restrain, curb**

step *NOUN*

❶ *The baby took her first **steps** yesterday.*
• **footstep, pace, stride**

❷ *Be careful not to trip on the **step**.*
• **doorstep, stair**

A set of steps going from one floor of a building to another is a **staircase.**
A folding set of steps is a **stepladder.**
The steps of a ladder are the **rungs.**

❸ *The first **step** in making a cake is to weigh the ingredients.*
• **stage, phase, action**

step *VERB*

*Don't **step** in the puddle!*
• **put your foot, tread, walk, stamp, trample**

➤ **to step something up**

*They have **stepped up** security at the airport.*
• **increase, intensify, strengthen, boost**

sterile *ADJECTIVE*

❶ *Very little grows in the **sterile** soil of the desert.*
• **barren, dry, arid, infertile, lifeless**

OPPOSITE **fertile**

❷ *The nurse put a **sterile** bandage on the wound.*
• **sterilised, disinfected, germ-free, antiseptic, hygienic, clean,**

OPPOSITE **infected**

stern *ADJECTIVE*

*The coach gave each of the players a **stern** look.*
• **disapproving, unsmiling, severe, strict, hard, harsh, grim**

OPPOSITE **lenient**

stew *VERB*

for ways to cook food see **cook**

stick *NOUN*
❶ *They collected **sticks** to make a fire.*
• twig, branch, stalk
❷ *The old lady walked with a **stick**.*
• cane, rod, staff, pole
A stick used by a conductor is a **baton**.
A stick carried by a police officer is a **truncheon**.
A magic stick used by a fairy, witch or wizard is a **wand**.

stick *VERB* **sticks, sticking, stuck**
❶ *He **stuck** his fork into the potato.*
• poke, prod, stab, thrust, dig, jab
❷ *She tried to **stick** the broken pieces of china together.*
• glue, paste, cement, bond, join, fasten
❸ *The stamp wouldn't **stick** to the envelope.*
• adhere, attach, cling
❹ *The wheels of the caravan **stuck** fast in the mud.*
• jam, wedge, become trapped
❺ *(informal) I can't **stick** people who're always complaining.*
• put up with, stand, tolerate, bear, abide, endure
➤ **to stick out**
*The shelf **sticks out** too far.*
• jut out, poke out, project, protrude
➤ **to stick up for someone** *(informal)*
*She **stuck up for** him when he was in trouble.*
• support, defend, side with, stand up for, speak up for

sticky *ADJECTIVE*
❶ *Someone had left a blob of **sticky** toffee on the chair.*
• tacky, gummy, gluey
(informal) gooey, icky
❷ *I don't like hot **sticky** weather.*
• humid, muggy, clammy, close, steamy, sultry
OPPOSITE dry
❸ *(informal) The pirates came to a **sticky** end.*
• grisly, gruesome, horrible, nasty, unpleasant

stiff *ADJECTIVE*
❶ *Stir the flour and water to a **stiff** paste.*
• firm, hard, solid
A common simile is **as stiff as a poker**.
OPPOSITE soft
❷ *He mounted the picture on **stiff** card.*
• rigid, inflexible, thick
OPPOSITE pliable
❸ *Her muscles were **stiff** after the long walk.*
• aching, achy, painful, taut, tight
OPPOSITE supple
❹ *The team will face **stiff** competition in the final.*
• strong, powerful, tough, difficult
OPPOSITE easy
❺ *His **stiff** manner made him hard to talk to.*
• unfriendly, cold, formal, awkward, wooden
OPPOSITE relaxed
❻ *The judge imposed a **stiff** penalty.*
• harsh, severe, strict, hard
OPPOSITE lenient
❼ *A **stiff** breeze was blowing.*
• strong, brisk, fresh
OPPOSITE gentle

stifle *VERB*
❶ *We were almost **stifled** by the fumes from the exhaust pipe.*
• choke, suffocate, smother
To kill someone by stopping their breathing is to **strangle** or **throttle** them.
❷ *She tried to **stifle** a yawn.*
• suppress, muffle, hold back, repress, restrain

still *ADJECTIVE*
❶ *The prisoner sat **still** and said nothing.*
• motionless, unmoving, stationary, static, inert
❷ *It was a beautiful **still** evening.*
• calm, peaceful, quiet, tranquil, serene, hushed, silent, noiseless, windless

still *VERB*
*I breathed deeply to try to **still** my nerves.*
• calm, quieten, soothe, lull
OPPOSITE agitate

stimulate *VERB*
❶ *Her travels **stimulated** her to write a book.*
• encourage, inspire, spur
❷ *The exhibition **stimulated** my interest in painting.*
• arouse, rouse, stir up, kindle, excite, provoke, trigger
OPPOSITE discourage

sting *VERB* **stings, stinging, stung**
❶ *One of the campers was **stung** by a wasp.*
• bite, nip
❷ *The smoke made our eyes **sting**.*
• smart, hurt, prick, prickle, tingle

stingy *ADJECTIVE (informal)*
*He's too **stingy** to give anyone a birthday card.*
• mean, miserly, selfish, uncharitable
(informal) tight-fisted, penny-pinching
OPPOSITE generous

stink *VERB*
*The dungeon **stank** of unwashed bodies.*
• reek, smell
see also **smell**

stink *NOUN*
*The mouldy cheese gave off a dreadful **stink**.*
• odour, stench, reek, bad smell

stir *VERB*
❶ ***Stir** the mixture until it is smooth.*
• mix, beat, blend, whisk
❷ *The giant **stirred** in his sleep.*
• move slightly, shift, toss, turn
➤ **to stir something up**
*The bandits were always **stirring up** trouble.*
• arouse, encourage, provoke, set off, trigger, whip up

stir *NOUN*
*The news caused quite a **stir**.*
• fuss, commotion, excitement, hullabaloo

stock *NOUN*
❶ ***Stocks** of food were running low.*
• supply, store, reserve, hoard, stockpile
❷ *The shopkeeper arranged his new **stock**.*
• goods, merchandise, wares
❸ *The duke is descended from royal **stock**.*
• descent, ancestry, family, line

stock *VERB*
*Most supermarkets now **stock** organic food.*
• sell, carry, trade in, deal in, keep in stock

stocky *ADJECTIVE*
*The wrestler had a strong **stocky** body.*
• dumpy, squat, thickset, solid, sturdy
OPPOSITE thin

stodgy *ADJECTIVE*
❶ *The pudding was rich and **stodgy**.*
• heavy, solid, starchy, filling
OPPOSITE light
❷ *I'm finding the book a bit **stodgy**.*
• boring, dull, uninteresting, slow, tedious
OPPOSITE lively

stole *VERB past tense see* **steal**

stomach *NOUN*
*He rolled over and lay on his **stomach**.*
• belly, gut, paunch
(informal) tummy
The part of the body that contains the stomach is the **abdomen**.

stomach *VERB*
*I can't **stomach** watching horror films.*
• stand, bear, put up with, tolerate, take

stone *NOUN*
*The columns of the temple were carved from **stone**.*
A large lump of stone is a **rock**.
A large rounded stone is a **boulder**.
Small rounded stones are **pebbles**.
A mixture of sand and small stones is **gravel**.
Pebbles on the beach are **shingle**.
Round stones used to pave a path are **cobbles**.
for precious stones see **jewel**

stony *ADJECTIVE*
❶ *The waves broke over the* ***stony*** *beach.*
• **pebbly, rocky, shingly**
OPPOSITE **sandy**
❷ *There was a* ***stony*** *silence in the room.*
• **unfriendly, cold, hostile, frosty, icy**
OPPOSITES **warm, friendly**

stood *past tense see* **stand**

stoop *VERB*
We had to ***stoop*** *to go through the tunnel.*
• **bend, duck, bow, crouch**

stop *VERB*
❶ *I'll go into town when the rain* ***stops****.*
• **end, finish, cease, conclude, terminate**
OPPOSITE **start**
❷ *Can you* ***stop*** *talking for a minute?*
• **give up, cease, suspend, quit, leave off, break off**
(informal) **knock off, pack in**
OPPOSITES **continue, resume**
❸ *Guards,* ***stop*** *that man!*
• **hold, detain, seize, catch, capture, restrain**
❹ *You can't* ***stop*** *me from going.*
• **prevent, obstruct, bar, hinder**
❺ *How do you* ***stop*** *this machine?*
• **turn off, immobilise**
❻ *The bus will* ***stop*** *at the school gates.*
• **come to a stop, halt, pull up, draw up**
❼ *If you tighten the valve, it will* ***stop*** *the leak.*
• **close, plug, seal, block up, bung up**

stop *NOUN*
❶ *Everything suddenly came to a* ***stop****.*
• **end, finish, conclusion, halt, standstill**
❷ *They drove down through France, with a short* ***stop*** *in Paris.*
• **break, pause, stopover, rest**

store *VERB*
Squirrels need to ***store*** *food for the winter.*
• **save, set aside, stow away, hoard, reserve, stockpile**
(informal) **stash**

store *NOUN*
❶ *The building is now used as a grain* ***store****.*
• **storeroom, storehouse, repository, vault**
A store for food is a **larder** or **pantry**.
A store for weapons is an **armoury** or **arsenal**.
❷ *He kept a large* ***store*** *of wine in the cellar.*
• **hoard, supply, quantity, stock, stockpile, reserve**
❸ *He's the manager of the local grocery* ***store****.*
see also **shop**

storey *NOUN*
The new building has six ***storeys****.*
• **floor, level, tier**

storm *NOUN*
❶ *Crops were damaged in the heavy* ***storms****.*
• **squall, blizzard, gale, thunderstorm, hurricane, typhoon**
An old word for storm is **tempest**.
When a storm begins to develop it is **brewing**.
see also **weather**
❷ *Plans to close the library caused a* ***storm*** *of protest.*
• **outburst, outcry, uproar, clamour**

storm *VERB*
The soldiers ***stormed*** *the castle.*
• **charge at, rush at, attack**

stormy *ADJECTIVE*
❶ *It was a dark,* ***stormy*** *night.*
• **blustery, squally, tempestuous, wild, windy, rough, choppy, gusty, raging**
OPPOSITE **calm**
❷ *Fighting broke out at the end of a* ***stormy*** *meeting.*
• **bad-tempered, quarrelsome, turbulent, violent**

story *NOUN*
Peter Pan is a ***story*** *about a boy who never grew up.*
• **tale**
(informal) **yarn**

WORD WEB

VARIOUS KINDS OF STORY:

• **adventure story, bedtime story, crime story, detective story, fable, fairy tale, fantasy, folk tale, ghost story, horror story, legend, love story, mystery, myth, narrative poem, novel, parable, romance, saga, science fiction** or *(informal)* **sci-fi, short story, spy story, thriller**

Invented stories are **fiction**.

for other types of writing see **writing**

❶ *The book tells the* ***story*** *of her childhood in New York.*

• **account, history, narrative**

A story of a person's life is a **biography**.

The story of your life, told by you, is your **autobiography**.

❷ *It was the front-page* ***story*** *in all the papers.*

• **article, item, feature, report, piece**

❸ *(informal) Have you been telling* ***stories*** *again?*

• **lie, fib**

stout *ADJECTIVE*

❶ *The doctor was a* ***stout*** *man with grey hair.*

• **fat, plump, chubby, dumpy, tubby, portly, stocky, beefy, burly**

OPPOSITE **thin**

❷ *You will need a pair of* ***stout*** *walking boots.*

• **strong, sturdy, tough, robust, sound, substantial**

OPPOSITE **weak**

❸ *The enemy put up a* ***stout*** *resistance.*

• **brave, courageous, spirited, plucky, determined, staunch, resolute, firm**

OPPOSITE **cowardly**

stow *VERB*

They ***stowed*** *the boxes in the attic.*

• **store, put away, pack, pile, load**

straight *ADJECTIVE*

❶ *They walked in a* ***straight*** *line.*

• **direct, unswerving**

A common simile is **as straight as an arrow**.

OPPOSITE **crooked**

❷ *It took a long time to get the room* ***straight****.*

• **neat, orderly, tidy**

OPPOSITE **untidy**

❸ *She found it difficult to get a* ***straight*** *answer from him.*

• **honest, plain, frank, straightforward**

OPPOSITES **indirect, evasive**

straightforward *ADJECTIVE*

The cake recipe is fairly ***straightforward****.*

• **simple, plain, uncomplicated, easy, clear, direct**

OPPOSITE **complicated**

strain *VERB*

❶ *The dog was* ***straining*** *at its lead.*

• **pull, tug, stretch, haul**

❷ *People were* ***straining*** *to see what was going on.*

• **struggle, strive, make an effort, try, attempt**

❸ *Take it easy and don't* ***strain*** *yourself.*

• **weaken, exhaust, wear out, tire out, tax**

strain *NOUN*

The ***strain*** *of her job was making her ill.*

• **stress, tension, worry, anxiety, pressure**

strand *NOUN*

The ***strands*** *of the wool began to unravel.*

• **fibre, filament, thread**

stranded *ADJECTIVE*

❶ *A whale lay* ***stranded*** *on the beach.*

• **run aground, beached, marooned**

❷ *He was* ***stranded*** *in London without any money.*

• **abandoned, deserted, helpless, lost, stuck**

(informal) **high and dry**

strange *ADJECTIVE*

❶ *A **strange** thing happened this morning.*
• **funny, odd, peculiar, unusual, abnormal, curious, extraordinary, remarkable, singular, uncommon**
OPPOSITES **ordinary, everyday**
❷ *Did you hear **strange** noises in the night?*
• **mysterious, puzzling, baffling, mystifying, perplexing, bewildering, inexplicable**
❸ *The professor showed us his **strange** inventions.*
• **weird, eccentric, peculiar, bizarre**
(informal) **oddball, wacky**
❹ *I find it hard to get to sleep in a **strange** bed.*
• **unfamiliar, unknown, new, alien**
OPPOSITE **familiar**

stranger *NOUN*

*A **stranger** stopped us and asked for directions to the castle.*
• **newcomer, outsider, visitor, foreigner**

strangle *VERB*

*The victim had been **strangled**.*
• **throttle**

strap *NOUN*

*The trunk was fastened with a leather **strap**.*
• **belt, band**

strategy *NOUN*

*The school has a **strategy** to deal with bullying.*
• **plan, policy, procedure, approach, scheme, programme**

stray *VERB*

*Some sheep had **strayed** on to the road.*
• **wander, drift, roam, rove, straggle, meander, ramble**

streak *NOUN*

❶ *The horse had a white **streak** on his muzzle.*
• **band, line, stripe, strip, smear, stain**
❷ *There is a **streak** of meanness in his character.*
• **element, trace**

streak *VERB*

❶ *Rain had begun to **streak** the window.*
• **smear, smudge, stain, line**
❷ *A group of motorbikes **streaked** past.*
• **rush, speed, dash, fly, hurtle, flash, tear, zoom**

stream *NOUN*

❶ *The climbers dipped their feet in the cool mountain **stream**.*
• **brook, rivulet**
(Scottish) **burn**
❷ *The raft was carried along with the **stream**.*
• **current, flow, tide**
❸ *A **stream** of water poured through the hole.*
• **cataract, flood, gush, jet, rush, torrent**
❹ *The museum had a steady **stream** of visitors.*
• **series, string, line, succession**

stream *VERB*

*Warm sunlight **streamed** through the window.*
• **pour, flow, flood, issue, gush, spill**

street *NOUN*

see **road**

strength *NOUN*

❶ *Hercules was said to have enormous **strength**.*
• **power, might, muscle, brawn, toughness, force, vigour**
❷ *The main **strength** of the team is in scoring goals.*
• **strong point, asset, advantage**
OPPOSITE **weakness**

strengthen *VERB*

❶ *Regular exercise **strengthens** your muscles.*
• **make stronger, build up, toughen, harden**
❷ *Concrete was used to **strengthen** the tunnel.*
• **fortify, reinforce, bolster, prop up**
OPPOSITE **weaken**

strenuous *ADJECTIVE*
❶ *We are making* ***strenuous*** *efforts to recycle our rubbish.*
• **determined, strong, vigorous, energetic, resolute**
OPPOSITE **feeble**
❷ *The doctor told him to avoid* ***strenuous*** *exercise.*
• **hard, tough, difficult, demanding, tiring, exhausting**
OPPOSITE **easy**

stress *NOUN*
❶ *The hospital staff were working under a lot of* ***stress****.*
• **strain, pressure, tension, worry, anxiety**
❷ *My piano teacher puts great* ***stress*** *on the need to practise.*
• **emphasis, importance, weight**

stress *VERB*
She ***stressed*** *the need for absolute secrecy.*
• **emphasise, draw attention to, highlight, underline**

stretch *VERB*
❶ *He* ***stretched*** *the rubber band until it snapped.*
• **expand, extend, draw out, pull out, elongate, lengthen**
❷ *She* ***stretched*** *her arms wide.*
• **extend, open out, spread out**
❸ *The road* ***stretched*** *into the distance.*
• **continue, extend**

stretch *NOUN*
❶ *He had a two-year* ***stretch*** *in the army.*
• **spell, period, time, stint**
❷ *There are often accidents on this* ***stretch*** *of road.*
• **section, length, piece**
❸ *It's a beautiful* ***stretch*** *of countryside.*
• **area, tract, expanse, sweep**

strict *ADJECTIVE*
❶ *The club has* ***strict*** *rules about who can join.*
• **rigid, inflexible**
(informal) **hard and fast**
OPPOSITE **flexible**
❷ *The sergeant was known for being* ***strict*** *with his men.*
• **harsh, severe, stern, firm**
OPPOSITE **lenient**
❸ *He used the word in its* ***strict*** *scientific sense.*
• **exact, precise, correct**
OPPOSITE **loose**

stride *NOUN*
The robot took two ***strides*** *forward.*
• **pace, step**

strike *VERB* **strikes, striking, struck**
❶ *Roy* ***struck*** *his head on the low ceiling.*
• **bang, bump, hit, knock, thump, collide with**
(informal) **wallop, whack**
❷ *The enemy could* ***strike*** *again at any time.*
• **attack**
❸ *The clock* ***struck*** *one.*
• **chime, ring**

striking *ADJECTIVE*
The most ***striking*** *feature of the mermaid was her iridescent tail.*
• **conspicuous, noticeable, prominent, remarkable, memorable, extraordinary, outstanding, impressive**
OPPOSITE **inconspicuous**

string *NOUN*
❶ *She tied some* ***string*** *round the parcel.*
• **rope, cord, twine**
for musical instruments with strings see **music**
❷ *They have received a* ***string*** *of complaints.*
• **series, succession, chain, sequence**

string *VERB* **strings, stringing, strung**
We ***strung*** *the fairy lights on the Christmas tree.*
• **hang, arrange, thread**

stringy *ADJECTIVE*
*This meat is very **stringy**.*
• chewy, fibrous, tough
OPPOSITE tender

strip *VERB*
❶ *Lottie **stripped** the paper off her present.*
• peel, remove
OPPOSITES cover, wrap
❷ *He **stripped** and got into the bath.*
• get undressed, undress
OPPOSITE dress

strip *NOUN*
*In front of the house was a narrow **strip** of grass.*
• band, length, ribbon, piece, bit

stripe *NOUN*
*The tablecloth was white with blue **stripes**.*
• line, strip, band, bar

strive *VERB* **strives, striving, strove, striven**
*Each athlete **strives** to do his or her best.*
• try hard, aim, attempt, endeavour

stroke *NOUN*
❶ *He split the log with a single **stroke**.*
• blow, hit, action, movement, effort
❷ *She added a few quick pencil **strokes** to her drawing.*
• line, mark

stroke *VERB*
*Jess was curled up on the sofa, **stroking** the cat.*
• pat, caress, rub, touch, fondle, pet

stroll *VERB*
*The children **strolled** quietly home.*
• walk slowly, amble, saunter
see also **walk**

strong *ADJECTIVE*

OVERUSED WORD

Try to vary the words you use for **strong**. Here are some other words you could use.

FOR A STRONG PERSON OR STRONG BODY:
• powerful, muscular, mighty, well-built, beefy, brawny, burly, strapping
*Crocodiles have **powerful** jaws.*
A common simile is **as strong as an ox**.
OPPOSITES weak, puny

FOR STRONG MATERIAL:
• robust, sturdy, tough, hard-wearing, durable, stout, substantial
*The tent is made from **hard-wearing** material.*
OPPOSITES thin, flimsy

FOR A STRONG LIGHT OR STRONG COLOUR:
• bright, brilliant, dazzling, glaring
The glaring noonday sunlight was streaming in at our door, outside of which some kind of a band appeared to be playing.—THE VOYAGES OF DOCTOR DOLITTLE, Hugh Lofting
OPPOSITES weak, pale

FOR A STRONG FLAVOUR OR STRONG SMELL:
• overpowering, pronounced, pungent, piquant
*I smelt the **pungent** aroma of burnt toast.*
OPPOSITES faint, slight

FOR A STRONG ARGUMENT OR STRONG CASE:
• convincing, persuasive, effective, sound, solid, valid
*The police have **solid** evidence of his guilt.*
OPPOSITES weak, feeble, flimsy

FOR A STRONG INTEREST OR STRONG SUPPORTER:
• enthusiastic, keen, passionate, fervent, avid, zealous
*Viv takes a **keen** interest in fashion.*
OPPOSITE slight

struck *past tense see* **strike**

structure *NOUN*
❶ *The pagoda is a magnificent* ***structure****.*
• **building, construction, framework**
❷ *Can you explain the* ***structure*** *of the poem?*
• **design, plan, shape, arrangement, organisation**

struggle *VERB*
❶ *The captives* ***struggled*** *to get free.*
• **strain, strive, wrestle, writhe about, tussle, fight, battle**
❷ *The expedition had to* ***struggle*** *through a snowstorm.*
• **stagger, stumble, flounder, labour**

struggle *NOUN*
❶ *The rebels surrendered without a* ***struggle****.*
• **fight, battle, combat, clash, contest**
❷ *It was a* ***struggle*** *to keep going in the blazing heat.*
• **effort, exertion, problem, difficulty**

stubborn *ADJECTIVE*
She's too ***stubborn*** *to admit that she was wrong.*
• **obstinate, pig-headed, strong-willed, uncooperative, inflexible, wilful**
A common simile is **as stubborn as a mule.**
OPPOSITE **compliant**

stuck *past tense see* **stick**

stud *VERB*
➤ **studded with**
The lid of the chest was ***studded with*** *jewels.*
• **inlaid with, encrusted with**

student *NOUN*
A student at school is a **pupil.**
An old word for a pupil is **scholar.**

studious *ADJECTIVE*
Sadiq is a quiet, ***studious*** *boy.*
• **hard-working, diligent, scholarly, academic, bookish**

study *VERB*
❶ *He went to university to* ***study*** *medicine.*
• **learn about, read, research into**
❷ *The spy* ***studied*** *the document carefully.*
• **examine, inspect, analyse, investigate, look closely at, scrutinise, survey**
❸ *She has to* ***study*** *for her exams.*
• **revise, cram**
(informal) **swot**

stuff *NOUN*
❶ *What's that sticky* ***stuff*** *on the carpet?*
• **matter, substance**
❷ *You can put your* ***stuff*** *in one of the lockers.*
• **belongings, possessions, things, gear**

stuff *VERB*
❶ *We managed to* ***stuff*** *everything into the boot of the car.*
• **pack, push, shove, squeeze, ram, compress, force, cram, jam**
❷ *The cushions are* ***stuffed*** *with foam rubber.*
• **fill, pad**

stuffy *ADJECTIVE*
❶ *Open a window—it's* ***stuffy*** *in here.*
• **airless, close, muggy, humid, stifling, musty, unventilated**
OPPOSITE **airy**
❷ *I found the book a bit* ***stuffy****.*
• **boring, dull, dreary, pompous, stodgy**
OPPOSITE **lively**

stumble *VERB*
❶ *He* ***stumbled*** *on a tree root and twisted his ankle.*
• **trip, stagger, totter, flounder, lurch**
❷ *The actress* ***stumbled*** *over her words.*
• **stammer, stutter, falter, hesitate**
➤ **to stumble across something**
I ***stumbled across*** *some old photos.*
• **come across, encounter, find, unearth, discover**

stump *VERB*
The detective was ***stumped*** *by the case.*
• **baffle, bewilder, perplex, puzzle, fox, mystify, outwit, defeat**
(informal) **flummox**

stun *VERB*
❶ *The pilot was alive but **stunned**.*
• daze, knock out, knock senseless, make unconscious
❷ *The whole town was **stunned** by the news.*
• amaze, astonish, astound, shock, stagger, stupefy, bewilder, dumbfound

stunt *NOUN*
*The acrobats performed breathtaking **stunts**.*
• feat, exploit, act, deed, trick

stupid *ADJECTIVE*
❶ *Trolls are often very **stupid**.*
• foolish, unintelligent, dense, dim, dim-witted, brainless, dumb, slow, thick, feeble-minded, half-witted, simple, simple-minded, dopey, dull
❷ *It would be **stupid** to go snowboarding without a helmet.*
• senseless, mindless, idiotic, unwise, foolhardy, silly, daft, crazy, mad
OPPOSITE intelligent

sturdy *ADJECTIVE*
❶ *Shetland ponies are short and **sturdy**.*
• stocky, strong, robust, athletic, brawny, burly, healthy, hefty, husky, muscular, powerful, vigorous, well-built
OPPOSITE weak
❷ *She bought some **sturdy** walking boots.*
• durable, solid, sound, substantial, tough, well-made
OPPOSITE flimsy

stutter *VERB*
*He tends to **stutter** when he's nervous.*
• stammer, stumble, falter

style *NOUN*
❶ *I don't like that **style** of jeans.*
• design, pattern, fashion
❷ *The book is written in an informal **style**.*
• manner, tone, way, wording
❸ *The actress always dresses with great **style**.*
• elegance, stylishness, taste, sophistication

stylish *ADJECTIVE*
*Jacqueline always wears **stylish** clothes.*
• fashionable, elegant, chic, smart, sophisticated, tasteful
(informal) trendy, snazzy
OPPOSITE unfashionable

subdue *VERB*
❶ *The army managed to **subdue** the rebels.*
• beat, conquer, defeat, overcome, overpower, crush, vanquish
❷ *Jason tried hard to **subdue** his anger.*
• suppress, restrain, repress, check, hold back, curb, control

subject *NOUN*
❶ *Do you have any strong views on the **subject**?*
• matter, issue, question, point, theme, topic
❷ *Her passport shows that she is a British **subject**.*
• citizen, national

subject *VERB*
*The press **subjected** him to a string of questions.*
• expose, submit, lay open

submerge *VERB*
❶ *The submarine **submerged** slowly.*
• dive, go down, go under
OPPOSITE surface
❷ *The tsunami **submerged** several coastal villages.*
• engulf, flood, drown, immerse, inundate, swallow up

submit *VERB*
❶ *The swordsman finally **submitted** to his opponent.*
• give in, surrender, yield
❷ *You need to **submit** a membership form to join the club.*
• give in, hand in, present

subordinate *ADJECTIVE*
*He began as a police officer of **subordinate** rank.*
• junior, lesser, lower, inferior
OPPOSITES superior, higher

subscribe *VERB*

➤ **to subscribe to**

She ***subscribes to*** *several good causes.*

• contribute to, donate to, give to, support

subsequent *ADJECTIVE*

I missed the first episode and two ***subsequent*** *ones.*

• later, succeeding, following, ensuing, next

OPPOSITE previous

subside *VERB*

❶ *One side of the old cottage has started to* ***subside****.*

• sink, settle

❷ *After three days, the flood waters began to* ***subside****.*

• go down, fall, recede, decline, ebb

❸ *The pain will eventually* ***subside****.*

• decrease, diminish, lessen, die down, dwindle

substance *NOUN*

❶ *The spacecraft was made from an alien* ***substance****.*

• material, matter, stuff

❷ *What was the* ***substance*** *of the book?*

• theme, essence, gist, subject matter

substantial *ADJECTIVE*

❶ *They have made* ***substantial*** *improvements to the city.*

• considerable, significant, sizeable, worthwhile, big, large, generous

OPPOSITE small

❷ *There is a* ***substantial*** *fence to keep out wild animals.*

• strong, sturdy, solid, robust, hefty, durable, sound, well-built

OPPOSITE flimsy

substitute *VERB*

You can ***substitute*** *margarine for butter in the recipe.*

• exchange, swap, switch

You can also say: Margarine can **take the place of** butter, or You can **replace** butter with margarine.

➤ **to substitute for someone**

He ***substituted for*** *the injured goalkeeper.*

• stand in for, take the place of, deputise for

substitute *NOUN*

The manager brought on a ***substitute*** *during extra time.*

• replacement, reserve, standby, stand-in

A substitute for a sick actor is an **understudy**.

subtle *ADJECTIVE*

❶ *There was a* ***subtle*** *smell of roses in the air.*

• faint, slight, mild, delicate

❷ *His jokes are too* ***subtle*** *for most people.*

• ingenious, sophisticated

❸ *I tried to give her a* ***subtle*** *hint.*

• gentle, tactful, indirect

OPPOSITE obvious

subtract *VERB*

If you ***subtract*** *5 from 20, you will have 15 left.*

• take away, deduct, remove

OPPOSITE add

succeed *VERB*

❶ *You have to work hard if you want to* ***succeed****.*

• be successful, do well, prosper, flourish, thrive

(informal) make it

❷ *Everyone hoped that the plan would* ***succeed****.*

• be effective, produce results, work

(informal) catch on

OPPOSITE fail

❸ *Edward VII* ***succeeded*** *Queen Victoria.*

• come after, follow, take over from, replace

success *NOUN*

❶ *She talked about her* ***success*** *as an actress.*

• achievement, attainment, fame

❷ *They congratulated the team on their* ***success****.*

• victory, win, triumph

❸ *The group's last CD was a great **success**.*
• **hit, bestseller**
(informal) **winner**
❹ *The **success** of the mission depends on the astronauts.*
• **effectiveness, successfulness, successful outcome, completion**
OPPOSITE **failure**

successful *ADJECTIVE*
❶ *She owns a very **successful** chain of restaurants.*
• **thriving, flourishing, booming, prosperous, profitable, popular**
❷ *The supporters cheered the **successful** team.*
• **winning, victorious, triumphant**
OPPOSITE **unsuccessful**

succession *NOUN*
*Arthur received a **succession** of mysterious emails.*
• **series, sequence, run, string, chain**

successive *ADJECTIVE*
*It rained on seven **successive** days.*
• **consecutive, uninterrupted**
You can also say: It rained on several days in succession.

suck *VERB*
➤ **to suck something up**
*A sponge will **suck up** water.*
• **soak up, draw up, absorb**

sudden *ADJECTIVE*
❶ *Maria felt a **sudden** urge to burst into song.*
• **unexpected, unforeseen, impulsive, rash, quick**
OPPOSITE **expected**
❷ *The bus came to a **sudden** halt.*
• **abrupt, sharp, swift**
OPPOSITE **gradual**

suffer *VERB*
❶ *He **suffers** terribly with his back.*
• **feel pain, hurt**
❷ *He will **suffer** for his crime.*
• **be punished, pay**
❸ *The home team **suffered** a humiliating defeat.*
• **experience, undergo, go through, endure, withstand, bear, tolerate**

suffering *NOUN*
*The people endured great **suffering** during the war.*
• **hardship, deprivation, misery, anguish, pain, distress**

sufficient *ADJECTIVE*
*The castaways had **sufficient** food for few days.*
• **enough, adequate, satisfactory**
OPPOSITE **insufficient**

suffix *NOUN*
OPPOSITE **prefix**

suffocate *VERB*
*The firefighters were nearly **suffocated** by the fumes.*
• **choke, stifle**
To stop someone's breathing by squeezing their throat is to **strangle** or **throttle** them.
To stop someone's breathing by covering their nose and mouth is to **smother** them.

suggest *VERB*
❶ *Mum **suggested** going to the zoo.*
• **propose, advise, advocate, recommend**
❷ *Her comments **suggest** that she's not happy.*
• **imply, hint, indicate, signal**

suggestion *NOUN*
*They didn't like his **suggestion**.*
• **proposal, plan, idea, proposition, recommendation**

suit *VERB*
❶ *Would it **suit** you to stay here overnight?*
• be convenient for, be suitable for, please, satisfy
OPPOSITE displease
❷ *His new haircut doesn't **suit** him.*
• look good on, become, flatter

suitable *ADJECTIVE*
❶ *Please wear clothes **suitable** for wet weather.*
• appropriate, apt, fitting, suited (to), proper, right
OPPOSITE unsuitable
❷ *Is this a **suitable** time to have a chat?*
• convenient, acceptable, satisfactory
OPPOSITE inconvenient

sulk *VERB*
*I was **sulking** because I wasn't allowed to play outside.*
• be sullen, mope, brood, pout

sulky *ADJECTIVE*
*Ron had turned into a **sulky** teenager.*
• moody, sullen, brooding, moping, mopey

sullen *ADJECTIVE*
*Beth slouched on the sofa, looking **sullen**.*
• sulky, moody, bad-tempered, mopey, morose, surly, sour
OPPOSITES cheerful, good-tempered

sum *NOUN*
❶ *The **sum** of 2 and 2 is 4.*
• total, result
❷ *They lost a large **sum** of money.*
• amount, quantity
➤ **sums**
*Desmond is good at doing **sums**.*
• adding up, arithmetic
(informal) maths
for other mathematical terms see **mathematics**

sum *VERB*
➤ **to sum up**
• summarise

summarise *VERB*
*Can you **summarise** the main points of the story?*
• sum up, outline, review
(informal) recap

summary *NOUN*
*We each wrote a **summary** of the poem.*
• synopsis, precis, outline

summit *NOUN*
*The **summit** of the mountain was shrouded in mist.*
• top, cap, peak, tip
OPPOSITE base

summon *VERB*
*The king **summoned** his knights from far and wide.*
• call, send for, order to come, bid to come
To ask someone politely to come is to **invite** them.

sun *NOUN*
*They went out into the garden to sit in the **sun**.*
• sunshine, sunlight
To sit or lie in the sun is to **sunbathe**.

sunlight *NOUN*
*Most plants can only grow in **sunlight**.*
• daylight, sun, sunshine
Rays of light from the sun are **sunbeams**.

sunny *ADJECTIVE*
❶ *It was a beautiful **sunny** day.*
• fine, clear, cloudless
OPPOSITE cloudy
❷ *The flat has a large, **sunny** living room.*
• bright, sunlit, cheerful
OPPOSITE gloomy
A place that gets a lot of sunshine is **sunbaked**.
see also **weather**

sunrise *NOUN*
*The magic spell wears off at **sunrise**.*
• dawn, daybreak
OPPOSITE sunset

sunset *NOUN*
*They arranged to meet in the churchyard at **sunset**.*
• **sundown, dusk, twilight, evening, nightfall**
OPPOSITE **sunrise**

superb *ADJECTIVE*
*Brazil scored another **superb** goal.*
• **excellent, outstanding, exceptional, remarkable, impressive, magnificent, marvellous, splendid, tremendous, wonderful**
(informal) **brilliant, fantastic, terrific, fabulous, sensational, super**
for other ways to describe something good see **good**

superficial *ADJECTIVE*
❶ *The scratch on his leg was only **superficial**.*
• **on the surface, shallow, slight**
OPPOSITE **deep**
❷ *The book gives a very **superficial** view of history.*
• **simple, trivial, lightweight, shallow, frivolous, casual**
OPPOSITES **thorough, profound**

superhero *NOUN*

WORD WEB

The arch-enemy of a superhero is a **super-villain** or **nemesis**.
A story with drawings featuring a superhero is a **comic book** or **comic strip**.

THINGS A SUPERHERO MIGHT WEAR OR USE:

• **belt, bodysuit, cape, costume, force field, laser beam, logo, mask, gadget, invisibility, superhuman strength, superpower, X-ray vision**
Zack had a force field and we had to know how powerful it was. Clearly the easiest way to find out was to throw things at him.—MY BROTHER IS A SUPERHERO, David Solomons

SOUNDS MADE BY SUPERHEROES:

• **pow, whoosh, zap, zoom**

superior *ADJECTIVE*
❶ *A colonel is **superior** in rank to a captain.*
• **senior, higher, greater**
❷ *They only sell chocolate of **superior** quality.*
• **first-class, first-rate, top, top-notch, choice, select, better**
❸ *I don't like her **superior** attitude.*
• **arrogant, haughty, snobbish, stuck-up, self-important**
(informal) **snooty**
OPPOSITE **inferior**

supernatural *ADJECTIVE*
*The fortune-teller claimed to have **supernatural** powers.*
• **magic, magical, miraculous**
OPPOSITE **natural**

supervise *VERB*
*Children must be **supervised** by an adult in the park.*
• **oversee, superintend, watch over, be in charge of, be responsible for, direct, manage**
To supervise candidates in an exam is to **invigilate**.

supple *ADJECTIVE*
*The moccasins are made of **supple** leather.*
• **flexible, pliable, soft**
OPPOSITES **stiff, rigid**

supplementary *ADJECTIVE*
*There is a **supplementary** charge for postage.*
• **additional, extra**

supply *VERB*
*The art shop can **supply** you with brushes and paints.*
• **provide, equip, furnish**

supply *NOUN*
*They had a good **supply** of fuel for the winter.*
• **quantity, stock, store, reserve**
➤ **supplies**
*We bought **supplies** for the camping trip.*
• **provisions, stores, rations, food, necessities**

A B C D E F G H I J K L M N O P Q R S T U V W X Y Z

support *NOUN*

❶ *She thanked them for their **support**.*

• **assistance, backing, aid, cooperation, encouragement, help**

❷ *The cinema was reopened with **support** from local businesses.*

• **donations, contributions, sponsorship**

❸ *The **supports** prevented the wall from collapsing.*

• **prop, brace**

A support for a shelf is a **bracket**.
A support built against a wall is a **buttress**.
A support for someone with an injured leg is a **crutch**.
A bar of wood or metal supporting a framework is a **strut**.
A support put under a board to make a table is a **trestle**.

support *VERB*

❶ *The rope couldn't **support** his weight.*

• **bear, carry, stand, hold up**

❷ *The beams **support** the roof.*

• **prop up, strengthen, reinforce**

❸ *His friends **supported** him when he was in trouble.*

• **aid, assist, help, back, encourage, stand by, stand up for, rally round**

❹ *She had to work to **support** her family.*

• **maintain, keep, provide for**

❺ *He **supports** several local charities.*

• **donate to, contribute to, give to**

❻ *Which team did you **support** in the World Cup?*

• **be a supporter of, follow**

supporter *NOUN*

❶ *The home **supporters** cheered their team.*

• **fan, follower**

❷ *She is a well-known **supporter** of animal rights.*

• **champion, advocate, backer, defender**

suppose *VERB*

❶ *I **suppose** you want to borrow some money.*

• **expect, presume, assume, guess, believe, think**

❷ ***Suppose** a spacecraft landed in your garden!*

• **imagine, pretend, fancy**

➤ **to be supposed to do something**

*The bus is **supposed to** leave at 9 o'clock.*

• **be meant to, be due to, be expected to, ought to**

suppress *VERB*

❶ *He managed to **suppress** his anger.*

• **check, hold back, contain, control, repress, restrain, curb, bottle up, stifle**

To suppress ideas for political or moral reasons is to **censor** them.

❷ *The army **suppressed** the rebellion.*

• **crush, quash, quell, put down, stamp out, stop, subdue**

supreme *ADJECTIVE*

*Her **supreme** achievement was winning a gold medal.*

• **greatest, highest, best, outstanding, top**

sure *ADJECTIVE*

❶ *I'm **sure** that I'm right.*

• **certain, convinced, confident, definite, positive**

OPPOSITES **unsure, uncertain**

❷ *He's **sure** to phone tonight.*

• **bound, certain**

OPPOSITE **unlikely**

❸ *A high temperature is a **sure** sign of illness.*

• **clear, definite, true, undoubted, undeniable**

OPPOSITES **unclear, doubtful**

surface *NOUN*

❶ *The **surface** of Mars is barren and rocky.*

• **exterior, outside**

The surface of something may be covered with a **crust** or **shell** or **skin**.
A thin surface of expensive wood on furniture is a **veneer**.

OPPOSITE **centre**

❷ *A dice has dots on each **surface**.*

• **face, side**

OPPOSITE **inside**

❸ *Oil floated on the **surface** of the water.*
• top
OPPOSITE bottom

surface *VERB*
❶ *The road is **surfaced** with cobbles.*
• cover, coat
❷ *The head of an alligator **surfaced** in the river.*
• rise to the surface, come up, emerge, appear
(informal) pop up

surge *VERB*
❶ *Massive waves **surged** around the tiny raft.*
• rise, roll, swirl, heave, billow
❷ *The crowd **surged** forward.*
• rush, push, sweep

surpass *VERB*
*It will be hard to **surpass** last year's performance.*
• beat, exceed, do better than, outdo

surplus *NOUN*
*Farmers have produced a **surplus** of apples this year.*
• excess, glut, surfeit, oversupply
OPPOSITES shortage, lack

surprise *NOUN*
*The news that Sara was married came as a **surprise**.*
• shock, revelation
(informal) bombshell

surprise *VERB*
❶ *I was **surprised** by how well she could sing.*
• amaze, astonish, astound, stagger, startle, stun, take aback, take by surprise, dumbfound
(informal) bowl over, flabbergast
❷ *He **surprised** the burglars as they came through the window.*
• discover, come upon, catch unawares, catch off guard, catch red-handed

surprised *ADJECTIVE*

WRITING TIPS

SOMEONE WHO FEELS SURPRISED MIGHT:

• have eyes bulging out of their head, have eyes on the end of stalks, jump out of their skin, stare wide-eyed
The Queen... simply sat there staring wide-eyed and white-faced at the small girl who was perched on her window-sill in a nightie.
—THE BFG, Roald Dahl

SOMETHING WHICH SURPRISES YOU MIGHT:

(informal) knock you for six, knock your socks off, knock you sideways, make your eyes pop
for things you might say when surprised see **exclamation**

surprising *ADJECTIVE*
*There are a **surprising** number of errors in the book.*
• amazing, astonishing, astounding, extraordinary, remarkable, incredible, staggering, startling, stunning, unexpected
OPPOSITE predictable

surrender *VERB*
❶ *The band of outlaws refused to **surrender**.*
• admit defeat, give in, yield, submit, capitulate
❷ *Please **surrender** your ticket to the driver.*
• give, hand over

surround *VERB*
❶ *The garden was **surrounded** by a stone wall.*
• enclose, fence in, wall in
❷ *The pack of wolves **surrounded** its prey.*
• encircle, ring, hem in, besiege

surroundings *PLURAL NOUN*
*The hotel is set in very pleasant **surroundings**.*
• setting, location, environment

a b c d e f g h i j k l m n o p q r s t u v w x y z

survey *NOUN*
❶ *They did a **survey** of local leisure facilities.*
• **review, investigation, study**
A survey to count the population of an area is a **census**.
❷ *The builders did a **survey** of the house.*
• **inspection, examination**

survey *VERB*
❶ *You can **survey** the whole valley from the top of the tower.*
• **view, look over, look at, observe**
❷ *They **surveyed** the damage done by the storm.*
• **inspect, examine, scrutinise, study**
❸ *The builders will need to **survey** the area.*
• **map out, plan out, measure**

survive *VERB*
❶ *He managed to **survive** alone on the island for six months.*
• **stay alive, last, live, keep going, carry on, continue**
OPPOSITE **die**
❷ *Ada **survived** her husband by twenty years.*
• **outlast**
❸ *Will the birds **survive** this cold weather?*
• **endure, withstand, live through, weather**

suspect *VERB*
❶ *The police **suspected** his motives.*
• **doubt, mistrust, have suspicions about**
❷ *I **suspect** that the shop will be closed on Sundays.*
• **expect, imagine, presume, guess, sense, fancy**

suspend *VERB*
❶ *The meeting was **suspended** until the next day.*
• **adjourn, break off, discontinue, interrupt**
❷ *For the party, we **suspended** balloons from the ceiling.*
• **hang, dangle, swing**

suspense *NOUN*
*The film was a thriller, full of action and **suspense**.*
• **tension, uncertainty, anticipation, expectancy, drama, excitement**

suspicion *NOUN*
*I have a **suspicion** that he is lying.*
• **feeling, hunch, inkling, intuition, impression**

suspicious *ADJECTIVE*
❶ *There is something about him which makes me **suspicious**.*
• **doubtful, distrustful, mistrustful, unsure, uneasy, wary**
OPPOSITE **trusting**
❷ *What do you make of his **suspicious** behaviour?*
• **questionable, suspect, dubious, shady** *(informal)* **fishy**

sustain *VERB*
❶ *Squirrels store nuts to **sustain** them through the winter.*
• **keep going, nurture, provide for**
❷ *The runners couldn't **sustain** the high speed.*
• **keep up, maintain**
❸ *Will the bridge **sustain** his weight?*
• **support, bear, carry, stand**

swagger *VERB*
*The lead actor **swaggered** about on stage.*
• **strut, parade**

swallow *VERB*
*The bread was so dry that it was hard to **swallow**.*
• **gulp down**
for other ways to eat and drink see **eat, drink**
➤ **to swallow something up**
*As it climbed higher, the rocket was **swallowed up** by the clouds.*
• **envelop, engulf, cover over, absorb**

swam *past tense see* **swim**

swamp *VERB*
*A huge wave threatened to **swamp** the ship.*
• **overwhelm, engulf, inundate, flood, submerge**

swamp *NOUN*
Much of the land near the coast is ***swamp****.*
• **marsh, bog, mire, fen, quicksand, quagmire**

swan *NOUN*
A female swan is a **pen**.
A male swan is a **cob**.
A young swan is a **cygnet**.

swap or **swop** *VERB*
We ***swapped*** *seats so I could sit in the aisle.*
• **change, exchange, switch, substitute**

swarm *VERB*
Hundreds of people ***swarmed*** *around the film star.*
• **crowd, flock**
➤ **to swarm with**
The garden is ***swarming with*** *ants.*
• **be overrun by, be crawling with, be infested with, teem with**

sway *VERB*
The tall grass ***swayed*** *in the breeze.*
• **wave, swing, rock, bend, lean**

swear *VERB* **swears, swearing, swore, sworn**
❶ *The knight* ***swore*** *that he would protect the unicorn.*
• **pledge, promise, vow, give your word, take an oath**
❷ *The player* ***swore*** *when he bashed his knee.*
• **curse**

sweat *VERB*
He ***sweats*** *a lot in hot weather.*
• **perspire**

sweaty *ADJECTIVE*
When I'm nervous, my palms get ***sweaty****.*
• **sweating, perspiring, clammy, sticky, moist**

sweep *VERB*
❶ *She* ***swept*** *the floor with an old broom.*
• **brush, clean, dust**
❷ *The bus* ***swept*** *past.*
• **shoot, speed, zoom**
➤ **to sweep something away**
He tried to ***sweep away*** *the rubbish.*
• **clear away, get rid of, remove**
The flood ***swept away*** *several houses.*
• **destroy, flatten, level**

sweet *ADJECTIVE*
❶ *The pudding is too* ***sweet*** *for me.*
• **sickly, sugary, sweetened, syrupy**
OPPOSITES **acid, bitter, savoury**
❷ *The* ***sweet*** *smell of roses filled the room.*
• **fragrant, pleasant**
OPPOSITE **foul**
❸ *We heard the* ***sweet*** *sound of a harp.*
• **melodious, pleasant, soothing, tuneful**
OPPOSITE **ugly**
❹ *What a* ***sweet*** *little cottage!*
• **attractive, charming, dear, lovely, pretty, quaint**
OPPOSITE **unattractive**

sweet *NOUN*
❶ *The bag contained a mixture of* ***sweets****.*
A North American word is **candy**.
A formal word for sweets is **confectionery**.
❷ *We had rhubarb crumble as our* ***sweet****.*
• **dessert, pudding**

sweet *NOUN*

WORD WEB

SOME KINDS OF SWEET:

• **barley sugar, boiled sweet, bubblegum, butterscotch, candyfloss, caramel, chewing gum, chocolate, fruit pastille, fudge, jelly baby, liquorice, lollipop, marshmallow, marzipan, mint** or **peppermint, nougat, rock, tablet, toffee, Turkish delight**

A B C D E F G H I J K L M N O P Q R S T U V W X Y Z

swell *VERB* **swells, swelling, swelled, swollen** or **swelled**
*The balloon **swelled** as it filled with hot air.*
• **expand, inflate, bulge, grow, enlarge, puff up, billow**
OPPOSITE **shrink**

swelling *NOUN*
*He had a painful **swelling** on his foot.*
• **inflammation, lump, bump, growth**
A **tumour** is a serious swelling on the body.

swerve *VERB*
*The car **swerved** to avoid a hedgehog.*
• **turn aside, veer, dodge, swing**

swift *ADJECTIVE*
❶ *They set off at a **swift** pace.*
• **fast, quick, rapid, speedy, brisk, lively**
❷ *She received a **swift** reply to her email.*
• **quick, fast, immediate, instant, prompt, speedy, snappy**
OPPOSITE **slow**

swim *VERB* **swims, swimming, swam, swum**
*We **swam** in the sea on our holiday.*
• **go swimming, bathe, take a dip**

WORD WEB

VARIOUS SWIMMING STROKES:
• **backstroke, breaststroke, butterfly, crawl, doggy-paddle**

PLACES WHERE YOU CAN SWIM:
• **baths, leisure pool, lido, paddling pool, swimming baths** or **swimming pool**

CLOTHING FOR SWIMMING:
• **bathing costume, bathing suit, bikini, swimming cap, swimming costume, swimsuit, trunks**

OTHER EQUIPMENT FOR SWIMMING:
• **armbands, flippers, float, goggles, nose-clip, rubber ring, snorkel**

swindle *VERB*
*He **swindled** them out of a lot of money.*
• **cheat, trick, dupe, fleece**
(informal) **con, diddle**

swing *VERB* **swings, swinging, swung**
❶ *A glass chandelier **swung** from the ceiling.*
• **hang, dangle, sway, flap, wave about**
❷ *She **swung** round when I called her name.*
• **turn, twist, veer, swerve**

swipe *VERB*
*The polar bear **swiped** the seal with its paw.*
• **swing at, hit, strike, slash**
for other ways to hit things see **hit**

swirl *VERB*
*Clouds of dust **swirled** up in the desert wind.*
• **spin, twirl, whirl, churn**

switch *VERB*
❶ *Please remember to **switch** off the light.*
• **turn**
❷ *The teams will **switch** ends at half-time.*
• **change, swap, exchange, shift**

swivel *VERB*
*The dentist **swivelled** round in her chair.*
• **spin, turn, twirl, pivot, revolve, rotate**

swollen *ADJECTIVE*
*My feet were **swollen** from walking all day.*
• **inflamed, bloated, puffed up, puffy**

swoop *VERB*
*The owl **swooped** and caught the mouse.*
• **dive, drop, plunge, plummet, descend, pounce**

swop *VERB*
see **swap**

sword *NOUN*
*Athena raised her shield and drew her **sword**.*
• **blade**

WORD WEB

SOME TYPES OF SWORD:

• **broadsword, claymore, cutlass, foil, rapier, sabre, scimitar**
Fighting with swords is **fencing** or **swordsmanship.**
for other weapons see **weapon**

swore *past tense see* **swear**

symbol *NOUN*
The dove is a ***symbol*** *of peace.*
• **sign, emblem, image, motif**
The symbols we use in writing are **characters** or **letters.**
The symbols used in ancient Egyptian writing were **hieroglyphics.**
The symbol of a club or school is their **badge.**
The symbol of a firm or organisation is their **logo.**

symbolise *VERB*
The dove ***symbolises*** *peace.*
• **represent, stand for, signify, indicate, mean, denote**

sympathetic *ADJECTIVE*
They were ***sympathetic*** *when my mother was ill.*
• **understanding, compassionate, concerned, caring, comforting, kind, supportive**
OPPOSITE **unsympathetic**

sympathise *VERB*
➤ **to sympathise with**
We ***sympathised with*** *those who had lost their homes.*
• **be sympathetic towards, be sorry for, feel for, commiserate with**

sympathy *NOUN*
Did you feel any ***sympathy*** *for the characters in the story?*
• **understanding, compassion, pity, fellow-feeling, tenderness**

synonym *NOUN*
'Cheerful' is a ***synonym*** *of 'happy'.*
OPPOSITE **antonym**

synthetic *ADJECTIVE*
Nylon is a ***synthetic*** *material.*
• **artificial, man-made, manufactured, imitation**
OPPOSITE **natural**

system *NOUN*
❶ *The city has an archaic transport* ***system.***
• **organisation, structure, network, framework**
(*informal*) **set-up**
❷ *Do you understand the new cataloguing* ***system?***
• **procedure, process, scheme, arrangement, method, routine**

systematic *ADJECTIVE*
Inspector Giles works in a ***systematic*** *way.*
• **methodical, logical, orderly, organised, scientific**
OPPOSITE **unsystematic**

a b c d e f g h i j k l m n o p q r s t u v w x y z

Tt

table *NOUN*
for items of furniture see **furniture**

tablet *NOUN*
❶ *The doctor prescribed some* ***tablets*** *for the pain.*
• **pill, capsule, pellet**
❷ *There was a stone* ***tablet*** *above the entrance to the tomb.*
• **slab, plaque**
❸ *He put a* ***tablet*** *of powder in the washing machine.*
• **block, piece, bar, chunk**

tack *VERB*
❶ *The carpet needs to be* ***tacked*** *down.*
• **nail, pin**
❷ *She* ***tacked*** *up the hem of her skirt.*
• **sew, stitch**

tackle *VERB*
❶ *They left him to* ***tackle*** *the washing-up.*
• **cope with, deal with, attend to, handle, manage, grapple with**
❷ *Another player* ***tackled*** *her and got the ball.*
• **challenge, intercept, take on**

tackle *NOUN*
❶ *The referee said it was a fair* ***tackle.***
• **challenge, interception**
❷ *He kept his fishing* ***tackle*** *in a special case.*
• **gear, equipment, apparatus, kit**

tactful *ADJECTIVE*
She gave him a ***tactful*** *reminder about her birthday.*
• **subtle, discreet, diplomatic, sensitive, thoughtful**
OPPOSITE **tactless**

tactics *PLURAL NOUN*
They discussed their ***tactics*** *for the next game.*
• **moves, manoeuvres, plan of action**
An overall plan for a game or battle is a **strategy.**

tag *NOUN*
The price is marked on the ***tag.***
• **label, sticker, ticket**

tag *VERB*
Every item is ***tagged*** *with a price label.*
• **identify, label, mark**
➤ **to tag along with someone**
She ***tagged along*** *with them when they left.*
• **accompany, follow, go with, join**
➤ **to tag something on**
He ***tagged on*** *a PS at the end of his letter.*
• **add, attach, tack on**

tail *NOUN*
He joined the ***tail*** *of the queue.*
• **end, back, rear**

tail *VERB*
The detective ***tailed*** *the suspect to this address.*
• **follow, pursue, track, trail, shadow, stalk**
➤ **to tail off**
The number of tourists ***tails off*** *in October.*
• **decrease, decline, lessen, diminish, dwindle, wane**

take *VERB* **takes, taking, took, taken**
❶ *Naomi* ***took*** *her sister's hand.*
• **clutch, clasp, take hold of, grasp, grip, seize, snatch, grab**
❷ *The soldiers* ***took*** *many prisoners.*
• **catch, capture, seize, detain**
❸ *Someone has* ***taken*** *my pen.*
• **steal, remove, make off with** *(informal)* **swipe, pinch**
❹ *The guide will* ***take*** *you to the edge of the forest.*
• **conduct, escort, lead, accompany**
❺ *The bus* ***took*** *us right to the station.*
• **bring, carry, convey, transport**
❻ *It'll* ***take*** *two people to lift that table.*
• **need, require**

❼ *The caravan can **take** six people.*
• hold, contain, accommodate, have room for
❽ *He couldn't **take** the heat of the midday sun.*
• bear, put up with, stand, endure, tolerate, suffer, stomach
❾ *He **took** their names and addresses.*
• make a note of, record, write down
❿ *The magician asked me to **take** a card.*
• pick, choose, select
⓫ *Take 2 from 8 and you get 6.*
• subtract, take away, deduct

➤ to take someone in
*Everyone was **taken in** by his disguise.*
• fool, deceive, trick, cheat, dupe, hoodwink

➤ to take off
*Our flight **took off** on time.*
• depart, lift off

➤ to take something off
*Please **take off** your coat.*
• remove, strip off, peel off

➤ to take part in something
*Would you like to **take part in** the show?*
• participate in, be involved in, join in

➤ to take place
*When did the accident **take place**?*
• happen, occur, come about

➤ to take something up
*She has recently **taken up** tap-dancing.*
• begin to do, start learning

tale *NOUN*
*Pinocchio is a **tale** about a boy made of wood.*
• story, narrative, account
(informal) yarn
for various kinds of story see **story**

talent *NOUN*
*She has a great **talent** for music.*
• gift, ability, aptitude, skill, flair, knack
Unusually great talent is **genius**.

talented *ADJECTIVE*
*He's a very **talented** dancer.*
• gifted, able, accomplished, capable, skilled, skilful, clever, brilliant
If you are talented in several ways, you are **versatile**.

talk *VERB*
❶ *Doug was trying to teach his parrot to **talk**.*
• speak, say things, communicate, express yourself
❷ *The two old friends had a lot to **talk** about.*
• discuss, converse, chat, chatter, gossip
(informal) natter
❸ *The prisoner refused to **talk**.*
• give information, confess
for other ways to say things see **say**

talk *NOUN*
❶ *I need to have a **talk** with you soon.*
• conversation, discussion, chat
The talk between characters in a story is the **dialogue**.
❷ *There is a **talk** about Egyptian art at lunchtime.*
• lecture, presentation, speech, address
A talk in church is a **sermon**.

talkative *ADJECTIVE*
*You're not very **talkative** this morning.*
• chatty, communicative, vocal, forthcoming, articulate
An informal name for a talkative person is a **chatterbox**.

tall *ADJECTIVE*
❶ *Jasmine is **tall** for her age.*
• big
OPPOSITE short
❷ *Singapore has many **tall** buildings.*
• high, lofty, towering, soaring, giant
Buildings with many floors are **high-rise** or **multi-storey** buildings.
OPPOSITE low

tally *VERB*
➤ to tally with
*Her story didn't **tally with** her husband's.*
• agree with, correspond with, match

tame *ADJECTIVE*
❶ *The guinea pigs are **tame** and used to people.*
• domesticated, broken in, docile, gentle, obedient, manageable
OPPOSITE wild

A B C D E F G H I J K L M N O P Q R S T U V W X Y Z

❷ *The film seems very **tame** nowadays.*
• **dull, boring, tedious, bland, unexciting, uninteresting**
OPPOSITE **exciting**

tame *VERB*
*They were trying to **tame** a wild horse.*
• **break in, subdue, master, control**

tamper *VERB*
➤ **to tamper with something**
*Someone has been **tampering with** the lock.*
• **meddle with, tinker with, fiddle about with, interfere with**

tan *VERB*
*Do you **tan** easily in the sun?*
• **get a tan, go brown**
If your skin goes red in the sun, you get **sunburn**.

tang *NOUN*
*You can taste the **tang** of oranges in the soup.*
• **sharpness, zest, zing**

tangle *VERB*
❶ *Her sewing threads were all **tangled** together.*
• **entangle, twist, knot, jumble, muddle**
Tangled hair is **dishevelled** or **matted** hair.
❷ *Dolphins can get **tangled** in fishing nets.*
• **catch, trap, ensnare, entangle**

tangle *NOUN*
*The computer cables have got into a **tangle**.*
• **muddle, jumble, knot, twist, confusion**

tap *VERB*
*Someone **tapped** three times on the door.*
• **knock, rap, strike**

tape *NOUN*
*The stack of old letters was tied up with **tape**.*
• **ribbon, braid, binding**

target *NOUN*
❶ *Her **target** was to swim thirty lengths.*
• **goal, aim, objective, intention, purpose, hope, ambition**
❷ *She was the **target** of his jokes.*
• **object, victim, butt**

tarnish *VERB*
❶ *The bronze sculptures had **tarnished** with age.*
• **discolour, corrode**
When iron corrodes it **rusts**.
❷ *The scandal **tarnished** his reputation.*
• **stain, taint, blot, spoil, mar**

tart *ADJECTIVE*
*Lemons have a **tart** taste.*
• **sharp, sour, acid, tangy**
OPPOSITE **sweet**

task *NOUN*
❶ *The robot was given a number of **tasks** to do.*
• **job, chore, exercise, errand**
❷ *The soldiers' **task** was to capture the hill.*
• **assignment, mission, duty, undertaking**

taste *VERB*
❶ *Taste the soup to see if it needs salt.*
• **sample, try, test, sip**
❷ *The curry **tastes** quite mild.*
for ways to describe how food tastes see **food**

taste *NOUN*
❶ *I love the **taste** of ginger.*
• **flavour**
❷ *May I have a **taste** of the cheese?*
• **mouthful, bite, morsel, nibble, bit, piece, sample**
❸ *Her **taste** in clothes is a bit odd.*
• **choice, preferenee, discrimination, judgement**

tasteful *ADJECTIVE*
*The room was decorated in **tasteful** colours.*
• **refined, cultivated, smart, stylish, artistic, elegant, attractive**
OPPOSITE **tasteless**

tasteless *ADJECTIVE*
❶ *He apologised for making a **tasteless** remark.*
• **crude, tactless, indelicate, inappropriate**
OPPOSITE **tasteful**
❷ *The sprouts were overcooked and **tasteless**.*
• **flavourless, bland, insipid**
OPPOSITE **flavourful**

tasty *ADJECTIVE*
*That pie was very **tasty**.*
• **delicious, appetising**
see also **food**
OPPOSITE **unappetising**

tattered *ADJECTIVE*
*Some of the blankets were worn and **tattered**.*
• **ragged, ripped, torn, frayed, tatty, threadbare**
OPPOSITE **smart**

taught *past tense see* **teach**

taunt *VERB*
*The gladiator **taunted** his opponent.*
• **barrack, insult, jeer at, laugh at, make fun of, mock, ridicule, sneer at**

taut *ADJECTIVE*
*Make sure the rope is **taut**.*
• **tight, tense, stretched**
OPPOSITE **slack**

teach *VERB* **teaches, teaching, taught**
*My dad is **teaching** me to play the guitar.*
• **educate, inform, instruct**
To teach people to play a sport is to **coach** or **train** them.
To teach one person at a time or a small group is to **tutor** them.

teacher *NOUN*
*We have a new ballet **teacher**.*
• **tutor, instructor, trainer**
Someone who teaches you to play a sport is a **coach**.
In the past, a woman who taught children in a private household was a **governess**.

team *NOUN*
*She's been picked for the junior hockey **team**.*
• **side**

tear *VERB* **tears, tearing, tore, torn**
❶ *The tree branch **tore** a hole in our kite.*
• **rip, snag, gash, shred, split, slit**
❷ *He **tore** home to watch his favourite TV programme.*
• **run, rush, dash, hurry, race, sprint, speed**
see also **run**

tear *NOUN*
*There was a **tear** in one of the sails.*
• **cut, rip, rent, split, gash, hole, opening, slit, gap**

tease *VERB*
*They **teased** him about his new haircut.*
• **taunt, make fun of, poke fun at, mock, ridicule, laugh at**

technical *ADJECTIVE*
*The computer manual uses **technical** language.*
• **specialised, scientific, advanced**

technique *NOUN*
❶ *The archaeologists use modern **techniques**.*
• **method, procedure, approach**
❷ *The pianist's **technique** was flawless.*
• **skill, expertise, art, craft**

tedious *ADJECTIVE*
*It was a **tedious** journey by bus.*
• **boring, dreary, dull, tiresome, monotonous, unexciting, uninteresting**
OPPOSITE **exciting**

teem *VERB*
➤ **to teem with**
*The pond **teemed with** tadpoles.*
• **be overrun by, be crawling with, be infested with, swarm with**

teenager *NOUN*
*The film is designed to appeal to **teenagers**.*
• **adolescent, youth**

telephone *NOUN, VERB*
see **phone**

tell *VERB* **tells, telling, told**
❶ *Tell us what you can see.*
• **describe, explain, reveal, report, say, state**

A B C D E F G H I J K L M N O P Q R S T U V W X Y Z

❷ *Tell me when you are ready.*
- **let you know, inform, notify, announce, communicate**

❸ *He* ***told*** *them to stop making so much noise.*
- **order, command, direct, instruct**

❹ *We* ***told*** *each other scary ghost stories.*
- **narrate, relate**

❺ *He* ***told*** *me he would buy the tickets.*
- **assure, promise**

❻ *She couldn't* ***tell*** *where she was in the dark.*
- **make out, recognise, identify, perceive**

❼ *Can you* ***tell*** *one twin from the other?*
- **distinguish, separate**

➤ to tell someone off
She ***told themoff*** *for being late.*
- **scold, reprimand, reproach**

(informal) **tick off**

temper *NOUN*

❶ *Mr Black had been in a bad* ***temper*** *all morning.*
- **mood, humour, state of mind**

❷ *The chef is always flying into a* ***temper****.*
- **rage, fury, fit of anger, tantrum**

➤ to lose your temper
When she ***loses her temper****, her cheeks go red.*
- **get angry, get annoyed, fly into a rage**

see also **angry**

temperature *NOUN*
for units for measuring temperature see **measurement**

tempestuous *ADJECTIVE*
There was a ***tempestuous*** *storm at sea.*
- **stormy, squally, rough, raging, turbulent, wild**

OPPOSITE **calm**

temple *NOUN*
for places where people worship see **building**

temporary *ADJECTIVE*
They made a ***temporary*** *shelter for the night.*
- **makeshift, provisional**

OPPOSITE **permanent**

tempt *VERB*
Can I ***tempt*** *you to have more pudding?*
- **coax, entice, persuade, attract**

To tempt someone by offering them money is to **bribe** them.
To tempt an animal into a trap is to **lure** it.

tend *VERB*

❶ *She* ***tends to*** *worry too much.*
- **be inclined to, be liable to, be apt to**

❷ *One of the campers was left to* ***tend*** *the fire.*
- **mind, watch over, maintain**

❸ *Ned spends a lot of time* ***tending*** *his garden.*
- **take care of, cultivate, manage**

❹ *Nurses* ***tended*** *those who were injured.*
- **care for, attend to, look after, nurse, treat**

tendency *NOUN*
He has a ***tendency*** *to be lazy.*
- **inclination, leaning, predisposition**

tender *ADJECTIVE*

❶ *Frost may damage* ***tender*** *plants.*
- **delicate, fragile**

OPPOSITES **hardy, strong**

❷ *Cook the meat slowly until it is* ***tender****.*
- **soft, succulent, juicy**

OPPOSITE **tough**

❸ *The bruise is still* ***tender****.*
- **painful, sensitive, sore**

❹ *She gave him a* ***tender*** *smile.*
- **affectionate, kind, loving, caring, warm-hearted, compassionate, sympathetic, fond**

OPPOSITE **uncaring**

tennis *NOUN*

WORD WEB

WAYS TO HIT A TENNIS BALL:
- **lob, serve, slice, smash, volley drop shot, backhand, forehand**

SCORING USED IN A TENNIS MATCH:

• **love, deuce, advantage, break point, match point, tie-break, game, set**

OTHER TERMS USED IN TENNIS:

• **ace, ballboy** or **ballgirl, court, doubles, net, racket** or **racquet, service, singles, umpire**

tense *ADJECTIVE*
❶ *The muscles in her shoulders were* ***tense****.*
• **taut, tight, strained, stretched**
❷ *The crowd were* ***tense*** *as they waited to hear the results.*
• **anxious, nervous, apprehensive, edgy, on edge, fidgety, jumpy**
(informal) **uptight, jittery**
❸ *It was a* ***tense*** *moment for all of us.*
• **nerve-racking, stressful, worrying**
OPPOSITE **relaxed**

tension *NOUN*
❶ *Can you check the* ***tension*** *on the guy ropes?*
• **tightness, tautness**
❷ *The* ***tension*** *of waiting was almost unbearable.*
• **stress, strain, anxiety, nervousness, suspense, worry**

tent *NOUN*

WORD WEB

SOME KINDS OF TENT:

• **dome tent, frame tent, marquee, pop-up tent, tepee, tunnel tent, yurt**
The ropes which hold down a tent are the **guy ropes.**

term *NOUN*
❶ *He was sentenced to a* ***term*** *in prison.*
• **period, time, spell, stretch, session**
❷ *The book has a glossary of technical* ***terms****.*
• **word, name, expression**

terrible *ADJECTIVE*
We heard there had been a ***terrible*** *accident.*
• **awful, dreadful, horrible, appalling, shocking, ghastly, horrific, frightful**
for other ways to describe something bad see **bad**

terrific *ADJECTIVE (informal)*
❶ *The footprint of the yeti was a* ***terrific*** *size.*
• **big, huge, immense, enormous, giant, gigantic, colossal, massive**
see also **big**
❷ *She's a* ***terrific*** *tennis player.*
• **excellent, first-class, first-rate, superb, marvellous, wonderful**
(informal) **brilliant, fantastic, fabulous**

terrify *VERB*
The dogs were ***terrified*** *by the thunder.*
• **frighten, scare, startle, alarm, panic, horrify, petrify**

territory *NOUN*
We had now entered uncharted ***territory****.*
• **land, area, ground, terrain, country, district, region, sector, zone**
A territory which is part of a country is a **province.**

terror *NOUN*
Her eyes filled with ***terror*** *as she described the ghost.*
• **fear, fright, horror, panic, alarm, dread**

test *NOUN*
How did you do in the maths ***test****?*
• **exam, examination, assessment, appraisal, evaluation**
A set of questions you answer for fun is a **quiz.**
A test for a job as an actor or singer is an **audition.**
A test to find the truth about something is an **experiment** or **trial.**

a b c d e f g h i j k l m n o p q r s t u v w x y z

test *VERB*

❶ *I made an appointment to have my eyes **tested**.*

• **examine, check, evaluate, assess, screen**

❷ *He is **testing** a new formula for invisible ink.*

• **experiment with, try out, trial**

text *NOUN*

❶ *The lawyer studied the **text** of the document.*

• **wording, words, content**

❷ *She quoted a **text** from Shakespeare.*

• **passage, extract, quotation**

textiles *PLURAL NOUN*

see **fabric**

texture *NOUN*

*Silk has a smooth **texture**.*

• **feel, touch, quality, consistency**

for ways to describe texture see **feel**

thankful *ADJECTIVE*

➤ **to be thankful for something**

*The travellers **were thankful for** our help.*

• **grateful for, appreciative of, pleased about, relieved about**

OPPOSITE **ungrateful**

thanks *PLURAL NOUN*

*She sent them a card to show her **thanks**.*

• **gratitude, appreciation**

thaw *VERB*

❶ *The snowman gradually began to **thaw**.*

• **melt, dissolve**

❷ *Leave frozen food to **thaw** before cooking it.*

• **defrost, unfreeze**

OPPOSITE **freeze**

theatre *NOUN*

WORD WEB

PARTS OF A THEATRE:

• **auditorium, balcony, bar, boxes, box office, circle, dress circle, dressing rooms, foyer, gallery, orchestra pit, stage, stalls**

PEOPLE WHO PERFORM OR WORK IN A THEATRE:

• **actor, actress, ballerina, dancer, director, dresser, make-up artist, musician, producer, prompter, scene shifter, stage manager, understudy, usher or usherette**

A person who writes plays for the theatre is a **dramatist** or **playwright**.

PERFORMANCES YOU MIGHT SEE AT A THEATRE:

• **ballet, comedy, dance, drama, farce, mime, musical, opera, pantomime, play, puppet show**

theft *NOUN*

*He was found guilty of **theft**.*

• **robbery, stealing**

for various kinds of theft see **stealing**

theme *NOUN*

*What is the **theme** of the poem?*

• **subject, topic, idea, gist, argument**

theory *NOUN*

❶ *The detective has a **theory** about the case.*

• **explanation, hypothesis, view, belief, idea, notion, suggestion**

❷ *She bought a book about musical **theory**.*

• **laws, principles, rules**

therapy *NOUN*

*She tried several **therapies** to cure her headaches.*

• **treatment, remedy**

thick *ADJECTIVE*

❶ *The Roman wall was about 2 metres* ***thick****.*
• **wide, broad**
❷ *The cabin was made from* ***thick*** *logs of wood.*
• **stout, chunky, heavy, solid, substantial**
OPPOSITES **thin, slender**
❸ *The explorers hacked their way through the* ***thick*** *jungle.*
• **dense, close, compact**
❹ *His boots got stuck in a* ***thick*** *layer of mud.*
• **deep, heavy**
OPPOSITES **thin, shallow**
❺ *The guide spoke with a* ***thick*** *Polish accent.*
• **heavy, noticeable**
OPPOSITE **slight**
❻ *(informal) Fortunately, the giant was rather* ***thick****.*
• **stupid, brainless, foolish**
OPPOSITE **intelligent**

thief *NOUN*

The police managed to catch the ***thief****.*
• **robber**
Someone who steals from people's homes is a **burglar** or **housebreaker.**
Someone who steals from people in the street is a **pickpocket.**
Someone who steals from shops is a **shoplifter.**
Someone who used to steal from travellers was a **highwayman.**

thin *ADJECTIVE*

❶ *The prisoners were dreadfully* ***thin****.*
• **lean, skinny, bony, gaunt, spare, slight, underweight**
Someone who is thin and tall is **lanky.**
Someone who is thin but strong is **wiry.**
Someone who is thin but attractive is **slim** or **slender.**
Thin arms or legs are **spindly.**
A common simile is **as thin as a rake.**
OPPOSITE **fat**
❷ *The fairy wore a* ***thin*** *cloak of spider's silk.*
• **fine, light, delicate, flimsy, sheer, wispy**
A thin line is a **fine** or **narrow** line.
A thin book is a **slim** book.
OPPOSITE **thick**
❸ *The icing should be* ***thin*** *enough to spread.*
• **runny, watery**
OPPOSITE **thick**

thin *VERB*

You can ***thin*** *the paint with a little water.*
• **dilute, water down, weaken**

➤ to thin out
The crowd ***thinned out*** *later in the day.*
• **diminish, disperse**

thing *NOUN*

❶ *What's that green* ***thing*** *on the floor?*
• **item, object, article**
❷ *We had a lot of* ***things*** *to talk about.*
• **matter, affair, detail, point, factor**
❸ *Some strange* ***things*** *have been happening.*
• **event, happening, occurrence, incident**
❹ *I have only one* ***thing*** *left to do.*
• **job, task, act, action**
❺ *Put your* ***things*** *in one of the lockers.*
• **belongings, possessions, stuff, equipment, gear**

think *VERB* **thinks, thinking, thought**

❶ ***Think*** *before you do anything rash.*
• **consider, contemplate, reflect, deliberate, reason**
To think hard about something is to **concentrate** on it.
To think quietly and deeply about something is to **meditate.**
To keep thinking anxiously about something is to **brood** on it.
❷ *Do you* ***think*** *this is a good idea?*
• **believe, feel, consider, judge, conclude**
❸ *What do you* ***think*** *this ring is worth?*
• **reckon, suppose, imagine, estimate, guess, expect**

➤ to think about something
I need some more time to ***think about*** *it.*
• **consider, reflect on, ponder, muse on, mull over**

➤ to think something up
They ***thought up*** *a good plan.*
• **invent, make up, conceive, concoct, devise**

A B C D E F G H I J K L M N O P Q R S T U V W X Y Z

thirsty *ADJECTIVE*
*They were **thirsty** after their long walk.*
• dry, parched
If someone is ill through lack of fluids, they are **dehydrated.**

thorn *NOUN*
*The florist cut the **thorns** off the rose stems.*
• prickle, spike, needle, barb

thorny *ADJECTIVE*
❶ *He scratched his arm on a **thorny** rose bush.*
• prickly, spiky, spiny, sharp, bristly, scratchy
❷ *They discussed the **thorny** problem for hours.*
• tricky, difficult, complicated, hard, perplexing, ticklish

thorough *ADJECTIVE*
❶ *The doctor gave him a **thorough** examination.*
• comprehensive, full, rigorous, careful, methodical, systematic, meticulous, painstaking, conscientious
OPPOSITE superficial
❷ *He's made a **thorough** mess of things!*
• complete, total, utter, absolute, downright

thought *past tense see* **think**

thought *NOUN*
❶ *She gave a lot of **thought** to the problem.*
• consideration, deliberation, study
❷ *The detective was lost in **thought**.*
• thinking, contemplation, reflection, meditation
❸ *What are your **thoughts** on modern art?*
• opinion, belief, idea, notion, conclusion

thoughtful *ADJECTIVE*
❶ *Mr Levi had a **thoughtful** expression on his face.*
• pensive, reflective, absorbed, preoccupied
OPPOSITES blank, vacant
❷ *She added some **thoughtful** comments in the margin.*
• well-thought-out, careful, conscientious, thorough
OPPOSITE careless
❸ *It was very **thoughtful** of you to visit me in hospital.*
• caring, considerate, kind, friendly, good-natured, unselfish
OPPOSITE thoughtless

thoughtless *ADJECTIVE*
*It was **thoughtless** of him to mention her dead husband.*
• inconsiderate, insensitive, uncaring, unthinking, negligent, ill-considered, rash
OPPOSITE thoughtful

thrash *VERB*
❶ *The rider **thrashed** and spurred his horse to go faster.*
• hit, beat, whip, flog
(informal) whack, wallop
❷ *The crocodile **thrashed** its tail in the mud.*
• swish, flail, jerk, toss
❸ *(informal) The visitors **thrashed** the home side 6–0.*
• beat, defeat, trounce

thread *NOUN*
❶ *There was a loose **thread** hanging from her dress.*
• strand, fibre
❷ *Do you sell embroidery **thread**?*
• cotton, yarn, wool, silk
Sewing thread is wound on to a **reel** or **spool**.

threat *NOUN*
❶ *She made a **threat** about phoning the police.*
• warning
❷ *Earthquakes are a constant **threat** in California.*
• danger, menace, hazard, risk

threaten *VERB*
❶ *The bandits **threatened** him when he tried to escape.*
• make threats against, menace, intimidate, terrorise, bully, browbeat
❷ *The forecast **threatened** rain.*
• warn of
❸ *Wild tigers are **threatened** with extinction.*
• endanger, put at risk

three *NOUN*
A group of three musicians is a **trio**.
Three babies born at the same time are **triplets**.
A shape with three sides is a **triangle**.
To multiply a number by three is to **triple** it.

threw *past tense see* **throw**

thrifty *ADJECTIVE*
*Wendy had been **thrifty** and saved her pocket money.*
• **careful, economical, frugal, prudent, sparing**
OPPOSITE **extravagant**

thrill *NOUN*
*Kim loves the **thrill** of rock climbing.*
• **adventure, excitement, sensation, tingle**
(informal) **buzz, kick**

thrill *VERB*
*The thought of seeing a real shark **thrilled** him no end.*
• **excite, exhilarate, electrify, rouse, stir, stimulate**
OPPOSITE **bore**

thrilled *ADJECTIVE*
*I was **thrilled** to be invited to the wedding.*
• **delighted, pleased, excited, overjoyed, ecstatic**

thrive *VERB* **thrives, thriving, thrived** or **throve, thrived** or **thriven**
*Tomato plants **thrive** in greenhouses.*
• **do well, flourish, grow, prosper, succeed**

throb *VERB*
*She could feel the blood **throbbing** through her veins.*
• **beat, pound, pulse, pulsate**

throng *NOUN*
*There were **throngs** of people on the street.*
• **crowd, swarm, horde**

throttle *VERB*
*My tie was so tight that it nearly **throttled** me!*
• **strangle, choke**

throw *VERB* **throws, throwing, threw, thrown**
❶ *I **threw** some bread into the pond for the ducks.*
• **fling, cast, pitch, sling, toss**
(informal) **bung, chuck**
To deliver the ball in cricket or rounders is to **bowl**.
To throw the shot in athletics is to **put** the shot.
To throw something high in the air is to **lob** it.
To throw something heavy is to **heave** it.
To throw something with great force is to **hurl** it.
If someone throws a lot of things at you, they **pelt** you.
❷ *The horse **threw** its rider.*
• **throw off, shake off, dislodge**
➤ **to throw away**
*We **threw away** a pile of old junk.*
• **get rid of, dispose of, discard, scrap**
(informal) **dump, ditch**

thrust *VERB*
❶ *Drew **thrust** his hands into his pockets.*
• **push, force, shove**
❷ *The bandit **thrust** at him with a dagger.*
• **lunge, jab, prod, stab, poke**

thump *VERB*
*'Silence!' he rasped, **thumping** his fist on the table.*
• **bang, bash, pound, hit, strike, knock, rap**
(informal) **whack, wham**

thunder *NOUN, VERB*
*We could hear **thunder** in the distance.*
A burst of thunder is a **clap, crack, peal** or **roll** of thunder.
see also **weather**

tick *VERB*
*A clock was **ticking** in the background.*
for various ways to make sounds see **sound**

➤ **to tick someone off** *(informal)*
*She **ticked him off** for talking in class.*
• **tell off, reprimand, reproach, scold**

ticket *NOUN*

❶ *They got free **tickets** for the concert.*
• **pass, permit, token, voucher, coupon**
❷ *What does it say on the price **ticket**?*
• **label, tag, tab**

tide *NOUN*

*The beach is completely covered at high **tide**.*
When the tide is coming in it is **flowing** or **incoming**.
When the tide is going out it is **ebbing** or **outgoing**.
The tide is fully in at **high tide** and fully out at **low tide**.

tidy *ADJECTIVE*

*Mr Rackham likes to keep his office **tidy**.*
• **neat, orderly, uncluttered, trim, smart, spruce, straight**
OPPOSITE **untidy**

tie *VERB*

❶ *Zoe **tied** a pink ribbon round the parcel.*
• **bind, fasten, hitch, knot, loop, secure**
To tie up a boat is to **moor** it.
To tie up an animal is to **tether** it.
OPPOSITE **untie**
❷ *The two teams are still **tied**.*
• **be equal, be level, draw**

tight *ADJECTIVE*

❶ *The lid was too **tight** for him to unscrew.*
• **firm, fast, secure**
If something is so tight that air cannot get through, it is **airtight**.
If something is so tight that water cannot get through, it is **watertight**.
OPPOSITE **loose**
❷ *They squeezed into the **tight** space.*
• **cramped, compact, small, narrow, poky, snug**
OPPOSITE **spacious**
❸ *Make sure that the ropes are **tight**.*
• **taut, tense, stretched, rigid**
A common simile is **as tight as a drum**.
OPPOSITE **slack**
❹ *He can be very **tight** with his money.*
• **mean, miserly, stingy**
OPPOSITE **generous**

tighten *VERB*

❶ *She **tightened** her grip on his hand.*
• **increase, strengthen, tense, stiffen**
❷ *You need to **tighten** the guy ropes.*
• **make taut, pull tighter, stretch**
❸ *He tried to **tighten** the screw.*
• **make tighter, screw up**
OPPOSITE **loosen**

till *VERB*

*Farmers use tractors to **till** the land.*
• **cultivate, farm, plough, dig**

tilt *VERB*

*The caravan **tilted** to one side.*
• **lean, incline, tip, slant, slope, angle**
When a ship tilts to one side, it **lists**.

timber *NOUN*

*He bought some **timber** to build a shed.*
• **wood, lumber, logs, planks**

time *NOUN*

❶ *Is this a convenient **time** to talk?*
• **moment, occasion, opportunity**
❷ *Autumn is my favourite **time** of the year.*
• **phase, season**
❸ *He spent a short **time** living in China.*
• **period, while, term, spell, stretch**
❹ *Shakespeare lived in the **time** of Elizabeth I.*
• **era, age, days, epoch, period**
❺ *Please try to keep **time** with the music.*
• **tempo, beat, rhythm**

WORD WEB

UNITS FOR MEASURING TIME:

• **second, minute, hour, day, week, fortnight, month, year, decade, century, millennium**

INSTRUMENTS USED TO MEASURE TIME:

- clock, egg timer, hourglass, pocket watch, stopwatch, sundial, timer, watch, wristwatch

➤ on time
*Please try to be **on time**.*
- punctual, prompt

timid *ADJECTIVE*
*At first, the mermaid was too **timid** to say anything.*
- shy, bashful, modest, nervous, fearful, shrinking, retiring, sheepish

A common simile is **as timid as a mouse**.
OPPOSITES brave, confident

tingle *VERB*
*My ears were **tingling** with the cold.*
- prickle, sting, tickle

tingle *NOUN*
❶ *She felt a **tingle** in her foot.*
- prickling, stinging, tickle, tickling, pins and needles

❷ *He felt a **tingle** of excitement.*
- thrill, sensation, quiver, shiver

tinker *VERB*
*He **tinkered** with the computer to get it to work.*
- fiddle, play about, dabble, meddle, tamper

tint *NOUN*
*The paint was white with a faint **tint** of blue.*
- colour, hue, shade, tone

for names of colours see **colour**

tiny *ADJECTIVE*
*The ladybird was so **tiny** that you could hardly see it.*
- little, minute, miniature, microscopic, minuscule

(informal) teeny, titchy
OPPOSITES big, large

tip *NOUN*
❶ *The **tip** of his nose felt cold.*
- end, point

The tip of an ink pen is the **nib**.
❷ *The **tip** of the mountain was covered in snow.*
- cap, peak, top, summit, pinnacle, crown

❸ *He gave them some useful **tips** on first aid.*
- hint, piece of advice, suggestion, clue, pointer

❹ *They took a load of rubbish to the **tip**.*
- dump, rubbish heap

tip *VERB*
❶ *The caravan **tipped** to one side.*
- lean, tilt, incline, slope, slant

When a ship tips slightly to one side, it **lists**.
When a ship tips right over, it **capsizes**.
❷ *Sophie **tipped** the box of crayons on to the table.*
- empty, turn out, dump, unload

❸ *Have you **tipped** the waiter?*
- give a tip to, reward

➤ to tip over
*He **tipped** the milk jug **over** by accident.*
- knock over, overturn, topple, upset

tiptoe *VERB*
for various ways to walk see **walk**

tire *VERB*
➤ to tire someone out
*Running in the playground had **tired** us all **out**.*
- exhaust, wear out

OPPOSITES refresh, invigorate

tired *ADJECTIVE*
*Have a lie-down if you're **tired**.*
- exhausted, fatigued, weary, worn out, listless, sleepy, drowsy

(informal) all in

➤ to be tired of something
*I'm **tired of** watching TV.*
- bored with, fed up with, sick of

If you are not interested in anything, you are **apathetic**.

tiring *ADJECTIVE*
*Digging the garden is **tiring** work.*
- exhausting, fatiguing, demanding, difficult, hard, laborious, tough

OPPOSITE refreshing

title *NOUN*

❶ *She couldn't think of a* ***title*** *for the story.*

• **name, heading**

The title above a newspaper story is a **headline.**

A title or brief description next to a picture is a **caption.**

❷ *The form asks you to fill in your name and* ***title.***

• **form of address, designation, rank**

The ordinary title used before a man's name is **Mr.**

The ordinary title used before a woman's name is **Miss** or **Mrs** or **Ms.**

A polite way to address someone whose name you don't know is **sir** or **madam.**

for royal titles see **royalty**

together *ADVERB*

❶ *They walked to school* ***together.***

• **side by side, hand in hand**

❷ *The choir sang the first verse* ***together.***

• **all at once, at the same time, simultaneously, in chorus, in unison**

OPPOSITES **independently, separately**

toil *VERB*

They had been ***toiling*** *all day in the fields.*

• **work hard, labour, sweat, slave**

(informal) **grind, slog**

toilet *NOUN*

Can you tell me where the ***toilet*** *is?*

• **lavatory, WC, bathroom**

(informal) **loo**

token *NOUN*

❶ *You can exchange this* ***token*** *for a free drink.*

• **voucher, coupon, ticket, counter**

❷ *They gave her a card as a* ***token*** *of their thanks.*

• **sign, symbol, mark, expression, indication, proof, reminder**

told *past tense see* **tell**

tolerant *ADJECTIVE*

Molly was very ***tolerant*** *towards other people.*

• **understanding, easy-going, open-minded, sympathetic, charitable, forgiving, lenient, indulgent, long-suffering**

OPPOSITE **intolerant**

tolerate *VERB*

❶ *He won't* ***tolerate*** *sloppy writing.*

• **accept, permit, put up with**

❷ *Cactus plants can* ***tolerate*** *extreme heat.*

• **bear, endure, stand, abide, suffer, stomach**

(informal) **stick**

tomb *NOUN*

Inside the ***tomb*** *were several ancient skeletons.*

• **burial chamber, crypt, grave, mausoleum, sepulchre, vault**

An underground passage containing several tombs is a **catacomb.**

A tomb is often marked by a **tombstone, gravestone** or **headstone.**

see also **pyramid**

tone *NOUN*

❶ *There was an angry* ***tone*** *to her voice.*

• **note, sound, quality, intonation, manner**

❷ *The room is painted in subtle* ***tones.***

• **colour, hue, shade, tint**

❸ *Eerie music created the right* ***tone*** *for the film.*

• **feeling, mood, atmosphere, spirit, effect**

took *past tense see* **take**

tool *NOUN*

There's a box of ***tools*** *in the garage.*

• **implement, utensil, device, gadget, instrument**

WORD WEB

TOOLS THAT ARE USED FOR WOODWORK:

• awl, chisel, clamp, drill, gimlet, hammer, jigsaw, plane, rasp, sander, saw, set square, T-square, vice

TOOLS THAT ARE USED IN THE HOME:

• broom, brush, ladder, mop, needle, pliers, scissors, screwdriver, tape measure, tweezers
for cooking utensils see **cook**

TOOLS THAT ARE USED FOR GARDENING OR FARMING:

• dibber or dibble, fork, hoe, lawnmower, pitchfork, rake, roller, scythe, secateurs, shears, shovel, sickle, spade, strimmer, trowel

TOOLS YOU MIGHT USE ON A BIKE OR CAR:

(trademark) Allen key, jack, lever, pump, spanner, wrench

OTHER TOOLS:

• axe, chainsaw, crowbar, file, hacksaw, hatchet, mallet, paintbrush, palette knife, penknife, pick, pickaxe, punch, sledgehammer, stapler

tooth *NOUN*

WORD WEB

TEETH IN A PERSON'S MOUTH:

• canine tooth, eye tooth, incisor, molar, wisdom tooth
A dog's or wolf's canine tooth is a **fang**.
A long tooth that sticks out of an animal's mouth is a **tusk**.

THINGS A DENTIST MIGHT FIT TO YOUR TEETH:

• braces, bridge or bridgework, crown, dentures, plate

SOME PROBLEMS PEOPLE HAVE WITH THEIR TEETH:

• cavity, decay, plaque, tartar, toothache
see also **dentist**

WRITING TIPS

You can use these words to describe teeth or jaws:
• jagged, needle-sharp, pincer-like, razor-sharp, serrated
I knew of the Hydra ... A monstrous dragon creature of the marshes, with nine great heads, each one full of razor-sharp teeth.—MEASLE AND THE DOOMPIT, Ian Ogilvy

TEETH MAY:

• bite, chew, chomp, clench, gnash, grind, munch, puncture, rip, snap, tear; chatter (with cold), flash, gleam
A fierce animal or creature might **bare its teeth** or **bare its fangs**.

top *NOUN*

❶ *They climbed to the* **top** *of the hill.*
• peak, summit, tip, crown, crest, head
OPPOSITES bottom, base
❷ *The* **top** *of the cabinet was covered with dust.*
• surface
❸ *The* **top** *of the jar was screwed on tightly.*
• lid, cap, cover, covering

top *ADJECTIVE*

❶ *Their office is on the* **top** *floor.*
• highest, topmost, uppermost, upper
OPPOSITES bottom, lowest
❷ *She got* **top** *marks in her exam.*
• most, best, highest
❸ *The skiers set off at* **top** *speed.*
• greatest, maximum
❹ *He is one of Europe's* **top** *chefs.*
• best, leading, finest, foremost, principal, superior
OPPOSITE junior

top *VERB*
❶ *Mum **topped** the cake with fudge icing.*
• **cover, decorate, garnish, crown**
❷ *The athlete is hoping to **top** her personal best.*
• **beat, better, exceed, outdo, surpass**

topic *NOUN*
*What was the **topic** of the conversation?*
• **subject, talking point, issue, matter, question**

topical *ADJECTIVE*
*The website often discusses **topical** issues.*
• **current, recent, up-to-date**

topple *VERB*
❶ *The books were piled too high and **toppled** over.*
• **fall, tumble, overbalance, collapse**
❷ *The gale **toppled** their TV aerial.*
• **knock down, overturn, upset**
❸ *The rebels plotted to **topple** the king.*
• **overthrow, bring down, remove from office**

tore *past tense see* **tear**

torment *VERB*
❶ *He was **tormented** by bad dreams.*
• **afflict, torture, plague, distress**
❷ *He told them to stop **tormenting** the other children.*
• **annoy, bother, harass, pester, tease, bully**
To torment someone continually is to **persecute** or **victimise** them.

torrent *NOUN*
*A **torrent** of water flowed down the hill.*
• **flood, gush, rush, stream, cascade**

toss *VERB*
❶ *He **tossed** a coin into the wishing well.*
• **throw, cast, hurl, fling, pitch, sling**
(informal) **chuck**
❷ *Let's **toss** a coin to see who'll go first.*
• **flip, spin**
❸ *The little boat **tossed** about in the storm.*
• **lurch, pitch, roll, heave, rock, bob**
❹ *She **tossed** and turned, unable to get to sleep.*
• **thrash about, flail, writhe, wriggle**

total *NOUN*
*You need a **total** of fifty points to win.*
• **sum, whole, entirety, amount**

total *ADJECTIVE*
❶ *The bill shows the **total** amount due.*
• **full, complete, whole, entire**
❷ *The party was a **total** disaster.*
• **complete, utter, absolute, thorough, downright, sheer**

total *VERB*
*The donations **total** almost 300 euros.*
• **add up to, amount to, come to, make**

totter *VERB*
*The child **tottered** across the floor.*
• **stagger, stumble, reel, wobble**
for various ways to walk see **walk**

touch *VERB*
❶ *Some animals don't like to be **touched**.*
• **feel, handle, stroke, fondle, caress, pat, pet**
❷ *The car just **touched** the gatepost.*
• **brush, graze, contact**
❸ *The speed of the racing car **touched** 200 miles per hour.*
• **reach, rise to**
❹ *I was **touched** by the poem that she wrote.*
• **move, affect, stir**
➤ **to touch on something**
*Your letter **touched on** the issue of payment.*
• **refer to, mention, raise**

touch *NOUN*
❶ *I felt a light **touch** on my arm.*
• **pat, stroke, tap, caress, contact**
❷ *Working with animals requires a special **touch**.*
• **sensitivity, understanding, feel, knack, manner**
❸ *There's a **touch** of frost in the air.*
• **hint, trace, suggestion**

touchy *ADJECTIVE*
*Be careful what you say—he's very **touchy**.*
• easily offended, sensitive, irritable, quick-tempered

tough *ADJECTIVE*
❶ *You'll need **tough** shoes for hiking.*
• strong, sturdy, robust, durable, stout, hard-wearing, substantial
Common similes are **as tough as nails** and **as tough as old boots.**
OPPOSITE **flimsy**
❷ *The meat was very **tough**.*
• chewy, leathery, rubbery
OPPOSITE **tender**
❸ *They played against **tough** opposition.*
• strong, stiff, powerful, resistant, determined, stubborn
OPPOSITES **weak, feeble**
❹ *The police deal with some **tough** criminals.*
• rough, violent, vicious, hardened
❺ *It was a **tough** job to clean the oven.*
• demanding, laborious, strenuous, gruelling, tiring, exhausting
OPPOSITE **easy**
❻ *The crossword puzzle was too **tough** for him.*
• difficult, hard, puzzling, baffling, knotty, thorny
OPPOSITE **easy**

tour *NOUN*
*They went on a sightseeing **tour**.*
• journey, trip, excursion, expedition, outing, drive, ride

tourist *NOUN*
*The cathedral was full of **tourists**.*
• sightseer, holidaymaker, traveller, visitor

tournament *NOUN*
*She reached the semi-final of the chess **tournament**.*
• championship, competition, contest, series

tow *VERB*
*Horses used to **tow** barges up and down the river.*
• pull, tug along, drag, haul, draw

tower *NOUN*
A small tower on a castle or other building is a **turret**.
A church tower is a **steeple**.
The pointed structure on a steeple is a **spire**.
The part of a tower with a bell is a **belfry**.
The tall tower of a mosque is a **minaret**.

tower *VERB*
➤ **to tower above something**
*The castle **towers above** the village.*
• rise above, stand above, dominate, loom over

town *NOUN*
A town with its own local council is a **borough**.
A large and important town is a **city**.
Several towns that merge into each other are a **conurbation**.
A word meaning 'to do with a town or city' is **urban**.
The people who live in a town are the **townspeople**.
see also **city**

toxic *ADJECTIVE*
*The flask contained a **toxic** gas.*
• poisonous, deadly, lethal, harmful
OPPOSITE **harmless**

toy *NOUN*

WORD WEB

SOME TOYS YOU MIGHT PLAY WITH:
• ball, balloon, bicycle, board game, boomerang, building bricks, computer or video game, doll, doll's house, frisbee, go-kart, hoop, jigsaw, kaleidoscope, kite, *(trademark)* Lego, marbles, model, playing cards, puppet, puzzle, rattle, rocking horse, *(trademark)* Rollerblades, roller skates, scooter, skateboard, skipping rope, teddy bear, top, train set, trampoline, water pistol, yo-yo
see also **game**

trace *NOUN*
❶ *The burglar left no **trace** of his presence.*
• **evidence, sign, mark, indication, hint, clue, track, trail**
A trace left by an animal might be its **footprint** or **scent** or **spoor**.
❷ *They found **traces** of blood on the carpet.*
• **tiny amount, drop, spot**

trace *VERB*
*She is trying to **trace** her distant ancestors.*
• **track down, discover, find, uncover, unearth**

track *NOUN*
❶ *A rough **track** leads past the farm.*
• **path, pathway, footpath, trail**
❷ *They followed the deer's **tracks** for miles.*
• **footprint, footmark, trail, scent**
❸ *They are laying the **track** for a new railway.*
• **line, rails**
❹ *The athletes are warming up on the **track**.*
• **racetrack, circuit, course**

track *VERB*
*Astronomers are **tracking** the path of the comet.*
• **follow, trace, pursue, chase, tail, trail, hunt, stalk**
➤ **to track someone** or **something down**
*They **tracked down** the owner of the car.*
• **find, discover, trace, hunt down, sniff out, run to ground**

tract *NOUN*
*They had to cross a **tract** of desert.*
• **area, expanse, stretch**

trade *NOUN*
❶ *The **trade** in antiques has been booming recently.*
• **business, dealing, buying and selling, commerce, market**
❷ *He is still learning his **trade** as a plumber.*
• **craft, skill, occupation, profession, business**

trade *VERB*
➤ **to trade in something**
*The company **trades in** second-hand computers.*
• **deal in, do business in, buy and sell**
for people who sell things see **shop**

tradition *NOUN*
*It's a **tradition** to sing 'Auld Lang Syne' on New Year's Eve.*
• **custom, convention, habit, routine, shion**

traditional *ADJECTIVE*
❶ *The African drummers wore **traditional** costumes.*
• **national, regional, historical**
❷ *They chose to have a **traditional** wedding.*
• **conventional, customary, established, time-honoured, habitual, typical, usual**

traffic *NOUN*
for types of traffic see **vehicle**

tragedy *NOUN*
❶ *'Romeo and Juliet' is a **tragedy**.*
OPPOSITE **comedy**
❷ *The accident at sea was a terrible **tragedy**.*
• **disaster, catastrophe, calamity, misfortune**

tragic *ADJECTIVE*
❶ *He died in a **tragic** accident.*
• **catastrophic, disastrous, calamitous, terrible, appalling, dreadful, unfortunate, unlucky**
❷ *She had a **tragic** expression on her face.*
• **sad, sorrowful, mournful, grief-stricken, pitiful, woeful, wretched, pathetic**
OPPOSITES **comic, happy**

trail *NOUN*
❶ *We walked along a **trail** through the woods.*
• **path, pathway, track, route**
❷ *The police were on the **trail** of the bank robbers.*
• **track, chase, hunt, pursuit**
The trail left in the water by a ship is its **wake**.

trail *VERB*
❶ *The detective* ***trailed*** *the suspect all day.*
• **follow, chase, tail, track, pursue, shadow, stalk, hunt**
❷ *She* ***trailed*** *her suitcase behind her.*
• **pull, tow, drag, draw, haul**
❸ *He is already* ***trailing*** *behind the front runners.*
• **fall behind, lag, straggle, dawdle**

train *NOUN*
❶ *They travelled to Johannesburg by* ***train.***
for words to do with trains see **railway**
❷ *It was a strange* ***train*** *of events.*
• **sequence, series, string, chain, succession**

train *VERB*
❶ *He* ***trains*** *the football team every Saturday.*
• **coach, instruct, teach, tutor**
❷ *They are* ***training*** *hard for the Commonwealth Games.*
• **practise, exercise, prepare yourself**
(informal) **work out**
❸ *The archer* ***trained*** *his arrow on the target.*
• **aim (at), point (at), level (at)**

trainer *NOUN*
❶ *Their* ***trainer*** *makes them work hard.*
• **coach, instructor, teacher, tutor**
❷ *These* ***trainers*** *are for indoor use.*
for types of shoe or boot see **shoe**

tramp *VERB*
They ***tramped*** *across the muddy fields.*
• **march, hike, trek, trudge, plod, stride**
for other ways to walk see **walk**

trample *VERB*
Don't ***trample*** *the flowers!*
• **crush, flatten, squash, tread on, walk over, stamp on**

trance *NOUN*
The fortune-teller was lost in a ***trance.***
• **daydream, daze, dream**
One way to be in a trance is to be **hypnotised.**
Unconsciousness caused by an illness or accident is a **coma.**

tranquil *ADJECTIVE*
❶ *They led a* ***tranquil*** *life in the country.*
• **calm, peaceful, quiet, restful, serene, sedate**
(informal) **laid-back**
OPPOSITES **eventful, busy**
❷ *The sea was* ***tranquil*** *after the storm had passed.*
• **calm, placid, still, undisturbed, unruffled**

transfer *VERB*
Some paintings have been ***transferred*** *to the new gallery.*
• **move, remove, shift, relocate, convey, hand over**

transform *VERB*
They ***transformed*** *the attic into an office.*
• **change, alter, turn, convert, adapt, modify**

translate *VERB*
She ***translates*** *Russian poetry into English.*
• **interpret, convert**
A person who translates a foreign language is an **interpreter** or **translator.**
An expert in languages is a **linguist.**

transmit *VERB*
❶ *The spy* ***transmitted*** *her messages in code.*
• **send, communicate, relay, emit**
To transmit a programme on radio or TV is to **broadcast** it.
OPPOSITE **receive**
❷ *Can the disease be* ***transmitted*** *to humans?*
• **pass on, spread, carry**

transparent *ADJECTIVE*
The box had a ***transparent*** *lid.*
• **clear**
(informal) **see-through**
Something which is not fully transparent, but allows light to shine through, is **translucent.**

transport *VERB*
The goods are ***transported*** *to Europe by sea.*
• **take, carry, convey, ship, transfer, move, bring, fetch, haul, shift**

A B C D E F G H I J K L M N O P Q R S T U V W X Y Z

transport *NOUN*

WORD WEB

TRANSPORT BY AIR:

• **aeroplane, airship, helicopter, hot-air balloon**
see also **aircraft**

TRANSPORT BY ROAD:

• **bicycle, bus, car, coach, horse, jeep, lorry, minibus, taxi, van**
see also **vehicle**

TRANSPORT BY RAIL:

• **monorail, train, tram, underground**
see also **railway**

TRANSPORT BY WATER:

• **barge, boat, canoe, ferry, punt, raft, ship, yacht**
see also **boat**
for various ways to travel see **travel**

trap *NOUN*

❶ *The animal was caught in a* ***trap****.*
• **snare, net, noose, booby trap**
❷ *The police set up a* ***trap*** *to catch the robbers.*
• **ambush**

trap *VERB*

They tried to ***trap*** *the mouse.*
• **capture, catch, snare, corner**

trash *NOUN*

❶ *He put the* ***trash*** *into the bin.*
• **rubbish, waste, garbage, junk, litter, refuse**
❷ *Don't listen to that* ***trash****!*
• **nonsense**

travel *VERB*

She prefers to ***travel*** *to work by bus.*
• **go, journey, move along, proceed, progress**

WORD WEB

VARIOUS WAYS TO TRAVEL:

• **cruise, cycle, drive, fly, go by rail, hike, hitch-hike, motor, pedal, ramble, ride, roam, row, sail, tour, trek, voyage, walk, wander**
When birds travel from one country to another they **migrate**.
When people travel to another country to live there they **emigrate**.
for methods of transport see **transport**

PEOPLE WHO TRAVEL AS A WAY OF LIFE:

• **itinerant, nomad, traveller**

OTHER PEOPLE WHO TRAVEL:

• **astronaut, commuter, cyclist, driver** or **motorist, explorer, hitch-hiker, holidaymaker, motorcyclist, passenger, pedestrian, pilot** or **aviator, rambler** or **walker, sailor, tourist**
A person who travels to a religious place is a **pilgrim**.
A person who travels illegally on a ship or plane is a **stowaway**.
A person who likes travelling round the world is a **globetrotter**.

treacherous *ADJECTIVE*

❶ *His* ***treacherous*** *plan was to ambush them as they escaped.*
• **disloyal, traitorous, deceitful, double-crossing, faithless, false, unfaithful, untrustworthy**
A treacherous person is a **traitor**.
OPPOSITE **loyal**
❷ *The roads are often* ***treacherous*** *in winter.*
• **dangerous, hazardous, perilous, unsafe, risky**
OPPOSITE **safe**

tread *VERB*

Please ***tread*** *carefully.*
• **step, walk, proceed**

➤ **to tread on**
*Don't **tread on** the wet cement!*
• **walk on, step on, stamp on, trample, crush, squash**

treasure *NOUN*
*The **treasure** was buried somewhere on the island.*
• **hoard, riches, wealth, fortune**
A hidden store of treasure is a **cache**.
for things you might find as treasure see **coin, jewel**

treasure *VERB*
*She **treasures** the photograph of her grandmother.*
• **cherish, prize, value**

treat *VERB*
❶ *The old woman had always **treated** him kindly.*
• **behave towards, deal with**
❷ *She is being **treated** for minor injuries.*
• **give treatment to**
To treat a wound is to **dress** it.
To treat an illness or wound successfully is to **cure** or **heal** it.
❸ *Let me **treat** you by buying you dinner.*
• **give you a treat, pay for**

treatment *NOUN*
❶ *The hospital is for the **treatment** of sick animals.*
• **care, nursing, healing**
❷ *He is trying a new **treatment** for back pain.*
• **remedy, therapy, medication**
Emergency treatment at the scene of an accident is **first aid**.
for kinds of medical treatment see **medicine**
❸ *The sculpture has been damaged by careless **treatment**.*
• **handling, use, care, management**

treaty *NOUN*
*The two sides signed a peace **treaty**.*
• **agreement, pact, contract**

tree *NOUN*

WORD WEB

Trees which lose their leaves in winter are **deciduous**.
Trees which have leaves all year round are **evergreen**.
Trees which grow cones are **conifers**.
A young tree is a **sapling**.
Small, low trees are **bushes** or **shrubs**.
Miniature trees grown in very small containers are **bonsai** trees.

SOME VARIETIES OF TREE:

• **alder, ash, aspen, baobab, banyan, bay, beech, birch, cedar, chestnut, cypress, elder, elm, eucalyptus, fir, flame tree, hawthorn, hazel, holly, juniper, larch, lime, maple, monkey puzzle, oak, olive, palm, pine, plane, poplar, redwood, rowan, spruce, sycamore, tamarind, willow, yew**
for names of fruit trees see **fruit**

PLACES WHERE TREES GROW:

• **forest, grove, jungle, plantation, spinney, thicket, wood, woodland**
An area covered with trees is a **wooded** area.
A small group of trees is a **copse** or **coppice**.
An area planted with fruit trees is an **orchard**.

tremble *VERB*
*The little fairy was **trembling** with cold.*
• **shake, shiver, quake, quiver, shudder**

tremendous *ADJECTIVE*
❶ *They heard a **tremendous** roar issuing from the cave.*
• **big, enormous, great, huge, immense, massive, mighty, fearful**
❷ *Winning the cup was a **tremendous** achievement.*
• **marvellous, magnificent, wonderful, superb, terrific, sensational, spectacular, stupendous, extraordinary, outstanding**

a b c d e f g h i j k l m n o p q r s t u v w x y z

tremor *NOUN*
*A **tremor** in her voice showed she was nervous.*
• **trembling, shaking, quavering, quivering, vibration, wobble**

trend *NOUN*
❶ *There is a general **trend** towards healthier eating.*
• **tendency, movement, shift, leaning**
❷ *This type of computer game is the latest **trend**.*
• **fashion, style, craze, fad, vogue**

trial *NOUN*
❶ *Scientists are conducting **trials** on a new space probe.*
• **test, experiment**
❷ *The **trial** will be heard in a crown court.*
• **case, hearing**
A military trial is a **court martial**.

triangular *ADJECTIVE*
A triangular shape is **three-cornered** or **three-sided**.

tribe *NOUN*
see **family**

trick *NOUN*
❶ *Stephie played a **trick** on her brother.*
• **joke, practical joke, prank**
Tricks which a magician performs are **conjuring tricks**.
❷ *The Trojans never guessed that the wooden horse was a **trick**.*
• **deception, pretence, fraud, cheat, hoax** *(informal)* **con**

trick *VERB*
*He **tricked** them into believing he was a police officer.*
• **deceive, dupe, fool, hoodwink, cheat, swindle** *(informal)* **con**

trickle *VERB*
*Water **trickled** from the tap.*
• **dribble, drip, leak, seep, ooze**
OPPOSITE **gush**

tricky *ADJECTIVE*
❶ *There were a couple of **tricky** questions in the exam.*
• **difficult, complicated, awkward, intricate, involved, ticklish**
OPPOSITES **straightforward, easy**
❷ *Redbeard is a **tricky** person to deal with.*
• **crafty, cunning, sly, wily**

trigger *VERB*
*The burnt toast **triggered** the smoke alarm.*
• **activate, set off, switch on, start**

trim *ADJECTIVE*
*Mr Stanley always keeps his garden **trim**.*
• **neat, orderly, tidy, well-kept, smart, spruce**
OPPOSITE **untidy**

trim *VERB*
❶ *He asked the barber to **trim** his beard.*
• **cut, clip, shorten, crop, neaten, tidy**
❷ *The cuffs of the blouse are **trimmed** with lace.*
• **edge, decorate, adorn**

trip *NOUN*
*They went on a **trip** to the seaside.*
• **journey, visit, outing, excursion, jaunt, expedition**

trip *VERB*
❶ *I nearly **tripped** on the stairs.*
• **catch your foot, stumble, fall, slip, stagger**
❷ *We heard her **tripping** along the corridor.*
• **run, skip**

triumph *NOUN*
*The team celebrated their **triumph** at the Olympic Games.*
• **victory, win, success, conquest**

triumphant *ADJECTIVE*
❶ *They cheered the **triumphant** team.*
• **winning, victorious, conquering, successful**
OPPOSITE **unsuccessful**
❷ *'I've solved the riddle!' said Nat with a **triumphant** smile.*
• **elated, exultant, joyful, gleeful, jubilant**

trivial *ADJECTIVE*
*Don't bother me with **trivial** details.*
• **unimportant, minor, insignificant, trifling, negligible, petty, silly, slight, frivolous**
OPPOSITE **important**

troop *NOUN*
*A **troop** of horse riders crossed the river.*
• **group, band, party, body, company**

troop *VERB*
*The children **trooped** along the road.*
• **march, parade, walk, proceed**
To walk one behind the other is to file along.

troops *PLURAL NOUN*
see **armed forces**

trophy *NOUN*
*My friend, Marnie, won a **trophy** for gymnastics.*
• **award, prize, cup, medal**

trouble *NOUN*
❶ *The family has had a lot of **trouble** recently.*
• **difficulty, hardship, suffering, unhappiness, distress, misfortune, pain, sadness, sorrow, worry**
❷ *The police dealt with **trouble** in the crowd.*
• **disorder, unrest, disturbance, commotion, fighting, violence**
❸ *The **trouble** with this computer is that it's very slow.*
• **problem, difficulty, disadvantage, drawback**
➤ **to take trouble**
*He **took trouble** to remember all our names.*
• **bother, make an effort, take pains**

trouble *VERB*
❶ *What's **troubling** you?*
• **distress, upset, bother, worry, concern, pain, torment, vex**
❷ *I don't want to **trouble** her if she's busy.*
• **disturb, interrupt, bother, pester**
❸ *Nobody **troubled** to tidy up the room.*
• **bother, make an effort, take trouble**

troublesome *ADJECTIVE*
❶ *Do you find the heat **troublesome**?*
• **annoying, irritating, trying, tiresome, bothersome, distressing, inconvenient, upsetting**
❷ *There are two **troublesome** teenagers in the family.*
• **badly behaved, disorderly, rowdy, unruly, disobedient**

trousers *PLURAL NOUN*
for items of clothing see **clothes**

truce *NOUN*
*The two sides agreed on a **truce**.*
• **ceasefire, armistice, peace**

true *ADJECTIVE*
❶ *Do you think the newspaper report is **true**?*
• **accurate, correct, right, factual, authentic, undeniable**
OPPOSITES **untrue, false**
❷ *This is a **true** copy of my birth certificate.*
• **genuine, real, actual, faithful, exact**
OPPOSITE **false**
❸ *Esther has always been a **true** friend.*
• **faithful, loyal, constant, devoted, sincere, steady, trustworthy, dependable, reliable**
OPPOSITE **unreliable**

trunk *NOUN*
❶ *The **trunk** of a palm tree can bend in the wind.*
• **stem, stock**
❷ *Push up from the ground, keeping your **trunk** straight.*
• **torso, body, frame**
❸ *The magician kept his things in a huge travelling **trunk**.*
• **chest, case, box, crate, suitcase, coffer**

trust *VERB*
❶ *I **trusted** her to keep my identity a secret.*
• **rely on, depend on, count on, bank on, believe in, be sure of, have confidence in, have faith in**
❷ *I **trust** you are well.*
• **hope**

a b c d e f g h i j k l m n o p q r s t u v w x y z

A B C D E F G H I J K L M N O P Q R S T U V W X Y Z

trust *NOUN*
❶ *The director has **trust** in her acting ability.*
• belief, confidence, faith
❷ *They put their lives in the **trust** of the pilot.*
• responsibility, safekeeping, hands

trustworthy *ADJECTIVE*
*Sir Boldwood was a **trustworthy** ally of the king.*
• reliable, dependable, loyal, trusty, true, honourable, responsible
OPPOSITE untrustworthy

truth *NOUN*
❶ *The detective doubted the **truth** of her story.*
• accuracy, authenticity, correctness, genuineness, reliability, truthfulness, validity
OPPOSITE inaccuracy, falseness
❷ *Are you sure you're telling the **truth**?*
• facts
OPPOSITE lies

truthful *ADJECTIVE*
❶ *She is normally a **truthful** person.*
• honest, frank, sincere, straight, straightforward, reliable, trustworthy
❷ *He gave a **truthful** answer.*
• accurate, correct, proper, right, true, valid
OPPOSITE dishonest

try *VERB*
❶ *I'm going to **try** to beat my dad at chess.*
• aim, attempt, endeavour, make an effort, strive, struggle
❷ *Would you like to **try** a larger size?*
• test, try out, evaluate, experiment with

try *NOUN*
❶ *We may not succeed, but it's worth a **try**!*
• attempt, effort, go, shot
❷ *Would you like a **try** of my mango smoothie?*
• trial, test, taste

trying *ADJECTIVE*
*The way he keeps asking questions is very **trying**.*
• tiresome, irritating, annoying, wearing, wearisome

tub *NOUN*
*We shared a large **tub** of popcorn between us.*
• pot, drum, barrel, cask, vat

tube *NOUN*
*Roll the paper into a **tube**.*
• cylinder, pipe
A flexible tube is a **hose**.
A tube which liquid pours out of is a **spout**.

tuck *VERB*
*He **tucked** his t-shirt into his jeans.*
• push, insert, stuff

tuft *NOUN*
*The goat stood munching on a **tuft** of grass.*
• clump, bunch

tug *VERB*
❶ *It annoys me when my brother **tugs** my hair.*
• pull, yank, jerk, pluck, wrench
❷ *We **tugged** the sledge up the hill.*
• drag, pull, tow, haul, lug, draw, heave

tumble *VERB*
*The boy slipped and **tumbled** into the water.*
• topple, drop, fall, pitch, flop, stumble, plummet

tumult *NOUN*
*He had to shout to be heard above the **tumult**.*
• noise, uproar, commotion, clamour, din, racket, rumpus, hubbub, cacophony

tune *NOUN*
*Can you play the **tune** to 'Happy Birthday'?*
• melody, song, air, theme

tunnel *NOUN*
A tunnel dug by rabbits is a **burrow**.
A system of burrows is a **warren**.
A tunnel in a mine is a **gallery**.
A tunnel beneath a road is a **subway** or **underpass**.

tunnel *VERB*
*Badgers use their strong front paws to **tunnel** for food.*
• **burrow, dig, excavate**

turmoil *NOUN*
*The whole country was in **turmoil**.*
• **chaos, upheaval, uproar, disorder, unrest, commotion, disturbance, pandemonium**
OPPOSITES **calm, peace**

turn *VERB*
❶ *A wheel **turns** on its axle.*
• **go round, revolve, rotate, roll, spin, swivel, pivot, twirl, whirl**
❷ *The van **turned** into a side street.*
• **change direction, corner**
To turn unexpectedly is to **swerve** or **veer off** course.
If you turn to go back in the direction you came from, you **do a U-turn**.
If marching soldiers change direction, they **wheel**.
❸ *He **turned** a curious shade of green.*
• **become, go, grow**
❹ *They **turned** the attic into a spare bedroom.*
• **convert, adapt, change, alter, modify, transform, develop**
➤ **to turn something down**
*She **turned down** the offer of a part in the play.*
• **decline, refuse, reject**
➤ **to turn something on** or **off**
*He **turned on** the radio.*
• **switch on or off**
➤ **to turn out**
*Everything **turned out** well in the end.*
• **end up, come out, happen, result**
➤ **to turn over**
*The boat **turned over**.*
• **capsize, overturn, turn upside down, flip over, keel over**
➤ **to turn up**
*A friend **turned up** unexpectedly.*
• **arrive, appear, drop in**

turn *NOUN*
❶ *She gave the handle a **turn**.*
• **twist, spin, whirl, twirl**
A single turn of a wheel is a **revolution**.
The process of turning is **rotation**.
❷ *The house is just past the next **turn** in the road.*
• **bend, corner, curve, angle, junction**
A sharp turn in a country road is a **hairpin bend**.
❸ *It's your **turn** to do the washing up.*
• **chance, opportunity, occasion, time, slot, go**
❹ *Everyone had to do a **turn** in the show.*
• **act, performance, scene, sketch**
❺ *(informal) Seeing the skeleton gave her quite a **turn**.*
• **fright, scare, shock, start, surprise**

turret *NOUN*
see **tower**

twig *NOUN*
*They gathered **twigs** to make a fire.*
• **stick, branch, stalk, stem, shoot**

twin *NOUN*
*This vase is a **twin** of the one in the museum.*
• **double, duplicate, lookalike, match, clone**

twinkle *VERB*
*The stars **twinkled** in the sky.*
• **sparkle, shine, glitter, glisten, glimmer, glint**

twirl *VERB*
❶ *The dancers **twirled** faster and faster.*
• **spin, turn, whirl, revolve, rotate, pirouette**
❷ *He paced up and down, **twirling** his umbrella.*
• **twiddle, twist**

twist *VERB*
❶ *She **twisted** a bandage round her wrist.*
• **wind, loop, coil, curl, entwine**
❷ *Twist the handle to open the door.*
• **turn, rotate, revolve, swivel**

A B C D E F G H I J K L M N O P Q R S T U V W X Y Z

❸ *The road **twists** through the hills.*
• wind, weave, curve, zigzag
❹ *He **twisted** and turned in his sleep.*
• toss, writhe, wriggle
❺ *I tried to **twist** the cap off the bottle.*
• unscrew
❻ *Heat can **twist** metal out of shape.*
• bend, buckle, warp, crumple, distort

twisted *ADJECTIVE*
*The trunk of the olive tree was **twisted** with age.*
• warped, gnarled, buckled, misshapen, deformed

twitch *VERB*
*The dog **twitched** in his sleep.*
• jerk, jump, start, tremble

two *NOUN*
Two musicians playing or singing together are a **duet** or a **duo**.
Two people or things which belong together are a **couple** or a **pair**.
To multiply a number by two is to **double** it.

type *NOUN*
❶ *What **type** of films do you like to watch?*
• kind, sort, variety, category, class, genre
❷ *The book was printed in large **type**.*
• print, lettering, letters, characters

typical *ADJECTIVE*
❶ *The weather is **typical** for this time of year.*
• normal, usual, standard, ordinary, average, predictable, unsurprising
OPPOSITE unusual
❷ *The pointed arch is **typical** of Gothic architecture.*
• characteristic, representative
OPPOSITE uncharacteristic

Uu

ugly *ADJECTIVE*
❶ *The princess had to kiss a fat, **ugly** toad.*
• grotesque, hideous, unattractive, repulsive, revolting, monstrous
OPPOSITE beautiful
❷ *The room was filled with **ugly** furniture.*
• unattractive, unsightly, displeasing, tasteless, horrid, nasty
OPPOSITE beautiful
❸ *The crowd was in an **ugly** mood.*
• unfriendly, hostile, menacing, threatening, angry, dangerous
OPPOSITE friendly

ultimate *ADJECTIVE*
*Her **ultimate** goal is to be a writer.*
• eventual, final
OPPOSITE initial

umpire *NOUN*
see **referee**

un- *PREFIX*

WRITING TIPS

There are so many words which begin with **un-** that there is not enough space to include them all below, but you can still find synonyms for them using your thesaurus. First, take away the prefix **un-** to find the positive word (e.g. **able** from **unable**), then add **un-** or **not** to the synonyms listed in that entry to make their opposites (for example, **not allowed** or **unwilling**).

unanimous *ADJECTIVE*
*It was a **unanimous** decision.*
• collective, joint, united
A decision where most, but not all, people agree is a **majority** decision.

unattractive *ADJECTIVE*
see **ugly**

unavoidable *ADJECTIVE*
The accident was ***unavoidable****.*
• **inevitable, bound to happen, certain, destined**

unaware *ADJECTIVE*
➤ **unaware of**
They were ***unaware of*** *the dangers that lay ahead.*
• **ignorant of, oblivious to, unconscious of**

unbearable *ADJECTIVE*
The stench in the cave was ***unbearable****.*
• **unendurable, intolerable, impossible to bear**

unbelievable *ADJECTIVE*
❶ *The account of the UFO sighting was* ***unbelievable****.*
• **unconvincing, unlikely, far-fetched, improbable, incredible**
❷ *She scored an* ***unbelievable*** *goal.*
• **amazing, astonishing, extraordinary, remarkable, sensational, phenomenal**

uncertain *ADJECTIVE*
❶ *I was* ***uncertain*** *what to do next.*
• **unsure, doubtful, in two minds, unclear**
❷ *They are facing an* ***uncertain*** *future.*
• **indefinite, unknown, undecided, unpredictable**

unclean *ADJECTIVE*
see **dirty**

unclear *ADJECTIVE*
see **uncertain**

uncomfortable *ADJECTIVE*
❶ *She complained that her shoes were* ***uncomfortable****.*
• **restrictive, cramped, hard, stiff, tight, tight-fitting**
❷ *He spent an* ***uncomfortable*** *night sleeping on the floor.*
• **restless, troubled, disagreeable, uneasy**
OPPOSITE **comfortable**

uncommon *ADJECTIVE*
see **unusual**

unconscious *ADJECTIVE*
❶ *The patient had been* ***unconscious*** *for two days.*
If you are unconscious because of a hit on the head, you are **knocked out.**
If you are unconscious for an operation, you are **anaesthetised.**
If you are unconscious because of an accident or illness, you are **in a coma.**
❷ *She's* ***unconscious*** *of the effect she has on other people.*
• **ignorant, unaware**
❸ *They laughed at her* ***unconscious*** *slip of the tongue.*
• **accidental, unintended, unintentional**
OPPOSITE **conscious**
➤ **unconscious of**
He's ***unconscious of*** *all the trouble he's caused.*
• **unaware of, ignorant of, oblivious to**

uncover *VERB*
❶ *Archaeologists have* ***uncovered*** *two more skeletons.*
• **dig up, unearth, expose, reveal, show, disclose**
To uncover your body is to **strip** or **undress.**
❷ *He* ***uncovered*** *the truth about his family's past.*
• **detect, discover, come across**
OPPOSITES **cover up, hide**

undergo *VERB*
Wizards have to ***undergo*** *rigorous training.*
• **go through, be subjected to, experience, put up with, endure**

undermine *VERB*
Losing the race could ***undermine*** *her confidence.*
• **weaken, lessen, reduce, destroy, ruin**
OPPOSITES **support, boost**

A B C D E F G H I J K L M N O P Q R S T U V W X Y Z

understand *VERB* **understands, understanding, understood**

❶ *I don't* ***understand*** *what you mean.*
• **comprehend, grasp, follow, see, take in, realise, appreciate, recognise, work out, fathom**
❷ *Can you* ***understand*** *this writing?*
• **read, interpret, make out, make sense of**
To understand something in code is to **decode** or **decipher** it.
❸ *I* ***understand*** *they're moving to Sydney.*
• **believe, hear**

understanding *NOUN*

❶ *The robot has limited powers of* ***understanding.***
• **intelligence, intellect, sense, judgement**
❷ *The book will increase your* ***understanding*** *of science.*
• **appreciation, awareness, knowledge, comprehension, grasp**
❸ *The two sides reached an* ***understanding.***
• **agreement, deal, settlement, arrangement, accord**
❹ *She treats her patients with* ***understanding.***
• **sympathy, compassion, consideration**

understanding *ADJECTIVE*

Martha is an ***understanding*** *person.*
• **sympathetic, caring, friendly, kind, helpful, open-minded, tolerant**

undertake *VERB*

❶ *She was asked to* ***undertake*** *a secret mission.*
• **take on, accept, tackle, handle**
❷ *He* ***undertook*** *to pay all the costs.*
• **agree, consent, promise, guarantee, commit yourself**

underwear *NOUN*

• **underclothes, underclothing, undergarments**
(informal) **undies**
Women's underclothes are **lingerie.**
for items of underwear see **clothes**

undo *VERB* **undoes, undoing, undid, undone**

❶ *I'll have to* ***undo*** *this row of knitting.*
• **unfasten, untie, unravel, loosen, release**
To undo stitching is to **unpick** it.
❷ *Sue* ***undid*** *the wrapping on the parcel.*
• **open, unwrap, unfold, unwind, unroll, unfurl**
❸ *The good witch tried to* ***undo*** *the spell.*
• **reverse, cancel out, wipe out**

undoubtedly *ADVERB*

She is ***undoubtedly*** *our best player.*
• **definitely, certainly, surely, doubtless, of course**

undress *VERB*

He ***undressed*** *quickly and got into bed.*
• **get undressed, take off your clothes, strip**
OPPOSITE **dress**

unearth *VERB*

❶ *The dog* ***unearthed*** *an old bone.*
• **dig up, uncover**
❷ *She* ***unearthed*** *some old diaries in the attic.*
• **find, discover, come across, stumble upon, track down**

uneasy *ADJECTIVE*

❶ *I had an* ***uneasy*** *feeling that something was wrong.*
• **anxious, nervous, apprehensive, tense, troubling, upsetting, worrying**
OPPOSITE **confident**
❷ *Our guest passed an* ***uneasy*** *night.*
• **restless, unsettled, uncomfortable, disturbed**
OPPOSITE **comfortable**

unemployed *ADJECTIVE*

Since the factory closed, he has been ***unemployed.***
• **out of work, jobless**
(informal) **on the dole**
To be unemployed because there is not enough work to do is to be **redundant.**
OPPOSITES **employed, working**

uneven *ADJECTIVE*
❶ *The ground was very **uneven** in places.*
• **rough, bumpy, rutted**
OPPOSITE **smooth**
❷ *Their performance has been **uneven** this season.*
• **erratic, inconsistent, irregular, variable, unpredictable**
OPPOSITE **consistent**
❸ *It was a very **uneven** contest.*
• **one-sided, unbalanced, unequal, unfair**
OPPOSITE **balanced**

unexpected *ADJECTIVE*
*Her reaction was totally **unexpected**.*
• **surprising, unforeseen, unpredictable, unplanned**
OPPOSITE **expected**

unfair *ADJECTIVE*
❶ *Do you think that the umpire's decision was **unfair**?*
• **unjust, unreasonable, wrong, one-sided, unbalanced, impartial, biased**
OPPOSITES **fair, just**
❷ *I felt that her criticism of my work was **unfair**.*
• **undeserved, unmerited, uncalled for, unjustified**
OPPOSITES **fair, deserved**

unfaithful *ADJECTIVE*
see **disloyal**

unfamiliar *ADJECTIVE*
*The astronauts looked on an **unfamiliar** landscape.*
• **strange, unusual, curious, novel, alien**
➤ **unfamiliar with**
*They were **unfamiliar with** the local customs.*
• **unaccustomed to, unused to, unaware of**

unfit *ADJECTIVE*
❶ *She used to be **unfit** before she took up swimming.*
• **out of condition, unhealthy**
OPPOSITE **fit**
❷ *He is **unfit** to be left in charge of the house.*
• **unsatisfactory, unsuitable, incompetent, inadequate**

unfortunate *ADJECTIVE*
❶ *The **unfortunate** couple had lost all their possessions.*
• **unlucky, poor, unhappy, hapless, wretched, ill-fated**
❷ *The goalkeeper made one **unfortunate** error.*
• **disastrous, calamitous, unwelcome**
OPPOSITES **fortunate, lucky**
❸ *He made an **unfortunate** remark about her cooking.*
• **regrettable, inappropriate, tactless, unsuitable, untimely**

unfriendly *ADJECTIVE*
*The housekeeper greeted us with an **unfriendly** glare.*
• **unwelcoming, inhospitable, unsympathetic, unkind, impolite, uncivil, unhelpful, hostile, cold, cool, distant, stand-offish, aloof, unsociable, unneighbourly**
OPPOSITES **friendly, amiable**

ungrateful *ADJECTIVE*
*Don't be so **ungrateful**.*
• **unappreciative, unthankful**
OPPOSITE **grateful**

unhappy *ADJECTIVE*
❶ *You look **unhappy**—what's the matter?*
• **sad, miserable, depressed, downhearted, despondent, gloomy, glum, downcast, dejected, forlorn, woeful, crestfallen**
(informal) **down in the dumps, down in the mouth**
OPPOSITES **happy, cheerful**
❷ *I'm still **unhappy** with my score.*
• **dissatisfied, disappointed, displeased, discontented**
OPPOSITES **satisfied, pleased**

A B C D E F G H I J K L M N O P Q R S T U V W X Y Z

unhealthy *ADJECTIVE*
❶ *One of the calves has been* ***unhealthy*** *since birth.*
• **unwell, ill, sick, diseased, infirm, sickly, poorly, weak, delicate, feeble, frail**
OPPOSITES **healthy, strong**
❷ *He eats an* ***unhealthy*** *diet of junk food.*
• **unwholesome, unnatural, harmful, unhygienic**
OPPOSITES **healthy, wholesome**

unhelpful *ADJECTIVE*
The shop assistant was most ***unhelpful****.*
• **uncooperative, unfriendly, inconsiderate, reluctant to help**
OPPOSITE **helpful**

unidentified *ADJECTIVE*
An ***unidentified*** *aircraft was spotted at night.*
• **unknown, unrecognised, unspecified, unnamed, anonymous, nameless**
OPPOSITE **named**

uniform *NOUN*
The guards at the Tower of London wear fancy ***uniforms****.*
• **costume, outfit, regalia, livery**

uniform *ADJECTIVE*
The greenhouse is kept at a ***uniform*** *temperature.*
• **consistent, regular, even, unvarying, identical, similar, the same**
OPPOSITES **different, varying**

unify *VERB*
The new president tried to ***unify*** *the country.*
• **unite, bring together, harmonise, combine, integrate, join, merge, amalgamate**
OPPOSITE **separate**

unimportant *ADJECTIVE*
Don't worry about ***unimportant*** *details.*
• **insignificant, minor, trivial, trifling, irrelevant, secondary, slight, small, negligible, worthless, petty**
OPPOSITE **important**

uninhabited *ADJECTIVE*
The island had been ***uninhabited*** *for centuries.*
• **unoccupied, empty, deserted, abandoned**
OPPOSITES **inhabited, populated**

uninteresting *ADJECTIVE*
see **boring**

union *NOUN*
The city was formed by the ***union*** *of two neighbouring towns.*
• **uniting, joining, integration, combination, merger, amalgamation, fusion**
A union of two rivers is a **confluence.**
A union of two countries is their **unification.**
A union of two people is a **marriage** or **partnership.**

unique *ADJECTIVE*
Each person's fingerprints are ***unique****.*
• **distinctive, different, individual, special, peculiar**
(informal) **one-off**

unit *NOUN*
The bookcase is built up from separate ***units****.*
• **piece, part, bit, section, segment, element, component, module**
for units of measurement see **measurement**

unite *VERB*
❶ *King Bluetooth* ***united*** *the kingdoms of Denmark and Norway.*
• **combine, join, merge, link, integrate, unify, amalgamate, bring together**
OPPOSITE **separate**
❷ *People of all ages* ***united*** *to celebrate Chinese New Year.*
• **collaborate, cooperate, join forces**
OPPOSITE **compete**
To unite to do something bad is to **conspire.**

universal *ADJECTIVE*
Scientists have made a discovery of ***universal*** *importance.*
• **general, widespread, global, worldwide**

unjust *ADJECTIVE*
see **unfair**

unkind *ADJECTIVE*
*It was a thoughtless and **unkind** remark.*
• callous, hard-hearted, cruel, thoughtless, heartless, uncaring, unfeeling, inconsiderate, unsympathetic, unfriendly, uncharitable, harsh, mean, nasty, selfish, spiteful, vicious, malicious
OPPOSITE kind

unknown *ADJECTIVE*
❶ *The letter was in an **unknown** hand.*
• unidentified, unrecognised
OPPOSITE known
❷ *The author of the story is **unknown**.*
• anonymous, nameless, unnamed, unspecified
OPPOSITE named
❸ *The explorers entered **unknown** territory.*
• unfamiliar, alien, foreign, undiscovered, unexplored, uncharted
OPPOSITE familiar
❹ *The part was played by an **unknown** actor.*
• little known, unheard of, obscure
OPPOSITE famous

unlike *ADJECTIVE*
*The food was **unlike** anything I had tasted before.*
• different from, distinct from
OPPOSITE similar (to)

unlikely *ADJECTIVE*
*No-one believed her **unlikely** excuse.*
• unbelievable, unconvincing, improbable, implausible, incredible, far-fetched
OPPOSITE likely

unlucky *ADJECTIVE*
❶ *Some people think that 13 is an **unlucky** number.*
• unfavourable, ill-omened, ill-starred, jinxed
❷ *By an **unlucky** chance, their plan was discovered.*
• unfortunate, unwelcome, untimely
OPPOSITE lucky

unmarried *ADJECTIVE*
If you are unmarried, you are **single**.
If your marriage has been legally ended, you are **divorced**.
An unmarried man is a **bachelor**.
An unmarried woman is a **spinster**.

unmistakable *ADJECTIVE*
*There was an **unmistakable** smell of burnt toast.*
• distinct, distinctive, clear, obvious, plain, telltale

unnatural *ADJECTIVE*
❶ *It's **unnatural** for it to snow in April.*
• unusual, abnormal, odd, strange, weird, bizarre
❷ *Some of the acting in the film was a bit **unnatural**.*
• stiff, stilted, unrealistic, forced, self-conscious
❸ *Her hair was an **unnatural** orange colour.*
• artificial, synthetic, man-made, manufactured
OPPOSITE natural

unnecessary *ADJECTIVE*
*I'm deleting any **unnecessary** files from my computer.*
• inessential, non-essential, uncalled for, unwanted, excessive, superfluous, surplus, extra, redundant
OPPOSITE necessary

unoccupied *ADJECTIVE*
❶ *Since the fire, the flats have been **unoccupied**.*
• empty, uninhabited, deserted, unused, vacant
OPPOSITE occupied
❷ *The bathroom is **unoccupied**.*
• available, vacant
OPPOSITE engaged

unpleasant *ADJECTIVE*
❶ *Mr Smallweed was a thoroughly **unpleasant** man.*
• **disagreeable, unfriendly, unkind, bad-tempered, nasty, malicious, spiteful, hateful**
❷ *Being lost in the jungle had been an **unpleasant** experience.*
• **uncomfortable, disagreeable, awful**
❸ *The smell from the drain was very **unpleasant**.*
• **disgusting, foul, repulsive, revolting, horrible, horrid, repellent, offensive, objectionable**
see *also* **bad**
OPPOSITE **pleasant**

unpopular *ADJECTIVE*
*The new manager was **unpopular** at first.*
• **disliked, hated, despised, unloved**
OPPOSITE **popular**

unreal *ADJECTIVE*
*Everything seemed **unreal**, as if in a dream.*
• **imaginary, made-up, fictitious, false, pretend**
OPPOSITE **real**

unsafe *ADJECTIVE*
see **dangerous**

unsatisfactory *ADJECTIVE*
*The repairs to the roof were **unsatisfactory**.*
• **unacceptable, inadequate, disappointing, displeasing, poor, incompetent, insufficient**
OPPOSITE **satisfactory**

unseen *ADJECTIVE*
see **invisible**

unsteady *ADJECTIVE*
*The table was a bit **unsteady**.*
• **unstable, shaky, wobbly, insecure, unbalanced, rickety**
OPPOSITES **stable, steady**

unsure *ADJECTIVE*
see **uncertain**

untidy *ADJECTIVE*
❶ *Our house is the one with the **untidy** garden.*
• **messy, disorderly, cluttered, jumbled, tangled, littered, chaotic**
(informal) **higgledy-piggledy, topsy-turvy**
❷ *His work was **untidy** and full of mistakes.*
• **careless, disorganised, slapdash**
(informal) **sloppy**
❸ *She arrived looking **untidy** and flustered.*
• **dishevelled, bedraggled, rumpled, unkempt, scruffy, slovenly**

untrue *ADJECTIVE*
see **false**

unusual *ADJECTIVE*
❶ *The weather was **unusual** for the time of year.*
• **abnormal, out of the ordinary, exceptional, remarkable, extraordinary, odd, peculiar, singular, strange, unexpected, irregular, unconventional, unheard of**
OPPOSITE **ordinary**
❷ *Ebenezer is an **unusual** name.*
• **uncommon, rare, unfamiliar**
OPPOSITE **common**

unwell *ADJECTIVE*
see **ill**

unwilling *ADJECTIVE*
see **reluctant**

unwise *ADJECTIVE*
see **foolish**

upheaval *NOUN*
*Moving to a new house causes such an **upheaval**.*
• **disruption, disturbance, upset, commotion, fuss**

uphill *ADJECTIVE*
❶ *The last part of the road is* ***uphill****.*
• upward, ascending, rising
❷ *Finding a job proved to be an* ***uphill*** *struggle.*
• hard, difficult, tough, strenuous, laborious, arduous, exhausting, gruelling, taxing

upkeep *NOUN*
The ***upkeep*** *of a car can be expensive.*
• care, maintenance, running

upper *ADJECTIVE*
My bedroom is on the ***upper*** *floor.*
• higher, upstairs
OPPOSITE lower

upright *ADJECTIVE*
❶ *The car seat should be in an* ***upright*** *position.*
• erect, perpendicular, vertical
OPPOSITE horizontal
❷ *He is an* ***upright*** *member of the local community.*
• honest, honourable, respectable, reputable, moral, virtuous, upstanding, principled, trustworthy
OPPOSITE corrupt

uproar *NOUN*
The meeting ended in ***uproar****.*
• chaos, confusion, disorder, commotion, turmoil, pandemonium, mayhem, rumpus, furore

upset *VERB*
❶ *Something in the letter had* ***upset*** *her.*
• distress, trouble, disturb, displease, unsettle, offend, dismay, grieve, fluster, perturb
❷ *Bad weather* ***upset*** *the train timetable.*
• disrupt, interfere with, interrupt, affect, throw out
❸ *The baby* ***upset*** *a whole bowl of cereal.*
• knock over, spill, tip over, topple
❹ *A fallen tree branch* ***upset*** *the canoe.*
• overturn, capsize

upset *NOUN*
❶ *He is off school with a stomach* ***upset****.*
• illness, ailment
(informal) bug
❷ *They caused a major* ***upset*** *by winning 7–0.*
• shock, surprise, upheaval

upside down *ADJECTIVE*
❶ *I can't read the writing if it's* ***upside down****.*
• wrong way up, inverted
(informal) topsy-turvy
❷ *(informal) Everything in her life seemed to be* ***upside down****.*
• in a mess, chaotic, disorderly, jumbled
(informal) higgledy-piggledy
OPPOSITE orderly

up-to-date *ADJECTIVE*
❶ *The spacecraft uses* ***up-to-date*** *technology.*
• new, modern, present-day, recent, current, the latest, advanced, cutting-edge
OPPOSITE out of date
❷ *Her clothes are always* ***up to date****.*
• fashionable, stylish, contemporary
(informal) trendy, hip
OPPOSITE old-fashioned

upward *ADJECTIVE*
He started on the steep, ***upward*** *climb.*
• uphill, ascending, rising
OPPOSITE downward

urban *ADJECTIVE*
Most of the population live in ***urban*** *areas.*
• built-up, densely populated
OPPOSITE rural

urge *VERB*
He ***urged*** *her to reconsider her decision.*
• advise, counsel, appeal to, beg, implore, plead with, press
To urge someone to do something is to **advocate** or **recommend** it.
➤ **to urge someone on**
The fans tried to ***urge on*** *their team.*
• encourage, spur on, egg on discourage

urge *NOUN*
*I had a sudden **urge** to burst into song.*
• **impulse, compulsion, longing, wish, yearning, desire, itch**
(informal) **yen**

urgent *ADJECTIVE*
❶ *She had **urgent** business in New York.*
• **pressing, immediate, essential, important, top-priority**
OPPOSITE **unimportant**
❷ *He spoke in an **urgent** whisper.*
• **anxious, insistent, earnest**

usable *ADJECTIVE*
❶ *The lift is not **usable** today.*
• **operating, working, functioning, functional**
OPPOSITE **unusable**
❷ *This ticket is **usable** only on certain trains.*
• **valid, acceptable**
OPPOSITE **invalid**

use *VERB*
❶ *She **used** a calculator to add up the figures.*
• **make use of, employ, utilise**
To use your knowledge is to **apply** it.
To use your muscles is to **exercise** them.
To use a musical instrument is to **play** it.
To use an axe or sword is to **wield** it.
To use people or things selfishly is to **exploit** them.
❷ *Can you show me how to **use** the photocopier?*
• **operate, work, handle, manage**
❸ *You've **used** all the hot water.*
• **use up, go through, consume, exhaust, spend**

use *NOUN*
❶ *Would these books be any **use** to you?*
• **help, benefit, advantage, profit, value**
❷ *A sonic screwdriver has many **uses**.*
• **function, purpose, point**

useful *ADJECTIVE*
❶ *A flask is **useful** for keeping food warm.*
• **convenient, handy, effective, efficient, practical**
❷ *The website offers some **useful** advice.*
• **good, helpful, valuable, worthwhile, constructive, invaluable**
OPPOSITE **useless**

useless *ADJECTIVE*
❶ *This old vacuum cleaner is **useless**.*
• **ineffective, inefficient, impractical, unusable**
OPPOSITES **useful, effective**
❷ *Her advice was completely **useless**.*
• **worthless, unhelpful, pointless, futile, unprofitable, fruitless**
OPPOSITE **useful**
❸ *(informal) I'm **useless** at drawing.*
• **bad, poor, incompetent**
(informal) **rubbish, hopeless**
OPPOSITE **good**

user-friendly *ADJECTIVE*
*The computer manual isn't very **user-friendly**.*
• **easy to use, straightforward, uncomplicated, understandable**

usual *ADJECTIVE*
❶ *I'll meet you at the **usual** time.*
• **normal, customary, familiar, habitual, regular, standard**
❷ *It's **usual** to knock before entering.*
• **common, accepted, conventional, traditional**
OPPOSITE **unusual**

utensil *NOUN*
*A row of cooking **utensils** hung on the wall.*
• **tool, implement, device, gadget, instrument, appliance**
for various tools see **tool**

utter *VERB*
*The robot could only **utter** a few phrases.*
• **say, speak, express, pronounce, put into words**

utter *ADJECTIVE*
*They stared at the unicorn in **utter** amazement.*
• **complete, total, absolute, sheer, downright, out and out**

vacancy *NOUN*
They have a ***vacancy*** *for a trainee journalist.*
• **job, opening, post, position, situation**

vacant *ADJECTIVE*
❶ *The house over the road is still* ***vacant****.*
• **unoccupied, uninhabited, deserted, empty**
OPPOSITE **occupied**
❷ *The receptionist gave me a* ***vacant*** *stare.*
• **blank, expressionless, mindless, absent-minded, deadpan**
OPPOSITE **alert**

vague *ADJECTIVE*
❶ *The directions she gave me were rather* ***vague****.*
• **indefinite, imprecise, broad, general, ill-defined, unclear, woolly**
OPPOSITES **exact, detailed**
❷ *A* ***vague*** *shape could be seen through the mist.*
• **blurred, indistinct, obscure, dim, hazy, shadowy**
OPPOSITE **definite**

vain *ADJECTIVE*
❶ *The duchess was* ***vain*** *about her appearance.*
• **arrogant, proud, conceited, haughty, self-satisfied**
OPPOSITE **modest**
❷ *He made a* ***vain*** *attempt to tidy the room.*
• **unsuccessful, ineffective, useless, worthless, fruitless, futile, pointless**
OPPOSITE **successful**

valid *ADJECTIVE*
❶ *The ticket is* ***valid*** *for three months.*
• **current, legal, approved, authorised, official, permitted, suitable, usable**
❷ *She made several* ***valid*** *points.*
• **acceptable, reasonable, sound, convincing, genuine, legitimate**
OPPOSITE **invalid**

valley *NOUN*
A rocky path meandered through the ***valley****.*
• **vale, dale, dell, gorge, gully, hollow, pass, ravine, canyon**
(Scottish) **glen**

valuable *ADJECTIVE*
❶ *Apparently the painting is very* ***valuable****.*
• **expensive, costly, dear, precious, priceless**
❷ *He gave her some* ***valuable*** *advice.*
• **useful, helpful, constructive, good, worthwhile, invaluable**
OPPOSITE **worthless**
WHICH WORD? Note that **invaluable** is not the opposite of **valuable**. A piece of invaluable advice is very good, but a piece of bad advice is worthless.

value *NOUN*
❶ *The house has recently increased in* ***value****.*
• **price, cost, worth**
❷ *He stressed the* ***value*** *of taking regular exercise.*
• **advantage, benefit, merit, use, usefulness, importance**

value *VERB*
❶ *He had always* ***valued*** *her advice.*
• **appreciate, respect, esteem, have a high opinion of, set great store by**
To value something highly is to **prize** or **treasure** it.
❷ *A surveyor was sent to* ***value*** *the house.*
• **price, cost, rate, evaluate, assess**

van *NOUN*
for various vehicles see **vehicle**

vanish *VERB*
With a flick of his wand, the wizard ***vanished*** *into thin air.*
• **disappear, go away, fade, dissolve, disperse**
OPPOSITE **appear**

vanity *NOUN*
His ***vanity*** *is such that he never admits he's wrong.*
• **arrogance, pride, conceit, self-esteem, self-importance**

a b c d e f g h i j k l m n o p q r s t u v w x y z

vapour *NOUN*

*Thick clouds of **vapour** poured from the volcano.*

• **smoke, fumes, steam, gas**

Vapour hanging in the air is **haze, fog, mist** or **smog.**

When something turns to vapour it **vaporises.**

variable *ADJECTIVE*

*The temperature is **variable** at this time of year.*

• **changeable, varying, fluctuating, erratic, inconsistent, uncertain, unpredictable, unsteady, unstable**

If your loyalty to friends is variable, you are **fickle.**

OPPOSITE **constant**

variation *NOUN*

*There are huge **variations** in age within the group.*

• **difference, alteration, change, fluctuation, shift**

variety *NOUN*

❶ *The centre offers a **variety** of leisure activities.*

• **assortment, mixture, array**

❷ *The supermarket has over thirty **varieties** of pasta.*

• **kind, sort, type, make, brand**

A variety of animal is a **breed** or **species.**

❸ *There is not much **variety** in her choice of words.*

• **variation, change, difference, diversity**

various *ADJECTIVE*

*The hats are available in **various** colours.*

• **different, assorted, several, varying, differing, a variety of, diverse**

vary *VERB*

❶ *The length of daylight **varies** with the seasons.*

• **change, alter, differ, fluctuate**

❷ *They **vary** the menu from week to week.*

• **change, modify, adjust, alter**

vast *ADJECTIVE*

❶ *The miser accumulated a **vast** fortune.*

• **large, huge, enormous, great, immense, massive**

❷ *A **vast** stretch of water lay between them and dry land.*

• **broad, wide, extensive, sweeping**

OPPOSITES **small, tiny**

vault *VERB*

➤ to vault over something

*He **vaulted over** the fence.*

• **jump over, leap over, bound over, spring over, clear, hurdle**

vault *NOUN*

*The gold was stored in the **vaults** of the bank.*

• **strongroom, treasury**

An underground part of a house is a **cellar.**

A room underneath a church is a **crypt.**

veer *VERB*

*The car suddenly **veered** to the left.*

• **change direction, swerve, turn**

vegetable *NOUN*

WORD WEB

GREEN VEGETABLES:

• **broccoli, Brussels sprout, cabbage, cauliflower, Chinese cabbage, kale, spinach**

ROOT VEGETABLES:

• **beetroot, carrot, parsnip, radish, swede, sweet potato, turnip**

LEGUMES OR PULSES:

• **broad bean, butter bean, chickpea, French bean, kidney bean, lentil, mangetout, sugar-snap, pea, runner bean, soya bean**

OTHER VEGETABLES:

• artichoke, asparagus, aubergine, celeriac, celery, courgette, garlic, leek, marrow, mushroom, okra, onion, pepper, potato, pumpkin, shallot, squash, sweetcorn, water chestnut, yam

vegetarian *NOUN*
A person who doesn't eat any animal products is a **vegan**.
The opposite—a person or animal that eats flesh—is a **carnivore**.
An animal that feeds only on plants is a **herbivore**.

vegetation *NOUN*
The rainforest is filled with lush ***vegetation****.*
• **foliage, greenery, growth, plants, undergrowth**

vehicle *NOUN*

WORD WEB

VEHICLES WHICH CARRY PEOPLE:

• buggy, bus, cab, car or motor car, caravan, coach, hovercraft, jeep, minibus, minicab, motorcycle or motorbike, taxi, train, tram
see also **aircraft, bicycle, boat, car, railway**
for space travel see **space**

VEHICLES USED FOR WORK:

• ambulance, bin lorry, bulldozer, fire engine, hearse, horsebox, lorry, removal van, pick-up truck, police car, steamroller, tank, tanker, tractor, truck, van

VEHICLES WHICH TRAVEL ON SNOW OR ICE:

• sled, sledge, sleigh, snowmobile, snowplough, toboggan

OLD HORSE-DRAWN VEHICLES:

• carriage, cart, chariot, coach, gig, stagecoach, trap, wagon

veil *VERB*
Her face was partly ***veiled*** *by a scarf.*
• **cover, conceal, hide, mask, shroud**

vein *NOUN*
A tube in the body that carries blood away from the heart is an **artery**.
Veins and arteries are **blood vessels**.
Delicate hair-like blood vessels are **capillaries**.

vengeance *NOUN*
The knight swore ***vengeance*** *on his enemies.*
• **revenge, retribution, retaliation**
OPPOSITE **forgiveness**

venomous *ADJECTIVE*
The adder is Britain's only ***venomous*** *snake.*
• **poisonous**
OPPOSITE **harmless**

vent *NOUN*
A ***vent*** *in the roof lets the smoke out.*
• **gap, hole, opening, outlet, slit**
➤ **to give vent to**
She ***gave vent to*** *her anger.*
• **express, let go, release**

venture *NOUN*
His first business ***venture*** *was a disaster.*
• **enterprise, undertaking, project, scheme**

venture *VERB*
They ***ventured*** *out into the snow.*
• **journey, set forth, dare to go**

verdict *NOUN*
What was the jury's ***verdict****?*
• **conclusion, decision, judgement, opinion**

verge *NOUN*
Don't park on the ***verge*** *of the road.*
• **side, edge, margin**
A stone or concrete edging beside a road is a **kerb**.
The flat strip of road beside a motorway is the **hard shoulder**.

a b c d e f g h i j k l m n o p q r s t u v w x y z

A B C D E F G H I J K L M N O P Q R S T U V W X Y Z

verify *VERB*
*Several witnesses **verified** his statement.*
• **confirm, prove, support**
(informal) **check out**

versatile *ADJECTIVE*
*He's a very **versatile** musician.*
• **adaptable, resourceful, many-sided, all-round, flexible**

verse *NOUN*
❶ *Most of the play is written in **verse**.*
• **rhyme**
The rhythm of a line of verse is its **metre**. Something written in verse is **poetry** or a **poem**.
see also **poem**
❷ *We need to learn the first two **verses** of the poem by heart.*
• **stanza**

version *NOUN*
❶ *The two newspapers gave different **versions** of the accident.*
• **account, description, story, report**
❷ *It's an English **version** of a French play.*
• **adaptation, interpretation**
A version of something which was originally in another language is a **translation**.
❸ *A new **version** of the computer game will be released in May.*
• **design, model, form, variation**

vertical *ADJECTIVE*
*The fence posts must be **vertical**.*
• **erect, perpendicular, upright**
A vertical drop is a **sheer** drop.
OPPOSITE **horizontal**

very *ADVERB*
*Carl is a **very** talented juggler.*
• **extremely, highly, enormously, exceedingly, truly, intensely, especially, particularly, remarkably, unusually, uncommonly, outstandingly, really**
(informal) **terribly**
OPPOSITE **slightly**

vessel *NOUN*
❶ *A fishing **vessel** has gone missing in the North Sea.*
• **boat, ship, craft**
for types of boat or ship see **boat**
❷ *Archaeologists found clay **vessels** at the site.*
• **pot, dish, bowl, jar, bottle, container**
➤ **blood vessels**
Blood vessels are your **arteries, capillaries** and **veins**.

vex *VERB*
*It **vexed** her that he'd forgotten her birthday.*
• **annoy, irritate, make you cross, upset, anger, exasperate**

vibrate *VERB*
*I pulled a lever and the whole engine began to **vibrate**.*
• **shake, shudder, tremble, throb, judder, quake, quiver, rattle**

vicious *ADJECTIVE*
❶ *This was once the scene of a **vicious** murder.*
• **brutal, barbaric, violent, bloodthirsty, cruel, merciless, pitiless, ruthless, callous, inhuman, malicious, sadistic, atrocious, barbarous, murderous, villainous, wicked**
❷ *Male baboons can be **vicious** if provoked.*
• **fierce, ferocious, violent, savage, wild**

victim *NOUN*
❶ *Ambulances took the **victims** to hospital.*
• **casualty**
Victims of an accident are also **the injured** or **the wounded**.
A person who dies in an accident is a **fatality**.
❷ *The hawk carried its **victim** in its talons.*
• **prey**

victor *NOUN*
*Who were the **victors** in the battle?*
• **winner, conqueror, champion**

victorious *ADJECTIVE*
*A trophy was presented to the **victorious** team.*
• **winning, triumphant, conquering, successful, top, first**
OPPOSITE **defeated**

victory *NOUN*
*Hannibal won several **victories** over the Romans.*
• **win, success, triumph**
OPPOSITE **defeat**

view *NOUN*
❶ *There's a good **view** from the top of the hill.*
• **outlook, prospect, scene, panorama, scenery**
❷ *What are your **views** on animal testing?*
• **opinion, thought, attitude, belief, conviction, idea, notion**
➤ **in view of something**
*In **view of** the circumstances, they gave her a refund.*
• **because of, as a result of, considering, taking account of**

view *VERB*
❶ *Thousand of tourists come to **view** Niagara Falls each year.*
• **look at, see, watch, observe, regard, contemplate, gaze at, inspect, survey, examine, eye**
❷ *Wanda **viewed** her cousin with extreme dislike.*
• **think of, consider, regard**

viewer *NOUN*
People who view a performance are the **audience** or **spectators**.
People who view something as they happen to pass by are **bystanders, onlookers** or **witnesses**.

vigilant *ADJECTIVE*
*A lookout has to be **vigilant** at all times.*
• **alert, watchful, attentive, wary, careful, observant, on the lookout, on your guard**
OPPOSITE **negligent**

vigorous *ADJECTIVE*
❶ *She does an hour of **vigorous** exercise every week.*
• **active, brisk, energetic, enthusiastic, lively, strenuous**
❷ *I gave the door a **vigorous** push.*
• **forceful, powerful, mighty**
❸ *He was a **vigorous** man in the prime of life.*
• **healthy, strong**
OPPOSITE **feeble**

vigour *NOUN*
*When they sighted land, they began to row with **vigour**.*
• **energy, force, spirit, vitality, gusto, verve, enthusiasm, liveliness, zeal, zest**

vile *ADJECTIVE*
❶ *The professor gave us a **vile** concoction to drink.*
• **disgusting, repulsive, revolting, foul, horrible, loathsome, offensive, repellent, sickening, nauseating**
OPPOSITE **pleasant**
❷ *Murder is a **vile** crime.*
• **dreadful, despicable, appalling, contemptible, wicked, evil**

villain *NOUN*
*Detectives are on the trail of an infamous **villain**.*
• **criminal, offender, rogue, wrongdoer**
An informal word for the villain in a story is **baddy**.
OPPOSITE **hero**
see also **criminal**

violate *VERB*
*The bowler was penalised for **violating** the rules.*
• **break, disobey, infringe, flout, disregard, ignore**

violation *NOUN*
*He's guilty of a **violation** of the rules.*
• **breach, breaking, offence (against)**
A violation of the rules of a game is a **foul** or an **infringement**.

violence *NOUN*
❶ *The marchers protested against the use of **violence**.*
• **fighting, might, war, brute force, barbarity, brutality, cruelty, savagery**
OPPOSITES **non-violence, pacifism**

a b c d e f g h i j k l m n o p q r s t u v w x y z

❷ *The **violence** of the storm uprooted trees.*
• **force, power, strength, severity, intensity, ferocity, fierceness, fury, rage**
OPPOSITES **gentleness, mildness**

violent *ADJECTIVE*
❶ *There were **violent** clashes in the streets.*
• **aggressive, forceful, rough, fierce, frenzied, vicious, brutal**
OPPOSITES **gentle, mild**
❷ *The bridge was washed away in a **violent** storm.*
• **severe, strong, powerful, forceful, raging, tempestuous, turbulent, wild**
OPPOSITES **weak, feeble**

virtually *ADVERB*
*It's **virtually** impossible to tell if the letter is genuine.*
• **almost, nearly, practically, as good as, in effect**

virtue *NOUN*
❶ *She has the **virtue** of a saint!*
• **goodness, decency, honesty, integrity, righteousness, uprightness, worthiness, morality**
OPPOSITE **vice**
❷ *One **virtue** of living in the country is that it's quiet.*
• **advantage, benefit, asset, good point, merit, strength**

virtuous *ADJECTIVE*
*She had always tried to lead a **virtuous** life.*
• **good, honest, honourable, innocent, just, law-abiding, moral, praiseworthy, pure, righteous, trustworthy, upright, worthy**
OPPOSITE **wicked**

visible *ADJECTIVE*
*There were no **visible** signs that the door had been forced.*
• **noticeable, obvious, conspicuous, clear, distinct, evident, apparent, perceptible, recognisable, detectable**
OPPOSITE **invisible**

vision *NOUN*
❶ *He began to have problems with his **vision**.*
• **eyesight, sight**
❷ *The soothsayer saw a **vision** of the future.*
• **apparition, dream, hallucination**
Something travellers in the desert think they see is a **mirage**.
❸ *As an artist, she has great **vision**.*
• **foresight, imagination, insight**

visit *VERB*
*They're **visiting** friends in Toronto for a few days.*
• **call on, come to see, drop in on, go to see, pay a call on, stay with**

visit *NOUN*
❶ *My grandmother is coming for a **visit**.*
• **call, stay**
❷ *We are planning a short **visit** to Paris.*
• **trip, excursion, outing**

visitor *NOUN*
❶ *They've got some Polish **visitors** staying with them.*
• **guest, caller**
❷ *Rome welcomes millions of **visitors** every year.*
• **tourist, holidaymaker, sightseer, traveller**

visualise *VERB*
*I can't **visualise** her with curly hair.*
• **imagine, picture, envisage, see**

vital *ADJECTIVE*
*It is **vital** that you remember the secret password.*
• **essential, crucial, imperative, important, necessary, indispensable**
OPPOSITE **unimportant**

vitality *NOUN*
*That painting of sunflowers bursts with **vitality**.*
• **energy, life, liveliness, spirit, animation, exuberance, vigour, zest**

vivid *ADJECTIVE*
❶ *Gauguin often painted in* ***vivid*** *colours.*
• **bright, colourful, strong, intense, vibrant, dazzling, brilliant, glowing, striking, showy**
❷ *He gave a* ***vivid*** *description of his travels in Mexico.*
• **lively, clear, powerful, evocative, imaginative, dramatic, lifelike, realistic, graphic**
OPPOSITE **dull**

voice *NOUN*
The robot spoke with a slow, metallic ***voice****.*
• **speech, tone, way of speaking**
for types of singing voice see **sing**

WRITING TIPS

You can use these words to describe a voice:
• **croaky, droning, gruff, high-pitched, husky, low, shrill, soft-spoken, squeaky, throaty**
It was a low, soft voice, plush as velvet, with sibilants as swashing as the sea.—PETER PAN IN SCARLET, Geraldine Mccaughrean

voice *VERB*
He ***voiced*** *several objections to the plan.*
• **express, communicate, put into words, speak**

volcano *NOUN*
Molten rock that builds up inside a volcano is **magma**.
Molten rock that pours from a volcano is **lava**.
Lava and ash pouring from a volcano is an **eruption**.
A volcano that often erupts is an **active volcano**.
A volcano that can no longer erupt is an **extinct volcano**.
A volcano that is neither active nor extinct is a **dormant volcano**.
A scientist who studies volcanoes is a **volcanologist**.

volume *NOUN*
❶ *We had to measure the* ***volume*** *of the jug.*
• **capacity, size, dimensions**
❷ *They struggle to cope with the* ***volume*** *of fan mail they receive.*
• **amount, quantity, bulk, mass**
❸ *The full encyclopedia consists of twenty* ***volumes****.*
• **book, tome**

voluntary *ADJECTIVE*
She does ***voluntary*** *work for a charity.*
• **optional, unpaid**
OPPOSITE **compulsory**

volunteer *VERB*
No-one ***volunteered*** *to do the washing-up.*
• **offer, put yourself forward, be willing**

vomit *VERB*
The seasickness made him want to ***vomit****.*
• **be sick, heave, retch**
(informal) **throw up**

vortex *NOUN*
see **spiral**

vote *VERB*
Everyone has a right to ***vote*** *in the election.*
• **cast your vote**
➤ **to vote for someone** or **something**
I haven't decided who to ***vote for****.*
• **choose, opt for, nominate, elect**

vote *NOUN*
The results of the ***vote*** *will be known tomorrow.*
• **ballot, election, poll, referendum**

voucher *NOUN*
You can exchange this ***voucher*** *for a free drink.*
• **coupon, ticket, token**

vow *VERB*
He ***vowed*** *never to reveal the genie's name.*
• **pledge, promise, guarantee, swear, give your word, take an oath**

a b c d e f g h i j k l m n o p q r s t u v w x y z

A B C D E F G H I J K L M N O P Q R S T U V W X Y Z

vow *NOUN*
*The mermaid took a **vow** to leave the sea forever.*
• **pledge, promise, oath, word**

voyage *NOUN*
A holiday voyage is a **cruise**.
A voyage across a channel or sea is a **crossing**.
A long voyage is a **sea passage**.
for other ways to travel see **travel**

vulgar *ADJECTIVE*
❶ *The new colour scheme just looks **vulgar** to me.*
• **tasteless, unsophisticated, cheap, tawdry**
(informal) **tacky**
OPPOSITE **tasteful**
❷ *The book sometimes uses **vulgar** language.*
• **indecent, offensive, rude, coarse**
OPPOSITE **decent**

vulnerable *ADJECTIVE*
*As night fell, the outlaws were in a **vulnerable** position.*
• **defenceless, exposed, unguarded, unprotected, at risk**
OPPOSITE **safe**

Ww

waddle *VERB*
*A pair of geese **waddled** along the path.*
• **toddle, totter, shuffle, shamble, wobble**

wade *VERB*
❶ *Is it safe to **wade** in the river?*
• **paddle, wallow**
❷ *She had piles of paperwork to **wade** through.*
• **toil, labour, work, plough**

wag *VERB*
*The dog was eagerly **wagging** its tail.*
• **move to and fro, shake, swing, wave, waggle, wiggle**

wage *NOUN*
*Her weekly **wage** was barely enough to live on.*
• **earnings, income, pay, pay packet**
A fixed amount someone is paid per year for work is a **salary**.

wage *VERB*
*The Greeks **waged** a long war against Troy.*
• **carry on, conduct, fight**

wail *VERB*
*Upstairs, the baby began to **wail**.*
• **cry, howl, bawl, cry, moan, shriek**

wait *VERB*
*Please **wait** here until I get back.*
• **remain where you are, stay, stop, rest, pause, linger**
(informal) **hang about** or **around, hold on**

wait *NOUN*
*There was a long **wait** before the show began.*
• **interval, pause, delay, hold-up**

wake or **waken** *VERB*
❶ *Hagor the giant **woke** from a deep sleep.*
• **awake, awaken, become conscious, come round, rise, arise, stir, wake up**
❷ *The alarm clock **woke** me at 6 a.m.*
• **rouse, arouse, awaken, disturb**

walk *VERB*

OVERUSED WORD

Try to vary the words you use for **walk**. Here are some other words you could use.

TO WALK SLOWLY:

• **amble, saunter, stroll, crawl, creep, pace, plod, step, wander**
*I **sauntered** down the lane, humming a tune.*

TO WALK UNSTEADILY:

stagger, stumble, totter, hobble, limp, lope, lurch, shamble, shuffle, toddle, waddle
Sleeping people are not fast. They stumble, they stagger; they move like children wading through rivers of treacle, like old people whose feet are weighed down by thick, wet mud.
—THE SLEEPER AND THE SPINDLE, Neil Gaiman

TO WALK HEAVILY OR LOUDLY:

• **stamp, tramp, clump, pound, traipse, trudge, wade**
The robot ***clumped*** *its way along the corridor.*

TO WALK QUIETLY:

• **pad, patter, tiptoe, slink, steal, prowl, stalk**
The burglar ***slunk*** *away into the shadows.*

TO WALK SMARTLY OR PROUDLY:

• **march, stride, strut, parade, swagger, trot**
Captain Flint ***swaggered*** *on board the ship.*

TO WALK A LONG DISTANCE:

• **hike, trek, ramble**
They are planning to ***trek*** *across the Himalayas.*

TO WALK IN A GROUP:

• **file, troop**
The children ***trooped*** *into the classroom.*

walk *NOUN*

❶ *We went for a* ***walk*** *in the country.*
• **stroll, ramble, hike, trek, tramp, trudge**
❷ *There are some lovely* ***walks*** *through the forest.*
• **path, route**

walker *NOUN*

When you walk along the street, you are a **pedestrian.**
If you go for long walks, you are a **hiker** or **rambler.**

wall *NOUN*

A crumbling stone ***wall*** *surrounded the cottage.*
• **barricade, barrier, fortification, embankment**
A wall to hold back water is a **dam** or **dyke.**
A low wall along the edge of a roof is a **parapet.**
A wall built on top of a bank of earth is a **rampart.**
A wall or fence made of sticks is a **stockade.**

wallow *VERB*

❶ *Hippos like to* ***wallow*** *in mud.*
• **roll about, flounder, wade, lie, loll**
❷ *He is* ***wallowing*** *in all the attention.*
• **revel, take delight, bask**

wand *NOUN*

The fairy gave a flick of her magic ***wand.***
• **stick, rod, baton, staff**
for other words to do with magic see **magic**

wander *VERB*

❶ *Sheep* ***wandered*** *about the hills.*
• **stray, roam, rove, range, ramble, meander, travel, walk**
❷ *We must have* ***wandered*** *off the path.*
• **stray, turn, veer, swerve**

wane *VERB*

❶ *At sunset, the light began to* ***wane.***
• **fade, fail, dim**
OPPOSITE **brighten**
❷ *Her enthusiasm* ***waned*** *after a while.*
• **decline, decrease, lessen, diminish, subside, weaken, dwindle**
OPPOSITE **strengthen**

want *VERB*

❶ *He desperately* ***wants*** *to win a medal.*
• **wish, desire, long, hope**
❷ *Gayle had always* ***wanted*** *a pony of her own.*
• **wish for, desire, fancy, crave, long for, yearn for, hanker after, pine for, set your heart on, hunger for, thirst for**
❸ *That floor* ***wants*** *a good scrub.*
• **need, require**

A B C D E F G H I J K L M N O P Q R S T U V W X Y Z

want *NOUN*
❶ *The hotel staff saw to all their* ***wants****.*
• **demand, desire, wish, need, requirement**
❷ *The plants died for* ***want*** *of water.*
• **lack, need, absence**

war *NOUN*
The ***war*** *between the two countries lasted many years.*
• **fighting, warfare, conflict, strife, hostilities**
see also **fight**

ward *VERB*
➤ **to ward off someone** or **something**
❶ *He put up his shield to* ***ward off*** *the blow.*
• **avert, block, check, deflect, turn aside, parry**
❷ *The charm was intended to* ***ward off*** *bad luck.*
• **fend off, drive away, repel, keep away, push away**

wares *PLURAL NOUN*
The market traders displayed their ***wares****.*
• **goods, merchandise, produce, stock, commodities**

warlike *ADJECTIVE*
The Picts were said to be a ***warlike*** *people.*
• **aggressive, fierce, violent, hostile, quarrelsome, militant**
OPPOSITE **peaceful**

warm *ADJECTIVE*
❶ *It was a* ***warm*** *September evening.*
Weather which is unpleasantly warm is **close** or **sultry**.
Water or food which is only just warm is **lukewarm** or **tepid**.
A common simile is **as warm as toast**.
OPPOSITE **cold**
❷ *Sandy put on a* ***warm*** *jumper.*
• **cosy, thick, woolly, snuggly**
OPPOSITE **thin**
❸ *The fans gave the singer a* ***warm*** *welcome.*
• **friendly, warm-hearted, welcoming, kind, affectionate, genial, amiable, loving, sympathetic**
OPPOSITE **unfriendly**

warm *VERB*
She sat by the fire, ***warming*** *her hands and feet.*
• **heat, make warmer, thaw out**
OPPOSITE **chill**

warn *VERB*
The guide ***warned*** *us to keep to the path.*
• **advise, caution, alert, remind**
To warn people of danger is to **raise the alarm**.

warning *NOUN*
❶ *There was no* ***warning*** *of the danger ahead.*
• **sign, signal, portent, indication, advance notice**
❷ *The traffic warden let him off with a* ***warning****.*
• **caution, reprimand**

warp *VERB*
The wheel had slightly ***warped*** *with age.*
• **bend, buckle, twist, curl, bend out of shape, distort**

warrior *NOUN*
see **fighter**

wary *ADJECTIVE*
The cat is always ***wary*** *when strangers are around.*
• **cautious, distrustful, suspicious, careful, watchful, attentive, vigilant, on your guard**
OPPOSITE **reckless**

wash *VERB*
❶ *It took Rapunzel a long time to* ***wash*** *her hair.*
• **clean**
To wash something with a cloth is to **mop**, **sponge** or **wipe** it.
To wash something with a brush is to **scrub** it.
To wash something in clean water is to **rinse**, **sluice** or **swill** it.
To wash yourself all over is to **bath** or **shower**.
❷ *Waves* ***washed*** *over the beach.*
• **flow, splash**

waste *VERB*
*Let's not **waste** any more time.*
• **squander, misuse, throw away, fritter away**
OPPOSITE **save**

waste *NOUN*
*A lot of household **waste** can be recycled.*
• **rubbish, refuse, trash, garbage, junk, litter**
Waste food is **leftovers**.
Waste metal is **scrap**.

wasteful *ADJECTIVE*
*It's **wasteful** to cook more food than you need.*
• **extravagant, uneconomical, prodigal, lavish, spendthrift**
OPPOSITES **economical, thrifty**

watch *VERB*
❶ *I could sit and **watch** the sea for hours.*
• **gaze at, look at, stare at, view, contemplate**
❷ ***Watch** how the batsman holds the bat.*
• **observe, take notice of, keep your eyes on, pay attention to, attend to, heed, note**
❸ *Could you **watch** my bag for a few minutes?*
• **keep an eye on, keep watch over, guard, mind, look after, safeguard, supervise, tend**
➤ **to watch out**
Watch out—there's a car coming!
• **be careful, pay attention, beware, take care, take heed**

watch *NOUN*
for instruments used to measure time
see **time**

watchful *ADJECTIVE*
*She kept a **watchful** eye on the baby.*
• **alert, attentive, observant, vigilant, careful, sharp-eyed, keen**

water *NOUN*

WORD WEB

SOME AREAS OF WATER:

• **brook, (*Scottish*) burn, canal, lake, lido, (*Scottish*) loch, ocean, pond, pool, reservoir, river, rivulet, sea, stream**
Animals and plants which live in water are **aquatic**.

SPORTS PLAYED IN OR NEAR WATER:

• **angling, canoeing, deep-sea diving, diving, kayaking, rafting, rowing, sailing, snorkelling, swimming, surfing, water polo, waterskiing, windsurfing**

WRITING TIPS

You can use these words to describe **how water moves**:
• **bubble, cascade, dribble, drip, flood, flow, froth, gurgle, gush, jet, ooze, overflow, ripple, roll, run, seep, shower, spill, spatter, splash, spout, spray, sprinkle, spurt, squirt, stream, surge, sweep, swirl, swish, trickle, well up**
see also **flow**
The water cascaded over the lip of the basin and dropped, in a miniature Niagara Falls, onto the kitchen floor.—MEASLE AND THE SLITHERGHOUL, Ian Ogilvy

water *VERB*
*Please remember to **water** the plants.*
• **wet, irrigate, sprinkle, dampen, moisten, soak, drench**

watery *ADJECTIVE*
❶ *The soup was **watery** and tasteless.*
• **weak, thin, runny, diluted, watered down**
❷ *Chopping onions makes my eyes **watery**.*
• **tearful, wet, damp, moist**

wave *VERB*
❶ *The tall grass **waved** in the breeze.*
• **move to and fro, sway, swing, flap, flutter**
❷ *I tried to get their attention by **waving** a newspaper.*
• **shake, brandish, flourish, twirl, wag, waggle, wiggle**

wave *NOUN*
❶ *We watched the **waves** break on the shore.*
• **breaker, roller, billow**
A very small wave is a **ripple**.
A huge wave caused by an earthquake is a **tidal wave** or **tsunami**.

A B C D E F G H I J K L M N O P Q R S T U V W X Y Z

A number of white waves following each other is **surf**.
The top of a wave is the **crest** or **ridge**.
❷ *A* ***wave*** *of anger spread through the crowd.*
• **surge, outbreak**

waver *VERB*

❶ *She* ***wavered*** *about whether to send the letter.*
• **hesitate, dither, falter, be uncertain, think twice**
❷ *The candle flame* ***wavered*** *in the draught.*
• **flicker, quiver, tremble, shake, shiver**

wavy *ADJECTIVE*

The mermaid combed her long ***wavy*** *hair.*
• **curly, curling, rippling, winding, zigzag**
OPPOSITE **straight**

way *NOUN*

❶ *Can you show me the* ***way*** *to the bus station?*
• **direction, route, road, path**
❷ *Is your house a long* ***way*** *from here?*
• **distance, journey**
❸ *This is the best* ***way*** *to make porridge.*
• **method, procedure, process, system, technique**
❹ *What a childish* ***way*** *to behave!*
• **manner, fashion, style**
❺ *In some* ***ways****, the brothers are very alike.*
• **respect, particular, feature, detail, aspect**
❻ *Things are in a bad* ***way****.*
• **state, condition**

weak *ADJECTIVE*

❶ *The footbridge was old and* ***weak*** *in places.*
• **fragile, flimsy, rickety, shaky, unsound, unsteady, unsafe, decrepit**
❷ *The patient was too* ***weak*** *to walk very far.*
• **feeble, frail, ill, sickly, infirm, delicate, puny**
❸ *The nobles plotted against the* ***weak*** *king.*
• **timid, spineless, ineffective, powerless, useless**
❹ *The film was fun, but the plot was a bit* ***weak****.*
• **feeble, lame, unsatisfactory, unconvincing**
❺ *He asked for a mug of* ***weak*** *tea.*
• **watery, diluted, tasteless, thin**
(informal) **wishy-washy**
OPPOSITE **strong**

weaken *VERB*

❶ *Too much water will* ***weaken*** *the flavour.*
• **reduce, lessen, diminish, sap, undermine**
❷ *The storm had* ***weakened*** *overnight.*
• **decrease, decline, die down, fade, dwindle, ebb away, wane**
OPPOSITE **strengthen**

weakness *NOUN*

❶ *He pointed out the* ***weakness*** *in their plan.*
• **fault, flaw, defect, imperfection, weak point**
❷ *Eve has a* ***weakness*** *for toffee apples.*
• **liking, fondness**
(informal) **soft spot**

wealth *NOUN*

The family had acquired its ***wealth*** *from coal.*
• **fortune, money, riches, affluence,prosperity**
OPPOSITE **poverty**

➤ **a wealth of**
There's ***a wealth of*** *information on the Internet.*
• **lots of, plenty of, an abundance of, a profusion of**

wealthy *ADJECTIVE*

They say that he comes from a very ***wealthy*** *family.*
• **rich, well-off, affluent, prosperous, moneyed, well-to-do**
(informal) **flush, loaded**
OPPOSITE **poor**

weapon *NOUN*

WORD WEB

Weapons in general are **weaponry** or **arms**.
A collection or store of weapons is an **armoury** or **arsenal**.

VARIOUS WEAPONS:

• bayonet, blowpipe, bomb, dagger, gun, hand grenade, harpoon, machine gun, missile, mortar, pistol, revolver, rifle, shell, sword, torpedo, truncheon
see also **sword**

SOME WEAPONS USED IN THE PAST:

• battering ram, battleaxe, blunderbuss, bow and arrow, cannon, catapult, crossbow, javelin, lance, longbow, musket, pike, spear, staff, tomahawk, trident

wear *VERB* **wears, wearing, wore, worn**
❶ *Can I* **wear** *my new dress to the party?*
• dress in, be dressed in, have on
❷ *The rug in the hallway is starting to* **wear**.
• fray, wear away, wear out
❸ *Those tyres have* **worn** *well.*
• last, endure, survive
➤ **to wear off**
The pain will **wear off** *soon.*
• die down, disappear, ease, fade, lessen, subside, weaken

weary *ADJECTIVE*
The children were **weary** *after the long walk.*
• tired, worn out, exhausted, fatigued, flagging
(informal) all in

weather *NOUN*

WORD WEB

The typical weather in a particular area is the **climate**.
A person who studies and forecasts the weather is a **meteorologist**.

SOME TYPES OF WEATHER:

• fog: mist, *(Scottish)* haar, haze, smog
• ice and snow: blizzard, frost, hail, ice, sleet, snowstorm
• light rain: drizzle, shower
• heavy rain: cloudburst, deluge, downpour, monsoon, torrent
• sun: drought, heatwave, sunshine
• storm: squall, tempest
• light wind: breeze, gust
• strong wind: cyclone, gale, hurricane, tornado, typhoon, whirlwind
see also **sky, wind**

WRITING TIPS

You can use these words to describe weather.

TO DESCRIBE CLOUDY WEATHER:

• dull, grey, overcast, sunless

TO DESCRIBE COLD WEATHER:

• arctic, bitter, chilly, frosty, icy, raw, snowy, wintry
(informal) nippy, perishing
It was one January morning, very early—a pinching, frosty morning—the cove all grey with hoar-frost.—TREASURE ISLAND, Robert Louis Stevenson

TO DESCRIBE SNOW:

• crisp, powdery, slushy

TO DESCRIBE HOT WEATHER:

• baking, humid, melting, roasting, sizzling, sticky, sultry, sweltering

TO DESCRIBE STORMY WEATHER:

• rough, squally, tempestuous, turbulent, violent, wild

THUNDER MAY:

• boom, crash, resound, roar, rumble

TO DESCRIBE SUNNY WEATHER:

• bright, cloudless, fair, fine, springlike, summery, sunny, sunshiny

TO DESCRIBE WET WEATHER:

• damp, drizzly, raining cats and dogs, showery, spitting, torrential

RAIN MAY:

• lash or pelt down, pour, pour down, teem
(informal) bucket, tip down
The sky rumbled loudly above them and the rain continued to pour down, bouncing on the lane and running into little streams.
—GOODNIGHT MISTER TOM, Michelle Magorian

TO DESCRIBE WINDY WEATHER:

• biting, blowy, blustery, breezy, gusty

WIND MAY:

• batter, blast, buffet, howl, moan, wail

weather *VERB*
*Somehow, the tiny ship **weathered** the storm.*
• survive, withstand, endure, come through

weave *VERB*
*A messenger **weaved** his way through the crowd.*
• wind, zigzag, twist and turn

web *NOUN*
*A **web** of tunnels lay under the castle.*
• net, network, mesh

wedding *NOUN*
*She was a bridesmaid at her cousin's **wedding**.*
• marriage
A formal word for a wedding is **nuptials**.

WORD WEB

PEOPLE WHO MAY BE INVOLVED IN A WEDDING:

• best man, bride, bridegroom, bridesmaid, groom, maid or matron of honour, page, registrar, usher, wedding guests
see also **marry**

wedge *VERB*
*The door was **wedged** open with an old shoe.*
• jam, stick

weep *VERB* **weeps, weeping, wept**
*Deirdre buried her face in her hands and began to **weep**.*
• cry, sob, shed tears
To weep noisily is to **bawl** or **blubber**.
To weep in an annoying way is to **snivel** or **whimper**.

weigh *VERB*
➤ **to weigh someone down**
❶ *Many troubles **weighed** him **down**.*
• bother, worry, trouble, distress, burden
❷ *She was **weighed down** with shopping.*
• load, burden, lumber
➤ **to weigh something up**
*The detective **weighed up** the evidence.*
• consider, assess, evaluate, examine, study, ponder

weight *NOUN*
*Take care when lifting heavy **weights**.*
• load, mass, burden
for units for measuring weight see **measurement**

weighty *ADJECTIVE*
❶ *He lifted a **weighty** volume off the shelf.*
• heavy, bulky, cumbersome
OPPOSITE light
❷ *They had **weighty** matters to discuss.*
• important, serious, grave, significant
OPPOSITES unimportant, trivial

weird *ADJECTIVE*
❶ ***Weird** noises have been heard in the tower at midnight.*
• eerie, ghostly, unearthly, mysterious, uncanny, unnatural
(informal) spooky, creepy
OPPOSITES ordinary, natural

❷ *My big sister has a **weird** taste in music.*
• **strange, odd, peculiar, bizarre, curious, quirky, eccentric, outlandish, unconventional, unusual**
(informal) **wacky, way-out**
OPPOSITE **conventional**

welcome *NOUN*
*The landlady gave us a friendly **welcome**.*
• **greeting, reception**

welcome *ADJECTIVE*
❶ *A cup of tea would be very **welcome**.*
• **pleasant, pleasing, agreeable, appreciated, desirable, acceptable**
OPPOSITES **unwelcome, unacceptable**
❷ *You're **welcome** to use my bike.*
• **allowed, permitted, free**
OPPOSITE **forbidden**

welcome *VERB*
❶ *An elderly butler **welcomed** us at the door.*
• **greet, receive, meet, hail**
❷ *We **welcome** suggestions from the public.*
• **appreciate, accept, like, want**

welfare *NOUN*
*Her only concern was the **welfare** of her children.*
• **well-being, good, benefit, interests**

well *ADVERB*
❶ *The whole team played **well** on Saturday.*
• **ably, skilfully, expertly, effectively, efficiently, admirably, marvellously, wonderfully**
OPPOSITE **badly**
❷ *It's cold outside, so you'd better wrap up **well**.*
• **properly, suitably, correctly, thoroughly, carefully**
❸ *I know her brother **well**.*
• **closely, intimately, personally**

well *ADJECTIVE*
*Mrs Orr looks surprisingly **well** for her age.*
• **healthy, fit, strong, sound, robust, vigorous, lively, hearty**
OPPOSITE **ill**

well-known *ADJECTIVE*
*A **well-known** athlete will open the new sports shop.*
• **famous, celebrated, prominent, notable, renowned, distinguished, eminent**
OPPOSITES **unknown, obscure**

went *past tense see* **go**

west *NOUN, ADJECTIVE, ADVERB*
The parts of a continent or country in the west are the **western** parts.
To travel towards the west is to travel **westward** *or* **westwards**.
A wind from the west is a **westerly** wind.

wet *ADJECTIVE*
❶ *Archie took off his **wet** clothes and had a hot bath.*
• **damp, soaked, soaking, drenched, dripping, sopping, wringing wet**
❷ *The pitch was too **wet** to play on.*
• **waterlogged, saturated, sodden, soggy, dewy, muddy, boggy**
❸ *Take care—the paint is still **wet**.*
• **runny, sticky, tacky**
❹ *It was cold and **wet** all afternoon.*
• **rainy, showery, pouring, drizzly, misty**
see also **weather**
OPPOSITE **dry**

wet *VERB* **wets, wetting, wet** or **wetted**
Wet the clay before you start to mould it.
• **dampen, moisten, soak, water**
OPPOSITE **dry**

wheel *NOUN*
A small wheel under a piece of furniture is a **caster**.

A B C D E F G H I J K L M N O P Q R S T U V W X Y Z

The centre of a wheel is the **hub**.
The outer edge of a wheel is the **rim**.

wheel *VERB*

❶ *A pair of seagulls **wheeled** overhead.*
• **circle, orbit**
❷ *The column of soldiers **wheeled** to the right.*
• **swing round, turn, veer, swerve**

whiff *NOUN*

*I caught a **whiff** of coffee as I walked past the cafe.*
• **smell, scent, aroma**

while *NOUN*

*You may need to wait a **while** for the next train.*
• **period, time, spell**

whimper or **whine** *VERB*

*A dog **whimpered** in the corner of the room.*
• **cry, moan**

whip *VERB*

❶ *The jockey **whipped** his horse to make it go faster.*
• **beat, hit, lash, flog, thrash**
❷ ***Whip** the cream until it is thick.*
• **beat, whisk**

whirl *VERB*

*The snowflakes **whirled** in the icy wind.*
• **turn, twirl, spin, twist, circle, spiral, reel, pirouette, revolve, rotate**

whisk *VERB*

***Whisk** the egg yolks together in a bowl.*
• **beat, whip, mix, stir**

whisper *VERB*

*What are you two **whispering** about?*
• **murmur, mutter, mumble**
OPPOSITE **shout**

whistle *NOUN, VERB*

for various sounds see **sound**

white *ADJECTIVE, NOUN*

WORD WEB

SOME SHADES OF WHITE:

• **cream, ivory, off-white, platinum, silvery, snow-white**

When coloured things become whiter they become **bleached** or **faded**.
When someone turns white with fear they **blanch** or **turn pale**.
Hair that is **hoary** is white with age.
Something which is rather white is **whitish**.
Common similes are **as white as a sheet, as white as chalk** and **as white as snow**.

whole *ADJECTIVE*

❶ *I haven't read the **whole** book yet.*
• **complete, entire, full, total, unabbreviated**
OPPOSITE **incomplete**
❷ *The dinosaur skeleton appears to be **whole**.*
• **in one piece, intact, unbroken, undamaged, perfect**
OPPOSITES **broken, in pieces**

wholesome *ADJECTIVE*

*Pets should be fed a **wholesome** diet.*
• **healthy, nutritious, nourishing**
OPPOSITE **unhealthy**

wholly *ADVERB*

*I'm not **wholly** convinced by his story.*
• **completely, totally, fully, entirely, utterly, thoroughly**
OPPOSITE **partly**

wicked *ADJECTIVE*

❶ *Snow White had a **wicked** stepmother.*
• **evil, cruel, vicious, villainous, detestable, mean, corrupt, immoral, sinful, foul, vile**
OPPOSITES **good, virtuous**
❷ *They hatched a **wicked** scheme to take over the world.*

• evil, fiendish, malicious, malevolent, diabolical, monstrous, deplorable, dreadful, shameful

❸ *The goblin had a **wicked** grin on his face.*

• mischievous, playful, impish, naughty

wide *ADJECTIVE*

❶ *The hotel is close to a **wide** sandy beach.*

• broad, expansive, extensive, large, spacious

OPPOSITE narrow

❷ *She has a **wide** knowledge of classical music.*

• comprehensive, vast, wide-ranging, encyclopedic

OPPOSITE limited

widely *ADVERB*

*The legend of King Arthur is **widely** known.*

• commonly, everywhere, far and wide

widespread *ADJECTIVE*

*There is **widespread** interest in the new engine design.*

• general, extensive, universal, wholesale

Something which spreads over the whole world is **global** or **worldwide**.

OPPOSITE uncommon

width *NOUN*

*The room is about eight feet in **width**.*

• breadth

The distance across a circle is its **diameter**.

wield *VERB*

*The lumberjack was **wielding** his axe.*

• brandish, flourish, hold, use

wife *NOUN*

*Katherine is Mr Gray's second **wife**.*

Another word for a person's wife or husband is **spouse**.

wild *ADJECTIVE*

❶ *I don't like seeing **wild** animals in captivity.*

• undomesticated, untamed

OPPOSITE tame

❷ *The hedgerow was full of **wild** flowers.*

• natural, uncultivated

OPPOSITE cultivated

❸ *To the west is a **wild** and mountainous region.*

• rough, rugged, uncultivated, uninhabited, desolate

OPPOSITE cultivated

❹ *The crowd was **wild** with excitement.*

• riotous, rowdy, disorderly, unruly, boisterous, excited, noisy, uncontrollable, hysterical

OPPOSITES calm, restrained

❺ *The weather looked **wild** outside.*

• blustery, windy, gusty, stormy, turbulent, tempestuous

OPPOSITE calm

wilful *ADJECTIVE*

❶ *He was very **wilful** as a child.*

• obstinate, stubborn, strong-willed, pig-headed

❷ *There is a fine for **wilful** damage to trees.*

• deliberate, intentional, planned, conscious

will *NOUN*

*They seem to have lost the **will** to win.*

• desire, wish, determination, resolution, willpower, resolve, purpose

willing *ADJECTIVE*

❶ *She is always **willing** to help.*

• eager, happy, pleased, ready, prepared

OPPOSITE unwilling

❷ *I need a couple of **willing** volunteers.*

• enthusiastic, helpful, cooperative, obliging

wilt *VERB*

*The flowers **wilted** in the heat.*

• become limp, droop, flop, sag, fade, shrivel, wither

OPPOSITE flourish

wily *ADJECTIVE*
*The player was outwitted by his **wily** opponent.*
• **clever, crafty, cunning, shrewd, scheming, artful, sly, devious**

win *VERB* **wins, winning, won**
❶ *Who do you think will **win**?*
• **come first, be victorious, succeed, triumph, prevail**
To win against someone is also to **beat, conquer, defeat** or **overcome** them.
OPPOSITE **lose**
❷ *She **won** first prize in the poetry competition.*
• **get, receive, gain, obtain, secure** *(informal)* **pick up, walk away with**

wind *NOUN (rhymes with* **tinned***)*
A gentle wind is a **breath, breeze** or **draught**.
A violent wind is a **cyclone, gale, hurricane** or **tornado**.
A sudden unexpected wind is a **blast, gust, puff** or **squall**.
see also **weather**
for wind instruments see **music**

wind *VERB (rhymes with* **find***)* **winds, winding, wound**
❶ *She **wound** the wool into a ball.*
• **coil, loop, roll, turn, curl**
❷ *The road **winds** up the hill.*
• **bend, curve, twist and turn, zigzag, meander**

window *NOUN*
The glass in a window is a **pane**.
A semicircular window above a door is a **fanlight**.
A window in a roof is a **skylight**.
A decorative window with panels of coloured glass is a **stained-glass window**.
A person whose job is to fit glass in windows is a **glazier**.

windy *ADJECTIVE*
❶ *It was a cold, **windy** day.*
• **breezy, blustery, gusty, squally, stormy**
OPPOSITE **calm**
❷ *This spot is too **windy** for a picnic.*
• **windswept, exposed, draughty**
OPPOSITE **sheltered**

wink *VERB*
❶ *My friend **winked** at me and smiled.*
To shut and open both eyes quickly is to **blink**.
❷ *The lights **winked** on and off.*
• **flash, flicker, sparkle, twinkle**

winner *NOUN*
*The **winner** was presented with a silver cup.*
• **victor, prizewinner, champion, conqueror**
OPPOSITE **loser**

winning *ADJECTIVE*
*The **winning** team went up to receive their medals.*
• **victorious, triumphant, conquering, successful, top-scoring, champion**
OPPOSITE **losing**

wintry *ADJECTIVE*
*It was a grey, **wintry** day.*
• **cold, frosty, freezing, bitter, icy, snowy**

wipe *VERB*
*I **wiped** the table with a cloth.*
• **rub, clean, polish, mop, swab, sponge**
➤ **to wipe something out**
*Pompeii was **wiped out** by the eruption of Mount Vesuvius.*
• **destroy, annihilate, exterminate, get rid of**

wire *NOUN*
*Several **wires** protruded from the robot's head.*
• **cable, lead, flex**
A system of wires is **wiring**.

wisdom *NOUN*
*She's a woman of great **wisdom**.*
• **sense, judgement, understanding, intelligence, common sense, good sense, insight, reason**

wise *ADJECTIVE*
❶ *The soothsayer was very old and **wise**.*
• **sensible, reasonable, intelligent, perceptive, knowledgeable, rational, thoughtful**
❷ *I think you made a **wise** decision.*
• **good, right, proper, sound, fair, just, appropriate**
OPPOSITE **foolish**

wish *NOUN*
*Her dearest **wish** was to travel to the Amazon.*
• **desire, want, longing, yearning, hankering, craving, urge, fancy, hope, ambition** *(informal)* **yen**

wish *VERB*
*I **wish** that everyone would sit still for a minute!*
If you wish something would happen, you can say that you **want** or **would like** it to happen.
➤ **to wish for**
*If you had three wishes, what would you **wish for**?*
• **desire, want, crave, fancy, long for, yearn for, hanker after**

wisp *NOUN*
*She blew a **wisp** of hair away from her face.*
• **shred, strand**

wistful *ADJECTIVE*
*She gave a **wistful** sigh as she read the letter.*
• **sad, melancholy, thoughtful, pensive**

wit *NOUN*
❶ *Ogres are creatures with very little **wit**.*
• **intelligence, cleverness, brains, sharpness, understanding**
❷ *The film script sparkled with **wit**.*
• **humour, comedy, jokes**
❸ *Charlie is regarded as the class **wit**.*
• **joker, comedian, comic**

witch and **witchcraft** *NOUN*
see **magic**

withdraw *VERB* **withdraws, withdrawing, withdrew, withdrawn**
❶ *The general **withdrew** his troops.*
• **call back, recall**
OPPOSITE **send in**
❷ *She **withdrew** her offer of help.*
• **take back, cancel, retract**
OPPOSITES **make, present**
❸ *The wolves **withdrew** into the forest.*
• **retire, retreat, draw back, fall back, back away**
OPPOSITE **advance**
❹ *He **withdrew** his hands from his pockets.*
• **draw back, pull back, take away, remove**
OPPOSITES **put out, extend**
❺ *Some competitors **withdrew** at the last minute.*
• **pull out, back out, drop out**
OPPOSITE **enter**

wither *VERB*
*The flowers had **withered** and died.*
• **shrivel, dry up, shrink, wilt, droop, sag, flop**
OPPOSITE **flourish**

withhold *VERB* **withholds, withholding, withheld**
*The police believe he is **withholding** information.*
• **hold back, keep back, refuse**
OPPOSITE **grant**

withstand *VERB* **withstands, withstanding, withstood**
*Penguins can **withstand** extreme cold.*
• **bear, endure, stand up to, tolerate, cope with, survive, resist, weather**

witness *NOUN*
*A **witness** said that the car was going too fast.*
• **bystander, observer, onlooker, eyewitness, spectator**

A B C D E F G H I J K L M N O P Q R S T U V W X Y Z

witty *ADJECTIVE*
He gave a ***witty*** *account of his schooldays.*
• **humorous, amusing, comic, funny**
OPPOSITE **dull**

wizard *NOUN*
❶ *The* ***wizard*** *cast a spell over the whole palace.*
• **magician, sorcerer, enchanter**
see also **magic**
❷ *My sister is a* ***wizard*** *with computers.*
• **expert, specialist, genius**
(informal) **whizz**

wobble *VERB*
❶ *The cyclist* ***wobbled*** *all over the road.*
• **sway, totter, teeter, waver, rock**
❷ *The jelly* ***wobbled*** *as I carried the plate.*
• **shake, tremble, quake, quiver, vibrate**

wobbly *ADJECTIVE*
❶ *The baby giraffe was a bit* ***wobbly*** *on its legs.*
• **shaky, tottering, unsteady**
❷ *This chair is a bit* ***wobbly****.*
• **loose, rickety, rocky, unstable, unsafe**
OPPOSITE **steady**

woman *NOUN*
A polite word for a woman is **lady**.
A married woman is a **wife**.
A woman who has children is a **mother**.
An unmarried woman is a **spinster**.
A woman whose husband has died is a **widow**.
A woman on her wedding day is a **bride**.
A woman who is engaged to be married is a **fiancée**.
Words for a young woman are **girl** and **lass**.
Old words for a young woman are **maid** and **maiden**.

won *past tense see* **win**

wonder *NOUN*
❶ *The sight of the Taj Mahal filled them with* ***wonder****.*
• **admiration, awe, reverence, amazement, astonishment**
❷ *It's a* ***wonder*** *that he is still alive.*
• **marvel, miracle**

wonder *VERB*
I ***wonder*** *why she left in such a hurry.*
• **be curious about, ask yourself, ponder, think about**
➤ **to wonder at**
People ***wondered at*** *the skill of the acrobats.*
• **marvel at, admire, be amazed by, be astonished by**

wonderful *ADJECTIVE*
❶ *It's* ***wonderful*** *what computers can do these days.*
• **amazing, astonishing, astounding, incredible, remarkable, extraordinary, marvellous, miraculous, phenomenal**
❷ *We had a* ***wonderful*** *time at the party.*
• **excellent, splendid, superb, delightful**
(informal) **brilliant, fantastic, terrific, fabulous, super, great**
OPPOSITE **ordinary**

wood *NOUN*
❶ *All the furniture in the room was made of* ***wood****.*
• **timber, lumber, planks, logs**
❷ *We followed a nature trail through the* ***wood****.*
• **woodland, woods, forest, trees**
see also **tree**

wood *NOUN*

WORD WEB

KINDS OF WOOD USED TO MAKE THINGS:

• **ash, balsa, beech, cedar, chestnut, ebony, elm, lime, mahogany, oak, pine, rosewood, sandalwood, spruce, teak, walnut**

A person who makes things from wood is a **carpenter** or **woodcarver**.
A person whose job is to cut down trees for wood is a **lumberjack**.

wooden *ADJECTIVE*
❶ *They sat down on a* ***wooden*** *bench.*
• **wood, timber**
❷ *The acting was a bit* ***wooden*** *at times.*
• **stiff, lifeless, awkward, unnatural, unemotional, expressionless**

woolly *ADJECTIVE*
❶ *He wore a* ***woolly*** *hat with a bobble on top.*
• **wool, woollen**
Clothes made of wool, such as hats and scarves, are **woollens**.
❷ *Mammoths were like elephants with* ***woolly*** *coats.*
• **thick, fleecy, furry, downy, fuzzy, hairy, shaggy, soft, cuddly**
❸ *Some parts of the plot were rather* ***woolly****.*
• **vague, confused, unclear, unfocused, hazy, indefinite, uncertain**

word *NOUN*
❶ *What's the French* ***word*** *for 'birthday'?*
• **expression, term**
All the words you know are your **vocabulary**.
❷ *You gave me your* ***word****.*
• **promise, assurance, guarantee, pledge, vow**
❸ *There has been no* ***word*** *from him for several weeks.*
• **news, message, information**

word *VERB*
I spent ages trying to ***word*** *the letter correctly.*
• **express, phrase, put into words**
The way that you word something is the **wording** or **phrasing**.

wore *past tense see* **wear**

work *NOUN*
❶ *Digging the garden involves a lot of hard* ***work****.*
• **effort, labour, toil, exertion**
❷ *Do you have any* ***work*** *to do this weekend?*
• **task, assignment, chore, job, homework, housework**
❸ *What kind of* ***work*** *does she do?*
• **occupation, employment, job, profession, business, trade, vocation**
for various kinds of work see **job**

work *VERB*
❶ *She's been* ***working*** *in the garden all day.*
• **be busy, exert yourself, labour, toil, slave**
❷ *He* ***works*** *in the bookshop on Saturdays.*
• **be employed, have a job, go to work**
❸ *My watch isn't* ***working****.*
• **function, go, operate**
❹ *Is the DVD player easy to* ***work****?*
• **operate, run, use, control, handle**
➤ **to work out**
Things didn't quite ***work out*** *as planned.*
• **turn out, happen, emerge, develop**
➤ **to work something out**
Can anyone ***work out*** *this sum?*
• **answer, calculate, solve, explain, figure out**

worker *NOUN*
The biscuit factory employs around 200 ***workers****.*
• **employee**
All the workers in a business or factory are the **staff** or **workforce**.
for people who do specific jobs see **job**

world *NOUN*
❶ *Antarctica is a remote part of the* ***world****.*
• **earth, globe**
❷ *Scientists are searching for life on other* ***worlds****.*
• **planet**

worried *ADJECTIVE*
You look ***worried****. Is something the matter?*
• **anxious, troubled, uneasy, distressed, disturbed, upset, apprehensive, concerned, bothered, tense, strained, nervous**
OPPOSITE **relaxed**

worry *VERB*
❶ *There's no need to* ***worry****.*
• **be anxious, be troubled, be disturbed, brood, fret**

A B C D E F G H I J K L M N O P Q R S T U V W X Y Z

❷ *It **worried** her that he hadn't replied to her letter.*
• **trouble, distress, upset, concern, disturb**
❸ *Don't **worry** her now—she's busy.*
• **bother, annoy, disturb, pester, harass**
(informal) **badger, bug**

worry *NOUN*
❶ *He's been a constant source of **worry** to her.*
• **anxiety, distress, uneasiness, vexation**
❷ *I don't want to add to your **worries**.*
• **trouble, concern, burden, care, problem**

worsen *VERB*
❶ *Moving the patient may **worsen** the pain.*
• **make worse, aggravate**
❷ *The weather had **worsened** overnight.*
• **get worse, deteriorate, degenerate**
OPPOSITE **improve**

worship *VERB*
❶ *Ancient Egyptians **worshipped** the sun god, Ra.*
• **pray to, glorify, praise**
for places where people worship see **building**
❷ *She adores her sons and they **worship** her.*
• **adore, be devoted to, look up to, love, revere, idolise**

worth *NOUN*
*This ring was once an object of great **worth**.*
• **value, merit, quality, significance, importance**

worthless *ADJECTIVE*
*It's nothing but a **worthless** piece of junk.*
• **useless, unusable, valueless**
(informal) **trashy**
OPPOSITE **valuable**

worthwhile *ADJECTIVE*
*It may be **worthwhile** to get a second opinion.*
• **helpful, useful, valuable, beneficial, profitable**
OPPOSITE **useless**

worthy *ADJECTIVE*
*They gave the money to a **worthy** cause.*
• **good, worthwhile, deserving, praiseworthy, admirable, commendable, respectable**
OPPOSITE **unworthy**

wound *(rhymes with* **sound***) past tense* see **wind** *VERB*

wound *NOUN (say* **woond***)*
*He is being treated in hospital for a head **wound**.*
• **injury, cut, gash, graze, scratch, sore**
for other types of wound see **injury**

wound *VERB (say* **woond***)*
*The fox was **wounded** in the leg and bleeding.*
• **injure, hurt, harm**

wrap *VERB*
❶ *She **wrapped** the presents in shiny gold paper.*
• **cover, pack, enclose, enfold, swathe**
To wrap water pipes is to **insulate** or **lag** them.
❷ *The mountain was **wrapped** in mist.*
• **cloak, envelop, shroud, surround, hide, conceal, wreathe**

wreathe *VERB*
*The tree was **wreathed** in fairy lights.*
• **encircle, festoon, surround, adorn, decorate**

wreck *VERB*
❶ *His bicycle was **wrecked** in the accident.*
• **demolish, destroy, crush, smash, shatter, crumple**
❷ *The injury **wrecked** her chances becoming a dancer.*
• **ruin, spoil**

wreckage *NOUN*
*Divers have discovered the **wreckage** of an old ship.*
• **debris, fragments, pieces, remains**
The wreckage of a building is **rubble** or **ruins**.

wrench *VERB*
The giant ***wrenched*** *the door off its hinges.*
• **pull, tug, prise, jerk, twist, force**
(informal) **yank**

wrestle *VERB*
He ***wrestled*** *with the thief as he tried to escape.*
• **struggle, tussle, grapple**

wretched *ADJECTIVE*
❶ *I lay in bed with flu feeling* ***wretched.***
• **miserable, unhappy, woeful, pitiful, unfortunate**
❷ *The* ***wretched*** *computer has frozen again!*
• **annoying, maddening, exasperating, useless**

wriggle *VERB*
The prisoner managed to ***wriggle*** *out of his bonds.*
• **twist, writhe, squirm, worm your way**

wring *VERB* **wrings, wringing, wrung**
❶ *She* ***wrung*** *the water out of her skirt.*
• **press, squeeze, twist**
❷ *He* ***wrung*** *her hand enthusiastically.*
• **shake, clasp, grip, wrench**
➤ **wringing wet**
Your socks are ***wringing*** *wet!*
• **soaked, drenched, dripping, sopping, saturated**

wrinkle *NOUN*
The old hag's face was covered in ***wrinkles.***
• **crease, fold, furrow, line, ridge, crinkle, pucker, pleat**
A small hollow on someone's skin is a **dimple.**

wrinkle *VERB*
The creature ***wrinkled*** *its nose and sniffed.*
• **pucker up, crease, crinkle, crumple, fold**
OPPOSITE **smooth**

write *VERB* **writes, writing, wrote, written**
❶ *My granny* ***wrote*** *a diary when she was a girl.*
• **compile, compose, draw up, set down, pen**
To write letters or emails to people is to **correspond** with them.
To write a rough version of a story is to **draft** it.
❷ *He* ***wrote*** *his address on the back of an envelope.*
• **jot down, note, print, scrawl, scribble**
To write on a document or surface is to **inscribe** it.
To write your signature on something is to **autograph** it.

writer *NOUN*
A person who writes books is an **author.**
A person who writes novels is a **novelist.**
A person who writes plays is a **dramatist** or **playwright.**
A person who writes scripts for films or television is a **scriptwriter** or **screenwriter.**
A person who writes poetry is a **poet.**
A person who writes about someone else's life is a **biographer.**
A person who writes for newspapers is a **correspondent, journalist** or **reporter.**
A person who writes music is a **composer.**
A person who writes a blog is a **blogger.**

writhe *VERB*
The wounded man was ***writhing*** *in agony.*
• **thrash about, twist, squirm, wriggle**

writing *NOUN*
❶ *Can you read the* ***writing*** *on the envelope?*
• **handwriting**
Untidy writing is a **scrawl** or **scribble.**
The art of beautiful handwriting is **calligraphy.**
❷ *The* ***writing*** *on the stone was very faint.*
• **inscription**
❸ *(often plural) She introduced me to the* ***writings*** *of Roald Dahl.*
• **literature, works**

A B C D E F G H I J K L M N O P Q R S T U V W X Y Z

WORD WEB

VARIOUS FORMS OF WRITING AND LITERATURE:

• autobiography, biography, blog, children's literature, classic, comedy, crime or detective story, diary, drama or play, essay, fable, fairy story or fairy tale, fantasy, fiction, film or TV script, folk tale, ghost story, historical fiction, history, journalism, legend, letters or correspondence, lyrics, myth, newspaper article, non-fiction, novel, parody, philosophy, poetry or verse, prose, romance, saga, satire, science fiction or *(informal)* sci-fi script, screenplay, spy story, thriller, tragedy, travel writing, western

I'm not really sure what makes a book a 'classic' to begin with, but I think it has to be at least fifty years old and some person or animal has to die at the end.—DIARY OF A WIMPY KID: DOG DAYS, Jeff Kinney

WRITING TIPS

You can use these words to describe a piece of writing.

TO DESCRIBE THE LANGUAGE OR STYLE IN A POSITIVE WAY:

• elegant, literary, ornate, poetic; colloquial, informal, slangy; formal, old-fashioned; hard-boiled, sparse

The author uses ***poetic*** *words, like 'cornucopia'.*

TO DESCRIBE THE LANGUAGE OR STYLE IN A NEGATIVE WAY:

• banal, dry, insipid, lacklustre, monotonous, plodding, prosaic

TO DESCRIBE A CHARACTER:

• hero, heroine, protagonist, narrator, villain; believable, convincing, lifelike, realistic, strong, well-drawn; feeble, thin, unbelievable, unconvincing, weak

Mr Scruggs is a thoroughly ***convincing*** *villain.*

TO DESCRIBE THE SETTING:

• atmospheric, moody; alien, exotic, fanciful, fantastic, fictitious, made-up, imaginary, strange, unfamiliar; eerie, spooky, weird; accurate, authentic, familiar, recognisable, true to life

The story is set on an ***imaginary*** *planet.*

TO DESCRIBE THE STORYLINE OR PLOT IN A POSITIVE WAY:

• action-packed, dramatic, dynamic, engrossing, entertaining, eventful, fast-paced, gripping, hair-raising, intriguing, mind-boggling, page-turning, rip-roaring, spellbinding, thrilling; creative, imaginative, moving, thought-provoking, well-crafted; amusing, diverting, entertaining, hilarious, humorous; romantic, sentimental

Finn's adventures are ***dramatic*** *and at times moving.*

TO DESCRIBE THE STORYLINE OR PLOT IN A NEGATIVE WAY:

• dull, insipid, uneventful, unimaginative; absurd, far-fetched, ludicrous, ridiculous, unbelievable, unlikely

TO DESCRIBE THE ENDING IN A POSITIVE WAY:

• cliffhanger, climax, conclusion, finale; electrifying, nail-biting, sensational, spectacular, surprising, unexpected

The book keeps you guessing until the ***sensational finale****.*

TO DESCRIBE THE ENDING IN A NEGATIVE WAY:

• abrupt, banal, clichéd, predicable, trite, unsatisfying

wrong *ADJECTIVE*
❶ *It was **wrong** to take the book without asking.*
• **bad, dishonest, irresponsible, immoral, sinful, wicked, criminal, unfair, unjust**
❷ *His calculations were all **wrong**.*
• **incorrect, mistaken, inaccurate**
❸ *Did I say the **wrong** thing?*
• **inappropriate, unsuitable, improper**
❹ *There's something **wrong** with the TV.*
• **faulty, defective, not working, out of order**
OPPOSITE **right**
➤ **to go wrong**
*The professor's plan began to **go wrong**.*
• **fail, backfire**
(informal) **flop, go pear-shaped**
succeed

wrote *past tense see* **write**

yacht *NOUN*
for types of boat or ship see **boat**

yard *NOUN*
*A solitary tree stood in the middle of the **yard**.*
• **court, courtyard, enclosure**

yearly *ADJECTIVE*
*I'm due for my **yearly** dental check-up.*
• **annual**

yearn *VERB*
➤ **to yearn for something**
*She **yearned for** some peace and quiet.*
• **want, wish for, desire, long for, pine for**
(informal) **be dying for**

yell *VERB*
*I **yelled** to attract their attention.*
• **call out, cry out, shout, roar, bawl, bellow**

yell *NOUN*
*The pirates gave a bloodcurdling **yell**.*
• **cry, roar, bellow**

yellow *ADJECTIVE, NOUN*

WORD WEB

SOME SHADES OF YELLOW:
• **amber, chrome yellow, cream, gold, golden, lemon, tawny**
Something which is rather yellow is **yellowish**.

yelp *VERB*
for sounds made by animals see **animal**

yield *VERB*
❶ *In the end, her parents **yielded** and let her go out.*
• **give in, give way, concede, surrender, admit defeat, submit, comply**

❷ *The apple trees **yielded** a good crop of fruit.*
• **bear, grow, produce, supply, generate**

yield *NOUN*
*They got a good **yield** from the orchard this year.*
• **crop, harvest, produce, return**

young *ADJECTIVE*
❶ *A lot of **young** people went to the concert.*
• **youthful, juvenile**
OPPOSITES **older, mature**
❷ *I think this book is a bit **young** for you.*
• **childish, babyish, immature, infantile**
OPPOSITES **adult, grown-up**
A young person is a **child** or **youngster**.
A young adult is an **adolescent** or **youth**.
A very young child is a **baby** or **infant**.
A young bird is a **chick**, **fledgling** or **nestling**.
Young fish are **fry**.
A young plant is a **cutting** or **seedling**.
A young tree is a **sapling**.
for other young animals and birds see **animal, bird**

young *PLURAL NOUN*
*The mother bird returned to feed her **young**.*
• **offspring, children, young ones, family**
A family of young birds is a **brood**.
A family of young cats or dogs is a **litter**.

youth *NOUN*
❶ *In her **youth**, she had been a keen tennis player.*
• **childhood, boyhood** or **girlhood, adolescence, teens**
❷ *The fight was started by a group of **youths**.*
• **adolescent, youngster, juvenile, teenager, young adult**

youthful *ADJECTIVE*
*The magic potion will keep you eternally **youthful**.*
• **young, youngish, vigorous, sprightly, young-looking**

Zz

zero *NOUN*
*Four minus four makes **zero**.*
• **nothing, nought**
A score of zero in football is **nil**; in cricket it is a **duck**, and in tennis it is **love**.

zest *NOUN*
*Uncle Arthur has a great **zest** for life.*
• **enthusiasm, eagerness, enjoyment**

zigzag *VERB*
*The road **zigzags** up the hill.*
• **wind, twist, meander**

zodiac *NOUN*

WORD WEB

THE SIGNS OF THE ZODIAC ARE:

• **Aquarius** (or the Water Carrier), **Aries** (or the Ram), **Cancer** (or the Crab), **Capricorn** (or the Goat), **Gemini** (or the Twins), **Leo** (or the Lion), **Libra** (or the Scales), **Pisces** (or the Fish), **Sagittarius** (or the Archer), **Scorpio** (or the Scorpion), **Taurus** (or the Bull), **Virgo** (or the Virgin)

zone *NOUN*
*No-one may enter the forbidden **zone**.*
• **area, district, region, sector, locality, neighbourhood, territory, vicinity**

zoo *NOUN*
*Which is your favourite animal in the **zoo**?*
• **menagerie, safari park, wildlife reserve, nature reserve, zoological gardens**
for animals you might see in a zoo see **animal**

Become a Word Explorer

You don't need a map and a compass to be an explorer. You can explore the world of **words** equipped with your thesaurus.
For example, you can:

- explore the differences between **synonyms**
- explore effects like **simile** and **alliteration**
- explore ways to **build words**
- explore ideas to improve your **stories** and other kinds of writing.

Use the following pages to help you.

Contents

Explore: Synonyms

The main job of a thesaurus is to list **synonyms**. Synonyms are words which mean the same—or nearly the same—as each other, like *big* and *huge*, or *horrible* and *nasty*.

Sometimes, you can choose between a few synonyms. A giant's nose might be *huge* or *immense* or *colossal* or *mammoth*: you can swap the words around and it makes no difference to the meaning.

Other synonyms are more limited and only fit in certain contexts.

For example:
- formal or informal synonyms (*yummy* is an informal synonym of *delicious*)
- synonyms which are special cases (*trunk* and *casket* are special types of box).

Examples
- In a piece of schoolwork, you might write:
  *The cake was **delicious** / **tasty**.*
- But in your diary or an email, you could write instead:
  *The cake was **scrumptious** / **yummy**!*
- In a story, you might write:
  *The magician carried his things in a **trunk**.*
  *The treasure was sealed in a wooden **casket**.*

Explorer tip:

You can easily spot **special synonyms** in the thesaurus. Look for the labels *formal, informal* or *old use*. Synonyms which are special cases are listed and defined in a separate paragraph.

Explore: Overused words

Words like *bad*, *big* and *nice* are very useful, but they can make your writing boring if you use them too often. If you choose a synonym which is more unusual, it will make your writing more interesting.

Examples

- Instead of making a mermaid simply ***beautiful***, try describing her as ***radiant*** or ***resplendent***.
- Is a ***big ogre*** scary enough? If not, transform it into a ***hulking*** or ***monstrous ogre***.

Note that you don't need to avoid overused words completely! There are some places where words like *bad* and *big* are the right words to use, for example in *big bad wolf* and *big toe*.

Explorer tip:

You can easily spot **OVERUSED WORDS** in the thesaurus, as they have their own panels. There is a complete list of **OVERUSED WORDS** at the front of the thesaurus.

Become a Word Explorer

Explore: Similes

This thesaurus notes common **similes** like *as fit as a fiddle*. But you can also make up your own, using your thesaurus for ideas.

Similes are useful for describing how a character looks or sounds, or how a landscape appears.

Examples

- *Miss Mullins had a face* ***like a soggy sponge***.
- *The dragon's eyes were* ***as dark as a moonless night***.
- *The waves crashed* ***like cymbals*** *on the shore*.

Similes allow you to mix and match. You can describe a person like an animal ***(Mr Scruggs scuttled off like a spider)***, or an animal like a thing ***(the snake sprang up like a jack-in-the-box)***.

Similes can also make your writing individual. Lots of people may describe a road as ***bumpy***, but you may be the only person to say it is ***as bumpy as the back of a crocodile***.

Explorer tip:

The **animal** and **bird** panels list ways to describe animals and birds. But you can also use these words in similes to describe people or things, for example ***as spiky as a stegosaur*** or ***as fluffy as a puffling***.

Explore: Idioms

An **idiom** is a phrase that doesn't mean exactly the same as the words in it. For example, *to be in hot water* is an idiom which means 'to be in trouble' (not to be in actual hot water).

Idioms can make your writing more lively. But be careful: your writing can look clichéd if you use too many!

Examples

A character in your story has just seen a ghost. How do you describe their reaction?

- *Anita **blanched** and stood **rooted to the spot**.*
- *She **had goosebumps** all over and began to **tremble like a leaf**.*

Explorer tip:

You will find suggestions for idioms and other words to use in the **WRITING TIPS** panels for **afraid**, **angry** and **surprised**.

Explore: Special names

A thesaurus can help you find the special names for certain things, for example the special names for young animals or birds, or for animal homes. Using these words can make your writing more accurate and interesting.

Special names for groups of people, animals or things are called **collective nouns**. For example, instead of simply ***a group of elephants*** or ***a group of whales***, you can say ***a herd of elephants*** or ***a pod of whales***.

Examples

- *There was a **vixen** and three fox **cubs** in the **earth**.*
- *We saw a **colony** of puffins perched on the cliffs.*

You can also make up your own collective nouns. For example, you could say ***a flutter of butterflies*** or ***a rumble of rhinoceroses***!

Explorer tip:

You will find special names and collective nouns listed in the **WORD WEB** panels for **animal**, **bird** and **group**.

Explore: Sound effects

Some words come with their own sound effects. These are called **onomatopoeic** words, and they sound like the thing they are describing. Using a sound-effect word can give an extra *zing* to your writing.

Examples

You are describing footsteps on a path.

- On a dry, stony path, the footsteps might ***crunch***, but on a muddy path, they would ***squelch***.
- A dog's paws might ***patter*** on the path, whereas a giant's feet would ***thud***.

Explorer tip:

You will find lots of sound-effect words in the **WORD WEB** panel for **sound**.

A sound effect that you can create yourself is **alliteration**, which means using two or more words which start with the same sound. This is especially useful in poetry, but can also be effective in story writing.

They went to sea in a Sieve, they did,
In a Sieve they went to sea.
—THE JUMBLIES, Edward Lear

Examples

You are writing a poem about food.

Use alliteration to make it ***crispy and crumbly***, ***gloopy and gooey***, or maybe ***sweet and sticky***.

If the food is disgusting, you might describe it as ***slimy and sloppy***, or even ***mouldy and mushy***!

Explorer tip:

You will find words to describe both delicious *and* disgusting food in the **WRITING TIPS** panel for **food**.

Explore: Word building

Have you ever thought about making up a word? You can add to the words in your thesaurus by creating your own.

Try building a new word by starting with a word you know, or a word you have found in the thesaurus, and adding one of these *suffixes* (endings) to it:

-ish	*purplish*, *shortish*, *hairyish*
-less or **-free**	a *flowerless* garden, a *chocolate-free* chin
-like	a *ghost-like* shadow, a *swan-like* neck
-proof	a *sword-proof* shield, a *magic-proof* castle
-y	a *lemony* pudding, a *herby* flavour

You can also build *compounds* by joining two whole words together. Here are a few suggestions for words to use, but you can also try out your own:

-feeling	*rough-feeling* skin
-looking	*scary-looking* teeth
-smelling	a *musty-smelling* room
-sounding	an *eerie-sounding* wail

Examples

You are describing a dragon.

You could give it: *lidless* eyes, *bat-like* wings, *sour-smelling* breath and *fire-emitting* nostrils.

Explore: Writing stories

Before you write:

1. Plan your story. Think about the setting, the characters and the action.
2. Share the story with a friend before you write. Would you want to read this story? Would your friend? Change your plan if necessary.

While you are writing:

3. Keep to your plan.
4. Write in sentences and think about punctuation.
5. Don't forget paragraphs. If you need to begin a sentence with an adverbial clause of time (e.g. ***Later that day . . . When it was all over . . .***) or place (e.g. ***Outside . . . In the woods . . .***) you probably need to start a new paragraph.

After you have written the first draft:

6. Use a dictionary to check your spelling.
7. Use a thesaurus to make sure you have chosen the best words.
8. Look at the **overused words** list on page viii. Try to use other words.
9. Can you add in some details about your characters to increase your reader's interest in them?
10. Can you add more information about your setting to help your reader 'see' it in their mind?

Creating a setting: Place

The first thing to decide is *where* your story takes place.

- Does the action happen *at sea* or *on a desert island*?
- Is it set in an *ancient castle* or in *outer space*?

Once you have a general setting, you can draw attention to details such as trees or buildings, animals or birds, or even mythological creatures.

Explorer tip:

Look up these entries and panels to help you describe your setting:
cave desert island jungle landscape mountain planet polar river sea seashore seaside pace

For words to describe *features* of your setting, look up **boat**, **castle**, **ice** and **tree**.

Creating a setting: Time

You also need to tell your readers *when* your story takes place.

- Does it take place in *late spring* or in *early autumn*?
- Does it begin at *dusk* or at *dawn*?
- Is it set in the *present* day, in *ancient* times, or even in the *future*?

Explorer tip:

Look up the entries for **day**, **night**, **season** and **time** to help you describe time.

Creating a setting: Atmosphere and weather

Once you've settled on the place and time, you can start to think about the atmosphere. What is the weather like?

- Is the sky *cloudy* or *cloudless*?
- Is the wind *blustery* or *breezy*?
- Is a storm *brewing*?

Explorer tip:

Look up the entries for ice, rain, sky, snow, sun and wind to help you describe weather.

You can also look up hot and cold for more ways to describe temperature.

Describing a character

Describing how your characters look, sound (and even smell!) will make them more believable and vivid. Think about the details which make people different from each other.

- Are your characters *lean* and *lanky*, or *short* and *squat*?
- Is their hair *straight* and *stringy*, or *fine* and *frizzy*?
- Are they more likely to *scowl* and *grimace*, or to *beam*?

Explorer tip:

Look up the entries for body, expression, eye, face, hair, nose and voice to help you describe your characters.

You can also look up the clothes panel for things that your characters might wear.

Typical characters

Some types of story require certain characters. For example, a detective story needs a detective, and a pirate story needs at least one pirate. A number of the **WORD WEB** panels focus on typical story characters like these. They are rather like dressing-up boxes with words (rather than costumes) with which to dress up your characters.

- **detective** lists things a detective might look for (*fingerprints, suspect*)
- **astronaut** lists places an astronaut might visit (*moonbase, spacelab*)

These **WORD WEB** panels don't list *everything* a detective or astronaut might do, but they do list *typical* things and can give you ideas for writing your own mystery story or space story.

Explorer tip:

Look up the entries for **astronaut**, **criminal**, **detective**, **explorer**, **fairy**, **ghost**, **knight**, **pirate**, **robot**, **spy** and **superhero** to help you create those characters.

The **magic** panel also has suggestions for **witches** and **wizards**.

Imaginary creatures

If your characters are not human, it is even more important to let your readers know how they look and sound. Not all aliens and ogres are alike, so be sure to describe *your* imaginary creatures in detail.

You can make an imaginary monster vivid by giving it body parts of real animals, for example the head of a snake, the wings of a bat, and the legs of a beetle.

Examples

You are writing a space story. How do you describe your alien creatures?

- *The aliens had* ***insect-like bodies****, with* ***spindly legs*** *and* ***spiky antennae****.*
- *Their* ***scaly backs*** *were patterned with* ***purple blotches****.*
- *They spoke to each other in* ***high-pitched screeches****.*

Describing action

When you describe what your characters do, try to be specific.

- How do your characters move? Do they ***scurry*** quickly, ***glide*** gracefully, or ***slink*** stealthily?
- Do they ***tap*** gently on a door, or ***pound*** it insistently?
- Do they ***nibble*** their food politely, or ***gobble*** it greedily?

There is nothing wrong with using simple words like *move*, *hit* and *eat*. But your writing will be more interesting if you sometimes use more colourful verbs.

Examples

You are writing a detective story. How does your main character act?

- *Inspector Giles* ***paced*** *slowly round the room,* ***twitching*** *his moustache. He* ***inspected*** *the broken window and* ***peered*** *closely at the stains on the carpet.*

Explorer tip:

Look up the entries for **eat**, **drink**, **look**, **move** and **walk** to help you describe action.

You will find even more action words in the entries for **hit** and **run**.

Look up the **animal** or **bird** panels for ways that creatures might move.

Writing dialogue

The words that your characters say in the story is the *dialogue*. When you are writing dialogue, try not to use the verb **say** each time. Your story will be more interesting if you vary the words which report what each character says.

Examples

- *'Stop that racket!'* ***snapped*** *Miss Grump.*
- *'Don't look now, but there's a ghost behind us,'* ***whispered*** *Evie.*

These sound far more interesting than simply *said Miss Grump* and *said Evie*.

Exclamations

Lively dialogue can bring the characters in your story to life. Try using *exclamations* at exciting moments in your story.

Examples

A character in your story suddenly gets angry or annoyed. What should he or she say?

- *'**Blast** that parrot!' said Captain Cutlass with an evil leer.*
- *'**Bother**! The magic potion is wearing off!' said Megan, frowning.*

Explorer tip:

The panels for **say** and **exclamation** have ideas that you can use to write dialogue.

Explore: Writing non-fiction

Your thesaurus can help you with **non-fiction** writing, too.

- How can you describe a *book* you have read, or a *place* you have visited?
- What words can you use to report a *sports match*?
- What words can you use in a *recipe* for cooking?

Examples

You are writing a book review. How do you describe the way that the book ends?

- *'Smugglers Cove' hurtles towards a* ***gripping finale****. The final chapter is a* ***nail-biting*** *description of a sea chase.*

You are writing a report of a football match. How do you describe the winning goal?

- *Martinez* ***dribbled*** *the ball past two* ***defenders****, then* ***chipped*** *it across to the* ***captain*** *who* ***blasted*** *it into the back of the net.*

Explorer tip:

You will find useful words and phrases to describe a book in the **WRITING TIPS** panel for **writing**.

Explorer tip:

You will find words that are used in various sports in the **WORD WEB** panels for **football**, **tennis**, etc. You can also get ideas for how a player might hit or throw a ball in the **WRITING TIPS** panel for **ball**.

The **WORD WEB** panels in the thesaurus include lists of related words which can give you ideas or information for a project on that topic.

Examples

You are writing a project on *animals*. Look up the **animal** panel to find:

- animals that live on land *(aardvark, zebra)* or in the sea *(dolphin, whale)*
- names of young animals *(cub, pup)*
- names of animal body parts *(claw, snout)*
- names of wild animal homes *(earth, warren)*

Explorer tip:

You can easily spot **WORD WEBS** in the thesaurus. They are treated in special panels and have this symbol next to them:

There is a complete list of **WORD WEB** panels at the front of the thesaurus.

Explore further . . .

Like a good explorer, be prepared to follow a trail. **Cross references** in the **WORD WEBS** will help you to find other panels with related information. For example, the panel for **dinosaur** points you also to **prehistoric**, where you will find a list of other prehistoric animals.

You may want to explore your topic further by looking up the listed words in a dictionary or an encyclopedia.

Explore: Writing letters

When you are writing a letter or email, think about *who* you are writing to, and *why*. This will help you decide what type of letter to write.

- You might write a formal letter to a teacher, but an informal email to a friend.
- You might send informal invitations to your birthday party, but receive a formal invitation to a wedding.

If a character in your story writes a letter, it should also fit with the person and situation you are describing.

- A medieval knight would write an elaborate, formal letter to a king.
- A spy might send a hasty, informal email to headquarters.

Here are some tips for writing both formal and informal types of letter.

Formal letters

In a **formal letter**, you should:

- write in complete sentences
- avoid short forms like *don't* and *I'm* (use *do not* and *I am*)
- avoid informal words and phrases, such as *thanks* (use *thank you* instead)
- begin with *Dear*, and end with *Yours sincerely* or *Yours truly*
- call the person you are writing to by their family name or title (if you don't know their name, call them *Sir* or *Madam*)

Dear Prince Charming,

Thank you for your invitation to the Palace Ball on Saturday. Unfortunately I am unable to come, as I must stay at home all evening to sweep the floors. Please accept my apologies.

Yours sincerely,
Cinderella

Informal letters

Informal letters and emails are often chatty in tone, as if you were speaking rather than writing the words.

- use incomplete sentences
- use short forms like *don't* and *I'm*
- use informal words and phrases, such as *terrific* or *thanks*
- use exclamation marks when you (or your characters) are excited
- begin with *Dear* or *Hello* or *Hi* (or just a name), and end with *Yours* or *Best wishes*
- call the person you are writing to by their first or given name, or by a nickname

Dear Cinders

Just had a terrific idea! Meet me at the kitchen door at 6pm on Sat. Bring a pumpkin and a few mice.

Yours
Fairy Godmother

Explorer tip:

Use the **WORD WEB** panel at **communication** to help you look for ways to address people you are speaking to or writing to.

Explore: Punctuation

Punctuation makes writing easier to read and understand. You should use these basic punctuation marks in your writing:

- a **full stop** (.) comes at the end of a sentence
- a **comma** (,) separates items in a list, or parts of a sentence:
  Hedgehogs eat slugs, snails and worms.
  After four days at sea, we sighted land.
- an **apostrophe** (') shows that a letter is missing, or tells you who something belongs to:
  Don't enter the dragon's lair! = Do not enter the lair of the dragon!

These punctuation marks are especially useful for writing dialogue in a story:

- **quotation marks** (' ' or " ") come before and after words that a character says:
  'My name,' said the knight, 'is Sir Joustalot.'
- a **question mark** (?) comes at the end of a question:
  'How old are you?' I asked the wizard.
  Note that you don't need a question mark if the question is reported, not spoken:
  I asked the wizard how old he was.
- an **exclamation mark** (!) comes after a shout, or shows that a character is excited:
  'Wow! Look at the size of that crater!'

Explorer tip:

The **WORD WEB** panel for **punctuation** lists various punctuation marks that you might use or come across. You will find more tips on writing **dialogue** and using **exclamations** in the **Explore: Writing stories** section above.